THE BEST PLAYS OF 1983–1984

THE
BURNS MANTLE
YEARBOOK

THE
BEST PLAYS
OF 1983-1984

EDITED BY OTIS L. GUERNSEY JR.

Illustrated with photographs and
with drawings by HIRSCHFELD

DODD, MEAD & COMPANY
NEW YORK

EDITOR'S NOTE

HERE is the 65th volume in the *Best Plays* series of theater yearbooks published since the 1919–20 edition by Dodd, Mead & Company and edited down through the years by Burns Mantle (28 volumes), John Chapman (5 volumes), Louis Kronenberger (9 volumes), Henry Hewes (3 volumes) and the incumbent, whose 20th volume this *The Best Plays of 1983–84* is. From the beginning this series has striven, with notable success, to capture the creative persona of each New York theater season (broadening its base beyond Broadway as the situation warranted) by including, in addition to credits and statistics, examples of the very heart of the theater: its best new scripts. Uniquely, *Best Plays* has applauded dramatists from the front row of its attention. We're proud to continue doing so in this volume, thanks to the extraordinary talent—and in almost all cases willing permission for the quoting of excerpts from the plays—which rekindles the fires of imagination, year after year, in the playhouses all over town. We are deeply grateful to these dramatists—not only the few Best Play authors but also the many whose work flashes in and out of the limelight. It isn't just their occasional success, but the sum total of their continuing, indomitable striving that keeps our theater aflame.

As we added off Broadway to our Best Plays eligibility and detailed factual listing, so we added and now Camille Croce maintains the most comprehensive record of off-off-Broadway activity, plus an overview of the OOB season by Mel Gussow, distinguished alternate drama critic of the New York *Times.* Our focus on cross-country theater has also widened continuously under the supervision of Ella A. Malin and with the assistance of the American Theater Critics Association, whose members annually provide reviews of notable new work all over the country and select an outstanding script to be presented in this volume in the same manner as the Best Plays. To concentrate on and deepen our coverage of new plays and musicals put on around the United States, in line with our special regard for the living, working dramatist, Miss Malin has reorganized that section this season to take in only *new* scripts produced by groups we have regularly listed, plus many other new-play-producing groups we weren't able to include previously.

A special feature of this volume is a special Best Play citation of the Peter Brook version of *Carmen*, with a review by Douglas Watt, drama critic of the New York *Daily News*. Our 1983–84 edition is also specially indebted to Jonathan Dodd of Dodd, Mead & Company for his supervisory assistance; to the editor's wife who has painstakingly supported this enterprise during almost half her married years; to Rue Canvin for her compilations of necrology and publications; to Stanley Green for his record of major cast replacements; to William Schelble for his Tony Awards and Allan Wallach for his Critics Awards data; and to Henry Hewes of ATCA, Ralph Newman of the Drama Book Shop, Robert Nahas of the Theater Arts Book Shop, Hobe Morrison of *Variety* and Thomas

T. Foose, with continuing gratitude to the scores of helpers in the theater's public relations departments who have tirelessly supplied us with information, and generously with material, and without whom there certainly would be no *Best Plays* volume as we have come to expect it.

Each of the 20 volumes we have edited has been adorned with the wonderful drawings of Al Hirschfeld, whose uncannily perceptive caricatures of each season's highlights have been a major attraction in these pages and in 1984 won him the Tony committee's first annual Brooks Atkinson Award for lifetime achievement in the theater. Other highly valued embellishments of our text are the examples of the year's most effective stage designs contributed by Peter Larkin and Theoni V. Aldredge, as well as the photos which so vividly record the "look" of the theater season, the work of Martha Swope and Joseph Abeles, Bert Andrews, Mark Avery, Chris Bennion, Ross Cameron/KLH, Susan Cook, Peter Cunningham, Gerry Goodstein, Ken Howard, Susan Piper Kublick, JWL, Brigitte Lacombe, Lascher, David MacKenzie, Inge Morath, Lanny Nagler, Carol Rosegg and Anita Feldman/Shevett. In photos, drawings, statistics and reviews, the many efforts coming together in *The Best Plays of 1983–84* are a celebration of a theater which annually lives up to the devotion of its admirers, thanks to the corresponding devotion of its artists.

OTIS L. GUERNSEY Jr.

July 1, 1984

CONTENTS

Drawings by HIRSCHFELD

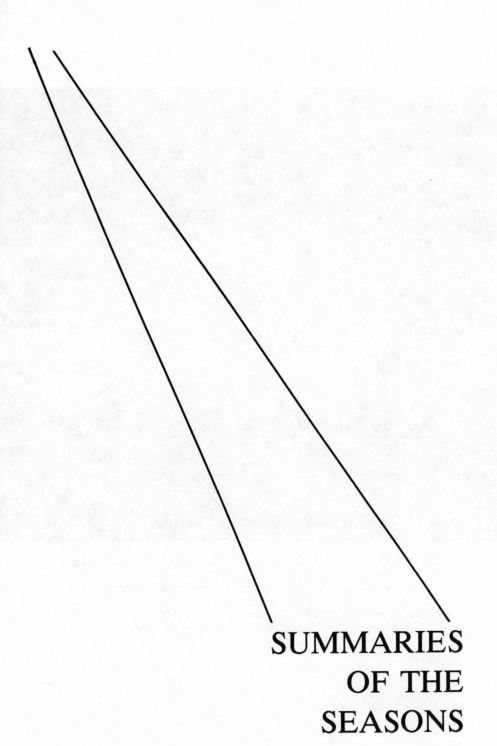

SUMMARIES
OF THE
SEASONS

A LONG, LONG CHORUS LINE—*Above* is a scene from the 3,389th performance of *A Chorus Line* Sept. 29, 1983, when it became the longest-running
Broadway production of all time, passing the record previously held by *Grease*.
On this special occasion, 330 past and present members of the musical's cast
assembled onstage at the Shubert Theater to participate in the performance, and
many of them are in the line reflected in the mirror in this photo

O
O
O

THE SEASON IN NEW YORK

O   *By Otis L. Guernsey Jr.*
O
O

MUSICALS, musicals, long-running musicals (*A Chorus Line* in the longest run in Broadway history and *The Fantasticks* in its 25th year off Broadway, the longest New York run of all time)... musicals, musicals, musicals about musicals (*La Cage aux Folles, The Tap Dance Kid*) . . . musicals, musicals, musicals everywhere dominating the 1983–84 theater season in New York. From the off-Broadway hit *Taking My Turn* in early June 1983 to the thrilling Broadway crescendo of *Sunday in the Park With George* in May 1984, this was a conspicuously musical year, with the likes of *La Cage aux Folles, The Human Comedy, Zorba, La Tragédie de Carmen, Doonesbury, Baby* and *The Tap Dance Kid* marching shoulder to shoulder behind the band and the holdovers *Cats, Dreamgirls, 42nd Street, Nine, My One and Only, Little Shop of Horrors* and *On Your Toes* (the latter, at 505 performances, second only to *Pal Joey* as Rodgers & Hart's longest-running hit).

No wonder, therefore, that our list of the ten Best Plays is weighted with musicals, two out of the ten for the second year in a row: *La Cage aux Folles*, with a Jerry Herman score and a Harvey Fierstein book based on the French movie and stage comedy, and the innovative *Sunday in the Park With George*, with book by James Lapine and score by Stephen Sondheim, plus a special eleventh Best Play citation to *La Tragédie de Carmen*, Peter Brook's creative remodeling of the Bizet classic.

"The shortest distance between two points is a hit review in London," observed the playwright Louis Phillips recently, and certainly it was the road taken by the two towering straight plays of 1983–84: Tom Stoppard's *The Real Thing* and David Mamet's *Glengarry Glen Ross*. Both started as London hits, Stoppard's a native product, Mamet's an American import at the National Theater. So did the hilarious *Noises Off* by Michael Frayn and the touching *And a Nightingale Sang* . . . by the late C.P. Taylor. The Samuel Beckett one-acts cited in this volume's list of Best Plays were produced in Europe, often in London, before appearing in New York, while *Carmen* was originally staged in Paris, in French, with a later English translation having been provided in New York by Sheldon Harnick. Sam Shepard's abrasive *Fool for Love* came to town in the Magic Theater of San Francisco production, and Beth Henley's *The Miss Firecracker Contest* was also produced four times in regional theater—and once in London—before appearing this season at Manhattan Theater Club. Of the eleven 1983–84 Best Plays, the only New-York-originating ones were Tina Howe's inimitable *Painting Churches*, which moved uptown from an off-off-Broadway debut last year, and

3

La Cage aux Folles, produced directly for Broadway via the out-of-town-tryout route.

The list of the 1983–84 Best Plays is evenly divided between Broadway (*La Cage, The Real Thing, Noises Off, Glengarry, Sunday in the Park*) and off Broadway (*Painting Churches, Nightingale, Miss Firecracker, Fool for Love* and the Beckett plays including *Rockaby*), with the extra fillip of *Carmen* at Lincoln Center. Among the shows that came close to making this list were *The Tap Dance Kid*, with a Charles Blackwell book about an upward-mobile black family, and plays that couldn't find an audience despite their evident quality: Shirley Lauro's *Open Admissions* and Joanna M. Glass's *Play Memory* on Broadway and Ted Tally's *Terra Nova* off. Also crowding the top ten were the Galt MacDermot musical *The Human Comedy*, the comedy-drama *Cinders* by Polish-born playwright Janusz Glowacki (both at New York Shakespeare Festival) and R.A. Shiomi's 1930s-style detective tale, *Yellow Fever*.

One of the more dramatic developments on Broadway in 1983–84 was the precipitous drop in the production of new plays, diminished by almost half from last year: 8 American playscripts where there were 15, 4 foreign ones where there were 8. Even revivals dropped off, from 14 to 11, and there was only one revue in place of two (only specialties showed a rise, from 3 to 4). With musicals holding steady at 10 shows for the third straight year, total Broadway production (not counting specialties) amounted to only 34 offerings, a new low, off from 49 last year, 45 in 1981–82, 51 the year before that, 58 in 1979–80 and the previous nadir, 47 in 1978–79.

Because of a sustained high level of quality among the recent shows, leading to longer runs, or continuing inflation, or a combination of the two, the year's total Broadway box office gross, was *up* from $203 million last year to a record $226,507,518 in 1983–84, according to *Variety* estimate (the League of New York Theaters and Producers estimate differed slightly but not materially). The road gross was up too, to $206 million from $184 million, and so was the average price of the Broadway admission, $29.75 in June 1984 as compared with $27.69 the year before. On the down side were total attendance, 7.9 million, declining from 8.1 million last year and 10.7 the year before, and playing weeks (if ten shows play ten weeks, that's 100 playing weeks), off sharply from 1,259 in 1982–83 to 1,119 in 1983–84. We should add that because of a calendar anomaly, these *Variety* totals were derived from a 53-week season.

Production costs were up—of course. The price tag on each of the ten musicals didn't always reach $5 million, but it did at *La Cage aux Folles*, which began to recoup rapidly at a $45 top (pretty much the going rate for a musical this year but expected to be headed toward an inevitable $50), bringing in a *Variety*-estimated $130,000 weekly profit from a $450,000 weekly gross. *La Tragédie de Carmen* came in from Paris for a mere $1.5 million, and the short-lived Marilyn Monroe musical, *Marilyn*, was estimated to have cost its backers about $3 million. Among the long runners the Broadway champ, *A Chorus Line*, is now estimated by *Variety* to have earned a net profit of $37 million, $16 million from the Broadway company. The marathon run of *The Fantasticks* off Broadway has profited those who put up the $16,500 to produce it $2.5 million so far, which is even more impressive when expressed as 7,674 per cent. But the Babe Ruth of this league is David Merrick who "hit a Broadway homer," as *Variety* put it, when he put up all the money for *42nd Street* and was collecting an estimated $500,000 weekly net profit from the Broadway and two touring companies.

The level of straight-play production costs and ticket prices in 1983–84 was more modest than that of the musicals, but still forbidding. $32.50 was a commonplace top-of-the-scale ticket, with $37.50 not unknown. At these prices, *The Real Thing*, an $825,000 hit, was estimated to be profiting $135,000 out of its $250,000 weekly gross. This year's $850,000 hit revival of *Death of a Salesman* came into town with a $1.8 million advance sale. *Torch Song Trilogy*, brought uptown at $400,000, was off the nut and making a profit in the second year of its run in a smallish house. On the road, a company of *Master Harold . . . and the Boys*, assembled for $200,000, collected a $300,000 profit on that investment.

At the economic levels illustrated by these examples, it wasn't surprising to find 1983–84 legitimate stage production spreading out over a group of producers widening to share the heavy risks, increasing in size as rapidly as the costs. A head count adds up to 90 producing individuals and organizations (not counting associates) billed above the titles of the 34 Broadway shows. *La Cage*, for example, listed seven, but in this respect, we believe, *Marilyn* topped them all with 12 producers and one associate, plus three more associates named in the below-title credits.

Most active of the season's producers was The Shubert Organization with participation in six Broadway shows, three of them Best Plays: *The Real Thing, Glengarry Glen Ross, Sunday in the Park With George, The Human Comedy, A Moon for the Misbegotten* and *The Wiz*. James M. Nederlander and his Organization came next with five, including two Best Plays: *La Cage aux Folles, Noises Off, Shirley MacLaine on Broadway, Oliver!* and the musical *Chaplin* which didn't make it to New York. Producers who distinguished themselves by taking part in three exceptional programs each were Emanuel Azenberg *(Real Thing, Misbegotten, Sunday in the Park)*, Elliot Martin *(American Buffalo, Glengarry* and, off Broadway, *Woza Albert!)*, the husband-and-wife team of Alexander H. Cohen and Hildy Parks *(Edmund Kean, Carmen, Play Memory)*, Kenneth-John Productions *(Zorba, Baby, The Rink)*, Arnold Bernhard *(Buffalo, Glengarry, Woza)* and the Roger L. Stevens-Robert Whitehead-Kennedy Center combination *(Noises Off, Death of a Salesman, End of the World)*. For the Lee Guber-Shelly Gross team *(Painting Churches, Shirley MacLaine)* and Roger Berlind *(Rink, Real Thing)* this can also be said to have been a good year. For the Elizabeth Taylor-Zev Bufman producing alliance it was time to call it quits after the close of their high-grossing *Private Lives* on the road and a short-lived revival of *The Corn Is Green*.

The director's chair left empty after the untimely death of Alan Schneider looks all the more poignant because he filled it with such conspicuous brilliance in this, his last season. He was the year's most active New York theater director with four programs of one-acters (the two by Samuel Beckett cited as a Best Play, one by Harold Pinter and one by a group of distinguished contemporary playwrights). Mike Nichols *(Real Thing)* and Gregory Mosher *(Glengarry)* shared 1983–84 straight-play-direction honors on Broadway, and certainly Michael Blake-

THE RINK—Chita Rivera *(above left)* and Liza Minnelli as mother and daughter in the Terrence McNally–John Kander–Fred Ebb musical. *On opposite page* is a sketch by Peter Larkin of his spectacular roller skating rink scene design for this show

more deserves special recognition for his direction of the snarled traffic of *Noises Off*. With the exception of Gerald Gutierrez *(Isn't It Romantic, Terra Nova)*, Allen R. Belknap *(The Killing of Sister George* and *The Flight of the Earls)*, Harold Prince *(Play Memory* and *End of the World)*, Elinor Renfield *(The Sea Gull, Open Admissions* and the Young Playwrights Festival) and Wilford Leach *(The Human Comedy, Non Pasquale)*, the directorial function was spread out like the production effort over a large number of one-time efforts on and off Broadway. Notable among these were, for musicals, Arthur Laurents *(La Cage)*, Peter Brook *(Carmen)*, Robert H. Livingston *(Taking My Turn)*, A.J. Antoon *(The Rink)* and James Lapine *(Sunday in the Park)*; and, for plays, Arvin Brown *(Buffalo)*, Raul Aranas *(Yellow Fever)*, John Madden *(Cinders)*, Terry Kinney *(Nightingale)* and Stephen Tobolowsky *(Miss Firecracker)*. Performers dabbling (but not often doubling) in direction included Robert Drivas, Donal Donnelly, Geoffrey Holder, Carroll O'Connor, Estelle Parsons, Phyllis Newman, John Lone, Lee Grant, Barbara Harris, John Malkovich and of course Christopher Martin with his CSC productions. Authors directing included Richard Maltby Jr., Maria Irene Fornes, John Bishop and Sam Shepard.

There have been seasons in which the director-choreographer (Tommy Tune, Jerome Robbins, the late Gower Champion, etc.) was king. Not so this season, in which only Ron Field *(Five-Six-Seven-Eight . . . Dance!* at the Music

Hall) and Tony Tanner (*Preppies* off Broadway) performed both functions with any mentionable degree of success. The season's most appealing choreography was provided by Scott Salmon *(La Cage)*, Graciela Daniele *(The Rink)* and Danny Daniels *(The Tap Dance Kid)*.

Like producers and directors, designers—133, count 'em, 133—were fruitfully occupied all over town, usually at the rate of one show per artist per season. Outstanding exceptions were William Ivey Long with five costume designs including *Play Memory* and *End of the World* and Judy Dearing with five. Ann Emonts *(Tap Dance Kid, Terra Nova)* did four, and so did Linda Fisher *(Painting Churches)*, Patricia McGourty *(Doonesbury)* and Jennifer Von Mayrhauser *(Baby, Miss Firecracker)*. Theoni V. Aldredge's memorable *La Cage* costumes were one of three assignments this season, as was Patricia Zipprodt's *Sunday in the Park* raiment (done in collaboration with Ann Hould-Ward). Others who did three shows were Jane Greenwood *(Heartbreak House)*, Ruth Morley *(Death of a Salesman)* and Rita Ryack *(The Human Comedy)*. Among other outstanding costuming this season was that of Nan Cibula *(Glengarry)*, Carla Kramer (the Beckett plays) and Lydia Tanji *(Sound and Beauty)*.

Standouts among the year's musical settings were *The Rink* (Peter Larkin, who also did *Doonesbury*), *Sunday in the Park* (Tony Straiges) and *Carmen* (Jean-Guy Lecat); and among straight plays, *Fen* (Annie Smart, who also did the costumes), *Noises Off* (Michael Annals, who also did the costumes) and *The Real Thing* (Tony Walton). The year's busiest scene designers and among the most accomplished were Marjorie Bradley Kellogg with four shows including *Buffalo* and *Heartbreak House*, David Jenkins (four including *Nightingale*), John Lee Beatty (four including *Baby* and *Miss Firecracker*), Clarke Dunham (three including *End of the World*), David Potts (three including *Full Hookup*), Heidi Landesman (three including *Painting Churches*), Loren Sherman (three including *The Harvesting*), Andrew Jackness (three including *Isn't It Romantic*) and Ray Recht (three including *The Babe*). Other notable sets were those for *The Tap Dance Kid* (Michael Hotopp and Paul dePass), *Yellow Fever* (Christopher Stapleton) and *Spookhouse* (Bill Stabile), a Maharam Award winner.

Happily, only a few among our cherished performers found themselves stranded in craft too frail for their talents this season. Such a fate befell Carroll O'Connor, Angela Lansbury (whose revived *Mame* proved less popular than in days of yore), Jack Lemmon, Cicely Tyson, Jack Klugman, Peggy Lee, Anthony Newley, Ann Reinking and Anne Meara. Others, however, shone like the stars they are or soon will be: Jeremy Irons as the confident playwright and suffering lover of *The Real Thing*. . . . George Hearn and Gene Barry basking in the warmth of *La Cage aux Folles* . . . Robert Prosky and Joe Mantegna portraying the life of a salesman in *Glengarry Glen Ross* . . . Liza Minnelli and Chita Rivera striving toward each other in *The Rink* . . . Samuel E. Wright holding his private fort and Hinton Battle besieging it in *The Tap Dance Kid* . . . Joan Allen shyly emerging from the British family ensemble of *And a Nightingale Sang* . . . Ben Kingsley as Kean, Anthony Quinn as Zorba, Al Pacino as Teach, a trio of forceful star turns . . . Bonnie Koloc and Rex Smith in the touching *The Human Comedy* . . . The *Cinders* ensemble, including Dori Hartley as a menacing Prince Charming . . . The *Fool for Love* duos (Kathy Baker and Ed Harris and their later replacements) bouncing each other off the walls in their star-crossed affair . . . George N. Martin and Marian Seldes, lovable eccentrics of *Painting Churches* . . . The reinterpretations of famous roles by Rex Harrison and Rosemary Harris *(Heartbreak House)*, Dustin Hoffman and John Malkovich *(Death of a Salesman)*, Jessica Tandy *(The Glass Menagerie)* and Kate Nelligan *(A Moon for the Misbegotten)* . . . Donald Li and later Mako impersonating a Humphrey Bogart-type private eye in *Yellow Fever* . . . Sandy Duncan stretching out and filling the vast Music Hall stage in *Five-Six-Seven-Eight* . . . *Dance!* . . . The solo creations of Billie Whitelaw *(Rockaby)*, Ian McKellen (excerpts from Shakespeare) and Estelle Parsons *(Orgasmo Adulto)* . . . Percy Mtwa and and Mbongeni Ngema in their satirical *Woza Albert!* . . . The whole zany ensemble of *Noises Off*, timing their frenzied non-stop action as precisely as the formations of a marching band . . . The handsome gestures of Bernadette Peters and the *Sunday in the Park With George* ensemble, and the Mississippi-accented antics of those in *The Miss Firecracker Contest* . . . These major character images of 1983–84 were vividly personified in a memorable group of performances.

The ultimate insignia of New York professional theater achievement (we insist) are the Best Plays citations in these volumes, 16 years older than the Critics Awards and only three years younger than the Pulitzer Prizes. Each Best Play selection is now made with the script itself as the first consideration, for the reason (as we've stated in previous volumes) that the script is the spirit of the theater's physical manifestation. It is not only the quintessence of the present, it is most of what endures into the future. So the Best Plays are the best scripts, with as little weight as humanly possible given to comparative production values. The choice is made without any regard whatever to a play's type—musical, comedy or drama—or origin on or off Broadway, or popularity at the box office, or lack of same.

We don't take the scripts of bygone eras into consideration for Best Play citation in this one, whatever their technical status as American or New York "premieres" which didn't happen to have a previous production of record. We draw the line between adaptations and revivals, the former eligible for Best Play selection but the latter not, on a case-by-case basis. We likewise consider the eligibility of borderline examples of limited-engagement and showcase production case by case, ascertaining whether they're probably "frozen" in final script version and no longer works-in-progress before considering them for Best Play citation (and in the case of a late-season arrival the determination may not be possible until the following year).

If a script influences the very character of a season, or by some function of consensus wins the Critics, Pulitzer or Tony Awards, we take into account its future historical as well as present esthetic importance. This is the only special consideration we give, and we don't always tilt in its direction, as the record shows.

The Best Plays of 1983–84 are listed here for visual convenience in the order in which they opened in New York (a plus sign + with the performance number signifies that the play was still running after May 31, 1984):

Fool for Love
(Off Broadway; 432+ perfs.)

Samuel Beckett One-Acts
(Off Broadway; 350 & 78 perfs.)

La Cage aux Folles
(Broadway; 327+ perfs.)

La Tragédie de Carmen
(Broadway; 187 perfs.)

Painting Churches
(Off Broadway; 206 perfs.)

And a Nightingale Sang . . .
(Off Broadway; 177 perfs.)

Noises Off
(Broadway; 199+ perfs.)

The Real Thing
(Broadway; 172+ perfs.)

Glengarry Glen Ross
(Broadway; 78+ perfs.)

The Miss Firecracker Contest
(Off Broadway; 35+ perfs.)

Sunday in the Park With George
(Broadway; 34+ perfs.)

Broadway

Sandy Duncan and the Rockettes tided Broadway over the summer with *Five-Six-Seven-Eight . . . Dance!*, a spectacular melange of musical and comedy numbers, Ron Field choreography and wide-stage showmanship at Radio City Music Hall. Before the end of August, however, more good musical news was being made with the arrival of *La Cage aux Folles*, based on the same Jean Poiret play about a homosexual couple and their Riviera night club as the popular French movie comedy. Harvey Fierstein, author of the long-running Best Play *Torch Song Trilogy*, wrote the book about the cabaret owner and his lover, the glamorous star of his floor show, who have raised a son (the result of a single heterosexual adventure in the cabaret owner's youth). The son, grown up, now wishes to marry the daughter of a notoriously prudish politician. The French-farcical possibilities of that situation were roundly realized in the script and in Arthur Laurents's direction, but as Fierstein remarked to someone while his show was in the crucible of preparation in its Boston tryout, "It's really about 'Honor thy father and mother.' " There is an undertow of feeling beneath the laughter in *La Cage* that tugs irresistably at the audience's sympathy for Georges (Gene Barry) and his drag-queen lover Albin (George Hearn in his Tony-winning performance), a respectable couple with the same sensibilities as any middle-aged married pair trying to adjust to their son's choice of a bride. Sexual identity was the running gag of this musical comedy, but it was family affection that was finally put to the test.

The embellishments were superb. Jerry Herman's score was loaded with shining take-home melodies ("Song on the Sand," "I Am What I Am," "Look Over There") and refreshingly singable, articulate lyrics. Theoni V. Aldredge's costumes were as outlandishly colorful as the drag chorus line they dressed. So was Scott Salmon's choreography featuring an athletic can-can performed by the mostly-male "Les Cagelles" dressed as female dancers. David Mitchell's sets were able to evoke St. Tropez, though most of them were home and night club interiors. Laurents's direction dominated the production with taste, style and wit, and the performances were impeccable—Barry's in a conspicuously masculine key of self-respect, Hearn's in that of proud effeminacy. Even in a busy year for musicals, *La Cage* stood far out as musical theater entertainment.

At the other end of the season, Stephen Sondheim ventured once more into musical *terra incognita,* this time in company with James Lapine, and they returned to place marvels on display in their *Sunday in the Park With George.* "George" is the painter Georges Seurat; the "park" is described in a Sondheim lyric as "a small suburban park" on an island in the Seine, the island named in Seurat's impressionist masterpiece "A Sunday Afternoon on the Island of La Grande Jatte." Strollers, fisher folk, picnickers, lovers, even the dogs in that painting are characterized and set in motion by Lapine's book and direction and Sondheim's music and lyrics. The painter himself (played by Mandy Patinkin) is seen as an artist so obsessed by his vision of a new approach to color and composition that he can't even look up from his drawing pad to see his newborn daughter by his mistress "Dot" (Bernadette Peters). His painting gradually comes together, though, and it is beautifully consummated in Act I, even as the lovers are being pulled apart. But their great grandson, the *raison d'etre* of Act II, is also an artist exploring new ground with light itself (the laser beam). He is helped to find his way by the example of his ancestor.

A *Sunday in the Park* program note stated that all the characters were "products of the authors' imagination," though "suggested" by the life of Georges Seurat. This musical was a show of many parts: Sondheim's pointillist arpeggios timed to the tip of Seurat's dotting paint brush, the notes then coming together in the ear of the audience (like Seurat's solid-color dots blending into subtle shades on the retina of the beholder) in aria-like harmonies for the singers, soaring mightily in the act finales entitled "Sunday"; the endless versatility of Sondheim's dynamic lyrics, expressing the highest aims of the artist or amusing themselves and the audience by imitating the yapping of a small dog; Lapine's staccato book, making up somewhat in variety for what it lacked in dramatic tension, and his staging of the stylized movements, gestures and poses of the bustle era; the Tony Straiges scenery with its clever use of cutouts; the Seurat-colored costumes by Patricia Zipprodt and Ann Hould-Ward; the spectacular laser effect in Act II by Bran Ferren; and of course the performances by and around Miss Peters, a three-dimensional presence within this musical tribute to two-dimensional art. Each of these contributions to *Sunday in the Park* was a remarkable example of its kind. They combined in the form and perspective of the musical stage in an effect even more remarkable than the sum of its parts, a Best Play and the Critics Award winner as best musical.

Another original and compelling musical theater concept was *La Tragédie de Carmen* as reshaped by Peter Brook, as though he had not already given us more than enough to think about with his *Marat/Sade* and his unique *A Midsummer Night's Dream.* His *Carmen* was very different from the opera, though in it Brook retained a goodly share of Bizet. It was a "written" work, so to speak, though not exactly in the words of the French libretto (translated into an English version by Sheldon Harnick during its New York run). Brook "writes" in stagecraft, a medium of expression and dramatization of which he is a master. To say that he "directed" this *Carmen* wouldn't adequately define his creative function.

THE TAP DANCE KID—In the title role of this musical, Alfonso Ribeiro demonstrates his dancing prowess for Hinton Battle and the chorus *(above)*. The boy's disapproving father is portrayed by Samuel E. Wright *(left)*

With the art of stagecraft, Brook "rewrote" *A Midsummer Night's Dream* without much altering Shakespeare's words, and he has similarly "rewritten" *Carmen*, realizing the drama in a magical series of stage images (carried out in Jean-Guy Lecat's design) and including highlights from Bizet's haunting score. Our view of this *Carmen*, however, is unsupported by any intimate knowledge of the opera medium, so that we have asked Douglas Watt, drama critic of the New York *Daily News* and a frequent contributor of music criticism to that and other publications, to describe and evaluate Peter Brook's new conception of *Carmen* in these pages. We are honored by its inclusion and direct the reader's attention to it in this volume's Best Plays section, where *La Tragédie de Carmen* receives a special citation.

A remarkable book by Charles Blackwell was in large measure responsible for the success of *The Tap Dance Kid*, which was not at first received with unbridled enthusiasm. By season's end, however, it was managing to make a run of it in the vasty Minskoff Theater. This musical richly deserved and finally found an audience for its family drama of a black lawyer (Samuel E. Wright, taut as a tuned violin string) who has struggled desperately to pull his family up into the middle class, only to find his sub-teen-age son reverting to stereotype, possessed with ambition to become a dancer like his uncle (Hinton Battle) and maternal grandfather. The emotional structure, as family members lined up one by one on the side of the child against his formidable father, was strong enough to carry a straight play, directed by Vivian Matalon for all it was worth in intensity.

The score was a fuller participant in two other appealing musicals, *The Rink* and *Baby*. In the former, John Kander and Fred Ebb provided an emotionalized group of songs to be sung by Liza Minnelli as a prodigal daughter and Chita Rivera as her skeptical mother, belting their animosities and affections out to each other. A spectacular Peter Larkin set depicting a run-down roller-skating rink next to the roller coaster at an Eastern amusement park was a metaphor for the drama of a deteriorated mother-daughter relationship moving painfully toward crisis in the book by Terrence McNally. Likewise, the David Shire-Richard Maltby Jr. score of *Baby* was a prime attraction of this musical celebration of childbirth in a book by Sybille Pearson dividing its attention among three college-town couples: a pair of undergraduate posslq's who face imminent parentage with chin up and thumbs down on marriage; a middle-aged faculty pair who, following an evening of too-careless rapture, find themselves becoming parents *again* just as they are breathing a sigh of relief that their children are grown and fled and they can settle down to easeful retirement; and an athletic pair trying so hard to have a baby (and failing) that they're willing to suffer the indignities of a clinical approach to their problem. Joy and wonder abounded onstage in *Baby*, both in the performances of the ensemble under Maltby's direction and in the matching score.

Even more of a *tour de force* of music was *The Human Comedy*, with William Saroyan's novel about a California family of the 1940s set hauntingly to music by Galt MacDermot. In a libretto (truly a libretto, all singing, no dialogue) by William Dumaresq, Bonnie Koloc dominated her scenes as a widow who never quits trying to keep her family going, even after she loses her oldest son to World War II. A large cast of neighbors served as a Greek chorus for the individuals

BEETHOVEN'S TENTH—George Rose and Peter Ustinov in the play
written by the latter and imported from the London stage

who stepped forward out of concert-style groupings to play their parts under
Wilford Leach's direction, which harmonized the performances, the sentimental-
ity of the score and the episodes of family life and death into a unified paean to
the faith and endurance of small-town America. *The Human Comedy* originated
off Broadway at New York Shakespeare Festival, where it was conspicuously
popular. It didn't find much of an audience in transfer to Broadway but seems
certain to be headed for future success elsewhere.

We also suspect that *Doonesbury*, with Garry Trudeau's famous cartoon characters doing their socially satirical thing in book and lyrics by Trudeau himself
and score by Elizabeth Swados, will have another life. The season's agenda also
included two other large-scale musicals: *Marilyn*, musicalizing Marilyn
Monroe's life, with Alyson Reed in the title role, and *Amen Corner*, the Philip
Rose-Peter Udell-Garry Sherman musical version of James Baldwin's play about
the lady pastor of a Harlem storefront church.

The number of new straight plays presented on Broadway this year was patheti-
cally and historically small, but among them were scripts of the first quality. Tom
Stoppard's *The Real Thing*, for example, the Critics Award best-of-bests winner,
glittered in language like his *Travesties* and sometimes shivered in despair like his
Rosencrantz and Guildenstern Are Dead. The play explored the ways of sexual
infidelity under the direction of Mike Nichols and as performed by Jeremy Irons as
a playwright who knows very well how a flippant husband-wife scene should be
written for the stage, but not how to make a game out of the agonies of "the real
thing" when his own beloved goes astray. Tony Walton's set accommodated this
play comfortably, even though it moved around a lot in space and time. The play
in turn challenged its audience with wit and moved it to pity and dismay.

Another British Best Play, Michael Frayn's *Noises Off*, was a masterpiece of

The 1983–84 Season on Broadway

PLAYS (8)

The Guys in the Truck
Brothers
Open Admissions
GLENGARRY GLEN ROSS
The Golden Age
Play Memory
A Woman of Independent Means
End of the World

MUSICALS (10)

LA CAGE AUX FOLLES
Amen Corner
LA TRAGEDIE DE CARMEN
Marilyn
Doonesbury
Baby
The Tap Dance Kid
The Rink
The Human Comedy (transfer)
SUNDAY IN THE PARK WITH GEORGE

FOREIGN PLAYS IN ENGLISH (4)

Edmund Kean
NOISES OFF
THE REAL THING
Beethoven's Tenth

REVUE (1)

Five-Six-Seven-Eight . . . . Dance!

REVIVALS (11)

Mame
The Corn Is Green
Zorba
American Buffalo
The Glass Menagerie
Circle in the Square:
  Heartbreak House
  Awake and Sing!
Death of a Salesman
Oliver!
A Moon for the Misbegotten
The Wiz

SPECIALTIES (4)

Peg
Ian McKellen Acting Shakespeare
Shirley MacLaine on Broadway
The Babe

HOLDOVERS WHICH BECAME HITS IN 1983–84

Brighton Beach Memoirs
Cats
My One and Only
Torch Song Trilogy

Categorized above are all the new productions listed in the Plays Produced on Broadway section of this volume.
Plays listed in CAPITAL LETTERS have been designated Best Plays of 1983–84.
Plays listed in *italics* were still running after May 31, 1984.
Plays listed in **bold face type** were classified as successes in *Variety's* annual estimate published June 6, 1984.

Here are examples of Theoni V. Aldredge's costume design sketches for the musical *La Cage aux Folles*. The completed costumes can be glimpsed in photos of the show's scenes in the Best Plays section

its farcical genre, masterfully directed by Michael Blakemore and played by a team of thespian athletes who must have broken the all-time record for exits and entrances within the limit of three acts. The play depicted the antics on and offstage of the members of a touring troupe performing a kinetic farce in a country-house setting with eight doors and a window; and, simultaneously, hammering at each other backstage in a tangle of jealous personal rages. The Michael Annals sets and costumes were marvels of engineering to fit this cleverly engineered script's special needs of comings and goings, of wrapping-on and ripping-off of clothing. The play-within-the-play being "performed" by these "actors" was also a farce, about trysts in a supposedly empty house. Its first act was seen being "rehearsed" in Act I of *Noises Off*, "played" in Act II but observed from the "actors'" point of view behind the scenes, and then "played" again in Act III (and become an absolute shambles of missed cues and careless improvisations) again from the audience's point of frontal view, all the while amusing itself with the slings, arrows and egos of the backstage personnel. Playing together with the precise timing of a baseball infield, and with as much physical energy, the ensemble led by Dorothy Loudon, Paxton Whitehead and Brian Murray were champions at their hilarious game.

Another import from the London stage, Raymund Fitzsimons's *Edmund Kean*, was a showcase for a Ben Kingsley performance of that gifted, harried 19th century tragedian in the great Shakespearean roles. Though this was a one-man

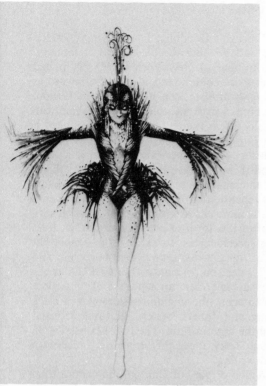 

performance alternating excerpts from the plays and from Kean's life, it was billed as a "play," and certainly Kingsley made it seem so, filling the stage with his characterization. And Shakespearean roles also came under scrutiny in the portrayals and comments by Ian McKellen in his one-man show *Ian McKellen Acting Shakespeare*, also imported. Finally, Peter Ustinov's comedy *Beethoven's Tenth*, starring the author as the composer come back to earth to advise and succor a music critic played by George Rose, could not repeat on Broadway the popular success it had enjoyed on the London stage before its appearance here.

An American playscript arriving—triumphantly—on Broadway by way of London was David Mamet's stinging *Glengarry Glen Ross*, a life-of-a-salesman comedy of real estate hustlers conniving their way through another day. When Mamet considered his completed script, he feared that its halves might be somewhat mismatched in style (Act I is a series of three two-man conversations in a Chinese restaurant, Act II sends the balloon up in the real estate office with the whole cast), and he took this problem to his friend Harold Pinter who read it, decided the only thing wrong with it was that it hadn't yet been produced and handed it to Peter Hall of the National Theater who promptly produced it. This wasn't a case, therefore, of an American play turned down by American producers until it was put on in London (which has happened). *Glengarry Glen Ross* won the best-play award of the Society of West End Theaters and was still running in London when it opened in Chicago and New York.

Mamet is a resident playwright of Chicago's Goodman Theater whose artistic director, Gregory Mosher, produced and directed the play there in January. When this Chicago production was brought to New York in March, it had already been seen by the 1984 Pulitzer Prize committee and won that award as a regional theater offering, just as *'night, Mother* won it last year in Boston. Mamet's play, cited by the New York Drama Critics Circle as the best American play of the season, was as broad-shouldered as the city which first produced it in America. As in Mamet's *American Buffalo*, its language is a painfully perfect expression of lower middle class characters who are more shrewd than articulate, ambitious beyond their education, and therefore have learned to express themselves by imaginative inflections and combinations of the few words they know and trust. For example, their copious repetition of four-letter obscenities shades every other word and phrase with a little more or less meaning that its dictionary definition. Mamet has made the most of this form of communication, as John O'Hara did with upper middle class speech forms, to express the simple but ferocious intentions of an ensemble of hungry real estate salesman vying and cheating each other for hot leads in a sales competition with a Cadillac as the prize. Mosher's direction made a frontal assault on the audience's cool, in particular with the performances of Joe Mantegna, the champion salesman, a sleek go-getter with an answer for everything, and Robert Prosky, old, tired, wily and trying desperately to keep his hold on the bottom rung. The play's construction *is* a bit uneven, but there was nothing shaky about this immensely successful collaboration of acting, directing and writing.

It's worth adding that it wasn't London origin but Chicago momentum that helped define the 1983–84 theater season in New York. This was a Chicago year in Manhattan, with *Glengarry Glen Ross* at the head of a parade of Chicago-originated productions and personalities including another Best Play (*And a Nightingale Sang . . .*, with Joan Allen in the season's outstanding performance by an actress); the first fully professional production of Lanford Wilson's 1965 off-off-Broadway play *Balm in Gilead*, brought to Circle Rep by Chicago's Steppenwolf Ensemble; the Second City troupe in their revue *Orwell That Ends Well*; and a number of other performers from Chicago in casts all over town.

It was a long time between the appearances of the few other new American playscripts making it to Broadway this season, and short shrift for all of them once they arrived. Shirley Lauro's *Open Admissions* dramatized the shortcomings of the well-intentioned policy of extending the opportunity of higher education to all comers, whether or not the system is equipped to deal with them or the student is qualified to profit from the experience. This candid and timely script, previously produced successfully OOB and in regional theater, survived only 17 performances on Broadway. A new A.R. Gurney Jr. play, *The Golden Age*, suggested by Henry James's *The Aspern Papers*, with Irene Worth as an elderly dowager in possession of a valuable manuscript coveted by a young scholar (Jeff Daniels), lasted for only 29. Arthur Kopit's *End of the World* (one of two straight plays staged by Harold Prince this season) confronted the menace of nuclear holocaust in a whimsical context but at a length too great for its breadth, though it had the advantage of performances by Barnard Hughes as a mystery millionaire commissioning a play to arouse the public to its danger, John Shea as the play-

BABY—Liz Callaway, Catherine Cox and Beth Fowler in a scene from the Sybille Pearson–David Shire–Richard Maltby Jr. musical

wright who accepts this challenge and Linda Hunt as his tiny but formidable agent, an affectionate caricature of Audrey Wood. Miss Hunt was nominated for a best-supporting-performance Tony, an accolade which carried this May production no farther than the ides of June. The other play staged by Harold Prince was Joanna M. Glass's *Play Memory*, scenes of family decline and disintegration, nominated for a best-play Tony even after it had departed after less than a week's run. Applause was muted, however, at the other short-lived American entries: *The Guys in the Truck*, about sports broadcasting; *Brothers*, with Carroll O'Connor as a tough union leader dominating his offspring (it opened and closed in only one performance); and *A Woman of Independent Means*, a one-performer play with Barbara Rush as a Texas matriarch of this century reviewing the events of her life.

Among the specialties, *Shirley MacLaine on Broadway* drew cheers late in the season with this year's Academy Award-winning star in a personalized, solo (with backup dancers) song-and-dance show. Earlier in the season, Peggy Lee's solo performance recalling events from her life and reprising songs from her glittering career, *Peg*, found no such support and closed after a brief run. Likewise, an attempt to memorialize Babe Ruth with a one-character play about his life and career, *The Babe*, with Max Gail playing the 1920s Sultan of Swat, couldn't draw his fans to 1984 Broadway in any significant numbers.

Here's where we list the *Best Plays* choices for the outstanding individual achievements of the season in New York, on and off Broadway. In the acting categories, clear distinction among "starring," "featured" or "supporting" players can't be made on the basis of official billing, which is as much a matter of contracts as of esthetics. Here in these volumes we divide acting into "primary" and "secondary" roles, a primary role being one which might some day cause a star to inspire a revival in order to appear in that character. All others, be they vivid as Mercutio, are classed as secondary. Furthermore, our list of individual bests makes room for more than a single choice when appropriate. We believe that no useful purpose is served by forcing ourselves into an arbitrary selection of a single best when we come upon multiple examples of equal quality (we couldn't imagine choosing this year between Stephen Sondheim and Jerry Herman, or Liza Minnelli and Chita Rivera, or why anyone would want to do so). We include them all in our list.

Here, then, are the *Best Plays* bests of 1983–84:

PLAYS

BEST PLAY: *The Real Thing* by Tom Stoppard

BEST AMERICAN PLAY: *Glengarry Glen Ross* by David Mamet

BEST REVIVAL: *Balm in Gilead* by Lanford Wilson, directed by John Malkovich

BEST ACTOR IN A PRIMARY ROLE: Jeremy Irons as Henry in *The Real Thing*

BEST ACTRESS IN A PRIMARY ROLE: Joan Allen as Helen Stott in *And a Nightingale Sang . . .*

BEST ACTOR IN A SECONDARY ROLE: Joe Mantegna as Richard Roma and Robert Prosky as Shelly Levene in *Glengarry Glen Ross*; special citation to the ensemble of *Noises Off*

BEST ACTRESS IN A SECONDARY ROLE: Linda Hunt as Audrey Wood in *End of the World*

BEST DIRECTOR: Gregory Mosher for *Glengarry Glen Ross*; Mike Nichols for *The Real Thing*; Alan Schneider for six Samuel Beckett one-acts

BEST SCENERY: Michael Annals for *Noises Off*; Annie Smart for *Fen*

BEST COSTUMES: Jane Greenwood for *Heartbreak House*

MUSICALS

BEST MUSICAL: *La Cage aux Folles*

BEST BOOK: Charles Blackwell for *The Tap Dance Kid*

BEST MUSIC AND LYRICS: Jerry Herman for *La Cage aux Folles*; Stephen Sondheim for *Sunday in the Park With George*

BEST REVIVAL: *Zorba* by Joseph Stein, John Kander and Fred Ebb, directed by Michael Cacoyannis

BEST ACTOR IN A PRIMARY ROLE: George Hearn as Albin in *La Cage aux Folles*

BEST ACTRESS IN A PRIMARY ROLE: Liza Minnelli as Angel and Chita Rivera as Anna in *The Rink*

BEST ACTOR IN A SECONDARY ROLE: Samuel E. Wright as William in *The Tap Dance Kid*

BEST ACTRESS IN A SECONDARY ROLE: Bonnie Koloc as Mrs. Kate Macauley in *The Human Comedy*

BEST DIRECTOR: Peter Brook for *La Tragédie de Carmen*

BEST CHOREOGRAPHER: Scott Salmon for *La Cage aux Folles*

BEST SCENERY: Peter Larkin for *The Rink*; Tony Straiges for *Sunday in the Park With George*

BEST COSTUMES: Theoni V. Aldredge for *La Cage aux Folles*

Off Broadway

Musicals also burgeoned off Broadway this season, their production total nearly doubling from 7 a year ago to 13, and in revue form growing from 5 to 7. There was some erosion in the total of straight-play production, but considering the shrinkage taking place uptown, off Broadway made an admirable showing in 1983-84 (see the one-page summary of the off-Broadway season accompanying this report). There were 57 new plays and musicals (including one extended engagement, one transfer and one revised version) produced off Broadway in 1983-84, as compared with 59 in 1982-83 and 58 in 1981-82. This season's contingent comprised 32 American straight-play programs, the 13 abovementioned musicals and 12 foreign plays as compared with the 39-7-13, 45-9-7, 33-14-8 and 39-7-12 in the past four seasons and the peak 38-15-12 of 1979. In addition to this year's 57, there were the 7 revues, plus 35 revivals and 11 specialties, making a grand total of 110 programs presented off Broadway during the past twelve months.

The inner strength of the 1983-84 off-Broadway season was also admirable, providing five Best Play citations, three American scripts and two foreign. And we must take pains to explain what we mean by "off Broadway," because its border lines are blurring at both the Broadway and off-off-Broadway ends. Most other publications apply the term loosely, sometimes to plays that are clearly OOB (weekend or Wednesday-to-Saturday performances only, reduced ticket prices, Equity concessions). We can't draw indelible lines, but we try to distinguish between professional and experimental theater; between what is probably a work-in-progress which may evolve as it rises to a higher level of commitment, and what is probably a "frozen" script facing the world for better or for worse as a finished work in production or publication. Only the latter is regularly considered for Best Play designation, for obvious reasons. Full off-Broadway plays and musicals are thus eligible for Best Play designation on the same terms as those classified under the Broadway heading, whereas works-in-progress are not.

By the lights of these *Best Plays* volumes, then, an off-Broadway production is one a) with an Equity cast b) giving 8 performances a week c) in an off-Broadway theater d) after inviting public comment by reviewers. And to the best of our information, an "off-Broadway theater" is a house eligible to operate under the off-Broadway contract because it is of a specific size in a specific area, i.e.: seating 499 or fewer and situated in Manhattan *outside* the area bounded by Fifth and Ninth Avenues between 34th and 56th Streets, and by Fifth Avenue and the Hudson River between 56th and 72d Streets.

Obviously, we make exceptions to each of these rules; no dimension of "off" or "off off" can be applied exactly. In each *Best Plays* volume we stretch somewhat in the direction of inclusion—never of exclusion. The point is, "off Broadway" isn't an exact location either geographically or esthetically, it's a state of the art, a level of expertise and professional commitment. In these volumes we'll continue to categorize it, however, as accurately as we can, as long as it seems useful for the record, while reminding those who read these lines that distinctions

FOREIGN PLAYS AT N.Y. SHAKESPEARE—Among this season's productions at Joseph Papp's headquarters were a restaging of Caryl Churchill's British play *Fen* with an American cast including *(above)* Pamela Reed, Linda Griffiths, Concetta Tomei and Robin Bartlett in Annie Smart's potato-field setting; and Janusz Glowacki's Polish play in translation, *Cinders*, with *(below)* Christopher Walken as a TV reporter, Robin Gammell as a commissar and Lucinda Jenney as a reform-school inmate

are no longer as clear as they once were—and elsewhere in this volume we offer the most comprehensive list of 1983–84 OOB productions anywhere, compiled by Camille Croce, plus a review of the OOB season by Mel Gussow.

Not a New York season in the 1970s and 1980s has gone by without something from Samuel Beckett—a revival of *Waiting for Godot* here, a new one-acter or an excerpt of a program of collected highlights there. This season we were treated to six new-to-New-York Beckett one-acters on two separate programs directed by the late Alan Schneider, an incomparable interpreter of Beckett's work, who met an untimely death in a London street accident this spring. This tragic event removed much of our pleasure but doubled our resolve, taken before the accident, to cite Beckett as a 1983–84 Best Play author. This we do with profound admiration for the work and profound regret that it is the last to be staged by Mr. Schneider.

In making this citation, we don't single out the first program of one-acters offered in June 1983 under the title *Samuel Beckett's Ohio Impromptu, Catastrophe, What Where*, nor the second one in February under the title of *Rockaby*, comprising *Enough, Footfalls* and the title play, and presenting Billie Whitelaw from the London stage in three aspects of womanhood. Each of these six works encompassed infinite riches of Beckett insight and imagery in the most compact and sparsely furnished room he could devise for his purposes, which ranged from an object lesson in tyrannous government to the last gasps of a dying crone. The latter is the subject of *Rockaby*, which we present in its entirety in the Best Plays section of this volume as a prime example of Beckett's playwriting brilliance, while repeating that it is the whole collection of his six Schneider-directed presentations that we salute with this 1983–84 Best Play citation.

Another off-Broadway Best Play from abroad was *And a Nightingale Sang . . .*, an affectionate study of a British family during World War II, written by the late C.P. Taylor whose *Good* was one of last season's Best Plays. This family is in no way heroic, nor does it cringe from events: Dad is an air raid warden, Mom places her trust in her church, Grandpa accepts his transient status of being shuttled between the households of his children, and younger daughter is a sweetheart of the armed forces. But it was the luminous performance of Joan Allen as the plain-Jane older daughter that lit the corners of this play with a growing brightness as the character gradually responds to the opportunity of romance offered by a soldier (Peter Friedman) stationed nearby. In her ugly duckling phase there is no hint of the swan to come, nor much of the duckling finally left at the end of the play, in a performance which seemed uncannily effortless and yet solidly true. Miss Allen came on from Chicago, where *And a Nightingale Sang . . .* had previously been produced, to provide New York with the year's best performance by an actress in one of its Best Plays.

The translation of a Polish play, *Cinders* (previously produced in London) by Janusz Glowacki, was a major achievement of Joseph Papp's New York Shakespeare Festival season. The play is set in a Polish reform school for girls, some of whom are staging their version of the Cinderella tale while a government deputy and TV crew eavesdrop on their project. All the TV reporter (Christopher Walken) cares about is getting a sensational story, and all the deputy (Robin Gammell) cares about is political obeisance, and neither cares much what he has

The 1983–84 Season Off Broadway

PLAYS (32)

Circle Rep:
FOOL FOR LOVE (extended run)
Full Hookup
Levitation
The Harvesting
American Place:
Great Days
The Danube
Terra Nova
Yellow Fever
A Weekend Near Madison
Basement Tapes
A Little Madness
Public Theater:
Sound and Beauty
Young Playwrights
Playwrights Horizons:
Baby With the Bathwater
Isn't It Romantic
Fables for Friends
PAINTING CHURCHES
Negro Ensemble:
Puppetplay
American Dreams
The Lady and the Clarinet
Manhattan Theater Club:
Friends
THE MISS FIRECRACKER CONTEST

Living Theater:
The Archeology of Sleep
The Yellow Methuselah
Street Theater
To Gillian on Her 37th Birthday
The Flight of the Earls
The Actors' Delicatessen
A Hell of a Town
The Vampires
'night, Mother (transfer)
Spookhouse

REVUES (7)

Serious Bizness
Sunset
Leftovers
One More Song/One More Dance
Babalooney
A . . . My Name Is Alice
Orwell That Ends Well

MUSICALS (13)

Taking My Turn
Non Pasquale
Public Theater:
Lenny and the Heartbreakers
The Human Comedy
American Passion
Dogs
The Brooklyn Bridge
Preppies
Blue Plate Special
Weekend
Tallulah
Love
Nite Club Confidential

REVIVALS (35)

LOOM:
Rose Marie (extended run)
(12 operettas in running repertory)
Roundabout
Ah, Wilderness!
The Knack
The Master Builder
The Killing of Sister George
Old Times
On Approval
King Richard III
Fen
The Philanthropist
CSC:
Hamlet
Dance of Death
Circle Rep:
The Sea Gull
Balm in Gilead
Mirror Theater:
Paradise Lost
Inheritors
Rain
Ghosts
The Hasty Heart

Living Theater
The Antigone of Sophokles
The One and the Many
Pieces of Eight
The Shadow of a Gunman

FOREIGN PLAYS IN ENGLISH (12)

Greek
BECKETT ONE-ACTS
Manhattan Theater Club:
Mensch Meier
Other Places
Big Maggie
Big and Little
Public Theater:
A Private View
Cinders
AND A NIGHTINGALE SANG . . .
ROCKABY
Woza Albert!
Dracula

SPECIALTIES (11)

Public Theater:
Goodnight Ladies!
Orgasmo Adulto Escapes From the Zoo
My Uncle Sam
An Evening With Quentin Crisp
Fun House
American Place:
The Vi-Ton-Ka Medicine Show
Do Lord Remember Me (return engagement)
Secret Honor
Dinah! Queen of the Blues
Nostalgic for the Future
Hey, Ma . . . Kaye Ballard

Categorized above are all the productions listed in the Plays Produced Off Broadway section of this volume. Plays listed in CAPITAL LETTERS have been designated Best Plays of 1983–84. Plays listed in *italics* were still running off Broadway after May 31, 1984.

to do to get it. The principal (George Guidall) is sensitive to the needs of of the girls in his charge; but in the end this doesn't do any of them much good, neither victimized Cinderella (Lucinda Jenney) nor the Prince (Dori Hartley), a survivor and reform-school ringleader. Under John Madden's direction the play developed a momentum that brought it very close to the inner circle of the Best Plays list.

Another important element of the New York Shakespeare Festival season was a group of three Czechoslovakian one-acters by Vaclav Havel offered in translation. The title, *A Private View*, suggested that these autobiographical sketches were written to be played in private homes because they were banned from public view in an authoritarian society which had once jailed their author for human rights activities and which was the butt of the injustices and failings portrayed and protested in these plays. The Papp organization also revived Caryl Churchill's *Fen*, an episodic drama of English farmers being dispossessed by big-capital conglomerates, with a marvelous set by Annie Smart featuring rows and rows of richly fertile potato-field soil pointing out at the audience like accusing fingers.

Manhattan Theater Club found room in its full season for two productions of new foreign works: *Other Places*, three Harold Pinter one-acts directed by the late Alan Schneider, and *Mensch Meier*, the translation of a German play by Franz Xaver Kroetz depicting workers on the West side of the wall as blue-collar slaves (Kroetz had three plays produced in New York this year, the two others OOB). MTC also presented a revival of a British script, Christopher Hampton's 1971 Best Play *The Philanthropist*.

The humor and skill of the performers, Percy Mtwa and Mbongeni Ngema (who had also helped develop the material), in the independently-produced *Woza Albert!* didn't lessen the impact of their two-man show's statements about the injustices, absurdities and cruelties of apartheid in their South African homeland. CSC (formerly Classic, now City Stage Company) mounted a Christopher Martin translation from the German of Botho Strauss's 1978 comment on modern society under the title of *Big and Little/scenes*. Other importations of this off-Broadway season were a British re-working of the Oedipus tragedy, *Greek* by Steven Berkoff; an Irish play about a resourceful widow, *Big Maggie* by John B. Keane; and a British version of the Dracula tale facetiously entitled *Dracula, or A Pain in the Neck*.

Among the best of the American scripts off Broadway was Tina Howe's *Painting Churches*, stepping up from a prizewinning off-off-Broadway production the season before at Second Stage, whose Carole Rothman also directed this version. The play's subject wasn't architectural refurbishment, as the title might imply, but the Church family of Boston: father (George N. Martin), a famous poet, lovable but on the edge of senility and becoming a problem; mother (Marian Seldes), bravely, competently and wittily making the best of increasingly difficult circumstances; and daughter (Elizabeth McGovern), a successful artist who has come home to help her parents in their hour of need and, incidentally, to paint their portrait. The father's decline and the daughter's memories of how hard it was to get started in her career were played in counterpoint on the sensitive instrument of the mother, in Tina Howe's first Best Play.

TAKING MY TURN—Tiger Haynes, Margaret Whiting, Marni Nixon, Cissy Houston and Mace Barrett in the musical by Robert H. Livingston, Gary William Friedman and Will Holt

"Abrasively comic" and "more of a collision than an embrace," we noted of Sam Shepard's *Fool for Love* in the 1982–83 Best Plays volume. In further consideration of this 1984 Obie Award-winner and 1983–84 Best Play, we find ourselves going back to those phrases to describe this kinetic script, in which a half-brother and half-sister practise emotional and physical violence on one another, as though punishing each other for their incestuous but irresistible love. They are hopelessly locked in a lifelong affair that began at first sight, before they knew they were related, and cannot be severed even by this knowledge. Their father observes and comments from the sidelines like a disembodied spirit, and an outsider intrudes on the lovers in a final scene that emphasizes both the black-comic and the passionate aspects of their relationship. Shepard directed his own script with total perception of its powerful content, while the cast served him boldly throughout the bruising action. Shepard is one of his generation's most prolific and successful American playwrights (his *Buried Child* won the Pulitzer Prize and his *True West* ran off Broadway for more than a year). *Fool for Love*, his first Best Play, is the equal in impact and the superior in style and depth of vision of any of his other work that we have seen.

Circle Rep brought the Shepard play to New York in the Magic Theater of San

VISITORS FROM CHICAGO—Mike Hagerty *(kneeling)* and Isabella Hofmann, Richard Kind, Rick Thomas, John Kapelos and Meagen Fay in the comedy revue *Orwell That Ends Well*

Francisco (where it originated) production, in what was to be a limited engagement; but, as the play gathered momentum, it was upped in status to an open-ended off-Broadway run, with the show moved to Theater Row uptown, to make room for the new season at the downtown facility. When Circle Rep resumed play-producing in November, it presented new American scripts in a revival sandwich. Warming up with a Jean-Claude van Itallie translation of Chekhov, the group proceeded to *Full Hookup* by Conrad Bishop and Elizabeth Fuller, another drama of violence between the sexes; *Levitation* by Timothy Mason, in which an aspiring playwright tries to heal his wounds in a homecoming visit to the Midwest; and *The Harvesting*, a detective drama written and directed by John Bishop. Circle Rep then put the finishing touches on its 1983–84 season with an important revival of Lanford Wilson's 1965 comedy *Balm in Gilead*, of which more in the next chapter of this report.

Beth Henley's *The Miss Firecracker Contest*, a comedy about very un-average small-town Mississippi folk, was one of only two American scripts to make it to opening night at Manhattan Theater Club this season, but it was a Best Play and a triumph of teamwork of authorship and production in MTC's small UpStage space. Like it's author's previous Best Play *Crimes of the Heart*, this one boldly silhouetted with eccentricities the kind of Southern characters Miss Henley either knows so well or invents so vividly: a competent, attractive young woman come home to take refuge and seemingly able to manage everything but her own life (an almost exact equivalent of one of the *Crimes of the Heart* sisters); a wild young female spirit trying to break loose and make her mark in a local beauty contest, paying a price at every turn (another close equivalent); the young man of the family who, judging from his aimless past, ought to be a wimp, but isn't; a family friend (in an outstanding performance by Belita Moreno) whose honesty is a delight as she plays the unpromising cards life dealt her and, suprisingly, wins almost every hand. With the help of Stephen Tobolowsky's hyperactive direction, Miss Henley stirs these people up with a small-town beauty contest. They are irresistibly—but not consistently—charming, and there are real horrors lurking at the edges of their lives. Miss Henley put a backspin on these follies that made them all the more entertaining, from an opening blast of super-patriotism to a curtain line that tops the comedy. The other American play offered by MTC was Lee Kalcheim's *Friends*, a reunion of two college pals in midlife crisis.

The good times in American playwriting off Broadway in 1983–84 didn't end where it was necessary to draw the line on Best Plays selections. R.A. Shiomi's *Yellow Fever* delightfully converted Humphrey Bogart-type private-eye cliches for a cast of orientals in a Vancouver setting, with Donald Li and later Mako turning up the collar of the trenchcoat in the leading role. A more poetic approach and style was successfully taken by David Henry Hwang in two one-acters with Japanese locales and characters directed by John Lone. The first, *The House of Sleeping Beauties*, introduced an aging novelist into a strange brothel where the girls are maintained in a state of drugged insensibility—an effort, a program note states, to create a fantasy around the suicide of the Japanese writer Yasunari Kawabata. The second play, *The Sound of a Voice*, featured Lone himself as a Samurai in a fateful love affair with a bewitched creature of the forest. This program of outstanding one-acters by an outstanding playwright, offered under the title *Sound and Beauty*, was the only new American straight play produced this season at Joseph Papp's Public Theater complex, other than the special Young Playwrights Festival of one-acters by teen-agers selected in the Foundation of the Dramatists Guild's third annual contest encouraging young people to write scripts.

Playwrights Horizons, on the other hand, expended all its energies in the American-play category. This Andre Bishop-Paul Daniels group's schedule included a new Christopher Durang comedy, *Baby With the Bathwater*, slashing at the immediate and long-term results of parental incompetence; and Mark O'Donnell's *Fables for Friends*, an assemblage of nine comedy sketches of friendship. A revised version of Wendy Wasserstein's comedy *Isn't It Romantic*, with

Cristine Rose as a girl managing to cope with the big city despite the attentions of her indulgent mother (Betty Comden), proved solidly popular with Theater Row audiences. Playwrights Horizons also helped bring in Ted Tally's South Pole adventure play, *Terra Nova* (much applauded in regional theater productions), with Robert Foxworth and Anthony Zerbe as the explorers Scott and Amundsen, in partnership with American Place. As for American Place itself, the Wynn Handman organization also offered on its schedule *Great Days* by Donald Barthelme, a cluster of conversations about our life and times; a Maria Irene Fornes play about a romance in the shadow of nuclear holocaust, *The Danube*; and a recreation of a famed old American entertainment form in *The Vi-Ton-Ka Medicine Show*, complete with down-home music combo, a bullwhip and six-shooter artist and the hawking of bottles of "tonic" to the members of an audience who, to an even greater degree than usual, permitted themselves a willing suspension of disbelief.

The Negro Ensemble Company presented Pearl Cleage's *Puppetplay*, contemplating a world in which people are turned into puppets, and *American Dreams* by Velina Houston, a drama of black vs. Asian racial frictions. And the Julian Beck-Judith Malina Living Theater of 1950s and 1960s fame made a brief return visit with a repertory schedule which included Beck's *The Archeology of Sleep*, directed by Malina, a series of dramatic images and comments on its title subject, with the performers moving into the aisles and making contact with members of the audience in the renowned but not always appreciated style of *Paradise Now* and other Living Theater presentations.

A worthwhile effort in independent production was *A Weekend Near Madison* by Kathleen Tolan on a subject recurring on our stages: the reunion of 1960s activists 20 years later, with a reassessment of their ideals. Later in the season, Michael Brady's *To Gillian on Her 37th Birthday* mixed contrasting colors of family conflict and undying family love in the retrospections of a widower grieving over his wife's death. And Michael Cristofer's *The Lady and the Clarinet* came in from California with high hopes, destined to be dashed, for a Gordon Davidson-directed play starring Stockard Channing as a lady reminiscing about her past loves for a clarinet player hired to play background music for her dinner date.

Since Harvey Fierstein, the author of two current Broadway hits, was unable to repeat his success with the black comedy *Spookhouse* (set in an apartment above the Coney Island horror show and starring Anne Meara), it's no wonder that a number of other 1983–84 efforts also fell far short of acclaim. Evocation of the Nixon era was twice attempted, once in the form of satire (*Basement Tapes*, an imaginary meeting of G. Gordon Liddy with the Messrs. Ford and Nixon) and once as a monologue with the former President telling his side of the Watergate story to a tape recorder in *Secret Honor*. Other subjects raised briefly in new American scripts off Broadway were a son placing his family in crisis by dabbling in the sale of armaments (*A Little Madness*), the 1959 Christopher Street gay bar riot (*Street Theater*), the present tragedies in Ireland (*The Flight of the Earls*), the days of vaudeville (*The Actors' Delicatessen*), survival of nuclear disaster (*A Hell of a Town*) and suburban family eccentricity (*The Vampires*).

The very first offering of the off-Broadway musical year, *Taking My Turn*,

SPOOKHOUSE—Anne Meara and Court Miller in a
scene from Harvey Fierstein's black comedy

proved to be its star attraction all season. Conceived and directed by Robert H.
Livingston, with a score by Gary William Friedman and Will Holt, it was a
comforting review of growing old, a theme musical with a great deal to say on
the subject of "the golden years," all of it basically upbeat and entertaining. New
York Shakespeare Festival soon followed suit with a warm-hearted musical ver-
sion of Saroyan's *The Human Comedy* which later moved to Broadway. Joseph
Papp's group also offered (at the Delacorte in Central Park) a pop opera called
Non Pasquale, based on *Don Pasquale* and starring Ron Leibman under Wilford
Leach's direction; and (at the Public Theater) a rock musical, *Lenny and the
Heartbreakers*. Also in organizational production was a country-Western musical
comedy soap opera, *Blue Plate Special*, at Manhattan Theater Club.

An early off-Broadway musical entry, *American Passion*, came and went after
a single performance. The notion of having the Mayor of New York City adopt
a dog from the city pound in *Dogs* didn't last much longer, nor did musical
homage to the massive *The Brooklyn Bridge* in its 100th anniversary year, nor
prep school quirks and culture in *Preppies*, nor young love in Manhattan in
Weekend. The Tony Lang-Arthur Siegel-Mae Richard musical *Tallulah* was a

little more substantial, with Helen Gallagher and Russell Nype in its cast and Tallulah Bankhead as its subject. The late-arriving musical *Love*, based on Murray Schisgal's comedy with the same title spelled in three letters, stepped forward with a book by Jeffrey Sweet (a contributor of Best Play synopses to this and other volumes) which won an Outer Critics Circle Award. Sweet's skillful adaptation kept faith with the style and the humor of the Schisgal work, and the show also had the advantage of an appealing score by Howard Marren and Susan Birkenhead. Finally, there was *Nite Club Confidential*, an arrival from OOB written and directed by Dennis Deal, with old and new musical numbers in night club settings from Sutton Place to the Village, from Hollywood to Paris.

The revue form was alive and well off Broadway this season. While *Forbidden Broadway* continued at Palsson's with revisions bringing its satire up-to-date with developments in the big theaters, O'Neals'/43d Street brought *Serious Bizness*, a collection of sketches on the contemporary scene staged by Phyllis Newman, from American Place (where it began in the American Humorists series) to the cabaret scene for a season-long run. Musical revues built around the life of the entertainer (*Sunset*), compulsive eating (*Leftovers*), ballet (*One More Song/One More Dance*) and company-developed music and comedy numbers (*Babalooney*) proved short-lived. Not so the subjects of feminism and society's eccentricities in the season's two final revue offerings, *A . . . My Name Is Alice* (which began as an American Place Women's Project and continued in full off-Broadway status, both as a theater and as a cabaret offering) and *Orwell That Ends Well* created and performed by Chicago's famed Second City troupe.

The highlights of the season's specialty programs off Broadway usually came from the reflected glow of their stars: Estelle Parsons in *Orgasmo Adulto Escapes From the Zoo*, a two-part new English version of Italian political satire by Franca Rame and Dario Fo; Quentin Crisp in one of his evenings; Eric Bogosian in sinister characterizations facetiously entitled *Fun House*; and Kaye Ballard in the story and songs of her life and career, *Hey Ma . . . Kaye Ballard*.

In April, Marsha Norman's 1982–83 Best Play and Pulitzer Prize drama *'night, Mother* was transferred from Broadway to off Broadway, intact, with its renowned performances by Anne Pitoniak and Kathy Bates. While there has always been considerable Broadway-to-off-Broadway traffic in *scripts* in revival or second productions, the traffic in whole *productions* like *A Chorus Line*, *Torch Song Trilogy*, etc., has been a one-way flow uptown, making this a most unusual, if not unique, occurrence. While Broadway was struggling like Laocoön to get new plays produced in its strangling 1983–84 circumstances, off Broadway gave a hearing to dozens of new playscripts and found room for *'night, Mother* too.

BALM IN GILEAD—Laurie Metcalf and Danton Stone
in the Circle Repertory revival of Lanford Wilson's play

Revivals on and off Broadway

The commercially appealing promise of Broadway musical hit potential in-
spired four attempts this season to do it all over again. Of the four, however, only
Zorba attracted a sizeable audience, thanks in large measure to Anthony
Quinn's starring portrayal of Nikos Kazantzakis's ebullient Greek. True, this
Joseph Stein-Fred Ebb-John Kander show proved durable (remember the songs
"No Boom Boom" and "Happy Birthday"?) as staged by Michael Cacoyannis and choreographed by Graciela Daniele. But it was Quinn's lusty characterization, fitting him as perfectly on the musical stage as it did when he played it
in the straight screen version *Zorba the Greek*, that electrified this handsome
revival.

The same might have been expected of Angela Lansbury's Mame in a revival
of the show of that title. Indeed, Miss Lansbury owns the part if anyone does and
operates it flawlessly—but without popular success this time in a full-scale
1983–84 Broadway incarnation. Patti LuPone fared no better as Nancy in a
re-run of *Oliver!*, nor did a Geoffrey Holder-directed ensemble in a revival of *The
Wiz*. Off Broadway, Light Opera of Manhattan was alone on the musical revival
scene and enhanced it as usual with Gilbert & Sullivan, Friml, Herbert,
Strauss et al—though for LOOM this was a tight-belt season, in that they
mounted no new productions in their repertory; and, finally, a sad one punctuated
by the death of their noted producer-director and inspiring mentor, William
Mount-Burke.

Over on the straight-play side, notes our corresponding theater historian

Thomas T. Foose, "A distinction of 1983–84 was the number of revivals of modern classics on Broadway itself." Most conspicuous of these was the Robert Whitehead-Roger L. Stevens production of Arthur Miller's *Death of a Salesman* with Dustin Hoffman as Willy Loman and John Malkovich, a gifted alumnus of Chicago's Steppenwolf troupe, as Biff, under the direction of Michael Rudman. In the Ben Edwards set, shadowy high-rises in the background threatened to engulf the Loman home with the very forces that built it—an accurate reflection of the play itself. Hoffman's performance was intelligently detailed, a young man masterfully assuming an old man's persona, with fury showing underneath and through his despair. Hoffman's Willy Loman was an acting *tour de force* certainly worthy of the support of an excellent cast in this first-rate revival of Miller's masterpiece.

The large group of Broadway revivals of modern classics also took in a Eugene O'Neill play, the difficult *A Moon for the Misbegotten*, with Kate Nelligan in a powerful portrayal of Josie under the direction of James Leveaux. In fact, stars shone everywhere in this reflection of Broadway's recent past in Broadway's busy present: Cicely Tyson as Miss Moffat, the Ethel Barrymore role, in Emlyn Williams's *The Corn Is Green*; Al Pacino bringing his justly renowned Teach to Broadway this season as he did off Broadway in 1982, in David Mamet's *American Buffalo* (nominated for a best-revival Tony, as was Mamet's *Glengarry Glen Ross* in the best-play category—probably the first time any playwright has been nominated for two plays in the same year); Jessica Tandy as Mother, the Laurette Taylor role, in Tennessee Williams's *The Glass Menagerie*; Rex Harrison and Rosemary Harris in George Bernard Shaw's *Heartbreak House*; and Nancy Marchand in Clifford Odets's *Awake and Sing!*, the latter two revivals comprising the entire season at Circle in the Square.

Modern classics were also abundantly available off Broadway in 1983–84. O'Neill was well represented by a John Stix-directed *Ah, Wilderness!* at Gene Feist's two-theater Roundabout company, whose programs were a major attraction of the season both in the appropriateness of the selections and the quality of their presentation. The Roundabout's 1983–84 schedule, honored by a special Outer Critics Circle Award, took in *The Knack* by Ann Jellicoe, *The Killing of Sister George* by Frank Marcus, *Old Times* by Harold Pinter, *On Approval* by Frederick Lonsdale (its first major New York revival since its original 1926 Broadway production), plus Ibsen's *The Master Builder* and the abovementioned O'Neill.

Circle Repertory probably didn't consider *Balm in Gilead* by Lanford Wilson (one of its playwriting regulars) a modern classic when the company decided to mount a revival of the play, but they may have turned it into one with the magic of a masterful production. The script looks into the lives and personalities of a number of patrons of a seedy all-night Upper Broadway coffee shop of the kind to be found on a corner near Wilson's "Hot l Baltimore" and catering to about the same trade. *Balm in Gilead* was Wilson's first full-length play, produced in 1965 at Cafe La Mama in the early days of OOB but never in major New York revival until the last day of this season, when it appeared with a large cast of Circle Rep regulars and aspirants under the direction of the abovementioned John Malkovich of Steppenwolf (who revived it in Chicago in 1980). It was well worth

ZORBA—Lila Kedrova and Anthony Quinn *(center)* in
a scene from the Broadway revival of the musical

waiting for; the vitality built into the script was fully realized in a presentation that opened on the last day of the season and gave a new meaning to the old expression "last but not least."

The season also witnessed a promising—and much-performing—attempt to establish a repertory company in New York, as the Mirror Theater under the artistic directorship of Sabra Jones came onto the scene with the stated purpose "To create an alternating company and to develop a formula of operation economically and artistically possible" and the stated goals "To play in alternating repertory, to return the artist to management and to preserve the art of acting through the development of an ensemble and the stylistic variety of repertory: actors both skilled and feelingful," the latter being a word we've never encountered before but which could be applied usefully to any number of this year's New York stage performances. The Mirror Theater expects to be searching for material of all periods, including new plays, in seasons designed to "provoke active thought" and "celebrate life." We earnestly hope they will succeed where so many other repertory efforts have found it impossible to make it in New York City. They have begun well with a quartet of modern classics—Susan Glaspell's *Inheritors* (1921), John Colton's *Rain* (1923), Clifford Odets's *Paradise Lost* (1935), John Patrick's *The Hasty Heart* (1945)—plus the Eva Le Gallienne translation of Ibsen's *Ghosts*.

The off-Broadway year's "modern classic" repertory also took in the Irish Arts Center's revival of Sean O'Casey's *The Shadow of a Gunman*, directed by Jim Sheridan and transferred from OOB; a collection of modern one-acters presented by the Acting Company in a brief guest appearance at the Public Theater; and a translation of Ernest Toller's 1920 expressionist German drama, *The One and the Many*, in Living Theater repertory. The historically classical canon was also represented on the latter group's schedule with *The Antigone of Sophokles*. New York Shakespeare Festival produced a *King Richard III* with Kevin Kline in the title role at the Delacorte; and Christopher Martin's City Stage Company (CSC) presented a free adaptation by Martin and Karen Sunde of *Hamlet*, with Noble Shropshire as the prince, and an English version by Martin of Strindberg's *Dance of Death*.

As in the other categories, the revival numbers were down slightly this year both on and off Broadway, but not the quality of the entertainment. With big musicals lumbering onto Broadway side by side with the "feelingful" star turns in *Buffalo*, *Salesman* and *Misbegotten*; with Circle in the Square, LOOM, Roundabout, CSC and even Circle Rep in full revival feather; and with the new Mirror Theater planting its feet on the scene, New York City in 1983–84, as in other seasons, was in and of itself an ambitious repertory of revivals of great theater of many eras and nations.

Offstage

A very large camel thrust its nose into the tent sheltering copyrighted legitimate stage material when, in January, the U.S. Supreme Court decided in the Sony Betamax case that the increasingly common practise of home videotaping for private use was not illegal, as a lower court had ruled. The 5-to-4 decision stated in part: "One may search the Copyright Act in vain for any sign that the elected representatives of the millions of people who watch television every day have made it unlawful to copy a program for later viewing at home."

This would not seem materially to affect the stage until one remembers the huge body of the beast behind that nose: the many other videotaping uses which threaten to erode authors' ownership of the material they themselves have created, and which take reflected encouragement from the Supreme Court decision in this particular case. "Piracy is the enemy," declared a prominent composer on the subject of videotaping in the Spring 1984 issue of *The Dramatists Guild Quarterly*, the stage authors' intercom. He had recently examined a mail order catalogue of taped musicals offered for sale at a post office box address. Two of the tapes on that list were of shows he himself had produced on TV. No deal for selling their tapes had been sought or permission obtained.

"Once a tape of show is made, there is no possibility of control of its production in whatever quantity, for whatever purpose," he concluded. Whether in private hands or in the most carefully negotiated contract, as soon as songs, dramatizations, film versions, etc. are recorded in the laboratory, the possibility—even the certainty, some believe—exists that copies will be made and *circulated*, let alone those that are made off the air by individuals for their own libraries.

The opposite point of view—that videotaping of stage material broadens its potential use and will therefore be of long-range benefit to authors—was expressed by a leading theatrical agent, who stated, "What it boils down to is, you don't have effective protection of the material. But if you can make a very good deal up front, and if you want a record of your show, I really think that the good balances out the bad." The recording companies will continue to explore possibilities of safeguarding product by means of new technologies, and it is expected that the U.S. Congress will eventually write laws to define the dos and don'ts of taping. In any case, the camel has settled in and is likely to remain for a very long time.

On Broadway, in modern times, the expression "The show must go on" has meant that it must be played eight times a week by the star as well as the supporting cast—especially the star in, say, a revival production linking audience interest to his/her presence in the leading role. In the case of an exceptionally demanding role, physically, it has become acceptable for a player to substitute for the star at matinees (as in the title role of *Evita* or the *Torch Song Trilogy* lead), but not as a rule. This season, however, according to a Richard Hummler article in *Variety*, "The tendency is increasing among legit stars in demanding roles to play fewer than the conventional 8 performances a week." The article cited the cases of Kate Nelligan, who was excused from playing the *A Moon for the Misbegotten* matinees during the first weeks of the run; Al Pacino, who played only 7 and later 6 performances of *American Buffalo*; and Dustin Hoffman, who played only 7 performances of *Death of a Salesman* during the last weeks of its spring run.

Federal antitrust lawsuits between the Dramatists Guild (the organization of playwrights, composers, lyricists and librettists) and the League of New York Theaters and Producers (the organization of Broadway producers and theater owners) in a controversy reported in this section in the two previous *Best Plays* volumes, dragged on, unsettled and unlitigated, through another season, though it did not seem greatly to affect the working relationship between these two inseparable groups of the collaborative theater art. In its June survey of the 1983–84 season, *Variety* reported that "Many productions are operating under new royalty formulas which obviously are agreeable to both producers and authors."

In other organizational developments, the Association of Theatrical Press Agents and Managers came to terms with the League which called for pay hikes rising over a three-year period to 7 per cent and a new minimum of $893 weekly for managers and 6 per cent and $1,018 for press agents. The Society of Stage Directors and Choreographers reached a new agreement with the off-Broadway League by which the flat fees of $1,300 for directors and $1,050 for choreographers were changed to a scale sliding in proportion to the seating capacity of the small theaters and rising to $3,250 and $2,600 in a 351-to-499-seat house, with 20 per cent royalty minimum for directors and 1.5 per cent for choreographers remaining unchanged.

The tenth anniversary of the Theater Development Fund's TKTS half-price ticket booth in Duffy Square was celebrated in style with Joseph Papp as master of ceremonies, Colleen Dewhurst and Eddie Albert as greeters and New York City Mayor Edward Koch congratulating TDF President Anna E. Crouse on this popular and valuable support project. TKTS booths are now also in operation in Fulton Mall, Brooklyn, and on the mezzanine of #2 World Trade Center in

Lower Manhattan. Their inventory was expanded this year to include matinee and Sunday tickets, previously unavailable at these locations.

The Theater Hall of Fame located in the Gershwin Theater inducted seven new members in 1984, as voted by the 275 play-reviewer members of the American Theater Critics Association. The inductees were Alfred de Liagre Jr., Arthur Laurents and the late Lehman Engel, E.Y. Harburg, Sam Levene, Donald Oenslager and Herman Shumlin. The Songwriters Hall of Fame has been moved out of its former Times Square headquarters (a building destined to be demolished when a proposed massive new Broadway area redevelopment scheme goes through) and is "on hold," according to its executive director, Randy Poe, with special exhibitions going on around the city and with its archives in a three-year computerization program at C.W. Post College. And the unofficial theater hall of fame—Sardi's Restaurant on 44th Street, whose walls are a who's who of theater notables, past and present, in caricature—was reported very close to a sale by Vincent Sardi, present owner and operator of the establishment founded by his father, after years of negotiations with interested parties.

Both the administrators of the Tony Awards and the members of the New York Drama Critics Circle altered somewhat the rules for selection of their annual bests. Only a few years ago, almost all the members of the Tony nominating committee were regularly published working critics (including the editor of the *Best Plays* volumes). By 1983, the panel comprised about half working critics and half bureaucrats, educators and retired critics. In 1984, it was decided to eliminate working critics entirely from this committee because, as a statement from the administration put it, it would "burden them with an obligation that might place them in a position of conflict," particularly with respect to other awards. It was also decided that the panel would meet and confer, whereas in recent years they had filed their ballots of nomination without consulting one another. *Variety* speculated that both these changes in Tony nominating procedure "may be related to" lack of a best-play nomination for Neil Simon's popular *Brighton Beach Memoirs* last year.

Certainly the change in the New York Drama Critics Circle voting procedure was a response to the protracted and peculiar balloting which last year ended in *Brighton Beach Memoirs* winning the Critics Award, which is selected in a point system of proportional voting when no candidate gets a majority of first-place votes on the first ballot. Under the old rules, the point-system ballots (3 for first choice, 2 for second, 1 for third) were repeated without limit until one play received a specified number of points. Under the 1984 rule change, there is now only one point-weighted ballot, followed by a third ballot on which the winner is to be decided by a simple plurality among the second ballot's top three point-getters. The new rule didn't come into play in this year's voting, because the winners in all three categories were decided by simple majorities on the first ballots.

A major change in New York's critical personnel was the retirement after last season and his 70th birthday of Walter Kerr from regular duty as drama critic of the Sunday New York *Times.* Starting in the 1950s when he first came to new York on the *Herald Tribune* after a stint as critic for the Roman Catholic

Daniel Gerroll as Oates, Ian Trigger as Bowers, Robert Foxworth as Scott
and Simon Jones as Wilson in Ted Tally's South Pole drama *Terra Nova,*
popular in cross-country production but short-lived this season off Broadway

bi-weekly *Commonweal,* Kerr's penetrating insights have influenced every aspect
of theater—especially criticism itself—with his conscientious, informed, superbly
articulate play-reviewing and general criticism. Kerr moved over to the *Times* in
1966 for one season as its daily and subsequent seasons as its Sunday critic,
maintaining throughout his career a combination of expertise and stylistic skill
that none in his generation of critics could equal. Kerr will keep in touch with
the New York theater and contribute articles to the *Times* occasionally. His
former post was manned this season by Benedict Nightingale, a British critic.

Around the playhouses, the Nederlander-owned 46th Street theater was renamed the Ethel Merman in honor of the late, great star of Broadway musicals,
and the Alvin was renamed the Neil Simon in honor of America's most successful
playwright. An effort to make a marquee out of Tennessee Williams's name fell
through, however, when the administrator of the late playwright's estate obtained
a court order against renaming the little Playhouse on West 48th Street for him.
The theater had been bought by Jack Lawrence and undergone a $1 million
facelift turning it into two auditoriums: a 499-seat Broadway house and a 199-seat

off-Broadway facility now comfortably named the Audrey Wood Theater after the noted agent for Tennessee Williams and other prominent authors (doubly celebrated this season when Arthur Kopit wrote her into his play *End of the World* as a character). The 499-seater under the same roof was deemed too small, however, to suit her client's reputation and now bears the name of its owner.

Work continued apace on refurbishing 42d Street theaters and the building of a 1,500-seat house, to be known as the Marquis Theater, within the huge new Marriott Marquis Hotel structure which is replacing the Morosco, Helen Hayes and Bijou Theaters on 45th-46th Streets (and the Little Theater on 44th Street was renamed the Helen Hayes to keep that distinguished lady's name glowing in Broadway lights). And in an effort to forestall any future demolition of theaters, New York City's Theater Advisory Council has outlined a plan for making real estate concessions to the owners of 44 legitimate playhouses, permitting them to increase the scale of nearby development projects, provided they promise to maintain their theaters.

The Vivian Beaumont and Mitzi E. Newhouse Theaters in Lincoln Center returned to action this season with *La Tragédie de Carmen* and *And a Nightingale Sang . . .* , respectively. Furthermore, as we went to press, the running conflict between the Beaumont and Lincoln Center boards of directors over whether to begin refurbishing the theater or proceed immediately to a new policy and production schedule seemed to be nearing resolution in favor of the the latter. In the absence of theater attractions, the Music Hall paid the major share of its 1983–84 attention to rock and other concert programs and special events, while the Nederlander filled in with "International Music Stars" concert bookings including Domenico Modugni and Enrico Macias; and Sammy Davis Jr. played the Gershwin.

Off Broadway, the new Playhouse 91 was busy with *Quartermaine's Terms* most of the season. The renovated 384-seat Promenade Theater at Broadway and 76th Street came into off-Broadway action, and the new, $1.8 million, 420-seat Minetta Lane Theater in Greenwich Village was getting ready for a summer 1984 debut under the same ownership as the Orpheum Theater on lower Second Avenue. Gene Feist's distinguished Roundabout Theater Company lost its West 23d Street home but found another 499-seat theater at Park Avenue and 17th Street which is being readied for the group's first fall production Oct. 10.

In a last, long look backward over our shoulder at the 1983–84 theater season on and off Broadway before it disappears over the horizon of history, we can't help the sinking feeling that rising production and ticket costs and changing public entertainment habits are slowly strangling the theater as we have known it for several generations. Broadway is settling deeper and deeper into the role of an "occasion," worth at least $50 a ticket for a big musical, a major award-winner or a star vehicle, but incapable of maintaining at those prices even admittedly superior plays like Shirley Lauro's *Open Admissions* (17 performances) or Joanna M. Glass's Tony-nominated *Play Memory* (5 performances). Off Broadway can still scrape up an audience for quality theater, usually (but not in the case of Ted Tally's excellent *Terra Nova*), though rising costs are beginning to limit play-producing and playgoing opportunities even there.

Out of these threatening flames, however, there have arisen at least two plans for a vital living-theater future, one from Joseph Papp of the New York Shakespeare Festival and the other from Roger L. Stevens of Broadway and Kennedy Center, putting forward two concepts of the same entity: a national theater. Papp suggested that a fund be established—$10 million to start with, rising to $50 million later—to finance subsidized non-profit productions on Broadway side by side with the commercial ones, thus broadening the base of quality attractions. The monies, Papp suggested, should come from sources having the greatest obligation to a healthy, creative, imaginative theater: "The City of New York, developers, builders and the theater industry. Additional financing should be sought from the state, the Federal government, the film and television industries, foundations, corporations and individuals."

Stevens's concept of a national theater, *Variety* commented, "is somewhat more tangible but still in the early planning stages." It calls for a joint formation by Kennedy Center and the American National Theater and Academy (ANTA) of an American National Theater Company funded by outlays of $1 million a year for five years by ANTA from monies received from the sale of its New York theater, and $1 million a year starting the second year by Kennedy Center, to stimulate a continuing series of productions originating at the Eisenhower Theater in Washington, with touring potential. By the end of the season, ANTA-Kennedy Center had already taken "the first steps toward the foundation and development of an American national theater company" by naming Peter Sellars, a 26-year-old who has already made a name for himself as a director of theater and opera, to the post of artistic director and chief operating officer of the venture.

The Messrs. Papp and Stevens have long since established themselves on the theater scene as Titans of their era by more than usually imaginative and resourceful means: Papp by stubbornly putting on admission-free performances of Shakespeare, Stevens by producing a string of Broadway hits after selling the Empire State Building to somebody. Things being as they are on the threshold of 1984–85, perhaps the time has finally come to implement their bold suggestions for continuing achievement in our theater's less and less promising commercial circumstances.

OFF OFF BROADWAY

By Mel Gussow

Off off Broadway encourages the widest range of theatrical expression. It is the place to find innovative works of the avant garde, stage-sweeping spectacles too expensive to produce in the commercial theater and new plays by new playwrights. One can see mini- and monodramas—and even, on occasion, well-made plays, the kind of popular fare that in a healthier economic time would have had a home on Broadway. Off off Broadway, more can be done for less money—and usually with more imagination. Paying a lower ticket price, theatergoers can also afford to take chances.

The most notable event of an active season was an epic musical, *The Gospel at Colonus*, an Obie Award winner, which crossbred Sophocles's tragedy *Oedipus at Colonus* with gospel music, and—against odds—became a joyful and cohesive musical celebration. With book and direction by Lee Breuer (a founding member of the Mabou Mines) and music by Bob Telson, the show filled the stage at the Brooklyn Academy of Music with some 60 actors and singers, including Brooklyn's Institutional Radio Choir and the Five Blind Boys of Alabama, singing for Oedipus.

On the opposite end of the spectrum—one person, no scenery, the most intimate surroundings—was Whoopi Goldberg, a brilliant stand-up monologist who appeared in *The Spook Show*, a performance piece of her own authorship presented in a late-night series of theatrical entertainments at the Dance Theater Workshop. Miss Goldberg, a young black actress, enraptured audiences with her shaggy sagas of growing up strange, of street drug culture and of taking a first, eventful trip to the Continent. She is a cross between Lily Tomlin and Richard Pryor, with the addition of her own idiosyncratic, iconoclastic attitude.

A good play can easily be overlooked by institutional theaters as well as commercial managements. Such was the case with *Split Second*, an incendiary study of a black police officer who kills a car thief and is tortured by his conscience. Written by Dennis McIntyre, the author of *Modigliani*, the drama explored warring impulses of vengeance and guilt. It was introduced at the miniscule Intar Stage Two, then moved off Broadway in June for an extended run.

As theater allies itself with experimental dance and music, it is increasingly difficult to draw the line between one form and another, as typified this season by the work of Ping Chong and Martha Clarke. Mr. Chong, who studied and collaborated with Meredith Monk, was represented by *A Race*, an otherworldly excursion in futurism, a graduation ceremony for a class of humanoids. The show was—characteristic of the director—visually and intellectually arresting. Miss Clarke, a choreographer, dancer and founding member of the Pilobolus dance company, has undertaken a new career as theatrical conceptualist. This year she presented a stage adaptation of Hieronymus Bosch's panoramic painting *The Garden of Earthly Delights*. In performance this became an impressionistic tableau of imagery with a vibrant score by Richard Peaslee and a high-flying aerial ballet that sent dancers swooping over the heads of theatergoers. The show was produced by the Music-Theater Group/Lenox Arts Center, a prolific generator of musical theater.

Ellen Stewart's La Mama continues to be a valuable home for international companies as well as American troupes, this year welcoming the Danish-based Odin Teatret making its American debut with a two-play series. *Brecht's Ashes 2* was a sardonic, critical commentary on the life and work of Brecht, *The Million* a vaudeville that dealt tangentially with the travels of Marco Polo. The director and author was Eugenio Barba, a former associate of Jerzy Grotowski. Among the many other events at La Mama were Andrei Serban's environmental *Uncle Vanya*, starring Joseph Chaikin and F. Murray Abraham; *Jerusalem*, an ecumenical oratorio by Elizabeth Swados about the Holy City; Len Jenkin's *Five of Us*, a wry comedy that dealt with an interlocked, mutually obsessive extended family of friends; and *Damnee Manon, Sacree Sandra*, Michel Tremblay's musings on the relationship between the sacred and the profane.

With his visceral language and imagery, the German playwright Franz Xaver Kroetz has quickly become an off-off-Broadway favorite, with three of his plays produced in New York this season, highlighted by *Through the Leaves* (directed by JoAnne Akalaitis at the Interart Theater). Charles Ludlam, the impresario of the Ridiculous Theatrical Company, recycles popular culture, this year setting his satirical sights on Maria Callas. His *Galas* was a tempestuous travesty, with the author reserving the role of the title primadonna for himself.

Plays can have a short shelf life, a fact that the Second Stage has been trying to rectify. This company is primarily devoted to the reinvestigation of plays from the recent past, renewing the life of Lanford Wilson's *Serenading Louie*, a tale of domestic violence, starring Dianne Wiest; and John Guare's *Landscape of the Body*, a grotesque view of the urban nightmare. A rediscovery of a very different sort appeared at the York Theater, which specializes in musicals from the recent past, in this case, Stephen Sondheim's *Pacific Overtures*. The striking new production starred Ernest Abuba in the leading role of the narrator and shogun. As actor, director and playwright, Mr. Abuba is one of many talented artists to emerge from the Pan Asian Repertory Theater. This year, the Pan Asian company produced Philip Kan Gotanda's *A Song for a Nisei Fisherman*, Wakako Yamauchi's *The Face Box* and Ruth Wolff's chronicle *Empress of China*. Other active ethnic communities were variously represented by Irish, Jewish, Greek and Hispanic theaters. One of the most resourceful in the latter category is Repertorio Español, offering, among other plays, Julio Mauricio's *La Valija*, a poignant story of infidelity, performed in Spanish.

The Ensemble Studio Theater, a prolific consortium of actors, directors and playwrights who move freely among the disciplines, presented two interesting works by playwrights of potential: Eduardo Machado's *Broken Eggs*, about unhappily resettled Cuban exiles in California, and Michael Brady's *To Gillian on Her 37th Birthday*, about a widower's obsession with his dead wife. The latter moved briefly into an off-Broadway engagement. The E.S.T.'s primary contribution is in nurturing playwrights, introducing many of them in an annual marathon of one-acts. Vivid short plays in this spring festival included Jane Willis's

TO GILLIAN ON HER 37TH BIRTHDAY—Noelle Parker, Sarah Jessica Parker, Jean DeBaer, Richmond Hoxie, David Rasche, Frances Conroy and Cheryl McFadden in a scene from the Ensemble Studio Theater production of the Michael Brady play

Slam! (two slam-dancers facing high school graduation); Ara Watson's *Bite the Hand* (two prostitutes looking for new life) and Katharine Long's *Ariel Bright* (a fanciful comedy set in a funeral parlor). Two one-acts from previous E.S.T. festivals, Romulus Linney's *Tennessee* and *Goodby, Howard* surfaced at the Manhattan Punch Line on a triple bill of effervescent Linney plays, entitled *Laughing Stock*. The evening starred Frances Sternhagen and Jane Connell, two of many name actors who work off off Broadway. One Linney play, *F.M.*, new to New York, dealt deftly with a novelist in the rough who takes a course in creative writing. The Punch Line also gave first stage to Mike Eisenberg, an MIT computer whiz and author of *Hackers*, a sharply programmed computer comedy.

The WPA slipped from last year's peak and had a mixed season of new plays, as did the Hudson Guild Theater and the Production Company, the latter offering the helter skelter Hope-Crosby spoof, *The Road to Hollywood* and the pithy *Second Lady*, a one-woman show in which Judith Ivey played the wife of a campaigning candidate. The CSC changed its name—but not its initials—from Classic Stage Company to City Stage Company, promising a divergence from a diet of classics. An intriguing production of Botho Strauss's *Big and Little/ scenes* was followed by an aberrant one of *Hamlet*, as rearranged by CSC director

Christopher Martin (his version began with Ophelia's funeral). Even in error, the CSC remained a significant repository for classics (a detailed listing of its 1983–84 programs appears in the Plays Produced Off Broadway section of this volume). In need of money, the company curtailed its season and at least temporarily ended its role in repertory. Other classical outfits continue—the Classic Theater with *A New Way to Pay Old Debts* and the Jean Cocteau Repertory with a rare production of *The Life and Death of King John*. In the theatrical outreaches of Brooklyn, the New Theater of Brooklyn opened its doors with the New York premiere of Alexander Ostrovsky's wistful, backstage *Artists and Admirers*.

The imaginative use of puppetry was evidenced in the work of Julie Taymor (*The Transposed Heads*), the Bread and Puppet Theater and Theodora Skipitares whose *Age of Invention* is a continuing series on American ingenuity. Touring American performance groups appeared briefly, with several groups at the Brooklyn Academy of Music's Next Wave Festival, including California's George Coates with *The Way of How*, a visual essay in the orchestration of human behavior. While the accent on various stages was more on the esthetic than the political, there were occasional demonstrations of public concern, as in Michael Picardie's South African dialogue, *Shades of Brown*, a co-production of the Chelsea Theater Center and the New Federal Theater; and *Freedom Days*, Steve Friedman's musical reflection on the birth of civil rights.

Hugh Leonard is one of Ireland's foremost playwrights, the author of several Broadway successes. His *The Patrick Pearse Motel*, a hit some seasons ago in London, found its way onto a small off-off-Broadway stage—with mirthful results. This was a door-slamming modern bedroom farce. Amlin Gray, author of *How I Got That Story*, was represented at the Theater for the New City by *Zones of the Spirit: Outlanders* and *Wormwood*, an arresting adaptation of the life and work of Strindberg. Ronald Tavel's *Success and Succession* was a promising attempt by an experimentally-inclined dramatist to write a straightforward family play. Literary figures were in vogue, with attempted one-person imitations of Herman Melville, Robert Frost and Zelda Fitzgerald.

The Mabou Mines, a creative community of theater artists, ended the season with two characteristically diverse works: *Pretty Boy*, Greg Mehrten's free adaptation of Wedekind's *Lulu*, and Ruth Maleczech's 14-minute holographic visualization of Samuel Beckett's prose fragment *Imagination Dead Imagine*.

In 1984, the Living Theater, a seminal off-off-Broadway company, returned for a New York season and seemed to have lost its artistic way during its self-imposed exile. But in the absence of the Living Theater—and sometimes inspired by its example—off off Broadway continues to thrive. This year was no exception.

○
○
○

THE SEASON
AROUND THE UNITED STATES

with

A DIRECTORY OF NEW-PLAY
PRODUCTIONS

and

OUTSTANDING NEW PLAYS
CITED BY
AMERICAN THEATER CRITICS
ASSOCIATION
○
○
○

THE American Theater Critics Association (ATCA) is the organization of more than 250 leading drama critics of all media in all sections of the United States. One of this group's stated purposes is "To increase public awareness of the theater as a *national* resource" (italics ours). To this end, ATCA has cited a number of outstanding new plays produced this season across the country, to be listed and briefly described in this volume; and has designated one of them for us to offer as an introduction to our coverage of "The Season Around the United States" in the form of a synopsis with excerpts, in much the same manner as the Best Plays of the New York season.

The process for the selection of plays, including Fred Gamel's *Wasted* in this volume, is as follows: Critics who are members of ATCA may nominate a play if it has been given a production in a professional house. It must be a finished play given a full production (not a reading or an airing as a play-in-progress). Nominated scripts were studied and discussed by an ATCA play-reading committee chaired by Ann Holmes of the Houston *Chronicle* and comprising Bernard Weiner of the San Francsico *Chronicle,* Julius Novick of the *Village Voice,* Damien Jaques of the Milwaukee *Journal* and John Habich of the Tallahassee *Democrat.* The committee members made their choices on the basis of script rather than production, thus placing very much the same emphasis as the editor of this volume in making his New York Best Play selections. There were no eligibility requirements (such as Equity cast or formal resident-theater status) except that a nominee be the first full professional production of a new work outside New York City within this volume's time frame of June 1, 1983 to May 31, 1984. The timing of nominations and openings prevented some works from being considered this year, but they will be eligible for consideration next year if they haven't moved on to New York production.

The list of 1983–84 plays nominated by members of ATCA as outstanding presentations in their areas, with descriptions written by the critics who saw and nominated them, follows the synopsis of *Wasted*, which was prepared by the *Best Plays* editor.

Cited by American Theater Critics
as an Outstanding New Play
of 1983–84

WASTED

A Play in Two Acts

BY FRED GAMEL

Cast and credits appear on page 63

*FRED GAMEL was born in Rockmart, Ga. in 1944, the son of a factory worker.
He was educated at Campbell High School in Smyrna, Ga. and at various colleges
in the late 1960s after a hitch in U.S. Marine Corps intelligence from 1963 to 1967,
which included a full tour of combat duty in Vietnam. He has been writing poetry
since age 13 and was a voracious reader. When he decided at about that age that
he had read everything worth reading, a Smyrna librarian challenged him, pointing
out that he had no experience reading plays. He began by dipping into a* Best Plays
volume and proceeded to great enjoyment of the theater as literature.

When Gamel's play Wasted *was produced at Seven Stages in Atlanta, it was only
the second performance its author had ever seen onstage (the first was a touring*
The Caine Mutiny Court-Martial *when he was a freshman in high school). His
script, here cited by ATCA as outstanding in 1983–84 cross-country theater, was
one of five or six he has started to write, and was the one he was encouraged to finish
by the drama critic Ernest Schier. It is about an incident in Vietnam but is not
autobiographical; rather, it is based on something he heard discussed and decided
was an important object lesson in our urgent need to stick together racially in order
to survive as a whole nation.*

*Until he began writing in earnest last year, Gamel wandered to and fro, holding
down an assortment of jobs. Looking back now, he sees that he was "picking up
stories" and that this was "maybe research." Then he joined Turner Broadcasting
in Atlanta, on the shipping dock, and was selected for training in telecommunica-
tions. Now, he hopes, he is permanently connected with the Turner organization in
that field, while at the same time he continues writing plays. Gamel is married, with
three children, and lives in Kennesaw, Ga.*

Time: The late afternoon of April 6, 1968

Place: A coastal base camp near ChuLai in Vietnam

ACT I

SYNOPSIS: The sound of helicopters is heard, as members of a Marine Corps rifle squad come onto the scene—*"in green jungle fatigues, armed to the teeth and unspeakably dirty."* They peel off layers of gear and tend to separate in groups, dividing along racial lines and settling into a pair of tents.

Sgt. Michael Kelly, the squad leader, white, *"never talked to a black man until he joined the Marine Corps,"* sees Cpl. Spider Evans, black, *"street-tough, entered Marines in lieu of serving jail sentence for assault,"* throw some empty C-ration cans onto the ground outside his tent, complaining that the previous occupants always leave a sloppy mess for their group to pick up. Kelly orders Spider to put the cans in the trash barrel. Reluctantly and angrily, Spider finally obeys.

Cpl. Bassett, the first fire team leader, black, *"college background, natural leader,"* takes Spider aside and reproaches him for giving Kelly, whose nickname is "Farm Boy," a hard time.

SPIDER: Fuck him, he's a asshole. Always gotta be the honcho.
BASSETT: And you always gotta give him some shit.
SPIDER: Gives him something to do. Fuck the asshole . . .
BASSETT: You didn't think he was such an asshole when we got hit last night . . .
SPIDER: Did I send us out on patrol, Hound? I'm supposed to be grateful . . . ?
BASSETT: Lighten up on Kelly. I don't want any hassles this trip in.
SPIDER: Don't worry 'bout me.
BASSETT: You're in my team. Hear?
SPIDER: Shit! *(Grins at Bassett, offers fist for dap.)* I hear.

In the tent at right, Kelly watches Cpl. "Mac" McNeil, white, *"baker's apprentice become a Marine,"* wrestling with the radio which he carries into combat and which isn't working properly. Mac is also concerned about Spider's attitude toward Kelly.

MAC: . . . . . How many times you gonna let that skinny nigger jump in your shit before you fuck him up?
KELLY: Spider's a dickhead when we get to the rear, but he's a damn good field Marine . . .
MAC: He's a smart-mouthed nigger in the field . . .
KELLY: He knows his shit . . . if he gets out of line, Bassett can handle him.
MAC: They're *all* niggers when we get outta the bush . . .

KELLY: I don't want to hear it. Besides, Spider's been shaky shit since he got wounded . . .

MAC: Don't gimme that. You been hit, Bassett's been hit. You guys aren't flaking out.

KELLY: We just don't show it yet.

MAC: That's right, mother Kelly, take up for your babies. . . . .

Kelly has noticed that this camp seems to be unusually quiet; nobody is moving around. Maybe something has happened that he doesn't know about, or maybe they are in "Condition Red" because of recent bombing. Kelly goes off to check with his lieutenant.

Mac joins Bassett, and they discuss the possibility of getting a beer soon, the ailing radio, the newcomers to the outfit, tonight's movie, how many days they have left in their tour of Vietnam duty (it's April 6, 1968, and Bassett has 105 more days to go). It seems they have a new platoon leader, a sergeant whom they characterize as a "dimwad" apt to get some of them killed.

Mac goes off to get the radio repaired. Cpl. "Slick" Acevedo, a machine gunner whose *"life has been a war from day one, smuggler before war with narrow escapes from police,"* comes out of a tent with his assistant, Pfc. "Father" Gomez. Acevedo, on his way to have his gun checked by the armorer, also expresses hatred for the new platoon leader, Sgt. Drew, before exiting.

In the tent with his own fire team, Bassett finds that Spider has been smoking something stronger than cigarettes and warns him that he'd be in no condition if, for example, they happened to draw guard duty tonight. Being thrown in the guardhouse is safer than regular duty here in Vietnam, Spider remarks, but Bassett reminds him that brig time wouldn't count as part of his 13-month tour, which he'd have to serve anyway. Bassett won't report Spider to his superiors, but he demands that Spider behave himself and stop antagonizing everyone from Kelly to Acevedo, who might take it into his head to kill him. Spider defies him, but Bassett brings him into line with a show of physical force.

BASSETT: . . . . . I will not hesitate to knock your black-assed dick right into the dirt if you fuck with me so much as one little bit. Do-you-read-me, man?

SPIDER *(backing away, cautious now):* I got me a little buzz . . . but I ain't stoned. I won't do no more . . . yet. Be cool, man. You gonna jack up a brother just because he got down on your white buddy? Well, fuck 'em, fuck everybody . . .

BASSETT: Fuck me too, Spider?

SPIDER: No man, Brothers got to take care of each other.

BASSETT: You make it hard to do . . . take care of each other.

SPIDER: Brothers got to take care of each other . . . dammit!

Bassett gives Spider a chore to perform, and Spider goes off to do it. Two of the new men, Roy and Thomas, join Bassett and ask about the platoon leadership. Bassett explains that their sergeant—Hamilton—was killed, and though Kelly was acting platoon sergeant for a while, he didn't have enough stripes for the position and was superseded by Staff Sgt. Drew.

Kelly joins Bassett. He has noticed that Spider is on hair trigger and advises Bassett to keep Spider and Acevedo apart. The subject of Sgt. Drew comes up. To Bassett's comment, "That asshole nearly got us killed," Kelly adds, "He's been out of the grunts too long. . . . . It's his first war, and he's got to unlearn fifteen years of Marine Corps training."

Bassett warns Kelly that Drew is "pissing the Brothers off." Kelly maintains that he is just as annoyed with Drew as any of the Brothers and intends to talk to the lieutenant about him. Drew has threatened to report the Brothers for shaking hands in their own special way ("doing daps") and writing black power slogans on their helmet covers.

BASSETT: . . . . . Drew uses the word "nigger" too often for his own good. He knows he's doing it, saying it. He makes damned sure we hear it. Says it a lot. And it ain't no slip of the lip or nothing. He's doing it on purpose. Fuck him, I write it off to the fact that he's a dumbass redneck. Some of the Brothers don't take it that good. Some of the Brothers want to waste him . . . seriously.

KELLY: Hound . . .

BASSETT: Let me finish . . . he might have got away with that cheap crap back in Bumfuck, Mississippi . . . but everybody is toting a gun over here. Not just the white citizen's council or the law or the KKK. We all are armed to the teeth. Some of the shit we use don't leave no fingerprints . . . don't leave much of goddamned anything as a matter of fact.

KELLY: Jesus. Why in the shit haven't you said something? I haven't heard him, Hound.

BASSETT: You're not black. You'd heard if you were.

KELLY: Listen, if everybody that talks fragging actually starts fragging we'd all be dead in a week.

Bassett wouldn't take part in such a thing himself, he assures Kelly, but he warns that it might happen. Kelly promises to see the lieutenant and reminds Bassett that Drew "don't count. We do, the survivors of this squad. Us dumb fucken grunts got to pull together and drag ourselves and as many kids as we can through." (Kelly, the oldest in the platoon except for Drew, is 23.) Kelly advises Bassett to keep everybody calm—including Spider when he gets back from his errand—until Kelly can check out the whole situation with the lieutenant.

Kelly is on his way to the showers when he is stopped by Mac with news as to why this base seems to be "wired down so tight. . . . . Somebody has wasted Suppernigger stateside. Martin Luther King, man." There are rumors of black mutiny in other branches of the service and of staff plans to disarm the black troops. Kelly, though shocked at the news of Martin Luther King's assassination, doesn't believe the rumors: "We're mostly black, and that'd take some god-damned serious disarming."

Kelly feels the platoon should be officially informed of this terrible event.

MAC: . . . . . What I wonder is if any of our niggers have heard yet.

KELLY: Mac, I'd watch my fucken mouth if I were you. The last thing you're going to need now in Vietnam is more enemies.

MAC: Guess you're right, watch the old lip . . . you surprised someone shot King?

KELLY: No. Not really. Growing up in Atlanta you hear all kinds of shit about King.

MAC: King from Atlanta?

KELLY: No shit.

MAC: I wonder what's going on in Jersey. They burned most of it down *last* summer.

KELLY: Our problem is what's going to happen here. Folks stateside don't have Victor Charley and the NVA working on ways to take advantage of our habitual national fuckups. The gooks know our politics better'n the average grunt. So watch your mouth until I at least get a chance to talk with Hound. . . . .

Acevedo and Gomez come back with the news about the assassination—Gomez mourning, Acevedo indifferent and commenting, "It's not a matter of who shot him but who had him shot." Kelly warns them to keep quiet until he can have a talk with Bassett.

Spider comes in—he has also heard the news and immediately picks a quarrel with Kelly and Acevedo (whom he calls a "spick," throwing a punch that hits Gomez by mistake). The others restrain Spider. Kelly tries to discuss the news with Bassett—but Spider, furious, drowns out all other conversation with screams of rage until the others fall silent. Then Spider tells Bassett, "Someone wasted Martin Luther King down in Dixie land. Blew the man away. The Brothers back home are going up against the man everywhere . . . government's sending regular troops into the cities and neighborhoods because the Brothers have flipped out. Going up against the man . . . and here we are fighting for the man . . . ain't that a fucken joke. You and Kelly like to shoot the shit so much, shoot the shit over that . . ."

Spider leaves center stage to Bassett (who hadn't heard the news and wonders whether reports of uprisings back home are true) and Kelly (who doesn't know the answer but to his own disgust finds himself placing a hand on his pistol holster when Bassett approaches him).

Spider is still on the ragged edge, swearing at Kelly and finally taking a swing at him which Bassett parries. The newcomers Roy and Thomas manage to overpower Spider and wrestle him to the ground, physically subdued but still volubly enraged.

SPIDER *(on the ground with Roy and Thomas, not resisting):* Hound! They goddamn hate us . . . can't you see? Are you too blinded by all this Marine Corps shit to see? . . . they act like our buddies, joke and slap our backs . . . but they call us niggers and hate our guts when we turn our backs . . . they hate us . . . and I hate them, I hate every goddamn one of these white motherfuckers . . .

ROY *(holding Spider down, gentle tone):* Easy man, easy. We know.

KELLY *(attempts to move past Bassett to Spider):* That's it . . .

BASSETT *(blocks Kelly):* I got it, Kelly. Calm down, Spider. We'll talk about it, talk about everything. Just be cool one minute. I want to find out what is going on . . .

KELLY: If you can't cool him down, I will.

BASSETT *(surprised, then angered):* Sergeant Kelly, I'll handle this. O.K.? Go get your shower, man . . .

KELLY: Hound, I'm sorry about King. I don't know what the fuck to say . . . but . . . this is still my squad . . .

BASSETT: You're sorry . . . back off. Back off just a hair, man. We got to talk, the Brothers got to talk and find out a thing or two.

KELLY: Yeah? And what are the fucken gooks going to do, Hound, call off the goddamn war while you people have a fucken meeting?

BASSETT: Kelly . . . let me take care of this. We need to talk. Blacks. Black Marines . . . we got to sort things out. I know you, Kelly. Just let me handle this. Just give us a minute.

Bassett also orders Spider to shut up, as Mac comes in with the message that the lieutenant wants to see Kelly. Kelly goes off, as the black contingent of Marines gathers in a group (observed by Mac) and listens to Bassett advise them all to stay cool and think things out. Spider, still hot, swears to kill Sgt. Drew at the first opportunity. If he can't wait until they go back out into the battle area, Bassett tells him, "Don't tell me about it. . . . . Do it . . . or don't do it. I don't give a fucken shit. Just don't talk about it and don't tell me nothing . . . nothing, do you hear? You're a fool not to wait until we're back out in the bush, but that's up to you. You hear? I don't want to hear about it either fucken way. Hear?"

Spider hears. The black Marines move away, as Bassett watches Mac strap on his .45 holster. Mac departs, leaving Bassett alone onstage to consider the situation. *Curtain.*

ACT II

That night, the tents are dimly lit and quiet. Spider is smoking what appears to be a joint, and *"the intensity of Spider's expression builds as he looks into knapsack."* Finally he picks up the knapsack and exits.

Thomas and Roy discuss King and Malcolm X, contrasting several Northern and Southern attitudes and values. They hate Sgt. Drew almost as much as Spider does, but they feel that Spider is "burnt out . . . . . in his own world." Thomas decides that "Kelly may be a white boy from Atlanta, but he looks like our best bet to make it outta here in one piece."

Bassett comes in. The fact that Spider is absent worries him, in the light of Spider's threats earlier. Bassett hasn't counted the grenades and doesn't know if Spider has any with him. He comments to the others, "Spider should have been sent home when he got hit. Hell, we all thought he would be, but they sent him back. They not only sent him back, they sent him back just in time for Tet." Bassett adds that in the bush Spider knows what he is doing, and they all need him. Still, Spider already had problems when he arrived here, and the war has exacerbated them. While their former platoon leader, "Crow" Hamilton, was alive, he kept Spider together because Spider trusted him. Now, however, Bassett is afraid that Sgt. Drew may push Spider too far.

Kelly and Mac return, Mac carrying his radio. Acevedo is playing cards with Gomez, who is lecturing him about brotherhood: "In the field, we are a band of brothers. We drink from the same cup, sleep side by side in the bush and trust each other each time we get hit that we will somehow hold up together . . . when the fire comes. Why are we so distant here . . . Sometimes I want to cry, it is all so wrong for us to hate each other even for one second when death is so close, always . . ."

Acevedo is unimpressed. He and Gomez continue their card game while Mac fiddles with the radio. Mac tunes in on some racist gibes between two units, as well as orders from Net Control to cease using the frequency for "unauthorized transmissions." Quickly, Kelly shuts off the radio—but Bassett has also heard the broadcast.

It seems, according to Mac, that they have closed the club this evening to reduce the possibility of friction between the black and white contingents.

KELLY: That makes it a good move.

MAC: Yeah? Dontcha think they're carrying this shit a little too far? That formation this afternoon, the little speech by the battalion commander. Fucken spooks gonna think they can get away with murder.

KELLY: I'm going to murder you if you call them spooks one more time. Bassett hear that shit on the radio, it's bad enough without him hearing you call them spooks . . .

MAC: Well, what the fuck do we call them, then? Black Marines, Afro-Americans, Blacks, Neeeegroes, Soul Brothers . . . ?

KELLY: Call them by their goddamn names . . . forget they're black.

MAC: They won't let you forget . . . like Bassett this afternoon, sticking up for that fucken idiot Spider . . . I thought I knew Hound. Shit, he's just another nigger . . .

KELLY: Bassett did the right thing, he kept the shit together. I played it wrong. I should have gone straight to Bassett when I learned about King. Instead, I hung with you and Slick. I just don't know how to talk race with him . . . we walk all around it.

MAC: Fuck 'em. You college boys sweat it too much.

KELLY: No, race is something we have to deal with . . . ignoring it is where I went wrong. You got to recognize it, deal with it, and then go on with the job.

MAC: Kelly, you're an idealist, a damn dreamer. The blacks are gonna just naturally stick the fuck together. . . . .

Mac feels that he knows blacks better than Kelly does and distrusts them, particularly in groups, with their special handshakes and Afro hairstyles and black power slogans. He also challenges Kelly on the subject of Spider, but even in this case Kelly tends to be understanding: "If Spider's coming unglued, he's no different from anybody else in this platoon." Kelly has seen Acevedo use water buffalos and even "gooks" in the paddies as targets for testing his weapons during a helicopter assault. Spider is Bassett's problem, Kelly insists. Mac insinuates that

Bassett isn't to be trusted and that right now Spider, who is absent, is probably up to no good.

Kelly goes over to Bassett and orders him to explain why he isn't keeping an eye on Spider. Bassett shrugs off Kelly's question, and Kelly wants to know what's wrong with him. Bassett replies, "What do you mean, Kelly? What's supposed to be eating me . . . a leader of my people gets wasted in the land of the big PX, nobody even sends word of it to us at the firebase . . . we get a deadhead nigger-hater for a platoon sergeant . . . I'm fighting a war for a country where I'm a second-class citizen . . . and I'm supposed to sail on like nothing's ever been wrong in my life."

Kelly promises to go all the way to the colonel if need be to take care of the Sgt. Drew situation. Bassett assures Kelly that Drew will be taken care of and advises Kelly to take care of himself.

KELLY: Hound, we got to stick together . . . we're all still in this thing together.

BASSETT: No, Kelly, some of us are in it a little more than others now. Some of us are going to give ourselves a little more room to deal with the *real* side of this shit.

KELLY: Have I ever fucked you over, hurt your feelings?

BASSETT: Kelly! You amaze me. Here the whole world is fucked slap up and you are worried about hurting my feelings. Shit! Rule Number Two over here ought to be don't make friends.

KELLY: What's Rule Number One?

BASSETT: Take care of your own goddamned self.

KELLY: You don't feel that way, Hound. Not after all the times you've saved Spider's ass . . . shit, you and I swam a river of fire to get Crow. We've seen too much together.

BASSETT: We've seen hell. Yeah, hell! Those bunkers at Khe Sanh, goddamn airwingers loading pallets of dead grunts onto C-130s with a fucken fork-lift . . .

KELLY: All you got to do is . . .

BASSETT: All I got to do is look around me. Damn, are you blind, Farm Boy? Grunts crackin' up at the firebase when the chopper crashed, laughing and say-ing "Fucken wing-wipers won't sleep in a bed tonight." Nobody gives a shit any more. King gets wasted and asses like Drew toss it right back into our faces . . .

KELLY: Bassett . . . James . . . I hate it about King getting wasted.

BASSETT: Wasted . . . ain't *that* the right word. King hated violence. Hated killing. What it get him? A bullet in Memphis. I can't figure out all that I'm feeling now but it ain't healthy . . . King hated violence but I feel violent as fucken hell inside right now. What choice do we have? The people in the project must be going apeshit. You never lived in a project, did you? Well, I did . . . just like Spider . . . and I probably will when I go back to . . . my country. My country, shit! I wonder what the fuck I've got to do for my country to feel like I got one. And I wonder if King's victories for our people aren't going to end up like these little empty victories we have over here. I'll have to fight in *my country* all my goddamn life. Home.

Kelly insists that there are laws on the books directed toward Bassett's problem and reminds him that they must maintain discipline if they are to survive out here. He won't allow Spider to disrupt it. Kelly is tired of hearing Bassett's excuses for Spider.

Lieutenant Blade, 26, *"starched and clean in contrast to the squad,"* comes to have a talk with the men, who gather around him. Blade notices that Spider is missing but declines Kelly's offer to go find him and bring him back. Blade tells his listeners that the death of Martin Luther King is a great loss to everyone because he "belonged to all Americans. . . . . Despite the feelings and emotions we all harbor, we are all Americans. American Marines. We still have a job to do here in Vietnam as Marines. How we feel politically about the issues and politics stateside is something we must consider only after we do that job. I think that you can all agree that our most important personal consideration right now is to make it through our thirteen-month tours and still do the job we came to do. We can do that best if we keep the job uppermost in our minds and remember that we are Marines. . . . . We are not black, not white, not tan . . . we are green, Marine Corps green."

Acevedo and others receive these words with obvious skepticism. Blade cautions the group against dissent and rumor and warns that any untoward incidents will be relentlessly prosecuted. Bassett interrupts Blade to ask him whether the rumors of riots, etc. back home are true. Blade reluctantly admits that there may be some truth to them. He will supply harder information as soon as he can. The group breaks up after Blade tells the men to stay in the area tonight.

Kelly takes this opportunity to complain privately to Lt. Blade about Sgt. Drew's exacerbating influence on the black troops. Blade admits Drew is a problem which he intends to do something about. Kelly emphasizes that the matter is urgent and should be attended to immediately.

BLADE: What's got you bugged, Kelly? These spooks or Drew's inexperience? We lost so many people during Tet that it only stands to reason that a few losers will get sent out here to us. Besides . . . I understand the blacks have been disrespectful to Drew because he's Southern . . . Mississippi, isn't he?

KELLY: Who told you that?

BLADE: Sergeant Drew . . . said that Spider was insubordinate out at the fire base . . .

KELLY: Spider popped off to the asshole when he got us ambushed . . .

BLADE: Was that an appropriate place to "pop off"? You are letting these blacks run slack. Corporal Bassett was bordering on being insubordinate tonight.

KELLY *(irritated, impatient):* Bassett's got a lot on his mind, wouldn't you agree . . . Lieutenant?

BLADE: Look, Kelly, I'll level with you. We can't cater to these black bas . . . black Marines forever. There has got to eventually be a limit. I halfway agree with Sergeant Drew that we are far too conciliatory with them. Reverse prejudice is still prejudice. Hell, you can't take over this platoon if you can't keep control of these people here in the rear area.

KELLY: Sir?

BLADE: You have got to handle these people tonight. Get us through tonight and I'll get rid of Sergeant Drew. You can not let these black Marines rattle you. Understand?

KELLY: Yes, sir.

And Blade wants to see Spider first thing in the morning, he tells Kelly before he leaves the area. When Blade has gone, Mac suggests to Kelly that Spider has gone to frag Sgt. Drew—he overheard something to this effect when Spider was talking to Bassett. Mac is reporting this to avoid blame in any investigation that might take place after such an incident. Kelly is angry that Bassett didn't report this to him. He is aware that in any such investigation they might *all* be considered accessories if they knew about Spider's intention beforehand, and Kelly will have to report to the lieutenant that Bassett, at least, knew.

Kelly sends Acevedo and Gomez looking for Spider, mostly to get them out of the way when he confronts Bassett, which he proceeds to do, demanding that Bassett tell him where Spider has gone.

KELLY: . . . . . I *know* that Spider told you he was going to waste Drew's ass tonight. I *know* he told you he had ordnance or a grenade . . . I *know! (Kelly is standing directly in Bassett's face now.)* Now tell me where the fuck he is and let's go get him or I go to the lieutenant and the MPs will take over and Spider's ass will have had it.

BASSETT: Bullshit, how do you know Spider wasn't just running his mouth like he . . .

KELLY: You asshole, Mac heard Spider tell you . . .

BASSETT: You told anybody? Is that what you and the lieutenant were talking about?

KELLY: No, I haven't told anybody yet.

BASSETT: Then fuck it, man. Drew ain't no great loss.

> *Kelly grabs Bassett. Bassett jerks free. The two Marines are squared off, ready to fight.*

KELLY: Goddamn it Bassett, you dumb fucken . . .

BASSETT: Dumb fucken what? You were going to call me a dumb fucken nigger, huh? Just do it, motherfucker . . .

KELLY: Motherfucker yourself, goddamn you. I don't believe this, you lied to me, you sonofabitch!

BASSETT: I am not going to let you burn a Brother!

KELLY: Damn you . . . *I am your brother!*

Even Drew is "one of us," Kelly insists, and he refuses to stand by while Spider kills him. Kelly reminds Bassett that they may all be liable as accessories for Spider's actions, and it is up to the squad to find him and "hold his ass down until he cools off." Kelly promises not to say anything if Drew is wasted the next time they go into the field—but not here and now.

The roar and rumble of a nearby explosion interrupts their conversation— probably an ARVN Claymore out in the wire, Bassett judges. It is followed by small arms and artillery fire, as Bassett (who doesn't know whether or not Spider has a grenade with him) agrees to help Kelly go find the missing man, as long as he is sure that Kelly means Spider no harm.

A clatter of beer cans arced into the area with a shout of "Grenade!" heralds the sudden appearance of Spider who is clutching his knapsack, swaying on his feet, having trouble focussing, obviously extremely unsettled, possibly (as Bassett says when he moves to cope with the situation) stoned. He hasn't fragged Drew yet (the explosion was indeed a Claymore, not an action of Spider's), but he apparently still means to do it. Bassett tries to take Spider's knapsack, but he refuses to give it up and prepares to defend himself and his knapsack against all comers, expecially Kelly, even Bassett. Spider defies them, screaming and waving his knapsack, as they make ready to rush him.

SPIDER (rams fist into knapsack): I'll blow your asses off . . .
> Acevedo appears with Gomez, draws pistol from pants pocket and watches previous interchange. As Spider moves to pull something from knapsack, Acevedo fires . . . grinning. Gomez knocks Acevedo down with body-block. Everybody hits the deck. Spider springs back up to grab a rifle, catches Kelly coming up and puts rifle to Kelly's face . . . Kelly, on hands and knees, is helpless. Spider works bolt on rifle. Bassett draws weapon. Chambers a round.

BASSETT: Drop it, Spider!
SPIDER: Goddammit!
> Pivots weapon, butt locked into his side to aim at Bassett's midsection.

BASSETT: Don't make me do it!
> Kelly attempts to spring up for Spider's weapon, missing. Spider is turning weapon to Kelly for keeps as Bassett fires three times. Spider flips over upon impact. There is a pause. Sporadic firing continues along with helicopter sound in distance. Kelly goes to Spider, Bassett stands stunned.

KELLY (hoarse whisper): God . . . Bassett . . .
> Thomas moves to where Spider dropped knapsack, picks it up, looks inside.

THOMAS: Oh shit, no . . . (Dumps orange out into spotlight.) Fucken wasted shit . . .
> Gomez retrieves orange, tosses to Acevedo. Acevedo will not catch it, walks away. Roy glares at Acevedo's departure.

KELLY: Just fucken beautiful . . .
BASSETT (dropping weapon, sits down, dying inside): Christ!
> Lt. Blade and Mac arrive onstage with large flashlight as lights are slowly dying.

BLADE: What happened here?
KELLY (not looking at lieutenant, staring into lights offstage as lights die): Fucken waste . . .
BLADE: Kelly?
KELLY (rages into darkening theater): It's a fucken waste!
> Darkness becomes total. Curtain.

Other Outstanding New Plays Cited
by American Theater Critics Association Members

The Ballad of Soapy Smith by Michael Weller (Seattle Repertory Theater)—A play with stronger connections to Seattle history could hardly have been commissioned by this theater for its opening salvo in its new Bagley Wright Theater.

Michael Weller, author of *Moonchildren*, has written a heroic piece, broad in scope, filled with humor and sarcasm, that focuses with considerable dramatic license on the adventures of Jefferson Randolph Smith, real life con artist of the Klondike gold rush. "Soapy" Smith, as he was called, comes to turn-of-the-century Skagway with old dreams of power and a dangerous new thirst for respectability. In Weller's eyes, this renegade is a complex fellow caught between the old reprobate he is and the man he'd like to be. He has been chased out of every outpost, and the Klondike is his last chance. Like a dying sinner seeking absolution, he tries for an unarticulated redemption by "doing good"—no matter how much violence is required to enforce it. "All I ever wanted," says Smith, "is everything. Is that too much to ask?" The paradox proves fatal.

Hidden in the folds of the sprawling specacle with its roustabouts, saloons, whores and vigilantes is a subtle existential question: Can man *will* himself to be good? In this regard *Soapy Smith* is linked to Jean Paul Sartre's *The Devil and God* which poses the same question in a different context and comes up with the same answer. That answer, of course, is no, but Weller has found a rambunctious and dramatically muscular way to explore it. His play provides fodder for every director's—and set designer's—dream of pyrotechnics, while chewing on quite a bit more than mere bluster and noise.

SYLVIE DRAKE
Los Angeles *Times*

Coyote Ugly by Lynn Seifert (San Francisco: Berkeley Stage)—The slightly outrageous story of a hard bitten, depraved family living in the Arizona desert unfolds in the crackling, wild dialogue of this young playwright who was runner-up in the Susan Smith Blackburn competition for women playwrights in 1984. Underneath its startlingly incestuous tale lie the fantasies of some little people struggling not to be forgotten in the world's haste. Its sizzling and highly original language embroiders a narrative that may or may not be true but that seems to parody other Western plays.

Driving force of *Coyote Ugly* is 12-year-old Scarlet Pewsy who, though physically impaired during what she describes as a lurid birth (her chin is nearly buried in her shoulder), is strangely aware, charismatic, forceful, incredibly uncontrolled and imaginative. She's a trapper of wild animals—coyotes and bobcats—and a healer who conjures her kind of magic with stones and old bones. Are the bizarre stories she tells true?

There's Andreas her mother, emotionally abandoned long ago by her father Red who pinches the girls and dreams of one thing: owning a Buick of his own.

LONG WHARF THEATER, NEW HAVEN—Katherine
Borowitz, Jon DeVries, Sam McMurray and Nancy Elizabeth
Kammer in a scene from *Homesteaders* by Nina Shengold

With the arrival of Dowd, their son who'd been away for 12 years, strange stories
unfold of an affair on the hide-a-bed between Andreas and Dowd. What happens
to Dowd as a result, and how Scarlet treats Dowd and his wife, make a string
of astonishing revelations in a play of much originality in word and scheme.

ANN HOLMES
Houston *Chronicle*

The Execution of Justice by Emily Mann (Actors Theater of Louisville)—The
shootings of San Francisco Mayor George Moscone and Supervisor Harvey Milk,
and the trial of their convicted killer Dan White, are Emily Mann's subjects in
The Execution of Justice. The play begins with a stylized scene in which a redneck
policeman personifies conservative community attitudes which condoned White's
light sentence, and a man dressed as a nun embodies the homosexual community
and liberal causes supported by the victims.

The epic drama then alternates between actual courtroom testimony, flash-
backs to the events leading to the murders and trial, diverse voices from the San
Francisco community, and explorations of Dan White's confused mental state.
The author clearly believes that justice was not done in White's mild punishment
and makes a forceful indictment through her arrangement of the evidence.

HOLLY HILL
New York Theater Correspondent
London *Times*

Homesteaders by Nina Shengold (Albany: Capital Repertory Company; Long Wharf Theater, New Haven, Conn.)—Is it possible to start all over again? To deny one's past, change one's name and make a clean, complete break? Probably not, but it's an intriguing thought, one that's explored with gutsy grittiness in *Homesteaders*. Unlike so many of today's young playwrights, Nina Shengold is able to write layered, textured dialogue and create roles that are equally layered and textured. The main reason her play holds our attention is that it's constantly peeling off its layers to reveal other unsuspected ones beneath. When it's roaring out at its tough best, its language as rough as its setting, it has a bold immediacy that's like a gust of Arctic air, brash and bracing. The setting is a tiny island fishing community in southeastern Alaska in 1979. The five characters are two brothers, flotsam of the Kerouac generation, the two women in their lives, and the troubled 14-year-old daughter of the elder brother. The play is raunchy and has a foul mouth. It also has vigor and a prickly veracity. It lives.

MARKLAND TAYLOR
The New Haven *Register*

Kingdom Come by Amlin Gray (Milwaukee Repertory Theater)—This is a warm and thoughtful play about the cold and thoughtless fury the Norwegian Lutheran Church unleashed on its members who emigrated to the New World.

Amlin Gray follows the immigrants from their different decisions to disobey their church and leave their impoverished country to the physical and mental hardships they endured when they settled in the upper Midwest. Based partly on O.E. Rolvaag's epic novel *Giants in the Earth*, *Kingdom Come* explores with poignancy and a vivid humanity the psychological anguish the Norwegian immigrants suffered.

Cut off from their church, relatives and culture, the settlers had little but their own courage to sustain them through howling blizzards, clouds of ravenous locusts and painful ordeals in childbirth or disease. Some survived the physical problems but succumbed to the mental strain of isolation and disapproval from the church. *Kingdom Come* is beautiful in its simplicity. The play is written with great intelligence and sensitivity and has a special ability to move audiences that is rare on the stage.

DAMIEN JAQUES
Milwaukee *Journal*

The Nerd by Larry Shue (Milwaukee Repertory Theater)—A wonderfully silly farce that leaves audiences riding a wave of rising giddiness, the play is a neatly crafted package that sustains and builds its humor with a natural ease.

While Shue's writing is packed with quick and witty repartee, his play is much more than a collection of jokes. Similar to some of the author's other work, *The Nerd* is a cry—no, a whimper—for understanding of the nice guy, the Caspar Milquetoasts of the world.

The play focuses on a good-natured bachelor architect from Terre Haute, Ind. who was saved from death in Vietnam by a good Samaritan he never met. His savior was a soldier who risked his life to drag his unconscious colleague to safety, and in a burst of gratitude, the architect writes the courageous fellow after the war: "As long as I am alive, you will have somebody on earth who will do anything for you." He lives to regret that letter. The architect is celebrating his 34th birthday and attempting to deal with his girl friend's decision to leave Terre Haute for a better job, when guess who drops in.

Rich Steadman—his savior—is an inspector at a Wisconsin chalk factory. He lacks all social grace, sensitivity and class. He is too dense to take a hint, too cloddish to realize his social gaffes. He moves in on the architect who is too nice a guy to kick him out, and the architect's life becomes a shambles. Shue has written some very funny circular dialogue, and the play ends with a nifty double twist.

DAMIEN JAQUES
Milwaukee *Journal*

Private Scenes by Joel Homer (San Francisco: Magic Theater)—The battle of the sexes is enacted in new and original ways in this shard-like drama, about a man and woman of the liberated 1980s. A young man, an artist, and young woman, who becomes his model, pick each other up, meet regularly for sex (much as in the manner of *Last Tango in Paris*); then, as the relationship gets more and more complicated, become entangled in all sorts of sexual power games, some of them incendiary in their passion, as she wants more commitment and he tries to keep the affair cooled down. At times the resulting battle resembles a mix between Shepard's *Fool for Love,* Oshima's *In the Realm of the Senses* and an esthetic dispute about the nature of art. The set is sparse, the two characters are nude for much of the action (though not in a way designed to titillate)—the result being a play that, at times, reaches the universal level in unearthing the male/female aspects battling in each of us.

BERNARD WEINER
San Francisco *Chronicle*

Secrets in the Sand, by the San Francisco Mime Troupe (major scriptwriter Robert Alexander, aided by the collective)—This play with music, performed in the usual outrageous pop-cartoon style of this *commedia-*based company, takes off from historical Hollywood fact: the 1956 John Wayne-Susan Hayward movie *The Conqueror* was shot in the Utah desert near where A-bombs had been regularly tested; an inordinately high number of cast and crew members later died of cancer. The Mime Troupe play tells the story of how the radiation facts were finally uncovered. The aim is to get audiences to realize that, armed with the facts, ordinary citizens can indeed fight city hall, the U.S. government, giant corporations, whomever—and emerge victorious. The play is wonderfully funny, pointed, informative and, above all, entertaining.

BERNARD WEINER
San Francisco *Chronicle*

A DIRECTORY OF NEW-PLAY PRODUCTIONS

Compiled by Ella A. Malin

Professional 1983–84 productions of new plays by leading resident companies around the United States, plus a selection of others on which information was available at Ella A. Malin's request, are listed below in alphabetical order of the locations of the producing organizations. This comprehensive Directory of new scripts appearing in professional circumstances in cross-country theater, with casts and credits of first productions, is as inclusive as possible (though some revised versions offered locally as "premieres" have been omitted on a case-by-case basis). Figures in parentheses following titles give number of performances and date given is opening date, both included whenever a record of these facts was obtainable from the producing managements.

Atlanta: Seven Stages Theater

(Artistic director, Del Hamilton)

WASTED (6). By Fred Gamel. March 22, 1984. Director, Joe Feldman; scenery, John Charlebois, Joe Feldman, R.J. McDermitt; sound, Michael Keck, Joe Feldman; lighting, Mitzi Alspach.

Evans	Michael Keck
Kelly	Jerry Griffin
Bassett	Tony Vaughn
MacNeill	Eddie King
Pruitt	Micah Penn

Thomas	Sidney Rhee
Acevedo	George D. Nikas
Gomez	John Goldman
Blade	Kent Whipple
Voice of Chris Noel	Nita Hardy
Radio Sequences	Fred Gamel, John Ballard

Time: The late afternoon of April 6, 1968. Place: A coastal base camp near ChuLai in Vietnam. One intermission. (See synopsis in introduction to this section.)

Baltimore: Center Stage

(Artistic director, Stan Wojewodski Jr.; managing director, Peter W. Culman)

CROSSING THE BAR (8). By Michael Zettler. September 30, 1983. Director, Stephen Zuckerman; scenery, Hugh Landwehr; lighting, Richard Winkler; costumes, Mimi Maxmen.

Rudolph Brunner	William Mooney
Peggy Mulhern	Betsey Sue Aidem
Jim Mulhern	Jay Devlin
Augustino Farentelli	Stan Lachow
John Gonzales	Irwin Ziff
Peter Dalton Gaughan	Bryan E. Clark
Anthony DePasquale	Tom Crawley
Friederick Manlich	Tom Bade
John Fitzpatrick	William R. Riker

Time: An autumn afternoon. Place: Mulhern's Deer Point Tavern in Windgap, Pennsylvania. Two intermissions.

THE SLEEP OF REASON (44). By Antonio Buero-Vallejo; translated by Marion Peter Holt. December 29, 1983. Director, Travis Preston; scenery and costumes, Kate Edmunds; lighting, Jennifer Tipton.

Francisco Tadeo

Calomarde	John Gould Rubin
King Ferdinand VII	Michael Tolaydo
Francisco de Goya	Emery Battis
Leocadia Zorrilla Weiss	Jennifer Harmon
Eugenio Arrieta	David O. Petersen
Gumersinda Goicoechea	Caris Corfman
Jose Duaso y Latre	Daniel Szelag
Voice of Maria Weiss	Shannon Rye

Royal Volunteers: Stevan Arbona, Steven Blanchard, Peter Crombie, Lance Lewman, John

Gould Rubin.
Time: December 1823. Place: Madrid. One intermission.

OHIO TIP-OFF (44). By James Yoshimura. May 4, 1984. Director, John Pasquin; scenery, Hugh Landwehr; lighting, Judy Rasmuson; costumes, Linda Fisher.

Gerald .... Tom Wright
Tico................. William E. Kennedy

Horace .... Bill Fagerbakke
Trumbo .... Jay O. Sanders
Erv .... Mark Kenneth Smaltz
Dwight .... Eugene Lee
Tony................... Samuel L. Jackson
Sawyer .... Walter Atamaniuk
Time: The present. Place: A locker room in an old run-down convention center in Xenia, Ohio. One intermission.

Berkeley, Calif.: Berkeley Repertory Theater

(Founding artistic directory, Michael Leibert; acting artistic director, Joy Carlin; managing director, Mitzi Sales)

SEASON'S GREETINGS (45). By Alan Ayckbourn. December 2, 1983. Director, Douglas Johnson; scenery, Karen Gjelsteen; lighting, Derek Duarte; costumes, Merrily Murray-Walsh.

Neville .... David Booth
Belinda .... Hope Alexander-Willis
Phyllis................... Michelle Morain
Harvey .... Irving Israel
Bernard................. Brian Thompson
Rachel .... Judith Marx
Eddie .... Michael Tulin
Pattie .... Emily Heebner
Clive...................... Charles Dean
Time: The present. Place: Somewhere in England; the home of Neville and Belinda Bunker. Act I, Scene 1: Christmas Eve, evening. Scene 2: Christmas day, noon. Scene 3: Christmas day, midnight. Act II, Scene 1: Dec. 26, Boxing Day,

afternoon. Scene 2: Dec. 27, 5:15 A.M.

THE MARGARET GHOST (38). By Carole Braverman. April 13, 1984. Director, Edward Hastings; scenery, Mark Donnelly; lighting, Greg Sullivan; costumes, Jeannie Davidson.

Margaret Fuller................. Joy Carlin
Anna Ward .... Hope Alexander-Willis
Nathaniel Hawthorne......... Charles Dean
Sophia Hawthorne............. Judith Marx
Ralph Waldo Emerson .... Dan Cawthon
Horace Greeley .... Irving Israel
James Nathan .... David Booth
Joseph Mazzini .... Richard Rossi
Angelo Ossoli.............. Tony Amendola
Act I: Margaret's home in Boston, 1846. Act II: The office of the Tribune, New York City, 1848. Act III: Margaret's apartment in Rome, 1850.

Boston: Huntington Theater Company, Boston University

(Producing director, Peter Altman; managing director, Michael Maso, artistic advisor, Zelda Fichandler)

ON THE RAZZLE (26). By Tom Stoppard; adapted from Johann Nestroy's Einen Jux Will er Sich Machen. May 19, 1984. Director, Thomas Gruenewald; scenery, James Leonard Joy; lighting, Jeff Davis; costumes, Mariann Verheyen; music composed and performed by Allen Cohen.

Weinberl...................... Gary Beach
Christopher .... Susan Pellegrino
Sonders................... David Staller
Marie .... Emily Heebner
Zangler...................... Reid Shelton
Gertrud; Lisette........ M. Lynda Robinson
Belgian Foreigner; Coachman ... Scott Rhyne
Melchior................. Sam Tsoutsouvas
Hupfer................... John Leighton
Mme. Knorr .... Ingrid Sonnichsen
Frau Fischer .... Valerie von Volz

Waiters.. Michael Pereira, William McManus
Phillipine; Miss Blumenblatt .... Bella Jarrett
Ragamuffin................ Douglas Murray
Customers, Restaurant Staff: Laurence Adden, Michael Chiklis, Dorothy Gallagher, Christopher Johnston, Christal Miller.
Time: About 1840. Place: A provincial Austrian town and Vienna. Act I, Scene 1: Zangler's office and grocery shop, lunchtime. Scene 2: A street in Vienna, later the same day. Scene 3: Mme. Knorr's Fashion House, immediately thereafter. Act II, Scene 1: Vienna, the Imperial Gardens Cafe, dinner time. Scene 2: Miss Blumenblatt's living room, later that evening. Scene 3: Miss Blumenblatt's garden, immediately thereafter. Scene 4: Zangler's shop, the next morning.

HUNTINGTON THEATER COMPANY, BOSTON—Emily
Heebner and David Staller in Tom Stoppard's *On the Razzle*

Buffalo, N.Y.: Studio Arena Theater

(Artistic director, David Frank; managing director, Michael P. Pitek III)

A PLACE TO STAY (29). By Richard Culliton. April 27, 1984. Director, Ron Lagomarsino; scenery and costumes, Lowell Detweiler; lighting, Curt Ostermann.
Ann..................... Deborah Taylor
David .... Steve Hofvendahl

Time: The present. Place: Ann's apartment in Chicago. Act I, Scene 1: Early September. Scene 2: Two weeks later. Scene 3: One month later. Scene 4: Mid-December. Act II, Scene 1: Early January. Scene 2: Mid-February. Scene 3: Two days later. Scene 4: A few days later.

Cambridge, Mass.: American Repertory Theater

(Artistic director, Robert Brustein; managing director, Robert J. Orchard)

TRAVELER IN THE DARK (28). By Marsha Norman. February 3, 1984. Director, Tom Moore; scenery, Heidi Landesman; lighting, James F. Ingalls; costumes, Robert Blackman.
Stephen.................. Damion Scheller
Sam..................... Sam Waterston
Glory .... Phyllis Somerville
Everett .... Hume Cronyn
One intermission.

BIG RIVER: THE ADVENTURES OF HUCKLEBERRY FINN (28). Book, William Hauptman; music and lyrics, Roger Miller. February 17, 1984. Director, Des McAnuff; musical director, orchestrator, vocal arranger, Michael S. Roth; scenery, Heidi Landesman; lighting, James F. Ingalls; costumes, Patricia McGourty. With Nina Bernstein, John Bottoms, Sandy Brown, Thomas Derrah, Mark Driscoll, Ben Evatt, Jeremy Geidt, Ben Halley Jr., Robert Joy, Jerome Kilty, Maren MacDonald, Harry S. Murphy, Marianne Owen, Tony Shalhoub, Alison Taylor.
Time: Sometime during the 1840s. Place: The Mississippi River. One intermission.

HOLY WARS (5). By Allan Havis. March 28, 1984. Director, Gerald Chapman; scenery, Kate Edmunds; lighting, Thom Palm; costumes, Lynn

Jeffery, Elizabeth Perlman.
Morocco
The Colonel................ Ben Halley Jr.
Mr. Kempler .... Tony Shalhoub
Time: The present, over a period of ten days. Place: Fez, Morocco. The Colonel's office in the jailhouse.
The Road From Jerusalem
Heinrich.................... Jeremy Geidt
Grace .... Lise Hilboldt
Ari .... Tony Shalhoub
Victims....... Sophie Geidt, Nicole Shalhoub
Time: The near future. Place: A bomb shelter on the outskirts of Jerusalem. One intermission.

STROKES (6). By Leslie Glass. April 7, 1984. Director, Phillip Cates; scenery, Kate Edmunds; lighting, Thom Palm; costumes, Elizabeth Perlman, Lynn Jeffery.
Lily....................... Shirley Wilber
Mitch .... Guy Strauss
Marsha.................... Lise Hilboldt
Teddy .... Thomas Derrah
Lorraine .... Maggie Topkis
Place: A suburban home. Act I, Scene 1: Last Tuesday afternoon. Scene 2: Ten minutes later. Act II, Scene 1: Wednesday, early evening. Scene 2: Thursday, noon.

Chicago: Goodman Theater

(Artistic director, Gregory Mosher; managing director, Roche Schulfer)

GLENGARRY GLEN ROSS (39). By David Mamet. January 27, 1984. Director, Gregory Mosher; scenery, Michael Merritt; lighting, Kevin Rigdon; costumes, Nan Cibula.
Levene .... Robert Prosky
Williamson.................. J. T. Walsh
Moss...................... James Tolkan
Aaronow.................. Mike Nussbaum
Roma .... Joe Mantegna

Lingk .... William L. Petersen
Baylen...................... Jack Wallace
Act I: Three scenes in a Chinese Restaurant.
Act II: A real estate office.

THE ROAD (42). Written and directed by Wole Soyinka. April 20, 1984. Scenery, Patricia Woodbridge; lighting, Stephen Strawbridge; costumes, Judy Dearing.

GOODMAN THEATER, CHICAGO—Cast members
perform a festival dance in Wole Soyinka's *The Road*

Murano............... Reggie Montgomery
Salubi .... Ving Rhames
Samson...................... Paul Bates
Professor.................... Bill Cobbs
Kotonu.................... Robert Jason
Chief................... Lorenzo Clemons
Say Tokyo Kid .... Steven W. J. Long
Particulars Joe............ Ernest Perry, Jr.
   Layabouts: Wilson Cain III, Johnny Lee
Davenport, Razz Jenkins, Jay Lawson, Ivory
Ocean, Tunji Ojevemi, Sammy Kunnle Oshin,
Jeris L. Poindexter, Sam Sanders, Tony
Stokes, Mark Townsend.
   One intermission.

HURLYBURLY (29). By David Rabe. March
23, 1984. Director, Mike Nichols; scenery, Tony
Walton; lighting, Jennifer Tipton; costumes, Ann
Roth.
Phil....................... Harvey Keitel
Eddie .... William Hurt
Mickey .... Christopher Walken
Artie........................ Jerry Stiller
Donna.................... Cynthia Nixon
Darlene................. Sigourney Weaver
Bonnie .... Judith Ivey
   Time: A little while ago. Place: A house in the
Hollywood Hills. Two intermissions.

Chicago: Wisdom Bridge Theater

   (Artistic director, Robert Falls; executive director, Jeffrey Ortmann)

KABUKI MEDEA (60). Conceived, designed
and directed by Shozo Sato, based on Euri-
pides's *Medea*; Kabuki version by William Mark
Strieb and Lou Anne Wright; edited by A. Doyle
Moore. December 8, 1983. Lighting, Michael S.
Phillips; scenery associate, Timothy P. Lynch.

Kokens.... John Barricklo, Gregory Franklin
Nurse........................ Janis Flax
Medea.............. Barbara E. Robertson
Jason..................... Dean Fortunato
Princess .... Roone O'Donnell
King of Korea............. Dean Fortunato
    Chorus: Judith Easton, Suzanna Fleck, John Hines, Gordon McClure, Michael C. Myszkowski, Milissa M. Pacelli, Rick Sparks, Joan Rundell.
    Place: Medieval Japan. Prologue: The tropical island of Ryukyu (Okinawa). Act I: Ten years later, in the foreign land of Kyushu. Act II: The island of Kyushu.

CARELESS LOVE (41). By John Olive. June 21, 1984. Directors, J. R. Sullivan, Robert Falls; scenery and lighting, Michael S. Phillips; costumes, Marjory Jakus.
Jack........................ Scott Jaeck
Martha .... Pamela Shaffer
    Time: The present, spring, summer and early fall. Place: Chicago, Jack's apartment and locations about town. One intermission.

Cincinnati: Playhouse in the Park

(Producing director, Michael Murray; managing director, Baylor Landrum)

THEY DANCE TO THE SUN (24). By Leigh Podgorski. November 4, 1983. Director, Gloria Musio Thayer; scenery, David Ariosa; lighting, Jay Depenbrock; costumes, Rebecca Senske.
Joe Gunnison.............. Donald Reeves
Kristin Tabor............. Jacklyn Maddux
Helen Hourihan................ Glynis Bell
Julie Kagel...... Catherine Ann Christianson
Ronnie DeForrester .... Tania Myren
Jaimie Tabor .... Dave Florek
    Time: The present. Place: Aspen, Colo. Act I, Scene 1: Middle of September. Scene 2: One week later. Scene 3: Two days later. Scene 4: Two weeks later. Act II, Scene 1: Two weeks later.

Scene 2: That night, 3 A.M. Scene 3: Later that day. Scene 4: The following morning.

LOVE AND HOURS (24). By Stephen Metcalfe. May 18, 1984. Director, Michael Murray; scenery, David Ariosa; lighting, Jay Depenbrock; costumes, Rebecca Senske.
Moon .... Margaret Gibson
Gale .... Don Toner
O'Neal .... Dave Florek
    Time: The present, fall. Place: A cafe on Martha's Vineyard. Act I: Early afternoon. Act II, Scene 1: Late afternoon. Scene 2: Evening.

Costa Mesa, Calif.: South Coast Repertory

(Producing artistic director, David Emmes; artistic director, Martin Benson)

BECOMING MEMORIES (40). By Arthur Giron; in collaboration with Illusion Theater Ensemble. January 10, 1984. Director, Martin Benson; scenery, Michael Devine; lighting, Greg Sullivan; costumes, Louise Hayter.
Rosina .... Anne Hearn
Albert..................... Wesley Grant
Ida .... Marnie Mosiman
Henry................... James R. Winker
John .... Richard Doyle
Margaret..................... Megan Cole
Sophie....................... Rita Zohar
Oscar................... Harvey Gold
Vinora.................. Martha McFarland
Linda .... Gabrielle Sinclair
Michael..................... James LeGros
Stephen.................... Brad Zerbst
    Time: 1915 to the present. Place: Various locations in the Midwest. One intermission.

MEN'S SINGLES (27). By D. B. Gilles. September 28, 1983. Director, Paul Rudd; scenery,

Mark Donnelly; lighting, Paulie Jenkins; costumes, Kim Simons.
Rob.................. Wortham Krimmer
Larry .... Richard Doyle
Kurt .... Jeff Allin
    Place: The men's locker room of a tennis club in Manhattan. Act I, Scene 1: A Tuesday in April, early evening. Scene 2: A week later. Scene 3: A week later. Scene 4: A week later. Scene 5: A week later. Scene 6: The next evening. Act II, Scene 1: The following Tuesday. Scene 2: A week later. Scene 3: A week later. Scene 4: A week later. Scene 5: Four weeks later. One intermission.

LIFE AND LIMB (20). By Keith Reddin. January 25, 1984. Director, Jules Aaron; scenery, Mark Donnelly; lighting, Paulie Jenkins; costumes, Barbara Cox.
Franklin .... Arliss Howard
Effie..................... Kristen Lowman
Tod..................... Geoffrey Donne

Jerry; Grandfather........ John-David Keller
Donna...................... Patti Johns
Sam; Erik................... Art Koustik
Chris........ Dennis Palmieri/Chad Tillner
  Time: 1952–1959. Place: Mostly in the Morris-
town, N.J. area. One intermission.

BING AND WALKER (23). By James Paul
Farrell. April 25, 1984. Director, Martin Ben-
son; scenery, John Ivo Gilles; lighting, Liz
Stillwell; costumes, Barbara Cox.
Ellie Walker.................. Lois Foraker
Eddie Bing............... Terrence Beasor
Diane Bing.................. Anne Hearn
Arthur Walker................ Troy Evans
  Time: Early summer, 1977. Place: The Walker
backyard in Woods Hole, Mass. One intermis-
sion.

Evanston, Ill.: Northlight Repertory Theater

(Artistic director, Michael Maggio; managing director, Eileen Tipton)

BALLERINA (51). By Arne Skouen. January
28, 1984. Director, Michael Maggio; scenery,
Linda Buchanan; lighting, Robert Shook; cos-
tumes, Carry Fleming.
Hanne................ Belinda Bremmer
Rutta .... Ann Dowd
Auden..................... John Greenleaf
Edith................. Dorothea Hammond
Berger..................... John Mahoney
Malin .... Marian Reiter
  One intermission.

Hartford, Conn.: Hartford Stage Company

(Artistic director, Mark Lamos; managing director, William Stewart)

AND A NIGHTINGALE SANG . . . (34). By
C.P. Taylor. October 4, 1984 Director, Terry
Kinney; scenery, David Jenkins; lighting, David
K. H. Elliott; costumes, Jess Goldstein.
Helen Stott................... Joan Allen
Joyce Stott................. Moira Harris
George Stott................ John Carpenter
Peggy Stott.................. Beverly May
Andie .... Robert Cornthwaite
Eric..................... Francis Guinan
Norman .... Peter Friedman
  Time: The years of World War II. Place: New-
castle-on-Tyne. Act I, Scene 1: "Oh, Johnnie,
How You Can Love" Sunday, September 3,
1939. Scene 2: "We'll Meet Again" June 20, 21,
1940. Scene 3: "Yours" August 12, 1940. Act II,
Scene 1: "That Lovely Weekend" November,
1942. Scene 2: "The White Cliffs of Dover" June
6, 7, 1944. Scene 3: "A Nightingale Sang in
Berkeley Square" May 8, 1945.

THE VALUE OF NAMES (40). By Jeffrey
Sweet. February 7, 1984 Director, Emily
Mann; scenery, Marjorie Bradley Kellogg; light-
ing, Pat Collins; costumes, Jennifer Von Mayr-
hauser.
Benny Silverman.............. Larry Block
Norma Silverman .... Robin Groves
Leo Greshen .... Alvin Epstein
  Time: Today. Place: A house in the Holly-
wood Hills. One intermission.

Houston: Alley Theater

(Artistic director, Pat Brown; managing director, Tom Spray)

AMATEURS (24). By Tom Griffin. May 20,
1984. Director, George Anderson; scenery,
Keith Belli; lighting, Richard W. Jeter; cos-
tumes, Fotini Dimou.
Charlie .... Jim Bernhard
Nathan Monroe........... Mitchell Patrick
Dorothy .... Bettye Fitzpatrick
Wayne Seabury .... Bob Burrus
Jennifer Collins .... Lawr Means
Irene Chilmark .... Bonnie Gallup
Ernie Chilmark .... J. Morgan Armstrong
Mona Williams .... Charlene Bigham
Paul Cortland .... John Woodson
  Time: The present. Place: New England. Act
I: A Friday evening, October. Act II: An hour
later. One intermission.

Staged readings

COLD FEET. By Diane Corley; director,
George Anderson; November 14, 1983.
Karen....................... Lawr Means
Reba....................... Donna Kane

NINA VANCE ALLEY THEATER, HOUSTON—Mitchell Patrick,
Bob Burrus and Charlene Bigham in *Amateurs* by Tom Griffin

Brun . . . . Sarah Jane Moody
Cheryl. . . . . Melissa Ann Gray
Moderator . . . . Ruth E. Adams
LITTLE BIRD. By Mary Gallagher; director, Jo
Allessandro Marks; January 9, 1984.
Kelly. . . . . Steve Brush
Dante DiLoreto. . . . . Clint
Maura. . . . . Melissa Ann Gray
Prandy . . . . Sarah Jane Moody
Narrator . . . . Anthony Hendrix

WORDS FROM THE MOON. By Tom
Ross. February 20, 1984. Director, Ken
Fowler. With Richard Hill, Melissa Ann
Gray, Sarah Jane Moody, Ruth E. Adams, An-
thony Hendrix, Steve Brush, Kent Johnson, Pat-
rick Nugent, Sheri Tyrell Brogdon.
CONVERSATIONS. By Gloria Parkinson.
April 2, 1984. Director, Beth Sanford.
Edith. . . . . Bettye Fitzpatrick
Ruth . . . . Lawr Means

Lansing, Mich.: BoarsHead Theater

(Artistic director, Richard Thomsen; managing director, Barbara Carlisle; producer, John
Peakes)

BARBARA AND KENNETH'S MUSICAL
DREAMHOUSE (16). By Richard Elizabeth
File. August 4, 1983. Director, John Peakes; scenery, Tim Stapleton, Gordon R. Phetteplace;
lighting, Gordon R. Phetteplace; costumes, Patricia K. Smith.
    Cast: Jim Burton, Claude David File, Nancy-
Elizabeth Kammer, Buck Schirner, BethAnne
McGuire, members of the apprentice company.
    Time and Place: The historic past. Any resem-
blance to real people was intended. One intermission.

THE COURTSHIP OF CARL SAND-
BURG (24). By Bob Gibson; music adapted and
arranged from *The American Songbook* and new
words and music by Bob Gibson. January 5,
1984. Director, Nancy-Elizabeth Kammer; scenery, Tim Stapleton; lighting, Tim Stapleton,
D.R. Sherman; costumes, Patricia K. Smith.
Carl Sandburg . . . . Eric Tull
Musicians . . . . Bob Gibson, Anne Hills
    Time: 1908–1920. Place: Mid-America and
certain far reaches of Carl Sandburg's mind. One
intermission.

TAKING COMFORT (26). By Glen Merzer. March 1, 1984. Director, John Peakes; scenery, Tim Stapleton; lighting, George Sherlock; costumes, Patricia K. Smith.

Devon........................ Mag Kelly
Nancy..................... Jeanne Michels
Elsa......................... Judith Klein
Larry .... Kyle Eukert
Alex .... Buck Schirner
    Time: In the near future. Place: An apartment in Berkeley, California. One intermission.

WHY AM I ALWAYS ALONE WHEN I'M WITH YOU (24). By Andrew Johns. March 29, 1984. Director, Barbara Carlisle, scenery, Tim Stapleton; lighting, George Sherlock; costumes, Patricia K. Smith.

Herbert Bracewell .... John Peakes
Florence Bracewell .... Carmen Decker
    Time: New Year's Eve. Place: Herbert Bracewell's study.

Los Angeles: Center Theater Group, Ahmanson Theater

(Artistic director, Robert Fryer)

BEETHOVEN'S TENTH (60). By Peter Ustinov. October 7, 1983. Director, Robert Chetwyn; musical sequences, Stephen Pruslin; scenery, Kenneth Mellor; lighting, Martin Aronstein; costumes, Madeline Ann Graneto.

Stephen Fauldgate............ Fritz Weaver
Jessica Fauldgate.............. Mary Jay
Pascal Fauldgate .... Adam Redfield
Irmgard .... Elizabeth Norment
Ludwig..................... Peter Ustinov
Dr. Collis Jagger........... Gwyllum Evans
Father....................... Brad O'Hare
Countess Giulietta Guiccardi... Leslie O'Hara
Count Robert Wenzel
    Gallenberg................. John Devlin.

Place: Stephen Fauldgate's London home. One intermission.

A SENSE OF HUMOR (60). By Ernest Thompson. December 4, 1983. Director, Robert Greenwald; scenery and lighting, Gerry Hariton, Vicki Baral; costumes, Len Marcus; Estelle Parsons's costumes, Ruth Morley.

Richard Dale................ Jack Lemmon
Elizabeth Dale.............. Estelle Parsons
Abe Manning................ Clifton James
Jean Manning .... Polly Holliday
    Act I, Scene 1: Late at night. Scene 2: The next morning. Act II, Scene 1: That afternoon.

Los Angeles: Center Theater Group, Mark Taper Forum

(Artistic director, Gordon Davidson; general manager, William P. Wingate)

AN AMERICAN COMEDY (54). By Richard Nelson. October 13, 1983. Director, John Madden; scenery, Andrew Jackness; lighting, James F. Ingalls; costumes, Julie Weiss.

Max Whitcomb .... Mark Blum
George Reilly................ Bob Gunton
Joe Williams .... Bill Macy
Julie Jackson .... Melora Marshall
Tony Ricardo................. Jack Hallett
Freddy Hart............... David Downing
Samuel Conklin.......... Lester C. Fletcher
Eva Rose .... Demetra Arliss
Col. Face .... Robert Ellenstein
    Time: 1936. Act I: A first class cabin of an ocean liner, morning. Act II: The same, later that afternoon. Act III: The same, later that evening.

THE GENIUS (54). By Howard Brenton. April 5, 1984. Director, Ben Levit; scenery, Douglas W. Schmidt; lighting, Tharon Musser; costumes, Csilla Marki.

Leo Lehrer.............. Andrew Robinson
Gilly Brown............. Mare Winningham
Richard Weight.............. Jack Gwillim
Graham Hay .... Roy Dotrice
Virginia Hay .... Suzanne Lederer
Cliff Jones .... Ralph Drischell
Andrea Long .... Alison Price
Tom Dicks............ Charles Shaughnessy
Skeleton .... Miriam Mayer
Guards .... Steve Nevil, Eric Trules
Greenham Woman .... Susan Zimmerman
    Time: The present. Place: An English University in the Midlands. Act I, Scene 1: The prize winner. Scene 2: Equations in the snow. Scene 3: Theories in a wood. Scene 4: Crisis in a garden. Act II, Scene 1: An accident. Scene 2: State moves. Scene 3: Treacheries. Scene 4: Embassy. Scene 5: Peace moves.

Taper, Too

WIRE (30). By Hayden Wayne. October 18, 1983. Director, Ben Levit; choreographer, Mary

Jane Eisenberg; musical director, David Anglin; scenery, Larry Fulton; lighting, Brian Gale; costumes, Karen Miller; clown sequences staged by Jimmy Briscoe.

Clown................... Pendleton Brown
Kid....................... Paul Beard II
Boy in Blue............. Daniel McDonald
Girl in Pink............ Sharon Jayne Scott
Roustabout............. Stuart K. Robinson
   Trio: Gretchen Almond, Lita Gaithers, Laurnea Laurae Wilkerson. Gypsies: Kai Ganado, Steve Hicks, William Pasley, Monica Valdez, Lynne Yoneyama. Musicians: David Anglin piano, Pat Carey bass, M. B. Gordy percussion, Joe Sorce woodwinds.
   Place: A circus. One intermission.

REGARD OF FLIGHT and THE CLOWN BAGATELLES (44). November 29, 1983. Written and performed by Bill Irwin, with Doug Skinner and M.C. O'Connor; music by Doug Skinner. Scenery, John Ivo Gilles; lighting, Joan Arhelger; original staging, Matthew Cohen.
   One intermission.

New Theater for Now

MADE IN AMERICA (6). By Alvin Boretz. February 23, 1984. Director, Steven Robman; scenery, D. Martyn Bookwalter; lighting, Paulie Jenkins; costumes, Molly Harris Campbell.
Matt AcAvoy.............. Brian Dennerhy
Frances McAvoy.......... Elizabeth Huddle
Steve..................... Patrick Stack
Eugene .... Earl Billings
Beckman............... Carmen Argenziano
Ruthie..................... Valerie Curtin
Paul McAvoy............... Mark Herrier
Vincent................... Pat McNamara
Jack Potter............... Michael Talbott

Ben Kittredge .... Dan Monahan
One intermission.

PASS/FAIL (7). By Peter Noah. February 29, 1984. Director, Robert Berlinger; scenery, D. Martyn Bookwalter; lighting, Paulie Jenkins; costumes, Garland W. Riddle.
Harry Anderson .... Steven Peterman
Jenny Tolbert............... Lisa Eichhorn
George Gordon............... Mike Farrell
Gail Edwards;
   T.V. Interviewer.......... Rhonda Aldrich
David Shaw................ Shaun Cassidy
   Time: The present. Place. Various classrooms and apartments in and around a New England university. Act I: Late winter. Act II: That spring. Epilogue: The following winter.

CAKEWALK (7). By Michael Genelin and Joseph Charney. March 7, 1984. Director, John Frank Levey; scenery, D. Martyn Bookwalter; lighting, Paulie Jenkins; costumes, Carol Brolaski.
Cakewalker................ Richard Lawson
Leo Frank .... Joel Polis
Lucille Frank............. Theresa DePaolo
Hugh Dorsey............... Gerrit Graham
Luther Rosser .... Michael Bond
Gov. John Slaton............ John Napierala
Stenographer; Mary Phagen; Conley's
   Lady; Mrs. McKnight .. Kathleen Salamone
Bailiff; George Epps; Demonstrator;
3d Lyncher .... Jay Louden
Newport Lanford; Collier's Man;
1st Lyncher........... Ralph Meyering Jr.
Judge Roan; 2d lyncher .... Wiley Harker
Mrs. Formby; Mrs. Webster;
   Sally Slaton.............. Anne Gee Byrd
   Time: 1913 and the years thereafter. Place: Atlanta, Ga. One intermission.

Los Angeles: East West Players

(Artistic director, Mako; producer, Keone Young; administrator, Janet Mitsui)

PAINT YOUR FACE ON A DROWNING IN THE RIVER (35). By Craig Kee Strete. May 16, 1984. Director, Mako; scenery, Will Guest, Terry Izumi, Virginia Galko; lighting, Rae Creevey; American Indian consultant, George American Horse.
Grandmother.............. Shizuko Hoshi
Tall Horse .... Jim Ishida/Ralph Brannen
Old Cat .... George American Horse/
                                Jose De Vega
Leon Brokeshoulder .... Jerry Craig/
                                Keone Young

Joseph Little Eagle ...... Wayne Waterman/
                                Sheldon Wolfchild
Nila................... Ellen Wakamatsu/
                                Momo Yashima

   Act I, Scene 1: 1969, a home on an American Indian reservation in the Southwest. Scene 2: Flashback, 18 months. Scene 3: Vision scene, four days later, on a hilltop. Scene 4: Later the same day. Act II, Scene 1: Back to 1969, a home on an American Indian Reservation in the Southwest.

Louisville, Ky.: Actors Theater of Louisville

(Producing director, Jon Jory)

1983 Shorts, 6 bills Nov. 1–20
Bill #1 (6 performances):
THE DEATH OF KING PHILIP. By Romulus Linney. Director, Ray Frye.

Mary Rowlandson, age 60	Anne Shropshire
Mary Rowlandson, age 30	Deborah Hedwall
Rev. Joseph Rowlandson	Frederic Major
King Philip	Michael Kevin

   Time: 1675. Place: New England. One intermission.
COUVADE by Sallie Bingham. Director, Frazier W. Marsh.

A	Dierk Torsek

A GOTHIC TALE. Written and directed by John Pielmeier.

Isaac	John C. Vennema
Morton	Michael Kevin
Eliza	Susan Kingsley

   Time: Spring of 1898. Place: The tower room of an old house off the Georgia Coast.

Bill #2 (6 performances):
BUSINESSMAN'S LUNCH. By Michael David Quinn. Director, Larry Deckel.

John	Fred Sanders
Nick	Dierk Torsek
Bentley	Steve Rankin
Waitress	Margo Martindale

   Place: Harrigan's Hideaway, a fern-and-quiche restaurant.
GRACELAND. By Ellen Byron. Director, Ken Jenkins.

Bev Davies	Margo Matindale
Rootie Mallert	Jan Leslie Harding

   Time: 5 A.M. three days before the Presley mansion, Graceland, opens to the public.
HUSBANDRY. By Patrick Tovatt. Director, Jon Jory.

Dee	Gloria Cromwell
Les	Ray Fry
Harry	Ken Jenkins
Bev	Deborah Hedwall

   Time: An evening in early Spring. Place: An old farmhouse.

Bill #3 (6 performances):
TROTSKY'S BAR MITZVAH. By Max Apple. Director, Frazier W. Marsh.

Larry	Will Oldham
Grandpa	Ray Fry
Baker's assistant	Thomas Martell Brimm

   Place: A bakery.
CHEEK TO CHEEK. By John Pielmeier. Director, Robert Spera

He	John C. Vennema
She	Ellen Tobie

CUFFS. By Lee Eisenberg. Director, Robert Spera.

Mort	Frederic Major
Tom	Fred Sanders
Dick	Michael Kevin
Harry	Vaughn McBride

   Place: the fitting room of a men's clothing store.
ARTS AND LEISURE. By Paul Rudnick. Director, Frazier W. Marsh

Woman	Ellen Tobie

   Place: Manhattan, New York City.
SWEET SIXTEEN. By David Bradley. Director, Frazier W. Marsh

Security Guard	Vaughn McBride
Jake Lewis	Frederic Major
Mark	John C. Vennema
Martha Lewis	Deborah Hedwall
Peter	Fred Sanders

FIVE IVES GETS NAMED. By Ray Blount Jr. Director, Robert Spera.

Reed Ives	Steve Rankin.

   Time: 1 A.M. Place: A New York singles bar.
AMERICAN TROPICAL. By Richard Ford. Director, Frazier W. Marsh

Sid	Steve Rankin
Cheryl	Ellen Tobie
Suzie	Blair Besten

   Place: A trailer park in Central Florida.
SHASTA RUE. By Jane Martin. Director, Jon Jory

Mama	Theresa Merritt

   One intermission.

Bill #4 (1 performance):
COASTAL WATERS. By Corey Beth Madden. Director, Ken Jenkins.

Willa Miller	Basia McCoy
Russell Miller	Frederic Major
Dottie Kroetz	Gloria Cromwell
Joann Miller Huffman	Deborah Hedwall

   Place: A condominium located between Ft. Lauderdale and Boca Raton, Florida.
GIRL IN GREEN STOCKINGS. By Kenneth Pressman. Director, Larry Deckel.

Madeline Dawkins	Anne Shropshire
Rena Jackson	Theresa Merritt
Linda Lee Foy	Ellen Tobie

   Time: A winter morning. Place: A screened-in porch. One intermission.

Bill # 5 (2 performances):
WHAT COMES AFTER OHIO? By Daniel Meltzer. Director, Vaughn McBride.
Phil .... J. E. Freeman
Murray .... Andy Backer
  Time: Spring of 1933. Place: A wooded area on the Ohio-Kentucky border.
APPROACHING LAVENDAR. By Julie Beckett Crutcher. Director, Robert Spera.
Wren .... Gwen Gautsch
Jennifer .... Ellen Tobie
Abigail .... Lee Anne Fahey
  Place: Outside the Monsignor's office.
THE RENOVATION by Susan Sandler. Director, Adale O'Brien.
Sylvie .... Margo Martindale
Caroline .... Storey Doughten
  Place: New York City. One intermission.

Bill # 6 (1 performance):
BUSINESSMAN'S LUNCH (see Bill #2)
WELL LEARNED. By Andrew J. Bondor. Director, Larry Deckel
Man .... Thomas Martell Brimm
  Time: The present
CREATIVE PLEAS. By Fred Sanders. Director, Robert Spera.
Wally .... Dierk Torsek
Louise .... Jan Leslie Harding
  Place: A school classroom in Washington, D. C. One intermission.
  Designers, 1983 Shorts: Scenery, Paul Owen; lighting, Karl Haas; costumes, Marcia Dixcy.

THE OCTETTE BRIDGE CLUB (12). By P. J. Barry. February 22, 1984. Director, Robert Spera.
Martha .... Sylvia Gassell
Mary Margaret Donavan .... Elizabeth Moore
Nora .... Ruth Livingston
Connie .... Gloria Cromwell
Alice .... Sally Parrish
Ann .... Lynn Cohen
Lil .... Mary Shelley
Betsy .... Beth Dixon
Robert Foster .... Jon Huffman
  Place: Living room in a Rhode Island home. Act I: A Friday night in late October 1934. Act II: The night before Halloween, 1944. One intermission.

DANNY AND THE DEEP BLUE SEA (12). By John Patrick Shanley. February 24, 1984. Director, Barnet Kellman.
Roberta .... June Stein
Danny .... John Turturro.
  Time: The present. Place: The Bronx.

INDEPENDENCE (10). By Lee Blessing. February 29, 1984. Director, Patrick Tovatt.
Jo .... Shelley Crandall
Kess .... Deborah Hedwall
Sherry .... Gretchen West
Evelyn .... Sylvia Gassell
  Time: Eleven days in Late May. Place: Independence, Iowa

LEMONS (10). Written and directed by Ken Broadhurst. March 1, 1984.
Wendall Kendall .... Hal Tenny
Mrs. Kendall .... Kaye Edsell
Wade Grady .... Michael Kevin
Bud Goodee .... Fritz Sperberg
Desenelle .... Shyrl Ryanharrt
Beri Fancher .... Ray Fry
Gus Popp .... Steve Rankin
Kyle Choat .... Andy Backer
Gern Choat .... Jason Milligan
Genisse Choat .... Lorri Holt
Vanda Goodee .... Marilyn Hamlin
Jessie Winter .... Adale O'Brien
Lloyd .... Bob Burris
  Time: The present. Place: Showroom of Beuchel Goodee Motors, a dealership for Edgarant Beamus Automobiles. One intermission.

COURTSHIP (6). By Horton Foote. March 4, 1984. Director, Frazier W. Marsh; scenery, Paul Owen; lighting, Jeff Hill; costumes, Marcia Dixcy.
Elizabeth .... Susan Bruyn
Laura .... Joan Shangold
Mr. Vaughn .... Lanny Flaherty
Mrs. Vaughn .... Beth Dixon
Aunt Lucy .... Ruth Livingston
Aunt Sarah .... Sally Parrish
Horace .... Joseph Adams
Stanley .... Angelo Tiffe
  Dancers: Mark Fredo, Brian Hotaling, Laura Holland Sametz, Gwen W. Gautsch
  Time: September 1914. Place: The Vaughns' home in Harrison, Texas. One intermission.

THE EXECUTION OF JUSTICE (10). By Emily Mann. March 8, 1984. Directors, Oskar Eustis, Anthony Taccone; scenery, Paul Owen; lighting, Jeff Hill; costumes, Marcia Dixcy.
  Cast: Witness (representing testimony of Ex-District Attorney Joseph Freitas and Gene Marine)—Andy Backer. Sister Boom Boom; Supervisor Harvey Milk; Witness (representing testimony of Dr. Donald Lunde)—Kent Broadhurst. Mayor George Moscone—Fritz Sperberg. Witness (representing testimony of Gwenn Craig)—Cheryl Lynn Bruce. Cop; Mr.

Aparicio; Witness (representing testimony of William Melia, Fire Chief Sherratt, Dr. Roland Levy, Richard Pabich)—Bob Burrus. Harry Britt; Witness (representing testimony of Dr. Martin Blinder)—Ray Fry. Witness (representing testimony of Woman; Laurie Parker)—Marilyn Hamlin. Witness (representing testimony of Supervisor Carol Ruth Silver); Mary Ann White —Lorri Holt. Witness (representing testimony of Gay Man)—Patrick Husted. Tom Norman, Attorney for the Prosecution—Frederic Major.

Also Juror; Witness (representing testimony of Cyr Copertini)—Adale O'Brien. Witness (representing testimony of Jim Denman)—Steve Rankin. Clerk of the Court; Witness (representing testimony of Denise Apcar)—Shyrl Ryanharrt. Juror; Witness (representing testimony of Mr. Rudy Nothenberg, Carl Henry Carlson; Police Officer Sullivan, Officer Byrne, Dr. George Solomon)—Fred Sanders. Daniel James White—John Spencer. Juror; Witness (representing testimony of Edward Erdelatz, Fireman Frediani, Dr. Richard Delman)—Robert Spera. The Judge —Hal Tenny. Douglas Schmidt, Defense Attorney—Dierk Torsek. Witness (representing testimony of Dr. Stephens, Inspector Frank Joseph Falzon, Supervisor Lee Dolson, Dr. Jerry Jones) —John C. Vennema. Joan McKintosh—Darcy Heller.

Place: San Francisco. Two intermissions. (See review in introduction to this section.)

007 CROSSFIRE (4). By Ken Jenkins. March 13, 1984. Director, Jon Jory; scenery, Paul Owen; lighting, Jeff Hill; costumes and puppets,

Marcia Dixcy, Sandra Strawn
Toby .... Dierk Torsek
Bonnie .... June Stein
Richard.................. John C. Vennema
Sue .... Tania Myren
Pamela .... Cheryl Lynn Bruce
Tom .... Ken Jenkins
Wanda .... Marilyn Hamlin
Eileen .... Lorri Holt
Litvanov................. Frederic Major
Izvolsky .... Andy Backer
Romanov .... John Spencer
Reynolds................. Clarence Felder
Hamilton .... Hal Tenny
Brown....................... Bob Burrus
Chorus .... Adale O'Brien, Fred Sanders,
                John Turturro
Mr. Blusoot .... Patrick Husted

Time and Place: Three separate realities with different time frames; on board KAL Flight 007 (several hours); inside and near a rehearsal hall (two days); the outside world (approximately one week).

THE UNDOING (3). By William Mastrosimone. March 16, 1984. Director, Jon Jory; scenery, Paul Owen; lighting, Jeff Hill; costumes, Marcia Dixcy.
Lorraine Tempesta .... Debra Monk
Lorr Tempesta................ Tania Myren
Berk .... Clarence Felder
Mrs. Corvo.................. Lynn Cohen
Mrs. Mosca .... Elizabeth Moore

Place: The back room of a poultry market. One intermission.

Milwaukee: Milwaukee Repertory Theater

(Artistic director, John Dillon; managing director, Sara O'Connor)

THE SPLINTERED WOOD (44). By William Stancil. December 9, 1983. Director, Sharon Ott; scenery, Laura Mauer, Tim Thomas; lighting, Dennis Parichy; costumes, Patricia M. Risser.
Mrs. Ella Sumner Dan .... Kathleen Chalfant
Jack Sumner .... Peter Silbert
Mr. Magowan .... James Pickering
Alma Cowart............... Rose Pickering
Mamie Dan .... Mary Fogarty
Felton James .... Laurence Ballard
Jared Sprowl .... Eric Hill
Caroline James Sprowl .... Ellen Lauren
Mr. Thomas................. Jack Bittner
Mrs. Bessie Hinds............. Lois Holmes
Voice.................... John Merriman

Place: Ella Dan's boarding house, Etowah City, Ga. Act I, Scene 1: Late afternoon, September 1938. Scene 2: Later that same evening. Act

II, Scene 1: The next afternoon at 5. Scene 2: A week later.

THE FOREST (44). By Alexander Ostrovsky; translated by Tom Cole. January 20, 1984. Director, John Dillon; scenery, Laura Maurer, Tim Thomas; lighting, Spencer Mosse; costumes, Carol Oditz.
Raisa Pavlovna
  Gurmyzhskaya .... Rosemary Prinz
Aksycha .... Ellen Lauren
Karp..................... James Pickering
Aleksei Sergeyich Bulanov .. Laurance Ballard
Evgeny Appollonych
  Milonov .... William Stancil
Uar Kirilyxh Bodaev .... Eric Hill
Ivan Petrov
  Vosmibratov .... Victor Raider-Wexler

MILWAUKEE REPERTORY THEATER—Mary Fogarty, Peter Silbert and Kathleen Chalfant in *The Splintered Wood* by William Stancil

Peter (Petya) .... Edward Nahhat
Ulita .... Rose Pickering
Terenka .... Jeremy Schneider
Gennady Demyanick........ Daniel Mooney
Arkady (Komediansky) .... Peter Silbert
   Time: 1870. Place: A rural estate in central
Russia. Act I, Scene 1: Raisa Pavlovna's manor
house drawing room. Scene 2: In the forest, later
that day. Scene 3: Raisa's garden, next morning.
Act II, Scene 1: The garden, that night. Scene 2:
The drawing room, next day.

ZONES OF THE SPIRIT: OUTLANDERS and
WORMWOOD (10). By Amlin Gray. March 8,
1984. Director, Eric Hill; scenery, Joseph M.
Sankey; lighting, Russell Swift; costumes, Gayle
M. Strege, Katherine E. Duckert.
Outlanders
Askanius............. Victor Raider-Wexler
Karin .... Ellen Lauren
The Apothecary........... John Merriman
Skerot .... James Pickering
   Time: the 1890's. Place: A converted riverside
pavilion in a small spa town in Sweden. Based on
characters from Strindberg's *The Scapegoat.*
Wormwood
Marika Borg .... Ellen Lauren
Johan Ekdahl................ John Starmer
Malachi .... Victor Raider-Wexler

Ossian Borg .... James Pickering
   Time: the 1890s. Place: The back room of a
disreputable tavern in Stockholm. Suggested by
Strindberg's *The Son of a Servant.*

ANTONY AND ME (10). By Andrew Johns.
March 29, 1984. Director, Rob Goodman; scenery, Laura Maurer, Tim Thomas; lighting, Miriam Hack; costumes, Mary Piering.
Antony .... Victor Raider-Wexler
Jim .... Jonathan Smoots
Rosalinda .... Miki Kim
Meyer .... James Pickering
Inez.................... Catherine Albers
   Time: The present. Place, New York City

THE FROG PRINCE and THE REVENGE
OF THE SPACE PANDAS, OR BINKY RU-
DICH AND THE TWO-SPEED CLOCK (10).
By David Mamet. April 19, 1984. Directors,
John Dillon, Kristine Thatcher; scenery, Laura
Maurer, Tim Thomas; lighting, Mark Nash; costumes, Sam Fleming, Cecelia Mason.
The Frog Prince
Prince....................... Larry Shue
Servingman .... James Pickering
Witch .... Catherine Albers
Milkmaid .... Kristine Thatcher
Musician.................... Wesley Savick
   Place: A wood. One intermission

The Revenge of the Space Pandas, or Binky Rudich and the Two-Speed Clock.
Bob .... James Pickering
Leonard (Binky) Rudich .... F. J. Pratt
Vivian Mooster .... Mary Louise Harmel
Mrs. Rudich .... Kristine Thatcher
Buffy; Executioner .... Catherine Albers
Boots; TV announcer .... Peter Callender
Hank; Jester .... Christopher Randolph

George Topax .... Victor Raider-Wexler
Edward Farpis .... Larry Shue
    Albert Einstein: Miki Kim, John Merriman, Dawn Pierce, John Starmer, Michelle J. Weinstock
    Time: The present. Place: Rudich House, Waukegan; Earth; Crestview; Fourth World in the Goolagong System.

New Haven, Conn.: Long Wharf Theater

(Artistic director, Arvin Brown; executive director, M. Edgar Rosenblum)

NOT QUITE JERUSALEM (88). By Paul Kember. October 25, 1983. Director, John Tillinger; scenery, Andrew Jackness; lighting, Judy Rasmuson; costumes, William Ivey Long.
Dave .... Anthony Fusco
Mike .... Daniel Gerroll
Carrie .... Cara Duff-MacCormick
Pete .... Greg Martyn
Ami .... Jon Korkes
Gila .... Caitlin Clarke
    Time: Spring and early summer. Place: An Israeli kibbutz. Act I, Scene 1: The culture hall/dining room at dawn. Scene 2: The refet (cowshed), a week later, early morning. Scene 3: Later, the same day. Act II, Scene 1: The swimming pool, a month later, late afternoon. Scene 2: The culture hall/dining room, a few days later, evening. Scene 3: The same, later the following evening.

HOMESTEADERS (42). By Nina Shengold. February 18, 1984. Director, John Pasquin; scenery, Michael Yeargan; lighting, Judy Rasmuson; costumes, Linda Fisher.
Neal .... Jon DeVries
Jack .... Sam McMurray
Edra .... Nancy Elizabeth Kammer

Jake .... Katherine Borowitz
Laurel .... Kelly Wolf
    Time: Summer, 1979. Place: An island fishing community in southeastern Alaska. Act I, Scene 1: June. Scene 2: July. Act II, Scene 1: August. Scene 2: Two days later. (See review in introduction to this section.)

THE BATHERS (38). By Victor Steinbach. March 31, 1984. Director, Steven Robman; scenery, Marjorie Bradley Kellogg; lighting, Pat Collins; costumes, Natasha Landau.
Veronica .... Bara-Cristin Hansen
Doukhno .... Merwin Goldsmith
Zimenko .... John Charles-O'Leary
Galina .... Robin Leary
Kaloyev .... William Swetland
Artyukhin .... Richard E. Council
Yakov .... Tom Batten
Korotkov .... Colin Fox
Lyudmilla .... Kristine E. Nielsen
Dobryakov .... Jack Davidson
Rakhlin .... Robert Lansing
Schelglove .... Colin Stinton
    Time: The recent past. Place: Pupkov, a provincial city on the Volga River. One intermission.

New Haven, Conn.: Yale Repertory Theater

(Artistic director, Lloyd Richards)

Winterfest (in repertory):
THE DAY OF THE PICNIC (15). By Russell Davis. January 16, 1984. Director, Tony Giordano; scenery, Peter Maradudin; lighting, Tom Roscher; costumes, Charles Henry McClennahan.
Betsey Fullbright .... Margaret Hilton
Denise Jones .... Theresa Merritt
Dinko Tasovac .... Ron Faber
Nani Nam Yum .... Lori Tan Chinn
Stanley Kronenberg .... Carl Low

Julius Nkumbi .... James Earl Jones
Staff .... Patricia Clarkson
    Time: September, the present. Place: A nursing home in the United States. One intermission.
THE SWEET LIFE (15). By Michael Quinn. January 17, 1984. Director, Robert Alford II; scenery, Andrew Carter; lighting, William J. Buck; costumes, James D. Sandefur.
Eddie Van Dam .... Joseph Siravo
Al .... David Jaffe

Joe......................... Alan Mixon
Charlie .... William Andrews
Peanut Butter Ron .... Al Mancini
Richard.................... Dennis Green
Fat Ron .... Tyrone Wilson
Esteban..................... Joseph Urla
Boss Ron .... John Finn
    Time: June, July and August of a recent summer. Place: Third floor of the Stars and Stripes Caramels candy factory in Wilson City, a small city in upstate New York. One intermission.
CHOPIN IN SPACE (15). By Philip Bosakowski. January 18, 1984. Director, James Simpson; scenery, Michael H. Yeargan; lighting, William B. Warfel; costumes, Candice Donnelly.
Frederic Chopin .... Dann Florek
Marya; Danuta .... Laila Robins
The Bear .... Allen Evans
The Tank ..... Tom Isbell/Jonathan Emerson
Stash; Hitler; Delacroix .... Bill Cohen
Beezo; George Sand .... Robin Bartlett
The Pope; FDR;
    Ronald Reagan............. Robert Lesser
Babci; Eleanor
    Roosevelt............ Christian Clemenson
Man With Hangover........... Tom Isbell
Man With Flower;
    Harry Truman .... Jonathan Emerson
    No intermission.

NIGHT IS MOTHER TO THE DAY (20). By Lars Noren, translated by Harry G. Carlson. March 6, 1984. Director, Göran Graffman; scenery, Richard F. Mays; lighting, Robert Wierzel; costumes, Catherine Zuber; choreographer, Wesley Fata.
Martin .... Keith Charles

Elin....................... Anita Gillette
George .... Christopher McHale
David .... Greg Germann
    Time: July 14, 1955. Place: A small provincial hotel in Sweden. One intermission.

MA RAINEY'S BLACK BOTTOM (20). By August Wilson. April 3, 1984. Director, Lloyd Richards; musical director, Dwight Andrews; scenery, Charles Henry McClennahan; lighting, Peter Maradudin; costumes, Daphne Pascucci.
Sturdyvant .... Richard M. Davidson
Irvin....................... Lou Criscuolo
Cutler...................... Joe Seneca
Toledo .... Robert Judd
Slow Drag .... Leonard Jackson
Levee .... Charles S. Dutton
Ma Rainey............... Theresa Merritt
Policeman............ David Wayne Nelson
Dussie Mae .... Sharon Mitchell
Sylvester.................. Steven R. Blye
    Time: Early March, 1927. Place: Bandroom and recording studio of a record company in Chicago. One intermission.

THE ROAD TO MECCA (20). Written and directed by Athol Fugard; suggested by the life and work of Helen Niemand. May 1, 1984. Scenery, Elizabeth Doyle; lighting, William B. Warfel; costumes, Derek McLane.
Helen .... Carmen Mathews
Elsa...................... Marianne Owen
Marius .... Tom Aldredge
    Time: The present. Place: Helen's home in a small village in the Great Karoo, a semi-desert region in the center of South Africa. One intermission.

Philadelphia: Philadelphia Drama Guild

(Producing director, Gregory Poggi)

THE FATHER (21). By August Strindberg; adapted by Oliver Hailey from a non-Anglicized translation by Ann B. Weissman. April 26, 1984. Director, William Woodman; scenery, Daniel P. Boylen; lighting, F. Mitchell Dana; costumes, Jess Goldstein.
Captain.................... Stephen Joyce
Pastor..................... Adrian Sparks
Orderly.................. James McConnell
Nojd .... Mark Lewis
Laura .... Betsy Palmer
Doctor .... Jonathan Moore
Nurse .... Ruth Nelson
Bertha.................... Katherine Leask
    Time: Early December 1890. Place: The living

room of the Captain's home at a regimental cavalry post in a remote country district of Sweden. One intermission.

Playwright's project: Staged Readings

(Project director, Steven Schachter)

MOONLIGHT AND LOVE SONGS. By Marc Zagoren. December 5, 6, 1983. Director, Kay Matschullat.
Esmi Spiegel.............. Florence Stanley
Flora Joy Baum................. Alex Elias
Sophie Schaeffer......... Delphi Harrington
Malcolm Stebbins .... Colin Fox
James Berman .... Jeff Natter

David Spiegel............ Mark Fleischman
Phil Berman.................. Ed Conery
Betsy Stanton............ Kathleen Layman
Pianist...................... Amy Sicular
   Time: Early October. Place: The living room
of Sophie and Phil's large house in Purchase,
N. Y.
VERDI FOREVER. By Stephen Hanan; director, Jerry Felix. March 16, 1984.
Tessa...................... Valerie Perri
Peppina................. Elizabeth Hubbard
Giuseppe Verdi .... Stephen Newman
Antonio Barezzi............ Richard Woods
Bagasset .... Dillon Evans
Nino Rossi................. Stephen Hanan
Fanny Sax .... Anna Mathias
   Time: August 1959. Place: Villa Verdi at Sant
Agata, Parma.
STATUES. By Kevin M. Arkadie. Director,

Richard Romagnoli. March 17, 1984.
Jean....................... Carla Belver
Hank...................... Tom Valletta
Jennifer.................... Sally Mercer
Millie .... Suzanne Roberts
Aaron..................... Hank Deluca
Axel .... Joseph Walsh
   Place: Living room of an upper middle class
house in a Philadelphia suburb.
FINISH LINES by Karolyn Nelke; director Kay
Matschullat. March 27, 1984.
George Coddington...... Christopher Cooper
Hattie Turner................. Kaiulani Lee
Attilio Zampieri................ Mark Blum
Adam Coddington............ John Glover
Lily Coddington .... Polly Draper
   Place: George's 4th floor walk-up tenement
apartment in Brooklyn.

Portland, Me.: Portland Stage Company

(Artistic director, Barbara Rosoff; managing director, Patricia Egan)

NATIVE AMERICAN (18). By Constance
Congdon. December 30, 1983. Director, Barbara
Rosoff; scenery, John Döepp; lighting, Jackie
Manasee; costumes, Martha Hally.
Frank Shirley.............. Jonathan Fuller
Arieta.................... Elizabeth Perry
Eugenia..................... Dori Arnold
Hart Wills .... Walter Flanagan
   Time: Now. Place: The prairie in Southeastern
Colorado. Act I, Scene 1: An August morning.
Scene 2: 11 p.m. that night. Act II, Scene 1: The
next day. Scene 2: An hour later.

MADONNA OF THE POWDER ROOM (19).
By Paula Cizmar. March 23, 1984. Director,
Barbara Rosoff; scenery, Patricia Woodbridge;

lighting, Arden Fingerhut; costumes, Amanda
Aldridge.
Bessie Puleski.............. Lenka Peterson
Martie Puleski .... Leigh Curran
Violet Sovik .... Keliher Walsh
Linda DelVecchio
   Robinson.............. Marylou DiFilippo
Theresa DelVecchio .... Sarah Melici
Irma Sovik .... Deirdre Sullivan
   Film sequences from The Life and Times of
Rosie the Riveter produced and directed by Connie Field.
   Time: A hot Monday in August, 1982. Place:
Bessie Puleski's kitchen in a Midwestern mill
town. One intermission.

Princeton, N.J.: McCarter Theater

(Artistic director, Nagle Jackson; managing director Alison Harris)

PLAY MEMORY (14). By Joanna M. Glass.
October 5, 1983. Director, Harold Prince; scenery, Clarke Dunham; lighting, Ken Billington; costumes, William Ivey Long; incidental
music, Larry Grossman.
Cam MacMillan .... Donald Moffat
Ruth MacMillan .... Jo Henderson
Jean MacMillan........... Valerie Mahaffey
Billy; Ross .... Jerry Mayer
Roy...................... James Greene
Ken; Duncan......... Edwin J. McDonough
Mike Melzewski.......... George Sperdakos
Miss Halverson .... Marilyn Rockafellow

Ernest..................... Steven Moses
   Time: 1939 to 1968. Place: Saskatoon, Saskatchewan, Canada. One intermission.

AT THIS EVENING'S PERFORMANCE
(14). Written and directed by Nagle Jackson.
March 28, 1984. Scenery, Elizabeth K.
Fischer; lighting, Richard Moore; costumes,
Emelle Holmes.
Saskia .... Stacy Ray
Oskar .... Robin Chadwick
Piers .... Greg Thornton
Gunther Posnik............... Barry Boys

Hippolyta Posnik............ Penelope Reed
Valdez................... Gerald Lancaster
Pankoff........................ Jay Doyle
    Time: The present. Place: The dressing rooms
and stage of a provincial theater in Strevia. One
intermission.

JUDEVINE: A VERMONT ANTHOLOGY
(14). By David Budbill. January 17, 1984. Direc-

tor, Robert Lanchester; scenery, Lisa Martin
Cameron; lighting, Richard Moore; costumes,
Barb Taylorr.
    Cast: Poet, Antoine—Tony Campisi; Poet,
Postmaster, Doug, Raymond—Gerald Lancas-
ter; Poet, Clerk, Alice, Ann—Mary Martello;
Poet, Jerry, Arnie, Granny—Nat Warren-
White.
    One intermission.

Providence, R.I.: Trinity Square Repertory Company

(Director, Adrian Hall)

JONESTOWN EXPRESS (34). By James Res-
ton Jr. May 18, 1984. Director, Adrian Hall;
scenery and lighting, Eugene Lee; costumes, Wil-
liam Lane; choreographer, Sharon Jenkins; musi-
cal director, Daniel Birnbaum.
Rev. Jim Jones.......... Richard Kneeland
Grace Garcia........... Sylvia Ann Soares
Richard Tropp............. Timothy Crowe
Lucy Ann Barak.............. Becca Lish
Milan Barak............... David C. Jones
Larry Layton.............. Richard Ferrone
Carolyn................... Rose Weaver
Stanley Clayton........ Ricardo Pitts-Wiley
Christine Miller............ Barbara Orson

Jerry Joe Snipes......... Richard Kavanaugh
Millie..................... Barbara Meek
Lupe Santiago .... Ed Hall
Marcilline.............. Cynthia Strickland
Bonny Bouquet .... Patricia Ann Thomas
Cong. Leo J. Ryan .... Keith Jochim
Don Harris............ William Damkoehler
John Victor .... Seth Monahan
    Temple Members, Soldiers, Newsmen, etc.:
Michael Cobb, Estelle Reed, Frederick Sullivan
Jr., John Thayer, Brian Tivnan, Dan Welch.
    Time: 1960s to the present. Place: In the mind
and memory of the people of Jonestown. One
intermission.

St. Paul: Actors Theater of St. Paul

(Artistic director, Michael Andrew Miner; managing director, Jan Miner)

THE GRAND HUNT (24). By Gyla Her-
nadi; adapted by Suzanne Grossman. November
4, 1983. Director, David Ira Goldstein; scenery,
Dick Leerhoff; lighting, Chris Johnson; cos-
tumes, Nayna Ramey.
Antal Lehar................. Paul Boesing
Gustav Gratz.............. Alan Woodward
Istban Rakovsky .... David Lenthall
Lt. Stephan Elias............. David Conner
Capt. Gabor Pimasz .... Mark Davis
Count Erdody .... David M. Kwiat
Lt. Sandor Boross........ Steve D. Estenson
Eva Aldoboi................ Sally Wingert
Georges Schrei............. D. Scott Glasser
Guards ..... Kurt Crocker, David Hodnefield
    Time: Spring 1921. Place: A room in Count
Erdody's castle in western Hungary, moving to
King Charles IV of Hungary, his chateau in

Switzerland and then the Flandorffer Street barracks in Sopron, Hungary. One intermission.

NICE PEOPLE DANCING TO GOOD
COUNTRY MUSIC (22). By Lee Blessing.
March 24, 1984. Director, James Cada; scenery,
Dick Leerhoff; lighting, Nayna Ramey; cos-
tumes, Christopher Beesley.
Jim Stools.................. David Lenthall
Roy Manual................ David M. Kwiat
Jason Wilfong .... Arthur Phillips
Catherine Empanger.......... Louise Goetz
Eve Wilfong.............. Barbara Kingsley
    Time: The present. Place: A bar in Houston.
Act I: "Toys for Men"—a parking lot in front of
the bar, one morning in September. Act II: "Sex-
ual Advice for Teens"—an outside deck above
the bar, late afternoon.

San Francisco: American Conservatory Theater

(General director, William Ball)

THE DOLLY (28). By Robert Locke. May 8,
1984. Director, Lawrence Hecht; scenery, Ralph

Funicello; lighting, Robert Peterson; costumes,
Cathleen Edwards.

Byron .... Ray Reinhardt	Inez....................... DeAnn Mears
Jim .... John Hertzler	Susan .... Hilary Ginsburg Walker
Laird.................... Bruce Williams	Two intermissions.
Deborah .... Barbara Dirickson	

San Francisco: One Act Theater Company of San Francisco

(Artistic director, Ric Prindle; general manager, Steve Sigel)

THE DEAD END KID (28). Book by Michael Lynch, based on his book *A Letter From Leo Gorcey*; music by Steve Sigel and Andy Kulberg; lyrics by Steve Sigel. December 9, 1983. Director, Simon L. Levy; musical directors, Steve Sigel, Andy Kulberg; choreographer, Rodger Henderson; scenery, Jeffer Whitman; lighting, Rhonda Birnbaum; costumes, Gael Russell.

Bryan; Leo Gorcey .... Steve Cotten
Huntz Hall.................... Dan Hiatt
Gabriel Dell................ Stephen Sloane
Bobby Jordan.............. Grant Machan
Helen .... Priscilla Alden
Ema Moztek .... Leslie Buchbinder
Stacey Moztek................. Tina Sigel
Time: The present, winter. Place: A condominium in Pacific Heights, San Francisco. Act I: Saturday afternoon. Act II, Scene 1: Sunday afternoon, one week later. Scene 2: Saturday afternoon, one week later.

Musical numbers: Overture; "A Letter/Stacy," "Top of the Hill," "An American Mother," "What A Star!", Entr'acte, "Dilemma," "Best of Friends," "All These Years," "It's Just a Movie," "Sheena, Queen of the Jungle," "Until I Found You," "Me, Bryan."

LAST CALL AT PARADISE TAVERN (28). By Terry Mack Murphy. May 18, 1984. Director, Larry Russell; scenery, Bruce Brisson; lighting, James A. McCracken; costumes, Suzanne Raftery.

May .... Laurellee Westway
Mitch .... Gerald Winer
Les .... Robert Lerman
Bonnie .... Maureen Coyne
Time: An hour before closing, the present. Place: a neighborhood bar in a suburb of Chicago.

THREE MORE SLEEPLESS NIGHTS by Caryl Churchill. Director, Susan Marsden; designers, same as for *Last Call at Paradise Tavern*.

Margaret................... Jean Schiffman
Frank .... Ric Prindle
Pete..................... Douglas Leach
Dawn .... Nancy Palmer Jones

TAPS AT 8:23 (28). By Holly Kern. May 20, 1984. Director Tom McDermott; scenery, Peggy McDonald; lighting, William Simonds; costumes, Suzanne Raftery.

Eva Bess................ Carol McElheney
Ruby.................... Maureen Coyne
Joni........................ Stacey Jack
Time: August 1983, almost sunset. Place: Eva Bess's house in Augusta, Ga.

Seattle: Seattle Repertory Theater

(Artistic director, Daniel Sullivan; producing director, Peter Donnelly)

THE BALLAD OF SOAPY SMITH (28). By Michael Weller. October 26, 1983. Director, Robert Egan; scenery, Eugene Lee; lighting, Spencer Mosse; costumes, Robert Blackman; songs, Michael Weller; musical score, Norman Durkee.

Pianoman................. Norman Durkee
Man on Boat;
  Photographer .... James Brousseau
Paul Anthony MacAleer.. Christopher Cooper
Tripod Schultz.............. J. V. Bradley
Jefferson Randolph
  (Soapy) Smith.............. Denis Arndt
George Wilder.............. John Aylward

Frenchie Villiers; Cpl. Egan... Frank Corrado
Maj. James Strong........... Paul Hostetler
William Whitmore............ Robert Riehle
Frank Reid.................. Kevin Tighe
Calvin Barkdull............. Scott Caldwell
Michael C. Sherpy........... Michael Santo
Kitty Strong................ Kate Mulgrew
Mattie Silks .... Marjorie Nelson
Burke Gallagher;
  Gov. of Alaska.............. Ted D'Arms
Charlie Bowers .... Lee Corrigan
William Jackson .... Mark Jenkins
Syd Dixon .... Kurt Beattie
Red Gibbs .... Michael J. Smith

Townswomen... Toni Cross, Kathleen Worley
Fritz .... Roderick Aird
Reverend Dickey .... Clayton Corzatte
Tagish Sam .... William P. Ontiveros
Violet .... Gretchen Rumbaugh
Pearl .... Tina Marie Goff
Sick Man .... Corky Dexter
Mollie Fewclothes .... Karen Kay Cody
District Commissioner; Jensen... Rod Pilloud
J. D. Stewart .... Brian Martin
  Miners, Skagway Militiamen, Townspeople,
Alaska Militiamen, Guards, Mattie's Girls, Vigi-
lantes and Their Wives: Company.
  Time: 1897–98. Place, Skagway, Alaska. (See
review in introduction to this section.)

THE ADVENTURES OF HUCKLEBERRY
FINN (37). By Mark Twain; adapted by James
Hammerstein and Christopher Harbon; music by
Ralph Affoumado. November 30, 1983. Direc-
tors, James Hammerstein, Christopher Har-
bon; musical director, Daniel Birnbaum; musical
stager, Nancy Cranbourne.
  Cast: Jo, Charlotte Grangerford, Mrs. Shack-
leford—Karen Kay Cody; Cardplayer, Man
With Gun, Tom Grangerford, Hines, Earl—
Frank Corrado; Riverman, Judge Thatcher,
King—Ted D'Arms; Violinist, William Wilkes,
Farmer—Corky Dexter; Ben, Buck Granger-
ford, Boy in Traveling Clothes, Boy in Canoe—
Brian Faker; Riverman—Michael Geer; Lula,
Betsy, Bessie, Lize—Tamu Gray; Cardplayer,
Singing Canoeist, Rev. Shackleford, Doctor—
Mark Jenkins; Miss Watson, Widow Bartley—
Susan Ludlow; Huckleberry Finn—Robert
Macnaughton.
  Also Pap Finn, Col. Grangerford, Dr. Robin-
son; Silas Phelps—Glen Mazen; Aunt Polly,
Judith Loftus, Mrs. Grangerford, Mary Jane
Wilkes—Kathryn Mesney; Widow Douglas,
Miss Rucker—Marjorie Nelson; Riverman—
Keith Nicholai; Tom Sawyer, Emmeline—Wil-
liam O'Leary; Riverman, Bob Grangerford,
Duke—John Procaccino; Banjo Player, Harney
Sheperdson, Auctioneer, Jed—Carl August
Sander; Dancing Riverman, Ferryboat Captain,
Parker, Judge, Harvey Wilkes, Luke—Michael
Santo; Steve, Shadrach—Steve Sneed; Jim—
David Toney; Hank, Sophia Grangerford,
Joanna Wilkes, Aunt Sally—Sharon Ullrick.
  Time: March to late October, 1836. Place:
1,200 miles on or near the Mississippi River. One
intermission.

SHIVAREE (16). By William Mastrosimone.
November 9, 1983. Director, Daniel Sullivan;
scenery, Robert Dahlstrom; lighting, Michael
Davidson; costumes, Sally Richardson.

Chandler .... Steven Flynn
Scagg .... John Procaccino
Mary Ann .... Diane Kagan
Laura .... Lori Larsen
Shivaree .... Maggie Baird
  Time: The present. Place: The South. One in-
termission.

COMING OF AGE IN SOHO (5). Written
and directed by Albert Innaurato. January,
1984. Scenery, Alex Hutton; lighting, James
Verdery; costumes, Lisa Cerveny, Sarah Hal-
pern.
Gioconda Palcotrinieri .... Mary Lou Rosato
Odysseus MacDowell ...... William O'Leary
Pasquale Foscari .... Mark Jenkins
Mad Max .... Morgan Strickland
Danny Amato .... Tony Soper
Beatrice Dante .... John Procaccino
Antoinette Palcotrinieri ..... Marjorie Nelson
Puer Schlussnuss .... Brian Faker
  Time: The present. Place: New York City. Act
I, Scene 1: Lobby of a SoHo building containing
lofts. Scene 2: Gioconda's loft, a few days later.
Act II, Scene 1: Beatrice's loft, a week later.
Scene 2: Giocanda's loft, a week later. Act III,
Scene 1: Giocanda's loft, another week later.
Scene 2: Beatrice's loft, a week later. Scene 3:
Beatrice's loft, a few days later. Scene 4: Pas-
quale's duplex, later the same day. Scene 5: Bea-
trice's loft, late afternoon of the same day. Scene
6: Gioconda's loft, that evening.

SPLITTN' HAIRS: BOUFFANTE JR: 23
PIGTAILS: PERMANENT WAVE (5). Writ-
ten and performed by Rebecca Wells. February
17, 1984. Director, Robert Loper; scenery and
lighting, Cynthia Bishop; Costumes, Sarah
Halpern.
Loretta Sue Endless .... Rebecca Wells.
  Two intermissions.

BETWEEN EAST AND WEST (5). By Richard
Nelson. March 23, 1984. Directors, Ted
D'Arms, Richard Nelson; scenery, David
Logan; lighting, Rick Kennedy-Paulsen; cos-
tumes, Lisa Cerveny, Sarah Halpern.
Gregor Hasek .... Sean G. Griffin
Erna Hasek .... Megan Cole
  Time: The present. Place: An apartment in
New York City. Scene 1: Culmination. Scene 2:
Eight months earlier. Scene 3: The context. Scene
4: Before. Scene 5: And after. Scene 6: Dustin
Hoffman. Scene 7: Land of opportunity. Scene 8:
Shadows. Scene 9: The free world. Scene 10: Si-
beria. Scene 11: His memory. Scene 12: Her
memory. Scene 13: What's left. Scenes 14a and
14b: Erna recalls two earlier scenes. Scene 15:

Going places. Scene 16: Remainders. No intermission.

ABINGDON SQUARE (5). Written and directed by Maria Irene Fornes. April 27, 1984. Scenery and costumes, Tom Fichter; lighting, Martin Pavloff; original music, Paige Wheeler.
Marion . . . . Lianne Pattison

Michael. . . . . Carl Sander
Juster . . . . John Aylward
Minnie . . . . Anne O'Connell
Mary. . . . . Faye B. Summers
Frank . . . . Brian Faker
Glazier . . . . David W. Schaub
    Time: Between 1905 and 1912. Place: New York City. One intermission.

Stamford, Conn: Hartman Theater

(Producing artistic director, Edwin Sherin; executive director, Harris Goldman)

THE CHAIN (28). Written and directed by Elia Kazan. November 4, 1983. Scenery, Tony Straiges; lighting, Allen Lee Hughes; costumes, Jane Greenwood.
Watchman . . . . Jack Waltzer
Orestes . . . . Joseph Ragno
Stage Manager. . . . . Richard Bly
Aegisthus . . . . Salem Ludwig
Alexandros's Wife. . . . . Nancy Berg
Electra . . . . Corinne Neuchateau
Priestess . . . . Geraldine Baron
Clytemnestra . . . . Barbara Covington
Messenger. . . . . Robert Heller
Messenger's Wife. . . . . Eulalie Noble
Alexandros. . . . . J. J. Quinn
Diomedes . . . . Martin Priest
Cassandra. . . . . Sharon Chatten
Iphegenia . . . . Dianne Hull
Old Nurse . . . . Katherine Squire
    Chorus of Women: Anna Galiena, Susan Burns, Sally Moffet, Cathleen Leslie, Denise Lute, Frances Fisher. Chorus of Elders: Harry Davis, Nick La Padula, Dino Condos, Ed Setrakian.
    Time: The present. Place: A theater being used for a rehearsal. One intermission.

BEDROCK (28). By David Epstein. January 6, 1984. Director, Melvin Bernhardt; scenery and costumes, Steven Rubin; lighting, Craig Miller.
Jess . . . . John Rubinstein
Mary. Anne Twomey
Faith. . . . . Jean DeBaer

Act I: A cabin on a lake in upstate New York, a spring morning. Act II: Four years later, summer. Act III: Almost two years later, a fall afternoon.

CANTORIAL (28). By Ira Levin. February 3, 1984. Director, Edwin Sherin; cantorial singer, Paul Zim; scenery, Marjorie Bradley Kellogg; lighting, Jeff Davis; costumes, Ann Roth.
Warren Ives. . . . . Kristoffer Tabori
Lesley Arenstein . . . . Blanche Baker
Morris Lipkind . . . . Woody Romoff
Lyle Hathaway . . . . Dion Anderson
Victoria Kraus. . . . . Christine Jones
Howard Balaban . . . . Harris Laskawy
William Ives. . . . . Rex Robbins
    Time: The present. Place: A home that was formerly a synagogue, on the lower East Side of Manhattan. Act I: Late summer, early fall. Act II: Late fall, early winter.

STEM OF A BRIAR (28). By Beddow Hatch. March 23, 1984. Director, Leonard Peters; scenery, Hugh Landwehr; lighting, Richard Winkler; costumes, Carol Oditz.
Roderick Denner IV. . . . . . Dennis Boutsikeris
Roy McClure. . . . . David Romero
Nancy Denner. . . . . Donna Bullock
Margaret Denner. . . . . Michael Learned
Roderick Denner III. . . . . John McMartin
Blakely, bailiff . . . . James Doerr
Judge Barnes . . . . Robert Dale Martin
Carl Sanders . . . . Jack Sims
    Time: Mid-1940s to mid-1950s. Place: Texas. One intermission.

Syracuse, N.Y.: Syracuse Stage

(Producing director. Arthur Storch; managing director, James A. Clark)

THE DOUBLE BASS (28). By Patrick Susskind. April 20, 1984. Director, Arthur Storch; scenery, Charles Cosler; lighting, F.

Mitchell Dana; costumes, Maria Marrero. With Alan Brasington.

SYRACUSE STAGE—Alan Brasington in *The Double Bass* by Patrick Susskind

Washington, D.C.: Arena Stage

(Producing director, Zelda Fichandler; executive director, Thomas Fichandler; associate producing director, Douglas C. Wager)

ACCIDENTAL DEATH OF AN ANARCHIST (46). By Dario Fo; adapted by Richard Nelson from a literal translation by Suzanne Cowan. February 3, 1984. Director, Douglas C. Wager; scenery, Karl Eigsti; lighting, Allen Lee Hughes; costumes, Marjorie Slaiman.

Fool	Richard Bauer
Sergeant	Michael Jeter
Inspector Bertozzo	Joe Palmieri
Captain	Tom Hewitt
Police Chief	Raymond Serra
Reporter	Susan Plaksin
Stagehand	Terry Hinz

Act I, Scene 1: Rome, Italy, central police headquarters, 2d floor office. Scene 2: The same building, 4th floor office. Act II: The same, later the same day.

Waterford, Conn.: Eugene O'Neill Theater Center

(President, George C. White; artistic director, Lloyd Richards)

New works in progress: 2 performances each, July 14–Aug. 6, 1983.

DANNY AND THE DEEP BLUE SEA. By John Patrick Shanley; director, Amy Saltz.

STREGA (THE WITCH) By Anna Theresa Cascio: director, Dennis Scott.

NIGHT AND DAY. By Lars Noren; translated from the Swedish by Harry G. Carlson; director, Göran Graffman.

THE ORDINARY by Michel Vinaver; translated and directed by Gideon Y. Schein.

DAY OF THE PICNIC (THE WITCH DOCTOR'S REVENGE). By Russell Davis; director, Tony Giordano.

INDEPENDENCE. By Lee Blessing; director, Barnet Kallman.

OHIO TIP-OFF. By James Yoshimura; director, Walton Jones.

LIFE AND LIMB. By Keith Reddin; director, John Pasquin.

THE ABLE-BODIED SEAMAN. By Alan
Bowne; director, Dennis Scott.
THE MELODY SISTERS. By Anne Com-
mire; director, Walton Jones.
FENCES. By August Wilson; director, William
Partlan.
THE GREAT DIVIDE. By Robert Litz; direc-
tor, Dennis Scott.
OPEN HEART. By William Di Canzio; direc-
tor, Amy Saltz.

Company: Mary Alice, Chris Ard, Daniel
Barton, Frances Bay, Julie Boyd, Richard
Brooks, Tony Campisi, Frances Chaney, Lori
Tan Chinn, Bryan Clark, Carolyn Coates, Bill
Cobbs, Maury Cooper, Caris Corfman, Tandy

Cronyn, Alma Cuervo, Jill Eikenberry, Ray
Fry, Megan Gallagher, Kevin Geer, Lydia
Hamilton, Jo Henderson, Leonard Jackson,
Brent Jennings, Michael Lombard, Beverly
May, Nancy Mette, Mary McDonnell, Sam
McMurray, Vic Polizos, James Ray, Howard E.
Rollins, Joe Seneca, Ben Siegler, Sloan Shel-
ton, Pat Skipper, Michael Tucker, John Tur-
turro, Ken Welsh, Carla White, Tom Wright.

Designers: Bernard B. Berner, G. Russell
Christian, Kate Edmunds, Fred Voelpel, Ann
Wrightson.

Dramaturgs: Michael Feingold, Edith Oliver, Ernest Schier.

West Springfield, Mass.: StageWest

(Producing director, Stephen E. Hays)

HANNIBAL BLUES (28). By Bernard
Sabath. February 16, 1984. Director, Thomas
Gruenewald; scenery, James Leonard Joy; light-
ing, Barry Arnold; costumes, Mariann Ver-
heyen.
Roy Fulton .... Gregory Chase

Ben Fulton.................. Jon Matthews
Rebecca Setterdahl .... Jane Hoffman
Arabella Winchell .... Betty Williams
Place: A small Missouri Town. Act I: May,
1925. Act II: Late that evening.

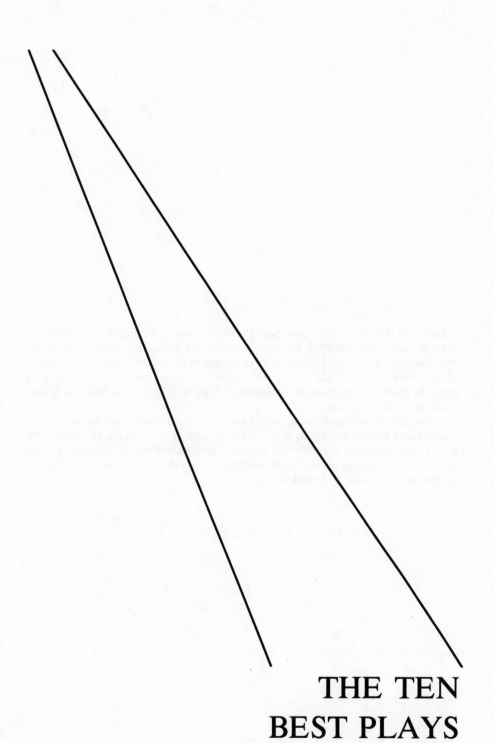

THE TEN
BEST PLAYS

Here are details of 1983–84's Best Plays—synopses, biographical sketches of authors and other material. By permission of the publishing companies which own the exclusive rights to publish these scripts in full in the United States, most of our continuities include substantial quotations from crucial/pivotal scenes in order to provide a permanent reference to style and quality as well as theme, structure and story line.

In the case of such quotations, scenes and lines of dialogue, stage directions and descriptions appear *exactly* as in the stage version or published script unless (in a very few instances, for technical reasons) an abridgement is indicated by five dots (. . . . .). The appearance of three dots (. . .) is the script's own punctuation to denote the timing of a spoken line.

FOOL FOR LOVE

A Full-Length Play in One Act

BY SAM SHEPARD

Cast and credits appear on page 349

SAM SHEPARD was born Samuel Shepard Rogers on Nov. 5, 1942 in Fort Sheridan, Ill. After attending Duarte High School and Mount San Antonio Junior College (1961–62) in California he embarked upon a playwriting career which has become one of the foremost in the world. It began in 1963 OOB at Theater Genesis with Cowboys *and* Rock Garden. *His first off-Broadway production was the one-acter* Up to Thursday *in 1965 in the Theater 1965 (Richard Barr, Clinton Wilder, Edward Albee) New Playwrights Series. His only full-scale New York production has been* Operation Sidewinder *by the Repertory Theater of Lincoln Center March 12, 1970 for 52 performances. In the tributary theater, however, his works have brought him numerous Obies, grants and other accolades including the 1979 Pulitzer Prize and Obie for* Buried Child *and an Obie and Best Play citation for* Fool for Love *which opened off Broadway May 26, 1983 in its Magic Theater of San Francisco production, directed by Shepard, and enriched the entire 1983–84 season in its long off-Broadway run.*

Shepard is playwright-in-residence at the Magic Theater and, indeed, most of his recent plays have originated there under the supervision of their author. The long list of his scripts which have appeared off Broadway and OOB includes the following: the one-acter Chicago *(1966, Obie),* La Turista *(1967, Obie), the one-acter* Red Cross *(1968),* Forensic and the Navigators *and* Melodrama Play *(1968, Obie), a segment of* Oh! Calcutta! *(1969),* The Unseen Hand *(1970), portions of* Terminal *(1970),* Back Bog Beast Bait *(1971),* Mad Dog Blues *(1971),* The Tooth of Crime *(1973, Obie), the one-acters* The Holy Ghostly *and* Icarus's Mother *(1973, Obie), portions of* Nightwalk *(1973), the one-acter* The Blue Bitch *(1973), the one-acters* Killer's Head *and* Action *(1975, Obie),* Geography of a Horse Dreamer *(1976),* Cowboys 2 *(1976),* Suicide in B Flat *(1977),* Curse of the Starving Class *(1977, Obie),* Angel City *(1977), the one-acter* Hawk Moon #1

(1978), Seduced *(1979), the collaborations* Tongues *and* Savage/Love *(1979, in the season Shepard received an Obie for sustained achievement) and* True West *(1980), a revival of which has been running off Broadway at the same time as* Fool for Love.

Shepard is also the author of the screen plays Zabriski Point *and* Me and My Brother *and has acted in several films including the recent* The Right Stuff. *He has been the recipient of grants from the Guggenheim and Rockefeller Foundations and Yale University. He lives in California with his wife, O-Lan Johnson, and son.*

Time: The Present

Place: A motel room on the edge of the Mojave Desert

SYNOPSIS: The motel room is drab and barren, with a metal four-poster in the center and metal table and chairs down left. The bathroom door is at right, the hall door at left and a picture window center with a street light shining beyond it. Merle Haggard's "Wake Up" is playing as the lights come up revealing, at left, a black stage-level platform on which an Old Man is seated, in a rocking chair, with a bottle of whiskey and styrofoam cup on the floor beside him. Sitting on the edge of the bed facing the audience is May, *"feet on floor, legs apart, elbows on knees, head hanging forward, face staring at floor,"* barefoot and dressed in denim skirt and T-shirt. She is in her early 30s.

Eddie, in his late 30s, sits at the table. He is dressed in worn and taped cowboy boots, dirty jeans and Western shirt, with spurs dangling from his belt. *"When he walks, he limps slightly and gives the impression he's rarely off a horse. There's a peculiar broken-down quality about his body in general, as though he's aged before his time."* Finished working resin into a bucking glove, he takes it off and puts it on the table with a bucking strap. He rises, strokes May's head and assures her he's not going to leave.

> *May suddenly grabs his closest leg with both arms and holds tight, burying her head between his knees.*

EDDIE: . . . . . I'm not gonna leave. Don't worry. I'm not gonna leave. I'm stayin' right here. I already told ya that.

> *She squeezes tighter to his leg, he just stands there, strokes her head softly.*

May? Let go, okay? Honey? I'll put you back in bed. Okay?

> *She grabs his other leg and holds on tight to both.*

Come on. I'll put you in bed and make you some hot tea or somethin'. You want some tea?

> *She shakes her head violently, keeps holding on.*

With lemon? Some Ovaltine? May, you gotta let go of me now, okay?

> *Pause, then she pushes him away and returns to her original position.*

Now just lay back and try to relax.

> *He starts to try to push her back gently on the bed as he pulls back the blankets. She erupts furiously, leaping off bed and lashing out at him*

Ed Harris as Eddie and Kathy Whitton Baker as May in *Fool for Love*

> *with her fists. He backs off. She returns to bed and stares at him*
> *wild-eyed and angry, faces him squarely.*

(After a pause.) You want me to go?

MAY *(shakes her head):* No!

EDDIE: Well, what do you want then?

MAY: You smell.

EDDIE: I smell.

MAY: You do.

EDDIE: I been drivin' for days.

MAY: Your fingers smell.

EDDIE: Horses.

MAY: Pussy.

EDDIE: Come on, May.

MAY: They smell like metal.

EDDIE: I'm not gonna start this shit.

MAY: Rich pussy. Very clean.

"I don't need you," May exclaims, but when Eddie grabs his glove and bucking strap, goes to the door, exits and slams it behind him, she screams, "Don't go!" She clutches a pillow hysterically and is standing facing the door when Eddie returns, having left his leather outside. He tries to calm May down by assuring her he'll take care of her. May still relishes the thought of how she is going to murder Eddie and his lover—whom she calls "the Countess"—with sharp knives.

They circle the motel room, backs pressed against the walls, glaring at each other like beasts in a cage, as Eddie tries to impress May by telling her he missed her so much—every part of her, but for some unknown reason her neck in particular—that he drove more than 2,000 miles to be here with her. He means to take her back, to Wyoming, where he's bought a site for his trailer. May is perfectly contented here, she says, with a job as a cook, and she locks herself in the bathroom to escape Eddie's persistent description of the idyllic life they'll lead. Behind the door, May shouts that she would hate this "Lame country dream life with chickens and vegetables."

EDDIE: You'll get used to it.

MAY *(enters from bathroom):* You're unbelievable!

> *She slams bathroom door, crosses upstage to window.*

EDDIE: I'm not lettin' go of you this time, May.

> *He sits in chair upstage of table.*

MAY: You never had a hold of me to begin with. *(Pause.)* How many times have you done this to me?

EDDIE: What.

MAY: Suckered me into some dumb little fantasy and then dropped me like a hot rock. How many times has that happened?

EDDIE: It's no fantasy.

MAY: It's all a fantasy.

EDDIE: And I never dropped you either.

MAY: No, you just disappeared!

EDDIE: I'm here now, aren't I?

MAY: Well, praise Jesus God!

EDDIE: I'm gonna take care of you, May. I am. I'm gonna stick with you no matter what, I promise.

Lamely, May orders him to go away but finds herself accused of having deserted Eddie after he left her by herself in the trailer for a long stretch. He'd supplied her with a large stack of French fashion magazines to keep her company, but she walked out on him even though she knew he'd be back looking for her. Now he plans to fetch his things from the truck and spend the night here with her in her room. Soon they find themselves embracing: *"Long, tender kiss. They are very soft with each other. She pulls away from him slightly. Smiles. She looks him straight in the eyes, then suddenly knees him in the groin with tremendous force."*
Eddie falls to the floor, as May exits into the bathroom, slamming the door (both doors are equipped with drums concealed in the frames, with amplifiers, exaggerating and prolonging this sound). As Eddie lies helpless, the Old Man speaks for the first time, declaring to no one in particular that in his mind he is married to Barbara Mandrell.

With Eddie still on the floor, May comes in from the bathroom and changes into red dress and black high-heeled shoes, as she tells Eddie she doesn't understand her own feelings: "I don't understand how I could hate you so much after so much time. How, no matter how much I'd like to not hate you, I hate you even more. It grows." May is obsessed with a vision of Eddie together with an unnamed "her" which comes into her mind as a kind of repeated torture.

When Eddie learns that May is getting ready for a date who is coming here to pick her up, he is instantly angry and goes out, slamming the door. When he returns he is carrying a shotgun and a bottle of tequila (in his absence, May threw some of her things into a suitcase which she has now hidden under the bed). May is obviously worried about the shotgun, as Eddie pours himself a tumblerful of tequila and sits at the table down left. She cautions him that the man coming here is "very friendly." He isn't of much concern to Eddie, because May called him a "man"; if she were deeply involved with him, she'd call him a "guy".

MAY: . . . . . He's a very gentle person.

EDDIE: Is that right. Well, I'm a very gentle person myself. My feelings get easily damaged.

MAY: What feelings.

> *Eddie falls silent, takes a drink, then gets up slowly with glass, leaves bottle on table, crosses to bed, sits on bed, sets glass on floor, picks up shotgun and starts dismantling it.*

MAY *(watches him closely):* You can't keep messing me around like this. It's been going on too long. I can't take it any more. I get sick every time you come around. Then I get sick when you leave. You're like a disease to me. Besides, you got no right being jealous of me after all the bullshit I've been through with you.

> *Pause.*

EDDIE *(keeps his attention on shotgun as he talks to her):* We've got a pact.

MAY: Oh, God.

EDDIE: We made a pact.

MAY: There's nothing between us now!

EDDIE: Then what're you so excited about?

MAY: I'm not excited.

EDDIE: You're beside yourself.

MAY: You're driving me crazy. You're driving me totally crazy!

EDDIE: You know we're connected, May. We'll always be connected. That was decided a long time ago.

MAY: Nothing was decided! You made all that up.

EDDIE: You know what happened.

MAY: You promised me that was finished. You can't start that up all over again. You promised me.

EDDIE: A promise can't stop something like that. It happened.

MAY: Nothing happened! Nothing ever happened!

EDDIE: Innocent to the last drop.

May asks Eddie to leave. He declares that she will never be able to replace him; nevertheless he does leave, taking the shotgun with him. May calls out his name and hugs the wall, weeping, moving toward the corner, as the lights concentrate on the Old Man telling a story about driving across Southern Utah with his wife and child (presumably May, who moves toward the bed on her knees, grabs a pillow and embraces it, rocking back and forth). The child wouldn't stop crying, and the Old Man remembers that he stopped the car, carried her outside to get some air and found himself surrounded by a herd of lowing cattle.

May hears Eddie coming back (as the lights come up in the playing area), swigs a drink from the bottle and sits contemplating it as Eddie enters carrying two steer ropes, throwing one on the bed and building a loop on the other, spinning it and roping each of the bedposts. He has come back, he says (as each of them takes another swig from the bottle), to see for himself whether someone is really coming to take her out on a date. He continues roping bedposts, and May accuses him of childish behavior, showing off for her the way he used to do in high school. When her date arrives, Eddie will "nail his ass to the floor," he promises, roping a chair and dragging it along.

> *May suddenly stands, goes to bedpost, grabs her purse, slings it on her shoulder and heads for stage left door.*

MAY: I'm not sticking around for this.

> *She exits, leaving door open. Eddie runs offstage after her.*

EDDIE: Where're you goin'?

MAY *(offstage):* Take your hands off a me!

EDDIE *(offstage):* Wait a second, wait a second. Just a second, okay?

> *May screams. Eddie carries her back onstage screaming and kicking. He sets her down, slams door shut. She walks away from him, straightening her dress.*

EDDIE: Tell ya what. I'll back off. I'll be real nice. I will. I promise. I'll be just like a little ole pussy cat, okay? You can introduce me to him as your brother or something. Well—maybe not your brother.

MAY: Maybe not.

EDDIE: Your cousin. Okay? I'll be your cousin. I just wanna meet him is all. Then I'll leave. Promise.

MAY: Why do you want to meet him? He's just a friend.

EDDIE: Just to see where you stand these days. You can tell a lot about a person by the company they keep.

May decides to go call her date and tell him not to come, just as headlights flash across the window. Eddie takes the pair of spurs from his belt—*"old and used, with small rowels"*—and puts them onto his boot heels. May warns Eddie not to hurt her friend. Sarcastically, he promises he won't. As May looks outside she sees that the headlights are not her friend's. They belong to a big, black Mercedes Benz with a woman in the front seat staring back at May. Eddie warns May to get away from the door. *"Suddenly the white headlight beams slash across the stage through the open door. Eddie rushes to the door, slams it shut and pushes May aside. Just as he slams the door the sound of a large caliber magnum pistol explodes off left, followed immediately by the sound of shattering glass, then a car horn blares and continues on one relentless note."*

Eddie turns out the room lights and pulls May to the safety of the floor beside the bed, as the horn continues to blare and the lights are flicked from high to low beam. Whoever the occupant of the Mercedes Benz may be, she has obviously followed Eddie here and, as May says, is driving "the kind of car a Countess drives. That's the kind of car I always pictured her in."

The headlights finally disappear, to the sound of squealing rubber. Eddie takes a cautious look outside and sees that the visitor has shot out the windshield of his truck. He warns May to pack and get ready to leave with him because his crazy friend is sure to be back. May doesn't see any reason why she should leave, this being Eddie's problem and not hers, Eddie tells her, "I came here to get you! Whatsa matter with you! I came all this way to get you! Do you think I'd do that if I didn't love you! Huh? That bitch doesn't mean anything to me! Nuthin'. I got no reason to be here but you." But May still refuses to go with him.

Again a light comes up on the Old Man whose comment, this time, directly concerns the two young people on the periphery of whose lives he has been occupying a special place as an observer.

OLD MAN: Amazing thing is, neither one a you look a bit familiar to me. Can't figure that one out. I don't recognize myself in either one a you. Never did. 'Course your mothers both put their stamp on ya. That's plain to see. But my whole side a the issue is absent, in my opinion. Totally unrecognizable. You could be anybody's. Probably are. I can't even remember the original circumstances. Been so long. Probably a lot a things I forgot. Good thing I got out when I did, though. Best thing I ever did.

The light fades on the Old Man and comes up in the room where Eddie, coiling his rope, vows that he will never give up his pursuit of May, no matter what.

EDDIE: . . . . . I don't care if you hate my guts. I don't care if you can't stand the sight of me or the sound of me or the smell of me. I'm never leavin'. You'll never get rid of me. You'll never escape me either. I'll track you down no matter where you go. I know exactly how your mind works. I've been right every time. Every single time.

MAY: You've gotta give this up, Eddie.

EDDIE: I'm not giving it up!

Pause.

MAY *(calm):* Okay. Look. I don't understand what you've got in your head any more. I really don't. I don't get it. *Now,* you desperately need me. *Now,* you can't live without me. *NOW* you'll do anything for me. Why should I believe it this time?

EDDIE: Because it's true.

MAY: It was supposed to have been true every time before. Every other time. Now it's true again. You've been jerking me off like this for fifteen years. Fifteen years I've been a yo-yo for you. I've never been split. I've never been two ways about you. I've either loved you or not loved you. And now I just plain don't love you. Understand? Do you understand that? I don't love you. I don't need you. I don't want you. Do you get that? Now if you can still stay then you're either crazy or pathetic.

Headlights slash again across the window, and this time May is determined to go out and deal with "the Countess" herself, "tear her damn head off!" Eddie holds her back, and in the midst of their struggle Martin *("mid-30s, solidly built, wears a green plaid shirt, a blue baseball cap, baggy work pants with suspenders, heavy work boots")* comes crashing through the front door and tackles Eddie. He heard them yelling and assumed May was being attacked. May tries to explain, saying Eddie is her cousin, and Eddie makes it as difficult as possible for her by accusing her of lying.

Martin is a straightforward person, answering all questions as though they were sincerely posed, therefore an easy target for Eddie's mockery to hit, but not so easy to penetrate. May wants to run right off to the movies with Martin and goes into the bathroom to get ready. Eddie, still on the floor, prods Martin on his choice of a movie and his occupation (yard work). Returning to the subject of whether or not May was lying when she said they were cousins, Eddie makes Martin feel that perhaps he is intruding on something he doesn't understand and had better leave. But when Martin moves toward the door Eddie bars his way, and Martin's exit turns into an attempt to escape, frustrated by Eddie, who leads Martin into sitting at the table with glass filled, waiting for May to come out of the bathroom. Eddie sits too, drinking from the bottle. The Old Man's presence at this table is not perceived by Martin, but Eddie pours him a drink. Eddie explains to Martin that May is in a state of shock.

MARTIN: Shock? How come?

EDDIE: Well, we haven't seen each other in a long time. I mean—me and her. We go back quite a ways, see. High school.

MARTIN: Oh. I didn't know that.

EDDIE: Yeah. Lotta miles.

MARTIN: And you're not really cousins?

EDDIE: No. Not really. No.

MARTIN: You're—her husband?

EDDIE: No. She's my sister. *(He and the Old Man look at each other then he turns back to Martin.)* My half-sister.

Pause. Eddie and Old Man drink.

MARTIN: Your sister?

EDDIE: Yeah.

MARTIN: Oh. So—you knew each other even before high school then, huh?

EDDIE: No, see, I never even knew I had a sister until it was too late.

MARTIN: How do you mean?

EDDIE: Well, by the time I found out we'd already—you know—fooled around.
Old Man shakes his head, drinks. Long pause. Martin just stares at Eddie.

EDDIE *(grins):* Whatsa matter, Martin?

MARTIN: You fooled around?

EDDIE: Yeah.

MARTIN: Well-um—that's illegal, isn't it?

EDDIE: I suppose so.

OLD MAN *(to Eddie):* Who is this guy?

MARTIN: I mean—is that true? She's really your sister?

EDDIE: Half. Only half.

MARTIN: Which half?

EDDIE: Top half. In horses we call that the "topside."

OLD MAN: Yeah, and the mare's what? The mare's uh—"distaff," isn't it? Isn't that the bottom half? "Distaff." Funny I should remember that.

MARTIN: And you fooled around in high school together?

EDDIE: Yeah. Sure. Everybody fooled around in high school. Didn't you?

MARTIN: No, I never did.

EDDIE: Maybe you should have, Martin.

MARTIN: Well, not with my sister.

EDDIE: No, I wouldn't recommend that.

MARTIN: How could that happen? I mean—

EDDIE: Well, see— *(Pause. He stares at the Old Man.)* —our daddy fell in love twice. That's basically how it happened. Once with my mother and once with her mother.

OLD MAN: It was the same love. Just got split in two, that's all.

Eddie explains to Martin that his father led a double life with two separate families, neither aware of the other's existence. Even when his father would disappear for months at a time, his mother was glad to see him when he came back. She asked no questions.

After years of appearing and disappearing, the time came when his father stayed home for a long period, sitting in his chair and then going for long walks, day and night. ("I was making a decision," the Old Man comments.) One night he took Eddie on one of his walks, for miles into the center of town where Eddie's father bought a bottle at the liquor store. They kept going, through town and out the other side, still wordless, drinking the bottle dry.

Finally they reached a house with a red awning, and Eddie's father walked up onto the porch and rang the doorbell. "And then this woman comes to the door," Eddie continues, telling the tale to Martin, "This real pretty woman with red hair. And she throws herself into his arms. And he starts crying. He just breaks down right there in front of me. And she's kissing him all over the face and holding him real tight and he's just crying like a baby. And then through the doorway, behind them both, I see this girl. *(The bathroom door very slowly and silently swings open revealing May, standing in the door frame, back-lit with yellow light, in her red dress. She just watches Eddie as he keeps telling story. He and Martin are unaware of her presence.)* She just appears. She's just standing there, staring at me and I'm staring back at her and we can't take our eyes off each other. It was like we knew each other from somewhere but we couldn't place where. But the second we saw each other, that very second, we knew we'd never stop being in love."

May slams the bathroom door and assures Martin that the story is a pack of lies made up by Eddie and told differently every time. May tries to take Martin off to the movies, but Eddie insists they stay and hear him out. May takes over, however; she has decided to finish Eddie's story herself, "Without any little tricks added on to it." Her mother, the red headed woman, was obsessed with love for her father and would go looking for him when he went away. Her father, afraid that his two women would "find out about each other and devour him whole," tried to maintain a certain distance. But May's mother persisted and finally discovered the town where he lived with his other family. May and her mother patrolled the streets, looking through windows, until they found him at supper with Eddie and Eddie's mother.

May does not describe the encounter except to say that her father just kept on eating his chicken, ignoring the women. A couple of weeks later he disappeared again, for good, to her mother's intense grief. May was now joyously in love with Eddie: "We couldn't take a breath without thinking of each other. We couldn't eat if we weren't together. We couldn't sleep. We got sick at night when we were apart. Violently sick. And my mother even took me to see a doctor. And Eddie's mother took him to see the same doctor but the doctor had no idea what was wrong with us. He thought it was the flu or something. And Eddie's mother had no idea what was wrong with him. But my mother—my mother knew exactly what was wrong. She knew it clear down to her bones. She recognized every symptom. And she begged me not to see him but I wouldn't listen. Then she begged Eddie not to see me but he wouldn't listen. Then she went to Eddie's mother and begged her. And Eddie's mother— *(Pause. She looks straight at Eddie.)* Eddie's mother blew her brains out. Didn't she, Eddie? Blew her brains right out."

The Old Man doubts this version of the story, but Eddie comments that his mother used his father's shotgun, the first time she'd ever fired it. The Old Man admits he was away at the time but feels that somebody could have found him so that he could come back and deal with the situation. As for May's mother (the Old Man tells May), she loved him so much that he couldn't help responding: "How could I turn away from her? We were completely whole."

Very slowly Eddie and May move toward each other.

OLD MAN *(to Eddie):* Stay away from her! What the hell are you doin'! Keep away from her! You two can't come together! You gotta hold up my end a this deal. I got nobody now! Nobody! You can't betray me! You gotta represent me now! You're my son!

    Eddie and May come together center stage. They kiss each other tenderly. Headlights suddenly arc across stage again from up right, cutting across the stage through window then disappearing off left. Sound of loud collision, shattering glass, an explosion. Bright orange and blue light of a gasoline fire suddenly illuminates upstage window. Then sounds of horses screaming wildly, hooves galloping on pavement, fading, then total silence. Light of gas fire continues now till end of play. Eddie and May never stop holding each other through all this. Long pause. No one moves. Then Martin stands and moves upstage to window, peers out through Venetian blinds. Pause.

MARTIN: *(upstage at window, looking out into flames):* Is that your truck with the horse trailer out there?

EDDIE *(stays with May):* Yeah.

MARTIN: It's on fire.

EDDIE: Yeah.

MARTIN: All the horses are loose.

EDDIE *(steps back away from May):* Yeah, I figured.

MAY: Eddie—

EDDIE *(to May):* I'm just gonna go out and take a look. I gotta at least take a look, don't I?

MAY: What difference does it make?

EDDIE: Well, I can't just let her get away with that. What am I supposed to do? *(Moves toward stage left door.)* I'll just be a second.

MAY: Eddie—

EDDIE: I'm only gonna be a second. I'll just take a look at it and I'll come right back, okay?

Eddie exits stage left door. May stares at door, stays where she is. Martin stays upstage. Martin turns slowly from window upstage and looks at May. Pause. May moves to bed, pulls suitcase out from underneath, throws it on bed and opens it. She goes into bathroom and comes out with clothes. She packs the clothes in a suitcase. Martin watches her for a while, then moves slowly downstage to her as she continues.

MARTIN: May—

May goes back into the bathroom and comes back out with more clothes. She packs them.

Do you need some help or anything? I got a car. I could drive you somewhere if you want.

Pause. May just keeps packing her clothes.

Are you going to go with him?

She stops. Straightens up. Stares at Martin. Pause.

MAY: He's gone.

MARTIN: He said he'd be back in a second.

MAY *(pause):* He's gone.

May exits carrying her suitcase, leaving the door open and Martin staring after her. The Old Man is rocking in his chair and staring into space at an imaginary picture of the woman of his dreams. Merle Haggard's "I'm the One Who Loves You" is heard, swelling in volume as the lights fade slowly to black. *Curtain.*

○○○
○○○
○○○
○○○
○○○
○○○

LA CAGE AUX FOLLES

A Musical in Two Acts

BOOK BY HARVEY FIERSTEIN

MUSIC AND LYRICS BY JERRY HERMAN

BASED ON THE PLAY BY JEAN POIRET

Cast and credits appear on page 317

HARVEY FIERSTEIN (book) was born June 6, 1954 in the Bensonhurst section of Brooklyn, where he still resides and where he was educated, receiving a Fine Arts degree from Pratt Institute. At 15 he was a drag performer (female impersonator) at Club 82 in the East Village. In 1971 he made his professional stage acting debut at La Mama ETC. He had taken writing classes in high school but did not set pen to paper with any professional intent until, in 1972, he wrote a short play with parts in it for all the playwrights who had been writing parts for him (it was called In Search of the Cobra Jewels *and was put on at Playwrights' Workshop Club, Fierstein's first New York production). There followed* Freaky Pussy *in 1974 and* Flatbush Tosca *in 1975 at New York Theater Ensemble.*

The first one-acter in Fierstein's acclaimed Torch Song Trilogy *was* The International Stud, *produced at Theater for the New City in 1976, at La Mama in 1978 and then off Broadway that same season, with Fierstein in the leading role of Arnold, which he carried through the second of the* Torch Song Trilogy *plays,* Fugue in a Nursery, *at La Mama and then off Broadway in 1979, and the third,* Widows and Children First!, *at La Mama in 1979. In combination, as* Torch Song Trilogy, *this program of three plays about a "drag queen," intensely portrayed in the author's Tony Award-winning performance, climbed all the way to the top of the production ladder, beginning OOB at the Richard Allen Center October 16, 1981; moving to full off-Broadway status January 15, 1982 for 117 performances and a citation as a Best Play of its season; then to Broadway June 10, 1982 and a number of Tonys including that for the best Broadway play of the season, plus the Dramatist Guild's Hull-Warriner Award and many other honors.*

La Cage aux Folles, *adapted by Fierstein from the French play of the same title on which the French movie comedy hit also was based, opened on Broadway August 21, 1983 after an acclaimed Boston tryout and wins its author his second Best Play citation. Fierstein has been the recipient of a Rockefeller Foundation grant in playwriting, a Ford Foundation grant for new American plays, a CPS Fellowship and a Public Broadcasting grant. His acting career has included more than 60 appearances on stage and screen, and he is pursuing his playwriting career, his latest work having been* Spookhouse *off Broadway this season.*

JERRY HERMAN (music, lyrics) was born in New York City July 10, 1932 and received his B.A. in 1953 from the University of Miami, which awarded him its Order of Merit in 1971. The first professional production of a Herman score was the off-Broadway revue I Feel Wonderful *(1958), followed off Broadway by* Nightcap *(1958, setting an off-Broadway revue record of 400 performances),* Parade *(1960),* Madame Aphrodite *(1961, a book musical with book by Tad Mosel) and a Joe Masiell revue (1978) to which he contributed special material. That same year a revue of his songs,* Tune the Grand Up!, *was produced off off Broadway, as was the revue* Jerry's Girls *in 1981.*

On Broadway, Herman's long and distinguished career began with the score of Milk and Honey *(1961, 543 performances) and proceeded to the now-legendary* Hello, Dolly! *which opened January 16, 1964, won both the Critics and Tony Awards and is the sixth longest-running Broadway show of all time with an initial run of 2,844 performances. There have already been two major Broadway revivals of this work, one in 1975 with Pearl Bailey in the title role and one in 1978 with Carol Channing, the original Dolly.*

Herman's Broadway scores continued with Mame *in 1966 for 1,508 first-run performances, revived this season (see its entry in the Plays Produced on Broadway section of this volume);* Dear World *(1969), based on* The Madwoman of Chaillot; *contributions to the revue* From A to Z *(1969);* Mack & Mabel *(1974);* The Grand Tour *(1979); and the opening song of* A Day in Hollywood/A Night in the Ukraine *(1980), "Just Go to the Movies." Herman's second Best Play,* La Cage aux Folles *settled in for a long Broadway run early this season on August 21.*

In addition to his Hello, Dolly! *awards, Herman has received numerous Grammys and other citations for his songs and scores. In 1964 he set new lyrics to his most famous tune, turning it into "Hello, Lyndon" for Pres. Lyndon B. Johnson's campaign. In New York City, where he lives, Herman was recently inducted into the Songwriters Hall of Fame.*

JEAN POIRET (original play) is a French actor and playwright born August 17, 1926. After studying at the Rue Blanche drama school in Paris he began combining writing and acting, creating sketches for himself. His first Paris-produced play was

Douce Amère (Bittersweet, *1970). He starred in his second,* Féfé de Broadway, *and co-starred with Michel Serrault in his third,* La Cage aux Folles *(1973), which opened at the Théâtre du Palais Royale, proved immensely popular and ran for seven years, has received many productions around the world and was made into the world-famous movie comedy of the same title. Poiret's latest work is* Joyeuses Pacques *(Happy Easter, 1980), which is still running in Paris and in which he created the leading role.*

Our method of synopsizing La Cage aux Folles *in these pages differs from that of the other Best Plays. In order to illustrate the distinctive "look" of its characters and production numbers, the musical is represented here partly in photographs, with continuity and short excerpts from the book and lyrics to portray its textual style and flavor. These photographs of* La Cage aux Folles *depict scenes as produced August 21, 1983 at the Palace Theater by Alan Carr, Kenneth D. Greenblatt, Marvin A. Krauss, Stewart F. Lane, James M. Nederlander, Martin Richards, Barry Brown and Fritz Holt, and as directed by Arthur Laurents, with scenery by David Mitchell and costumes by Theoni V. Aldredge.*

Our special thanks are tendered to the producers and their press representatives, Shirley Herz, Sam Rudy and Peter Cromarty, for making available these selections from Martha Swope's excellent photographs of the show.

Time: Summer

Place: St. Tropez, France

ACT I

1. Georges (Gene Barry, *left*) is the owner of a St. Tropez night club called La Cage aux Folles, and Albin (George Hearn, *right*) is his lover and the star of his show in female garb as "the great Zaza."

2. The night club revue's chorus of 12, "Les Cagelles" *(above),* is composed of ten female impersonators and two women. They come onstage and establish themselves with the opening number, "We Are What We Are":

We are what we are
And what we are is an illusion
We love how it feels
Putting on heels
Causing confusion
We face life
Though it's sometimes sweet
          and sometimes bitter
Face life
With a little guts and lots of glitter

Look under our frocks
Girdles and jocks
Proving we are what we are!

We are what we are
Half a brassiere
Half a suspender
Half real and half fluff
You'll find it tough
Guessing our gender. . . . .

3. In the apartment they share, Albin is feeling a bit neglected. Georges tries to reassure him, even agreeing to let Albin appear as Salome again.

In his dressing room at the club, Albin becomes glamorous Zaza *(right),* singing "A Little More Mascara:"

. . . . . When my little road
                                has a few bumps again
And I need something level to lean upon
I put on my sling pumps again
And wham—this ugly duckling is a swan!
So when my spirit starts to sag
I rustle out my highest drag
And put a little more mascara on. . . . .

4. Georges's beloved son Jean-Michel (John Weiner, *below right*), result of a youthful adventure, announces that he means to marry Anne, daughter of a renowned moralist. She's bringing her parents to meet Georges. Jean-Michel hopes Albin will make himself scarce so that Georges can invite his real mother to join them during the visit. "So it's farewell to Albin! Just like that," Georges accuses, "The man raises you for twenty years like a mother. . . . . Judas!" But Jean-Michel pleads in song—while Anne (Leslie Stevens, *below center*) appears in his mind's eye—"I'm simply a man / Who walks on the stars / Whenever it's Anne on my arm."

5. Georges gives his son his blessing. They're worried about telling Albin, but Albin has already been told by their eavesdropping "maid," Jacob. *"The door flies open,"* and Albin enters *"in a rage."*

ALBIN: What have we raised, Georges? An animal? Snakes live male and female together. Cats live male and female together. We're human beings. We know better! What would you talk about?

GEORGES: There's no use arguing when he's like this. Run, fool, run.

JEAN-MICHEL: I love her, Albin.

ALBIN: Why didn't you tell me yourself? Why do I have to hear about my son on the streets? Look how thin you are. You haven't been eating. It's that girl!

JEAN-MICHEL: It's not the girl.

GEORGES: Her name is Anne.

JEAN-MICHEL: You always say I'm too thin.

ALBIN: Because you always are. Now just march yourself into the kitchen and have Claudine make you some soup.

JEAN-MICHEL: Albin . . .

GEORGES: I'll talk to him.

JEAN-MICHEL: Albin, I'm sorry.

ALBIN: He's sorry. He's sorry: Oh, Georges, what are we to do? Our baby is getting married! Oh, Georges, where did we go wrong?

Georges reassures Albin that their affectionate relationship will see them through this crisis, reprising his son's song "With Anne on My Arm" as "With You on My Arm" *(below):* "Life is a celebration / With you on my arm / It's worth the aggravation / With you on my arm."

6. On a midnight promenade, Albin learns that Jean-Michel's mother, Sybil, is coming to the wedding, and he erupts to Georges, "Do you refer to that woman who seduced you one night backstage at the Lido in Paris? That harlot who once every three or four years thinks to send her flesh and blood son a birthday card? Always, I might add, on the wrong day. . . . . What right has that woman to butt into the boy's life now?" At a cafe table *(above),* in the moonlight, Georges sings his love song to Albin, "Song on the Sand":

Do you recall that windy little beach we walked along?
That afternoon in fall / That afternoon we met
A fellow with a concertina sang . . . what was the song?
It's strange what we recall / And odd what we forget . . .

I heard la da da da da da da da as we walked on the sand
I heard la da da da . . . I believe it was early September
Through the crash of the waves I could tell that the words were romantic
Something about sharing / Something about always.

Though the years race along I still think of our song on the sand
And I still try and search for the words I can barely remember
Though the time tumbles by there is one thing that I am forever certain of
I hear la da da da da da da da da da da da da
And I'm young and in love. . . . .

Albin rushes off to a performance before Georges can tell him that he is to absent himself while the bride's parents are here.

7. The midnight show includes a can-can *(above)* and Albin on a trapeze *(below)*, with the title tune: "It's slightly 40s, and a little bit 'New Wave' / You may be dancing with a girl who needs a shave/Where both the riffraff and the royalty are patrons / At La Cage aux Folles. . . . ."

Meanwhile, Jean-Michel reminds his father to speak to Albin. Georges chides his son: "Look at him. The man who has dedicated these last twenty years to making a home for us. . . . . I want you to look at him and consider what it is you're doing; throwing him out of the home he has made for us." But Jean-Michel insists, and Georges promises to explain everything to Albin.

8. Through a screen behind which Albin is changing for the next number, Georges reveals the wedding plan: "I told you about Sybil coming. What I failed to tell you is that you're not. You've heard about that politician who wants to impose his morality on the coast? Well, he is the girl's father. . . . . And so, for one night. . . . . Sybil will be my wife. And after they've gone we can all have a good laugh about how we pulled one over on them."

Albin comes out, stares coldly at Georges and begins the "We Are What We Are" number with Les Cagelles. He can't go through with it, however *(right),* and orders the dancers and musicians off the stage.

Alone and a capella, Albin transforms the song into a personal affirmation, "I Am What I Am" *(below).*

9. I am what I am
I don't want praise
I don't want pity
I bang my own drum
Some think it's noise
I think it's pretty. . . . .

I am what I am
And what I am
Needs no excuses
I deal my own deck
Sometimes the ace
Sometimes the deuces
There's one life
And there's no return
           and no deposit
One life
So it's time
       to open up your closet
Life's not worth a damn
Till you can say—"Hey, world,
I am what I am!"

Albin doffs his wig, throws it at Georges, exits. Georges reaches out to Albin. *Curtain.*

ACT II

10. In town, Georges searches for Albin, who has been out all night, and finally catches up with him near their favorite cafe.

GEORGES: Albin.

ALBIN: I have nothing to say to you, Georges.

GEORGES: I apologize. All right?

ALBIN: I'm sorry, it's not all right. To think I'd live to see the day when Jean-Michel, who I raised as my own, would cast me out . . .

GEORGES: He's a kid. He wasn't thinking. He's in love.

ALBIN: And you?

GEORGES: I'm an old fool. Who also wasn't thinking. Who's also in love.

Albin begins to soften as the music of a concertina is heard and Georges reprises an excerpt from their love song, "Song on the Sand."

ALBIN: The fact remains I am unwanted.

GEORGES: But, my love, you are wanted. It's all you bring with you that's questionable. Now, you have certain mannerisms, albeit charming mannerisms, which could shock people who haven't been forewarned.

ALBIN: Et tu? (Imitating Georges.) ". . . which could *shock* people who haven't been forewarned."

GEORGES: Ah, but my mannerisms can translate as tasteful affectation. While yours are no less than suspicious. . . . . Albin, the point is if you wish to attend tonight's affair, you may do so simply by donning the proper attire and appropriately straightening up your act. You will assume the role of Jean-Michel's dear Uncle Al.

Georges coaches Albin for the role of heterosexual Uncle Al: "You must tell yourself, '. . . . . I am a man. I am strong. I will climb back up that mountain.' Now, drop your shoulders. Let them go round and beaten. Stop holding in your stomach. Let it pour over your lap, a testimonial to the nights out drinking with the boys. Now spread your legs! . . . . . You're wearing pants, not a skirt. Spread them!" Soon, others join them in instructing Albin (at top of opposite page) with the song "Masculinity":

GEORGES: Grunt like an ape / And growl like a tiger
           Give us a roaring, snoring, masculine laugh. . . . .
           Try and remember that John Wayne was not soprano
           Try keeping it gruff, and rough and low

ALBIN: Ha, ha

GEORGES: Try more of John Wayne and less of Brigitte Bardot. . . . .

ALL: Think of Ghengis Khan and think Taras Bulba
       Think of Attila's huns and Robin Hood's men
       And try not to weaken or collapse
       If they discover the pantyhose under your chaps
       You can climb back up the mountain once again!

11. At home *(left),* Albin appears as Uncle Al, but Jean-Michel still deplores his presence: "I ask for one lousy favor from him, and look. I should've known better. My whole life I've had to put up with his nonsense. When I think of what I've had to go through because of him. The razzings I took at school."

Georges counters, "What about what he's given up for you? . . . . . The hours spent on your homework. The nights sitting up in your sickroom." In song, he directs Jean-Michel to "Look Over There" at Albin:

How often is someone concerned with
        the tiniest thread of your life?
Concerned with whatever you feel
        and whatever you touch
Look over there / Look over there
Somebody cares that much!

(continued on the next page)

"Look Over There" (continued)

When your world spins too fast / And your bubble has burst
Someone puts himself last / So that you can come first

So count all the loves who will love you from now to the end of your life
And when you have added the loves who have loved you before
Look over there / Look over there
Somebody loves you more!

12. Jean-Michel, torn between his loves for Anne and Albin, leaves the room. Then a telegram arrives from his mother saying she won't be coming to the wedding after all. When Jean-Michel returns to announce the arrival of Anne and her parents, M. and Mme. Dindon, Albin rushes offstage.

The parents (Jay Garner and Merle Louise, *above center*) are admitted by the "maid" Jacob (William Thomas Jr., *above left*). Then Jacob passes plates of hors d'oevres while Georges declares he knows nothing about the conspicuous night club next door and pretends to have served in the hyper-masculine Foreign Legion. Bride and groom hear these four join voices in "Cocktail Counterpoint" (*above* and *top of opposite page*).

13. "Cocktail Counterpoint"

GEORGES:	MME. DINDON:	DINDON:	JACOB:
I joined the	Oh what lovely	This is	It's appalling
Foreign Legion	Dishes	Even	To confess
With a sabre	They're so	Worse	Our new
In my hand	Delicate	Than I feared	In-laws
And crawled	And frail	The son is	Are a mess
Across the desert	Mine have	Strange	
With my belly	Naked children	The father	She's a
In the sand	I believe	Is weird	Prude
With	They're on-	To meet	He's a
Men who loved	Ly male	The wife	Prig
Their camel	Oops, I think	I'm actually	She's a
And their	They're playing	Afraid	Pill
Brandy and	Some exotic lit-	I prefer	He's a
I swear—	Tle game	That	Pig
Nobody dished	Oops,	You	
Nobody swished	I think	Remain	So zis
When I was a	That	An	Zis
Foreign	Leapfrog	Old	Zis
Legionnaire.	Is its name.	Maid.	For your papa! . . . . .

14. *"Suddenly the front door flies open. A fortyish woman, neatly dressed, enters. It is a mother. It is Albin," (right),* leaping into the breach, masquerading as Jean-Michel's absent mother. The Dindons are taken in, but not Anne, who has *"noticed Albin's five o'clock shadow. At first she is shocked, then she laughs to herself."* Anne obviously approves of the deception.

The evening's difficulties continue: Jacob burns the dinner, so they are all obliged to go out to a restaurant, Chez Jacqueline, run by *"a handsome, very stylish woman,"* a close friend of Georges and Albin.

At the restaurant, Anne tells Jean-Michel, "I love your mother. I think he is incredible." Dindon talks of his daughter's dowry. Jacqueline insists that Albin favor them with a song, and he cannot refuse *(next page).*

15. Albin's infectious song, "The Best of Times," draws others to join in *(above)*, including Jacqueline herself (Elizabeth Parrish):

The best of times is now
What's left of summer but a faded rose?
The best of times is now
As for tomorrow, well, who knows, who knows, who knows?

So hold this moment fast
And live and love as hard as you know how
And make this moment last
Because the best of times is now / Is now/ Is now!

    The applause is triumphant. *"Zaza, ever the star, back in her element, curtsies and curtsies, and ends, as she always does, with her habitual gesture: she takes off her wig. And freezes in horror."* Albin cries "Oh, merde!" as he realizes that he has given himself away. Dindon also freezes in horror, then explodes in disapproval. The scene ends in pandemonium.

16. Back at the apartment, Dindon rages, but Anne is determined to marry Jean-Michel, who affirms his filial loyalty to Albin in a reprise of "Look Over There." Jacqueline arrives, bringing the press to interview Dindon—but he can't afford to be seen with these notorious night club types. Albin offers to help Dindon escape if he'll bless the marriage with a dowry and promise never to attend family gatherings. Grudgingly, Dindon agrees. Peace is thus restored, with romance triumphant *(below)*.

17. Albin sets up an ironic ruse, slipping the Dindons past the reporters in disguise as Les Cagelles, he in drag, she in the almost-nude. The stage empties, leaving Georges and Albin to their "Song on the Sand":

GEORGES: Though the time tumbles by there is one thing that I
                                                                        am forever certain of
               I hear la da da da da da da
ALBIN: La da da da da da da
GEORGES & ALBIN: And I'm young and in love!
               They are dancing now. . . . . Lights glow in the buildings, twinkle in
               the boats in the harbor. . . . . Little slivers of moonlight float down on
               them, and—the curtain falls.

PAINTING CHURCHES

A Play in Two Acts

BY TINA HOWE

Cast and credits appear on page 372

TINA HOWE was born in New York City in 1937, the daughter of newscaster Quincy Howe. She received her B.A. at Sarah Lawrence in 1959 and pursued graduate studies in secondary education at Columbia Teachers College in New York and Chicago Teachers College. But playwriting was already in her blood after her first one-acter (Closing Time, about the end of the world) was put on in a production directed, produced and starred in by Jane Alexander at Sarah Lawrence. Her first professional outing was the short-lived The Nest off Broadway in 1970. Her next major production did not take place until 1976, when her play Museum appeared at the Los Angeles Actors Theater and then at New York Shakespeare Festival in 1977 (as an OOB offering) and 1978 (for 78 off-Broadway performances). She won further acclaim with The Art of Dining at Kennedy Center in 1979, following a short off-Broadway run at New York Shakespeare Festival.

Painting Churches, its author's first Best Play, was produced off off Broadway by Second Stage in February 1983 for 30 performances, winning Miss Howe a Rosamond Gilder award for creative achievement, then moving off Broadway Nov. 22, 1983 in this same Second Stage production. Other plays by Miss Howe include Birth and After Birth published by Vintage Books in the anthology New Women's Theater and the one-acter Appearances produced OOB in 1982. She is the recipient of a 1982–83 Obie Award for distinguished playwriting for Museum, The Art of Dining and Painting Churches, published in a single volume by Avon.

Tina Howe is married to the novelist Norman Levy, and they have two teen-aged children. They live in New York City, where Miss Howe teaches playwriting at New

York University and is the recipient of a Rockefeller playwriting grant for residency at Second Stage.

In the following synopsis of Painting Churches, *the occurrence of capital letters in dialogue excerpts is taken from the off-Broadway script, in which the author used this typographical device for emphasis, not necessarily denoting a materially raised voice.*

Time: *Several years ago*

Place: *Beacon Hill—Boston, Mass.*

ACT I

Scene 1: A bright spring morning

SYNOPSIS: Fanny Church, *"a Bostonian from a fine old family, in her 60s,"* is sitting on the living room sofa packing family silver into a box. The room, in copious sunlight through a wall of three arched windows at right, is littered with packed cartons, and all the furniture—*"Oddities from second-hand stores are mixed in with fine old furniture, and exotic hand-made curios vie with tasteful family objects d'art"*—is tagged for removal. It is one week before everything will be moved out of this house to a house on Cape Cod.

Upstage, the living room gives through an archway onto a hall, beyond which Fanny's husband Gardner Church, *"an eminent New England poet from a finer family, in his 70s,"* can be heard at the typewriter. Fanny comes upon her grandmother's Paul Revere teaspoons, determined never to sell them no matter what but remembering a museum's onetime attempt to acquire them. She shouts to her husband, who comes in scattering papers on the floor. He is wearing mismatched tweeds. Fanny is still in her bathrobe but is crowned with a Lily Dache hat she found in a thrift shop for 85 cents and is wearing in honor of their daughter's imminent visit.

Gardner comments that the Lily Dache label is identical to the one in his bathrobe. Fanny believes this is just one of her husband's frequent delusions, but Gardner goes to get the robe and brings it back to prove his point. He puts the robe on over his clothes and exits; but soon the sound of the doorbell is heard. Fanny rushes off to change into a dress while Gardner answers the door offstage and returns to the room with their daughter Mags, a painter in her early 30s. She *"comes staggering in carrying a suitcase and an enormous duffle bag. She wears wonderfully distinctive clothes and has very much her own look."*

Mags bubbles over with explanations of why she has arrived a bit later than expected. Soon her mother comes back, struggling with a recalcitrant zipper.

MAGS *(to Gardner):* You look wonderful!
GARDNER: Well you don't look so bad yourself!

Marian Seldes *(standing)* as Fanny Church, Elizabeth McGovern as Margaret Church and George N. Martin as Gardner Church in *Painting Churches*

MAGS: I love your hair. It's gotten so . . . white!
  Fanny grunts and struggles.
(Waves at her.) Hi Mum . . .

FANNY: Just a minute, dear, my zipper's . . .

GARDNER *(picks up Mags's bags):* Well, come on in and take a load off your feet . . .

MAGS: I was so afraid I'd never make it . . .

GARDNER *(wandering around with her bags):* What have you got in here? Lead Weights?

MAGS: I can't believe you're finally letting me do you.

FANNY *(flings her arms around*   GARDNER *(walking in circles):* Now
Mags, practically knocking her over):   let's see . . . where should I put
OH DARLING . . . MY PRECIOUS   these?
MAGS, YOU'RE HERE AT LAST!

Fanny gets Mags's luggage away from Gardner, sets it down and puts him to work on her zipper. He can't get it to close, so she simply pulls the dress off. Mags looks around at the chaos of her parents' living room.

MAGS: . . . . . So, you're finally doing it . . . selling the house and moving to Cotuit year round. I don't believe it. I just don't believe it!

GARDNER: Well how about a drink to celebrate Mags's arrival?

MAGS: You've been here so long. Why move now?

FANNY: Gardner, what are you wearing that bathrobe for . . . ?

MAGS: You love this house. *I* love this house . . . this room . . . the light. You can't move. I won't let you!

FANNY *(softly, to Gardner):* Really, darling, you ought to pay more attention to your appearance.

GARDNER: So Mags, how about a little . . . *(He drinks from an imaginary glass.)* to wet your whistle?

FANNY: We can't start drinking now, it isn't even noon yet!

MAGS: I'm starving. I've got to get something to eat before I collapse! *(She exits toward the kitchen.)*

FANNY: What *have* you done to your hair, dear? The color's so queer and all your nice curl has gone.

GARDNER: It looks to me as if she dyed it.

FANNY: Yes, that's it. You're absolutely right! It's a completely different color. She dyed it bright red!

Mags, returning, tells her parents she has merely added highlights to her natural hair color (Gardner likes it this way). In her eagerness to get started with their portrait, Mags sets up her easel at left, opposite the tall windows. Fanny has misgivings about the timing, but Mags assures her, "It's a perfect opportunity. there'll be no distractions, you'll be completely at my mercy." Also, Fanny promised "You can paint us, you can dip us in concrete, you can do anything you want with us, just so long as you help us get out of here!"
And Mags has some wonderful news: she is to be given a one-woman show in

New York at a gallery that has shown Rauschenberg, Johns, ". . . . . ALL THE
HEAVIES . . . It's incredible, beyond belief . . . I mean, at my age . . . Do you
know how good you have to be to get in there? It's a miracle . . . an honest-to-God,
star spangled miracle!"

Mags is a portraitist at a time when no one is doing portraits ("I'm so out of
it, I'm in.") The portrait of her parents will be included in her show. Gardner
thinks a portrait of Fanny in all her handsomeness would be fine, and Fanny
would like to have a new portrait of Gardner to replace the one in the National
Gallery ("He looks just like an undertaker!"). But Mags means to paint them side
by side in this room where they have lived so much of their lives.

Gardner suddenly misses some papers he'd been carrying and exits to find
them, giving Fanny the opportunity to talk privately with Mags.

FANNY: . . . . . I'm very worried about Daddy.

MAGS: Mummy, please, I just got here.

FANNY: He's getting very gaga. You haven't seen him in almost a year. Two
weeks ago he walked through the front door of the Codmans' house, kissed Emily
on the cheek and settled down in the maid's room, thinking he was home!

MAGS: Oh come on, you're exaggerating.

FANNY: He's mad as a hatter and getting worse every day! It's this crazy new
book of his. He works on it around the clock. I've read some of it, and it doesn't
make one word of sense, it's all at sixes and sevens . . .

GARDNER (poking his head back in the room, spies some of his papers on the
sofa and grabs them): Ahh, here they are. (Exits.)

FANNY (voice lowered): Ever since this dry spell with his poetry, he's been
frantic, absolutely . . . frantic!

Mags disagrees with Fanny, believing her father to be as sane as anybody. But
he's writing criticism, Fanny argues, without having any gift for it, and he stays
by himself in his study with his pet parakeet Toots, alternately typing away and
teaching the bird parts of Gray's Elegy. "Things are getting very tight around
here, in case you haven't noticed," Fanny informs Mags. "Daddy's last Pulitzer
didn't even cover our real estate tax, and now that he's too doddery to give
readings any more, that income is gone . . ."

Gardner comes in and out looking for a poem he was reading. Fanny finds
herself shouting at him because on top of everything else he is growing deaf. She
shows Mags a lighting effect she has created by perforating bits of a picture pasted
on a lamp shade, impressing Mags with her ingenuity. Gradually the idea of the
portrait begins to grow on Fanny, though for Mags it will mean a good deal of
study and planning of lighting before she can even begin. As Mags works on the
setup, Fanny and Gardner "settle down next to each other" and experiment with
poses.

> They stare straight ahead, trying to look like suitable subjects, but they
> can't hold still. They keep making faces, lifting an eyebrow, dropping
> one corner of the mouth. It's not huge faces, just flickering little
> changes; a half smile here, a self-important frown there. They steal
> glances at each other every so often.

GARDNER: How am I doing, Fan?

FANNY: Brilliantly, absolutely brilliantly!

MAGS: But you're making faces.

FANNY: *I'm* not making faces, *(Turning to Gardner and making a face.)* are *you* making faces, Gar?

GARDNER *(instantly making one):* Certainly not! I'm the picture of restraint!
     *Without meaning to, they get sillier and sillier. They start giggling, then
     laughing.*

MAGS *(can't help but join in):* You two are impossible . . . completely impossible! I was crazy to think I could ever pull this off! *(Laughing away.)* Look at you
. . . just . . . look at you!
     Blackout.

Scene 2: Two days later

About 5 p.m., the room is now cluttered with overflowing cartons as the Churches are fully occupied with packing up their belongings, everything from pots and pans to a pair of old galoshes. The latter remind Fanny of the snowstorms of her childhood, when her father would take her sledding on the Common.

Mags picks up a crimson tablecloth and drapes it over her mother to check the coloring ("It makes you glow like a pomegranite"), then tacks it up as a backdrop for the portrait. Gardner comes in after having gone for a walk and drops his raincoat on the floor. He cannot keep straight the various diseases suffered by friends he happens to meet, and he can't remember where to hang up his raincoat until Fanny directs him to the closet. He takes out a hanger and then, discussing family friends and their ailments, hands Fanny the hanger and puts his coat back on. Finally Fanny gets him straightened out and hangs up the coat herself.

Fanny and Gardner happen to be sitting in the portrait's posing chairs, and Mags feels their positions are just about right, when, to Gardner's delight, Fanny announces it's cocktail time (they have stocked some Dubonnet for Mags). Gardner fixes the drinks, and after he and Fanny *"take that first life-saving gulp"* they whisper conspiratorially.

> *Fanny grabs a large serving fork and they fly into an imitation of Grant
> Wood's "American Gothic."*

MAGS: . . . and I wonder why it's taken me all these years to get you to pose for me. You just don't take me seriously! Poor old Mags and her ridiculous portraits . . .

FANNY: Oh darling, your portraits aren't *ridiculous!* They may not be all that one *hopes* for, but they're certainly not . . .

MAGS: Remember how you behaved at my first group show in SoHo? Oh, come on, you remember. It was a real circus! Think back. . . . It was about six years ago . . . Daddy had just been awarded some Presidential medal of achievement, and you insisted he wear it around his neck on a bright red ribbon, and you wore this . . . *huge* feathered hat to match! I'll never forget it! It was the size of a giant pizza with twenty-inch red turkey feathers shooting straight up into the air . . . Oh come on, you remember, don't you . . . ?

FANNY *(leaping to her feet):* HOLD EVERYTHING! THIS IS IT! THIS IS REALLY IT! Forgive me for interrupting, Mags darling, it'll just take a minute. *(She whispers excitedly to Gardner.)*

MAGS: I had about eight portraits in the show, mostly of friends of mine, except for this old one I'd done of Mrs. Crowninshield.

GARDNER: All right, all right . . . let's give it a whirl.

> *A pause, then they mime Michelangelo's "Pieta" with Gardner lying across Fanny's lap as the dead Christ.*

MAGS *(depressed):* The "Pieta." Terrific.

FANNY *(jabbing Gardner in the ribs):* Hey, we're getting good at this.

GARDNER: Of course it would help if we didn't have all these modern clothes on.

Mags persists in reminding her parents of their behavior at the SoHo exhibition. Fanny collared the leading art critic, took him over to one of Mags's portraits and told him, "THAT'S MILLICENT CROWNINSHIELD! I GREW UP WITH HER. SHE LIVES RIGHT DOWN THE STREET FROM US IN BOSTON. BUT IT'S A VERY POOR LIKENESS, IF YOU ASK ME! HER NOSE ISN'T NEARLY THAT LARGE AND SHE DOESN'T HAVE SOMETHING QUEER GROWING OUT OF HER CHIN! THE CROWNINSHIELDS ARE REALLY QUITE GOOD LOOKING, STUFFY, BUT GOOD LOOKING NONETHELESS!"

Paying little attention to Mags, Fanny and Gardner are plotting another tableau which ends with them stretched out with their forefingers nearly touching, like Jehovah and Adam in Michelangelo's "The Creation." Mags applauds them but goes on with her reminiscence: Fanny set out to show the art critic a photo of Mrs. Crowninshield but was unable to find it in the "ocean of junk" which Fanny pulled out of her handbag and spread all over the art gallery floor, to Mags's acute embarrassment. "And that was my *first* show," Mags comments, as the scene blacks out.

Scene 3: Twenty-four hours later

Now the Churches' clothing is piled in the living room for sorting and packing. Gardner, in the process of rescuing old favorites from the discard, *"is wearing several sweaters and vests, a Hawaiian holiday shirt and a variety of scarves,"* over which he puts on an overcoat and a jacket in his effort to prevent Fanny from throwing anything out.

Mags startles her parents by taking them unawares with a flash camera, recording natural expressions. Mags goes out to the kitchen and comes back with a bowl of tapioca (she seems to become perpetually hungry while she's at home). They discuss the clothes for the portrait (as Gardner gets tangled in the excess clothing he's trying to take off). Fanny opts for the elegance of a long black dress and a tuxedo for Gardner. Incidentally, she feels that Mags lets herself look so "forlorn" that she would have great difficulty attracting a desirable Boston husband. But Mags wants no part of any Boston prospects. Her tastes run to "that dreadful Frenchman who smelled of sweaty socks . . . . . and that peculiar Oriental fellow."

Elizabeth McGovern, George N. Martin and Marian Seldes in a scene from *Painting Churches*

It's again time for cocktails. Mags joins in, accepting a Dubonnet. Fanny and Mags get to laughing about the excessive tallness and other characteristics of Boston girls. "The only hope for us . . . 'Boston girls' is to get as far away from our kind as possible," Mags has decided. She avoids her former friends because they remind her too much of herself.

MAGS: I mean . . . look at me! . . . . . Awkward . . . plain . . . I don't know how to dress, I don't know how to talk. When people find out Daddy's my father, they're always amazed . . . "Gardner Church is YOUR father?! Aw come on, you're kidding?!"

FANNY *(in a whisper):* Isn't she divine.

MAGS: Sometimes I don't even tell them. I pretend I grew up in the midwest somewhere . . . farming people . . . we work with our hands.

GARDNER *(to Mags):* Well, how about a little refill . . . ?

MAGS: No, no more thanks.

     Pause.

FANNY: What did you have to go and interrupt her for? She was just getting up a head of steam . . . ?

MAGS *(walking over to her easel):* The great thing about being a portrait painter, you see, is it's the *other* guy that's exposed, you're safely hidden behind the canvas and easel.

FANNY: Why, I never thought of it that way!

MAGS *(standing behind it):* You can be as plain as a pitchfork, as inarticulate as mud, but it doesn't matter because you're completely concealed: your body, your face, your intentions. Just as you make your most intimate move, throw open your soul . . . they stretch and yawn, remembering the dog has to be let out at five . . . To be so invisible while so enthralled . . . it takes your breath away!

GARDNER: Well put, Mags. Awfully well put!

MAGS: That's why I've always wanted to paint you, to see if I'm up to it. I mean, we know each other so well. It's quite a risk . . . Remember how you reacted to the first big thing I did as a child, my great masterpiece?

FANNY: You painted a masterpiece when you were a child . . . ?

MAGS: Well, it was a masterpiece to me.

Fanny doesn't remember any such thing. She's ready for another drink and sends Gardner to get it, insisting that Mags have another too. Gardner soon returns with the drinks, iceless, because the ice suddenly disappeared and he couldn't find it.

Mags continues her childhood reminiscence. It seems she developed a habit of pushing her food out between her front teeth in little curliques, like a tube of toothpaste. She did it, she says, because she didn't want to eat it and was afraid she might choke and make some kind of a scene: "You were awfully strict about table manners. I was always afraid of losing control." This way, Mags at least was in control, even though she was sent away to her bedroom to eat by herself, from a tray. Here she simply flushed food down the toilet—but she noticed that crayons left on the radiator melted into colorful blobs. She pressed the red crayon to the radiator and held it determinedly, with blistering fingers, until it bubbled like raspberry jam.

MAGS: Once I'd melted one, I was hooked! I finished off my entire supply in one night, mixing color over color until my head swam . . . ! The heat, the smell, the brilliance that sank and rose . . . I'd never felt such exhilaration! . . . Every week I spent my allowance on crayons. I must have cleared out every box of Crayolas in the city!

GARDNER *(gazing at Mags):* You know, I don't think I've ever seen you looking prettier! You're awfully attractive when you get going!

FANNY: Why, what a lovely thing to say.

MAGS: AFTER THREE MONTHS THAT RADIATOR WAS . . . SPEC-TACULAR! I MEAN, IT LOOKED LIKE SOME COLOSSAL FRUIT CAKE, FIVE FEET TALL . . . !

FANNY: It sounds perfectly hideous.

MAGS: It was a knockout; shimmering with pinks and blues, lavenders and maroons, turquoise and golds, oranges and creams . . . For every color, I imagined a taste . . . YELLOW: lemon curls dipped in sugar . . . RED: glazed cherries laced with rum . . . GREEN: tiny peppermint leaves veined with chocolate . . . PURPLE: . . .

FANNY: That's quite enough!

MAGS: And then the frosting . . . ahhhh, the frosting! *(All low and secretive.)*

A satiny mix of white and silver . . . I kept it hidden under blankets during the day . . . My huge . . . *(She starts laughing.)* . . . looming . . . teetering sweet . . .

FANNY: I ASKED YOU TO STOP! GARDNER, WILL YOU PLEASE GET HER TO STOP!

GARDNER: See here, Mags, Mum asked you to . . .

MAGS: I was so . . . *hungry* . . . losing weight every week. I looked like a scarecrow, what with the bags under my eyes and wax all over my hands. It's a wonder you didn't notice. But finally you came to my rescue . . . If you could call what happened a rescue. It was more like a rout!

Her parents try to stop her, but Mags continues: her mother came into her room one night, the radiator happened to be uncovered, and Fanny could see it in the moonlight. She cried out, "It's food!", thinking that Mags had used her uneaten meals. Gardner simply fainted at the sight of Mags's "masterpiece." Fanny immediately attacked it with some kind of a blow torch.

MAGS: . . . . . Of course, in a sense you were right. It *was* a monument of my cast-off dinners, only I hadn't built it with food . . . I found my own materials. I was languishing with hunger, but oh, dear Mother . . . I FOUND MY OWN MATERIALS . . . !

FANNY: Darling . . . *please?!*

MAGS: I tried to stop you, but you wouldn't listen . . . OUT SHOT THE FLAME! . . . I remember these waves of wax rolling across the room and Daddy coming to, wondering what on earth was going on . . . Well, what did you know about my abilities . . . ?

GARDNER: I just remember waking up with all this . . . wax in my slippers.

MAGS: You see, I had . . . I mean, I *have* abilities . . .

GARDNER: It was the dickens to get off. You should have seen my toe-nails . . .

MAGS: I have abilities. I have . . . strong abilities. I have . . . very strong abilities. They are very strong . . . very, very strong . . .

> *She rises and runs out of the room as Fanny and Gardner watch her, speechless. Curtain.*

ACT II

Scene 1: Three days later

Most of the clutter has now been packed up and taken out of the living room, in which Fanny and Gardner, dressed in their evening clothes, are posing for Mags, who has reached the stage of sketching the portrait. To pass the time, Gardner recites Yeats's *The Song of Wandering Aengus*. Fanny remembers that reciting the great love poems of the ages was Gardner's technique of wooing: "When you got going with them, there was nothing left of me! You could have had your pick of any girl in Boston! Why you chose me, I'll never understand.

I had no looks to speak of and nothing much in the brains department . . . Well, what did you know about women and the world? . . . What did any of us know?"

To Gardner, the posing is enjoyable (he recites more Yeats), but it bores Fanny, who is nervous partly because they haven't yet tackled Gardner's office—"books and papers up to the ceiling!"—in their packing. There won't be room for all his books in the Cotuit cottage, but Gardner insists he must take everything, and no one beside himself must touch his things—"There's a lifetime of work in there."

Nevertheless, Fanny breaks the pose and exits to survey the situation in the study, leaving Gardner to pose by himself. She begins carrying in armloads of books, while Garder confesses that this business of moving is giving him nightmares in which his mother stands directing streams of moving men carrying familiar objects and even people, perfect strangers, brought into their house to take over their possessions. It ends with their beds being carried in with Fanny lying in hers but Gardner's empty "as if I were dead or had never existed."

Fanny comes in with another load of books, exclaiming about the huge quantity of loose papers in Gardner's office. Meanwhile, Gardner wants his memory refreshed on exactly why they are going through this turmoil of moving.

FANNY: Because life is getting too complicated here.
GARDNER (remembering): Oh yes . . .
FANNY: And we can't afford it any more.
GARDNER: That's right, that's right . . .
FANNY: We don't have the . . . income we used to!
GARDNER: Oh yes . . . income!
FANNY (falling into her pose again): Of course we have our savings and various trust funds, but I wouldn't dream of touching those!
GARDNER: No, no, you must never dip into capital!
FANNY: I told Daddy I'd be perfectly happy to buy a gun and put a bullet through our heads so we could avoid all this, but he wouldn't hear of it!
MAGS (sketching away): No, I shouldn't think so.
        Pause.
FANNY: I've always admired people who kill themselves when they get to our stage of life. Well no one can touch my Uncle Edmond in that department . . .
MAGS: I know, I know . . .
FANNY: The day before his seventieth birthday he climbed to the top of the Old North Church and hurled himself face down into Salem Street! They had to scrape him up with a spatula! God, he was a remarkable man . . . state senator, president of Harvard . . .

Seeing that the others are preoccupied, Mags with her painting and Gardner with his books, Fanny tries sorting the books by colors. An oddly-striped one that she wants to throw away turns out to have been inscribed by Robert Frost; a dusty one was a gift from Malraux. She turns her attention to Gardner's papers and goes out to fetch an armful of them, calling back "WE NEED A STEAM SHOVEL FOR THIS!" Mags finally joins Fanny in the study-clearing project.

Gardner protests vigorously, particularly against disturbing his manuscript. Fanny is close to tears of frustration as Gardner wrests pages from her.

GARDNER *(rescues the rest of his papers from the carton):* YOU DON'T JUST THROW EVERYTHING INTO A BOX LIKE A PILE OF GARBAGE! THIS IS A BOOK, FANNY. SOMETHING I'VE BEEN WORKING ON FOR TWO YEARS . . . !
> *Trying to assemble his papers, but only making things worse, dropping them all over the place.*
You show a little respect for my things . . . you don't just throw them around every which way . . . It's tricky trying to make sense of poetry, it's much easier to write the stuff . . . that is, if you've still got it in you . . .
MAGS: Here, let me help . . .
> *Taking some of the papers.*
GARDNER: Criticism is tough sledding. You can't just dash off a few images here, a few rhymes there . . .
MAGS: Do you have these pages numbered in any way?
FANNY *(returning to her posing chair):* HA!
GARDNER: This is just the introduction.
MAGS: I don't see any numbers on these.
GARDNER *(exiting to his study):* The important stuff is in my study.
FANNY *(to Mags):* You don't know the half of it . . . *Not the half . . . !*
GARDNER *(offstage, thumping around):* HAVE YOU SEEN THOSE YEATS POEMS I JUST HAD . . . ?
MAGS *(reading over several pages):* What is this . . . ? It doesn't make sense. It's just fragments . . . pieces of poems.
FANNY: That's it, honey! That's his book. His great critical study! Now that he can't write his own poetry, he's trying to explain other people's. The only problem is, he can't get beyond typing them out. The poor lamb doesn't have the stamina to get beyond the opening stanzas, let alone trying to make sense of them.

Gardner returns, complaining that he now can't find anything; his best work has been thrown out or mislaid. But he is comforted when Mags reads him a couple of the scraps of poetry typed on pages, and reassured that his treasured "manuscript"—such as it is—is intact. Mags is touched to the heart by her father's passion for these excerpts from the poems of others, while Fanny comments under her breath, "He can't give up the words. It's the best he can do . . . . . Of course no one will ever publish this."

What's more, Fanny tells her daughter ruefully (as Gardner exits to his study in search of more "manuscript" pages), her father has become incontinent, so that they can't go out any more. Coincidentally, but in graphic proof of her point, Gardner has a large stain on his trousers when he returns.

Fanny goes to make herself a drink while Gardner recites Emily Dickinson to Mags. Returning, Fanny can't help treating the whole situation as a kind of joke. Her efforts to look on the funny side rather shock Mags, who interprets her mother's attitude as a form of cruelty: "YOUR DISDAIN REALLY TAKES

MY BREATH AWAY! YOU'RE IN A CLASS BY YOURSELF WHEN IT
COMES TO HUMILIATION . . . !" But Fanny persists in turning their predica-
ment into a sort of game, showing Gardner that dropping his pages into a packing
box is a make-believe bombing excercise. Gardner soon enters into the spirit of
fun, picking up pages and making bombing noises, while Fanny pretends to be
hit and falls to the floor.

MAGS: THIS IS HOW YOU PACK HIS THINGS . . . ?

FANNY (reviving, back on her feet, dusting herself off): I get involved. I keep
him company . . . which is more than you do!

MAGS: BUT YOU'RE MAKING A MOCKERY OF HIM . . . YOU TREAT
HIM LIKE A CHILD OR SOME DIM-WITTED SERVING BOY. HE'S
JUST AN AMUSEMENT TO YOU . . . !

FANNY: . . . and to you who see him once a year, if that . . . What is he to
you? . . . I mean, what do you give him from yourself that costs you something
. . . ? (Imitating her.) "Oh, hi Daddy, it's great to see you again. How have you
been? . . . Gee, I love your hair. It's gotten so . . . white!" . . . What color do
you expect it to get when he's this age . . . ? I mean, if you care so much how
he looks, why don't you come and see him once in a while? . . . But oh no
. . . you have your paintings to do and your shows to put on. You just come and
see us when the whim strikes. (Imitating her.) "Hey, you know what would be
really great? . . . To do a portrait of you! I've always wanted to paint you, you're
such great subjects!" . . . Paint us . . . ?! What about opening your eyes and really
seeing us . . .? Noticing what's going on around here for a change! It's all over
for Daddy and me. This is it! "Finita la commedia!" . . . All I'm trying to do is
exit with a little flourish, have some fun . . . What's so terrible about that? It can
get pretty grim around here, in case you haven't noticed . . . Daddy tap, tap,
tapping out his nonsense all day; me traipsing around to the thrift shops trying
to amuse myself . . . He never keeps me company any more, never takes me out
anywhere . . . I'd put a bullet through my head in a minute, but then who'd look
after him? . . . What do you think we're moving to the cottage for . . . ? So I can
watch him like a hawk and make sure he doesn't get lost. Do you think that's
anything to look forward to? . . . Being Daddy's nursemaid out in the middle of
nowhere? I'd much rather stay here in Boston with the few friends I have left,
but you can't always do what you want in this world! "L'homme propose, dieu
dispose!" . . . if you want to paint us so badly, you ought to paint us as we really
are. There's your picture . . . ! (She points to Gardner who's quietly playing with
a paper glider.) . . . Daddy spread out on the floor with all his toys and me
hovering over him to make sure he doesn't hurt himself! (She goes over to him.)
YOO HOO . . . GAR . . . ? . . . HELLO? . . .

GARDNER (looks up at her): Oh, hi there, Fan. What's up?

FANNY: How's the packing coming . . . ?

GARDNER: Packing . . . ?

FANNY: Yes, you were packing your manuscript, remember?
    She lifts a page and lets it fall into the carton.

GARDNER: Oh yes . . .

FANNY: Here's your picture, Mags. Face over this way . . . turn your easel over here . . .

> *She lets a few more papers fall.*

Up, up . . . and away . . .

> *Blackout.*

Scene 2: The last day

Everything is now packed, and the room is empty except for Mags's backdrop and portrait, now finished and covered with a cloth. Mags takes down the backdrop, while offstage Fran is making a last-minute check of the empty rooms, reminding Gardner that he hasn't yet taken away his typewriter or his pet parakeet, Toots, though they are leaving in 15 minutes.

Gardner enters carrying Toots in his cage and encouraging the bird to recite a little of Gray's *Elegy*. To Mags's astonishment, the bird recites four lines loud and clear, with Gardner's accent. Fanny enters wearing her travelling clothes and carrying suitcase and typewriter, Cotuit-bound, bringing to Mags's mind thoughts of her happy childhood there with her parents, and especially of the phosphorus which so often flashed around them when they swam in the sea.

Mags has worked all night on the portrait, and it's now finished. Panicking with the knowledge that the time has come to show her work to her parents, Mags takes the painting and hugs it to her chest, telling them, "Oh God, you're going to hate it! You're going to hate it! How did I ever get into this? . . . Listen, you don't really want to see it . . . it's nothing . . . just a few dabs here and there . . . It was awfully late when I finished it. The light was really impossible and my eyes were hurting like crazy . . . . ."

Gardner takes the painting from her and places it on the easel as Mags tries to control her diffidence, *"wrapping her arms around herself and making little whimpering sounds."* Fanny and Gardner study the work for what seems an eternity. Finally they begin to comment: Fanny complains that she is depicted with "purple skin and bright orange hair," but Gardner finds it "becoming . . . awfully clever . . . . . quite remarkable . . . . . it sparkles somehow." Fanny gradually admits that she likes her smile, and that Gardner's likeness is "absolutely darling." As they compare the portrait favorably to work of French impressionists, Mags tells herself joyfully, "They like it . . . they like it!"

The portrait reminds Fanny of a dancing couple in a Renoir painting; she illustrates by going to Gardner, and they dance around the room. The sound of a horn outside signals that their transportation to Cotuit has arrived, but they don't hear it and Mags ignores it, watching her parents dance and listening to them as they remember details of the French painting of the dancing couple, the woman in a flowered dress, a little band playing.

FANNY: . . . and there's a man in a dark suit playing the violin and someone's conducting, I think . . . And aren't Japanese lanterns strung up . . . ?

> *They pick up speed, dipping and whirling around the room.*

GARDNER: Oh yes! There are all these little lights twinkling in the trees . . .

FANNY: . . . and doesn't the woman have a hat on . . . ? A big red hat . . . ?

GARDNER: . . . and lights all over the dancers too. Everything shimmers with this marvelous glow. Yes, yes . . . I can see it perfectly! The whole thing is absolutely extraordinary!

> *The lights become dreamy and dappled as they dance around the room. Mags watches them, moved to tears. Curtain.*

AND A NIGHTINGALE
SANG . . .

A Play in Two Acts

BY C.P. TAYLOR

Cast and credits appear on page 376

CECIL (C.P.) TAYLOR was born in Glasgow Nov. 6, 1929, the son of a salesman and part-time journalist. He died Dec. 9, 1981, about two months after his play Good *was first presented by the Royal Shakespeare Company at The Warehouse but before its subsequent presentations at the Aldwych Theater in April 1982 and on Broadway later that year. Taylor began writing plays at 30 and completed at least 70 works produced in the West End, throughout England and on television before his death at 52. He wrote most frequently for the highly-regarded Live Theater Company at Newcastle, where he was resident dramatist. He also served as literary advisor to the Northumberland Youth Theater Association (1967–79), Tyneside Theater Trust (1971–74), Everyman Theater in Liverpool (1971–73) and Traverse Theater (1971–74). He was known for his work with mentally and physically handicapped and other deprived persons, applying drama therapy at the Northgate Hospital Arts Center, which he helped to establish, and in many other places and instances.*

The highlights of Taylor's playwriting career included Bread and Butter *(1969),* Black and White Minstrels *(1972),* Bandits *(produced by RSC in 1977 and off off Broadway at the Labor Theater April 19, 1979 for 12 performances) and* Schippel *(1981).* Good, *his first major American production and Best Play, opened on Broadway Oct. 13, 1982 for a 125-performance run. His second Best Play, this season's* And a Nightingale Sang . . . , *was first presented in Newcastle-on-Tyne, its setting, in 1977 and was produced in London in 1979. Its American debut took place Nov. 27 at Lincoln Center.*

Taylor was twice married, with four children. At the time of his death he lived at Long Horsely, near Newscastle.

The following synopsis of And a Nightingale Sang . . . *was prepared by Sally Dixon Wiener.*

Time: The years of World War II.

Place: Newcastle-on-Tyne.

ACT I

Scene 1: "Oh, Johnnie, How You Can Love"—Sunday, Sept. 3, 1939

SYNOPSIS: The tiered set is an unprepossessing, lived-in, drab working-class home: upstage right, a coat rack and piano; upstage center, a stove, kitchen cupboard and wall calendar; upstage left, two areas, a table and bench, and a bedroom with a statue of the Virgin Mary and candles on a small table; above the kitchen area, sandbags; center stage right, a parlor area with two armchairs, table with radio; and center stage, dining table with chairs. The set is basically realistic except for a downfront area, with bench, that represents a number of places in the town, a park, a flat, etc. It is a memory play, with a narrator, and the action moves fluidly both in time and between the playing areas (and much of the dialogue overlaps). Evocative of the mood of the play also are the onstage piano-playing and singing of the popular songs of the era.

As the play begins, Helen Stott, early 30s, with a slight limp and a defeated but resigned look about her that is reflected in her manner of dress and her prim hairstyle, speaks, as narrator. George Stott, in his 50s, her father, is at the piano.

HELEN: That Sunday . . . we were too busy to notice the war . . . So many things were happening to us . . . "The Coalman," me Da, was playing "Oh, Johnnie" . . . . . Me Mam . . . She gave everybody nicknames . . . I was "The Cripple" . . . Me Granda was "The Old Soldier" . . . Our Joyce was "The Babe in the Wood" . . . We called our Mam back "The Saint" . . .

GEORGE *(singing at the piano):* "Oh, Johnnie/Oh, Johnnie/How you can love," etc.

HELEN: Me Mam was making Sunday dinner . . . Joyce was making up her mind to say 'yes' or 'no' to Eric . . . And Granda was getting ready for Jackie's funeral . . .

Andie, her grandfather, in his 70s, doughty and philosophical, has Jackie, his dog that has died, in a sack. He is waiting for Helen, the sole mourner, to accompany him to services for Jackie. But Peggy Stott, Helen's mother, 50s, dowdy, settled into comfortable middle age, is preoccupied with affairs at the church; and Joyce, Helen's sister, early 20s, somewhat pretty, concerned with her appearance and very indecisive, has nothing but her young man on her mind. Helen's mother wants to go back to the chapel because Father Monaghan is apparently having a breakdown. Andie has no patience with this, because the priest would have nothing to do with the dog's service. Joyce is in a state because her young man Eric is coming with a ring and she wants her mother's advice—but her mother is determined to go to Father Monaghan.

HELEN *(To audience):* They were all kind of stuck there . . . The Old Soldier with Jackie in his sack . . . The Coalman . . . At his piano . . . The Saint . . . with her coat on . . . The Babe in the Wood . . . Making herself up . . . just in case she was going to take him . . . Everybody waiting for me as usual . . . to make up their minds for them . . . I was just going to take everything in hand as usual . . . And tell me Mam to go off to the Manse . . . And take Grandad to Walker with the dog . . . When the doorbell rang . . . And Joyce went white . . . Dad got up to answer it . . . Mam stopped him . . .

MAM: Wait a minute, man . . . Where you going . . .

GEORGE: Going to answer the bloody door . . .

JOYCE: It's *him,* Da . . . It's Eric . . .

MAM: We haven't decided what's to be done . . . Have we . . .

GEORGE: Ye not think it would be easier just to say "yes," and get it over with . . . This is bloody worse than Chamberlain running back and forwards to Germany . . . waiting for Hitler to make up his mind . . . *Will* I kick their teeth in . . . will I not . . .

JOYCE: I don't know if I love him . . .

GEORGE: I don't know if I love yer Mam . . . but I'm bloody married to her . . .

MAM: Now . . . That's not true . . . You know that . . . That's just an act . . . That's confusing the lass altogether.
    The bell rings again.

HELEN: I'll take him in the front room . . . You can't leave him at the door . . . like that . . . till you make up your mind about taking him or not . . .

JOYCE: Tell him I'm still getting dressed . . .

HELEN *(to audience):* Eric was there, all his brasses shining . . . like he'd been up all night polishing them for the great day . . . And his cap tucked in his epaulets . . .

ERIC: This is it . . . Eh, Helen . . .

HELEN: Is it? What? . . .

ERIC: Be on the wireless. Eleven o'clock . . . Chamberlain . . .

Eric, early 20s, a presentable enough young man, tells Helen that he has a "nice" ring he got in Glasgow. Mam comes to tell Helen that Joyce wants to see her. Eric tells Mam he'll be on his way shortly, "to fight old Adolf." He tries in vain to show the ring and is offered a cup of tea. Mam goes off to get it, and he's left alone, nobody wanting to see the ring. Helen is in the bedroom with Joyce.

JOYCE: I don't like him . . . Helen . . . Do you like him . . . I looked through the door . . . at him coming in . . . He smells of *bacon* doesn't he?

Joan Allen as Helen Stott and Peter Friedman as Norman in *And a Nightingale Sang . . .*

HELEN: Send him packing . . . If you don't like him . . . then . . .

JOYCE: Eee . . . You don't think I should do that . . . He might be going to his death . . . If I sent him away like that . . . It would be on my conscience the rest of my life . . . wouldn't it . . . Just at his hour of need . . . When all I needed to say was one word . . . To make him happy . . . I kept it back . . .

HELEN: Do you *believe* that . . . Joyce . . .

JOYCE: He could go away to France, happy . . .

HELEN: Joyce . . . Stop it . . . will you.

JOYCE: Stop what . . . man . . .

HELEN: Stop being in a picture . . . will you . . .

JOYCE: Do you like me hair this way . . .

HELEN: Not particularly . . .

JOYCE: I'd better change it . . . Helen, what would *you* do?

HELEN *(to audience):* What would *I* bloody do . . . I've never had the chance . . . have I? . . . With a face like mine . . . and my body all out of shape . . . If I walked down Shields Road . . . naked . . . no man would look at us twice . . . I don't know what I'd do . . . I'd given up thinking of having somebody to love us . . . I wasn't bothered . . . I could do *without* bloody men . . . Plenty other things to give you a lift in life . . . wasn't there . . .

Being tied to Eric for life worries Joyce, but Helen tells her she won't be if he's going to die in France tomorrow. Joyce goes to the statue of the Virgin Mary and prays he be brought safely back from the war. Andie opines that Eric will be an old man by then, anyway, because the wars get longer. Andie's put out because his dog Jackie's funeral is being so delayed. He's got Eric's tea but wants Helen to take it in to him. Joyce is still vacillating. Andie compares human emotions to the tide—he read that in one of Mam's magazines, and he goes on about the war. He sees everything as all finished, and a quick end to it all as the best way, because living is just a way to pass the time.

Joyce is more concerned about the color of Eric's eyes. It seems Mam thinks Eric's eyes are green, and Joyce is disappointed. Helen asks Eric to get out his Army Card to see if his eye color is on it. While he's checking, George goes on and on about how he thinks for himself, "about Hitler or anything else," that he can see Hitler's point about the Poles. (George thinks the Poles are very dodgy because a former mate of his, a Pole, did him out of a horse back in 1937, which resulted in George losing his coal business.) The card says Eric's eyes are olive green.

Suddenly there are sirens, throwing everyone into confusion, but Eric comes in and takes over, telling everyone to get their gas masks. He herds everyone into the kitchen, stuffs up the cracks and says to put the fire out. George is looking for last night's *Chronicle* that contained instructions about what to do in raids, but Eric tells him he knows what to do. Joyce is reacting favorably to Eric's taking charge of the situation. Andie, as usual, is philosophical.

Eric stuffs a blanket up the chimney to keep the gas out. He tells them the first thing they will hear is anti-aircraft guns. George says that when they hear the planes they should throw themselves on the ground, but Eric explains that that's when there is no cover. George doesn't like being argued with and goes on, from the *Chronicle,* that the bomb will make a "rushing sound" when it is approaching. He tells them that when they hear the sound to throw themselves down.

As the tension mounts, Mam insists she must get to her statue, and she wants Helen and Joyce to go with her; but before she can get out there is a whining sound, and all including Andie throw themselves down. Then Helen goes to the scullery and comes back with the kettle. She has realized the whining sound was the kettle, boiling.

Joyce wants to know if they want to see her ring.

HELEN *(to audience):* God knows when she got it . . . I found out later . . . when they were lying on the ground . . . She just said "yes" to him . . . So that was how our Joyce got engaged . . . and how Hitler changed my life too . . . .

Scene 2: "We'll Meet Again"—June 20, 21, 1940

Helen has agreed to meet a friend of Eric's, Norman, in Eldon Square on a Sunday afternoon. She has bought a turban especially for this occasion and feels that she looks terrible in it. She was nervous as she saw Norman coming across the square, she tells the audience. The family had already nicknamed him "The Tailor's Dummy" because he always looks so scrubbed and well-kept.

Norman, in his late 20s, in uniform and appealing-looking, has brought Helen chocolates and wants to know what she'd like to do. He's the straightforward type, he informs her, and he comments that the new turban fails to do her justice. Helen declares that even if she had a Paris designer outfit she'd still look like "something out of a jumble sale," but Norman assures her he wouldn't have asked her out if he hadn't thought she looked nice. He suggests going for coffee, but Helen would prefer to go see the barrage balloons in the Leazes Park—but would like to sit for a bit first. He suggests that they call it *our* square. She agrees to take the turban off. Norman takes her hand and this part of the scene ends with Helen remembering that he held it as they left the park, Helen limping badly and sure that he won't ask her out again.

This was not their first meeting, and Helen recalls how Eric first brought Norman to the house in mid-June in a week when her father was playing "I Love to Ride the Ferry" over and over. She was on the night shift, at Parsons, as was her father at the Neptune Yard.

HELEN *(to audience):* . . . That first time Norman came into my life. It was one of *those* perfect June days . . . I was sitting out on the step, in the back yard . . . Eric had disappeared to France, after two days honeymoon with Joyce in Walker . . . and we'd never heard from him since . . . I could get nowt out of Joyce . . . *How* she felt . . . Everybody was sure he was dead . . . The last of them had got out of Dunkirk three weeks back . . . and *still* we hadn't heard from Eric . . . First thing that happened was the Old Soldier turned up . . . Two weeks early . . . from Auntie Marge's . . . With all his luggage . . .

ANDIE: I stood out there . . . Listen to us . . . George . . . I stood out there . . . *Entranced* with the music . . .

HELEN: Granda . . . You're two weeks *early* . . .

ANDIE: No use asking me . . . if I'm two weeks early . . . or two weeks late . . .

GEORGE: You're two weeks early . . .

ANDIE: There's a war on . . . Different routines in wartime . . . Where's The Saint? . . .

GEORGE: I was thinking of putting a mattress in the shelter . . . We've got a shelter, now . . . Did you know? When I'm on nightshift . . . It's the best place . . . Nobody disturbs us there . . .

HELEN: Does me Mam know you're coming . . . She doesn't, Granda . . . Does she? . . .

GEORGE: She's gone to the chapel . . . There's a new Father . . . Monaghan's gone to be a chaplain . . . Did you hear . . .

ANDIE: I told you, Helen, man . . . It's out of me hands . . . Not for me to reason why . . . They work it out between them . . . Where me next pillow is . . . George . . . You should never have daughters . . . Take your whole life over, daughters . . . I know . . . Ye've got them . . . Don't say you haven't been warned . . .

Andie begins to cook some fish for his cat, Tibbie, that's come back with him, but he disappears to lie down when he gets the warning signal that Mam is returning, leaving it up to Helen to break the news that he's back. Mam comes in but goes directly in to the statute. She's convinced that Our Lady has changed her expression and is smiling now. She tells Helen that when she was at the chapel she was praying for Eric and that she felt herself glowing and rushed back. She believes Helen must be able to see that the statue is smiling, but her preoccupation is broken when she smells the fish and realizes that Andie must be back. Mam says that it isn't fair, his coming back early. Andie tries to smooth things over by telling her she's his favorite daughter.

The front door must have been left open, because suddenly The Lost Boy (Eric's nickname now) and another soldier are standing there, Eric immediately asking for Joyce. The other soldier is Norman—from Birmingham, Eric says. Eric has a gift, some soap powder, for Mam, and a gift for Joyce too.

Joyce is very nervous about seeing Eric again. She's worried about whether he'll stay at the house overnight. She doesn't mind "going to the pictures" with him, but can't stand it "when he's all over us . . ." Helen tries to reassure her. Mam tells George to stop playing the piano and asks Joyce if she isn't going to give Eric a kiss. Eric has three days' leave, and Andie offers to go off and return after that, but Joyce insists he should stay. Eric can go to Heaton to his mother's.

GEORGE: How about a double mattress in the shelter . . . with a hot water bottle . . . That was what I was thinking of . . .

MAM: Don't be daft, George, man . . . What would they be doing in the bloody shelter . . .

GEORGE: Bloody more than they'd be doing, with him in Heaton and her in Walker . . .

Joyce goes to the scullery ostensibly to get herself a cup of tea, but in reality to escape Eric's attentions. Helen goes out on an errand to the butcher's, and when she returns she finds that Andie has decided to go away again with his cases and his cat, and her parents have gone shopping with Norman. From the scullery, Helen overhears some of the conversation between Joyce and Eric—he kissing her and she asking him to stop. Eric presents Joyce with a pair of French knickers and suggests they go into the bedroom to try them on. Joyce ignores this suggestion but does concede that she is glad and relieved that he is back. She asks him to give her a little time, and to not push her, and says she's still his sweetheart.

The others come back, George with a new piece of music he begins to play and sing. Norman goes into the scullery to Helen. He gives her a bottle of scent he's bought for her, as George continues playing.

NORMAN: Fancy going out some time . . . Two of us . . .

HELEN: *Me . . . ?*

NORMAN: I don't need to go back till tomorrow night . . .

HELEN: Where to like . . .

NORMAN: Meet you in town . . . I know Eldon Square . . . You know Eldon Square . . . Could meet you there . . .

HELEN: If you *want* . . .

NORMAN: Do *you* want . . . ?

HELEN: I don't mind . . . *(to audience.)* That bloody song The Coalman was singing . . . And him looking at us . . . I had this feeling . . . Like I was in one of them films . . . With all the music playing . . .

GEORGE *(singing at the piano):* "The moon that lingered over London town," etc.

HELEN *(to audience):* I went into the kitchen . . . Joyce and Eric were sitting there . . . Not looking at each other . . . The Coalman was singing his bloody heart out . . . Both of them had this really sad look on their faces . . .

GEORGE *(singing at the piano):* "Poor puzzled moon . . . He wore a frown . . ." etc.

HELEN: Norman kept looking at me . . . Nobody had ever looked as us like that before . . . In my whole life . . .

Scene 3: "Yours"—Aug. 12, 1940

Eric and Joyce, now married, are dancing a tango as George, at the piano, is playing and singing "Yours." Eric wants Helen to come and dance too, but Joyce says Helen can't dance because of her foot, and to let her alone (Helen tells the audience it makes her jealous, not being able to dance).

Helen is anxious to see Norman. She was supposed to meet him again that day, in Eldon Square. He was to get leave, but there are raids, and they've heard all leaves are cancelled. Eric has been called back too; and the telegram coming for Eric, as it turned out, frightened Helen, who was worried that it was about Norman.

Helen can see that Joyce is relieved that Eric won't be there overnight. Mam is going to make him something for the train.

HELEN *(to audience):* And then the Old Soldier comes in with all his gear . . . and the cat basket . . . and a baby's gas mask . . .

GEORGE: Here he comes . . . Britain's Secret Weapon . . .

ANDIE: August fourteenth . . . it's in the papers . . . He's arriving in London . . . Adolf . . . Am I right? . . . you not read the papers . . .

GEORGE (with the papers): Wrong . . . August fifteenth . . . It's only the thirteenth today . . . So you've two days . . . And he'll take another day from London to Newcastle . . .

ANDIE: It's all over . . . Bar the shouting . . . Next year, this time, we'll all be singing "Deutschland Uber Alles" . . . and speaking German . . . I've always meant to learn a foreign language anyway . . .

JOYCE: Helen . . . You speak to him . . . He's going to end up behind bars . . . You are . . .

ANDIE: Have you got me ration books, Peggy . . . I'll need me ration books . . .

MAM: Where's he going? Where are you going, man . . .

ANDIE: Not bloody staying here for Hitler to find us . . . I'm going to Wooler . . .

ERIC: He's not coming . . . That's defeatist talk, Mr. Ryan . . .

GEORGE: If the whole British army's dancing around with their lasses like you, son, I wouldn't be too bloody sure.

ANDIE: I want me ration books, Peggy . . .

MAM: Sit down, you daft old bugger . . . I'm making everybody scrambled egg sandwiches . . .

The sirens go off, and George puts on his Warden's helmet and tells everybody to get into the shelter. Mam doesn't want to, she's sure she saw a rat in there, and it's flooded, too.

A long argument ensues when Andie produces the baby's gas mask for his cat. George claims it's government property, for babies, and that Andie can be charged on two counts. It's black market, and the authorities, in an emergency, could shoot him for less than that. As Block Warden, George demands it, but Andie refuses. The anti-aircraft guns have started up, and Mam is sure the church will be hit this time. Helen tells the audience she's "let down" because she's sure Norman won't get away from Tynemouth now.

Andie suggests George get to his post. Eric thinks the rest of them ought to be in the shelter. Mam says she just doesn't know where they should be. Joyce suggests she pray, but Mam can't look Our Lady in the eyes—she's very upset and doesn't want to talk about it. George is still after Andie about the baby's gas mask. Andie says he'll be in Wooler before George can do anything to him.

The planes start coming over. George is going to leave, being Block Warden, but Mam doesn't want him to go out. Andie philosophizes that "nothing matters . . . In the end . . ." Since the raid might last for hours, Eric could say he missed the train. Joyce is concerned that he's up for stripes and shouldn't disobey orders. He interrupts her to ask if she doesn't want him to spend the night. She says she does.

In the end, Helen tells the audience, a bomb fell nearby and they all ran into the shelter, Andie first with the cat basket, George hurrying them along. Mam complains of the water. Helen has brought a candle. Joyce and Eric are bickering again. George starts to leave but Mam holds him back. Then Andie tries to go back for the cat's gas mask. George finally says nobody is leaving, but agrees to go get the mask for Andie. Meanwhile another bomb has fallen. George comes back with the mask for Andie but says he's not to take it to Wooler. George would still like to go to his post, but Mam says no.

The planes are right over them now. Mam is praying as the bombs drop closer and closer. She's convinced they've hit the church, and she says it's all her fault. She is so distressed George offers to go look, but Mam tells him to loan his helmet to Eric and that Eric should go.

George is playing his mouth organ, and Andie joins him in singing "You Are My Sunshine," until George breaks off playing because of a smell. It's not gas, they discover. It's the cat, in his basket.

HELEN *(to audience):* There was just going to be another fight . . . About throwing out Tibbie . . . when the All Clear sounded . . . Eee . . . I was so happy . . . I could go down to see if Norman was coming . . . Even if he wasn't . . . Just going down to Eldon Square . . . sitting on our seat . . . Me Mam came in to us . . . When I was in the kitchen . . . She shut the door behind her . . .

MAM: Listen, Helen . . . On Sunday . . . After Mass . . . Father Kennelly . . . You know how they stand at the door . . . as you go out . . . He said to us: He couldn't help seeing us saying the Lord's Prayer . . . You could see . . . He'd never seen anybody say it like that before . . . Like I believed in it with my whole body and soul . . .

HELEN: You do, Mam . . .

MAM: I haven't finished yet, man . . . He touched us . . . the back of my hand . . . Standing there in his lovely priest's vestments . . . You know what I mean . . . And the light through the glass windows . . . That picture of Jesus . . . The light was coming through the windows . . . shining on his face . . . He touched my hand . . . It gave us a funny feeling . . . You know what I mean . . . You probably wouldn't . . . Joyce would . . . But I couldn't tell Joyce . . . I don't want Joyce to hear this . . . You listening to me Helen . . .

HELEN: I *know* what you mean, Mam . . .

MAM: It was a real sinful thought . . . The feeling was sinful . . . And I never told him at Confession . . . How could I? . . . It was him that was in the Confessional . . . Father Kennelly . . . But that feeling . . . It was like sometimes when you hear a choir and an organ bursting into a lovely hymn . . . Or you go in the park . . . on a lovely summer day . . . It made us really feel glad to be living . . . Looking at his face . . . and knowing there was such a person in the world . . .

HELEN: That's not sinful, Mam . . . Don't be daft . . . That's lovely . . .

MAM: It is, Helen, man . . . You don't know the half of it . . .

HELEN: It isn't . . . It's lovely . . . . .

Eric has come back with Joyce, who had gone out to look for him, worried about him; they look "a bit more together." Eric may as well stay, because the train he would have to get would make him miss his supper. He tells Mam that some shrapnel went through the roof of the church, and a couple of windows were blown in. Mam takes it as her warning.

Helen goes off to Eldon Square, where Norman is waiting, asleep. He has 24 hours' leave, but he's been up five nights in a row. He couldn't budge when the sirens went off, but he did put his helmet on.

Norman finally persuades Helen to take her hair down and tells her it's lovely. He wants to take her dancing. She says that upsets her. He wants to know what the matter is with her leg. She explains that it was noticed too late that one leg was shorter than the other—too late to get an operation. He persists, convinced that she could waltz, that they could dance the slow dances at least. He promises her they'll leave after ten minutes if she hates it.

She wants to know why he's got to dance with her, and he says it's like faith healing, to make her leg better. He puts his arms around her and kisses her and tells her she's walking better already. They're singing as they begin to dance. He starts to explain the waltz, but Helen says she knows, she's seen Joyce doing it and the foxtrot also. They go on singing "A Nightingale Sang in Berkeley Square," but Norman changes it to Eldon Square.

Helen wonders if he has a place for the night. Norman says he's staying with her, he doesn't want them to be separated during his 24 hours' leave. He suggests they find a private hotel off Osborne Road with a vacancies sign.

Helen says she'll be over in the morning for him, but Norman doesn't want Helen to leave. She doesn't want to leave him either, but she tells him she'll come back to have breakfast. Norman suggests they get rooms next to each other, but she tells him her mother would be waiting for her.

HELEN (to audience): We must've been talking louder than we thought . . . Because the wife from the hotel opened the door and asked what we wanted . . . I have no idea, to this day, what came over us . . . Because I just said: . . . We want a room for tonight . . . A double room . . . Yes we're married . . . The wife looked at us . . . And said something like "That's up to you" . . . Norman couldn't say anything . . . He was so surprised . . . We just signed the book . . . And went upstairs . . . The wife said she could maybe give us a Spam sandwich and a cup of tea . . . I was really starving . . . We had it in our room . . . It was nice . . . Nice chintzy curtains and matching bed cover . . .

NORMAN: I didn't mean you to come in the same room . . .

HELEN: I know that . . . It's a lovely room, isn't it . . . Clean and fresh . . .

NORMAN: She's put a hot water bottle in the bed . . . Bit dry—the sandwiches . . .

HELEN: They're all right . . . I phoned me Dad's Warden post . . . They're going to tell him . . .

NORMAN: I wasn't trying anything on . . . You know that, Helen, love . . .

HELEN: I know, Norman . . .

NORMAN: But I love you . . .

HELEN: I love you . . .

NORMAN: Will I sleep on the chair then . . .

HELEN: If you want . . .

NORMAN: I don't mind . . .

HELEN: Don't be daft, man . . . (Taking his hand and kissing him.) . . . I trust you . . . You trust me . . . We trust each other don't we . . . (To audience.)

. . . I didn't even have a nightie with us . . . I had to go to bed in my petticoat
. . . It was a good job I'd borrowed Joyce's . . . It was a nice yellow one . . . And
we didn't do anything . . . in the night . . . or the morning . . . We kissed and
cuddled a bit and went to sleep with our arms round one another . . . It was lovely
. . . Having his arms round us . . . Going to sleep . . . and waking up . . . with
him beside us . . . And the sun shining through the curtains . . .
    The song "Yours" up as lights fade. Curtain.

ACT II

Scene 1: "That Lovely Weekend"—November 1942

George and Joyce are singing "That Lovely Weekend" and Helen, with her
rosary, is saying a litany to Our Lady.

HELEN *(to audience):* . . . The week me Mam went to London . . . for her
Auntie's funeral . . . I stopped going to Mass . . . I still said my rosary . . . I always
felt better after saying it . . . I'd given up going to Confession, months ago
. . . I had to confess to adultery with Norman . . . and I didn't believe I *was*
committing adultery . . . I wasn't . . . But the whole thing blew up that weekend
. . . Me Mam came back from London . . . The Coalman was organizing a party
. . . He was always having parties . . . from then on . . . Everything began to turn
. . . Rommel had been beaten in Africa . . . and papers were all full of it . . . Pictures
of Monty . . . and the tanks in the desert . . . Me Dad was in trouble, too, with
me Mam . . . That was the week he'd joined the Communist Party . . . At the
yard . . . It started with us finding this flat . . . For Norman and me . . . in Elswick
. . . Clifton Road . . .
    NORMAN: It's nice . . . I like it . . .
    HELEN: Norman, love . . . I don't want you to feel I'm pushing you or anything
. . . Do you hear me . . .
    NORMAN: I know, Helen . . .
    HELEN: I'm not pushing you to marry us or anything, Norman . . . I mean that
. . . I'm just sick of having nowhere of our own . . . It'd be lovely . . . wouldn't
it . . . Having a weekend together in our own place . . .
    NORMAN: Helen . . . Look . . . I'm sorry . . . I love you.
    HELEN *(to audience):* When he came out with it at last . . . I felt that I'd known
all the time . . . I wasn't angry with him . . . I could understand how he hadn't
been able to tell me . . . It wasn't *his* fault, anyway . . . It was me pushing
him . . .
    NORMAN: I mean . . . I was just a kid . . . when I married her . . .
    HELEN: It's all right Norman . . . Honest . . .
    NORMAN: I love *you* . . . I bloody hate that . . . Hurting you like this . . . I
couldn't help it . . .
    HELEN: It's all right, love . . . Only thing that gets us . . . Is you spending your
leaves with her . . . That's all . . . It's understandable . . .
    NORMAN: I'll spend the next one with you, Helen . . . I mean . . . If there's

a next one for us to spend together . . . I mean . . . If you don't finish with us . . .

HELEN: Norman . . . Why should I finish with you . . . I love you . . .

Helen tries to distract him from going on about it by telling him she's bought ginger beer and pasties for them to eat in the flat. But Norman goes on apologizing, saying that he's tried to tell her about it often, that he didn't like lying to her. She doesn't want to hear any more. She knows all she wants to know for now.

George has been playing and singing "The Cossack Patrol" and is offering drinks and urging Communist literature on Norman and teasing Andie, who has answered an advertisement in the *Chronicle* about an elderly woman with a spare room, a widow (Andie's tired of being shuttled between his daughters and says his cat needs to settle down).

Joyce finally gets Helen alone in the scullery and tells her she's pregnant, but she doesn't know who the father is. She's not certain whether Eric's last leave was when he came home only for the day. Joyce tells Helen she just "fell into it" with a young man in the Air Force and confides that it was the first time she'd enjoyed herself with a man. She hadn't used protection.

Mam comes in, returning from her aunt's funeral in London on a train that was three hours late.

GEORGE: What did she leave you . . .

MAM: She left me Da her piano . . .

ANDIE: That's nice of her . . . Bring it with you . . . Did you?

MAM: Eee . . . You should've seen me and yer Auntie Marge . . . In this Rolls Royce . . . Going to the funeral . . . Joyce . . . You know what your Auntie Marge is like when she's had a sherry . . . She was putting her hand out the window . . . Like the Queen . . . Waving, to the crowds . . . Look at this cake . . . The shops are full of them . . .

HELEN *(to audience):* She started emptying her bag . . . Full of all kinds of rubbish . . . It was a shame for her . . . The cream cake . . . had that artificial cream in it . . . Like zinc ointment . . . And she'd bought some pies . . . and they'd turned in the train . . . The only decent thing she'd bought was some material . . .

George is celebrating the victory at Tobruk, and he wants to tell Mam about joining the Communist Party. Andie wants to tell her about the room at the widow's. Joyce is trying to get her mother's attention to help her figure out about Eric's last leave. Before she can take any of it in, Mam sees the Communist literature, assumes it's Norman's and is upset because Communists don't believe in God. Helen tries to tell her the literature is not Norman's. George is trying to show Mam his Communist card, Mam wants George to open his present, Andie is still trying to tell her about the room, and Joyce is still trying to get her attention.

George's present is a pair of cuff links. He gives Mam a kiss, but she tells him to act his age and finally goes for the calendar as Andie goes on about his written conversation with the widow. Mam thinks Eric last came on leave from Pickering, with his corporal stripes, but Joyce thinks that was the time before. George is trying to get her to look at his card, but Mam is still busy at the calendar and wants to know why Joyce wants to know. Andie wants his ration books because he's going move to the widow's house. Helen decides her mother may as well hear from her, too. "Me and Norman," she says. Mam assumes they are going to get married, gives them her blessing and wishes them happiness. Helen explains that they aren't getting married, but she's 31 and she's going to live with Norman in a flat in Elswick.

Mam is confused. Andie starts to explain, but Mam tells him to stay out of it. Andie tells her to give him his ration books and he'll leave for Heaton.

GEORGE: Andie . . . Take it easy . . . Just take it easy a minute . . . Norman . . . You've lost us here, lad . . . I don't get your drift . . . I do not get your drift, son . . .

HELEN: It was *my* idea, Da . . . It's no use talking to him . . .

GEORGE: I'm bloody *talking* to him . . . I want something straight . . . Have you been messing about with . . .

MAM: Don't start acting the father with her after all them years, George . . . Helen, pet . . .

GEORGE: I bloody *am* her father. Am I? Mind *you*. The way things are going, now I'm not sure . . .

MAM: My God. He's not *married!* He's not a married man, is he?

HELEN: Just fell into it young, Mam. He's not *really* married.

MAM: Oh, dear God in heaven. He's a married man.

ANDIE: It doesn't matter, Peggy! . . . It'll all be nothing in a hundred years' time . . .

GEORGE: What the hell good does that do . . . We're bloody here *now,* aren't we, man . . . *How's* he not married, Helen?

HELEN: He got married very young . . .

GEORGE: Is he a Russian or something . . . Does he have to have an interpreter . . .

HELEN: I made up my mind . . . To go . . . This weekend, Mam . . . That's the best thing . . . A quick break . . . If you can lend us some curtains and blankets . . .

GEORGE: You see what you're doing, son . . . Do you? . . . You're breaking up a whole household . . .

NORMAN: I'm very sorry, Mr. Stott . . . I didn't mean . . .

Andie is already thinking that if things don't work out at the widow's he can move in with Helen in Elswick. Helen offers to make her mother a cup of tea, but Mam wants her to go with her to Father Kennelly. Helen refuses. "If he's getting divorced," George says, but Norman says there aren't divorces during wartime. Mam quotes the Bible about "What God has joined together," and George says there's not that problem in Russia. And Mam suddenly remembers that the last time Eric was there, he'd had to return the same night.

HELEN *(to audience):* They didn't believe I was going . . . Till the Sunday . . . When I came into the kitchen . . . with my cases and things . . . I felt a bit

Robert Cornthwaite (Andie), Joan Allen (Helen), Beverly May (Peggy),
John Carpenter (George), Francis Guinan (Eric, *in background*) and Moira
McCanna Harris (Joyce) in a scene from *And a Nightingale Sang* . . .

easier . . . because Joyce's period suddenly came . . . It was a false alarm . . . So
that was one problem less me Mam had to face . . .

GEORGE *(at the piano):* "You'd be so nice to come home to/You'd be so nice
by the fire/When the breeze on high/Sings a lullaby," etc.

MAM: Where are you going, pet?

HELEN: Mam . . . Don't start that all over again . . .

MAM: Helen . . . You can't leave us . . . man . . . In the middle of a war
. . . and everything . . . Helen . . . Pet . . .

HELEN: I'll come over and see you every day . . . From me work, Mam . . .

MAM: George . . . Our lass is going away . . .

GEORGE: It's that bloody Lost Boy's fault . . . Bringing The Tailor's Dummy
home . . . like that . . . Told you . . . first time I saw him . . . We'll have nothing
but trouble from that stupid swine . . .

MAM: Are you not even staying for your dinner, pet?

HELEN: I've got to get to the house and arrange everything . . .

MAM: I'll never step over your doorstep . . . You know that . . . I swear
that . . .

HELEN: Ta ra . . . Da' . . . Ta ra . . . Mam . . . I'm sorry I couldn't have had
a nice white wedding for you in St. Anthony's . . .

MAM: Don't Helen . . . I can't even bear thinking about it . . .

HELEN *(to audience):* I rushed out the house . . . Another minute and they'd
have me crying too . . . But me Mam came after us . . .

MAM: You forgot yer ration book . . .

HELEN: Eee . . . I did . . . *(to audience.)* Taking it from her . . . It was a funny feeling . . . Like it was the final break . . . from her . . . It was funny taking that ration book . . . It was harder to do than anything I'd done up till then . . .

When Helen and Norman were sitting down to their dinner of haddock, the bells for the Tobruk victory began to ring, and she felt as if it were a sign for the two of them, the first time she had felt hopeful.

Scene 2: "The White Cliffs of Dover"—June 6, 7, 1944

Mam has come to Helen's to tell her that George has been hit by a bomb. He's in the hospital, and she wants Helen to go there with her. She doesn't know how badly he's hurt. A policeman came to the door to tell her. George is on day shift, but it was his turn at firewatching tonight.

Mam talks about what a good Da he was, and Helen tries to reassure her that it will be all right. There had been a raid, but only one plane got through. D-Day, Helen tells the audience, wondering what a plane was doing over Newcastle.

But when they got to the hospital they were told George had gone home. When they got home, Joyce was there with Eric. He was explaining how he had lost his corporal's stripes, when Andie arrived. George is not there, and Mam is convinced he's dead, hit by a German bomb. Eric says he'd have been "smashed to smithereens" if he'd been hit by a bomb, and Mam tells Joyce to tell him to hold his tongue.

Mam wants to go back to the hospital, sure that when they said he'd gone they meant he was dead, but Helen tells her they said went home. Mam goes in to the statue, and then George comes in, with a little sticking plaster on the side of his head. Andie remarks that it must have been a smallish bomb. Mam is relieved.

Weeks ago, Lord Haw Haw knew the clock on the town hall was slow, George tells them, and he goes on about Lord Haw Haw, who claims Germany is "stronger than ever." Eric says that's a bluff, they should see what they've been putting on ships; but he stops, he's to say nothing about that. Andie asks him if that's the reason he lost his stripes. Eric replies that he lost them because he was taken for a spy.

George asks if they want to hear about his "encounter with Hitler" or not, and Mam says they are listening. He was up on the roof, he says, and Mam asks if he ate his Spam sandwiches. Joyce is more interested in hearing about how Eric was mistaken for a spy, but George wants to be listened to. He says he was there when a Heinkel came in. Eric interrupts to tell Joyce that in Sussex his Tyneside was thought to be a German accent—"Okey dokey?" Joyce says it isn't "Okey dokey".

GEORGE: This Heinkel . . . You could see him . . . He was looking for something . . .

MAM: For you . . .

GEORGE: Looking for the *Yard,* man . . . You could see . . . He was going backwards and forwards . . . Look . . . If they know Newcastle Town Hall clock's two minutes slow . . . They'll know all about the whole Communist cell in the Yard . . . They might even've been after me as party secretary . . . Wouldn't put it past them . . .

ERIC: From up there . . . Mr. Stott . . . They couldn't make out *who* you were from there . . .

GEORGE: They dived . . . I'm telling you . . . A hail of bullets at us . . . They were so low . . . I could read the number on the wings . . . See that bloody swastika . . . Diving straight at us . . . I threw me stirrup pump at him . . . Take that, you bastard! . . . Then I retreated . . . Down the ladder . . . Me helmet dropped off . . . In the heat of the fighting . . .

ANDIE: First rule of a soldier . . . Hold on to your rifle and your helmet . . .

GEORGE: That's how they got us . . . A bullet bounced off the wall . . . Got me here . . . See . . .

MAM: Dear God . . . Thank you . . . Thank you, dear God . . . For bringing my man back to us . . . I'm going to put thanks to the Sacred Heart in the *Catholic Herald* this week . . . I am . . .

GEORGE: Stunned us . . . Next thing I knew . . . I was in the General . . . Some lass putting a plaster on me head . . . I showed the bastards. Eh . . . Eric . . . son . . . One thing . . . anyway . . . son . . . Right . . . Nobody can say, when it's all over, *I* haven't done my bit for the old country . . .

HELEN *(to audience):* It would've been all right . . . If we'd had our supper and went to bed . . . But me Dad had to drag us all out to the pub on Welbeck Road . . . to celebrate . . . And that's where the trouble started . . . Eric went for the drinks . . . Me Mam and Da' sat at the table . . . When he came back . . . He had only two pints . . . I didn't want one anyway . . . As soon as me Mam saw that . . . She stood up . . . Pulled me Da' up too . . . And walked out the pub without speaking . . .

Eric explains about not bringing the right number of drinks, telling Joyce he got mixed up because somebody made a nasty remark about her mother and he was defending her. He won't say what the person said, and Joyce says maybe "he was a spy like you." Eric says they did think he was a spy, and that he got picked up in Sussex, at a dance. He got the third degree, and the M.P.'s took him back to camp "drunk and disorderly . . . and losing a rifle." He left his rifle in the bog, he tells her. Joyce is incensed that he was at a dance.

HELEN *(to audience):* . . . Back in the house . . . It was Battle Stations . . . Me Mam was sitting there, at the table . . . Her arms folded . . . Black . . . The Coalman was at the piano, hiding from the storm . . .

ANDIE: I'm just telling yer Mam, Helen . . . She wants us to get married . . . On August Bank Holiday . . . The Black Widow . . .

MAM: I have seen some mean, some miserable characters in my day . . . But my God! . . . I never thought my own son-in-law—

ERIC: Bloody let us tell you . . .

MAM: Joyce'll tell you . . . Whenever he was due home on leave . . . I saved our meat ration . . . and points . . . and everything . . . I said: I want that lad to come home to a decent meal . . . I even saved cigarettes for him . . . Every time he came back, there was twenty Woodbines on the mantelpiece waiting for him . . . Is that right, son?

ERIC: I'm just telling you what happened . . .

MAM: Am I telling you a lie . . . Tonight . . . Everybody was having heart and onion pie . . . What do you sit down to . . .

ERIC: This bloke in the pub . . .

MAM: Pork chop and apple sauce . . . Because I know . . . A lad who's been away fighting for his country wants to come home to a nice, cheerful, tasty meal . . .

ERIC: Look . . . I'm telling you . . .

MAM: I was even saving up coupons for his birthday . . . Did you know that, Da'?

ANDIE: What you're asking for is people not to be people, Peggy . . . That's where you're falling down . . . Gratitude . . . That's not people . . . It would be very nice if people were grateful . . . and human beings and that kind of thing . . . But that's not how they're made . . . People are not human beings . . . That's where you go wrong! . . .

MAM: I don't care so much for myself . . . But after his wife's father . . . Has been snatched from the jaws of death . . .

ERIC: It slipped me mind . . . in the heat of the minute . . . That's all . . . If you'd have waited another second . . . I would've . . .

MAM: I just cannot understand anybody like that . . .

ANDIE: Take that Black Widow . . . I've given her five bob a week since I moved in . . . Cleaned and lighted her fire every day . . . Brushed her shoes . . . After I've done with them . . . And then she pays us by wanting to marry us . . .

MAM: It was even *him* that suggested we go out for a drink . . .

HELEN (*to audience*): . . . It just got too much for Eric . . . He stuck his hands in his pockets . . . and threw all his silver and copper on to the table . . .

ERIC: There's yer bloody drink, you rotten old cow! . . . Bloody fill yerself up till it comes out yer rotten throat!

Eric goes off, and Mam asks George if he isn't going to do something about him. George thinks he'll go to bed, he's had a bad day. Eric returns with his pack and case and asks Joyce if she's coming with him. She refuses to go after "finding out what you're up to, when you're away from me."

ERIC: How do I know what *you're* up to . . . like . . . When *I'm* away . . . All these bloody Yanks all over the place . . .

JOYCE: What do you mean by that? . . .

ERIC: Funny thing . . . You're never short of stockings . . . are you . . . Where do you get them from . . . What have you got to do to get them . . .

JOYCE: Bloody take that back . . . Hear me!

MAM: What are you hinting at, Eric . . .

ANDIE: I must admit . . . Peggy . . . If I was a lass . . . The way them Yanks go about . . . Throwing their dollars all over the place . . .

MAM: Keep out of this, Da . . . Will you . . . Are you insinuating . . .

ERIC: Oh, go and have a shit to yourself . . . The lot of you!

HELEN *(to audience):* And he walked out . . . Right out of our lives . . .

ANDIE: Now . . . Eric's not staying . . . With me complications with the widow . . . You understand . . . You think you might take us back for a few weeks . . . Till I find somewhere else . . . I was going to ask Helen . . . But I can't take to Elswick . . . somehow . . . I mean . . . If you've been in Walker all yer life . . . I've nobody to talk to . . . in Elswick . . . I don't like the library, either . . .

HELEN *(to audience):* Joyce . . . Stood there . . . White . . . Looking at the door Eric had gone through . . .

JOYCE: I don't bloody care . . . I don't care . . . I don't care if he *never* bloody comes back! . . .

George is at the piano, singing "The White Cliffs of Dover." Helen tells the audience that the news of the Normandy landings came over the radio the next day—but all Helen was thinking about was meeting Norman after an absence of several weeks.

HELEN *(to audience):* . . . . . When he was away . . . Sometimes I couldn't stand it . . . I was packing his other tunic . . . to take to him . . . That morning . . . He could go right back to Durham . . . And I saw he'd left some papers . . . and his pay book . . . in his tunic . . . Eee . . . I said to myself . . . He's a careless bugger . . . Doesn't even look after his pay book . . . I just looked inside . . . I don't know why I looked . . . And it bloody hit us . . . His wife's name was there . . . who he was paying his marriage allowance to . . . and then . . . an allowance to one child . . . I kept going back to the page . . . To make sure . . . I couldn't believe it wasn't a mistake . . . But it was there, right enough . . . One child . . . Matthew Peter . . . I washed up the dishes . . . And went into Parsons . . . I just went through the day . . . I was acting full of it . . . The lasses in the Blade shop said to us . . . What had come over us . . . I was so cheery . . . I couldn't bear to go home to me Mam's . . . Instead . . . I went to the station . . . to wait for Norman's train . . . If he was coming . . . Waited for hours . . . Men kept looking at us . . . Especially the Yanks . . . One of them offered us a bar of chocolate . . . I just stared right through him . . . In the end . . . I gave up . . . I went to our bench in Eldon Square—and he was bloody there . . . Sitting on our bench . . .

Helen confronts Norman, who arrived on an earlier train, about the child, explaining that she hadn't meant to look in his pay book, but that she thought he stayed with his parents when he went to Birmingham. Norman is sorry, but explains that when he went to Birmingham he went to see his wife, and felt sorry for her. She asks him if he loves the child. He says he doesn't know. He tells Helen he loves her, she knows that—but Helen says she doesn't know. She knows she loves him but asks why he needed to go back to his wife, and couldn't he finish with his wife, for his wife's sake.

Norman calls himself an idiot who messes up his own life and everybody else's. Helen is impatient with him and his breast-beating. He assures her that he loves her, he should have told her, "it just happened" and doesn't make a difference between them. He wants Helen's forgiveness, but she says she's not God. Then, finally, he looks "so miserable . . . dejected . . . and guilty" that she kisses him.

Scene 3: "A Nightingale Sang in Berkeley Square"—May 8, 1945

It is V. E. Day and there is the sound of hooters. Mam is pleased at having gotten a brown loaf at Jackson's and hopes Helen will go to get another. George is making a guy for the evening. Mam wants to know where the bowler hat that he has came from. He says it was his wedding hat.

JOYCE: What should I do about Eric, Mam?

HELEN: One of these days, Joyce . . . You'll actually make up your own mind about something, won't you?

JOYCE: I'm just asking . . .

MAM: Give me that hat . . .

GEORGE: I *need* it . . . That's yer Capitalist . . . You burn Capitalism . . . That's the idea . . . That's the whole point of the war . . . isn't it . . . Finish the old system . . . once and for all . . .

JOYCE: Did you read *his* letter?

HELEN: I read his letter . . .

JOYCE: What do you think? You see, he's due in about an hour. Should I go meet him . . . ?

HELEN *(to audience):* That week . . . Eric had written her . . . First time since he walked out of our house . . .

JOYCE: It was a nice letter, wasn't it . . .

HELEN: Yes . . . It was all right . . . *(To audience.)* "Dear Joyce, I'm coming back from Sussex on eighth at six o'clock . . . If you want to meet us at the station . . . Hope you are keeping well . . . Eric . . ." He was going to put "love" . . . but you could see he'd had second thoughts . . .

JOYCE: I mean . . . For *Eric* to write a *letter* . . . *You* know him, Mam . . .

MAM: Meet him, if you want to . . . Is nobody going out to see if they can get some more bread . . .

JOYCE: Mam . . . You see . . . I thought we were finished . . .

Andie turns up, and George comments that the cat will be eligible for an old age pension. Mam asks Andie why he's there with his cases and the cat. He claims that she asked him to come when he saw her recently, and that he was "touched."

JOYCE: I think this time . . . If we had a place of our own . . . Like Helen . . . That's what we've got to do . . . We're going to find a place . . .

MAM: I meant . . . Come up for a bite or something . . . That's all I meant . . .

ANDIE: I made a mistake . . . I'm sorry . . .

MAM: It's Eric turning up . . .

ANDIE: Where is he? . . .

JOYCE: I'm meeting him at the station, Granda . . .

ANDIE: Taking up with him again . . . ?

JOYCE: I don't know . . .

ANDIE: Say you do know, and you'll know. *(Looking at the effigy.)* What the hell's that?

MAM: Well might you ask.

GEORGE: What do you think it is?

ANDIE: Looks like you on yer wedding day.

JOYCE: What do you mean, Granda? Say I know.

ANDIE: I don't know, Joyce. Sometimes I say owt . . . First thing that comes into me head . . . It doesn't matter in the end, does it, Joyce? He's as good as any other lad, isn't he, Eric? I mean . . . He has all his equipment . . .

George asks Andie if he doesn't think it's the "dawn of a new world," but Andie's noncommittal. George believes the people will take over the world that they fought for. Mam would like to have Andie stay, but there's Eric, and there's not enough bread. Andie says he'll get some, the widow has some.

Helen tells the audience that Norman was coming from Durham to be with her V.E. night, to see the lights and the bonfire at Walker Park. On her way to meet him she got a white loaf for her mother and one for them and felt it was a sign that everything would be all right for them, finally. She arrives at the Square before Norman does, and she doesn't notice that he is carrying a case when he comes. He has brought it with him to help him break it to her that he's going to Birmingham tonight, and that he's to be moved to Leicester, which is closer to Birmingham than Durham, and that he's getting a compassionate leave because his mother is "in a right state" over his brother who's been missing since Arnheim. Helen is disappointed that he'll miss the "bonfire, then . . . and everything . . ."

NORMAN *(Nearly breaking):* . . . I know, Helen . . . I'm going to miss everything, love . . .

HELEN: What's the matter, pet . . . Come on . . . What's wrong . . . love . . .

NORMAN: I love you . . .

HELEN: I know . . .

NORMAN: Just . . . I'm getting pulled . . . all ways . . .

HELEN: It'll be all right, love . . . I'll come and see you at Leicester, will I? . . . And when you're demobbed . . .

NORMAN: I'm telling you . . . That's it . . . Helen . . . I don't know if I'm *coming* back . . . That's what I'm saying . . .

HELEN: You going back to *her* . . . Is that what you mean?

NORMAN: I don't know . . . My mother wants me back . . . With what happened to Tony . . . She wants me near her . . .

HELEN: You going back to *her* . . . Are you? In Birmingham . . .

NORMAN: It's not that . . .

HELEN: Do you love *her* better than me . . . Is that what you've found out, Norman?

NORMAN: I don't know what I'm going to do in the end . . . It's the kid . . . isn't it? . . . I love him . . . He really needs me . . . You should see him

... When I'm with him ... I mean ... A kid ... he needs a father ... doesn't he? ...

HELEN: Yes ... A kid needs a father ... Yes ... I suppose he does ...

NORMAN: In a few months, it'll be clear ... Just now ... You don't know where you are ... do you?

HELEN: I know where I am ... Norman ... Yes ... I do ... I'm clear enough ...

NORMAN: I don't want to leave you, Helen ... I love you ... You not see that ...

HELEN: I don't know what I see, Norman ... I should've known that ... shouldn't I ... I mean ... I should've known ... we weren't going to kind of live together for the rest of our lives ... I shouldn't have got into thinking like that ... The two of us should be together till death parted us ... That was stupid ... wasn't it ... You've got things pulling you away from us ... All the time ...

NORMAN: I think ... in the end ... when it's all clear ... I'll come back to you ... I'll write to you ... I'll send you an address where you can write to me ...

HELEN: Do you want some tea? I'm having some tea ... I was looking forward to walking round the town ... with all the lights on ... with you ... your train'll be away ... won't it ... Before it's dark ... I've a biscuit ...

NORMAN: I don't want a biscuit ... No ...

HELEN: I was even thinking ... now the war's finished ... If I could have a kid ...

NORMAN: Helen ... I'm sorry, love ... I bloody am ...

HELEN: I know ... It doesn't do any good, does it ... Me Mam made them biscuits ... They're horrible ...

NORMAN: Give them to the pigeons ...

HELEN: What'll we do, till your train's due ... ?

NORMAN: You're really good ... You deserve somebody really good ... Not a useless rotten bastard like me ...

HELEN: I said ... I do ... You're right ... I might go out and look for somebody now ... Now I know I deserve somebody worthwhile ... If Joyce and Eric take up again ... Should I give them the flat ... ?

NORMAN: I don't know ... love ...

HELEN: Come on then, Norman ... Cheer up ... We've won the war, haven't we ... ?

Joyce calls to Helen that Eric has brought her a banana from the Merchant Navy Yard, as Helen tells the audience that everyone is here in the house. Mam is making a bed for the Old Soldier in the kitchen. Eric and Joyce are dancing. Andie asks Helen if she's all right—she says yes and asks if he is. "Never think about it ... Doesn't matter ... does it? ... As good as I'll ever be," he tells her.

Eric tries to jolly Mam into going to the bonfire, but she won't "show meself" with that "bloody Communist dummy" representing Capitalism, not with the priests watching. Andie suggests they label it Lord Haw Haw instead.

GEORGE: Five years . . . Bloody fighting for yer freedom . . .

ANDIE: Told ye, didn't I . . . Exactly the same thing in 1918 . . .

HELEN *(to audience):* When we went out into the street . . . Everything was lit up . . . The whole world was lit . . . There was something burning really bright in the distance . . . I think it was the flares on the Eldon statue . . .

MAM: Eee . . . The lights . . . Look at them, Helen . . . Love . . . I can't get over them . . . Can you . . . Listen . . . There's a late Mass . . . tonight . . . Will you come with us, love . . .

HELEN: I might do, Mam . . . I might . . . *(To audience.)* Too many things had happened to us . . . that day . . . I was still drained inside us . . . whenever I thought of Norman . . . It was like a real pain in my body . . . It stabbed us . . . Every time I thought of him . . . They all went back into the house . . . I stood on the pavement taking everything in . . . The whole of Welbeck Road was a string of lights . . . People making their way to the park for the bonfire . . . Eric called out to us . . .

ERIC: Eh, Helen, man. Come and dance with us.

HELEN *(to audience):* . . . I was going to say to him . . . "Eric . . . I can't dance" . . . Then I remembered I did . . . I *could* . . . now . . . And I let him put his arms around us . . . And dance us away . . . *(To Eric.)* . . . Eric . . . I really enjoyed that banana . . . *(To audience.)* I really did, too . . .

They all sing "Roll Out the Barrel." Curtain.

NOISES OFF

A Play in Three Acts

BY MICHAEL FRAYN

Cast and credits appear on page 329

MICHAEL FRAYN was born in northwest London, the son of a sales representative. He attended Kingston Grammar School but left in 1952 and went into the Army, which assigned him to train for becoming an interpreter by studying Russian at Cambridge and in Moscow. He received a commission as an intelligence officer before his discharge in 1954, when he returned to Cambridge to study philosophy and—in 1957—to co-author a college-produced musical comedy, Zounds!

Frayn worked for the Manchester Guardian *as reporter and satirical columnist until 1962 and the London* Observer *until 1968, the year in which his first dramatic work,* Jamie, on a Flying Visit, *was televised on the BBC. His London stage debut took place in 1970 with* The Two of Us, *a program of four short works:* Black and Silver, The New Quixote, Mr. Foot *and* Chinamen. *There followed* The Sandboy *(1971 at the Greenwich Theater),* Alphabetical Order *(1975 in London and later in the U.S.A. at the Long Wharf Theater),* Donkey's Years *(1976, voted the best comedy of the year by the Society of West End Theater),* Clouds *(1978 in London),* Liberty Hall *(1980 in London) and* Make and Break *(1980 in Hammersmith and London). Frayn's* Noises Off *had its premiere at the Lyric Theater, Hammersmith Feb. 11, 1982 and soon transferred to the Savoy Theater in the heart of London, where it continued as a long-run hit while its American production was being staged on Broadway Dec. 11, 1983, its author's first Best Play.*

Subsequent (1984) Frayn playscripts at this writing are Number One *(an adaptation of Jean Anouilh's* Le Nombril) *and* Benefactors. *His published works*

include collections of his newspaper writings and the novels The Tin Men, The
Russian Interpreter *(for which he won the Hawthornden Prize),* Towards the End
of the Morning *and* A Very Private Life. *He has contributed many dramas and
documentaries to the BBC and has continued to contribute occasional pieces to the*
Observer, *for which he received a National Press Award in 1970. His translations
of* The Cherry Orchard *and* The Fruits of Enlightenment *have appeared at the
National Theater in London. Frayn is married, with three daughters, and lives near
Blackheath in southeast London.*

Time: *A Wednesday afternoon*

Place: *The living room of the Brents' country home*

ACT I

Grand Theater, Weston-Super-Mare, Monday, Jan. 14

SYNOPSIS: A high-ceilinged living room *"fully equipped with every aid to modern living"* features a sofa and tables in the center, a stairway at right winding
up to a gallery running the length of the room upstage, and numerous modes of
access. At ground level, the front door opens onto a garden and two other doors
lead to study and kitchen, and there is a lavatory door at left. Halfway up the
stairs another door opens to another bathroom. At gallery level are the doors to
the master bedroom and a linen closet and an exit at left to the rest of the house.

Into this country-house setting, *"a place where the discerning theatergoer will
feel instantly at home,"* enters Mrs. Clackett, *"a housekeeper of character,"* come
to answer the ringing telephone and carrying a plate of sardines. She puts down
the sardines and picks up the receiver.

MRS: CLACKETT: Hello . . . Yes, but there's no one here, love . . . No, Mr.
Brent's not here . . . He lives here, yes, but he don't live here now because he lives
in Spain . . . Mr. Philip Brent, that's right . . . The one who writes the plays, that's
him, only now he writes them in Spain . . . No, she's in Spain too, they're all in
Spain, there's no one here . . . Am I in Spain? No, I'm not in Spain, dear. I look
after the house for them, only I go home at one o'clock on Wednesday, so that's
where *I* am . . . No, because I've got a nice plate of sardines to put my feet up
with, and they've got color here . . . . .

She refers the caller to the real estate agents representing the house, then puts
the receiver down on the table beside the phone. She gets up and moves toward
the study carrying the plate of sardines but stops, wondering whether she should
be taking the sardines with her as she makes her exit.

At this point she is an actress stepping out of character, and we discover that
this is a rehearsal of a play (*"Nothing On,* by Robin Housemonger") at Grand

Dorothy Loudon, Victor Garber, Deborah Rush and Linda Thorson as performers rehearsing a scene from their play-within-the-play, with Brian Murray *(right)* as their director, in *Noises Off*

Theater, Weston-Super Mare; and that *"The living room of the Brents' Country home"* is a stage setting, the "real" setting being the interior of the theater where the rehearsal is taking place.

Dotty Otley, the actress playing Mrs. Clackett, wonders aloud what she is supposed to do with the sardines. The voice of the play's director, Lloyd Dallas, is heard from the rear of the auditorium.

LLOYD: You leave the sardines, and you put the receiver back.
DOTTY: Oh yes, I put the receiver back.
    She puts the receiver back and moves off again with the sardines.
LLOYD: And you leave the sardines.
DOTTY: And I *leave* the sardines?
LLOYD: You *leave* the sardines.
DOTTY: I put the receiver back and I leave the sardines.
LLOYD: Right.
DOTTY: We've changed that, have we, love?
LLOYD: No, love.

DOTTY: That's what I've always been doing?

LLOYD: I shouldn't say that, Dotty, my precious.

DOTTY: How about the words, love? Am I getting some of them right?

LLOYD: Some of them have a very familiar ring.

DOTTY: Only it's like a fruit machine in there.

LLOYD: I know that, Dotty.

DOTTY: I open my mouth, and I never know if it's going to come out three oranges or two lemons and a banana.

LLOYD: Anyway, it's not midnight yet. We don't open till tomorrow. . . . .

Thus coached, Dotty repeats the act of hanging up the phone and exiting but this time forgets that she's supposed to take a prop newspaper with her. Lloyd stops the action again, but not before Garry Lejeune (playing Roger Tramplemain, *"about 30 and has the well-appointed air of a man who handles high-class real estate"*) and Brooke Ashton (playing Vicki, *"a desirable property in her early 20s, well-built and beautifully maintained throughout"*) have made their entrance, having heard their cue.

Dotty apologizes for her mistakes. Lloyd is exasperated—this is supposed to be the dress rehearsal—but Garry tries to reassure Dotty.

GARRY: Listen, Dotty, your words are fine, your words are better than the, do you know what I mean? *(To Brooke.)* Isn't that right?

BROOKE: Sorry?

GARRY *(to Dotty):* I mean, O.K., so he's the, you know. Fine. But Dotty, love, you've been playing this kind of part for, well, I mean, Jesus, Dotty, you know what I mean.

LLOYD: All right? So Garry and Brooke are off, Dotty's holding the receiver . . .

GARRY: No, but here we are, we're all thinking, my God, we open tomorrow, we've only had a fortnight to rehearse, we don't know where we are, but my God, here we are!

DOTTY: That's right, my sweet. Isn't that right, Lloyd?

LLOYD: Beautifully put, Garry.

GARRY: No, but I mean, we've got to play Weston-Super-Mare all the rest of this week, then Yeovil, then God knows where, then God knows where else, and so on for God knows how long, and we're all of us feeling pretty much, you know . . . *(To Brooke.)* I mean, aren't *you?*

BROOKE: Sorry?

They go back to "Mrs. Clackett's" exit into the study (henceforth in this synopsis we will put quotation marks around the names of the characters in the play-within-the-play, for clarity's sake.) "Roger," a real estate agent carrying a cardboard box of files and a flight bag, and "Vicki" enter through the front door and prepare for what is clearly an assignation in this empty house, in the absence of owner and servants. "Vicki" exits into the bathroom just as "Mrs. Clackett" re-enters, to "Roger's" and her mutual surprise, making their excuses to each other: she just wanted to watch color TV, and he pretends that "Vicki" (as she re-enters the room) is a client to whom he's showing the house. But when "Mrs. Clackett" exits again, Dotty again forgets the sardines, precipitating another crisis. Poppy, the assistant stage manager, is called onstage. She is not at fault, but in her presence the performers let off steam, and the rehearsal recommences with "Mrs. Clackett's" exit, this time with the sardines.

"Vicki" is all for making straight for the bedroom upstairs, taking the champagne up there with them. "Roger" follows her lead; but after first trying the mezzanine bathroom door and the linen closet door, the actors find that the bedroom door upstairs on the gallery won't open.

At this moment "Philip Brent," owner of this house, *("in his 40s, with a deep suntan")* lets himself in the front door in company with "Flavia" *("in her 30s, the perfect companion piece to the above").* They believe they have the place to themselves, as this is supposed to be "Mrs. Clackett's" day off. But Frederick Fellowes (the actor playing "Philip") and Belinda Blair (the actress playing "Flavia") find that the front door to the set won't close, any more than the bedroom door upstairs will open.

LLOYD: And God said, Hold it. And they held it. And God saw that it was terrible.

GARRY *(to Frederick and Belinda):* Sorry, loves, the door won't open.

BELINDA: Sorry, love, this door won't close.

LLOYD: And God said, Poppy!

FREDERICK: Sorry, everyone. Am I doing something wrong? You know how stupid I am about doors.

BELINDA: Freddie, my sweet, you're doing it perfectly.

FREDERICK: As long as it's not me that's broken it.

Enter Poppy from the wings.

LLOYD: And there was Poppy. And God said, Be fruitful and multiply and fetch Tim to fix the doors.

Exit Poppy into the wings.

Lloyd takes a Valium as Tim *("The company stage manager. He is exhausted")* comes in and is told to fix the doors. During this pause in the play's action, Lloyd comes onto the stage to inform his troupe that they'll have to do without a real dress rehearsal, they won't have time for one after they get through the present "technical" rehearsal. He tells them to keep at it, "That's what it's all about. Doors and sardines. Getting on—getting off. Getting the sardines on—getting the sardines off. That's farce. That's the theater. That's life."

Lloyd notices that one of the acting company—Selsdon Mowbray, who is to play a burglar—is missing. This upsets everyone; apparently Selsdon is a problem. Poppy goes to look for him backstage, but he is nowhere to be found. Dotty apologizes for asking that he be cast in this play, in order to give him one last chance. As the conversation about Selsdon continues, Selsdon appears, walking down the aisle in his burglar costume. He stands watching the stage and listening, but the others don't see him. Brooke finally notices him, and they all exclaim at his presence. He'd been sleeping in the auditorium, waiting for his part in the rehearsal.

Tim, having finished the doors, is confused about what to do next (he's been on his feet for 48 hours). As the performers take their places, Belinda confides to Lloyd that Garry and Dotty are having an affair.

The rehearsal begins again from the point at which "Roger" and "Vicki" disappear into the bedroom and "Philip" and "Flavia" enter carrying flight bag and cardboard box of champagne and other supplies. They too are having an assignation in the last place, "Philip" believes, anyone will ever look for them—his own home. But they have to be careful: "If Inland Revenue find out we're in the country, even for one night, bang goes our claim to be resident abroad—bang goes most of this year's income. I feel like an illegal immigrant," declares "Philip."

They creep toward the gallery bedroom, but "Mrs. Clackett" enters and discovers them—she understands the situation, income tax and all. "Flavia" disappears into the mezzanine bathroom, as the housekeeper tells her employer that she has stored some unforwarded mail in the study. "Roger" and "Vicki" (now in her underwear) come out of the bedroom, having heard voices. "Mrs. Clackett" and "Philip," carrying box and flight bag, are supposed to have exited into the study, but for some reason "Philip" has failed to disappear on cue. Lloyd halts the rehearsal to find out what's wrong.

FREDERICK: . . . . . Why do I take the things off into the study? Wouldn't it be more natural if I left them on?

LLOYD: No.

FREDERICK: I just thought it might somehow be more logical.

LLOYD: No.

FREDERICK: Lloyd, I know it's a bit late in the day to go into all this . . .

LLOYD: No, Freddie, we've got several more minutes left before we open.

Enter Belinda from the mezzanine bathroom, to wait patiently.

FREDERICK: Thank you, Lloyd. As long as we're not too pushed. But I've never understood why he carries an overnight bag and a box of groceries into the study to look at his mail.

GARRY: Because they have to be out of the way for my next scene!

FREDERICK: I see that.

BELINDA: And Freddie, my sweet, Selsdon needs them in the study for *his* scene.

FREDERICK: I see that . . .

Lloyd admits he can think of no deeply underlying reason, adding, "I don't know. I don't think the author knows. I don't know why the author came into this industry in the first place. I don't know why any of us came into it." Frederick must take this for his answer until Belinda tells Lloyd that Frederick's wife has just left him. Lloyd takes pity on Frederick and explains, "You've had a great fright when she mentions income tax, and you feel very insecure and exposed, and you want something familiar to hold on to."

The rehearsal continues. "Roger" comes out of the bedroom, having heard voices and seen the door handle move. He looks over the gallery rail, sees the sardines and starts down to get them when "Mrs. Clackett" appears with still another plate of sardines. "Roger" hurriedly shoves scantily-dressed "Vicki" into the linen closet. "Mrs. Clackett" sees that the study door is open and closes it. "Roger," having picked up both plates of sardines, goes out the front door to look over another auto that seems to have turned up.

Meanwhile, "Flavia" comes out of the mezzanine bathroom swinging a hot water bottle. Heading for the bedroom, she notices that the linen closet door is open, closes it and locks it, unknowingly locking "Vicki" in.

"Philip" comes in from the study, and "Mrs. Clackett" exits into the kitchen. "Flavia" comes out onto the gallery, having found an unfamiliar dress ("Vicki's") in her room. "Philip" goes back into the study to re-seal a tax envelope he is going to pretend he's never received, and "Flavia" goes to put the dress in the attic, as "Roger" re-enters with only one plate of sardines. Hearing knocking upstairs, he goes and releases "Vicki" from her closet and ushers her back into the bedroom.

The rehearsal is suddenly halted when Brooke loses one of her contact lenses and all try to locate it. Brooke finds that it has merely slid around to the side of her eye, adjusts it, and the rehearsal continues. As "Roger" and "Vicki" disappear into the bedroom, "Philip" emerges from the study with the tax envelope and a tube of glue.

"PHILIP": Darling, this glue. It's not that special quick-drying sort, is it, that you can never get unstuck . . . ? Oh, Mrs. Clackett's made us some sardines.
> Exit "Philip" into the study with the tax demand, envelope, glue and one of the plates of sardines from the telephone table. Enter "Roger" from the bedroom, holding the hot water bottle. He looks up and down the landing. Enter "Vicki" from the bedroom.

"VICKI": Now what?

"ROGER": A hot water bottle! I didn't put it there!

"VICKI": I didn't put it there.

"ROGER": Someone in the bathroom, filling hot water bottles.
> Exit "Roger" into the mezzanine bathroom.

"VICKI" (anxious): You don't think there's something creepy going on?
> Exit "Vicki" into the mezzanine bathroom. Enter "Flavia" along the upstairs corridor.

"FLAVIA": Darling, are you coming to bed or aren't you?
> Exit "Flavia" into the bedroom. Enter "Roger" and "Vicki" from the mezzanine bathroom.

"ROGER": What did you say?

"VICKI": I didn't say anything.

"ROGER": I mean, first the door handle. Now the hot water bottle . . .

"VICKI": I can feel goose pimples all over.

"ROGER": Yes, quick, get something round you.

"VICKI": Get the covers over our heads.

"ROGER" (about to open the bedroom door): Just a moment. What did I do with those sardines?
> He goes downstairs. "Vicki" makes to follow.
You—wait here.

"VICKI" (uneasy): You hear all sorts of funny things about these old houses.

"ROGER": Yes, but this one has been extensively modernized throughout. I can't see how anything creepy would survive oil-fired central heating and . . .

"VICKI": What? What is it?

"Roger" stares at the telephone table in silence. The bedroom door opens, and "Flavia" puts "Vicki's" flight bag on the table outside without looking round. The door closes again.

"VICKI": What's happening?

"ROGER": The sardines. They've gone.

"VICKI": Perhaps there is something funny going on. I'm going to get into bed and put my head under the . . . *(She freezes at the sight of the flight bag.)*

"ROGER": I put them there. Or was it *there?*

"VICKI": Bag . . .

"Vicki" runs downstairs to tell "Roger" about the bag suddenly appearing, but by the time they get back up to the gallery "Flavia" has come out of the bedroom with "Roger's" box of files, picked up the bag and carried them both off towards the attic. They see that all their possessions including "Vicki's" dress have vanished. They run back downstairs to find out what's going on.

Exit "Roger" into the service quarters. "Vicki" opens the study door. There is a roar of exasperation from "Philip," off. She turns and flees.

"VICKI": Roger! There's something in there! Where are you?

There is another cry from "Philip," off. Exit "Vicki" blindly through the front door. Enter "Philip" from the study. He is holding the tax demand in his right hand and one of the plates of sardines in his left.

"PHILIP": Darling, I know this is going to sound silly, but . . .

He struggles to get the tax demand unstuck from his fingers, encumbered by the plate of sardines. Enter "Flavia" along the upstairs corridor, carrying various pieces of bric-a-brac.

"FLAVIA": Darling, if we're not going to bed I'm going to clear out the attic.

"PHILIP": Darling, I can't come to bed! I'm glued to a tax demand!

"FLAVIA": Darling, why don't you put the sardines down?

"Philip" puts the plate of sardines down on the table. But when he takes his hand away the sardines come with it.

"PHILIP": Darling, I'm stuck to the sardines!

"FLAVIA": Darling, don't play the fool. Get that bottle marked poison in the downstairs loo. That eats through anything.

Exit "Flavia" along the upstairs corridor.

"PHILIP" *(flaps the tax demand):* I've heard of people getting stuck with a *problem,* but this is ridiculous.

"Philip's" exit is Selsdon's cue to come on as the "Burglar" by breaking the glass in the mullioned window. Selsdon is a beat or two late, and Lloyd stops the action to correct his timing.

"Burglar" pours himself a drink and complains that houses are too easy to break into these days—there are no alarms in this one, and he has learned that the inhabitants are all away in Spain. He starts collecting pieces of loot and exits into the study just as "Roger" enters with "Mrs. Clackett," complaining about certain strange phenomena taking place in this house, such as the sudden appearance and disappearance of people and sardines. She assures him that nothing out of the ordinary happens here, and there is no one else in the house. "Mrs. Clackett" exits, and "Roger" and "Burglar" go in and out of various rooms without running into each other.

Finally, however, "Philip" emerges with the objects still stuck to his hands, in full view of "Roger," who at first takes him for an apparition and then for a sex criminal when his trousers fall down to his ankles. "Roger" phones the police; "Philip" shuffles out the front door; "Vicki" comes in through the window and discloses that she is in fact working for the Inland Revenue and then goes off with "Roger" in search of something to cover her near-nakedness; "Burglar" comes in from the study with a tape recorder; "Philip" comes back looking for "Flavia," who is finding treasures in the attic. Soon there are so many exits and entrances through the many openings in the set that that characters begin to encounter each other and are generally mystified as to who the others can be. Soon "Philip" wraps himself in a sheet to conceal his trouserless condition (he also has a nightdress stuck to his head and arranged like a burnoose), and "Vicki" has also found a sheet in which to wrap herself like an Arab. She encounters "Burglar" and finds that she's his long-lost daughter.

Adding to the complications, a real sheik arrives in his Arab robes. He has an appointment with "Roger" to look at the house, and he greatly resembles "Philip" because he is also played by Frederick. The action is halted when Tim, the stage manager, hiding behind the sofa, wrapped in a sheet and waiting to double for the "Philip" character while Frederick plays the "Sheik," misses his cue. Frederick takes the opportunity of this pause to speak to Lloyd.

FREDERICK: May I ask another silly question?

LLOYD: All my studies in world drama lie at your disposal, Freddie.

FREDERICK: I still don't understand why the Sheik just happens to be Philip's double.

GARRY: Because he comes in and we all think he's, you know, and we all, I mean, that's the joke.

FREDERICK: I see that.

BELINDA: My sweet, the rest of the plot depends on it!

FREDERICK: I see that. But it *is* rather a coincidence, isn't it?

LLOYD: It *is* rather a coincidence, Freddie, yes. Until you reflect that there was an earlier draft of the play, now unfortunately lost to us. And in this the author makes it clear that Philip's father as a young man had travelled extensively in the Middle East.

FREDERICK: I see . . . I *see!*

LLOYD: You see?

FREDERICK: That's very interesting.

LLOYD: I thought you'd like that.

FREDERICK: But will the audience get it?

LLOYD: You must tell them, Freddie. Looks. Gestures. That's what acting's all about. O.K.?

FREDERICK: Yes. Thank you, Lloyd. Thank you.

Lloyd gives them their cue, and they start again with the "Sheik's" entrance. The others think he is "Philip" who in the course of his comings and goings has offended or affronted each and every one of them in some way. They begin to tug at his robes, but Brooke, as "Vicki," misses a cue and leaves the stage in tears when Lloyd, tired and exasperated (it is now 1 A.M.), chides her. When Lloyd goes after her, Belinda confides to the others that Brooke and Lloyd are lovers. Finally, all are back in place, and Selsdon as "Burglar" repeats the cue: "But I'll tell you one thing, Vicki."

"VICKI": What's that, Dad?
"BURGLAR": When all around is strife and uncertainty, there's nothing like . . .
> He takes "Mrs. Clackett's" plate.
. . . a good old-fashioned plate of sardines!
LLOYD: And *curtain!*
> Pause. Then Tim realizes, and hobbles hurriedly into the wings. Curtain.

ACT II

Theater Royal, Goole, Wednesday Matinee, Feb. 13

Act I of *Nothing On* is about to begin again in another theater, where the touring company is playing about a month later—but this time the action is seen from backstage. *"The whole set has been turned through 180 degrees. All the doors can be seen—there is no masking behind them. Two stairways lead up to the platform which gives access to the doors on the upper levels. Some of the scene inside the living room is visible through the full-length window."* Exits at right and left lead to the dressing rooms and the "auditorium."

Poppy, onstage with Tim, warns the performers over the public address system to take their places. They have been having a problem with Dotty and hope she will be up for this performance.

Poppy exits and Lloyd enters, showing up unexpectedly from London, instructing Tim to get a large bunch of flowers without letting Poppy see them, and requesting two hours alone with Brooke in her dressing room between the matinee and evening performances. Tim tries to tell Lloyd about the Dotty crisis: she's having a lovers' quarrel with Garry and has locked herself in her dressing room.

TIM: I mean, they had the famous bust-up the week before last, when we were playing Workshop.
LLOYD: Right, right, you told me on the phone.
TIM: She went out with this journalist bloke . . .
LLOYD: Journalist—yes, yes . . .
TIM: But you know Garry threatened to kill him?
LLOYD: Kill him, yes, I know. Listen, don't worry about Dotty—she's got money in the show.
TIM: Yes, but now it's happened again! Two o'clock this morning I'm woken

Paxton Whitehead (Frederick), Dorothy Loudon (Dotty), Brian Murray (Lloyd), Linda Thorson (Belinda, holding axe) and Victor Garber (Garry) in a tense moment backstage during a performance of their play-within-a-play in *Noises Off*

up by this great banging on my door. It's Garry. Do I know where Dotty is? She hasn't come home.

LLOYD: Tim, let me tell you something about *my* life. I have the Duke of Buckingham on the phone to me for an hour after rehearsal every evening complaining that the Duke of Gloucester is sucking boiled sweets through his speeches. Catesby is off every afternoon doing a telly, and the Duke of Clarence is off for the entire week doing a commercial for Madeira. Richard himself—would you believe?—Richard III has now gone down with a back problem. Then last night Brooke rings me to say she's very unhappy here, and she's got herself a doctor's certificate for nervous exhaustion. I have no time to find or rehearse another "Vicki." I have just one afternoon, while Richard is fitted for a surgical corset and Lady Anne starts divorce proceedings, to cure Brooke of nervous exhaustion, with no medical aids except a little whiskey—you've got the whiskey?—a few flowers—you've got the money for the flowers?—and a certain fading bedside manner. So I haven't come to the theater to hear about other people's problems. I've come to be taken out of myself, and preferably not put back again.

Lloyd leaves by one door as Tim gives the audience the three-minute warning over the public address system and Poppy enters from the other door. She has seen Tim holding money and whiskey and takes the bottle from him and goes to hide it as Frederick and Belinda come in to announce Garry's state of great agitation (there is a possibility that neither Garry nor Dotty will show up for this performance). Belinda learns, with some chagrin, that Frederick spent the previous evening with Dotty listening to her troubles till 3 A.M. Now Belinda thinks she has reason to be jealous of Dotty.

Poppy comes in and repeats the three-minute warning over the p.a. system, not knowing that Tim has already done it. To add to the atmosphere of impending disaster, Selsdon is missing again. And when Tim enters with the flowers, Poppy assumes they're for her and gives them to Frederick to hold. Meanwhile, Belinda finds the hidden bottle of whiskey, so that Tim has to take it and hide it again.

After two one-minute warnings over the p.a. system, Lloyd comes in through the pass door to warn them they are whipping the audience into a state of confusion. Meanwhile, Brooke comes in with the bottle of whiskey, having also found it (they all assume that there are several bottles of whiskey, all of which Selsdon has hidden backstage). Lloyd kisses Brooke, who seems to be all right, but he can't give her the flowers because Poppy now thinks they're hers. Lloyd finally decides, "I think this show is beyond the help of a director, You just do it. I'll sit out there in the dark with a bag of toffees and enjoy it," and exits.

Selsdon comes in to report that Garry and Dotty have been having a row over someone named "Teddy" or "Neddy" (Belinda sees clearly that it's Freddy of whom Garry is now jealous). But Garry and Dotty do finally arrive and take their places for the opening scene, Dotty adopting the flagrant pose of *"a tragically misunderstood woman."* As the performers check their appearances in mirrors installed around the back of the set, Frederick reminds them that they are a team which must work together, but they pay scant attention to him. Lloyd comes back through the pass door.

LLOYD: *Now* what?

TIM: We're just going up.

LLOYD: We've been sitting there for an hour! They've gone quiet! They think someone's died!

FREDERICK: I'm sorry, Lloyd. It's my fault. I was just saying a few words to everyone.

LLOYD: Freddie, have you ever thought of having a brain transplant?

FREDERICK: Sorry, sorry. Wrong moment. I see that.

LLOYD: Anybody else have thoughts they feel they must communicate?

POPPY: Well, not now, of course, but . . .

LLOYD: *What?*

POPPY: I mean, you know, later . . .

LLOYD *(to Tim):* And you bought those flowers for Poppy?

TIM: No . . . well . . . yes . . .

LLOYD: And you didn't buy any flowers for me?

TIM: No . . . well . . . no . . .

LLOYD: Tim, have you ever heard of such a thing as jealous rage?

TIM: Yes . . . well . . . yes . . .

LLOYD: Then take five pounds of your own money, Tim, and go out to the florist's and buy some flowers for *me!* Gave Poppy the flowers! You two could have Freddie's old brain—you could have half each. *(Exits through the pass door.)*

FREDERICK: Oh dear.

BELINDA: Don't cry, Poppy, love.

SELSDON: Just get the old bus on the road.

POPPY: Act One. Curtain up.

　　　She presses a buzzer, and the act begins.

A *"somewhat condensed version"* of the act previously rehearsed takes place, from "Mrs. Clackett's" entrance with sardines to the meeting of "Vicki" with her long-lost father, the "Burglar." The actors are glimpsed and heard as they make their entrances "onstage" (upstage) to make the scenes, but it is their backstage (downstage) action—with its interpersonal strife mixing into the details of the performance—that is in full view now.

For example, as "Mrs. Clackett" goes through her scene of exposition with the telephone, Frederick (who has been holding the whiskey bottle but now puts it down on a chair) goes to Garry, who is waiting for his entrance, and *"gives Garry's arm a silently sympathetic squeeze . . . . . Garry shakes him off indignantly . . . . . Belinda hurries across to draw Frederick off. Frederick cannot understand what he has done to cause offense. He demonstrates what he did by giving Garry's arm another squeeze . . . . . Garry drops his props and threatens to hit Frederick. Frederick covers his nose. Belinda and Tim separate them and urge Garry back to the front door. Tim goes off towards the dressing rooms . . . . . Brooke makes her entrance . . . . . Frederick gives Dotty a sympathetic squeeze of the arm in her turn. As Garry turns back to collect the flight bag, he gets a fleeting glimpse of this . . . . . As Garry comes through the service quarters door, he sees Belinda glancing at him and hurriedly disconnecting Frederick from Dotty. He stamps on Frederick's foot."*

As the action of the play proceeds onstage, the players continue to take out their jealousies and animosities on each other backstage. Selsdon spots the whiskey bottle and goes off with it, Belinda running off after him while Frederick comforts a weeping Dotty and makes sure she has the right props when she goes back to the scene. When Dotty comes back she is more composed, and Frederick gives her a reassuring kiss, which Garry happens to see. Belinda gets back from the dressing rooms with the whiskey (which she hands to Dotty) just in time for her entrance with Frederick.

Backstage, Garry and Dotty are in a full quarrel, while Selsdon is trying to get the whiskey bottle, finally managing to do it after it is passed to Brooke. Tim enters with a somewhat smaller bunch of flowers. Belinda, backstage again, goes off after Selsdon and returns with the news that he's locked himself in with the bottle.

"Tim hands Belinda the flowers and dashes out to the dressing rooms. She gives the flowers to Frederick and fetches the fireman's axe from the fire point . . . . . She is going to rush off to the dressing rooms with it, when Poppy reminds her that she has an entrance coming up. Belinda runs up on the platform, finds she is still holding the axe and gives it to Brooke . . . . . But before she can explain what to do with it, Belinda has to make her entrance. Garry advances threateningly upon Frederick and gazes suspiciously at the flowers he is holding. Frederick has to hand Garry the flowers in order to make his entrance . . . . . Brooke comes down from the platform and asks Garry what she is supposed to do with the axe. Garry takes it thoughtfully and puts the flowers into her hands. He looks at the axe, then whirls it up over his head to wait for Frederick's exit."

As Belinda tries to get the axe from Garry, Dotty sees her with her arms around him and draws the obvious conclusion. While the play continues, there is a frantic juggling of the flowers and grappling for the axe behind the scenes. Tim finally gets hold of the axe and carries it off.

The time comes for "Roger" (Garry) to let "Vicki" (Brooke) out of the linen closet, but when Garry, onstage, opens the door, Brooke is not there. Garry improvises, while Poppy reads Brooke's lines from the script backstage and Lloyd comes in to find out what has gone wrong. Finally Brooke appears and is urged onstage, where to Garry's dismay she re-plays the scene Poppy has just read. Meanwhile, Lloyd has passed the flowers absent-mindedly to Dotty, who thinks they are for her and gives him a grateful kiss—which Garry happens to see.

The performers manage to get back into the play after dropping some of lines and business. But Tim brings back the axe and whiskey bottle together with Selsdon, who is holding up his trousers. Now they must juggle flowers, axe, whiskey and Selsdon, in a kind of counterpoint to the action of the play as they are passed from hand to hand, the whiskey being pretty much consumed in the process.

Here's an example of the coordination of onstage and offstage activity called for in the script. Below is a segment of the glue scene previously quoted in Act I of this synopsis and now staged with "offstage" action as described at left synchronized with the "play's" dialogue and business at right. The lines running across the page are in the script, denoting exact timing.

Frederick hastily conceals the whiskey under the chairs and makes his entrance.

There is (a) cry from "Philip," off. Exit "Vicki" blindly through the front door. Enter "Philip" from

---

Tim gives the axe to Lloyd and takes the flowers from Dotty, who snatches them right back, leaving Tim with only one. He hands this to Lloyd, who hands it to Brooke. She peers at it as it keels sadly over. Lloyd gives money to Tim, who exits wearily to the dressing rooms.

study. He is holding the tax demand in his right hand, and one of the plates of sardines in his left.

"PHILIP": Darling, I know this is going to sound silly, but . . .

He struggles to get the tax demand unstuck from his fingers, encumbered by the plate of sardines. Enter "Flavia" along the upstairs corridor, carrying various pieces of bric-a-brac.

"FLAVIA": Darling, if we're not going to bed I'm going to clear out the attic.

"PHILIP": Darling, I can't come to bed! I'm glued to a tax demand!

"FLAVIA": Darling, why don't you put the sardines down?

"Philip" puts the plate of sardines down on the table. But when he takes his hand away the sardines come with it.

"PHILIP": Darling, I'm stuck to the sardines!

"FLAVIA": Darling, don't play the fool. Get that bottle marked poison in the downstairs loo. That eats through anything.

Selsdon is explaining to everyone where he was, by a show of pulling a chain. This demonstration causes his trousers to fall down.

Exit "Flavia" along the upstairs corridor.

"PHILIP" (*flaps the tax demand*): I've heard of people getting stuck with a problem, but this is ridiculous.

Exit "Philip" into the downstairs bathroom.

Selsdon stoops to retrieve his fallen trousers and sees the whiskey that Frederick concealed beneath the chairs. He picks it up, and Lloyd snatches it out of his hand and gives it to Dotty.

"PHILIP": But this is ridiculous.

Frederick repeats the cue, and

---

slams the door again.

Exit "Philip" into the downstairs bathroom.

In the confusion, Selsdon continues to miss his repeated cue. The others realize what has happened and shove him onstage through the window, fallen trousers and all. Selsdon remembers most of his lines but at one point has to be prompted —loudly—while the others continue to juggle the props backstage, trying to smooth over their various distressed relationships but usually exacerbating them. Lloyd cannot quite manage to provide flowers for Brooke, no matter how many times he sends Tim out for a new bunch.

Aggressions flare. Garry dumps a plate of sardines over Dotty, who, in revenge, ties Garry's shoelaces together while he is taking a swig of whiskey. Everyone conspires to keep the bottle from Selsdon, passing it around (and drinking from it). Garry trips into an entrance and soon can be heard falling downstairs. Dotty hits Brooke, dislodging her lenses so she has to be guided blindly into her next entrance. Cues are missed and lines and business improvised as the confusion mounts.

This time Tim returns with a cactus which creates still another problem backstage as Garry uses it vengefully on Lloyd's backside and Brooke, at her next exit, is treated to the spectacle of Lloyd with his pants down and Dotty pulling out needles, so Brooke now imagines she has reason to be jealous of Dotty. Garry ties together the bedsheets which Frederick and Brooke will need to wear in the final scene. Lloyd manages to present Brooke with the cactus as a token of his affection, but she doesn't seem greatly pleased.

Frederick and Brooke find themselves tied together with the sheets as they try to enter through separate doors, causing a major crisis, much to Garry's satisfaction. To make matters worse, Selsdon is now drunk, so Tim will have to go on for him and Lloyd for Tim. But as they are preparing to do so, Selsdon enters and speaks his lines perfectly. They go into the final scene as follows:

Enter through the front door the

Lloyd picks up the whiskey from wherever Tim left it. He takes a weary swig and is just about to sit down on the cactus, when he springs up again guiltily, because Poppy is standing in front of him reproachfully. She begins to speak anxiously to him, at first in a completely inaudible whisper.

POPPY: Listen, I've got to talk to you *now*. I'm sorry, I know it's not a good moment—it's never a good moment. I keep trying to phone you, but you're never there. I know you're in rehearsals all day, but you're not there at night, either, you're not there in the morning —I don't know *where* you are.

Lloyd gestures that he can't hear and offers her a soothing sip of

most sought after of all properties today—a "Sheik." He is wearing Arab robes and bears a strong resemblance to "Philip," since he is played by the same actor.

"SHEIK": Ah! A house of peace! I rent it!

OMNES: You!

"FLAVIA": Is it?

"SHEIK" *(with dignity):* Is me? Certainly is me! Who else?

They all fall upon him.

"ROGER": You walk in asking to view a house like this, when you're nothing but a trouserless tramp!

He pulls up the "Sheik's" robes.

"SHEIK": What?

whiskey. She brushes it aside, becoming more and more agitated.

POPPY *(voicing the words, which are still drowned by the dialogue onstage):* No, no, no, I'm not going to be put off, I'm going to tell you, because as soon as that curtain's down you'll be round seeing her, I know that. Well, she's being difficult, isn't she—I saw you with that cactus—I'm not blind. And then you'll be on the next train back to London. I'm afraid I'm starting to know the way you operate, you see, Lloyd—and I bet there's someone else, in Richard III, isn't there, but you can't just walk away from it this time! *Lloyd wearily, smilingly, soothingly gestures that he can't hear a word.*

POPPY *(out loud):* Well, I'm sorry, but you've *got* to hear, because I'm *pregnant!*
A gasp from everyone on stage. They both become aware that the act has ended.

LLOYD *(Whispers):* And *curtain!*
Poppy runs back to the corner, Lloyd subsides, defeated, onto the cactus. Curtain.

"FLAVIA": You toss me aside like a broken china doll!
She hits him.
"SHEIK": What? What?
"MRS. CLACKETT": You take all the clean sheets!
Tries to pull the robes off him.
"VICKI": You snatch my nightdress!
Tries to pull the burnoose off him.
"SHEIK": What? What? What?
"BURGLAR": And what you're up to with my little girl down there in Basingstoke I won't ask. But I'll tell you one thing, Vicki.
"VICKI": What's that, Dad?
"BURGLAR": When all around is strife and uncertainty, there's nothing like . . . *(He takes Mrs. Clackett's plate.)* . . . a good old-fashioned plate of sardines!

Curtain.

ACT III

Municipal Theater, Stockton-on-Tees, Saturday, April 6

Act I of *Nothing On* is about to begin again in another theater, where the touring company is playing a couple of months later. This time we view the action from the front as in Act I of *Noises Off*, and we soon see that it is a different play from the one Lloyd was rehearsing originally. It has become a shambles of missed cues, improvised lines and business, carelessly managed props. The personal frictions have helped to create chaos, as is evident from the very beginning when "Mrs. Clackett" enters to answer the phone, carrying her plate of sardines—but limping because Belinda has kicked her just before her entrance, and letting the audience know about it by adding to her monologue, "No, I'm not in Spain, dear. I'm in agony. That's where I am. One moment I'm standing here with a plate of sardines, next moment she's kicked me on the kneecap and there's sardines all over the floor." Indeed, the sardines slip off the plate to the floor, and she covers them with the newspaper.

When "Mrs. Clackett" exits she mistakenly carries the telephone receiver with her, so that the phone falls off the table and travels toward the door as "Roger" and "Vicki" enter. They try to cope with the errant telephone, but there are so many other careless slips and alterations that the performance soon becomes a shambles. This does not faze the performers, who simply and individually adapt themselves to whatever circumstances or new dialogue and business they happen to encounter onstage. Gone is Lloyd's painstaking synchronization of words and actions—now it's catch-as-catch can, with the scenes virtually unrecognizable as the originals. For example, as "Philip" and "Flavia" enter, "Flavia" is carrying the mangled remains of the telephone.

"FLAVIA": . . . . . How odd to find the telephone in the garden!
"PHILIP": I'll put it back.
> *She hands him the phone—now in a very deteriorated condition—and he attempts to replace it on the telephone table. But it is still connected to its lead, which is too short, since it runs out through the downstairs bathroom door and back in through the front door.*
"FLAVIA": I thought I'd better bring it in.
"PHILIP": Very sensible.
> *He tugs discreetly at the lead.*
"FLAVIA": Someone's bound to want it.
"PHILIP": Oh dear.
> *Tugs.*
"FLAVIA": Why don't you put it back on the table?
"PHILIP": The wire seems to be caught.
"FLAVIA": Oh, look, it's caught round the downstairs bathroom.
"PHILIP": So it is.
> *"Flavia" turns and with discreet violence pulls the lead out of the junction-box where it originates. "Philip," meanwhile, takes the phone back out of the front door and re-emerges with it through the downstairs bathroom.*
"FLAVIA": I think I've disentangled it.
"PHILIP": I climbed through the bathroom window and . . . oh . . . oh . . .
> *He takes the parcel of sardines off the telephone table and puts the telephone in its place.*
"FLAVIA": Anyway, our little secret hideaway.
"PHILIP": The last place on earth anyone will . . .
> *Attempting to fold up the newspaper briskly and tidily, he becomes distracted by the contents that come oozing out over his hands.*
"FLAVIA": . . . look for us, yes, but it's rather funny, creeping in like this.
> *Pause.*

"PHILIP": Sorry?

"FLAVIA": I know what you're thinking. You're thinking, "It's damned serious!"

"PHILIP": Sorry. Yes. It's damned serious!

"FLAVIA": You're thinking about Inland Revenue.

"PHILIP": Absolutely. Inland Revenue. Well, to cut a long story short, I think I'm going to have a wash and go to bed.

> *He puts down the parcel of sardines on the sofa, picks up the bag and box and starts upstairs.*

"FLAVIA" *(hurriedly):* Yes, but Inland Revenue! We must have our little talk first about Inland Revenue! Because you're thinking something like, "If Inland Revenue finds out we're in the country, even for one night, bang goes our claim to be resident abroad, bang goes most of this year's . . ." Leave those!

> *"Philip" drops the bag and box, but by this time he is upstairs.*

To prevent cutting the whole first part of the act, they manage to get "Philip" downstairs again and into the study. "Roger" and "Vicki" are having a terrible time with the doors on the upper level. The performers try playing the scenes— what they can remember of them—but all the props are out of place, the cues are obscure, and soon accidents begin to happen. The moment arrives for the "Burglar's" entrance, and in he comes, played by Tim (apparently Selsdon is indisposed). Tim is part way into the scene when a second "Burglar," Selsdon, enters and takes it from the top. Soon the two are playing in unison, but not long before Lloyd, also entering as the "Burglar," makes it a trio.

In the utter confusion, Lloyd drinks from the onstage bottle and finds that it's real whiskey. The time has come for "Roger" to phone the police about the intruder. But they only have half a phone on the set, and by the time they have figured out what to do and how to get the two parts of the phone back together, Lloyd is hopelessly confused and disoriented.

LLOYD *(faintly):* I've got to get the 8:40 back to London.

> *Lloyd opens the door to flee, but recoils because there on the doorstep stands the "Sheik," played by Poppy.*

"MRS. CLACKETT": Oh, it's the other one! And in her wedding dress!

OMNES: Oh!

POPPY *(uncertainly):* A house of heavenly peace . . . ?

"FLAVIA": Yes! Yes! It's their wedding day! What a happy ending!

OMNES: Ah!

> *Lloyd and Poppy are hurriedly ushered down center.*

"MRS. CLACKETT": And what does she say to that?

"VICKI": Here are the sardines!

"MRS. CLACKETT": Never mind, love. *(Claps her on the back.)* You can't see nothing.

> *And indeed the clap on the back has dislodged "Vicki's" lenses.*

"FLAVIA": They just want to be alone in their new home. If only that window at the front had a curtain!

> *Enter Tim through the downstairs bathroom, dressed in black sheets.*

TIM: Curtain?

"MRS. CLACKETT": Oh, and here's the mother of the bride!

TIM: Sheet?

OMNES: Curtain!

> *Exit Tim into the wings.*

"BURGLAR" SELSDON: Last line?

OMNES: Last line!

"BURGLAR" SELSDON: But I'll tell you one thing, Vicki.

> *They all look at Vicki. She is looking for her lenses.*

OMNES: What's that, Dad?

"BURGLAR" SELSDON: When all around is strife and uncertainty, there's nothing like . . . *(Takes the sardines.)* . . . a good old-fashioned plate of . . .

OMNES: Sardines!

> *Curtain.*

THE REAL THING

A Play in Two Acts

BY TOM STOPPARD

Cast and credits appear on page 332

TOM STOPPARD was born in 1937 in Zlin, Czechoslovakia, where his family name was Straussler. When he was 18 months old his father, a physician, moved the family to Singapore, and from that time on Stoppard was brought up within the English-speaking culture. During World War II the doctor sent his wife and son to India for safety, and the boy attended an American school in Darjeeling. His father was killed in Singapore by the invading Japanese.

After the war Stoppard, age 9, and his mother (remarried to an English army major) moved to England, where Stoppard attended school until age 17 and then entered upon a writing career, first as a journalist and then as a free-lance whose credits included several TV and radio plays. His first stage play, A Walk on the Water *was produced in Hamburg and Vienna in 1964, after appearing on BBC-TV in 1963; then, under the new title* Enter a Free Man, *it was done in London in 1968 and off off Broadway in 1974. The first Stoppard play to appear on the New York stage began as a one-act verse burlesque written in Berlin on a Ford Foundation Grant in 1964,* Rosencrantz and Guildenstern. *The full-length version with the full-length title* Rosencrantz and Guildenstern Are Dead *was produced by the Oxford Theater Group at the 1966 Edinburgh Festival before moving on to London and then to Broadway Oct. 16, 1967 for a year's run, Stoppard's first Best Play citation and the Critics and Tony awards for the best play of the season.*

Stoppard's The Real Inspector Hound *was produced in London in 1969, and his* After Magritte *appeared there the following year. Combined on a single program, these two short plays were produced off Broadway for 465 performances, followed by a national U.S. tour under the auspices of Kennedy Center. His* Albert's Bridge, *a version of a Prix Italia-winning drama, was produced in London in 1971. A year later his* Jumpers *appeared at London's National Theater and, in the words of the critic Ossia Trilling, "introduced, unless I'm much mistaken, full frontal nudity for the first time on this august stage in the shape of the shapely Diana Rigg."* Jumpers *was produced in Washington in February, 1974 by Kennedy Center and came to Broadway April 22, 1974 for 48 performances and a Best Play citation.*

Stoppard's playwriting career continued with a new English version of Lorca's The House of Bernard Alba, *staged in Greenwich, England. His* Travesties *was produced by the Royal Shakespeare Company June 10, 1974 for 39 performances in repertory and crossed the Atlantic to Broadway Oct. 30, 1975 for 155 more performances, another Best Play citation and the Drama Critics and Tony awards for the best play of the season. Subsequent Broadway productions of Stoppard works have been* Dirty Linen & New-Found-Land *Jan. 11, 1977 for 159 performances;* Every Good Boy Deserves Favour *(written with Andre Previn) July 30, 1979 for 8 performances;* Dogg's Hamlet, Cahoot's Macbeth *Oct. 3, 1979 for 31 performances;* Night and Day *Nov. 27, 1979 for 95 performances; and, this season,* The Real Thing, *which came in from London Jan. 5 to win its author's fourth Best Play citation and the Critics and Tony awards for the best play of this 1983–84 season. Off-off-Broadway and in regional theater, he is one of the most frequently produced modern playwrights.*

Other work by Stoppard has included a translation of Arthur Schnitzler's Undiscovered Country *and an adaptation from Johann Nestroy,* On the Razzle, *both for the National Theater; the screen plays* Despair *and* The Human Factor; *the TV plays* The Engagement, Three Men in a Boat *(an adaptation) and* Professional Foul *and an "imaginary TV documentary" about Poland's Solidarity movement,* Squaring the Circle; *and the novel* Lord Malmquist and Mr. Moon. *Stoppard lives near London with his wife, Dr. Miriam Stoppard, a writer and broadcaster, and four sons.*

ACT I

Scene 1

SYNOPSIS: In a living room, Max *("40ish . . . . . doesn't have to be physically impressive, but you wouldn't want him for an enemy")* is sitting at the coffee table building a house of cards. Behind him, the door opens and slams shut, collapsing the cards, as Charlotte *("35-ish . . . . . doesn't have to be especially attractive, but you instantly want her for a friend")* enters the room and sets down a small suitcase and airport bag. She kisses the top of Max's head, as he inquires flippantly about her trip to Switzerland. He makes jokes about the failure of Japanese digital watches to panic the Swiss hand-and-dial watch industry. He goes on and on until Charlotte stops him; at which point he confronts her with the fact that in her absence he found her passport in her recipe drawer, so she couldn't have gone to Switzerland after all. And he noticed that it had no Dutch visa stamp, so she couldn't have gone to Amsterdam either, when she pretended to be going there recently and even brought Rembrandt place mats for her mother.

Charlotte warns Max that he had better drop the subject. She makes a move toward withdrawing, but Max will not let it go.

MAX: Aren't you going to tell me who it is?
CHARLOTTE: Who what is?
MAX: Your lover, lover.
CHARLOTTE: Which lover?
MAX: I assumed there'd only be the one.
CHARLOTTE: Did you?
MAX: Well, do you see them separately or both together? Sorry, that's not fair. Well, tell you what, nod your head if it's separately. *(She looks at him.)* Heavens. If you have an opening free, I'm not doing much at the moment. Or is the position taken? It is only two, is it? Nod your head. *(She looks at him.)* Golly, you are a dark horse. How do they all three get away at the same time? Do they work together, like the Marx Brothers?

Max goes on in this vein, mocking Charlotte, until she decides to leave, picks up her suitcase and moves toward the door. Max is still prodding her about her lover: "Is it anyone I know?" Charlotte replies, "You aren't anyone I know" and departs, leaving Max apparently impervious to any emotional impact as a result of her adventures.

Scene 2

Charlotte's living room is littered with the Sunday newspapers and features a record-player and shelves of records. Her husband Henry *("40-ish, is amiable but can take care of himself")* is choosing a record as Charlotte enters, wearing his dressing-gown. She would have preferred to stay in bed, but Henry has invited Max to come visit them. In the preceding scene, it seems, Charlotte and Max were not really wife and husband, but actress and actor portraying them on the stage.

Henry is a playwright who has been asked to provide a list of eight musical numbers he associates with major turning-points in his life and would like to have on a desert island. He is looking for a particular record he remembers hearing on a trip with Charlotte. Charlotte finds it for him—they were visiting Zermatt, and the number was "The Skater's Waltz."

Charlotte goes to get dressed, as Max arrives. Henry goes to the kitchen to fetch champagne and orange juice. Charlotte returns, dressed as casually as is her greeting to the acting colleague she works with every day in the play, which was written by Henry.

Charlotte comments that it may be a mistake for her to be appearing in her husband's play: people will probably think she got the part because she's the playwright's wife and that their real at-home conversation consists of crisp, witty exchanges. They discuss a couple of actors' problems with the script, but Henry ignores them. Max asks after Charlotte's and Henry's daughter Debbie.

CHARLOTTE: Daughter? Daughter? Must be some mistake. No place for children. Smart talk, that's the thing. Children are so unsmart. Before you know where you are, the chat is all about the price of sandals. Henry couldn't do that. He doesn't like research.

HENRY: True.

CHARLOTTE: Can't have a lot of kids complicating the clean exit with suitcase.

MAX *(to Charlotte):* Lots of people don't have children, in real life. Me and Annie . . .

HENRY: Oh, don't—I told her once that lots of women were only good for fetching drinks, and she became quite unreasonable.

> *Blithely, knowing what he is doing, Henry holds his empty glass towards Charlotte.*

Is there any more of that?

MAX *(glances at Charlotte and hastily tries to defuse the bomb):* Let me . . .

> *Max takes Henry's glass and fills it from the bottle and the jug.*

CHARLOTTE: Lots of *men* are only good for fetching drinks—why don't you write about them?

> *Max hands the glass back to Henry.*

HENRY: *(Smiling up at Max):* Terribly pleased you could come round.

CHARLOTTE: Oh, yes, you owe him a drink. I'm the victim of his fantasy, and you're quids on it. What an ego trip! Having all the words to come back with just as you need them. That's the difference between plays and real life—thinking time, time to get your bottle back. "Must say, I take my hat off to you, coming home with Rembrandt place mats for your mother." You don't really think that if Henry caught me out with a lover, he'd sit around being witty about place mats? Like hell he would. He'd come apart like a pick-a-sticks. His sentence structure would go to pot, closely followed by his sphincter. You know that, don't you, Henry? Henry? No answer. Are you there. Henry? Say something witty.

HENRY *(turns his head to her):* Is it anyone I know?

The doorbell rings—it's Max's wife, Annie, also an actress, bringing as a present a bag of vegetables for crudités. They discuss Henry's choice of desert-island records; it seems Henry prefers certain items of pop music ("I don't like *artists,* I like singles"). He was once taken to Covent Garden to hear Maria Callas in an effort to cure him of his addiction to pop, but it merely increased his belief that "The Righteous Brothers' recording of "You've Lost That Lovin' Feelin'" on the London label was possibly the most haunting, the most deeply moving noise ever produced by the human spirit."

Charlotte comes in with some dip for the crudités and is icily defensive when Henry decides it needs a little stronger seasoning. She exits with Max to chop the vegetables, leaving Henry and Annie alone in the room together.

HENRY: Are you all right?

ANNIE *(nods):* Are you all right? *(Henry nods.)* Touch me. *(Henry shakes his head.)* Touch me.

HENRY: No.

ANNIE: Come on, touch me. Help yourself. Touch me anywhere you like.

Jeremy Irons as Henry and Glenn Close as Annie in *The Real Thing*

HENRY: No.
ANNIE: Touch me.
HENRY: No.
ANNIE: Coward.
HENRY: I love you anyway.

Henry keeps repeating "I love you," and it is clear that Annie reciprocates his feeling, and that they have been lovers for some time. Annie suggests they walk out together right now, leaving the others chopping vegetables, but Henry can't bring himself to do that.

Max comes in, having cut his finger. Henry gives him a clean handkerchief to staunch the blood. When Max goes out to put it under the tap, Annie proposes that they reveal everything to whichever spouse comes back into the living room first. It's Charlotte who comes back first, but Henry can't bear to tell her. *"Annie and Henry continue to speak quite privately to each other in the interstices of the general conversation."* They manage to convey signals of love while Charlotte goes on about her daughter Debbie's preoccupation with ponies and riding school, where Henry is to pick her up later.

Somewhat roughly, Charlotte raises the subject of Max and Annie's lack of children. Henry changes it, inquiring about Annie's activities on the Brodie Committee. It seems Annie met Private Brodie on a train en route to a demonstration against American missiles (Brodie had recognized Annie from her appearances in a TV serial). Brodie got into a fight with two policemen at the demonstration and is now in jail, so that the Committee is working for his release. Annie is going from here to a protest meeting, and Max would accompany her except that he has a squash date and doesn't want to let his partner down. Henry characterizes this as "an interesting moral dilemma."

HENRY: . . . . . I ponder. On the one hand, Max's squash partner. Decent chap but not a deprivation of the first magnitude. And on the other hand, Brodie, an out-and-out thug, an arsonist, vandalizer of a national shrine, *but* mouldering in jail for years to come owing, *perhaps,* to society's inability to comprehend a man divided against himself, a pacifist hooligan.

MAX: I don't condone vandalism, however idealistic. I just—

HENRY: Yes, well, as acts of vandalism go, starting a fire on the Cenotaph using the wreath to the Unknown Soldier as kindling scores very low on discretion. I assumed he was trying to be provocative.

MAX: Of course he was, you idiot. But he got hammered by an emotional backlash.

HENRY: No, no, you *can't*—

MAX: Yes he bloody was!

HENRY: I mean "hammer" and "backlash." You can't *do* it!

MAX: Oh, for Christ's sake. This is your house, and I'm drinking your wine, but if you don't mind me saying so, Henry—

HENRY: *My* saying, Max.

MAX: Right. *(He puts down his glass definitively and stands up.)* Come on, Annie. *(To Henry.)* There's something wrong with you. You've got something missing. You may have all the answers, but having all the answers is not what life's about.

HENRY: I'm sorry, but it actually *hurts.*

MAX: Brodie may be no intellectual, like you, but he did march for a cause, and now he's got six years for a stupid piece of bravado and a punch-up, and he'd have been forgotten in a week if it wasn't for Annie. That's what life's about— messy bits of good and bad luck, and people caring and not necessarily having all the answers. Who the hell are you to patronize Annie? She's worth ten of you.

HENRY: I know that.

MAX: I'm sorry, Charlotte.

CHARLOTTE: Well done, Henry.

Max leaves toward the front door. Charlotte, with a glance at Henry, rolling her eyes in rebuke, follows him out of the room. Annie stands up. For the rest of the scene she is moving, hardly looking at Henry, perhaps fetching her handbag.

HENRY: It was just so I could look at you without it looking funny.

ANNIE: What time are you going for Debbie?

HENRY: Four o'clock. Why?

ANNIE: Three o'clock. Look for my car.

HENRY: What about Brodie?

ANNIE: Let him rot.
> *Annie leaves, closing the door. Pop music: Herman's Hermits, "I'm Into Something Good."*

Scene 3

Max is alone in his and Annie's living room, listening to the radio, which is playing Herman's Hermits as one of Henry's desert-island eight. Annie enters as they interview Henry on the program, but it is unintelligible under the conversation between Annie and Max.

Max is troubled because he found Henry's blood-stained handkerchief in their car. Max had returned it to Henry, so its presence indicates that Henry was in the car. Max makes the obvious inference.

MAX: . . . . . You filthy cow. You rotten filthy— *(He starts to cry, barely audible, immobile. Annie waits. He recovers his voice.)* It's not true, is it?
ANNIE: Yes.
MAX: Oh, God. *(He stands up.)* Why did you?
ANNIE: I'm awfully sorry, Max—
MAX *(interrupting, suddenly pulled together):* All right. It happened. All right. It didn't mean anything.
ANNIE: I'm awfully sorry, Max, but I love him.
MAX: Oh, no.
ANNIE: Yes.
MAX: Oh, *no.* You don't.
ANNIE: Yes, I do. And he loves me. That's that, isn't it? I'm sorry it's awful. But it's better really. All that lying.
MAX *(breaking up again):* Oh, Christ, Annie, stop it. I love you. Please don't—
ANNIE: Come on, please—it doesn't have to be like this.
MAX: How long for? And *him*—oh, *God.*
> *He kicks the radio savagely. The radio has gone into music again—the Righteous Brothers singing "You've Lost That Lovin' Feelin' "—and Max's kick has the effect of turning up the volume rather loud. He flings himself upon Annie in something like an assault which turns immediately into an embrace. Annie does no more than suffer the embrace, looking over Max's shoulder, her face blank.*

Scene 4

In still another living room—Henry's and Annie's—Henry is at work at a desk, writing, amid a clutter of cardboard boxes filled with books and papers, and with the radio playing pop music. Annie comes in, barefoot and wearing Henry's bathrobe. She finally breaks his concentration, and they embrace, after which Annie describes Max's feelings about the situation: "His misery just seems . . . not in very good taste. Am I awful? He leaves letters for me at rehearsal, you know, and gets me to come to the phone by pretending to be my agent and people.

He loves me, and he wants to punish me with his pain, but I can't come up with the proper guilt. I'm sort of irritated by it." She wishes Henry would write about *that* for a change, and Henry agrees: "Gallons of ink and typewriter ribbon expended on the misery of the unrequited lover; not a word about the utter tedium of the unrequiting."

Their talk is of love—theirs and love in the abstract. Henry has no difficulty making love but much difficulty writing about love properly. Their discussion of the relative physical attributes of a rival actress leads to some moderate horseplay; then they try to resume work, he writing and she reading a script. Soon, however, they are comparing notes on their engagements for later in the day— he to pick up his daughter Debbie, she to visit Brodie in jail. Henry still views Brodie as a common lawbreaker, but Annie sees him as a political martyr. It isn't Henry's opinion of Brodie that irritates Annie the most, however, it's his seeming lack of lover's jealousy where she is concerned.

ANNIE: . . . . . Why aren't *you* ever jealous?

HENRY: Of whom?

ANNIE: Of anybody. You don't care if Gerald Jones sticks his tongue in my ear —which, incidentally, he does whenever he gets the chance.

HENRY: Is that what this is all about?

ANNIE: It's insulting the way you just laugh.

HENRY: But you've got no interest in him.

ANNIE: I know that, but why should you assume it?

HENRY: Because you haven't. This is stupid.

ANNIE: But why don't you *mind?*

HENRY: I do.

ANNIE: No, you don't.

HENRY: That's true, I don't. Why *is* that? It's because I feel superior. There he is, poor bugger, picking up odd crumbs of ear wax from the rich man's table. You're right. I don't mind. I like it. I like the way his presumption admits his poverty. I like him, knowing that that's all there is, because you're coming home to me and we don't want anyone else. I love love. I love having a lover and being one. The insularity of passion. I love it. I love the way it blurs the distinction between everyone who isn't one's lover. Only two kinds of presence in the world. There's you and there's them. I love you so.

ANNIE: I love you so, Hen.

They kiss. The alarm on Henry's wrist watch goes off. They separate.

HENRY: Sorry.

ANNIE: Don't get kicked by the horse.

HENRY: Don't get kicked by Brodie.

He goes to the door to leave. At the door he looks at her and nods. She nods at him. He leaves. Annie goes slowly to Henry's desk and looks at the pages on it. She turns on the radio and turns it from pop to Bach. She goes back to the desk and, almost absently, opens one of the drawers. Leaving it open, she goes to the door and disappears briefly into the hall, then reappears, closing the door. She goes to one of the cardboard boxes on the floor. She removes the contents from the box. She places the pile of papers on the floor. Squatting down, she starts going through the pile, methodically and unhurriedly. The radio plays on. Curtain.

ACT II

Scene 5

Two years later, Henry and Annie's living room in a different house prominently features the record player (on which a Verdi opera is heard while Henry, at his desk, reads a script), a TV and video and a radio in addition to the usual furnishings. Annie comes in and turns off the machine because Henry is not really listening to the music. He can't tell one opera from another, just as Annie can't tell the Everly Brothers from the Andrews Sisters ("There isn't any difference," is her opinion).

Annie is thinking of accepting a part in a production of *'Tis Pity She's a Whore* to be staged in Glasgow but is reluctant to leave Henry alone for the five weeks it will take. Most of all, though, Annie wants to know what Henry thinks of the script he is reading. Henry reads aloud a couple of short scenes of two strangers meeting on a train, demonstrating the banality of its language and relationships. "It's not literary, and it's no good. He can't write," Henry declares. "You're a snob," Annie counters. "I'm a snob, and he can't write," Henry finishes.

It seems the play was written by Brodie, which accounts for Annie's special interest in it. She admires the effort it must have taken this semi-literate man to learn to write, and she feels that he has something to say, regardless of the shortcomings of his talent: "He's a prisoner shouting over the wall." At this point, his cause needs stimulation by something like a play, because people have become indifferent to it. When Henry criticizes Brodie's writing severely, Annie protests that he is exaggerating the importance of the writer's art, jealous of any outsider practising it, pretending it is so esoteric and mysterious that only the initiated can do it, shutting out the non-literate, like Brodie, who nevertheless may have something very important to say.

ANNIE: . . . . . You teach a lot of people what to expect from good writing, and you end up with a lot of people saying you write well. Then somebody who isn't in on the game comes along, like Brodie, who really has something to write about, something real, and you can't get through it. Well, *he* couldn't get through *yours*, so where are you? To you, he can't write. To him, write is all you *can* do.

HENRY: Jesus, Annie, you're beginning to appal me. There's something scary about stupidity made coherent. I can deal with idiots, and I can deal with sensible argument, but I don't know how to deal with you. Where's my cricket bat?

ANNIE: Your cricket bat?

HENRY: Yes. It's a new approach. *(He heads out into the hall.)*

ANNIE: Are you trying to be funny?

HENRY: No, I'm serious.

He goes out while she watches in wary disbelief. He returns with an old cricket bat.

ANNIE: You better not be.

HENRY: Right, you silly cow—

ANNIE: Don't you bloody dare—

HENRY: Shut up and listen. This thing here, which looks like a wooden club, is actually several pieces of particular wood cunningly put together in a certain way so that the whole thing is sprung, like a dance floor. It's for hitting cricket balls with. If you get it right, the cricket ball will travel two hundred yards in four seconds, and all you've done is give it a knock like knocking the top off a bottle of stout, and it makes a noise like a trout taking a fly . . . *(He clucks his tongue to make the noise.)* What we're trying to do is to write cricket bats, so that when we throw up an idea and give it a little knock, it might . . . *travel* . . . *(He clucks his tongue again and picks up the script.)* Now, what we've got here is a lump of wood of roughly the same shape trying to be a cricket bat, and if you hit a ball with it, the ball will travel about ten feet and you will drop the bat and dance about shouting "Ouch!" with your hands stuck in your armpits. *(Indicating the cricket bat.)* This isn't better because someone says it's better, or because there's a conspiracy by the MCC to keep cudgels out of Lords. It's better because it's better. You don't believe me, so I suggest you go out to bat with this and see how you get on. "You're a strange boy, Billy, how old are you?" "Twenty, but I've lived more than you'll ever live." Ohh, ouch!

He drops the script and hops about with his hands in his armpits, going "Ouch!" Annie watches him expressionlessly until he desists.

ANNIE: I hate you.

Nevertheless, Annie still hopes, can't Henry help out and turn Brodie's literary cudgel into a cricket bat? No, Henry believes, it is too heavy-handed in its moral propaganda against war, politics, finance, etc. Brodie and his work are not perceptive, they are merely prejudiced. Brodie's heroics don't count in his literary favor: "He's a lout with language . . . . . Words don't deserve that kind of malarkey. They're innocent, neutral, precise, standing for this, describing that, meaning the other, so if you look after them you can build bridges across incomprehension and chaos. But when they get their corners knocked off, they're no good any more, and Brodie knocks corners off without knowing he's doing it. So everything he builds is jerry-built. It's rubbish. An intelligent child could push it over. I don't think writers are sacred, but words are. If you get the right ones in the right order, you can nudge the world a little or make a poem which children will speak for you when you're dead."

Annie points out that the material in Henry's typewriter—a film script—is hardly the stuff of which poems are made. That's just pictures, not words, Henry argues. He offers to accompany her to Glasgow, but she has decided she wants to appear in Brodie's play, hoping that Henry will help her: "Don't *I* count, Hen?" But Henry is exasperated and suggests that Annie is determined to make this script work because she fancies its author. He sees that he shouldn't have made any such comment and tries to take it back, but Annie leaves the room saying, "Too late."

Scene 6

Annie is sitting on a train reading a paperback when she is interrupted by the entrance into her compartment of Billy, "*22-ish . . . . . He carries a zipped grip bag. He speaks with a Scottish accent.*" As he settles in, Annie recognizes him as a fellow-actor, en route to Glasgow where they are to play an incestuous brother and sister in the Elizabethan tragedy. Billy has read Brodie's play, too, and doesn't think much of it but believes he could do well with the lead part in it.

Billy insists on flirting with Annie, telling her he took this train because he knew she'd be on it. They discuss the class system (this is a first class compartment, and Billy doesn't have a first class ticket); Annie believes that people form groups because of common interests, not because of the system. Billy thinks her attitude is too casual: "I prefer Brodie. He sounds like rubbish, but you know he's right. You sound all right, but you know it's rubbish."

Billy will act in Brodie's play if Annie appears in it, though he knows Brodie is not a first-class writer like Henry, whose work Billy admires. They gravitate into a recital of a scene from the Elizabethan play, a love scene between brother and sister, and Billy becomes more and more impassioned.

>   *Now he stands up and opens his shirt.*
> ANNIE *(giggling):* Oh, leave off. *(She looks around nervously.)*
> BILLY *(starting to shout):*
>   And here's my breast; strike home!
>   Rip up my bosom; there thou shalt behold
>   A heart in which is writ the truth I speak.
> ANNIE: You daft idiot.
> BILLY: Yes, most earnest. You cannot love?
> ANNIE: Stop it.
> BILLY: My tortured soul
>   Hath felt affliction in the heat of death.
>   Oh, Annabella, I am quite undone!
> ANNIE: Billy!

Scene 7

Henry is visiting his daughter Debbie and his former wife Charlotte in Charlotte's living room. Henry is surprised to see Debbie light up a cigarette, but Debbie assures him she's been smoking ever since school days.

> DEBBIE: . . . . . Me and Terry used to light up in the boiler room.
> HENRY: *I* and Terry.
> DEBBIE: I and Terry. Are you sure?
> HENRY: It doesn't sound right but it's correct. I paid school fees so that you wouldn't be barred by your natural disabilities from being taught Latin and learning to speak English.
> CHARLOTTE: I thought it was so that she'd be a virgin a bit longer.
> HENRY: It was also so that she'd speak English. *Virgo syntacta.*

DEBBIE: You were done, Henry. Nobody left the boiler room virgo with Terry.

HENRY: I wish you'd stop celebrating your emancipation by flicking it at me like a wet towel. Did the staff know about this lout, Terry?

DEBBIE: He was on the staff. He taught Latin.

HENRY: Oh well, that's all right then.

CHARLOTTE: Apparently she'd already lost it riding anyway.

HENRY: That doesn't count.

CHARLOTTE: In the tackroom.

HENRY: God's truth. The groom.

CHARLOTTE: That's why he was bow-legged.

HENRY: I told you—I said you've got to warn her about being carried away.

DEBBIE: You don't get carried away in jodhpurs. It needs absolute determination.

Charlotte is looking through a bunch of old clippings and programs to find out who played Giovanni opposite her Annabella in *'Tis Pity She's a Whore* (he was the one to whom she surrendered her own virginity), but she can't seem to find it. Meanwhile, Henry is concerned because Debbie is going off on her own with a young man who plays the steam organ at fairs. Charlotte exits in the direction of the bath, as Debbie reassures her father—whom she insists on calling "Henry" —that she is going to be happy.

Debbie didn't much like Henry's last play. "Infidelity among the architect class," is how she describes it, but Henry adds, "It was about self-knowledge through pain." Debbie doesn't regard sexual fidelity as much of a virtue or infidelity as much of an sin—she used to be fascinated by it when she was twelve, but in the boiler room she found it was merely biology after all. Henry tries to explain to Debbie that the major importance of love is the sharing of total knowledge of each other: "Personal, final uncompromised. Knowing, being known. I revere that." When it disappears, all becomes painful.

HENRY: . . . . . Every single thing. Every object that meets the eye, a pencil, a tangerine, a travel poster. As if the physical world has been wired up to pass a current back to the part of your brain where imagination glows like a filament in a lobe no bigger than a torch bulb. Pain.
    Pause.

DEBBIE: Has Annie got someone else then?

HENRY: Not as far as I know, thank you for asking.

DEBBIE: Apologies.

HENRY: Don't worry.

DEBBIE: Don't you. Exclusive rights isn't love, it's colonization.

HENRY: Christ almighty. Another *ersatz* masterpiece. Like Michelangelo working in polystyrene.

DEBBIE: Do you know what your problem is, Henry?

HENRY: What?

DEBBIE: Your Latin mistress never took you into the boiler room.

HENRY: Well, at least I passed.

DEBBIE: Only in Latin.

Christine Baranski (Charlotte), Jeremy Irons (Henry) and Cynthia
Nixon (Debbie) in a scene from *The Real Thing*

Charlotte comes back with stamped and addressed postcards which Debbie is to send her weekly, in exchange for a forwarded allowance. Debbie's lover is somewhat frightened of Henry, so he isn't coming up to fetch her, nor are the parents to come down to see her off. She kisses her father, picks up her rucksack and exits.

Charlotte asks after Annie, whose Glasgow opening doesn't take place for a couple of weeks. Henry doesn't know or care who's playing opposite Annie, an indifference which Charlotte finds both typical and irritating, and which she at one time attributed—erroneously, it turned out—to Henry's having amorous relations with other women. On the contrary, Henry is "the last romantic" who has had only the one lover since their separation, whereas Charlotte has had nine: "No commitments, only bargains."

Charlotte even suggests that Henry might like to have a drink and stay awhile, but Henry prefers to remain totally committed to Annie: "I'd rather be an idiot. It's a kind of idiocy I like . . . . . It's no trick loving somebody at their *best.* Love is loving them at their worst. Is that romantic? Well, good. Everything should be romantic. Love, work, music, literature, virginity, loss of virginity . . ."

Charlotte comments, "You've still got one to lose, Henry."

Scene 8

Annie and Billy, in rehearsal clothes, are embracing as they recite part of a scene from their Elizabethan play. The scene ends in a kiss, which Annie returns in earnest.

Scene 9

Henry is seated in his living room, as Annie enters, dressed in a topcoat and carrying suitcase and traveling bag. She mentions how it went in Glasgow, and she has brought Henry a present.

Henry has been wondering why Annie didn't get home earlier, and he pursues this subject. She says she caught this morning's train, but Henry had phoned the hotel last night and found she had checked out. Annie admits she took the overnight sleeper; even so, she is quite late in arriving at the apartment—"Have you been to the zoo?" Henry asks pointedly. Annie warns Henry that such questioning reflects humiliation on him and tells him that she spent a morning in Euston station with a member of the cast. Henry seems to know or guess that it was Billy.

Annie sees that the bedroom is in quite a mess, as Henry has been rummaging through her things. Annie offers to straighten it up, but Henry tells her, "You can't put things back. They won't go back." He declares that he loves her, and Annie assures him that she is here because she loves him too.

HENRY: Tell me, then.
ANNIE: I love you.
HENRY: Not that.
ANNIE: Yes, that. That's all I'd need to know.

HENRY: You'd need more.

ANNIE: No.

HENRY: I need it. I can manage knowing if you did but I can't manage not knowing if you did or not. I won't be able to work.

ANNIE: Don't blackmail.

HENRY: You'd ask me.

ANNIE: I never have.

HENRY: There's never *been* anything.

ANNIE: Dozens. For the first year at least, every halfway decent looking woman under fifty you were ever going to meet.

HENRY: But you learned better.

ANNIE: No, I just learned not to care. There was nothing to keep you here so I assumed you wanted to stay. I stopped caring about the rest of it.

HENRY: I care. Tell me.

ANNIE *(hardening):* I did tell you. I spent the morning talking to Billy in a station cafeteria instead of coming straight home to you and I fibbed about the train because *that* seemed like infidelity—but all you want to know is did I sleep with him first?

HENRY: Yes. Did you?

ANNIE: No.

When Henry inquires further into whether she *wanted* to or not, Annie reminds him of her right to privacy and his dignity. But Henry has no use for such "debonair relationships" as the husband-wife scene in his play. Instead, he confesses, "I believe in mess, tears, pain, self-abasement, loss of self-respect, nakedness. Not caring doesn't seem much different from not loving."

With relentless poise, Annie informs Henry that she means to go right back to Glasgow this weekend to see Billy, who is interested in Brodie's play although he knows Brodie can't write. Annie warns him, "You have to find a part of yourself where I'm not important or you won't be worth loving." Henry preserves enough dignity to accept the fact of Annie's coming weekend in Glasgow—alone, without Henry accompanying her there.

Scene 10

Billy and Annie are filming a scene from Brodie's play, in which the two characters meet for the first time on a train. Billy is having trouble remembering some of Henry's rewrites and complains, "There's too many people writing this play. I liked it better before." Besides, Billy believes Annie loves him and should tell Henry about their relationship. "He knows," Annie tells Billy, who is thrown into confusion wondering how Henry took it, while the voice of the unseen film director insists that they go on with the scene in the script.

Scene 11

Henry is listening to the radio as Annie enters on her way to go out to the last day of acting in Brodie's script. The phone rings—it's Billy calling to find out why

Annie is late. Annie appreciates that Henry is now taking all this very coolly, and Henry tells her, "I don't get pathetic because when I got pathetic I could feel how tedious it was, how unattractive. Like Max, your ex. Remember Max? Love me because I'm in pain. No good. Not in very good taste." He admits, however that in spite of his debonair facade, "I can't *find* a part of myself where you're not important." He is even re-writing Brodie's "unspeakable drivel" because she thinks it's right for him to do so, not because he thinks it's right: "What you do is right. What you want is right." He just about worships her, and she tries to grasp the meaning of this relationship: "So you'll forgive me anything, is that it Hen? I'm a selfish cow but you love me so you'll overlook it, is that right? Thank you, but that's not it."

In any event, Annie is beginning to perceive that Billy may be more of a liability —"How can I need someone I spend half my time telling to grow up?"—than an asset. She tells Henry, "I don't feel selfish, I feel hoist. I send out waves, you know. Not free. Not interested. He sort of got in under the radar. Acting daft on a train. Next thing I'm looking round for him, makes the day feel better, it's like love or something." It didn't replace her love for Henry, but it gave her a good feeling which is now diminishing—but she won't drop Billy as though it were all finally meaningless. "This is the me who loves you, this me who won't tell Billy to go and rot," Annie finishes. "and I know I'm yours so I'm not afraid for you—I have to choose who I hurt and I choose you because I'm yours. I'm only sorry for your pain but even your pain is the pain of letting go of something, some idea of me which was never true . . . . ."

On the phone, Annie informs the director that she's on her way. She leaves, but not before asking Henry not to let his feelings for her be worn away. She promises not to be late getting back. After she goes, Henry puts on the record of Procol Harum's "A Whiter Shade of Pale," which he has noticed is a version of Bach's "Air on a G String." He is smiling, but then the smile vanishes and he says, "Oh, please, please, please, please *don't*" as the scene blacks out.

Scene 12

In Henry and Annie's living room, Brodie is watching the last scene of his play on television. Henry comes in with water for Brodie's whiskey and Annie enters bearing canapes. Brodie has been granted early release from his incarceration because of overcrowding in the prisons. He doesn't much like Billy's portrayal of him or Henry's rewrites.

BRODIE: . . . . . I don't owe you.

HENRY: Is it against your principles to say thank you for *anything,* even a drink?

BRODIE: Fair enough. You had a go. You did your best. It probably needed something, to work in with their prejudices.

HENRY: Yes, they are a bit prejudiced, these drama producers. They don't like plays which go "clunk" every time someone opens his mouth. They gang up against soap-box bigots with no idea that everything has a length. They think TV is a visual medium. *(To Annie, puzzled.)* Is this *him?*

BRODIE: Don't be clever with me, Henry, like you were clever with my play. I lived it and put my guts into it, and you came along and wrote it clever. Not for me. For her. I'm not stupid.

ANNIE *(to Henry):* No, this isn't him.

BRODIE: Yes, it bloody is. That was me on the train, and this is me again, and I don't think you're that different either.

ANNIE: And *that* wasn't him. *(She points at the TV.)* He was helpless, like a three-legged calf, nervous as anything. A boy on the train. Chatting me up. Nice . . . . .

When they got off the train at London, Brodie tagged along with her (Annie recalls), and when they passed the Cenotaph Brodie pulled out his lighter and, as Annie puts it, went "over the top to the slaughter, not an idea in his head except to impress me." Henry comments, "You should have told me. That one I would have known how to write."

Annie asks Brodie to finish his drink and leave, and when he replies in an insolent fashion, Annie presses the bowl of canape dip into his face. Brodie wipes his face, takes his coat from Annie and exits.

The phone rings, and Henry answers it. It's Annie's ex-husband Max with the news that he is going to be married again. While Henry is talking on the phone, Annie kisses him.

ANNIE: I've had it. Look after me.
        Henry covers the mouthpiece.
HENRY: Don't worry. I'm your chap. *(Into phone.)* Well, it's very decent of you to say so, Max. *(To Annie.)* "No hard feelings?" what does he mean? If it wasn't for me, he wouldn't be engaged *now.*
        Annie disengages herself from him with a smile and goes around turn-
        ing out the lights until the only light is coming from the bedroom door.
(Into phone.) No, I'm afraid she isn't . . . She'll be so upset when I tell her . . . No, I mean when I tell her she missed you . . . No, she'll be delighted. I'm delighted, Max. Isn't love wonderful?
        Annie finishes with the lights and goes out into the bedroom. Henry is
        being impatiently patient with Max on the phone, trying to end it.
Yes, well, we look forward to meeting her. What? Oh, yes?
        Absently he clicks on the little radio, which starts playing, softly, "I'm
        a Believer" by the Monkees. He is immediately beguiled. He forgets
        Max until the phone crackle gets back through to him.
Sorry. Yes, I'm still here.
        He turns the song up slightly. Curtain.

OHIO IMPROMPTU, CATASTROPHE AND WHAT WHERE

ENOUGH, FOOTFALLS AND ROCKABY

Two Programs of One-Act Plays

BY SAMUEL BECKETT

Casts and credits appear on pages 352 and 381

SAMUEL BECKETT, one of the outstanding writers of this century and the winner of the 1969 Nobel Prize for literature, was born in Foxrock near Dublin, Ireland, on April 13, 1906 and was educated at Portora Royal School, Enniskillen, and Trinity College, Dublin, where he lectured in French from 1930 to 1932. Just before World War II he established residence in France and has lived there ever since, serving for a time as a kind of secretary to James Joyce. He has written many of his plays, novels, stories and poems in the French language, including his first two plays which established him as a world-famous playwright: Waiting for Godot (En Attendant Godot) *and* Endgame (Fin de Partie).

Beckett's long list of New York theater productions of record began with the memorable Waiting for Godot *April 19, 1956 for 59 Broadway performances. It was named a Best Play of its season by Louis Kronenberger but was, in its time, too challenging a novelty to attract anything like the critical consensus required for such group citations as the Critics Award, which went that season to Giraudoux's* Tiger at the Gates *as best foreign play.* Waiting for Godot *was revived on Broad-*

way the following season by its original producer, Michael Myerberg, and director, Herbert Berghof. It has reappeared off and off off Broadway in numerous productions, at least one of them, in 1971, staged by the late Alan Schneider, who has interpreted so many of Beckett's subsequent stage writings for New York audiences.

First off-Broadway productions of Beckett plays have taken place as follows: Krapp's Last Tape *and* Embers *(1960),* Happy Days *(1961),* Endgame *(1962),* Play *(1964), a segment of* Oh! Calcutta! *(1969),* Act Without Words 1 *and* Not I *(1972),* That Time *and* Footfalls *(1977) and* Come and Go *(1983). An adaptation of his novel* Mercier and Camier *appeared off Broadway in 1979, and Beckett is also the author of the novels* Molloy, Malone Dies, The Unnamable *and* Watt *and the critical essay* Proust.

The first 1983–84 program of Beckett one-acters in their New York City premieres, directed by Schneider and produced off Broadway June 15, 1983 for 350 performances, was as follows, with dates of authorship: Ohio Impromptu *(1981, when it was staged at Ohio State University),* Catastrophe *(1982, homage to the Czechoslovakian playwright Vaclav Havel) and* What Where *(1983, making its world premiere). The second trio, also New York premieres and also directed by Schneider, produced off Broadway Feb. 16, 1984 for 78 performances, was* Enough *(1966, a Beckett short story),* Footfalls *(1976) and* Rockaby *(1980, staged in 1981 at the Center for Theater Research in Buffalo). Beckett received a special 1984 New York Drama Critics Circle citation for the body of his work for the theater, of which these programs were a prime example. Similarly, our Best Play citation, Beckett's second, is for the 1983–84 programs as a New York whole, five of whose parts are identified briefly below. The sixth—*Rockaby*—appears in its entirety as a symbol of Beckett's major contribution to this season.*

OHIO IMPROMPTU

"Little is left to tell," begins one of two characters reading from a book to the other, a listener. They are identical in appearance, dressed in black with flowing white hair. The reader is near the end of the tale, which very lightly touches now on a love remembered, now on a visitation from death. The reader comes to the end of the book and closes it with the statement, "Nothing is left to tell." The two sit motionless, staring into each other's expressionless eyes.

CATASTROPHE

An official of an obviously tyrannous government is showing his assistant how to prepare a "protagonist" for ceremonial exhibition for public edification. This "protagonist" is a physically and mentally dehumanized victim of oppression, posing like an articulated statue at the orders of the bureaucrat, who also is overbearing in his manner to his assistant. The "protagonist" is finally left staring in bewildered helplessness.

WHAT WHERE

Shadowy figures are under orders from a disembodied voice to put a prisoner to the torture in order to extract a confession. The figures repeat over and over that they have done so, and although their victim suffered greatly, he did not confess.

ENOUGH

Dramatic reading in monologue of a Samuel Beckett short story about a sometimes difficult, sometimes luminous, long-past but well-remembered relationship which might be construed as a love affair.

FOOTFALLS

Conversing with the offstage voice of her invalid mother as she paces a small rectangle of light which seems to limit her movement, a middle-aged woman reveals the sadness of a life cramped by circumstance and wasted in anguish.

ROCKABY

W = Woman in chair and V = Her recorded voice. Fade up on W in rocking chair facing front downstage slightly off center audience left. Long pause.

w: More.

Pause. Rock and voice together.

v: till in the end
the day came
in the end came
close of a long day
when she said
to herself
whom else
time she stopped
time she stopped
going to and fro
all eyes
all sides
high and low
for another
another like herself
another creature like herself
a little like

Billie Whitelaw in *Rockaby*

going to and fro
all eyes
all sides
high and low
for another
till in the end
close of a long day
to herself
whom else
time she stopped
time she stopped
going to and fro
all eyes
all sides
high and low
for another
another living soul
one other living soul
going to and fro
all eyes like herself
all sides
high and low
for another
another like herself
a little like
going to and fro
till in the end
close of a long day
to herself
whom else
time she stopped
going to and fro
time she stopped
time she stopped
    Together: echo of "time she stopped," coming to rest of rock, faint fade
    of light. Long pause.
w. More.
    Pause. Rock and voice together.
v: so in the end
close of a long day
went back in
in the end went back in
saying to herself
whom else
time she stopped
time she stopped
going to and fro

time she went and sat
at her window
quiet at her window
facing other windows
so in the end
close of a long day
in the end went and sat
went back in and sat
at her window
let up the blind and sat
quiet at her window
only window
facing other windows
other only windows
all eyes
all sides
high and low
for another
at her window
another like herself
a little like
another living soul
one other living soul
at her window
gone in like herself
gone back in
in the end
close of a long day
saying to herself
whom else
time she stopped
time she stopped
going to and fro
time she went and sat
at her window
quiet at her window
only window
facing other windows
other only windows
all eyes
all sides
high and low
for another
another like herself
a little like
another living soul
one other living soul

> *Together: echo of "living soul," coming to rest of rock, faint fade of*
> *light. Long pause.*

w: More.

> *Pause. Rock and voice together.*

v: till in the end
the day came
in the end came
close of a long day
sitting at her window
quiet at her window
only window
facing other windows
other only windows
all blinds down
never one up
hers alone up
till the day came
in the end came
close of a long day
sitting at her window
quiet at her window
all eyes
all sides
high and low
for a blind up
one blind up
no more
never mind a face
behind the pane
famished eyes
like hers
to see
be seen
no
a blind up
like hers
a little like
one blind up no more
another creature there
somewhere there
behind the pane
another living soul
one other living soul
till the day came
in the end came
close of a long day
when she said

to herself
whom else
time she stopped
time she stopped
sitting at her window
quiet at her window
only window
facing other windows
other only windows
all eyes
all sides
high and low
time she stopped
time she stopped
>   *Together: echo of "time she stopped, coming to rest of rock, faint fade*
>   *of light. Long pause.*

w: More.
>   *Pause. Rock and voice together.*

v: so in the end
close of a long day
went down
in the end went down
down the steep stair
let down the blind and down
right down
into the old rocker
mother rocker
where mother sat
all the years
all in black
best black
sat and rocked
rocked
till her end came
in the end came
off her head they said
gone off her head
but harmless
no harm in her
dead one day
no
night
dead one night
in the rocker
in her best black
head fallen
and the rocker rocking

rocking away
so in the end
close of a long day
went down
in the end went down
down the steep stair
let down the blind and down
right down
into the old rocker
those arms at last
and rocked
rocked
with closed eyes
closing eyes
she so long all eyes
famished eyes
all sides
high and low
to and fro
at her window
to see
be seen
till in the end
close of a long day
to herself
whom else
time she stopped
let down the blind and stopped
time she went down
down the steep stair
time she went right down
was her own other
own other living soul
so in the end
close of a long day
went down
down the steep stair
let down the blind and down
right down
into the old rocker
and rocked
rocked
saying to herself
no
done with that
the rocker
those arms at last

saying to the rocker
rock her off
stop her eyes
fuck life
stop her eyes
rock her off
rock her off

> *Together: echo of "rock her off," coming to rest of rock, slow fade out.*
> *Curtain.*

GLENGARRY GLEN ROSS

A Play in Two Acts

BY DAVID MAMET

Cast and credits appear on page 334

DAVID MAMET was born Nov. 30, 1947 in Flossmoor, Ill. He graduated from Goddard College in Vermont with a B.A. in English literature in 1969, after having observed creative theater at close quarters as a busboy at Second City in Chicago and having studied it at a professional school in New York. From 1971 to 1973 he was artist-in-residence at Goddard. In 1974 he became a member of the Illinois Arts Council faculty, and in 1975 he helped found and served for a time as artistic director of St. Nicholas Theater Company in Chicago, which mounted some of the first productions of his scripts including Reunion, Squirrels, Duck Variations *and* Sexual Perversity in Chicago.*

Mamet's first New York production was Duck Variations *off off Broadway at St. Clements in May 1975, followed by* Sexual Perversity *at the same group in September 1975. His* American Buffalo *moved from its world premiere at Chicago's Goodman Theater in October 1975 to St. Clements in January 1976. He received the 1975–76 Obie as best playwright for these latter two OOB productions, but his career on the professional New York stage began officially with the off-Broadway program of* Duck Variations *and* Sexual Perversity *at the Cherry Lane in June 1976, running for 273 performances. His* American Buffalo *was produced on Broadway in February 1977, was named a Best Play of its season, won the Critics Award for best American play, and has been widely produced elsewhere. It was revived in New York in June 1981 off Broadway for 262 performances and this season on Broadway for 102 performances.*

Mamet's second Best Play, A Life in the Theater, *opened off Broadway in October 1977 and ran for 288 performances. His third Best Play is the current*

Glengarry Glen Ross, *which opened on Broadway March 25 and won the 1984 Pulitzer Prize for its prior production at the Goodman Theater in Chicago and the Critics Award for best American play. Its nomination for the 1984 best-play Tony together with the nomination of* American Buffalo *in the best-revival category is a highly unusual, if not unique, instance of an author having two different plays cited for this competition in the same season.*

Mamet's other off-Broadway productions have included The Water Engine *(1977, transferred to Broadway with the curtain-raiser* Mr. Happiness*),* The Woods *(1979), a one-act play program comprising* The Sanctity of Marriage, Dark Pony *and* Reunion *(1979), and* Edmond *(1982). He has also put his hand to directing, staging a* Twelfth Night *at Circle Repertory in 1980. His long list of playwriting awards and grants includes, in addition to the abovementioned, many Joseph Jefferson Awards for distinguished Chicago shows, a New York State Council on the Arts Plays for Young Audiences grant, a Rockefeller playwriting-in-residence grant and a CBS Fellowship at Yale. At present he is playwright-in-residence and associate artistic director of the Goodman Theater.*

In addition to his plays, Mamet is the author of the screen plays The Postman Always Rings Twice *and* The Verdict *and the children's book* Warm and Cold. *He has taught acting and directing at New York University, the University of Chicago and the Yale Drama School. He is married to the actress Lindsay Crouse, with one child, and they divide their time among their New York City residence, Vermont and Chicago.*

The following synopsis of Glengarry Glen Ross *was prepared by Jeffrey Sweet.*

Time: Today

Place: A Chinese restaurant and a real estate office in Chicago

ACT I

Scene 1

SYNOPSIS: In a booth in a Chinese restaurant, Shelly Levene, a salesman in his 50s, is trying to get a younger man, John Williamson, to see things his way. Levene is one of an office full of salesmen hustling Florida real estate of dubious value called the Glengarry Highlands. Murray and Mitch, the bosses, have set up a competition among the salesmen. Whoever, by the 30th of the month, sells the most and thus comes in on the top of the contest board, will win a Cadillac. The two with the poorest sales records will get fired. At the moment, Shelly Levene is at the bottom of the board.

Levene believes he can turn his luck around. If he can just get some quality leads—which is to say names, addresses and phone numbers of people most likely to buy—he knows he can close some sales, get out of his slump and move up the board to the land of the living. But Murray has ordered Williamson to give the premium leads only to the guys at the top of the board like Roma. This means, of course, the higher you are on the board, the more likely you are to stay high on the board. If, on the other hand, you are down in the lower depths like Levene, you get leads likely to lead to zero, making it all but impossible to move up.

Levene is trying to persuade Williamson to bend the rules a little and give him some premium leads. Williamson is not being persuaded. As he explains to Levene, his job is "to marshal those leads." Levene interrupts.

LEVENE: Marshal the leads . . . marshal the leads? What the fuck, what bus did *you* get off of, we're here to fucking *sell. Fuck* marshaling the leads. What the fuck talk is that? What the fuck talk is that? Where did you learn that? In school? *(Pause.)* That's "talk," my friend, that's "talk." Our job is to *sell.* I'm the *man* to sell. I'm getting garbage. *(Pause.)* You're giving it to me, and what I'm saying is it's *fucked.*

WILLIAMSON: You're saying that I'm fucked.

LEVENE: Yes. *(Pause.)* I am. I'm sorry to antagonize you . . . . .

WILLIAMSON: You know what those leads cost?

LEVENE: The premium leads. Yes. I know what they cost. John. Because I, *I* generated the dollar revenue sufficient to *buy* them. Nineteen senny-*nine,* you know what I made? Senny-*nine?* Ninety-six thousand dollars. John? For *Murray* . . . For *Mitch* . . . look at the sheets . . .

Williamson tells Levene that he blew the last four premium leads he was given. Levene can explain that. But beyond the explanations . . . well, there are such things as streaks, and, okay, he's having a bad one. But he knows he can turn it around. He's proven himself in the past. He's made good dollars for this office in the past. He's due better treatment, earned it. He needs Williamson's help on this. Williamson says he can't help.

Levene offers to kick back to Williamson 10 per cent of what he sells. Williamson counters with a demand for 20, plus fifty bucks for each premium lead. This rankles Levene, but, okay, he agrees, it's a deal. Now he wants two hot ones. Williamson says he has to give the good stuff to Roma and Moss, who are at the top of the board, but Levene presses Williamson for the two leads. Okay, Williamson agrees. Only he wants the hundred for the two up front. Now.

Levene hasn't got a hundred on him. He has thirty. The rest, he swears, is back in the hotel. Will Williamson take the thirty on account against the hundred? He'll pay Williamson the rest tomorrow.

WILLIAMSON: I can't do it, Shelly.

LEVENE: Well, I want to tell you something, fella, wasn't long I could pick up the phone, call *Murray* and I'd have your job. You know that? Not too *long* ago. For what? For *nothing.* "Mur, this new kid burns my ass." "Shelly, he's out." You're gone before I'm back from lunch. I bought him a trip to Bermuda once . . .

WILLIAMSON: I have to go . . . *(Gets up.)*

Robert Prosky as Shelly Levene and Joe Mantegna as Richard Roma in *Glengarry Glen Ross*

LEVENE: Wait. All right. Fine. *(Starts going in pocket for money.)* The one. Give me the lead. Give me the one lead. The best you have.

WILLIAMSON: I can't split them.

       Pause.

LEVENE: Why?

WILLIAMSON: Because I say so.

LEVENE *(pause):* Is that it? Is that *it?* You want to do business that way . . . ?

       Williamson gets up, leaves money on the table.

LEVENE: You want to do business that way . . . ? All right. All right. All right. All right. What is there on the other list . . . ?

WILLIAMSON: You want something off the B list?

LEVENE: *Yeah.* Yeah.

WILLIAMSON: Is that what you're saying?

LEVENE: That's what I'm saying. Yeah. *(Pause.)* I'd like something off the other list. Which, very least, that I'm entitled to. If I'm still *working* here, which for the moment I guess that I am. *(Pause.)* What? I'm sorry I spoke harshly to you.

WILLIAMSON: That's all right.

LEVENE: The deal still stands, our other thing.

       Williamson shrugs. Starts out of the booth.

LEVENE: Good. Mmm. I, you know, I left my wallet back at the hotel.

Scene 2

Dave Moss and George Aaranow, two fiftyish salesmen, are talking in a booth after a meal in the restaurant. Aaranow is afraid of being one of the losers and getting fired. He's way down in the competition, and he's just missed making a sale. Moss says he should never have taken that lead, never should have expected to close a sale to a "Polack." Poles are bad news. Also bad news are Indians. The kind with names like Patel. "They keep coming up. I don't know. They like to talk to salesmen," says Moss. "They're *lonely,* something."

Moss hates the pressure of the contest. He remembers when he and Aaranow were in another office pushing Glen Ross Farms. That was more like it. Not this competition stuff, which brings with it the constant terror of being fired if maybe you have a bad month.

It's Mitch and Murray's fault it's this way, declares Moss. Jerry Graff has got the right idea. He's on his own, not sharing commissions with Mitch and Murray. Graff has spent some money, bought a list of nurses, whom he figured to have money tucked away they haven't touched and so would probably be hot leads. And Graff is doing very well, and, unlike the two of them, Graff isn't paying the likes of Mitch and Murray a big chunk of what he brings in. The hard part of what Graff has done is simply deciding to *do it*—to start off by himself.

MOSS: To say, "I'm going on my own." 'Cause what you do, George, let me tell you what you do: you find yourself in *thrall* to someone else. And we *enslave* ourselves. To *please.* To win some fucking *toaster . . .* to . . . to . . . and the guy who got there first made *up* those . . .
AARANOW: That's right . . .
MOSS: He made *up* those rules, and we're working for *him.*
AARANOW: That's the truth . . .
MOSS: That's the *God's* truth. And it gets me depressed. I *swear* that it does. At MY AGE. To see a goddamn: "Somebody wins the Cadillac this month. P.S. Two guys get fucked."

Moss thinks somebody should do something to Murray and Mitch. Get even. Hurt them. Aaranow wants to know what kind of something Moss has in mind. "Someone should rob the office," says Moss. Make a mess of the place, steal the premium leads, sell them to Jerry Graff.

AARANOW: . . . . . are you actually *talking* about this, or are we just . . .
MOSS: No, we're just . . .
AARANOW: We're just "*talking*" about it.
MOSS: We're just *speaking* about it. *(Pause.)* As an *idea.*
AARANOW: As an idea.
MOSS: Yes.
AARANOW: We're not actually *talking* about it.
MOSS: No.
AARANOW: Talking about it as a . . .
MOSS: *No.*

AARANOW: As a *robbery*.
MOSS: As a "robbery"?! No.
AARANOW: *Well.* Well . . .
MOSS: *Hey.*
          Pause.
AARANOW: So all this, um, you didn't, actually, you didn't actually go talk to Graff.
MOSS: Not actually, no.
          Pause.
AARANOW: You didn't?
MOSS: No. Not actually.
AARANOW: Did you?
MOSS: What did I say?
AARANOW: What did you say?
MOSS: Yes. *(Pause.)* I said, "Not actually." The fuck *you* care, George? We're just *talking* . . .
AARANOW: We are?
MOSS: Yes.
          Pause.
AARANOW: Because, because, you know, it's a *crime.*
MOSS: That's right. It's a crime. It is a crime. It's also very safe.
AARANOW: You're actually *talking* about this?
MOSS: That's right.

It comes out that Moss *has* talked to Graff and that Graff has said he'd buy the leads. That's five thousand leads at a buck a throw. And they'd split half and half: $2,500 for Moss and $2,500 for Aaranow, plus they'd both get jobs with Graff working those leads. But Aaranow's got to steal them tonight, because soon Mitch and Murray will move the leads elsewhere where they can't be gotten at.

Aaranow gets agitated at the idea of being assigned to break into the office. Moss tells him that's his part of the deal. It's logical. Moss can't be the one to do it; his hostility to the system is well known in the office, so he'd be an immediate suspect. Besides which, Moss has done his part by setting up the arrangement with Graff; Aaranow's got to pull his weight on this thing by doing the actual job. And while Aaranow's breaking in, Moss will be building an alibi by going to the movies with a friend and then going to the Como Inn. Aaranow is still concerned. How does Moss expect to explain his sudden move to Graff's operation? Moss will say that Graff has made him a better offer.

If Aaranow doesn't do this, then Moss himself will have to do it because he needs those leads tonight. And, says Moss, if he gets caught doing this, when they ask him for the names of his accomplices, Moss will name Aaranow, who is now an accessory before the fact, simply because Moss told him of his intentions.

MOSS: You *went* for it.
AARANOW: In the abstract . . .
MOSS: So I'm making it concrete.

AARANOW: Why?

MOSS: Why? Why *you* going to give me five grand?

AARANOW: Do you need five grand?

MOSS: Is that what I just said?

AARANOW: You need money? Is that the . . .

MOSS: Hey, hey, let's just keep it simple, what I need is not the . . . what do *you* need . . . ?

AARANOW: What is the five grand? *(Pause.)* What is the, you said that we were going to *split* five . . .

MOSS: I lied. *(Pause.)* All right? My end is *my* business. Your end's twenty-five. In or out. You tell me, you're out you take the consequences.

AARANOW: I do?

MOSS: Yes. *(Pause.)*

AARANOW: And why is that?

MOSS: Because you listened.

Scene 3

Again in the restaurant, Richard Roma, the top salesman on the board, is talking to a man named Lingk, who is sitting in the next booth. What Roma has to say is in the form of a spew of images, semi-philosophical pronouncements and profanity. A sample:

ROMA: . . . . . What I'm saying, what is our life? *(Pause.)* It's looking forward or it's looking back. And that's our life. That's *it*. Where is the *moment*? *(Pause.)* And what is it that we're afraid of? Loss. What else? *(Pause.)* The *bank* closes. We get *sick*, my wife died on a plane, the stock market collapsed . . . the house burnt down . . . what of these happen . . . ? None of 'em. We worry anyway. What does this mean? I'm not *secure*. How can I be secure? *(Pause.)* Through amassing wealth beyond all measure? No. And what's beyond all measure? That's a sickness. That's a trap. There is no measure. Only greed. How can we act? The right way, we would say, to deal with this: "There is a one-in-a-million chance that so and so will happen. . . . *Fuck* it, it won't happen to *me*. . . ." No. We know that's not the right way I think. *(Pause.)* We say the *correct* way to deal with this is "There is a one-in-so-and-so-chance this will happen . . . God *protect* me. I am powerless, let it not happen to me. . . ." But no to *that*. I say. There's something else. What is it? "If it happens, AS IT MAY for that is not within our powers, I will *deal* with it, just as I do *today* with what draws my concern today." I say *this* is how we must act. I do those things which seem correct to me *today*. I trust myself. And if security concerns me, I do that which *today* I think will make me secure. And every day I *do* that, when that day *arrives* that I need a reserve, (a) odds are that I have it, and (b) the *true* reserve that I have is the strength that I have of *acting each day* without fear. *(Pause.)* According to the dictates of my mind. *(Pause.)* Stocks, bonds, objects of art, real estate. Now: what are they? *(Pause.)* An opportunity. To what? To make money? Perhaps. To *lose* money? Perhaps. To "indulge" and to "learn" about ourselves? Perhaps. So *fucking what?* What *isn't?* They're an *opportunity*. That's all. They're an *event*. A guy comes up to you, you make a call, you send in a brochure, it doesn't matter, "There're these *properties* I'd like for you to see." What does it mean? What you *want* it to mean. *(Pause.)* Money? *(Pause.)* If that's what it signifies to you. Security? *(Pause.)* Comfort? *(Pause.)* All it is is THINGS THAT HAPPEN TO YOU. *(Pause.)* That's all it is . . . . .

Roma tells Lingk his name and buys him a drink—and suddenly it becomes clear that this guy Roma has been talking to is neither a colleague from the office nor a friend. Lingk is some guy whom Roma probably just happened to find himself seated next to in the restaurant, and Roma is working Lingk for a sale, pulling out a map of the Glengarry Highlands. *Curtain.*

ACT II

"The real estate office. Ransacked. A broken plate-glass window boarded up, glass all over the floor." A detective named Baylen is investigating.

Baylen is about to confer with Williamson in the inner office (offstage), when Roma steams in. Roma has heard that some of the contracts were stolen in the burglary. Was his newest one—the big sale he made to Lingk—among them? Roma has not received a satisfactory reply before Baylen takes Williamson offstage. Roma kicks a desk and barks in frustration, then pounds on the door to the inner office till Baylen opens it. Baylen doesn't appreciate his investigation being interrupted, but Roma doesn't care. Williamson comes out and assures Roma that the Lingk contract was filed before the break-in. Roma replies, "Then I'm over the fucking top and you owe me a Cadillac." Baylen gets Roma's name and tells him not to leave; he's going to want to talk to him. Baylen and Williamson return to the inner office.

Roma is now alone in the office with Aaranow, who is still in the down mood we saw him in the day before. His confidence is sapped. Roma tells him not to let it get to him, that he's a good man but he's been given ancient, worthless leads to chase. But Roma can't concentrate on Aaranow's problems for long. He is annoyed at the extra work this burglary will cause him. Yes, his big sale to Lingk may have been filed, but the contracts on smaller units were stolen, and he doesn't relish the idea of having to go out and reclose deals he's already closed. Roma sits down to make some phone calls, at which point he discovers the phones have been stolen, too.

Between the premium leads having been stolen and no phones, Roma despairs of getting any work done. He's about to leave when Williamson sticks his head out and asks him if he's planning on doing any work today. Roma wonders what he's supposed to work with if there are no leads. Williamson says, "I have the stuff from last year's . . ." Roma refers to them derisively as the "nostalgia" file, but agrees to take them; if he's going to work, he's going to have to work with *something* after all. Williamson is on his way back to the inner office when Aaranow asks if the leads were insured. Williamson doesn't know. Why does Aaranow ask? Lamely, Aaranow replies that Mitch and Murray are probably going to be upset. Williamson returns to the inner office.

AARANOW: He said we're all going to have to go talk to the guy.
ROMA: What?
AARANOW: He said we . . .
ROMA: To the cop?
AARANOW: Yeah.
ROMA: Yeah. That's swell. *Another* waste of time.
AARANOW: A waste of time? Why?
ROMA: *Why?* 'Cause they aren't going to find the guy.
AARANOW: The cops?
ROMA: Yes. The cops. No.
AARANOW: They aren't?
ROMA: No.
AARANOW: Why don't you think so?
ROMA: Why? Because they're *stupid.* "Where were you last night . . ."
AARANOW: Where were you?
ROMA: Where was I?
AARANOW: Yes.
ROMA: I was at home, where were *you?*
AARANOW: At home.
ROMA: *See . . . ?* Were you the guy who broke in?
AARANOW: Was I?
ROMA: Yes.
AARANOW: No.
ROMA: Then don't sweat it, George, you know why?
AARANOW: No.
ROMA: You have nothing to hide.
AARANOW: *(Pause):* When I talk to the police, I get nervous.
ROMA: Yeah. You know who doesn't?
AARANOW: No, who?
ROMA: Thieves.
AARANOW: Why?
ROMA: They're inured to it.
AARANOW: You think so?
ROMA: Yes. *(Pause.)*
AARANOW: But what should I *tell* them?
ROMA: The truth, George. Always tell the truth. It's the easiest thing to remember.

Williamson returns with three leads for Roma. Roma looks at the name on the first lead: Ravidam Patel. Roma hits the ceiling, saying that if *"Shiva* handed him a million dollars, told him 'sign the deal,' he wouldn't sign. And Vishnu, too. Into the bargain." Williamson tries to calm him down. He shouldn't worry about reclosing any of the contracts that were stolen; Murray will handle that himself. Roma is not mollified.

In the middle of this, an exultant Shelly Levene enters. He has just sold eight units of Mountain View—$82,000 worth—to a Bruce and Harriet Nyborg. This gives him a $12,000 commission and puts him on the board. He revels in the congratulations from Roma and Aaranow. He tells Williamson to get Mitch on the phone with the news.

Roma draws Levene's attention to the vandalized office and the resultant lack of telephones. Baylen has called for Aaranow to come in for interrogation. As he goes in, Moss comes out. Moss hasn't enjoyed his session with Baylen, of whom he says, "Cop couldn't find his dick two hands and a map." The news that the Machine (Shelly Levene's nickname) has sold eight units doesn't cheer him up any. Moss refuses to be an audience for what he calls Shelly's "war stories." What he wants to know is if the burglars got the contracts. Roma, irritated by Moss's attitude, shoots back a comment to the effect that whether they were stolen or not is of no importance to Moss because Moss hasn't closed one in a month, so he didn't have anything to be stolen. This just riles Moss more. He is in a frenzy of vituperation, accusing Roma of lording it over the others just because he's got the lead in the contest.

MOSS: . . . . . Decide who should be dealt with how? Is that the thing? I come into the fuckin' office today, I get humiliated by some jagoff cop. I get accused of . . . I get this *shit* thrown in my face by you, you genuine shit, because you're top name on the board . . .

ROMA: Is that what I did? Dave? I humiliated you? My *God* . . . I'm *sorry* . . .

MOSS: Sittin' on top of the *world,* sittin' on top of the *world,* everything's fucking *peach* fuzz . . .

ROMA: Oh, and I don't get a moment to spare for a bust-out *humanitarian* down on his luck lately. Fuck *you,* Dave, you know you got a big *mouth,* and *you* make a close the whole *place* stinks with your *farts* for a week. "How much you just ingested," what a big *man* you are, "Hey, let me buy you a pack of gum. I'll show you how to *chew* it." Your *pal* closes, all that comes out of your mouth is *bile,* how fucked *up* you are . . .

MOSS: *Who's* my pal . . . ? And what are you, Ricky, huh, what are you, Bishop *Sheean?* Who the fuck are *you,* Mr. Slick . . . ? What are you, friend to the *workingman?* Big deal. Fuck *you,* you got the memory of a fuckin' *fly.* I never liked you.

ROMA: What is this, your farewell speech?

MOSS: I'm going home.

ROMA: Your farewell to the troops?

MOSS: I'm not going home. I'm going to Wis*con*sin.

ROMA: Have a good trip.

MOSS *(Simultaneously with "trip"):* And fuck *you.* Fuck the *lot* of you. Fuck you *all.*

Moss storms out. Alone with Levene, Roma encourages him to tell the story of how he made the sale to the Nyborgs. Levene is only too happy to oblige. Early on, he says, he decided to go for the whole shot. He told the Nyborgs:

LEVENE: ". . . . . I came here to do good for you and for me. For *both* of us. Why take an interim position? *The only arrangement I'll accept* is full investment. Period. The whole eight units. I know that you're saying "be safe," I know what you're saying. I know if I left you to yourselves, you'd say "come back tomorrow," and when I walked out that door, you'd make a cup of *coffee* . . . you'd sit *down* . . . and you'd think "let's be safe . . ." and not to disappoint me you'd go *one* unit or maybe two, because you'd become scared because you'd met possi-*bil*ity. But this won't do, and that's not the subject . . ." Listen to this, I actually said this. "That's not the subject of our *evening* together." Now I handed them the pen. I held it in my hand. I turned the contract, eight units eighty-two grand. "Now I want you to sign." *(Pause.)* I sat there. Five minutes. Then, I sat there, Ricky, *twenty-two minutes* by the kitchen *clock. (Pause.)* Twenty-two minutes by the kitchen clock. Not a *word,* not a *motion.* What am I thinking? "My arm's getting tired?" *No.* I *did* it. I *did* it. Like in the *old* days, Ricky. Like I was taught . . . Like, like, like I *used* to do . . . I did it.

ROMA: Like you taught me . . .

LEVENE: Bullshit, you're . . . No. That's raw . . . well, if I *did,* then I'm *glad* I did. I, *well.* I locked on them. All on them, nothing on me. All my thoughts are on them. I'm holding the last thought that I spoke: "Now is the time." *(Pause.)* They signed, Ricky. It was *great.* It was fucking great. It was like they wilted all at once. No *gesture* . . . nothing. Like together. They, I swear to God, they both kind of *imperceptibly slumped.* And he reaches and takes the pen and signs, he passes it to her, she signs. It was so fucking solemn . . . . .

A great sale, Roma agrees. Shelly, now exuding confidence, cries out for more leads. Williamson comes out of the office to tell him the leads will be coming in with Murray and Mitch in a little while, and he expresses skepticism that Shelly's sale will stick. Levene tears into Williamson: "You have no idea of your job. A man's his job and you're *fucked* at yours." Williamson advises him to cool down, but Levene keeps up the attack. Williamson doesn't know anything about *selling.* Williamson has never walked up to the door of some guy he didn't know to hawk something the guy didn't want and *made the sale.* This is what Levene has done for years and years. He's put a daughter through college like that. *He's* a salesman. Williamson? Williamson is a secretary. And if Williamson doesn't like it and wants to fire him, fine, he'll go work with Jerry Graff. Roma's comment: "He's right, Williamson." Williamson returns to the inner office.

Roma glances out the window. What he sees makes him turn to Levene for help. Lingk is coming in, and Roma needs Levene to help him create a diversion to keep Lingk from successfully engaging him on the subject Roma suspects Lingk is here to see him about. Roma tells Levene: "You're a client. I just sold you five waterfront Glengarry Farms. I rub my head, throw me the cue 'Kenilworth.'"

When Lingk enters, Levene is playing the part of a very contented customer, a Mr. D. Ray Morton, a big executive at American Express. Between Roma and Levene's elaborate fabrications, Lingk can't get a word in edgewise. Suddenly, Roma "realizes" he's got to get "Ray" to the airport. Lingk insists that he has to talk to Roma. Roma, rubbing his head, suggests that they talk that evening. "Ray" reminds him, "Kenilworth."

Roma takes Lingk aside and tells him he suddenly remembers five weeks ago he promised "Ray" to go to his wife's birthday party that night in Kenilworth. But that's okay, they'll find another time. Looking in his book, Roma says the

Joe Mantegna and James Tolkan in a scene from *Glengarry Glen Ross*

earliest time he can make it is Monday lunch. Lingk says that would be too late. Lingk and his wife have changed their minds. They don't want the land. According to the law, they have the right to change their minds and get their money back within three days of making the deal. Roma tells Lingk that three days haven't begun yet because he hasn't sent the check to the bank and, according to Roma, the three days don't begin until the check is cashed. So Monday is still in the clear. Roma goes on like this with deliberate obfuscations and side-tracking to the point at which he almost has Lingk snowed.

At this point, Detective Baylen appears and yells for Levene to come into the inner office. This is awkward, of course, because Levene is still pretending to be "Ray" and in a big hurry to get to the airport. But he can't walk out on Baylen, so he pretends that "Ray" is going in to confer with Baylen on something.

Meanwhile, Aaranow has emerged, spluttering with indignation over the treatment he's received at Baylen's hands in the inner office—the suspicion, the "Gestapo tactics," the suggestion he call his attorney, etc. Aaranow finally exits with his grievances.

Roma is now alone with Lingk. Uncomfortable as he is, Lingk won't back down. His wife sent him to get the money back, period. There's no room for negotiation. Roma pours on the solicitude.

ROMA: . . . . . This is *me*. . . . This is Ricky, Jim. Jim, anything you *want,* you *want* it, you *have* it. You understand? This is *me*. Something *upset* you. Sit down, now sit down. You tell me what it is. *(Pause.)* Am I going to help you fix it?

You're goddamned right I am. Sit down. Tell you something . . . ? *Sometimes* we need someone from *outside*. It's . . . no, sit down . . . Now *talk* to me . . . . .

LINGK *(rising):* I can't talk to you, *you* met my wife, I . . . *(Pause.)*

ROMA: What? *(Pause.)* What? *(Pause.)* What, Jim: I tell you what, let's get out of here . . . let's go get a drink.

LINGK: She told me not to talk to you.

ROMA: Let's . . . no one's going to know, let's go around the *corner* and we'll get a drink.

LINGK: She told me I had to get back the check or call the State's att . . .

ROMA: *Forget* the deal, Jimmy. *(Pause.) Forget* the deal . . . you know me. The deal's *dead.* Am I talking about the *deal?* That's *over.* Please. Let's talk about *you.* Come on. *(Pause. Roma rises and starts walking toward the front door.)* Come on. *(Pause.)* Come on, Jim. *(Pause.)* I want to tell you something. Your life is your own. You have a contract with your wife. You have certain things you do *jointly,* you have a *bond* there . . . and there are *other* things. Those things are yours. You needn't feel *ashamed,* you needn't feel that you're being *untrue* . . . or that she would abandon you if she knew. This is your life. *(Pause.) Yes.* Now I want to *talk* to you because you're obviously upset and that *concerns* me. Now let's go. Right now.

Just as they start to leave, Baylen calls from the inner office door that he now wants to see Roma. The police presence alarms Lingk. Williamson enters from the office and tries to reassure Lingk by telling him about last night's burglary and letting him know that his contract had already gone through.

WILLIAMSON: Your contract went out to the bank.

LINGK: You cashed the check?

WILLIAMSON: We . . .

ROMA: . . . Mr. Williamson . . .

WILLIAMSON: Your check was cashed yesterday afternoon. And we're completely insured, as you know, in *any* case. *(Pause.)*

LINGK *(to Roma):* You cashed the check?

ROMA: Not to my knowledge, no . . .

WILLIAMSON: I'm sure we can . . .

LINGK: Oh, Christ . . . *(Starts out the door.)* Don't follow me. . . . Oh, Christ. *(Pause. To Roma:)* I know I've let you down. I'm sorry. For . . . Forgive . . . for . . . I don't know anymore. *(Pause.)* Forgive me. *(Lingk exits. Pause.)*

And now Roma turns all of his invective guns on Williamson. By opening his stupid mouth, Williamson has blown Roma's sale, costing him six thousand dollars and a Cadillac. "What are you going to do about it? What are you going to do about it, asshole. You fucking *shit.* Where did you learn your *trade.* You stupid fucking *cunt.* You *idiot.* Whoever told you you could work with *men?*"

Baylen tries to get Roma to come into the inner office now. Roma virtually orders the cop to shut up until he's finished telling off Williamson. Baylen backs down. Roma tells Williamson that he's going to see to it that Williamson gets fired for this. Williamson's a menace. He doesn't understand the philosophy behind the business he's in. He doesn't know the *rules,* rule number one being, "You never open your mouth till you know what the shot is." Roma goes into the inner office with Baylen.

Levene has come out during this, and he's only too happy to pick up where Roma left off. In the middle of his attack, he tells Williamson if he's "going to make something up, be sure it will *help* or keep your mouth closed." "How do you know I made it up?" Williamson asks.

The worm turns. The only way Levene could have known that Williamson hadn't sent the contracts to the bank is if he had seen them on Williamson's desk last night. And the only way he could have seen them is if he—Levene—was the one who robbed the office.

Levene tries to laugh it off, but Williamson knows he's hit the truth here. Either Levene tells him what he did with the leads, or he's going to turn Levene over to the detective. "If you tell me what you did with the leads, we can talk."

Levene cracks. Yes, he did steal the leads. He sold them to Jerry Graff. Yes, someone was in on it with him. Moss.

LEVENE: Okay: I . . . look: I'm going to make it worth your while. I am. I turned this thing around. I closed the *old* stuff, I can do it again. *I'm* the one's going to close 'em. *I* am! *I* am! 'Cause I turned this thing a . . . I can do *that,* I can do *anyth* . . . last night. I'm going to tell you, I was ready to Do the Dutch. Moss gets me, "Do this, we'll get well . . ." Why not. Big fuckin' deal. I'm halfway hoping to get caught. To put me out of my . . . *(Pause.)* But it *taught* me something. What it taught me, that you've got to get *out* there. Big deal. So I wasn't cut out to be a thief. I was cut out to be a salesman. And now I'm back, and I got my *balls* back . . . and, you know, John, you have the *advantage* on me now. Whatever it takes to make it right, we'll make it right. We're going to make it right.

WILLIAMSON: I want to tell you something, Shelly. You have a big mouth.
        Pause.
LEVENE: What?
WILLIAMSON: You've got a big mouth, and now I'm going to show you an even bigger one.
        Starts toward the detective's door.
LEVENE: Where are you going, John? . . . you can't do that, you don't want to do that . . . hold, hold on . . . hold on . . . wait . . . wait . . . wait . . . *(Pulls money out of his pockets.)* Wait . . . uh, look . . . *(Starts splitting money.)* Look, twelve, twenty, two, twen . . . twenty-five hundred, it's . . . take it. *(Pause.)* Take it all. . . . *(Pause.)* Take it!
WILLIAMSON: No, I don't think so, Shel.
LEVENE: I . . .
WILLIAMSON: No, I think I don't want your money. I think you fucked up my office. And I think you're going away.

Levene tries to make a deal with Williamson. He's hot again, he insists. The Nyborgs are just the beginning. And if Williamson gives him a break, he'll cut him in on 50 per cent of his action. Williamson says there's not going to be any action. The Nyborgs aren't a real sale. Williamson happens to know they're nuts. "They just like talking to salesmen." The check is worthless. The hot streak Levene thought he was on does not exist. And Williamson heads for the inner office to tell Baylen about Levene's part in the burglary. "Don't," Levene pleads.

WILLIAMSON: I'm sorry.
LEVENE: *Why?*
WILLIAMSON: Because I don't like you.
LEVENE: John: John: . . . my *daughter* . . .
WILLIAMSON: Fuck you.
Roma comes out of the detective's door. Williamson goes in.
ROMA: *(to Baylen):* Asshole. *(To Levene.)* Guy couldn't find his fuckin' couch the *living room* . . . Ah, Christ . . . what a day, what a day . . . I haven't even had a cup of *coffee.* . . . Jagoff John opens his mouth he blows my Cadillac. . . . *(Sighs.)* I swear . . . it's not a world of men . . . it's not a world of men, Machine . . . it's a world of clock watchers, bureaucrats, officeholders . . . what it is, it's a fucked-up world . . . there's no adventure *to* it. *(Pause.)* Dying breed. Yes it is. *(Pause.)* We are the members of a dying breed. That's . . . that's . . . that's why we have to stick together. Shel: I want to talk to you. I've wanted to talk to you for some time. For a long time, actually. I said, "The Machine, there's a man I would work with. There's a man . . ." You know? I never said a thing. I should have, don't know why I didn't. And that shit you were slinging on my guy today was *so* good . . . it . . . it was, and excuse me, 'cause it isn't even my place to say it. It was admirable . . . it was the old stuff. Hey, I've been on a hot streak, so *what?* There's things that I could learn from you. You eat today?
LEVENE: Me?
ROMA: Yeah.
LEVENE: Mm.
ROMA: Well, you want to swing by the Chinks, watch me eat, we'll talk?
LEVENE: I think I'd better stay here for a while.

Baylen comes out and demands Levene's presence in the inner office. Roma notices that Baylen is treating Levene somewhat roughly but doesn't know why. Baylen takes Levene to the inner office and closes the door, leaving Williamson on the outside with Roma.

ROMA: Williamson: listen to me: when the *leads* come in . . . listen to me: when the *leads* come in I want my top two off the list. For *me.* My usual two. Anything you give *Levene* . . .
WILLIAMSON: . . . I wouldn't worry about it.
ROMA: Well, I'm *going* to worry about it, and so are you, so shut up and *listen.* *(Pause.)* I GET HIS ACTION. My stuff is *mine,* whatever *he* gets for himself, I'm taking half. You put me in with him.
Aaranow enters.
AARANOW: Did they . . . ?
ROMA: You understand?
AARANOW: Did they catch . . . ?

ROMA: Do you understand? My stuff is mine, his stuff is ours. I'm taking half of his commissions—now, *you* work it out.
WILLIAMSON: Mmm.
AARANOW: Did they find the guy who broke into the office yet?
ROMA: No. *I* don't know.
    Pause.
AARANOW: Did the leads come in yet?
ROMA: No.
AARANOW *(settling into a desk chair):* Oh, God, I hate this job.
ROMA: *(simultaneously with "job," exiting the office):* I'll be at the restaurant.
    Curtain.

SUNDAY IN THE PARK WITH GEORGE

A Musical in Two Acts

BOOK BY JAMES LAPINE

MUSIC AND LYRICS BY STEPHEN SONDHEIM

Cast and credits appear on page 339

JAMES LAPINE (book) was born in 1949 in Mansfield, Ohio, where his father was a sales representative. He was educated at Franklin & Marshall (B.A. in history, 1971) and the California Institute of the Arts (M.F.A. in design, 1973). After a year in New York he landed a job in 1975 as a graphic designer for Yale Drama School and their magazine Yale Theater. *He had become interested in writing several years before, and while at Yale he adapted Gertrude Stein's three-page poem* Photograph *for the stage, directing it in New Haven and in its Obie Award-winning production in 1977 off off Broadway at The Open Space in Soho.*

The following year, Lapine wrote and directed Twelve Dreams *for production OOB by Lyn Austin's Music-Theater Performing Group/Lenox Arts Center. His* Table Settings *was produced OOB in 1979 under its author's direction in the Manhattan Workshop Series at Playwrights Horizons before being brought to a full-scale, 264-performance off-Broadway production on Jan. 14, 1980, its author's professional New York theater debut and his first Best Play. The following season*

217

he directed William Finn's musical March of the Falsettos, *launching it into a 268-performance off-Broadway run. In late 1981 he directed his own* Twelve Dreams *off Broadway at New York Shakespeare Festival and staged the same group's outdoor production of* A Midsummer Night's Dream *in Central Park the summer of 1982. This season he has been occupied in collaboration as book writer and director with Stephen Sondheim, author of the score, of the musical* Sunday in the Park With George *produced in workshop at Playwrights Horizons and then on Broadway May 2, 1984, receiving Lapine's second Best Play citation and the Critics Award for the best musical of the season.*

Lapine acknowledges the support of the Millay Colony and the Albee Foundation in furthering his playwriting career. He lives in New York City.

STEPHEN SONDHEIM *(music, lyrics) was born March 22, 1930 in New York City. The Oscar Hammerstein IIs were family friends, and it was under Hammerstein's influence and guidance that young Sondheim became interested in the theater and was induced to write a musical for his school (George School, a Friends school in Bucks County, Pa.). At Williams College he won the Hutchinson Prize for musical composition. After receiving his B.A. he studied theory and composition with Milton Babbitt. He wrote scripts for the* Topper *TV series and incidental music for the Broadway productions of* Girls of Summer *(1956) and* Invitation to a March *(1961).*

It was as a lyricist that Sondheim first commanded major attention, however. He'd written a show called Saturday Night *which never made it to Broadway; but Arthur Laurents remembered it, liked the lyrics and took steps to bring Sondheim into collaboration on the great* West Side Story *(1957) as its lyricist. Sondheim then wrote both music and lyrics for the hit musical* A Funny Thing Happened on the Way to the Forum *(1962) and* Anyone Can Whistle *(1964), as well as for his five straight Best Plays and Critics Award winners directed by Harold Prince:* Company *(1970),* Follies *(1971),* A Little Night Music *(1973, and Sondheim's third straight Tony Award as best composer and lyricist),* Pacific Overtures *(1976) and* Sweeney Todd, the Demon Barber of Fleet Street *(1979, and another best-score Tony). Prince also directed the 1981 musical adaptation of George S. Kaufman's and Moss Hart's* Merrily We Roll Along *with Sondheim music and lyrics. This season's Sondheim collaboration with James Lapine, book writer and director of* Sunday in the Park With George, *is the composer-lyricist's sixth Best Play and Critics Award winner, in what has certainly been and continues to be one of the most distinguished American musical theater careers ever.*

Other major Sondheim credits include the lyrics for Gypsy *(1959) and* Do I Hear a Waltz? *(1965), additional lyrics for the 1974 revival of* Candide *(still another Sondheim-Prince winner of the Critics Award) and two anthology programs of his songs:* Side by Side by Sondheim *on Broadway in 1977 and* Marry Me a Little *off Broadway in 1981. Other works have included the incidental music for the play* Twigs, *co-authorship with Anthony Perkins of the movie script for* The Last of Sheila, *the scores of the movies* Stavisky *and* Reds, *the music and lyrics for Burt Shevelove's adaptation of Aristophanes's* The Frogs, *staged in the Yale University swimming pool, and songs for the TV production* Evening Primrose.

Sondheim is on the council of the Dramatists Guild, the professional association of playwrights, composers, lyricists and librettists, and served as its president from 1973 to 1981, during which period it greatly expanded services to its members. He is a member of the American Academy and Institute of Arts and Letters and lives in New York City.

Act I: *A series of Sundays from 1884 to 1886, alternating between a park on an island in the Seine outside of Paris and George's studio*

Act II: *1984 at an American art museum and on the island*

ACT I

SYNOPSIS: This musical characterizes in dialogue and song 16 of the persons in Georges Seurat's "A Sunday Afternoon on the Island of La Grande Jatte" (see the illustrations on the next two pages of this synopsis) and, finally, poses them in a composition and setting which looks like that painting. These invented James Lapine-Stephen Sondheim characters who duplicate many of the painting's subjects onstage are identified in the photo caption on page 221 and numbered for cross-reference in this text.

The opening curtain rises on an expanse of white, suggesting a new canvas, framed by the proscenium arch at the top, sides and bottom too. George, an artist, enters and sits downstage with a large drawing pad and a box of chalk. *"He is . . . . . tall, dark beard, wearing a soft felt hat with a very narrow brim crushed down at the neck, and a short jacket. He looks rather intense."* As he reflectively considers "Order . . . . . design . . . . . composition . . . . . balance . . . . . light . . . . . harmony," the whiteness is replaced by a green riverside park scene. Trees and a strolling couple in two-dimensional cut-out silhouette are tracked onstage, as though George were adding them to his canvas. The scene is lit for early morning, and music is heard.

George summons his model Dot (#16 in tableau on page 221), wearing *"a traditional 19th century outfit: full-length dress with bustle."* He poses her for sketching. He commands her to stand still and concentrate on her pose, though she is uncomfortable in her fashionable dress.

> DOT *(sigh):* I read they're even wearing them in America.
> GEORGE: They are fighting Indians in America—and you cannot read.
> DOT: I can read . . . a little.
> > *Pause.*
> Why did we have to get up so early?
> GEORGE: The light.
> DOT: Oh.
> > *George lets out a moan.*
> What's the matter?

GEORGE *(erasing feverishly):* I hate this tree.
    A tree rises back into the fly space. Music stops.
DOT *(hurt):* I thought you were drawing me.
GEORGE *(muttering):* I am. I am. Just stand still.

    The landscape changes as George sketches it. An Old Lady (#6 in tableau) and her Nurse (#5 in tableau) enter and take their places under their usual tree. Boats appear on the river, as Dot grows more and more uncomfortable in the heat of the sun (George is in the shade). Music returns in the form of arpeggios, and soon Dot is singing "Sunday in the Park With George."

    DOT *(sings):*
        Artists are bizarre, fixed. Cold.
        That's you, George, you're bizarre. Fixed. Cold.
        I like that in a man. Fixed. Cold.
        God, it's hot out here.

        Well, there are worse things
        Than staring at the water on a Sunday.
        There are worse things
        Than staring at the water
        As you're posing for a picture
        Being painted by your lover
        In the middle of the summer
        On an island in the river on a Sunday . . . . .

    In fantasy, Dot wriggles out of her dress, leaving it standing there by itself. George continues drawing as though Dot were still in it, and Dot continues

On opposite page is a photo of Georges Seurat's painting "A Sunday Afternoon on the Island of La Grande Jatte." *Above* is the tableau suggested by that painting and posed onstage in the Act I finale of *Sunday in the Park With George.* The tableau characters as imagined in James Lapine's book and Stephen Sondheim's score (and identified by number in the accompanying synopsis) are as follows, *left to right:* 1) Boatman (William Parry, reclining); 2) Franz, a servant (Brent Spiner in top hat); 3) Frieda, a cook (Nancy Opel, sitting); 4) Celeste #1 (Melanie Vaughan, fishing); 5) Nurse (Judith Moore, back to camera) attending (6) an Old Lady, the artist's mother (Barbara Bryne, seated and holding parasol); 7) Soldier (Robert Westenberg); 8) Louise, a child (Danielle Ferland) with 9) Yvonne, her mother (Dana Ivey, holding parasol); 10) Woman (Sue Anne Gershenson, seated, wearing dark hat); 11) Man (John Jellison, seated, wearing black bowler); 12) Celeste #2 (Mary D'Arcy, seated, hatless); 13) Louis, a baker (Cris Groenendaal, holding baby); 14) "Mr." (Kurt Knudson, wearing light suit); 15) Jules, an artist (Charles Kimbrough, wearing black topper; and 16) Dot (Bernadette Peters, holding parasol). The two dogs and the monkey are two-dimensional cut-out silhouettes, as are the figures of a man (partly hidden behind fisherwoman), a woman with parasol standing in background *left* and one seated in foreground *right center,* a child in front of "Mr." and a woman seated at extreme right.

singing about modeling and being in love with an artist, posing to the music's rhythms and finally getting back into the dress, as George, continuously sketching, cautions her to hold still.

The Nurse opens the Old Lady's parasol for her as Franz (#2 in tableau) enters. The Nurse, obviously interested in him, tries to strike up a conversation, but the Old Lady demands attention.

There is a commotion from across the river, and a wagon trucks in portraying a tableau-vivant of Seurat's "Bathing at Asnières." Jules, a fellow-artist

(#15 in tableau), and Yvonne (#9 in tableau) enter. They criticize George's painting.

JULES *(sings):*
    It has no presence.
YVONNE *(sings):*
    No passion.
JULES:
    No life. *(They laugh.)*
    It's neither pastoral
    Nor lyrical.
YVONNE *(giggling):*
    You don't suppose that it's satirical?
        They laugh heartily.
JULES:
    Just density
    Without intensity—
YVONNE:
    No life . . . . .
    It's so mechanical.
JULES:
    Methodical.
YVONNE:
    It might be in some dreary
    Socialist peri-
    Odical.
JULES *(approvingly):* Good.
YVONNE:
    So drab, so cold.
JULES:
    And so controlled.
BOTH:
    No life.

Jules, a painter of reputation, tips his hat to the Old Lady and exchanges pleasantries with George but avoids direct comment on George's painting, which he and Yvonne have just been ridiculing ("I hate them," says Dot, sensing their condescension). Jules and Yvonne depart with Franz, their servant.

Dot is proud of her concentration on this morning's poses, but George seems indifferent, sending her off alone when she expected they'd leave the park together. She is so obviously disappointed that he promises to take her to the Follies that evening. After Dot leaves, George goes over to greet the Nurse and Old Lady who, it turns out, is his mother.

The scene shifts to a studio where George, on a ladder, is painting a large canvas while Dot is at the makeup table, looking like the painting "La Poudreuse," rhythmically powdering her face and talking to herself about the impor-

tance of concentration (as George has taught her) and George's habit of sometimes spending a whole night painting.

> *Lights down on Dot, up on George. A number of brushes in his hand,*
> *he is covering a section of the canvas—the face of the woman in the*
> *foreground—with tiny specks of paint, in the same rhythm as Dot's*
> *powdering.*

GEORGE *(pauses, checks):* Order. *(Dabs with another color, pauses, checks, dabs*
palette.) Design. *(Dabs with another brush.)* Composition. Tone. Form. Symme-
try. Balance. *(Sings "Color and Light.")*

More red. *(Dabs with more intensity.)*
And a little more red. *(Switches brushes.)*
Blue blue blue blue
Blue blue blue blue
Even even . . . *(Switches quickly.)*
Good . . .
(Humming.) Bumbum bum bumbumbum
Bumbum bum . . . *(Paints silently for a moment.)*

More red . . . *(Switches brushes again.)*
More blue . . . *(Again.)*
More beer . . .
> Takes a swig from a nearby bottle, always eyeing the canvas, puts the
> bottle down.

More light!
> *He dabs assiduously, delicately attacking the area he is painting.*

Color and light.
There's only color and light.
Yellow and white.
Just blue and yellow and white.
> *Addressing the woman he is painting.*

Look at the air, Miss—
> *Dabs at the space in front of her.*

See what I mean?
No, look over there, Miss—
> *Dabs at her eye, pauses, checks it.*

That's done with green . . .
> *Swirling a brush in the orange cup.*

Conjoined with orange . . .

Dot, at her vanity, picks up the song in the same rhythm, but her lyrics
concern her appearance and how, if it were improved here and there, she might
be a much-admired Follies girl. George talks to the figures in his painting,
saying to the man in the right foreground, "And you, sir. Your hat so black. So
black to you, perhaps. So red to me." He proceeds to another verse of "Color
and Light."

GEORGE *(muttering, trance-like, as he paints):*
Red red red red
Red red orange
Red red orange
Orange pick up blue
Pick up red
Pick up orange
From the blue-green blue-green
Blue-green circle
On the violet diagonal
Di-ag-ag-ag-ag-ag-o-nal-nal
Yellow comma, yellow comma
    Humming, massaging his numb wrist.
Numnum num numnumnum
Numnum num
    Sniffs, smelling Dot's perfume.
Blue blue blue blue
Blue still sitting
Red that perfume
Blue all night
Blue-green the window shut
Dut dut dut
Dot Dot sitting
Dot Dot waiting
Dot Dot getting fat fat fat
More yellow
Dot Dot waiting to go
Out out out but
No no no George
Finish the hat finish the hat
Have to finish the hat first
Hat hat hat hat
Hot hot hot it's hot in here . . .
    Whistles a bit, then joyfully
Sunday!

Color and light!

Dot watches George, impressed by his concentration on his work, alternating with him in singing additional "Color and Light" lyric lines. They are fascinated looking at each other—she with lover's eyes, he with painter's eyes. And it seems they're not going to the Follies after all, because George insists on finishing the hat. Dot, grievously disappointed, leaves the studio.

On another Sunday in the park, George is sketching the Boatman (#1 in tableau), who dresses as he does to repel people. The Nurse and the Old Lady are present, as are Celeste #1 (#4 in tableau) and Celeste #2 (#12 in tableau), who are gossiping.

Dot comes in on the arm of Louis the baker (#13 in tableau). Jules and Yvonne arrive and stand posed to one side.

>*Music continues under, slow and stately.*
JULES: They say he is working on an enormous canvas.
YVONNE: I heard somewhere he's painting little specks.
JULES: You heard it from me! A large canvas of specks. Really . . .
YVONNE: Look at him. Drawing a slovenly boatman.
JULES: I think he is trying to play with light.
YVONNE: What next?
JULES: A monkey cage, they say.
>*They laugh.*
BOATMAN: Sunday hypocrites. That's what they are. Muttering and murmuring about this one and that one. I'll take my old dog for company any day. A dog knows his place. Respects your privacy. Makes no demands. Right, Spot?
GEORGE *(as Spot):* Right.

The music continues, and the visitors to the park sing "Gossip," the Celestes commenting on George's habit of walking the streets at night, others making remarks about each other.

Dot has brought a red grammar textbook to the park and is reading laboriously about pronouns. Yvonne's daughter Louise (#8 in tableau) comes in and tries to pat the dog. The Boatman, furious, orders her to get away, and she leaves in tears. George starts to remonstrate, but the Boatman turns on him: "Who are you, with your fancy pad and crayons. You call that work? You smug goddamn holier-than-thou shitty little men in your fancy clothes—born with pens and pencils, not pricks. You don't know!"

The Boatman stalks off, and George turns to sketching the dog Spot. The Celestes come to see what he's doing and learn to their irritation that they have already been sketched by George unawares.

George goes over to greet Dot.

GEORGE: Good afternoon.
DOT: Hello.
GEORGE: Lesson number eight?
DOT: Yes. Pronouns. My writing is improving. I even keep notes in the back.
GEORGE: Good for you.
DOT: How is your painting coming along?
GEORGE: Slowly.
DOT: Are you getting more work done now that you have fewer distractions in the studio?
GEORGE *(a beat):* It has been quiet there.
>*Louis bounds onstage with a pastry tin.*
LOUIS: I made your favorite—
>*He stops when he sees George.*
GEORGE: Good day.

> *George moves downstage to Spot and sits. Dot watches him, then turns
> to Louis.*
> LOUIS *(opens the tin):* Creampuffs!

The lights change, and soon George is alone with the dog, trying to work him
into the composition on his sketch pad. George imagines what Spot is thinking
and what his life is like in the song "The Day Off."

> GEORGE *(as Spot, barks):*
> Ruff! Ruff!
> Thanks, the week has been
> *(Barks.)* Rough!
> When you're stuck for life on a garbage scow—
> *Sniffs around.*
> Only forty feet long from stern to prow,
> And a crackpot in the bow—wow, rough!
> *Sniffs.*
> The planks are rough
> And the wind is rough
> And the master's drunk and mean and—
> *Sniffs.*
> Grrrruff! Gruff!
> With the fish and scum
> And planks and ballast . . .
> *Sniffs.*
> The nose gets numb
> And the paws get calloused.
> And with splinters in your ass,
> You look forward to the grass
> On Sunday.
> The day off.
> *(Barks.)* Off! Off!
> Off!

A lap dog, Fifi, also appears (as a cut-out), and George assumes this little dog's
personality too.

> GEORGE *(as Fifi):*
> Yap! Yap!
> *(Pants.)* Yap!
>
> Out for the day on Sunday,
> Off of my lady's lap at last.
> Yapping away on Sunday
> Helps you forget the week just past—
> *(Yelps.)* Yep!
> Everything's worth it Sunday,

The day off.
Yep!
Stuck all week on a lady's lap.
Nothing to do but yawn and nap.
Can you blame me if I yap?
(As Spot.) Nope.

Some of the people stroll back: first the Nurse, then the Celestes, who have spotted a pair of Soldiers (#7 in tableau and his silent companion, a cut-out) and manage to attract their attention. Louise wants Frieda the cook (#3 in tableau) to play with her, but Franz wants Frieda's attention—after all, it's their day off. They notice that George is sketching them. Franz, continuing the song "The Day Off," tells Frieda in lyrics, "While he 'creates'/We scrape their plates/And dust their knickknacks/Hundreds to a shelf/Work is what you do for others/Liebchen/Art is what you do for yourself."
    Jules comes over to advise George to take some time off, meet people, have fun. George replies by asserting that Jules doesn't like his painting.

JULES: I did once.
GEORGE: You find it too tight.
JULES: People are talking about your work. You have your admirers, but you—
GEORGE: I'm using a different brushstroke.
JULES *(getting angry):* Always changing! Why keep changing?
GEORGE: Because I do not paint for your approval.
        Beat.
JULES: And I suppose that is why I like you.

George invites Jules to his studio for further consultation on George's work. As Jules drifts off, George again busies himself with sketching the Boatman, then exits, while Dot considers her relationship with Louis the baker in the song "Everybody Loves Louis."

DOT *(sings):*
    . . . . . Louis' always so pleasant.
    Louis' always so fair.
    Louis makes you feel present,
    Louis' generous.
    That's the thing about Louis:
    Louis always is "there."
    Louis' thoughts are not hard to follow,
    Louis' art is not hard to swallow.

    Not that Louis' perfection—
    That's what makes him ideal,
    Hardly anything worth objection:
    Louis drinks a bit,

Louis blinks a bit.
Louis makes a connection,
That's the thing that you feel . . .

We lose things.
And then we choose things.
And there are Louis's
And there are Georges—
Well, Louis's
And George.
But George has George
And I need—
Someone—
Louis—

A tourist couple—"Mr." (#14 in tableau) and "Mrs."—comes into the park, followed by George busily sketching them. They like nothing in this country but the pastries, and they decide to book passage home immediately, taking a baker with them.

The Soldier and his cut-out companion make friends with the Celestes and promenade off.

George, alone onstage, muses in song about Dot's leaving him because she did not understand "How you have to finish the hat" no matter what other distractions are claiming your attention. "And how you're always turning back too late/From the grass or the stick/Or the dog or the light," George continues in the lyrics of the song "Finishing the Hat."

GEORGE (sings):
. . . . . Studying the hat,
Entering the world of the hat,
Reaching through the world of the hat
Like a window,
Back to this one from that.
Studying a face,
Stepping back to look at a face
Leaves a little space in the way like a window,
But to see—
It's the only way to see.

And when the woman that you wanted goes,
You can say to yourself, "Well, I give what I give."
But the woman who won't wait for you knows
That, however you live,
There's a part of you always standing by,
Mapping out the sky,
Finishing a hat . . .
Starting on a hat . . .
Finishing a hat . . .

Shows sketch to Fifi.
Look, I made a hat . . .
Where there never was a hat . . .

Mr. and Mrs. return—they are lost and wandering, and when they ask directions of the Boatman he is deliberately rude to them. They see Louis the baker
and go after him. The park scene ends with characters singing fragments of songs
and watching as Dot confronts George and silently turns her dress around with
the bustle facing front, pantomiming a pregnancy.

In the studio, the big painting of the park is just about finished, and Dot, who
has only two more months of her pregnancy to go, has come to ask George for
a souvenir of their relationship: the painting of Dot at her vanity, powdering. Dot
means to go through with marrying Louis, who will have her in spite of her
condition, even though, as George comments, Louis is probably not what Dot
really wants. "I don't think I can have what I really want," Dot tells him, "Louis
is what I think I need."

Jules and Yvonne come in, and Jules studies the new painting while Yvonne
joins Dot. Dot is very cool to Yvonne, believing that they don't like George's
work and that Jules is actually jealous of it. George is too obsessive about his
work, Jules and Yvonne believe—even an artist ought to have a life outside his
work. On this point, Dot agrees.

Looking at the painting, Jules doesn't quite know what to make of it.

GEORGE: What is the dominant color? The flower on the hat?
JULES: Is this a school exam, George?
GEORGE: What is that color?
JULES *(bored):* Violet.
        George takes him by the hand and moves him closer to the canvas.
GEORGE: See? Red and blue. Your eyes made the violet.
JULES: So?
GEORGE: So, your eye is perceiving both red and blue *and* violet. Only eleven
colors—no black—divided, not mixed on the palette, mixed by the eye. Can't you
see the shimmering?
JULES *(approaches the canvas):* George . . .
GEORGE: Science, Jules. Fixed laws for color, like music.
JULES: You are a painter, not a scientist! You cannot even see these faces!
GEORGE: I am not painting faces! . . . . .

George is trying to go in a direction uniquely his own, and he hopes Jules will
help him get this painting into the next group show. Jules agrees to think it over
before departing with Yvonne.

Dot has something to tell George: she is planning to go to America with Louis
after the baby arrives. Dot senses that George doesn't really care whether she
stays or goes, and George finds it difficult to explain that he is living in his painting
and—at the very least—would care about her because she is in it too. Dot
expresses her feelings in the song "We Do Not Belong Together," singing to
George, "You could tell me not to go." But on George's part, "There's nothing

to say/I cannot be what you want." Dot realizes that she and George are uniquely
themselves and "We do not belong together/And we'll never belong—!/You have
a mission/A mission to see/Now I have one too, George/And we should have
belonged together/I have to move on."

Dot departs, as the scene changes to the park, where George is sketching the
Old Lady, his mother, and she is reminiscing about his childhood. In the song
"Beautiful," the Old Lady regrets the passing of natural beauty to make way for
man-made structures. George, on the other hand, is convinced that "All things
are beautiful" to those who can open their eyes and see.

Others come into the park including Mr. and Mrs. with their trunk and
acquisitions, Celese #2 and Soldier (who have ditched their companions),
Louise, Boatman, Louis and Dot—carrying in her arms her newborn baby,
Marie. Dot brings the baby over to George, who is sketching.

DOT: . . . . . George, we are about to leave for America. I have come to ask
for the painting of me powdering again. I would like to take it with me.
GEORGE *(stops for a moment):* Oh? I have repainted it.
      He draws.
DOT: What?
GEORGE: Another model.
DOT: You knew I wanted it.
GEORGE: Perhaps if you had remained still—
DOT: Perhaps if you would look up from your pad! What is wrong with you,
George? Can you not even look at your own child?
GEORGE: She is not my child. Louis is her father.
DOT: Louis is not her father.
GEORGE: Louis is her father now. Louis will be a loving and attentive father.
I cannot because I cannot look up from my pad.
      She stands speechless for a moment, then begins to walk away.
Dot. I am sorry.

George continues sketching the Old Lady, who fears that George is such a
dreamer he is detached from the rest of the world despite all efforts to get through
to him. George ceases drawing long enough to advise himself ruefully, "Connect,
George. Connect . . ."

Frieda comes in with Jules, having evaded their usual companions Franz and
Yvonne, looking for a place to make love. But Louise has spied on them and tips off
her mother and Franz as to what is going on. Soon *"all hell breaks loose and the
arguments erupt into total chaos,"* in a large melee observed by George and his
mother. At the sound of an arpeggiated chord, all suddenly freeze. Then, at
George's direction "Order . . . . . Design . . . . . Tension . . . . . Balance . . . . .
Harmony," they move toward the places he has assigned to them, while he himself
makes final adjustments to the positioning of the cut-outs. They are singing about
their "perfect park" with its "green elliptical grass" in the song "Sunday."

ALL *(sing):*
      . . . . . By the blue

Purple yellow red water
On the green
Orange violet mass
Of the grass
In our perfect park,
Made of flecks of light
And dark,
And parasols:
People strolling through the trees
Of a small suburban park
On an island in the river
On an ordinary Sunday . . .

A horn sounds. Chimes. They all reach their positions.

Sunday . . .

The horn again. Everyone turns, into their final poses, as George freezes them. He comes out to the apron.

Sunday . . .

The horn. They all suddenly shut their mouths. The picture is complete. At the last moment, George rushes back into the frame and removes Louise's eyeglasses. As he dashes back on to the apron, the completed canvas flies in. Final chord. Blackout. Curtain.

ACT II

The tableau is as it was at the end of Act I, with the characters in the painting frozen in a long pause; then Dot breaks silence with the first line of the song "It's Hot Up Here." The others begin arguing with each other and complaining in song, "It's hot up here/A lot up here/It's hot up here/Forever."

DOT *(sings):*
Hello, George.
I do not wish to be remembered
Like this, George,
With them, George.
My hem, George:
Three inches off the ground
And then this monkey
And these people, George—

They'll argue till they fade
And whisper things and grunt.
But thank you for the shade,
And putting me in front.
Yes, thank you, George, for that . . .

And for the hat . . .

The characters in the painting continue arguing and complaining about the heat. Then they turn to reminiscing about the past, breaking their poses and exiting one after the other. Dot remembers that she was in Charleston when she heard about George's death at the age of 31. Jules admits that George had "great promise . . . . . an unusual flair for color and light." Yvonne suggests that most women, including herself, fancied him. "But they hated him too," the Boatman observes, "Hated him because he only spoke when he absolutely had to. Most of all they hated him because they knew he would always be around."

Soon the painting's characters have all exited, the cut-outs have been dispersed and the stage returned to its white condition as at the beginning of Act I. *"Lights change. Electronic music. It is 1984."* The scene is the auditorium of the American museum which owns and displays the now-famous painting of the park. The painter's great grandson George, 32, clean-shaven (and played by George), enters with his grandmother, Marie (Dot's daughter, played by Dot), 98 and confined to a wheelchair.

George's assistant Dennis rolls onto the stage an immense white machine, "Chromolume #7," a creation of George's to be introduced here as part of a special ceremony honoring his ancestor's, Georges Seurat's, painting "A Sunday Afternoon on the Island of La Grande Jatte." Marie too has been invited to take part in this celebration of the work of both her father and her grandson. It begins with a film about Seurat, narrated by George and Marie.

GEORGE: Georges Seurat.

MARIE: Born December 2, 1859.

GEORGE: It was through his mother that the future artist was introduced to the lower-class Parisian parks. Seurat received a classical training at the Beaux Arts.

MARIE: Like his father, he was not an easy man to know.

GEORGE: He lived in an age when science was gaining influence over romantic principles.

MARIE: He worked very hard.

GEORGE: His first painting, at the age of twenty-four, "Bathing at Asnières," was rejected by the Salon, but was shown by the Group of Independent Artists.

MARIE: They hung it over the refreshment stand. Wasn't that awful?

GEORGE: On Ascension Day 1884, he began work on his second painting, "A Sunday Afternoon on the Island of La Grande Jatte." He was to work two years on this painting.

MARIE: He always knew where he was going before he picked up a paint brush.

GEORGE: He denied conventional perspective and conventional space . . . . . Having studied scientific findings on color, he developed a new style of painting. He found by painting tiny particles, color next to color, that at a certain distance the eye would fuse the specks optically, giving them greater intensity than any mixed pigments.

MARIE: He wanted to paint with colored lights.

GEORGE: Beams of colored light, he hoped.

MARIE: It was shown at the eighth and last Impressionist Exhibition.

GEORGE: Monet, Renoir and Sisley withdrew their submissions because of his painting.

Mandy Patinkin as George *(foreground)*, William Parry as Boatman (with eye patch), Cris Groenendaal as Louis (fourth from *right*) and Bernadette Peters as Dot (third from *right*) and others in a scene from *Sunday in the Park With George*

Seurat's painting was not a popular success. He painted six more major works (selling none) before he died. Now his great grandson, George, pays homage to "La Grande Jatte" with his latest Chromolume, which he proceeds to activate. It gives off light and color, but the electricity fails in a puff of smoke. George and his assistants fiddle with the apparatus while the museum director reminds the audience that after the presentation and dinner, condominiums built with the air rights over the museum will be available for inspection.

George announces that his Chromolume is now readjusted, and he turns it on once again. It emits blazes and shafts of light, to musical accompaniment, with various spectacular effects including strobes and lasers and spreading a pointillist pattern over its surroundings.

Meanwhile, Marie is telling the audience of her kinship with the painter and her possession of a red grammar book her mother gave her, with handwritten notes mentioning George in the back.

The Chromolume display ends with a final burst of light, after which the scene changes and the painting itself is the backdrop for a reception. The discussion of George's light show is a mixture of pros and cons in the language of art connoisseurs, expressed partly in song lyrics to the music of the Act I number, "The Day Off."

The museum director introduces George to an influential couple who admire his work, which he considers a combination of sculpture and invention. He reminds himself in the form of a song—"Putting it Together"—that he'd better make an effort with these well-heeled guests at the reception, because "Art isn't easy/Even when you're hot/Advancing art is easy/Financing it is not." Marie tells one of the guests that she and George have been invited to France for a Chromolume demonstration on the island, and that the contraptions "take a year to make . . . . . the minute he finishes one, he starts raising money for the next."

George is encouraged by enthusiasm for his work expressed by the representative of a lucrative family foundation and the agent for a well-endowed Texas museum. He leaves life-sized cutouts of himself with groups of guests while he steps forward for more of the song "Putting It Together," which is about "the art of making art."

GEORGE *(sings):*
　　Link by link,
　　Making the connections . . .
　　Drink by drink,
　　Fixing and perfecting the design.
　　Adding just a dab of politician
　　(Always knowing where to draw the line),
　　Lining up the funds but in addition
　　Lining up a prominent commission,
　　Otherwise your perfect composition
　　Isn't going to get much exhibition.

　　Art isn't easy.
　　Every minor detail
　　Is a major decision,
　　Have to keep things in scale,
　　Have to hold to your vision—
　　　　Pauses for a split second.
　　Every time I start to feel defensive,
　　I remember lasers are expensive.
　　What's a little cocktail conversation
　　If it's going to get you your foundation,
　　Leading to a prominent commission
　　And an exhibition in addition?

George chats with various other people including his technical assistant Dennis (who is feeling the pressure and wants to quit) and an art critic who believes that three or four Chromolumes were enough: "We have been there before, you know." George manages to keep his temper and concludes, "The art of making art/Is putting it together/Bit by bit—/Link by link—/Drink by drink—/Mink by mink—/And that/Is the state/Of the art."

Marie is positioned near the painting and discusses a detail of it with one of the guests, to whom she finally declares, "There are only two worthwhile things to leave behind when you depart this world: children and art." Elaine—George's divorced wife—goes over to George and encourages him—in vain—to enjoy his success. Marie then sings to Dot in the painting about her great grandson George in the song "Children and Art."

MARIE *(sings:)*
>   He should be happy—
>   Mama, he's blue.
>   What do I do?
>
>   You should have seen it,
>   It was a sight!
>   Mama, I mean it—
>   All color and light—!
>   I don't understand what it was,
>   But, Mama, the things that he does—
>   They twinkle and shimmer and buzz—
>   You would have liked them . . .
>   It . . .
>   Him . . .

George comes over, and in the guise of quoting her mother Dot, Marie advises her grandson, "It's not so much do what you like/As it is that you like what you do." Marie falls asleep, and Elaine wheels her offstage, leaving George to contemplate the painting and tell himself, "Connect, George. Connect."

"The painting flies out and the island is once again revealed, though this time it is barely recognizable because it is the present, and the trees are now replaced by high-rise buildings." George and Dennis are planning the placing and plugging-in of their Chromolume. George, it seems, has turned down the Texas museum commission, and he wants to know the real reason why Dennis is leaving after this show.

DENNIS: George. I love the Chromolumes. People really enjoy them. But I've helped you build the last five, and now I want to do something different.
GEORGE: I wish you had told me that in the first place.
DENNIS: I'm sorry.
GEORGE: Why do you think I turned down the commission? I don't want to do the same thing over and over again either.
DENNIS: There are other things you could do.
GEORGE: I know that. I just want to do something I care about.
DENNIS: Yeah . . . I see you brought the red book.
GEORGE: Since Marie died, I thought I would at least bring something of hers along.

Dennis exits to go back to the hotel. George leafs through the book, reciting some of its grammar examples, beginning the song "Lesson #8." He starts inserting his own name into simplified sentences: "George looks ahead/George sees the dark/George is afraid/Where are the people/Out strolling on Sunday?" He has been looking for a family connection, but all he can see is one old tree that may have been in his great-grandfather's painting. He concludes, "George looks around/George is alone/No use denying/George is aground/George has outgrown/What he can do/George would have liked to see/People out strolling on Sunday . . ."

George looks up to see that Dot has joined him—Dot who recognizes her red grammar in his hand and speaks to him as though he were her long-ago lover: "You taught me concentration . . . . . I worried too much about tomorrow. I thought the world could be perfect. I was wrong." George confesses that he isn't working on anything and doesn't know what to do next. Dot advises in song, "Move On."

DOT *(sings):*
. . . . . Look at what you want,
Not at where you are,
Not at what you'll be.
Look at all the things you've done for me:

Opened up my eyes,
Taught me how to see,
Notice every tree—
GEORGE *(sings):*
. . . Notice every tree . . .
DOT *(sings):*
Understand the light—
Just keep moving on.

Anything you do,
Let it come from you.
Then it will be new.

Give us more to see . . .

George is impressed with the notes handwritten in the back of the grammar and asks Dot about them. She explains to George that they are words her George would repeat over and over to himself at work, beginning with "Order." As George reads aloud this word in the grammar, the Old Lady appears and asks him if the park is as he expected it would be.

GEORGE: Well, the greens are a little darker . . . the sky a little greyer . . . mud tones in the water . . .
OLD LADY *(disappointed):* Well, yes, I suppose—
GEORGE: But the air seems rich and full of light.
OLD LADY: Good.
Chord. As the Old Lady leaves. George reads the next word.
GEORGE: "Design."
He raises his hand to the downstage right building and it begins to rise.

Music begins. One of the characters from the painting appears and begins to cross the stage.

"Tension."

He raises two buildings stage right and left. More people appear and begin to promenade.

"Composition. Balance."

Two more buildings rise. More people.

"Light."

The large opaque building in the back rises.

Dot. I cannot read this word.

DOT: Harmony.

The company begins to sing "Sunday."

GEORGE *(reads):* "So much love in his words . . . forever with his colors . . . how George looks . . . he can look forever . . . what does he see? . . . his eyes so dark and shiny . . . so careful . . . so exact . . ."

Dot takes George by the arm and they begin to stroll amongst the people. When the strollers reach the word "forever," they stop and bow to George. Then, their singing diminishing, they start to exit very slowly. George remains on the apron, and Dot is the only one left in the park. The white canvas drop begins to descend in front of her.

(Reads from the book.) "White. A blank page or canvas. His favorite. So many possibilities . . ."

George looks up and sees Dot fade behind the canvas. Lights fade to black. Curtain.

THE MISS FIRECRACKER
CONTEST

A Play in Two Acts

BY BETH HENLEY

Cast and credits appear on pages 361, 362

BETH HENLEY was born in Jackson, Miss. in 1932, the daughter of a lawyer. After graduation from high school she attended Southern Methodist University, receiving her B.S.A. in 1974 and going on to the graduate program in acting at the University of Illinois. She had written a play and the book for a musical while still in college. The world premiere of her first professionally-produced playscript, Crimes of the Heart, *took place in regional theater at the Actors Theater of Louisville in February 1979. The play was repeated at the California Actors' Theater in Los Gatos in April 1979, at the Loretto-Hilton Theater in St. Louis in October 1979 and at Center Stage, Baltimore in April 1980, finally reaching New York Dec. 9, 1980 for 35 performances at Manhattan Theater Club, where it was named a Best Play of its season and won the Critics Award for best American play and the Pulitzer Prize. On Nov. 4, 1981* Crimes of the Heart *was transferred to Broadway for an additional New York run of 535 performances.*

Miss Henley's second play, The Miss Firecracker Contest, *did not reach New York until after her third,* The Wake of Jamey Foster, *had been produced on Broadway in October 1982 for 12 performances, following its world premiere at Hartford Stage in January of that same year. Miss Firecracker premiered at the Studio Arena Theater in Buffalo in September 1981 and moved on to three more regional stagings and a production at the Bush Theater in London before making its New York bow to considerable applause and a Best Play citation, Miss Henley's second, at Manhattan Theater Club May 1, 1984.*

Still another of Miss Henley's plays, the one-acter Am I Blue, has been seen at Hartford Stage and in the 1979–80 Festival of One-Acts at Circle Rep in New York, and it is included in the anthology The Best Short Plays of 1983. Miss Henley is single and lives in Los Angeles.

The following synopsis of The Miss Firecracker Contest was prepared by Sally Dixon Wiener.

Time: The end of June and the beginning of July

Place: Brookhaven, Mississippi, a small Southern town

ACT I

Scene 1

SYNOPSIS: It is late on a hot Monday afternoon, but the sun barely penetrates the tall etched glass windows of the late Ronelle Williams's old-fashioned Victorian living room with its heavy drapes and *"endless clutter,"* which includes an old spinning wheel. Off to the right is the front door, beyond the tall windows. Upstage, a divided stairway leads off to the bedrooms. To the left of the stairway is the door to the kitchen.

As the play begins we hear "The Star-Spangled Banner" on a phonograph, and the lights go up on Carnelle Scott. At 24, she is *"tallish with an oddly attractive face and very bright dyed red hair"* and is attired in a leotard and fishnet tights. With more energy than aptitude, she is working out a routine that includes tap dancing and marching, dummy Roman candles, a fake gun, and two small American flags substituting for lighted sparklers. Frequent "Booms!" punctuate this strenuous activity as she imagines the Roman candles going off.

Carnelle is interrupted by the arrival of Popeye Jackson, 23, a fey *"small glowing person"* in a many-pocketed dressmaker's smock and thick glasses. Carnelle has sketches of the costume she wants Popeye to make for her for the Miss Firecracker Contest, Brookhaven's traditional Fourth of July beauty contest. "It's a famous contest," she explains to Popeye, who is new in town.

Popeye, with her tape measure, and with the help of a magnifying glass, takes Carnelle's measurements and assures Carnelle that she's experienced (she began sewing clothes at 4, "making little outfits for the bullfrogs that lived out around our yard"). When Carnelle is in the kitchen getting the snack she's prepared for them, Popeye looks around the room. Going over to the spinning wheel, she pretends to prick her finger on it and pantomimes a momentary swoon. Popeye thinks the house, which belonged to Carnelle's aunt who died recently of cancer, is "scary."

While they have iced tea and saltines, Carnelle describes the tragedy of her aunt's death, "a famous medical case." The monkey gland that replaced her

Holly Hunter as Carnelle Scott in *The Miss Firecracker Contest*

pituitary made her grow long black hair all over, but she was so saintly and brave she even allowed the newspapers to photograph her.

CARNELLE: It was awfully hard on me losing my Aunt Ronelle—though I guess I should be used to it by now.

POPEYE: What's that?

CARNELLE: People dying. It seems like people've been dying practically all my life, in one way or another. First my mother passed when I was barely a year old. Then my daddy kinda drug me around with him till I was about nine and he couldn't stand me any longer, so he dropped me off to live with my Aunt Ronelle and Uncle George and their own two children: Elain and Delmount. They're incredible those two. They're just my ideal. Anyhow, we're happy up until the time when Uncle George falls to his death trying to pull this bird's nest out of the chimney.

POPEYE: He fall off from the roof?

CARNELLE: That's right. Tommy Turner was passing by throwing the evening paper, and he caught sight of the whole event.

POPEYE: How awful.

CARNELLE: Anyhow, my original daddy appears back here to live with us looking all kinda fat and swollen. And after staying on about two years, he suddenly drops dead in the summer's heat while running out to the Tropical Ice Cream truck. Heart failure, they said it was. Then this thing with Aunt Ronelle dying right before Christmas. It's been hard to bear.

POPEYE (after a moment): I had a brother who was bit by a water moccasin down by the Pearl River, and he died.

CARNELLE: Well, you know, they say everyone's gonna be dying some day. I believe it too.

POPEYE: Yeah. May as well.

Carnelle goes off to get the red, blue and silver costume fabric, and Popeye becomes intrigued with one of the many photographs on the wall. It's of Carnelle's cousin Delmount, who has "kind of a checkered past." Carnelle doesn't exactly know where Delmount is, but he has been released from a mental hospital that his lawyer had gotten him into to avoid his having to go to jail for hitting a man in the face with a broken bottle.

Unexpectedly, Elain Rutledge, Carnelle's cousin and Delmount's sister, arrives, with luggage and a gift box. She is 32, "dressed in elegant pastels" and is "beautiful, but her looks are now more strained and anxious than they once were." It seems Elain wasn't expected until the weekend but decided to "cut off short" her visit to her mother-in-law by just beeping twice as she went through Hollybluff. Her gift, for Carnelle, is a bizarre Mardi Gras mask. Popeye asks to hold it, too, and Elain impulsively takes off her earrings and gives them to Popeye for a present. Popeye, never having had any "earbobs," is delighted.

As Popeye gathers up the fabric for the costume, ready to leave, Elain realizes that Carnelle is actually registered for the Miss Firecracker Contest and is disparaging about it, although she herself was a Miss Firecracker years ago. Elain has already commented on Carnelle's crimson-red hair.

Popeye goes off, promising to have the costume ready in time for the audition on Saturday. Carnelle is disappointed that Elain doesn't seem to have brought the red ante-bellum dress she'd asked her to bring for her to wear for the contest. Elain suggests she wait until after the audition to see if she gets into the pageant.

CARNELLE: I know why you're worried. You think I've ruined my chances, 'cause—'cause of my reputation.

ELAIN: I don't know what you mean—you're perfectly sweet.

CARNELLE: Well, everyone knew I used to go out with lots of men and all that. Different ones. It's been a constant thing with me since I was young and—

ELAIN: Let's not discuss it in all a this heat.

CARNELLE: I just mention it 'cause it's different now, since Aunt Ronelle died and since—I got that disease.

ELAIN: Please, Carnelle, nobody's profiting by this information!

CARNELLE: Anyway, I go to church now, and I'm signed up to where I take an orphan home to dinner once a week or to a movie; and—I work on the cancer drive here just like you do in Natchez.

ELAIN: That's all very admirable, I'm sure.

CARNELLE: My life has meaning. People aren't calling me Miss Hot Tamale any more like they used to. Everything's changed. And being in that contest— it would be such an honor to me . . . I can't explain the half of it.

ELAIN: Well, if you don't make it to the finals, just try to remember that Mama was at her most noblest when she was least attractive.

CARNELLE: I wish you had about a drop a faith in me. I'm not all that ugly.

ELAIN: And I wish you would stop fishing for compliments—'cause I'm sick and worn out with giving people compliments about themselves!

CARNELLE: I'm sorry. I'm so, so sorry. I make such stupid blunders. I know you don't think I'm ugly.

ELAIN: I'm not myself—I'm just not myself.

The telephone rings. It's Franklin, Elain's husband, but she adamantly refuses to speak to him. It seems she has left him, but she hasn't told anyone yet—not even Franklin.

CARNELLE: I just can't believe this. You were so in love. It seemed like Franklin loved you so much. I thought I wanted a man to love me that much.

ELAIN: Yes, he did love me. But it just caused him to follow me around asking, "Do you love me? How much do you love me? Tell me how you love me," till I could shake him till he rattled.

CARNELLE: Then you don't love him any more?

ELAIN (taking off her jewelry): No. He makes me ill.

CARNELLE: How awful.

ELAIN: Yes.

CARNELLE: But what about your two little boys. They need a mother.

ELAIN: Oh, children manage in this world. Don't ask me about them.

She shuts her cosmetic case.

CARNELLE: Gosh, Aunt Ronelle said you had it all up there in Natchez; everything—just like a queen in a castle.

ELAIN: I know. I did. I only hope I can stand to give it all up. *(Deeply moved.)* We had such beautiful clocks . . . . .

Elain is going upstairs to take a bath, and Carnelle helps her up with her things. The room is empty briefly until Delmount Williams, 28, *"tall and thin with piercing blue eyes and a sallow complexion,"* enters. He has left the door ajar. Shortly thereafter, Popeye comes in, having forgotten to take Carnelle's measurements. She recognizes Delmount from his photograph, and he assumes she's a friend of Carnelle's.

POPEYE: Yes. I just met her recently. I'm Popeye Jackson.

DELMOUNT: Popeye? That's an unusual name.

POPEYE: Oh, well . . . It's not my original name. I wasn't born with it. *(Embarrassed, she begins to run on.)* See, what happened was my brother Lucky, he threw a handful of gravel in my eyes and they started stinging and then he give me this brown bottle a drops t'put inside my eyes and telling me it's eye drops but, in fact, it's drops for the ears and then this burning sensation come into my eyes, causing me t'scream out and cry like the devil and after that I got me a pair of glasses and my eyes was bulged out a bit, so folks was calling me Popeye and the name just stuck with me—Popeye. That's how I got the name.

DELMOUNT *(after a moment):* Well, that's a mighty tragic tale.

POPEYE: Ah, no. Actually, the fortunate part is I can now hear voices through my eyes.

DELMOUNT: Through your eyes.

POPEYE: Well, now and then I hear 'em—laughing and—carrying on.

Delmount calls to Carnelle and is appalled at the color of her hair when she comes down to greet him. Popeye has taken the measurements and left. Delmount tells Carnelle that he's come to Brookhaven to sell the house—it was left to him. He's tired of working at "disgusting" jobs.

When Elain comes downstairs Delmount confronts her, claiming that she, his sister, wouldn't help to get him out of "a dirty lunatic asylum." He explains to Carnelle that he could have been released into Elain's custody after two months, but she refused to sign the papers.

ELAIN: Please, Delmount. I'm sorry, but we thought you needed the professional help. You were so upset about Mama dying—

DELMOUNT: Oh, Lord! She knows I wasn't upset 'cause of that! She knows that!

ELAIN: And Franklin just thought, 'cause of the children—

DELMOUNT *(under his breath):* Franklin—that sheep-pussy.

ELAIN *(angry):* I mean, after all, Delmount, you did commit a violent act—hitting that poor man in the face with a bottle—

DELMOUNT *(to Carnelle):* Do you actually think I'm of such base character? I challenged that man to a duel! I can't help it if the weapons he chose were broken bottles! It was an honorable act in defense of a woman with beautiful, warm bronze skin. I do not regret it.

ELAIN *(trying to break in between Carnelle and Delmount):* Well, besides all of that, you know good and well, you've always had a checkered past!

DELMOUNT: What checkered past? No, I'm not speaking to you!

ELAIN: For one thing, you tried to choke Carnelle's poor father to death right in there at the dining room table!

DELMOUNT: Why, I never!

ELAIN: You did! It was right on New Year's Day!

CARNELLE: That's right, 'cause I found the dime in the black-eyed peas—

DELMOUNT: All right, I did! I did it! But he was boring me to death! I just wanted to shut him up!

ELAIN: Now, see! See! That's not reasonable behavior! It's just not reasonable. And how you almost got run out of town on a rail 'cause of what happened with T. S. Mahoney's two young virgin daughters! It's no wonder you have bad dreams! It's no wonder!

DELMOUNT: Rub my face in it, why don't you! You're so damn perfect and I'm such a no account failure! Rub my face in it!

Elain flounces off, leaving Carnelle and Delmount alone. Delmount tells Carnelle that it was ironic about the Mahoney girls—they were "dying for it," and he was doing them a favor. He also tells Carnelle that he's going to give her half of what he gets for the house and furnishings so they can both leave Brookhaven.

CARNELLE: Well, Delmount. I don't know! I've never thought about leaving Brookhaven.

DELMOUNT: Well, think about it. There's never been anything here for you but sorrow.

CARNELLE: Yes, that's true. Still . . . I don't know. (After a moment.) Maybe if I could, if I could leave in a blaze of glory. Yes! That's what I'd like to do— leave this town in a blaze of glory!

DELMOUNT: How do you mean?

CARNELLE: Well, if I won the Miss Firecracker Contest—see, I'm a contestant in it and if I could just win first prize then I would be able to leave this town in a crimson blaze of glory!

DELMOUNT: The Miss Firecracker Contest—hell and damnation!
        He gets up.

CARNELLE: Where are you going?

DELMOUNT: For a walk!
        He exits out the front door.

CARNELLE (upset): Well, what in the world is eating him? (After a moment.) Hmm, yes . . . a crimson blaze of glory!
        She goes slowly into her routine which she performs with solemn beauty as the lights begin to fade . . . . .

Scene 2

The following Saturday "about 8 o'clock in the evening" there are now a number of bouquets of long-stemmed red roses in the living room and price tags are on much of the furniture. Delmount is writing out another price tag, for the spinning wheel, when Elain comes in with a tray with plum wine and three glasses. Elain is "somewhat tipsy." There is an atmosphere of tension because this is the night Carnelle was to hear if she's been chosen as one of the five Miss Firecracker contestants.

When the telephone rings Delmount answers, but Carnelle is in the kitchen door, listening. She removes Delmount's supper tray from the desk as he talks to a member of the D.A.R. who wants him to donate the spinning wheel to them, then retreats to the kitchen again, close to tears. The Miss Firecracker call was to have come by 6 o'clock; and on top of that, Elain tells Delmount, "they had the worst turnout in history."

They reminisce about how Carnelle's father left her with them, a little girl with her head full of ringworms, and how she grew up without any self-esteem and sleeping with everybody to try to prove she was attractive—a "degrading stage" according to Elain.

The phone rings again. Carnelle hurries from the kitchen to answer, but it's Elain's husband Franklin. She hands the phone to Elain and again goes back to the kitchen. Elain, on the phone, acknowledges receipt of the roses—"very fragrant"—but tells Franklin that she's not coming home, that the children will manage, and that she doesn't want to discuss it.

Delmount is surprised, Elain seems a little surprised at herself but insists that she means it. Delmount accuses her of often saying she's going to do something and then changing her mind because of what other people say—she wants everybody to think she's perfect. Elain lashes out at him, calling him selfish and saying that their mother always loved him best, whereas she had to win contests and enter pageants to get attention. When she graduated from junior college, their mother had said to her that "she'd had her spoonful of gravy" and to go get a rich husband. And she did. Delmount believes their mother was mean; Elain believes she was sweet to Delmount. To convince Elain how mean their mother was he relates an incident from their childhood involving their mother throwing lemon rinds out the kitchen door to the family dog who was expecting table scraps.

Elain goes on drinking wine. There's another phone call for Carnelle, but it's just "some creep" she used to date. "It was nobody." There's a knock at the door. Carnelle goes off to get some money, because she knows it's Popeye coming to get paid for making the costume. Delmount elects to disappear into the kitchen, leaving Elain to deal with Popeye. Elain tells Popeye it seems that Carnelle didn't make it into the finals for the contest. Elain gives Popeye a glass of wine, and Delmount interrupts their conversation by coming in from the kitchen to inquire about brownies. There are none left—Carnelle has apparently eaten them all, a "compulsive eater" when she is unhappy.

Delmount says hello to Popeye, admires her earrings, and goes back to the kitchen to see if there's any ice cream.

POPEYE (weakly): Oh. Oh. Oh.
    She begins fanning her heart and blowing air onto it.
ELAIN: What's the matter? Are you all right?
POPEYE: My heart—it's—hot. It's hot. It's burning. (*Blowing air onto her*

heart.) Puff, puff, puff. *(She puts the wine glass against her heart.)* There. Ah. It's better now. It's better.

ELAIN: My word, you look faint.

POPEYE: Tell me, when your heart gets hot, does that mean you're in love?

ELAIN: Darlin', are you in love?

POPEYE: I reckon.

ELAIN: Not—not with Delmount?!

POPEYE: Yes. *(Puff, puff.)* Yes.

ELAIN: How astonishing! Why, his complexion's so sallow—and he's got a rude, irritable disposition.

POPEYE: It does seem like it.

ELAIN: How utterly odd. Tell me, Popeye, have you ever been in love before?

POPEYE: Well, my heart's never been hot or nothing, but I did have me a boyfriend once.

ELAIN: And what was he like?

POPEYE: Not much. He liked t'pet me like I was a cat or something. He's asking me to purr and meow. Like "meow, meow, purr, purr, purr." I don't know, he's crazy. I's expecting him t'give me a box a catnips for Christmas.

ELAIN: What did he give you?

POPEYE: . . . Nothing.

ELAIN *(pouring them both wine):* Well, if you want my opinion, that is just about what Delmount will give you. He's an unstable character, and he's had a very checkered past.

POPEYE: I know 'bout that.

ELAIN: Well, did you know about his strange, obsessive eye for beauty? *(Popeye shakes her head.)* How he's been known to follow a normal looking woman through the streets all day and all night because he finds the mere shape of her nose exotic or beautiful; or perhaps he finds the texture of her lips to be unusually soft and smooth. You don't want anything to do with him. I worry about him. He's not right. He's obsessed.

Afraid that Carnelle is crying, Elain goess off to find her. Popeye is alone with her wine as Delmount comes back on with a dish of ice cream and sits down at the desk, writing.

POPEYE: Are you writing poems?

DELMOUNT: What?

POPEYE: Carnelle said you write poems.

DELMOUNT: Oh. Well, on occasion I have.

POPEYE: I'd like to read 'em.

DELMOUNT *(embarrassed):* They're personal.

POPEYE: Oh. *(She starts to run on.)* 'Course, I never read many poems before. There weren't all that many poem books you could get off a the traveling book mobile. Most books I got was about animals. Farm animals, jungle animals, Arctic animals and such. 'Course they was informative, I learned some things; they's called a gaggle a geese, a pride a lions, a warren a rabbits, a host a whales. That's my personal favorite one: a host a whales!

They look at each other.

Carnelle says you can wiggle your ears.

DELMOUNT: Does she?

POPEYE: Yes.

DELMOUNT *(straightening his hair):* It's an old trick.

POPEYE: I would liked t'have seen it.

DELMOUNT: I don't do it any more.

He takes a comb out and starts combing his hair.

POPEYE: What d'ya dream about at nights?

DELMOUNT *(taken aback):* Why do you ask?

POPEYE: I don't know, your face looks tired. I thought maybe you was having bad dreams.

DELMOUNT: What are you saying? You make me uncomfortable. A gaggle of geese! What's that?! What are you talking about? This whole night is unbearable! Oooh! Now the ice cream has given me a headache. Lord Jesus! A gaggle of geese! Oh, my head! My head!

He exits to the bedroom, holding his head. Popeye watches him leave, then she puts both of her hands over her heart and starts to sob as she falls to the floor.

Carnelle returns with a purse and Kleenex and finds Popeye crying. Popeye loves Delmount and has lost him, and Carnelle begins to cry because she's lost too—"didn't even make the finals"—and nobody loves her and she hates her hair. Elain comes back to find them both in hysterics and pours them some wine. Elain tries to calm them by telling them that their lives aren't over, like hers is. She can't believe she's really left Franklin and that there will be no more roses, and she begins to throw the roses around the living room.

When the telephone rings again, they are all crying, but Carnelle recovers herself enough to answer. She is told she *is* a finalist. The woman calling her was so late because her little dog Turnip was hit by a van and died.

Elain proposes a toast, and they call Delmount, who is in the middle of giving his hair a hot oil treatment, to join them. "Oh—my—miserable—God!" says Delmount as they click glasses. *Curtain.*

ACT II

Scene 1

It is the Fourth of July, *"about three o'clock in the afternoon."* The setting is an outside area, with a bench and a garbage can, behind a striped carnival tent; and, stage left, a backstage dressing room, with a makeshift dressing table and mirror. There are two entrances stage right to the outside area, and the dressing room can be entered by going up one step from the outside area or, upstage left, from the backstage of the beauty contest area.

Mac Sam, a carnival balloon man, *"mid-30s . . . . . thin . . . . . in drastically poor health . . . . . something extraordinarily sensual about him,"* comes on,

Margo Martindale (Tessy), Mark Linn-Baker (Delmount) and Belita
Moreno (Popeye) in a scene from *The Miss Firecracker Contest*

coughing, with a lot of balloons. Finding that Carnelle is not there, he finishes his cigarette and goes off. When Carnelle comes on, with all her paraphernalia for the contest, she's accompanied by Tessy Mahoney, *"the uglier of T. S. Mahoney's two ugly daughters,"* who is the contest coordinator. It's getting late, and Carnelle is nervous—the red dress doesn't fit right, it's too tight, and Popeye is nowhere to be found to help fix it. And now Carnelle's hairpiece is falling down. Tessy's sister is also one of the five finalists for Miss Firecracker, but Tessy confides to Carnelle that Carnelle and Caroline Jeffers are "the only real contenders" and Caroline Jeffers has yellow teeth.

Tessy is very interested in the fact that Delmount is back in town. Before she goes off, she asks Carnelle to tell Delmount that she's forgiven him. She understands now "that some men just don't have any self control." Carnelle is *"fooling with her hair"* in the mirror when Mac Sam comes on again and looks into the dressing room.

CARNELLE *(catching her breath):* Mac Sam. What are you doing here?

MAC SAM: Just came t'wish you well. Heard you were in the beauty contest and came by t'wish you well.

CARNELLE *(breathlessly):* Thanks. I'm nervous.

MAC SAM: Sure y'are. Well, good luck. I wish y'well.
> *He starts to leave.*

CARNELLE: I—didn't think I'd be seeing you again.

MAC SAM: Yeah, well, wonders never do quite cease.
> *He looks at her with his magnetic eyes, then starts to leave again.*

CARNELLE: I tried to notify you. After I found out. Couldn't . . . locate you though.

MAC SAM: Oh, "that." Yeah, well, I'm enjoying, "that." Find it most fascinating.

CARNELLE: But didn't you get the shots?

MAC SAM: Nah.

CARNELLE: But all you do is—they give you these shots and you're cured. It cures you.

MAC SAM: I don't care t'be cured.

CARNELLE: What do you mean? You've got to be.

MAC SAM *(taking out a cigaret):* Listen, Honey, this life a mine is strictly on the house. Strictly a free roll a the eternal dice. I was almost choked to death by my mama's umbilical cord at birth. Spent three days purple and gasping for breath. I'm tired out of gasping. *(He lights his cigaret and blows out the match.)* Mmm. Your hair looks really nice. I like that color. It looks good on you.

CARNELLE: It doesn't seem too loud?

MAC SAM *(smelling her hair):* Not a bit. No, Sugar, not a bit.

As Mac Sam leaves, he assures Carnelle he will be back. Delmount, meanwhile, has come back with a big toy dog for Carnelle that he won pitching dimes. *"There is a lightness to him that was not there in Act I."* He reports that the furniture is selling "like hot cakes" at the auction and things seem to be looking up for them. Carnelle just hopes she'll win the contest so she can leave in that blaze of glory. In the course of their conversation, Carnelle tells him Tessy Mahoney was inquiring about him, and she also reveals to Delmount that Popeye is in love with him.

Elain appears, wearing *"a flowing summer dress,"* very excited because she's been asked, as a former Miss Firecracker, to speak on "My Life as a Beauty" before the contest starts. She's been unable to find Popeye but has come up with the idea that Carnelle can carry the Mardi Gras mask to hide the fact that the dress doesn't fit.

Delmount hurriedly hides under the tent when Tessy comes on with a shoe box for Carnelle. Elain and Tessy renew acquaintance. The box is from Mac Sam. In it is a frog in a pink outfit, which convinces Carnelle Mac Sam must know where Popeye is, and she and Elain rush off to find him.

Tessy out of the way, Delmount comes out from under the tent as Popeye comes on, dancing and humming, wearing a summer dress and the earrings. She is looking at Carnelle's dress as Carnelle, Elain and Mac Sam return. Popeye needs scissors, but there are none, and anyway, it's too late to fix the dress now. Carnelle is even having trouble trying to get into the pantaloons. After a frantic struggle she finally succeeds and is looking for the hoopskirt when there is a *"fast blackout."*

Scene 2

It's a few minutes later. Mac Sam and Delmount are in the outside area, as before. They are both nervous about how things are going out front. Mac Sam has a flask, and his balloons are tied to the bench.

DELMOUNT: She look all right to you in that big, red thing?

MAC SAM: Oh, yeah.

DELMOUNT: God. How she can put herself through this I'll never understand. Never.

MAC SAM: Well, women are funny about their looks. My granpapa used to say to me, "Sammy, all ya have to do is tell a woman she's beautiful and she goes like that!"

He makes a horizontal victory sign with his fingers.

DELMOUNT: How pithy.

MAC SAM: Well, of course I try not to abuse the knowledge but it has come in handy in some borderline cases.

DELMOUNT: Well, fortunately, I have yet to make advances to any woman who did not possess at least one classically beautiful characteristic. It's sort of a romantic notion I've had. I don't know. Perhaps it's caused me to be fragmented in love. Perhaps it's been obsessive. What do you think?

MAC SAM: Well, what I like is a woman who can take it right slap on the chin. That's what I like.

He begins to cough, spreading germs all over his flask. He takes a slug, relieving his cough, then he says—

Care for a slug?

DELMOUNT *(aghast):* No, thank you.

Elain and Popeye come on from the right, very upset. "A travisty!" Elain moans. Carnelle tripped on the skirt of the red dress and fell down, and people were laughing at her and calling her "Miss Hot Tamale." Someone named Ronnie Wayne was throwing "peanuts and trash and ice" onto the stage. A peanut hit Carnelle in the face, Elain reports. Delmount rushes off, calling "He dies!"

Carnelle comes back into the dressing room in a state. Popeye and Elain go in to help her get the red dress off. She's convinced that if the dress had come sooner she could have fixed it and wouldn't have had to use the mask. Elain wants her to calm down—she's all wet and collapsing but stuffs the hot dog Popeye offers her into her mouth.

Meanwhile, Delmount is off, fighting with Ronnie Wayne. Tessy comes on, frantic. Carnelle, still in her hoop, sends Mac Sam off to stop Delmount.

Delmount's leg has been hurt, and there is blood on his face when Mac Sam brings him back. Elain goes for disinfectant, and Popeye goes for ice. They threw rocks at Delmount, but he claims to have enjoyed the whole thing. Mac Sam agrees, but he's spitting up blood. "Happens all the time," he shrugs.

Tessy enters the dressing room area again, calling to Carnelle.

TESSY (stepping outside, spotting Delmount): Why, will you look at you! I just hope you're proud of yourself. Causing all of that racket! Here, Carnelle, Tommy Turner wants you to show him which song on this record you want played for your routine.

CARNELLE: All right.

       She takes the record, goes through the dressing room and exits left.

TESSY: So how's life been treating you?

DELMOUNT: Oh, fair.

TESSY: Well, I just thought you should know that I'm still bearing emotional scars because of the time you took unfair advantage of me up in the attic. They're deep scars, Delmount. They hurt.

DELMOUNT (quietly as he squirms): Have a little mercy. I'm bleeding here. Look—blood.

       He mops off his head with a handkerchief.

TESSY: Well, you don't have to worry. I've already forgiven you. It's my religion: First Presbyterian. And to show you I mean it, tonight I'll let you take me to watch the fireworks.

DELMOUNT: What—

TESSY (she starts to leave): I'll even trust you to sit by me all alone in the dark! See you back here at 7:45 P.M. on the nose!

DELMOUNT: No, wait—

       He tries to get up but flinches in pain.

TESSY (as she exits through the dressing room and out left): I've got to run now! There's a show on!

DELMOUNT (overlapping, he crawls after her): Please—Don't forgive me! Don't! It was rotten behavior! I stink, I tell ya! I stink! (Dropping to the ground.) Christ.

MAC SAM (after a long moment): Classically—beautiful—characteristics?

DELMOUNT: She was an exception.

MAC SAM: I'll say.

Popeye has brought ice (actually a purple snow cone) for Delmount's leg, and Elain returns with disinfectant. When Elain's eyes meet Mac Sam's they seem instantly attracted to each other, and to keep up the conversation, *"primarily for Mac Sam's benefit"*, she tells Popeye that she's heard she lost her job and wants to know what happened. It seems Popeye took a compact case at the dress store where she was working to give to a child who didn't know what color her own eyes were. Mac Sam starts showing off, blowing smoke rings, etc., Delmount tries his old trick of wiggling his ears—but, to Popeye's disappointment, can't seem to manage it any more.

Carnelle has been off watching another contestant's act but must get ready for her own act now. In her red, blue and silver costume that Popeye made and in her tap shoes she goes off again when Tessy calls the time to do her routine to "The Star-Spangled Banner".

Popeye and Mac Sam have gone off to watch Carnelle's act, when Tessy comes on with more roses for Elain. Delmount asks to read the card. He's disgusted, because they're from Franklin. Elain has called Franklin, and he's picking her up the next morning. Elain excuses herself by saying that their mother left everything to Delmount. He offers her all the money he will make from the house and furnishings if she'll leave Franklin, but she's "used to better things now" and needs someone who adores her.

Carnelle, Popeye and Mac Sam return, jubilant. The act was a hit, Carnelle reports, and she must quickly change into her bathing suit for the crowning—it's time for the lineup. Then everyone except Delmount goes off to watch. Ridiculous though he believes the whole thing to be, he sincerely hopes she'll win. But in a few moments Mac Sam returns with the news that Carnell has *not* won —far from it. The "crowning blow," as Elain puts it when they've returned, is that she ended up in last place.

> *Carnelle enters the dressing room. They all stare at her. She wears a fifth place banner. She looks at herself in the mirror, then she bravely turns to face her family and friends, hoping for acceptance.*

DELMOUNT: Well, it was a stupid contest.

MAC SAM: Laughable.

ELAIN: Mama always said that what's really important in life is—

CARNELLE *(becoming angry):* I—don't—want—to—hear—it!! I wanted to win that contest. I cared about it. It was important to me. *(To Delmount.)* And I don't care how stupid and idiotic you think it was!! *(To Elain.)* And what are you looking at?! You never wanted me to win! You think I'm ugly—that's why you told me to wear that stupid mask over my face! I can't believe I ever wanted to be like you or that mean old monkey either! *(Turning to Mac Sam.)* And why don't you get well!?! You make me *sick* you're so *sick!!* You look like shit!!! I tell you, I'm so mad I could spit! *(Spit.)* There! *(Spit, spit.)* There, I spit! *(Spit.)* Die, you monkey! Die!

TESSY: Carnelle! *(She enters the dressing room left.)* Carnelle, come on! You and Saphire are gonna follow along alongside the Grand Float carrying these American flags. You better get out there; everyone's waiting.

> *She holds out a large American flag on a pole.*

CARNELLE *(grabbing the flag):* Thanks! *(She starts to leave right.)*

DELMOUNT: Wait. You don't have to do that. You don't have to follow that float.

CARNELLE: Look, if you come in last, you follow the float. I took a chance and I came in last; so, by God, I'm gonna follow that float!! *(She starts to leave again.)*

MAC SAM: Hey!

CARNELLE *(stopping):* What?!

MAC SAM: You're beautiful when you're mad!

CARNELLE *(looks at him, spits, then turns to exit right, carrying the American flag):* Aah!!!

As the scene ends, Elain is insisting she is not like her mother, Tessy is counting the hours until her date for the fireworks with Delmount, and Delmount this time accepts Mac Sam's offer of a slug from his flask.

Scene 3

It's evening and growing darker as Elain appears in Carnelle's dressing room. She's carrying a wine bottle and is *"a bit drunk."* Neither she nor Delmount, who comes on shortly after her, has seen Carnelle since the parade, and Elain doesn't think Carnelle wants to see her anyway. Elain has just come to get the red dress.

DELMOUNT: I don't understand you. I know you're probably a kind person. You can cheer sick people up; you gave Popeye your earrings; you have a need to be excited by life. But why do you go back to him? Why do you go back to being perfect? Why do you go back to being what Mama wanted? You know she was mean!

ELAIN *(turning to him angrily):* Yes, I know she was mean and you know it, too. So why do you straighten your wild hair! Why do you only fall in love with women who are partly perfect, partly beautiful? Why do you have horrible, sickening dreams about pieces of women's bodies? Some all beautiful; some all mutilated and bloody! I hate those dreams. I wish you didn't tell me about them. They scare me.

DELMOUNT: I'm sorry. I'm sorry.

ELAIN: It's okay.

DELMOUNT *(to soothe her):* I—I don't have those dreams any more. I've stopped having them.

ELAIN *(smiling):* You have?

DELMOUNT: Yes.

ELAIN: Well, good. That's good. Do you want some wine?

DELMOUNT: Sure. Give me some wine.

> She hands him the bottle—he takes a drink. He hands the bottle back to her—she takes a long drink.

ELAIN: You know about those earrings I gave Popeye . . .

DELMOUNT: Yeah?

ELAIN: I hated the damn things. They pinched my ears. I was glad to get rid of them.

Elain goes off, with the dress, telling Delmount she's going to have some fun —she's meeting someone "in the grove down under the wisteria trees." As they are saying goodbye, Popeye has come on, with a pair of binoculars and a sack of peanuts, and they both wait for Carnelle. Popeye supposes she'll be leaving Brookhaven and Delmount is leaving, too, he tells her.

POPEYE: You is? Where was you planning to go?

DELMOUNT: I thought I'd be going to New Orleans—get back to the University and learn to be a philosopher. That way, after I have time to study and think it all through, I'll be able to let everyone know why we're living. It'll be a great relief. I believe; and where are you going to go? When you leave Brookhaven. I mean.

POPEYE: Well, I don't know the particulars. But I heard a this place name of Elysian Fields.

DELMOUNT: Elysian Fields?

POPEYE: Right. See, they got this ambrosia t'eat and wine and honey t'drink and all sorts of people carrying on. Do you know what state it's located in?

DELMOUNT: It—isn't in a state.

POPEYE: It ain't?

DELMOUNT: No. It isn't even in the world. It's—it's fictional. It's a made-up place. Why, it's only in books and stories.

POPEYE: Oh. Well, shoot. Guess I won't be going there.

When Tessy appears, expecting Delmount to watch the fireworks with her, Delmount says he's promised to go with Popeye to see the fireworks. Tessy leaves, telling him she hopes he'll rot in "H". Popeye knows he was lying, and he goes off, briefly, only to return to ask Popeye if she *will* watch the fireworks with him. She agrees, and they go off. She's already picked out a good place from which to watch.

Carnelle, in a trench coat and bathing suit, comes out from beneath the tent and goes toward the dressing room as Mac Sam shows up. "I didn't want to see anyone," she tells him. He comments on how angry she was earlier, and she admits she'd never been so angry before. He follows Carnelle into the dressing room.

MAC SAM: You know, I went looking for you after the parade. Where'd you get off to?

CARNELLE: Oh, nowhere. Just out walking by the railroad tracks.

MAC SAM: What were you doing down there?

CARNELLE (as she gathers up her belongings): Kicking rocks. Thinking. I thought maybe I was a victim of broken dreams, but then I thought maybe I wasn't. I was trying so hard t'belong all my life and . . . Oh, looks like Elain came for her red dress. Anyway, I just don't know what you can, well, reasonably hope for in life.

MAC SAM: Not much, baby, not too damn much.

CARNELLE: But something—

MAC SAM: Sure. There's always eternal grace.

CARNELLE: It'd be nice. *(Holding up the shoe box.)* Look here, my frog's gone.

MAC SAM: Yeah. That Popeye set it loose.

CARNELLE: Oh, well, at least I still have the suit.
    She holds up the pink suit. They look at each other and smile.

MAC SAM: God, you're beautiful. I wouldn't trade those times we had together, not for anything.

CARNELLE: Really?

MAC SAM: Not for a golden monkey.
    She throws her arms around him.

She picks up all her things and leaves, refusing Mac Sam's invitation to watch the fireworks and "spend a fine night together."

Popeye and Delmount have climbed onto the tent roof. Delmount is looking through the binoculars when Popeye throws popcorn in front of them, pretending it's snow. They spot Carnelle coming back for something she's forgotten in the dressing room and beg her to come up on the roof with them, but she refuses. It's the toy dog she's forgotten.

CARNELLE *(looking around the room):* Grace. Eternal grace. Grace.
    Her voice breaking, she finds Grace. She picks up the dog and runs out of the dressing room, ablaze with excitement.
Hey! Hey, how do I get up there?! I wanna come up! I've changed my mind! I wanna come.

DELMOUNT *(overlapping):* Oh, child, you're coming up!

POPEYE *(overlapping):* Hurray! Hurray! It's easy! You just run around there and jump off of them piled-up boxes and climb up the pole!

CARNELLE: Great! I'm on my way! I'm coming up!
    She exits up right.

POPEYE: *Wow!* She's coming up! I'm so happy! I'm happy!

DELMOUNT: Oh, Popeye! *(He grabs her and kisses her full on the mouth.)* I've been dreaming about you at night. I see you riding across the sea with a host of green whales. I love you.

POPEYE *(past ecstasy):* I feel like m'teeth is gonna fall outta my head.
    Carnelle appears on the roof; she is carrying the dog.

CARNELLE: Hey! I'm up here! I made it! I'm up.

DELMOUNT: That's right! Now just slide on out here. That's it. Good. You made it.

CARNELLE: Oh, will you look at all those stars in the sky.

POPEYE: Yeah.

DELMOUNT: Oh, yeah.

CARNELLE: Listen, I—I don't know what I was thinking about this afternoon —when I was screaming and all.

DELMOUNT: Please, it's all right. You don't have to say anything. Everything's all right.

CARNELLE: It's just I was upset about not being able to leave in the blaze of glory. Of course, I know it doesn't matter. I mean, the main thing is—well, the main thing is . . . Gosh; I don't know what the main thing is. I don't have the vaguest idea.

Carnelle laughs, and the fireworks turn the night into colors of gold and red, much to Popeye's excitement. It's a nice night—"As nice as they come," comments Delmount. *Blackout. Curtain.*

Special Citation

○○○
○○○
○○○
○○○
○○○
○○○ # LA TRAGÉDIE DE CARMEN

A Full-Length Musical in One Act

ADAPTED FROM THE OPERA *CARMEN* BY
PETER BROOK, JEAN-CLAUDE
CARRIÈRE AND MARIUS CONSTANT

Cast and credits appear on page 322

PETER BROOK (co-adaptor and director) was born in London of Russian parentage March 21, 1925 and was educated at Gresham's School and Magdalen College, Oxford. In 1943, at age 19, he directed his first London production, Dr. Faustus *at the Torch, entering upon one of the most active and distinguished careers on the international stage. In the intervening years, Brook has directed dozens of plays, operas and motion pictures, also composing music and creating the designs for many of them. He became co-director of the Royal Shakespeare Theater, for which he did some of his acclaimed productions, in 1962 and was named a Commander of the British Empire in 1965.*

The list of Brook-directed plays that originated in or reached New York begins with Nancy Mitford's adaptation of Roussin's The Little Hut *for 29 Broadway performances in 1953 and continues with the Truman Capote-Harold Arlen musical* House of Flowers *(1954), Duerrenmatt's Best Play* The Visit *(1958), Anouilh's* The Fighting Cock *(1959),* Irma La Douce *(1960), Royal Shakespeare's* King Lear *(1964, cited in the annual* Variety *poll for Brook's costume designs), Duerrenmatt's Best Play* The Physicists *(1964), Marat/Sade *(1965, a Best Play and the Critics and Tony Award winner, with Brook also winning a Tony for its direction) and the Royal Shakespeare* A Midsummer Night's Dream *(1971, with Brook again winning the Tony for direction. It became evident to American audiences, especially in the latter Shakespeare production, that Brook was bringing more to the stage than "direction" or "staging" in the conventional meaning of those terms. He was observing and handling his source material in new and imaginative ways, "rewriting" not in words but in stagecraft, becoming, if any director ever has, an*

257

"auteur" (to use an overworked expression) of the final work. This is especially true of his latest, La Tragédie de Carmen, which opened in New York Nov. 17, 1983, played 187 performances in French and in an English version prepared by Sheldon Harnick, receiving our special citation as a 1983–84 Best Play "created" if not written by Brook with his co-adaptors.

In 1970 Brook founded the Centre International de Créations Théâtrales (International Center of Theater Research) with Micheline Rozan in Paris at Les Bouffes du Nord with the help of the French Ministry of Culture and the Ford, Anderson and Calouste Gulbenkian Foundations, bringing artists of many nations together to explore forms of dramatic expression, putting on public performances at their home base beginning with a Timon of Athens in 1974 and touring throughout the world. CICT visited New York at the La Mama Experimental Theater Club April 30–June 15, 1980 with Ubu, L'Os, The Ik and The Conference of the Birds, (the latter co-adapted and directed by Brook), a repertory which received a special New York Drama Critics Circle citation. And this season's Carmen originated as a co-production of the Paris Opera and CICT at Les Bouffes du Nord.

Brook is married to Natasha Parry, an actress, and they have a 20-year old daughter and a 17-year old son who have embarked upon acting careers. The Brooks make their home in Paris.

JEAN-CLAUDE CARRIÈRE (co-adaptor) is a script writer of 20 years' experience in theater and films. Louis Malle, Milos Forman and Andrzej Wajda have directed his work on the screen, and a long association with Louis Bunuel resulted in six movies and the book My Last Sign. He began writing plays in 1968 and worked with Peter Brook on CICT's first public production, Timon of Athens, in 1974. He has since taken part in adapting CICT's Measure for Measure, The Cherry Orchard, The Conference of the Birds, La Tragédie de Carmen and a stage version of the Mahabharata now in preparation at the Paris headquarters of the group.

MARIUS CONSTANT (co-adaptor and musical director) is a composer whose first symphonic work, Twenty-four Preludes for Orchestra, was conducted by Leonard Bernstein. He studied with Enesco, Nadia Boulanger, Arthur Honnegger and Olivier Messiaen. Among his many compositions of symphonies, concertos, chamber music, operas and ballets have been Candide at the Hamburg Opera, Nana at the Paris Opéra and Paradise Lost at the Metropolitan Opera under his own direction—and the theme for The Twilight Zone. He is the chief conductor of the National Youth Orchestra of Canada; founder of the ensemble Ars Nova; professor of orchestration at the Paris Conservatory; and former musical director of the Paris Opéra and lecturer at Stanford. He has won the Italia (1952), Koussevitzky (1962) and Marzotto (1967) Prizes for composition, and his music has been recorded several times on the Erato, Philips and Deutsche Grammophon labels.

Our special citation of La Tragédie de Carmen as a Best Play includes, below, the synopsis of its events as performed at Lincoln Center and as printed in its program; plus an evaluation of the creative forces and changes in this opera-become-musical-drama by Douglas Watt, drama critic of the New York Daily News and frequent contributor of musical criticism to various publications.

Peter Brook, director of *La Tragédie de Carmen,* is surrounded by the five actresses who alternated as Carmen in his version of the Bizet opera *(clockwise from lower left):* Cynthia Clarey, Eva Saurova, Hélène Delavault, Emily Golden and Patricia Schuman

PETER BROOK AND *CARMEN*

By Douglas Watt

Lincoln Center's controversial and long-neglected Beaumont Theater was brilliantly fulfilled in November by Peter Brook's fascinating production, *La Tragédie de Carmen,* an 80-minute distillation, in the form of a chamber opera, of the customary three-hour grand opera version of Bizet's masterpiece. It was utterly intoxicating.

Brook, who put it together in his Paris workshop and then presented it in that city for a sizeable run followed by a lengthy European tour, has restored some of the harsher and more lurid elements of the Prosper Mérimée novella that Bizet's proficient librettists, Meilhac and Halévy, excised in order to soften the work (but not sufficiently, as it happened) for the conventional tastes of the Opéra Comique audience. For *Carmen,* with spoken dialogue between musical numbers, was the late 19th century equivalent of what we call a musical. In fact, it wasn't until 1959 that it made it to the Paris Opéra in a circusy production replete with animals.

While *Carmen* has long been one of the most popular of all operas (*Aida, La Bohème* and *Carmen* constitute the Met's ABC of hits) and has often been called "the perfect opera," there is no denying that it has tended to drag at times, especially in the third of its four acts, in the innumerable routine performances it has endured in the assumption that its sock numbers would inevitably put it across.

In the original production, and on many occasions since then, particularly in Paris, the recitative that Ernest Guirard added following Bizet's early death, in order to create a musical whole, has been discarded in favor of added dramatic incisiveness. An East Berlin version in 1971 offered it as drama with music. Just the year before, on the contrary, Regina Resnik, who had sung Carmen at the Metropolitan Opera on several occasions in the 1950s and 1960s, produced a West German treatment in which all the recitatives were restored.

Never before, however, could the work have unfolded in sparer terms than Brook's, and all this makes the carping of the music critics (as opposed to the enthusiasm expressed by most of the drama critics) rather amusing. For it has never been determined just what the composer himself had in mind. *Carmen,* even with the Mérimée story toned down for the Opéra Comique, was a failure in its 1875 premiere—a fact that, along with physical ailments and a marital breakup, may have contributed to Bizet's death three months later at 37. He certainly wanted to retain as much of the bite of Mérimée's story (a combination of truth and anecdote filtered through his French consciousness during a trip to Spain; a trip, by the way, Bizet saw no reason to duplicate) as possible, as witness his own rewriting of the words to the Habanera to fit a song by the Spanish composer Yradier.

At any rate, Brook's knifelike paring of the opera may almost be said to have followed logically from Leonard Bernstein's electric 1972 Met production, inspired by Goeran Gentile, the Met's newly-appointed artistic director and general manager who died that summer in an auto accident abroad before his *Carmen* and the new season opened. Then, too, Guirard's recitatives were dispensed with.

Peter Brook's *La Tragédie de Carmen* (note his care in altering the title) utilized four singers, three speaking parts and a huge thrust stage covered, discounting a few props, solely with "dirt"— brown with reddish areas tapering off into gray rubble, the whole giving a sunbaked blood-and-sand effect. Dead center, what appeared to be a bundle of rags until a hand slipped out to present a playing card to the passing Don Jose, then to reach for the hand of the newly-arrived Micaëla to read its fortune, and then to sweep aside the covering to reveal the wanton, amoral, cruel, impetuously loving, mercurial heroine, was—well, Carmen.

From that moment on, events proceeded swiftly; and although along the general—indeed, inevitable—lines of the grand opera, not with the same details. The spectacle, panoply, chorus numbers, even quintets and trios were dispensed with as, through the irresistible set pieces for solo and duet, we moved rapidly and songfully through the four acts with minor prop changes—a throw rug, a few rude wood chairs, some burlap sacks bunched together to make a pallet for José and Carmen.

And instead of the one murder—Carmen's at the finish, with a sudden knife-thrust as the music of the Habanera is softly intoned again (in José's mind, of course) to fade out with the lights—there were now four. First, José's superior officer, Lt. Zuniga, was throttled by the lovesick country boy on discovering that Zuniga had been having it on with Carmen (Lillas Pastia, by the way, functioned both as innkeeper, briefly addressing us in English for an amusing few moments, and Carmen's pimp). Then, when Carmen's husband, Garcia (a figure omitted in the Meilhac-Halévy libretto), turned up, José polished him off with the leg knife he would eventually plunge into Carmen's back. And Escamillo, instead of triumphing in the ring to the cheers of the crowd, is gored to death by the bull, his glitteringly costumed corpse carried across the stage and off, the point being that not even his death could make Carmen return to José.

Brook's staging, ranging from the highly dramatic to the highly farcical (there were even two doors, one on either side, and with nothing behind them, for slamming entrances and exits) was so explicit, whether tender or lubricious, that, thank heavens, no translation was required for music that sings properly only in French—though the interpolation, late in the run, of a fluent English translation by Sheldon Harnick, to alternate with the French version, did no appreciable harm to the overall impact.

Even the dialogue passages, most of them underscored by the 14-piece, partially hidden orchestra, were so staged and acted as to be perfectly clear to the uninitiated.

This being an unusually intimate *Carmen,* operatic voices of a size required by the Met and other large houses were not required. And though the three Carmens, Don Josés, Escamillos and Micaëlas whose performances were attended by this writer were not of the top rank, their voices were entirely adequate for the

Beaumont, whose acoustics, with all the action taking place on what amounted to the theater's thrust fore stage, proved exceptional.

La Tragédie de Carmen was not intended as a substitute for *Carmen,* just as a fresh slant on a great work. It was surely such a transcendent "musical" that, had I been offered the opportunity of seeing it every week it was in New York, I'd have considered an otherwise largely lackluster Broadway musical season one of the most memorable.

Much has been and will continue to be written and speculated about Bizet's and his librettists' extraordinary work, and henceforth Brook's own remarkable recreation will have to be taken into account.

LA TRAGÉDIE DE CARMEN

SYNOPSIS (reprinted by permission from the playbill of the Vivian Beaumont Theater at Lincoln Center): Micaëla, a young country girl, arrives in Seville looking for her childhood sweetheart, Don José. She brings him a letter from his mother. A gypsy, Carmen, throws a flower to the young corporal and sings an erotic love song.

The two girls fight, and José's superior office, Zuniga, appears. Unable to control Carmen, he orders José to take her to jail. En route, Carmen promises José that if he lets her escape she will meet him at the inn of her friend Lillas Pastia. José lets Carmen go, whereupon Zuniga locks him up and takes away his corporal's rank.

Carmen arrives at the inn with stolen goods. Zuniga comes to see Carmen and offers money for her favors. Carmen accepts, but shortly thereafter José enters.

Carmen abandons Zuniga and sings for José. At this moment, the bugles blow, summoning José back to the barracks. Carmen is furious and taunts him; the situation becomes tense. José discovers Zuniga, loses control and kills the officer.

The body is quickly hidden as Escamillo, a famous bullfighter, enters. Buying drinks all around, he announces that he, too, wants Carmen. José, jealous, picks a fight with Escamillo. Carmen separates them and Escamillo withdraws, inviting all to his next bullfight.

José, who has now killed for Carmen, sings of his love for her. They go to the mountains where an old gypsy woman unites them.

While they are sleeping, Garcia appears at the camp. He is Carmen's husband, though she has hidden his existence from José. The two men challenge each other, and as they go off to fight, Carmen reads her tragic fate in the cards. The song ends, Garcia returns wounded and falls dead at Carmen's feet.

Micaëla appears again searching for José; the two women seem to understand each other. They sing while José, twice a murderer and abandoned by Carmen, flees.

Carmen becomes Escamillo's mistress. José returns to persuade her to leave with him to start a new life. She refuses, knowing she is putting her life in jeopardy.

Escamillo is killed in the bullring. Carmen still refuses José's offer, but she goes with him as far as the place where the cards have foretold that she will die.

A GRAPHIC GLANCE

Priscilla Lopez in *Non Pasquale*

Bernadette Peters in *Sunday in
the Park With George*

Louis Zorich, Kate Reid, Dustin Hoffman, John Malkovich, Stephen Lang, David Chandler and David Huddleston in the revival of *Death of a Salesman*

(Lower left clockwise) Patricia Schuman, Eva Saurova, Emily Golden, Hélene Delavault and Cynthia Clarey as the five alternating Carmens in *La Tragédie de Carmen*

Jessica Tandy and Amanda Plummer in the revival of *The Glass Menagerie*

Holly Hunter in *The Miss Firecracker Contest*

Charles Ludlam in *Galas*

Ian Bannen, Jerome Kilty and Kate Nelligan in the revival of *A Moon for the Misbegotten*

Elizabeth McGovern in *Painting Churches*

Sada Thompson in *Wednesday*

Mary Elizabeth Mastrantonio in *The Human Comedy*

George Hearn in
La Cage aux Folles

Robert Prosky in
Glengarry Glen Ross

HIRSCHFELD

Chita Rivera and Liza Minnelli in *The Rink*

Glenn Close and Jeremy Irons in *The Real Thing*

Peter Gallagher in *The Real Thing*

Edward Duke in *Jeeves Takes Charge*

Margaret Whiting in *Taking My Turn*

Bernadette Peters and Mandy Patinkin in *Sunday in the Park With George*

Alfonso Ribeiro in *The Tap Dance Kid*

Hinton Battle in *The Tap Dance Kid*

Estelle Parsons in *Orgasmo Adulto*
Escapes from the Zoo

HIRSCHFELD

Betty Comden in *Isn't It Romantic*

Richard Thomas in the revival
of *The Sea Gull*

Linda Hunt, John Shea and Barnard Hughes in *End of the World*

Chita Rivera in *The Rink*

Shirley MacLaine in *Shirley MacLaine on Broadway*

Gene Barry and George Hearn
in *La Cage aux Folles*

HIRSCHFELD 3
BOSTON

Liz Callaway in *Baby*

Percy Mtwa and Mbongeni Ngema
in *Woza Albert!*

J. J. Johnston in the revival
of *American Buffalo*

(Upper left clockwise) Amy Wright, Deborah Rush, Jim Piddock, Paxton Whitehead, Victor Garber, Douglas Seale, Brian Murray, Linda Thorson and *(center)* Dorothy Loudon in *Noises Off*

Marian Seldes in *King Richard III*

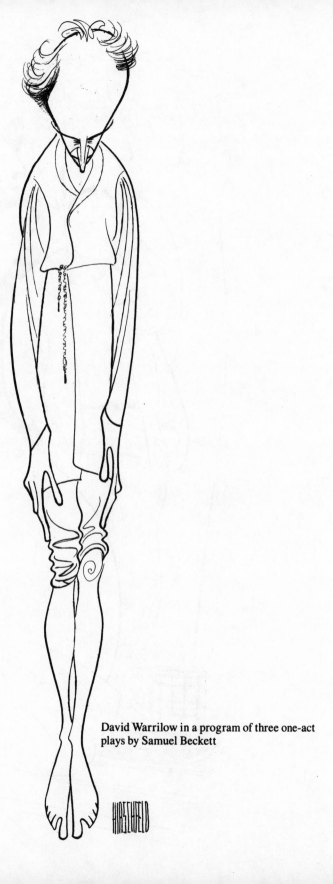

David Warrilow in a program of three one-act
plays by Samuel Beckett

HIRSCHFELD

Pat McNamara, Gary Klar, Carroll O'Connor, Frank Converse and Dennis Christopher in *Brothers*

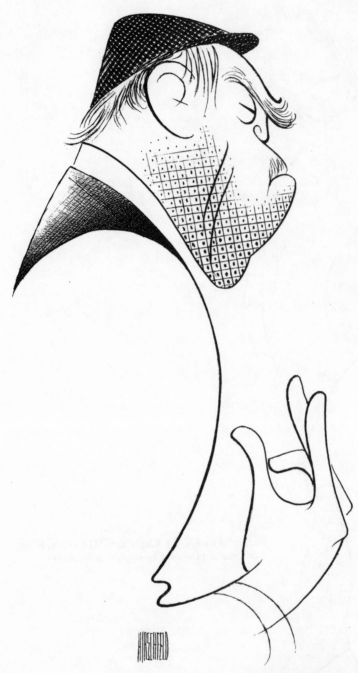

Anthony Quinn in the revival of *Zorba*

Lila Kedrova in the revival of *Zorba*

James Hayden, Al Pacino and J. J. Johnston in the revival of *American Buffalo*

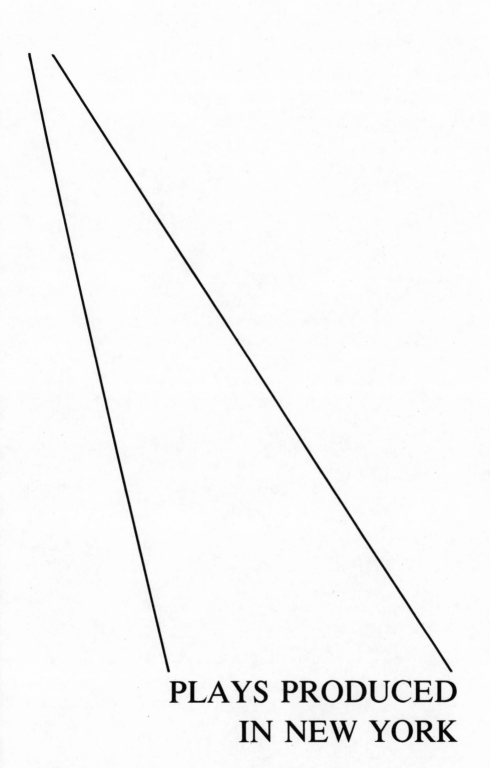

PLAYS PRODUCED
IN NEW YORK

PLAYS PRODUCED ON BROADWAY

Figures in parentheses following a play's title give number of performances. These figures are acquired directly from the production offices and do not include previews or extra non-profit performances. In the case of a transfer, the off-Broadway run is noted but not added to the figure in parentheses.

Plays marked with an asterisk (*) were still running on June 1, 1984. Their number of performances is figured through May 31, 1984.

In a listing of a show's numbers—dances, sketches, musical scenes, etc.—the titles of songs are identified wherever possible by their appearance in quotation marks (").

HOLDOVERS FROM PREVIOUS SEASONS

Plays which were running on June 1, 1983 are listed below. More detailed information about them appears in previous *Best Plays* volumes of appropriate years. Important cast changes since opening night are recorded in the Cast Replacements section of this volume.

*A Chorus Line (3,669; longest run in Broadway history). Musical conceived by Michael Bennett; book by James Kirkwood and Nicholas Dante; music by Marvin Hamlisch; lyrics by Edward Kleban. Opened April 15, 1975 off Broadway where it played 101 performances through July 13, 1975; transferred to Broadway July 25, 1975.

*Oh! Calcutta! (3,308). Revival of the musical devised by Kenneth Tynan; with contributions (in this version) by Jules Feiffer, Dan Greenberg, Lenore Kandel, John Lennon, Jacques Levy, Leonard Melfi, David Newman and Robert Benton, Sam Shepard, Clovis Trouille, Kenneth Tynan and Sherman Yellen; music and lyrics (in this version) by Robert Dennis, Peter Schickele and Stanley Walden; additional music by Stanley Walden and Jacques Levy. Opened September 24, 1976 in alternating performances with *Me and Bessie* through December 7, 1976, continuing alone thereafter.

Evita (1,567). Musical with book by Andrew Lloyd Webber; lyrics by Tim Rice. Opened September 25, 1979. (Closed June 25, 1983)

*42nd Street (1,572). Musical based on the novel by Bradford Ropes; book by Michael Stewart and Mark Bramble; music and lyrics by Harry Warren and Al Dubin; other lyrics by Johnny Mercer and Mort Dixon. Opened August 25, 1980.

Amadeus (1,181). By Peter Shaffer. Opened December 17, 1980 (date listed erroneously in some previous *Best Plays* volumes). (Closed October 16, 1983.)

*Dreamgirls (1,019). Musical with book and lyrics by Tom Eyen; music by Henry Krieger. Opened December 20, 1981.

Joseph and the Amazing Technicolor Dreamcoat (747). Revival of the musical based on the Old Testament story; music by Andrew Lloyd Webber; lyrics by Tim Rice. Opened

November 18, 1981 off Broadway where it played 77 performances; transferred to Broadway January 27, 1982. (Closed September 4, 1983)

Pump Boys and Dinettes (573). Musical with music and lyrics by Jim Wann, John Foley, Mark Hardwick, Debra Monk, Cass Morgan and John Schimmel. Opened October 1, 1981 off Broadway where it played 112 performances; transferred to Broadway February 4, 1982. (Closed June 19, 1983)

Agnes of God (599). By John Pielmeier. Opened March 30, 1982. (Closed September 4, 1983)

Nine (739). Musical with book by Arthur Kopit; music and lyrics by Maury Yeston; adaptation from the Italian by Mario Fratti. Opened May 9, 1982. (Closed February 4, 1984)

*Torch Song Trilogy (827). By Harvey Fierstein. Opened January 15, 1982 off Broadway where it played 117 performances through May 30, 1982; transferred to Broadway June 10, 1982.

*Cats (689). Musical based on *Old Possum's Book of Practical Cats* by T.S. Eliot; music by Andrew Lloyd Webber. Opened October 7, 1982.

A View From the Bridge (149). Revival of the play by Arthur Miller. Opened February 3, 1983. (Closed June 12, 1983)

Merlin (199). Musical based on an original concept by Doug Henning and Barbara De Angelis; book by Richard Levinson and William Link; songs and incidental music by Elmer Bernstein; lyrics by Don Black; magic illusions created by Doug Henning. Opened February 13, 1983. (Closed August 7, 1983)

On Your Toes (505). Revival of the musical with book by Richard Rodgers, Lorenz Hart and George Abbott; music by Richard Rodgers; lyrics by Lorenz Hart. Opened March 6, 1983. (Closed May 20, 1984)

*Brighton Beach Memoirs (486). By Neil Simon. Opened March 27, 1983.

K2 (85). By Patrick Meyers. Opened March 30, 1983. (Closed June 11, 1983)

'night, Mother (380). By Marsha Norman. Opened March 31, 1983. (Closed February 26, 1984 and transferred to off Broadway; see its entry in the Plays Produced Off Broadway section of this volume)

You Can't Take It With You (312). Revival of the play by Moss Hart and George S. Kaufman. Opened April 4, 1983. (Closed January 1, 1984)

Show Boat (73). Musical revival based on the novel by Edna Ferber; book and lyrics by Oscar Hammerstein II; music by Jerome Kern. Opened April 24, 1983. (Closed June 26, 1973)

*My One and Only (450). Musical with book by Peter Stone and Timothy S. Mayer; music by George Gershwin from *Funny Face* and other shows; lyrics by Ira Gershwin. Opened May 1, 1983.

The Caine Mutiny Court-Martial (213). Revival of the play by Herman Wouk. Opened May 5, 1983. (Closed November 6, 1983)

Private Lives (63). Revival of the play by Noel Coward. Opened May 8, 1983. (Closed July 17, 1983)

The Flying Karamazov Brothers (40). Variety revue devised by the performers. Opened May 10, 1983. (Closed June 12, 1983)

Passion (97). By Peter Nichols. Opened May 15, 1983. (Closed August 7, 1983)

Breakfast With Les and Bess (159). By Lee Kalcheim. Opened May 19, 1983. (Closed October 30, 1983)

PLAYS PRODUCED JUNE 1, 1983–MAY 31, 1984

Five-Six-Seven-Eight . . . Dance! (156). Musical revue written by Bruce Vilanch; original songs by David Zippel and Wally Harper. Produced by Radio City Music Hall Productions (also see note), Bernard Gersten executive producer, at Radio City Music Hall. Opened June 15, 1983. (Closed September 5, 1983)

CAST: Sandy Duncan, Don Correia, Bill Irwin, Armelia McQueen, Ken Sacha, Marge Champion.

The Rockettes: Joyce Dwyer, Carol Harbich, Joan Peer Kelleher, Gerri Presky, Susan Boron, Dee Dee Knapp, Deniene Fenn, Barbara Ann Moore, Judy Little, Phyllis Wujko, Barbara Ann Cittadino, Leslie McCarthy, Eileen M. Collins, Cindy Peiffer, Pauline A. Tzikas, Cynthia Hughes, Susanne Doris, Carol Toman, Pam Kelleher, Jackie Fancy, Gunny Hounsell, Prudence Gray Demmler, Terry Spano, Dottie Belle, Sonya Livingston, Rose Ann Woolsey, Susan Theobald, Carol Beatty, Catherine Beatty, Brie Daniels, Lynn Newton, Darlene Wendy, Lynn Sullivan, Alexis Ficks, Jennifer Hammond, Kerri Pearsall, Patricia Tully, Susan Cleland, Elizabeth Chanin.

Dancers: Robin Alpert, Christine Colby, Carol Estey, Edyie Fleming, Blanche, Sonya Hensley, Jodi Moccia, Gayle Samuels, Gregory Brock, Ciscoe Bruton II, Daniel Esteras, Douglas Graham, Michael Lafferty, Dan McCoy, Rodney Pridgen, Adrian Rosario.

Singers: Freida A. Williams, Holly Lipton Nash, Lois Sage, Roger Berdahl, Michael Halpern, Wayne Mattson, Wes Skelley, Paul Solen.

Orchestra: Louann Montesi concertmaster; Gilbert Bauer, Carmine Leleo, Howard Kaye, Joseph Kowalewski, Julius Kunstler, Nannette Levi, Samuel Marder, Holly Overton violins; Morris Sutow, Barbara Harrison violas; Frank Levy, Pamela Frame cellos; Dean Crandall bass; Kenneth Emery flute; Gerard J. Niewood, Edward Lucas, Joseph Camilleri, Joshua Siegel, Kenneth Arzberger reeds; George Bartlett, Nancy Freimanis French horns; Fernando Pasqualone, Richard Raffio, Norman Beatty trumpets; John Schnupp, C. David Jett, Donald Wittekind trombones; John Bartlett tuba; Thomas Oldakowski drums; James Saporito, Mario DeCiutiis percussion; Anthony Cesarano guitar; Raymond Viola piano; Jeanne Maier harp; Susanna Nason keyboards; Robert Swan music administrator; Fernando Pasqualone assistant conductor.

Directed and choreographed by Ron Field; musical supervisor, Wally Harper; musical director, Thomas Helm; scenery, Tom H. John; costumes, Lindsay W. Davis; lighting, Richard Nelson; film sequences, Christopher Dixon; orchestrations, Bill Byers; dance arrangements, Mark Hummel, Donald York; associate director, David Rubinstein; associate choreographer, Marianne Selbert; production stage manager, Raymond Chandler; stage managers, Howard Kolins, Jon Morton, Nelson K. Wilson; press, Gloria M. Ciaccio, Neil S. Friedman.

Series of musical and other numbers designed principally as a showcase for the singing, dancing and personality of Sandy Duncan.

ACT I

5-6-7-8 . . . Dance!

Half Hour (produced by Christopher Dixon); "Life Is a Dance" (by Gavin Christopher), "Five-Six-Seven-Eight . . . Dance!" (by Wally Harper and David Zippel), "Dance" (by Paul Jabara)—Sandy Duncan, Rockettes, Dancers, Singers.

LA TRAGÉDIE DE CARMEN—Carl Johan Falkman as Escamillo and Patricia Schuman as Carmen

5-6-7-8 . . . Band!
"It's Better With a Band" (by Wally Harper and David Zippel)—Duncan, Dancers.
5-6-7-8 . . . Husband!
Meet Don (produced by Christopher Dixon); "You Mustn't Kick It Around" (by Richard Rodgers and Lorenz Hart)—Don Correia Dancers, Rockettes; "It Only Happens When I Dance With You" (by Irving Berlin)—Duncan, Correia, Dancers, Singers.
5-6-7-8 . . . Protest!
"Singers Protest" (by Wally Harper and David Zippel), "One Step" (by Richard Maltby Jr. and David Shire)—Armelia McQueen, Rockettes, Singers.
5-6-7-8 . . . Victory!
"Bad Habits" (by Billy Field and Tom Price), "It's Not What You Weigh" (by Wally Harper and David Zippel), "Sing, Sing, Sing" (by Louis Prima), "Make Way for Tomorrow" (by Ira Gershwin, Yip Harburg and Jerome Kern)—Company.

ACT II

5-6-7-8 . . . Entr'acte!
5-6-7-8 . . . Marilyn!
Don's Fantasy (produced by Christopher Dixon); "I Go to Rio" (by Peter Allen and Adrienne Anderson), "I'm Flying" (by Mark Charlap and Carolyn Leigh)—Duncan, Correia, Rockettes, Singers.
5-6-7-8 . . . Sandy!
"She Just Loves Las Vegas!" (by Wally Harper and David Zippel), "Dance With Me" (by R. Parker Jr. and David Rubinson), "Neverland" (by Mark Charlap and Carolyn Leigh)—Duncan, Male Dancers.
5-6-7-8 . . . Audition!
"Tea for Two" (by Vincent Youmans)—Bill Irwin.
5-6-7-8 . . . Inspirations!
Dance Teams Medley of "I Love to Dance" (by Marilyn and Alan Bergman and Billy Goldenberg), "Tres Moutarde" (by Cecil Macklin), "La Cumparcita" (by G.H. Matos Rodriquez), "The Continental" (by Con Conrad), "Our Love Is Here to Stay" (by George Gershwin)—Dancers; "Where Did You Learn to Dance" (by Joe Myrow and Mack Gordon)—Duncan, Marge Champion; "I Love to Dance" (by Marilyn and Alan Bergman and Billy Goldenberg)—Champion, Correia, Dancers.
5-6-7-8 . . . Finale!
"Broadway Rhythm" (by Arthur Freed and Nacio Herb Brown), "Body Language" (by Steve Sperry and Barry Fasman)—Company.

Note: Radio City Music Hall also presented a return engagement of *The Magnificent Christmas Spectacular* for 92 performances 11/18/83–1/4/84 at Radio City Music Hall, conceived, produced and directed by Robert F. Jani; scenery, Charles Lisanby; costumes, Frank Spencer; lighting, Ken Billington; principal staging, Frank Wagner; staging and choreography, Violet Holmes, Linda Lemac, Frank Wagner; choral arrangements, Tom Bahler, Don Pippin; orchestrations, Elman Anderson, Robert M. Freedman, Michael Gibson, Arthur Harris; with a cast of Thomas Ruisinger, Edward Prostak, Kimberley Moke, Amy Dolan, Sky Ashley Berdahl, Rickie Cramer, Patricia Ward, Joan Cooper-Mirabella, David Roman, Michael Lott, Lou Ann Csaszar, Jeff Johnson, Ron Chisholm, Michael Graham, John Cunningham, The Rockettes and The New Yorkers.

The Guys in the Truck (1). By Howard Reifsnyder. Produced by James Conley at the New Apollo Theater. Opened and closed at the evening performance, June 19, 1983.

Al Klein	Harris Laskawy	Les Hammond	Robert Trumbull
Louie DeFalco	Lawrence Guardino	Nick Caruso	Lloyd Battista
Charlie Johnson	Geoffrey C. Ewing	Billie Fenstermacher	Bobbi Jo Lathan
Doug Frischetti	Mike Starr	Hugo Broonzy	Gary Klar
Harvey Olmstead	James Gleason		

Directed by David Black; scenery and costumes, John Falabella; lighting, John Gleason; sound, T. Richard Fitzgerald; associate producer, Paul Levine; production stage manager, Frank Marino; press, Burnham-Callaghan Associates, Jay D. Schwartz.
Comedy centering on sports broadcasting. The play was presented in two parts.

Mame (41). Revival of the musical based on the book *Auntie Mame* by Patrick Dennis and the play by Jerome Lawrence and Robert E. Lee; book by Jerome Lawrence and Robert E. Lee; music and lyrics by Jerry Herman. Produced by the Mitch Leigh Company at the Gershwin Theater. Opened July 24, 1983. (Closed August 28, 1983)

Patrick Dennis (age 10)	Roshi Handwerger	Bishop	Merwin Foard
Agnes Gooch	Jane Connell	M. Lindsay Woolsey	Donald Torres
Vera Charles	Anne Francine	Ito	Sab Shimono
Mame Dennis	Angela Lansbury	Doorman	Brian McAnally
Ralph Devine	Jacob Mark Hopkin	Elevator Boy	Marshall Hagins

Messenger................... David Miles
Dwight Babcock .... Willard Waterman
Bubbles the Clown; Gregor ..... Ken Henley
Dance Teacher;
  Mrs. Upson.............. Louise Kirtland
Bird Dancers.............. Suzanne Ishee,
                      Patrick Sean Murphy
Leading Man; Uncle Jeff .... Kenneth Kantor
Stage Manager............. Richard Poole
Mme. Branislowski;
  Mother Burnside............ Fran Stevens

Beauregard Jackson
  Pickett Burnside............ Scot Stewart
Cousin Fan................... Carol Lurie
Sally Cato.................. Barbara Lang
Patrick Dennis (age 19–29) .... Byron Nease
Junior Babcock .... Patrick Sean Murphy
Mr. Upson................. John C. Becher
Gloria Upson............. Michaela Hughes
Pegeen Ryan .... Ellyn Arons
Peter Dennis .... Daniel Mahon

Mame's Friends: Ellyn Arons, Alyson Bristol, Merwin Foard, Marshall Hagins, Ken Henley, Jacob Mark Hopkin, Michaela Hughes, Suzanne Ishee, Kenneth Kantor, Harry Kingsley, Melinda Koblick, David Loring, Carol Lurie, Brian McAnally, David Miles, Patrick Sean Murphy, Viewma Negromonte, Michele Pigliavento, Cissy Rebich, Richard Poole, Joseph Rich, Mollie Smith.

Understudies: Mr. Handwerger—Daniel Mahon; Miss Connell—Cissy Rebich; Miss Francine—Barbara Lang; Messrs. Torres, Shimono, Waterman, Becher—Kenneth Kantor; Miss Stevens—Louise Kirtland; Mr. Stewart—Donald Torres; Miss Lang—Carol Lurie; Mr. Murphy—Merwin Foard; Miss Kirtland—Fran Stevens; Mr. Mahon—Roshi Handwerger; Mr. Shimono—Ken Henley.

Directed by John Bowab; choreography recreated by Diana Baffa Brill from original choreography by Onna White; musical direction, Jim Coleman; production supervision, Jerry Herman; scenery, Peter Wolf, based on original designs by William and Jean Eckart; costumes by Robert Mackintosh, Miss Lansbury's furs by Maximilian; lighting, Thomas Skelton; sound, Christine Voellinger; orchestrations, Philip J. Lang; vocal arrangements, Donald Pippin; executive producer, Michael Lynne; associate producer, Manny Kladitis; stage manager, Paul Phillips; press, John A. Prescott.

Time: 1928–1946. Place: Mame's Beekman Place apartment and various locales in which she becomes involved.

Mame was first produced on Broadway 5/24/66 for 1,508 performances. This production was its first major New York revival.

ACT I

Scene 1: Somewhere in New York, 1928
  "St. Bridget".. Agnes, Patrick
Scene 2: Mame's apartment
  "It's Today" .... Mame, Company
Scene 3: Hallway of Mame's apartment
Scene 4: Mame's bedroom
Scene 5: Mame's living room (and all around New York)
  "Open a New Window"... Mame, Company
Scene 6: Mame's apartment
Scene 7: Shubert Theater—New Haven
  "The Man in the Moon".................................... Vera, Mame, Company
  "My Best Girl".. Patrick, Mame
Scene 8: Salon Pour Messieurs
Scene 9: Mame's apartment
  "We Need a Little Christmas" .... Mame, Patrick, Agnes, Ito, Beau
Scene 10: Peckerwood
  "The Fox Hunt".............. Uncle Jeff, Patrick, Cousin Fan, Mother Burnside, Cousins
  "Mame"... Beau, Company

ACT II

Scene 1: Prep school and college (and Singapore)
  "Mame" (Reprise) .... Patrick
  "My Best Girl" (Reprise) .... Patrick

Scene 2: Mame's apartment
"Bosom Buddies" .... Mame, Vera
Scene 3: Mame's apartment (six months later)
"Gooch's Song" .... Agnes
Scene 4: Upson farm
"That's How Young I Feel" .... Mame, Company
"If He Walked Into My Life".. Mame
Scene 5: Mame's apartment
"It's Today" (Reprise).. Mame, Company
"My Best Girl" (Reprise) .... Patrick
Scene 6: Mame's apartment—1946
"Open a New Window" (Reprise) .... Mame

*La Cage aux Folles (327). Musical based on the play *La Cage aux Folles* by Jean
Poiret; book by Harvey Fierstein; music and lyrics by Jerry Herman. Produced by Allan
Carr with Kenneth D. Greenblatt, Marvin A. Krauss, Stewart F. Lane, James M.
Nederlander, Martin Richards, and Barry Brown and Fritz Holt executive producers, at
the Palace Theater. Opened August 21, 1983.

Georges	Gene Barry	Albin	George Hearn
"Les Cagelles":		Jean-Michel	John Weiner
Chantal	David Cahn	Anne	Leslie Stevens
Monique	Dennis Callahan	Jacqueline	Elizabeth Parrish
Dermah	Frank DiPasquale	Renaud	Walter Charles
Nicole	John Dolf	St. Tropez Townspeople:	
Hanna	David Engel	Mme. Renaud	Sydney Anderson
Mercedes	David Evans	Paulette	Betsy Craig
Bitelle	Linda Haberman	Hercule	Jack Neubeck
Lo Singh	Eric Lamp	Etienne	Jay Pierce
Odette	Dan O'Grady	Babette	Marie Santell
Angelique	Deborah Phelan	Colette	Jennifer Smith
Phaedra	David Scala	Tabarro	Mark Waldrop
Clo-Clo	Sam Singhaus	Pepe	Ken Ward
Francis	Brian Kelly	Edouard Dindon	Jay Garner
Jacob	William Thomas Jr.	Marie Dindon	Merle Louise

Swing performers: Robert Brubach, Drew Geraci, Jan Leigh Herndon, Leslie Simons.
Understudies: Messrs. Hearn, Barry, Garner—Walter Charles; Mr. Thomas—Ken Ward; Mr.
Weiner—Drew Geraci; Miss Stevens—Jan Leigh Herndon; Miss Louise—Betsy Craig; Miss Parrish
—Sydney Anderson; Mr. Kelly—Robert Brubach; Mr. Charles—Jack Neubeck.
Directed by Arthur Laurents; choreography, Scott Salmon; musical direction and vocal arrange-
ments, Don Pippin; scenery, David Mitchell; costumes, Theoni V. Aldredge; lighting, Jules
Fisher; sound, Peter J. Fitzgerald; orchestrations, Jim Tyler; dance music arrangements, G. Har-
rell; assistant choreographer, Richard Balestrino; produced in association with Jonathan Farkas, John
Pomerantz, Martin Heinfling; production stage manager, Fritz Holt; stage manager, James Pente-
cost; press, Shirley Herz, Sam Rudy, Peter Cromarty.
Time: Summer. Place: St. Tropez, France.
Night club owner and his star performer, longtime homosexual lovers, in family crisis when the
former's son decides to marry the daughter of a straitlaced politician.
Jamie Ross replaced Gene Barry 2/20/84. Gene Barry replaced Jamie Ross 2/27/84.
A Best Play; see page 100.

ACT I

Overture
"We Are What We Are".. Les Cagelles
"A Little More Mascara" .... Albin, Friends
"With Anne on My Arm".. Jean-Michel
"With You on My Arm" .... Georges, Albin

"The Promenade"... Townspeople
"Song on the Sand" .... Georges
"La Cage aux Folles" .... Albin, Les Cagelles
"I Am What I Am".. Albin

ACT II

Entr'acte
"Song on the Sand" (Reprise)... Georges, Albin
"Masculinity".. Georges, Albin, Townspeople
"Look Over There" .... Georges
"Cocktail Counterpoint" .... Georges, Dindon, Mme. Dindon, Jacob
"The Best of Times" .... Albin, Jacqueline, Patrons
"Look Over There" (Reprise).. Jean-Michel
Grand Finale

The Corn Is Green (32). Revival of the play by Emlyn Williams. Produced by the Elizabeth Theater Group, Zev Bufman and Elizabeth Taylor producers, at the Lunt-Fontanne Theater. Opened August 22, 1983. (Closed September 18, 1983)

John Goronwy Jones........	Frank Hamilton	Robbart Robbatch..........	Ciaran O'Reilly
Miss Ronberry..............	Elizabeth Seal	Morgan Evans.............	Peter Gallagher
Idwal Morris.................	Neal Jones	Glyn Thomas............	Michael Nostrand
Sarah Pugh	Myvanwy Jenn	John Owen................	Robert McNeill
Groom; Dix.............	Michael Rothhaar	Will Hughes...............	Loris Sallahian
The Squire....................	Gil Rogers	Old Tom....................	John Eames
Mrs. Watty..............	Marge Redmond	A Mother................	Kristin Linklater
Bessie Watty	Mia Dillon	Knox.....................	Donald Buka
Miss Moffat.................	Cicely Tyson	Myfanwy	Connie Roderick

The Ash Grove Quartet: Myvanwy Jenn, Neal Jones, Kristin Linklater, Robert McNeill. Welsh Chorus: Donald Buka, John Eames, Myvanwy Jenn, Neal Jones, Kristin Linklater, Robert McNeill, Michael Nostrand, Ciaran O'Reilly, Connie Roderick, Michael Rothhaar, Loris Sallahian.

Standbys: Miss Tyson—Kristin Linklater; Mr. Gallagher—Neal Jones. Understudies: Miss Dillon, Messrs. McNeill, Nostrand—Connie Roderick; Misses Seal, Redmond—Myvanwy Jenn; Mr. Hamilton—John Eames; Miss Jenn—Kristin Linklater; Messrs. Eames, Rogers—Donald Buka; Messrs. O'Reilly, Jones, Sallahian—Michael Rothhaar.

Directed by Vivian Matalon; scenery, William Ritman; costumes, Theoni V. Aldredge; lighting, Richard Nelson; sound, Jack Mann; production stage manager, Charles Blackwell; stage manager, Henry Velez; press, Fred Nathan & Associates, Eileen McMahon, Anne Abrams.

Time: The latter part of the last century over a period of three years. Place: The living room of a house in Glensarno, a small village in the remote Welsh countryside. Act I, Scene 1: An afternoon in June. Scene 2: A night in August, six weeks later. Act II: An early evening in August, two years later. Act III, Scene 1: A morning in November, three months later. Scene 2: An afternoon in July, seven months later.

The Corn Is Green was first produced on Broadway 11/26/40 for 477 performances and was named a Best Play of its season and won the Critics Award for best foreign play. It has subsequently been revived on Broadway 5/3/43 for 56 performances and 1/11/50 for 16 performances, and off Broadway in the 1953–54 and 1961–62 seasons.

Edmund Kean (29). One-man performance by Ben Kingsley in a play by Raymund Fitzsimons. Produced by Alexander H. Cohen and Hildy Parks at the Brooks Atkinson Theater. Opened September 27, 1983. (Closed October 29, 1983)

Directed by Alison Sutcliffe; design, Martin Tilley; lighting, John Watt; choreography, Cleoné Rive; coordinating producer, Roy A. Somlyo; produced in association with Duncan C. Weldon, Paul Gregg, Lionel Becker, Peter Wilson; production stage manager, Alan Hall; stage manager, Ruth E. Rinklin; press, Merle Debuskey Associates, David Roggensack.

Ben Kingsley in excerpts from the life and major roles of Edmund Kean, the 19th century tragedian. The play was presented in two parts. A foreign play previously produced in London.

*Zorba (262). Revival of the musical based on the novel by Nikos Kazantzakis; book by Joseph Stein; music by John Kander; lyrics by Fred Ebb. Produced by Barry and Fran Weissler and Kenneth-John Productions, Inc. at the Broadway Theater. Opened October 16, 1983.

The Woman............... Debbie Shapiro	Mimiko.................... Aurelio Padron
Konstandi; Turkish Dancer;	Katapolis; Monk............. Peter Kevoian
Russian Admiral............. Frank DeSal	Yorgo;
Thanassai; French Admiral;	Italian Admiral...... Richard Warren Pugh
Monk...................... John Mineo	Sophia; Crow............. Pamela Trevisani
Constable.............. Raphael LaManna	Mavrodani.................. Charles Karel
Athena; Crow .... Suzanne Costallos	Pavli................ Thomas David Scalise
Niko.................. Robert Westenberg	Manolakas.............. Michael Dantuono
Zorba.................... Anthony Quinn	Widow...................... Taro Meyer
Despo; Crow................ Panchali Null	Priest; English Admiral........ Paul Straney
Marika; Crow .... Angelina Fiordellisi	Madame Hortense............ Lila Kedrova
Katina..................... Susan Terry	Marsalias; Monk............. Rob Marshall
Vassilakas.................. Chip Cornelius	Anagnosti..................... Tim Flavin
Marinakos; Monk............ Peter Marinos	Maria; Cafe Whore........ Karen Giombetti

Musicians: Antony Geralis assistant conductor, keyboards; Foti Gonis onstage bouzouki; Eddie Kochak dumbeg; Angelo Saridis bouzouki; Charles Sauss accordion; David Tancredi percussion.

Standbys: Mr. Quinn—Charles Karel, James Lockhart; Miss Kedrova—Suzanne Costallos; Miss Shapiro—Angelina Fiordellisi; Mr. Westenberg—Michael Dantuono; Miss Meyer—Susan Terry; Mr. Karel—James Lockhart; Mr. Padron—John Mineo; Mr. Dantuono—Chip Cornelius; Swings—Jim Litten, Danielle R. Striker; Dance Captain—Jim Litten.

Directed by Michael Cacoyannis; choreography, Graciela Daniele; musical director, Randolph Mauldin; scenery, David Chapman; costumes, Hal George; lighting, Marc B. Weiss; sound system, T. Richard Fitzgerald; musical supervisor, Paul Gemignani; orchestrations, Don Walker; dance arrangements, Thomas Fay; associate producer, Alecia Parker; production stage manager, Peter Lawrence; stage manager, Jim Woolley; press, Fred Nathan & Associates, Anne Abrams, Leslie Anderson, Bert Fink.

Zorba was produced on Broadway 11/17/68 for 305 performances.

Vivian Blaine replaced Lila Kedrova 1/10/84. Lila Kedrova replaced Vivian Blaine 1/31/84.

ACT I

Scene 1: A market place, Piraeus
"Life Is" .... The Woman, Company
Scene 2: A cafe, Piraeus
"The First Time" .... Zorba
Scene 3: A Crete village
"The Top of the Hill" .... The Woman, Company
Scene 4: Hortense's garden
"No Boom Boom" .... Hortense, Admirals, Zorba, Niko
Scene 5: Interior of Hortense's inn
"Vive la Difference" .... Admirals
Scene 6: The mine site
"Mine Song" .... Company
Scene 7: A village street
"The Butterfly".. Widow, Niko, The Woman
"Goodbye Canavaro"................................... Hortense, Zorba, Niko
Scene 8: A bar in Piraeus
"Grandpapa".. Zorba, The Woman, Company
        (Additional choreography by Theodore Pappas)

HEARTBREAK HOUSE—Rex Harrison and Amy Irving in
the revival at Circle in the Square

Scene 9: A village street
  "Only Love" .... Hortense
  "The Bend of the Road" .... The Woman
  "Only Love" (Reprise).. The Woman

ACT II

Scene 1: Hortense's garden
  "Yassou"... Company
  "Woman" .... Zorba
Scene 2: The widow's house
  "Why Can't I Speak/That's a Beginning"...................... Widow, Niko, The Woman
Scene 3: The church square
  "Easter Dance"... Company
Scene 4: Entrance to the mine
  "Miner's Dance".. Men

Scene 5: Hortense's bedroom
"The Crow" .... The Woman, Crows, Monks
"Happy Birthday" .... Hortense
Scene 6: The port, Piraeus
"I Am Free" .... Zorba

American Buffalo (102). Revival of the play by David Mamet. Produced by Elliot Martin and Arnold Bernhard in the Long Wharf Theater production at the Booth Theater. Opened October 27, 1983. (Closed February 4, 1984)

Donny Dubrow .... J.J. Johnston   Walter Cole (Teacher) .... Al Pacino
Bobby .... James Hayden

Standbys: Mr. Hayden—John Shepard; Mr. Johnston—Ralph Monaco.
Directed by Arvin Brown; scenery, Marjorie Bradley Kellogg; costumes, Bill Walker; lighting, Ronald Wallace; production stage manager, Wally Peterson; press, Jeffrey Richards Associates, C. George Willard.
Place: Don's Resale Shop, a junkshop. Act I: One Friday, in the morning. Act II: About 11 o'clock that night.
American Buffalo was produced on Broadway 2/16/77 for 135 performances and was named a Best Play of its season and won the Critics Award for best American play. It was revived off Broadway in this Long Wharf Theater production, directed by Arvin Brown and starring Al Pacino, 6/3/81 for 262 performances.
Bruce MacVittie replaced James Hayden 10/11/83.

Brothers (1). By George Sibbald. Produced by Noel Pearson in association with Orion Television, Inc. and Carnan Productions, Inc. at the Music Box Theater. Opened and closed at the evening performance November 9, 1983.

Tommy .... Dennis Christopher   James .... Pat McNamara
Earl .... Gary Klar   Harry .... Frank Converse
Jim .... Carroll O'Connor

Directed by Carroll O'Connor; scenery, Thomas A. Walsh; costumes, Merrily Murray-Walsh; lighting, Craig Miller; production stage manager, Bethe Ward; press, Seymour Krawitz, Patricia Krawitz, Robert Larkin.
Time: A warm evening in late summer. Place: The back yard of a house in a solid working-class neighborhood in an eastern seaport city. The play was presented in two parts.
Tough union leader dominates his four sons. Previously produced in regional theater at Costa Mesa, Calif.

Amen Corner (29). Musical based on the play *The Amen Corner* by James Baldwin; book by Philip Rose and Peter Udell; music by Garry Sherman; lyrics by Peter Udell. Produced by Prudhomme Productions, Ltd., Edward Mann, Judith Henry, Joel Goldstein, Gil Gerard, at the Nederlander Theater. Opened November 10, 1983. (Closed December 4, 1983).

Margaret Alexander .... Rhetta Hughes   Sister Boxer .... Helena-Joyce Wright
Sister Moore .... Jean Cheek   Brother Boxer .... Chuck Cooper
Odessa .... Ruth Brown   Luke .... Roger Robinson
David .... Keith Lorenzo Amos

Members of the Congregation: Loretta Abbott, Leslie Dockery, Cheryl Freeman, Gene Lewis, Denise Morgan, Lewis Robinson, Renee Rose, Vanessa Shaw, Jeffery V. Thompson.
Dancers: Loretta Abbott, Leslie Dockery, Renee Rose. Swings: Venida Evans, Leonard Piggee.
Understudies: Miss Hughes—Denise Morgan; Miss Brown—Venida Evans; Miss Cheek—Vanessa Shaw; Miss Wright—Cheryl Freeman; Mr. Cooper—Jeffery V. Thompson; Mr. Amos—Lewis Robinson; Mr. Robinson—Gene Lewis.
Directed by Philip Rose; choreography, Al Perryman; musical direction, Margaret Harris; scenery,

Karl Eigsti; costumes, Felix E. Cochren; lighting, Shirley Prendergast; orchestrations, Garry Sherman, Dunn Pearson; vocal arrangements, Garry Sherman; dance arrangements, George Butcher; assistant musical director, Joseph Joubert; production stage manager, Mortimer Halpern; stage managers, Dwight R.B. Cook, Sherry Lambert; press, Fred Nathan & Associates, Anne Abrams, Leslie Anderson, Bert Fink.

Time: The early 1930s. Place: A sanctified storefront church in Harlem and in the adjoining apartment.

Family and congregation problems of a Harlem church's lady pastor, based on *The Amen Corner*, produced on Broadway 4/15/65 for 84 performances.

ACT I

Scene 1: Church, Sunday morning
"Amen Corner" .... Margaret
Scene 2: Apartment, later that morning
"That Woman Can't Play No Piano" .... David, Friends
"In the Real World" .... Brother Boxer
"You Ain't Gonna Pick Up Where You Left Off" .... Margaret, Luke
Scene 3: Apartment, late afternoon the following Saturday
"In the Real World" (Reprise) .... Sister Boxer
"We Got a Good Thing Goin' " .... Luke, David
Scene 4: Church, same afternoon
"In His Own Good Time" . Sister Boxer, Brother Boxer, Sister Moore, Odessa, Congregation
Scene 5: Apartment, same afternoon
"Heat Sensation" .... Luke
"Everytime We Call It Quits" .... Luke

ACT II

Entr'acte .... Orchestra
Scene 1: Apartment, early Sunday morning
"Somewhere Close By" .... Odessa
"Leanin' on the Lord" ..... Sister Moore, Brother Boxer, Sister Boxer, Odessa, Congregation
"I'm Already Gone" .... David
"Love Dies Hard" .... Margaret
"Everytime We Call It Quits" (Reprise) .... Luke, Margaret
"Rise Up and Stand Again" .... Margaret

La Tragédie de Carmen (187). Musical adapted in the French language from Georges Bizet's opera by Marius Constant, Jean-Claude Carrière and Peter Brook. Produced by Alexander H. Cohen and Hildy Parks in the Peter Brook production, as originally presented in Paris at the Bouffes du Nord by the Théâtre National de l'Opéra de Paris and the Centre International de Créations Théâtrales, Micheline Rozan producer, at the Vivian Beaumont Theater. Opened November 17, 1983 (see note). (Closed April 28, 1984)

(Carmen).... Cynthia Clarey, Hélene Delavault, Emily Golden, Eva Saurova, Patricia Schuman
(Don José)........ Evan Bortnick, Laurence Dale, Howard Hensel, James Hoback, Peter Puzzo
(Micaëla)............ Anne Christine Biel, Véronique Dietschy, Agnès Host, Beverly Morgan
(Escamillo) .... Carl Johan Falkman, Jake Gardner, Ronald Madden, John Rath
(Lillas Pastia) .... Andreas Katsulas, Alain Maratrat
(Zuniga).. Jean-Paul Denizon, Andreas Katsulas
(Garcia).. Andreas Katsulas, Tapa Sudana
Old Woman.. Andreas Katsulas
(Parentheses indicate roles in which the performers alternated)

Orchestra: Randall Behr, Roger Cantrell conductors; Dennis Cleveland, Francine Post violin; Sandra Robbins viola; Michael Goldschlager cello; Lewis Paer bass; Mary Landolfi flute; Diane Lesser oboe; Larry Guy clarinet; Andrew Schwartz bassoon; David Wakefield French horn; Chris

Gekker trumpet; Michael Powell trombone; Raymond Pool harp; Daniel Druckman percussion; Gerald Tarack music coordinator.

Directed by Peter Brook; musical director, Marius Constant; scenery, Jean-Guy Lecat; costumes, Chloé Obolensky; artistic advisor, Bernard Lefort; associate director, Maurice Benichou; co-produced by Roy A. Somlyo; presented in association with James Nederlander Jr. and Arthur Rubin; production stage manager, Robert L. Borod; stage manager, Christopher A. Cohen; press, Merle Debuskey Associates, David Roggensack.

The *Carmen* tragedy stripped down to its dramatic skeleton but retaining highlights of the Bizet score, presented without intermission. A foreign play previously produced in Paris.

Note: An English version of this production, translated by Sheldon Harnick, opened 3/19/84 and continued in repertory with the French version, with the same cast alternating performances in the two languages.

Special Best Play citation; see page 257.

Marilyn (16). Musical with book by Patricia Michaels; music and lyrics by Jeanne Napoli, Doug Frank, Gary Portnoy, Beth Lawrence and Norman Thalheimer. Produced by Malcolm Cooke, William May, Dolores Quinton, James Kabler, Joseph Dio-Guardi, John Ricciardelli, Arnold Bruck, Tom Kaye, Leo Rosenthal, Harper Sibley, June Curtis and Renee Blau in association with Jerome Minskoff at the Minskoff Theater. Opened November 20, 1983. (Closed December 3, 1983)

Young Norma Jean	Kristi Coombs	Agent	Mitchell Greenberg
Norma Jean; Marilyn Monroe	Alyson Reed	Studio Head	Alan North
Jim Dougherty	George Dvorsky	Director	Gary-Michael Davies
Babs; Sis	Lise Lang	Asst. Director; Actor	Ty Crowley
Pat	Debi Monahan	Cameraman	Ed Forsyth
Madge; Coach; Companion	Dooba Wilkins	Designer	Michael Rivera
Elda; Louella	Melissa Bailey	Junior	Kevin Cort
Dottie; Hedda	Mary Testa	Tommy	Willy Falk
Ramona; Hairdresser	Deborah Dotson	Joe DiMaggio	Scott Bakula
Virginia	Jodi Marzorati	Arthur Miller	Will Gerard
Photographer	James Haskins	Strasberg	Steve Schocket
Soldier	Mark Ziebell		

Destiny: Peggie Blue, Michael Kubala, T.A. Stephens.

Ensemble: Melissa Bailey, Eileen Casey, Andrew Charles, Kevin Cort, Ty Crowley, Gary-Michael Davies, Deborah Dotson, Mark Esposito, Ed Forsyth, Marcial Gonzalez, Christine Gradl, Marguerite Lowell, Jodi Marzorati, Debi Monahan, Michael Rivera, Steve Schocket, Mary Testa, Dooba Wilkins, Mark Ziebell. Swings: Ivson Polk, Maryellen Scilla.

Understudies: Miss Blue, Messrs. Kubala, Stephens (Destiny)—Deborah Dotson, Michael Rivera, Mark Ziebell; Miss Coombs—Sarah Litzsinger; Miss Reed—Marguerite Lowell; Mr. Dvorsky—James Haskins; Mr. Haskins—Andrew Charles; Messrs. Greenberg, North—Steve Schocket; Miss Lang—Christine Gradl; Mr. Falk—Mark Ziebell; Mr. Bakula—Gary-Michael Davies; Mr. Gerard—Mitchell Greenberg.

Directed and choreographed by Kenny Ortega; musical supervision, direction, vocal and orchestral arrangements, Steven Margoshes; scenery, Tom H. John; costumes, Joseph G. Aulisi; lighting, Marcia Madeira; sound, T. Richard Fitzgerald; orchestrations, Bill Brohn; dance arrangements and additional orchestrations, Donald Johnston; additional dance arrangements, Ronald Melrose; assistant director, Greg Smith; assistant choreographer, Veda Jackson; associate producers, Peter Duke, Paul Faske, France Weiner; production stage manager, Steve Zweigbaum; stage manager, Arturo E. Porazzi; press, Shirley Herz, Sam Rudy, Peter Cromarty.

Subtitled "An American Fable," the musicalized life and times of the movie star and sex symbol Marilyn Monroe.

ACT I

Scene 1: A soundstage, Hollywood land
"We Are the Ones" .... Company
(songs are by Beth Lawrence and Norman Thalheimer unless otherwise noted)

Scene 2: Under the Hollywood Hills 1934–1942
  "Close the Door, Norma" .... Destiny
    (by Beth Lawrence)
  "A Single Dream" .... Young Norma Jean, Destiny
    (by Jeanne Napoli and Doug Frank)
  "Jimmy Jimmy" .... Destiny, Norma Jean, Babs, Jim, Pat, Ensemble
    (by Jeanne Napoli and Doug Frank)
  "Church Doors" .... Destiny
Scene 3: The parachute factory, 1945
  "Miss Parachute" .... Photographer, Madge, Elda, Dottie, Ramona, Virginia
Scene 4: Overseas
  "The Golden Dream" .... Soldier
Scene 5: Agent's home, Hollywood
  "Uh-Huh" .... Agent
Scene 6: Studio's executive office
Scene 7: The soundstage, 1948–1953
  "Can't Keep My Heart From Racing" .... Marilyn
    (by Beth Lawrence)
  "Money, Men and More" .... Marilyn, Men
    (by Jeanne Napoli and Doug Frank)
Scene 8: A movie balcony
Scene 9: The soundstage, 1955
  "I'll Send You Roses" .... Joe, Marilyn
  "Church Doors" (Reprise) .... Destiny
Scene 10: Marilyn's dressing room
Scene 11: DiMaggio's Restaurant
  "I'll Send You Roses" (Reprise) .... Joe, Marilyn
Scene 12: Premiere night
  "It's a Premiere Night" .... Company
  "Stairway Leading Nowhere" .... Marilyn
    (by Jeanne Napoli and Doug Frank)

ACT II

Scene 1: Marilyn's bedroom
  "We'll Help You Through the Night" .... Destiny
    (by Jeanne Napoli, Dawsen and Turner)
Scene 2: Soundstage
  "Shootin' " .... Marilyn, Company
  "Run Between the Raindrops" .... Marilyn
    (by Jeanne Napoli and Gary Portnoy)
  "You Are So Beyond" .... Tommy
    (by Jeanne Napoli and Doug Frank)
Scene 3: New York City, 1956–1960
  "In Disguise" .... Marilyn, Arthur, Ensemble
    (by Doug Frank)
  "A Special Man" .... Destiny
    (by Jeanne Napoli and Doug Frank)
  "Church Doors" (Reprise) .... Destiny
Scene 4: New York penthouse
  "Don't Hang Up the Telephone" .... Joe, Marilyn
    (by Jeanne Napoli and Gary Portnoy)
Scene 5: New York to Hollywood
  "All Roads Lead to Hollywood" .... Marilyn, Company
Scene 6: Soundstage
  "My Heart's an Open Door" .... Marilyn, Joe
  "Miss Bubbles" .... Marilyn, Men's Ensemble
    (by Jeanne Napoli, Doug Frank and Gary Portnoy)
  "A Single Dream" (Reprise) .... Marilyn

THE HUMAN COMEDY—Bonnie Koloc and Josh Blake as mother and son in Galt MacDermot–William Dumaresq musical

Doonesbury (104). Musical based on the comic strip *Doonesbury* by Garry Trudeau; book and lyrics by Garry Trudeau; music by Elizabeth Swados. Produced by James Walsh in association with Universal Pictures at the Biltmore Theater. Opened November 21, 1983. (Closed February 19, 1984)

Roland	Reathel Bean	Duke	Gary Beach
Mike Doonesbury	Ralph Bruneau	Honey	Lauren Tom
Mark	Mark Linn-Baker	J.J.	Kate Burton
B.D.	Keith Szarabajka	Joanie	Barbara Andres
Boopsie	Laura Dean	Provost	Peter Shawn
Zonker	Albert Macklin	Voice of Pres. Reagan	Reathel Bean

Musicians: Jeff Waxman conductor, keyboards; David Sawyer drums, percussion; Steve Skinner assistant conductor, keyboards, synthesizer programmer; Seth Glassman bass guitar.

Understudies: Messrs. Bruneau, Linn-Baker, Szarabajka, Shawn—Max Cantor; Mr. Bean—Peter

Shawn; Mr. Macklin—Scott Evans; Misses Burton, Dean—Eve Bennett-Gordon; Miss Andres—Deborah Darr; Miss Tom—Janet Wong.

Directed by Jacques Levy; choreography, Margo Sappington; musical direction and arrangements, Jeff Waxman; scenery, Peter Larkin; costumes, Patricia McGourty; lighting, Beverly Emmons; sound, Tom Morse; orchestrations, Elizabeth Swados; production stage manager, Warren Crane; stage managers, Deborah Clelland, Scott Evans; press, Jeffrey Richards Associates, C. George Willard.

Time: Graduation weekend. Place: Walden, an off-off-campus house.

The *Doonesbury* 1960s-type characters on the eve of graduation from college and preparing to join the middle class mainstream.

ACT I

Walden—living room
"Graduation" .... Roland, Mike, B.D., Boopsie, Mark, Zonker
"Just One More Night" .... Mike
Walden—back porch
"I Came to Tan" .... Zonker, Ensemble
Los Angeles County Courtroom
"Guilty" .... Duke, Ensemble
Walden—living room
"I Can Have It All" .... Boopsie, Ensemble
Los Angeles County Courtroom
Walden—living room
"Get Together" .... J.J., Mike
WBBY—radio station
"Baby Boom Boogie Boy" .... Mark, Roland, Ensemble
Walden—living room
"Another Memorable Meal" .... Mike, B.D., Boopsie, Mark, Zonker, J.J., Joanie

ACT II

Walden—living room
"Just a House" .... Ensemble
Walden—front yard
"Complicated Man" .... Honey, Boopsie
Walden Puddle
"Real Estate" .... Duke, Zonker
Walden—living room
"Mother" .... J.J., Joanie
"It's the Right Time To Be Rich" .... B.D., Roland
"Muffy & The Topsiders" .... Boopsie, Mike, Mark, Zonker
"Just One Night" (Reprise) .... Mike, J.J.
Commencement Exercises
"Graduation" (Reprise) .... Ensemble

The Glass Menagerie (92). Revival of the play by Tennessee Williams. Produced by Elizabeth I. McCann, Nelle Nugent, Maurice Rosenfield, Lois E. Rosenfield and Ray Larsen at the Eugene O'Neill Theater. Opened December 1, 1983. (Closed February 19, 1984)

The Mother .... Jessica Tandy   Her Daughter .... Amanda Plummer
Her Son .... Bruce Davison   The Gentleman Caller .... John Heard

Standbys: Miss Tandy—Mary Doyle; Miss Plummer—Kymberly Dakin; Mr. Davison—Alfred Karl; Mr. Heard—Bennett Liss.

Directed by John Dexter; scenery, Ming Cho Lee; costumes, Patricia Zipprodt; lighting, Andy Phillips; sound, Otts Munderloh; music, Paul Bowles; production stage manager, William Chance; stage manager, Bonnie Panson; press, Solters/Roskin/Friedman, Inc., Josh Ellis, Louise Ment.

Time: The past. Place: An alley in St. Louis. Part I: Preparation for a gentleman caller. Part II: The gentleman calls.

The last major New York revival of *The Glass Menagerie* was by Circle in the Square on Broadway 12/18/75 for 78 performances.

*Baby (205). Musical based on a story developed by Susan Yankowitz; book by Sybille Pearson; lyrics by Richard Maltby Jr; music by David Shire. Produced by James B. Freydberg and Ivan Bloch, Kenneth-John Productions, Inc. and Suzanne J. Schwartz in association with Manuscript Productions at the Ethel Barrymore Theater. Opened December 4, 1983.

Lizzie Fields	Liz Callaway	Mr. Weiss	Philip Hoffman
Danny Hooper	Todd Graff	Dean Webber; Mr. Hart	Dennis Warning
Arlene MacNally	Beth Fowler	Intern	Lon Hoyt
Alan MacNally	James Congdon	1st Woman; 5th Woman	Judith Thiergaard
Pam Sakarian	Catherine Cox	2d Woman	Lisa Robinson
Nick Sakarian	Martin Vidnovic	3d Woman	Kirsti Carnahan
Nurse; 4th Woman	Barbara Gilbert	6th Woman	Kim Criswell
Doctor	John Jellison		

People in the town: Kirsti Carnahan, Kim Criswell, Barbara Gilbert, Philip Hoffman, Lon Hoyt, John Jellison, Lisa Robinson, Judith Thiergaard, Dennis Warning.

Understudies: Miss Callaway—Kirsti Carnahan; Mr. Graff—Lon Hoyt; Miss Fowler—Judith Thiergaard; Mr. Congdon—John Jellison; Miss Cox—Lisa Robinson; Mr. Vidnovic—Philip Hoffman; Mr. Jellison—Michael Waldron; Swings—Judith Bliss, Michael Waldron.

Directed by Richard Maltby Jr.; musical staging, Wayne Cilento; musical direction, Peter Howard; scenery, John Lee Beatty; costumes, Jennifer Von Mayrhauser; lighting, Pat Collins; film design, John Pieplow; film sequences, Lennart Nilsson, Bo G. Erikson, Carl O. Lofman and Swedish television; orchestrations, Jonathan Tunick; sound, Jack Mann; sound textures and electronic programming, Dan Wyman; associate producers, Ronald Licht, Robert A. Stewart, J.C. Associates, Elaine Yaker, Karen Howard, Lillian Steinberg; production stage manager, Peter B. Mumford; stage manager, Gary M. Zabinski; press, Judy Jacksina, Glenna Freedman, Susan Chicoine, Marcy Granata, Marc P. Thibodeau, Kevin Boyle.

The experiences of three couples, each of which is having or trying to have a baby.

ACT I

March to early April
  A college town
    "We Start Today".................... Danny, Lizzie; Alan, Arlene; Nick, Pam; People
Early April
  Danny and Lizzie's apartment
    "What Could Be Better?" .... Danny, Lizzie
  Alan and Arlene's bedroom
    "The Plaza Song"... Alan, Arlene
  Nick and Pam's bedroom
    "Baby, Baby, Baby"....................... Nick, Pam; Alan, Arlene; Danny, Lizzie
Mid-April
  A doctor's waiting room
    "I Want It All" .... Pam, Lizzie, Arlene
  The track
    "At Night She Comes Home to Me"................................ Nick, Danny
  On the campus
    "What Could Be Better?" (Reprise)................................ Danny, Lizzie
Early May
  A doctor's office
  A baseball field
    "Fatherhood Blues" .... Danny, Alan, Nick, Mr. Weiss, Dean Webber
  Alan and Arlene's bedroom

Mid-May
   A bus station; Alan and Arlene's house
   Nick and Pam's bedroom
      "Romance" .... Nick, Pam
      "I Chose Right" .... Danny
Early June
   Graduation
      "We Start Today" (Reprise) .... Ensemble
Mid-July
   Danny and Lizzie's apartment
      "The Story Goes On" .... Lizzie

ACT II

Late August
   The town
      "The Ladies Singin' Their Song" .... Lizzie, Women
Early September
   A doctor's office
   On the campus
      "Baby, Baby, Baby" (Reprise)... Arlene
   Nick and Pam's bedroom
      "Romance" (Reprise).. Nick, Pam
   Alan and Arlene's Porch
      "Easier to Love"... Alan
Mid-September
   Danny and Lizzie's apartment
      "Two People in Love" .... Danny, Lizzie
Mid-October
   Nick and Pam's bedroom
      "With You"... Nick, Pam
   Alan and Arlene's porch
      "And What If We Had Loved Like That" .... Alan, Arlene
Mid-November
   All three bedrooms
      "We Start Today" (Reprise) .... Danny, Lizzie, Nick, Pam, Alan, Arlene
      "The Story Goes On" (Reprise) .... Company

Circle in the Square. Schedule of two revivals. **Heartbreak House** (66). By George Bernard Shaw. Opened December 7, 1983. (Closed February 5, 1984) **Awake and Sing!** (61). By Clifford Odets. Opened March 8, 1984. (Closed April 29, 1984) Produced by Circle in the Square, Theodore Mann artistic director, Paul Libin managing director, at Circle in the Square Theater.

HEARTBREAK HOUSE

Ellie Dunn	Amy Irving	Mazzini Dunn	William Prince
Nurse Guiness	Jan Miner	Hector Hushabye.........	Stephen McHattie
Capt. Shotover..............	Rex Harrison	Boss Mangan	Philip Bosco
Ariadne Utterword	Dana Ivey	Randall Utterword	Bill Moor
Hesione Hushabye.........	Rosemary Harris		

   Directed by Anthony Page; scenery, Marjorie Bradley Kellogg; costumes, Jane Greenwood; lighting, Paul Gallo; fight staging, B.H. Barry; produced by arrangement with Duncan C. Weldon with Paul Gregg and Lionel Becker for Triumph Apollo Productions, Ltd.; production stage manager, Michael F. Ritchie; stage manager, Ted William Sowa; press, Merle Debuskey, David Roggensack.

Time: 1912. Place: The house of Capt. Shotover situated in the hilly country on the north edge of Sussex, England. Act I: Late afternoon. Act II: After dinner the same day. Act III: Immediately after. This production previously appeared in London at the Haymarket 3/10/83–6/11/83. The last major New York revival of *Heartbreak House* was by Roundabout off Broadway 4/29/80 for 31 performances.

AWAKE AND SING!

Ralph Berger	Thomas G. Waites	Schlosser	Luke Sickle
Myron Berger	Dick Latessa	Moe Axelrod	Harry Hamlin
Hennie Berger	Frances McDormand	Uncle Morty	Michael Lombard
Jacob	Paul Sparer	Sam Feinschreiber	Benjamin Hendrickson
Bessie Berger	Nancy Marchand		

Standbys: Miss Marchand—Phyllis Newman; Messrs. Lombard, Sparer, Latessa, Sickle—Roger Serbagi. Understudies: Messrs. Waites, Hamlin, Hendrickson—Jacob Harran; Miss McDormand—Kathryn C. Sparer.

Directed by Theodore Mann; scenery, John Conklin; costumes, Jennifer Von Mayrhauser; lighting, Richard Nelson.

Place: An apartment in the Bronx. Act I, Scene 1: 1933, late summer. Scene 2: One year later, winter. Act II, Scene 1: That night. Scene 2: A week later.

The last major New York revival of *Awake and Sing!* was by Roundabout off Broadway 4/19/79 for 45 performances.

*Noises Off (199). By Michael Frayn. Produced by James M. Nederlander, Robert Fryer, Jerome Minskoff, Kennedy Center and Michael Codron in association with Jonathan Farkas and MTM Enterprises at the Brooks Atkinson Theater. Opened December 11, 1983.

Dotty Otley	Dorothy Loudon	Frederick Fellowes	Paxton Whitehead
Lloyd Dallas	Brian Murray	Belinda Blair	Linda Thorson
Garry Lejeune	Victor Garber	Tim Allgood	Jim Piddock
Brooke Ashton	Deborah Rush	Selsdon Mowbray	Douglas Seale
Poppy Norton-Taylor	Amy Wright		

Standbys: Misses Loudon, Thorson—Patricia Kilgarriff; Misses Rush, Wright—Elizabeth Austin; Mr. Seale—Herb Foster; Messrs. Murray, Whitehead—Rudolph Willrich; Messrs. Garber, Piddock—Patrick Clear.

Directed by Michael Blakemore; scenery and costumes, Michael Annals; lighting, Martin Aronstein; production stage manager, Susie Cordon; stage manager, Laura deBuys; press, Fred Nathan & Associates, Anne Abrams, Leslie Anderson, Bert Fink.

Act I: The living room of the Brents' country home on a Wednesday afternoon (Grand Theater, Weston-Super-Mare, Monday, Jan. 14). Act I (sic): The living room of the Brents' country home on a Wednesday afternoon (Theater Royal, Goole, Wednesday matinee, Feb. 13). Act I (sic): The living room of the Brents' country home on a Wednesday afternoon (Municipal Theater, Stockton-on-Tees, Saturday, March 8). The play was presented in three parts.

Comedy, a British troupe tours a slapstick farce called *Nothing On* (the play-within-the-play) in small towns in England. A foreign play previously produced in London.

A Best Play; see page 154.

Peg (5). One-woman musical with story and new lyrics and performed by Peggy Lee; new music by Paul Horner. Produced by Zev Bufman, Marge and Irv Cowan and Georgia Frontiere at the Lunt-Fontanne Theater. Opened December 14, 1983. (Closed December 17, 1983.

Quartet: Michael Renzi piano; Grady Tate drums; Jay Leonhart bass; Bucky Pizzarelli guitar. Directed by Robert Drivas; creative consultant, Cy Coleman; musical direction, Larry Fallon;

scenery, Tom H. John; costumes, Florence Klotz; lighting, Thomas Skelton; sound, Jan Nebozenko; sound consultant, Phil Ramone; vocal arrangements, Ray Charles; orchestrations, Artie Butler, Larry Fallon, Dominic Frontiere, Bill Holman, Gordon Jenkins, Philip J. Lang, Johnny Mandel, Billy May, Leon Pendarvis, Don Sebesky, Larry Wilcox, Tore Zito; production stage manager, Larry Forde; stage manager, Mark Rubinsky; press, David Powers.

Subtitled "A Musical Autobiography," with Miss Lee playing herself in excerpts from her life and career and singing a collection of songs, some new and some previously popularized by her.

MUSICAL NUMBERS (music by Paul Horner, lyrics by Peggy Lee unless otherwise noted), ACT I: "Fever" (by Johnny Davenport and Eddie Cooley, special lyrics by Peggy Lee); "Soul"; "Daddy Was a Railroad Man"; "Mama"; "That Old Piano"; "One Beating a Day" (music and lyrics by Peggy Lee); "That's How I Learned to Sing the Blues"; "Goody, Goody" (by Johnny Mercer and Matt Malneck); "Sometimes You're Up"; "He'll Make Me Believe That He's Mine"; "Why Don't You Do Right?" (by Joe McCoy).

ACT II: Overture; "I Love Being Here With You" (by Peggy Lee); "The Other Part of Me"; "I Don't Know Enough About You" (by Peggy Lee and Dave Barbour); "Angels on Your Pillow"; "It's a Good Day" (by Peggy Lee and Dave Barbour); "Manana" (by Peggy Lee and Dave Barbour); "What Did Dey Do to My Goil?"; "Stay Away From Louisville Lou" (music by Milton Ager, lyrics by Jack Yellen); "No More Rainbows"; "Flowers and Flowers"; "Lover" (music by Richard Rodgers, lyrics by Lorenz Hart); "Big Spender" (music by Cy Coleman, lyrics by Dorothy Fields); "I'm a Woman" (by Jerry Lieber and Mike Stoller); "Is That All There Is?" (by Jerry Lieber and Mike Stoller); "There Is More"; Bows and Exit Music.

*The Tap Dance Kid (169). Musical based on the novel *Nobody's Family Is Going to Change* by Louise Fitzhugh; book by Charles Blackwell; music by Henry Krieger; lyrics by Robert Lorick. Produced by Stanley White, Evelyn Barron, Harvey J. Klaris and Michel Stuart at the Broadhurst Theater. Opened December 21, 1983.

Daddy Bates	Alan Weeks	Emma	Martine Allard
Dipsey	Hinton Battle	William	Samuel E. Wright
Willie	Alfonso Ribeiro	Mona	Karen Paskow
Dulcie	Barbara Montgomery	Carole	Jackie Lowe
Ginnie	Hattie Winston	Winslow	Michael Blevins

Little Rio Dancers and New Yorkers: Leah Bass, Kevin Berdini, Michael Blevins, Karen Curlee, Suzzanne Douglas, Rick Emery, Karen E. Fraction, D.J. Giagni, J.J. Jepson, Karen Paskow, Rodney Alan McGuire, Jackie Patterson, Mayme Paul, Jamie M. Pisano, Ken Prescott, James Young.

Swings: Lloyd Culbreath, Linda Von Germer.

Standby: Mr. Wright—Donny Burks. Understudies: Messrs. Battle, Weeks—Jackie Patterson; Miss Winston—Suzzanne Douglas; Miss Allard—Tracey Mitchem; Mr. Ribeiro—David Callaway, Jimmy Tate; Misses Lowe, Montgomery—Leah Bass; Mr. Blevins—D.J. Giagni; Miss Paskow —Jamie M. Pisano.

Directed by Vivian Matalon; dances and musical staging, Danny Daniels; musical supervision, orchestra and vocal arrangements, Harold Wheeler; musical and vocal direction, Don Jones; scenery, Michael Hotopp, Paul dePass; costumes, Ann Emonts; lighting, Richard Nelson; dance music arrangements, Peter Howard; sound, Jack Mann; associate choreographer, D.J. Giagni; scenic photography, Mark Feldstein; associate producers, Mark Beigelman, Richard Chwatt; produced in association with Michael Kleinman Productions; production stage manager, Joe Lorden; stage manager, Jack Gianino; press, Judy Jacksina, Glenna Freedman, Susan Chicoine, Marcy Granata, Marc P. Thibodeau, Kevin Boyle.

Time: The present. Place: New York City: Roosevelt Island and Manhattan. The play was presented in a prologue and two acts.

A youngster's ambition to make it as a dancer on the New York stage.

ACT I

Scene 1: Dining room

"Another Day" .... Ginnie, Emma, Dulcie

Scene 2: Little Rio Club

SHIRLEY MACLAINE ON BROADWAY—The star *(seated)* is backed up by dancers Antonette Yuskis, Larry Vickers, Mark Reina and Jamilah Lucas in this scene from her show

Scene 3: Willie's bedroom
  "Someday" .... Emma, Willie
  "Lullabye"... Ginnie
  "Tap Tap".. Daddy Bates, Willie, Dipsey
Scene 4: Manhattan tram station
  "Dance if It Makes You Happy" .... Willie, Dipsey, Daddy Bates, Carole, Dancers
Scene 5: William's study
Scene 6: Dipsey's loft
  "William's Song" .... William
Scene 7: Outside Dipsey's loft
  "Class Act" (Finale)... The Family

*The Real Thing (172). By Tom Stoppard. Produced by Emanuel Azenberg, The Shubert Organization, Icarus Productions, Byron Goldman, Ivan Bloch, Roger Berlind and Michael Codron at the Plymouth Theater. Opened January 5, 1984.

Max	Kenneth Welsh	Billy	Peter Gallagher
Charlotte	Christine Baranski	Debbie	Cynthia Nixon
Henry	Jeremy Irons	Brodie	Vyto Ruginis
Annie	Glenn Close		

Standbys: Messrs. Irons, Welsh—Edmond Genest; Misses Close, Baranski—Leslie Lyles; Miss Nixon—Yeardley Smith; Messrs. Gallagher, Ruginis—Todd Waring.

Directed by Mike Nichols; scenery, Tony Walton; costumes, Anthea Sylbert; lighting, Tharon Musser; sound, Otts Munderloh; production supervisor, Martin Herzer; production stage manager, Alan Hall; press, Bill Evans, Sandra Manley.

The play was presented in two parts, with two years elapsing between Acts I and II.

Facets of commitment and unfaithfulness in love and marriage. A foreign play previously produced in London.

A Best Play; see page 174.

Ian McKellen Acting Shakespeare (37). One-man performance by Ian McKellen in selections from and comments on the works of William Shakespeare. Produced by Arthur Cantor, Bonnie Nelson Schwartz and Rebecca Kuehn at the Ritz Theater. Opened January 19, 1984. (Closed February 19, 1984)

Associate producer, Harvey Elliott; lighting, Charles Bugbee; stage manager, Mitchell Erickson; press, Arthur Cantor Associates, Harvey Elliott.

Part I: Jacques in As You Like It; King Henry V; Polonius, Hamlet, First Player in Hamlet; Bully Bottom in A Midsummer Night's Dream; Chorus in Henry V; Duke of Gloucester in Henry VI, Part 3; Prince Hal, Sir John Falstaff in Henry IV, Part 1; Mrs Quickly in Henry V; Sonnet XX: Romeo and Juliet.

Part II: The Tragedy of King Richard II; Samuel Pepys; David Garrick; George Bernard Shaw; Macbeth; Prospero in The Tempest.

Excerpts from the plays presented in a context of commentary on them, with parody of other actors, personal reminiscence and historical references. Previously produced at the Edinburgh Festival in 1976 and elsewhere including two benefit performances in New York and (in this version) in Los Angeles.

Open Admissions (17). By Shirley Lauro. Produced by Stevie Phillips in association with Universal Pictures. Opened January 29, 1984. (Closed February 12, 1984)

Calvin Jefferson	Calvin Levels	Peter Carlsen	Kevin Tighe
Salina Jones	Nan-Lynn Nelson	Cathy Carlsen	Maura Erin Sullivan
Georgia Jones	Pam Potillo	Prof. Clare Block	Sloane Shelton
Ginny Carlsen	Marilyn Rockafellow	Kitty Shim	Una Kim

Nick Rizzoli............ Vincent D'Onofrio   Mrs. Brewster .... C.C.H. Pounder
Juan Rivera .... Evan Miranda

Standby: Miss Rockafellow—Joy Franz. Understudies: Misses Shelton, Pounder—Faith Geer; Mr. Tighe—Richard Fitzpatrick; Miss Kim—June Angela; Miss Potillo—Tahra Takeesha Brown; Messrs. D'Onofrio, Miranda—Al Ferrer. Miss Nelson—C.C.H. Pounder; Miss Sullivan—Jessica Rubinstein.

Directed by Elinor Renfield; scenery, David Gropman; costumes, Ann Roth, Gary Jones; lighting, Tharon Musser; sound, Chuck London Media/Stewart Werner; associate producer, Bonnie Champion; production stage manager, Paul Phillips; stage manager, Michael J. Frank; press, Shirley Herz Associates, Sam Rudy, Peter Cromarty.

Time: The present, one day in January. Place: In and near Calvin and Ginny's Manhattan apartments and in a public college in New York City. The play was presented in two parts.

Shortcomings of the open admissions public education policy suffered by both pupils and teachers. Previously produced off off Broadway and at the Long Wharf Theater, New Haven, Conn.

*The Rink (129). Musical with book by Terrence McNally; music by John Kander; lyrics by Fred Ebb. Produced by Jules Fisher, Roger Berlind and Joan Cullman, Milbro Productions, Kenneth-John Productions, Inc. in association with Jonathan Farkas at the Martin Beck Theater. Opened February 9, 1984.

CAST: Angel—Liza Minnelli; Little Girl—Kim Hauser; Anna—Chita Rivera; Lino, Lenny, Punk, Uncle Fausto—Jason Alexander; Buddy, Hiram, Mrs. Jackson, Charlie, Suitor, Junior Miller—Mel Johnson Jr.; Guy, Dino, Father Rocco, Debbie Duberman—Scott Holmes; Lucky, Sugar, Punk, Arnie, Suitor, Bobby Perillo, Danny—Scott Ellis; Tony, Tom, Punk, Suitor, Peter Reilly—Frank Mastrocola; Ben, Dino's Father, Mrs. Silverman, Sister Philomena—Ronn Carroll.

Standbys: Miss Rivera—Patti Karr; Miss Minnelli—Lenora Nemetz. Understudies: Messrs. Alexander, Ellis, Mastrocola—Rob Marshall; Mr. Holmes—Frank Mastrocola; Messrs. Carroll, Johnson —Jim Tushar; Miss Hauser—Kimi Parks.

Directed by A.J. Antoon; choreography, Graciela Daniele; musical director, Paul Gemignani; scenery, Peter Larkin; costumes, Theoni V. Aldredge; lighting, Marc B. Weiss; sound, Otts Munderloh; dance arrangements, Tom Fay; orchestrations, Michael Gibson; assistant choreographer, Tina Paul; associate producer, Tina Chen; executive producer Robin Ullman; produced in association with Jujamcyn Theaters Corp., Richard G. Wolff president; production stage manager, Ed Aldridge; stage manager, Craig Jacobs; press, Merle Debuskey, William Schelble.

Time: The 1970s. Place: A roller rink somewhere on the Eastern seaboard.

Reunion between an estranged daughter and mother who owns a roller skating rink.

ACT I

"Colored Lights" .... Angel
"Chief Cook and Bottle Washer".. Anna
"Don't Ah Ma Me".. Anna, Angel
"Blue Crystal" .... Dino
"Under the Roller Coaster" .... Angel
"Not Enough Magic".......... Dino, Angel, Anna, Sugar, Hiram, Tom, Lenny, Dino's Father
"We Can Make It" .... Anna
"After All These Years" .... Wreckers
"Angel's Rink and Social Center" .... Angel, Wreckers
"What Happened to the Old Days?" .... Anna, Mrs. Silverman, Mrs. Jackson
"Colored Lights" (Reprise).. Angel

ACT II

"The Apple Doesn't Fall".. Anna, Angel
"Marry Me" .... Lenny
"We Can Make It" (Reprise) .... Anna
"Mrs. A." .... Anna, Angel, Lenny, Suitors
"The Rink" .... Suitors

334 THE BEST PLAYS OF 1983–1984

"Wallflower" .... Anna, Angel
"All the Children in a Row" .... Angel, Danny
Coda. .... Anna, Angel

*Glengarry Glen Ross (78). By David Mamet. Produced by Elliot Martin, The Shubert Organization, Arnold Bernhard and the Goodman Theater at the John Golden Theater. Opened March 25, 1984.

Shelly Levene	Robert Prosky	Richard Roma	Joe Mantegna
John Williamson	J.T. Walsh	James Lingk	Lane Smith
Dave Moss	James Tolkan	Baylen	Jack Wallace
George Aaronow	Mike Nussbaum		

Directed by Gregory Mosher; scenery, Michael Merritt; costumes, Nan Cibula; lighting, Kevin Rigdon; production stage manager, Joseph Drummond; stage manager, Daniel Miller Morris; press, Jeffrey Richards Associates, C. George Willard.

Act I: Three scenes in a Chinese restaurant. Act II: A real estate office.

Real estate salesmen hustling and competing with each other for sales leads. Previously produced in London.

A Best Play; see page 201.

*Death of a Salesman (66). Revival of the play by Arthur Miller. Produced by Robert Whitehead and Roger L. Stevens at the Broadhurst Theater. Opened March 29, 1984.

Willy Loman	Dustin Hoffman	Uncle Ben	Louis Zorich
Linda	Kate Reid	Howard Wagner	Jon Polito
Happy	Stephen Lang	Jenny	Patricia Fay
Biff	John Malkovich	Stanley	Tom Signorelli
Bernard	David Chandler	Miss Forsythe	Linda Kozlowski
Woman From Boston	Kathy Rossetter	Letta	Karen Needle
Charley	David Huddleston	Waiter	Michael Quinlan

Understudies: Messrs. Malkovich, Lang—Andrew Bloch; Messrs. Hoffman, Huddleston, Zorich, Signorelli—Bruce Kirby; Misses Fay, Kozlowski, Needle—Anne McIntosh; Messrs. Chandler, Polito —Michael Quinlan.

Directed by Michael Rudman; scenery, Ben Edwards; costumes, Ruth Morley; lighting, Thomas Skelton; music, Alex North; production associate, Doris Blum; production stage manager, Thomas A. Kelly; stage manager, Charles Kindl; press, Patricia Krawitz.

Time: A 24-hour period. Place: Willy Loman's home and yard and various places he visits in New York and Boston. The play was presented in two parts.

The last major New York revival of *Death of a Salesman* was by Circle in the Square on Broadway with George C. Scott as Willy Loman, 6/26/75 for 64 performances.

The Human Comedy (13). Transfer from off Broadway of the musical based on the novel by William Saroyan; libretto by William Dumaresq; music by Galt MacDermot. Produced by Joseph Papp and The Shubert Organization in the New York Shakespeare Festival production at the Royale Theater. Opened April 5, 1984. (Closed April 15, 1984)

Trainman	David Lawrence Johnson	Spangler	Rex Smith
Ulysses Macauley	Josh Blake	Thief	Christopher Edmonds
Mrs. Kate Macauley	Bonnie Koloc	Mr. Grogan	Gordon Connell
Homer Macauley	Stephen Geoffreys	Felix	Daniel Noel
Bess Macauley	Mary Elizabeth Mastrantonio	Beautiful Music	Debra Byrd
Helen	Anne Marie Bobby	Mary Arena	Caroline Peyton
Miss Hicks	Laurie Franks	Mexican Woman	Olga Merediz

Voice of Matthew	Neighbor .... Kathleen Rowe McAllen
Macauley................ Grady Mulligan	Diana Steed .... Leata Galloway
Marcus Macauley .... Don Kehr	Minister .... Walter Hudson
Tobey .... Joseph Kolinski	

Musicians: Joel Derouin, Josh Rodriguez violin; Gregory Singer viola; Nestor Cybriwsky cello; Doug Shear double bass; Jimmy Madison percussion; Charles C. Brown III guitars; Seldon Powell, Allen Won sax, clarinet, flute; Allen Shawn keyboard; Mac Gollehan trumpet, flugelhorn; Eddie Bert trombone.

Soldiers: Kenneth Bryan, Louis Padilla, Michael Willson. Townspeople: Marc Stephen DelGatto, Lisa Kirchner, Vernon Spencer, Dan Tramon.

Standby: Miss Koloc—Cass Morgan. Understudies: Messrs. Johnson, Noel—Vernon Spencer; Master Blake—Marc Stephen DelGatto; Miss Koloc—Lisa Kirchner; Mr. Geoffreys—Dan Tramon; Misses Mastrantonio, Peyton—Donna Murphy; Misses Bobby, Galloway—Kathleen Rowe McAllen; Miss Franks—Debra Byrd; Mr. Kehr—Grady Mulligan; Mr. Smith—Walter Hudson, Grady Mulligan; Mr. Edmonds—Daniel Noel; Mr. Connell—David Vogel; Miss Byrd—David Lawrence Johnson; Miss Merediz—Lisa Kirchner; Mr. Kolinski—Louis Padilla; Swing—David Vogel.

Directed by Wilford Leach; musical direction and orchestrations, Galt MacDermot; scenery, Bob Shaw; costumes, Rita Ryack; lighting, James F. Ingalls; sound, Tom Morse; conductor, Tania Leon; associate producer, Jason Steven Cohen; production stage manager, Alan Fox; stage manager, K. Siobhan Phelan; press, Merle Debuskey, Richard Kornberg, Barbara Carroll, Bruce Campbell.

Time: 1943. Place: A little town in California.

Musical version of Saroyan's novel produced off Broadway by New York Shakespeare Festival at the Public Theater 12/28/83–3/4/84 for 79 performances before being transferred to Broadway.

ACT I

"In a Little Town in California" .... Company
At the train crossing
   "Hi Ya, Kid" .... Trainman, Ulysses
At home
   "We're a Little Family".......................... Mrs. Macauley, Homer, Ulysses, Bess
At school
   "The Assyrians" .... Helen, Miss Hicks
   "Noses".. Homer
At the telegraph office
   "You're a Little Young for the Job" .... Spangler, Homer
   "I Can Carry a Tune"... Homer
   "Happy Birthday" .... Homer
   "Happy Anniversary" .... Homer, Spangler, Mr. Grogan
   "I Think the Kid Will Do"..................................... Mr. Grogan, Spangler
   "Beautiful Music".. Beautiful Music, Company
   "Cocoanut Cream Pie" .... Mr. Grogan, Homer
   "When I Am Lost" .... Homer, Beautiful Music, Company
Message
   "I Said, Oh No"...................................... Bess, Mary, Mexican Woman
At home
   "Daddy Will Not Come Walking Through the Door".................... Mrs. Macauley
   "The Birds in the Sky" .... Bess
   "Remember Always to Give" .... Mrs. Macauley
   "Long Past Sunset" .... Voice of Matthew Macauley
Message
   "Don't Tell Me"............................. Mary Arena, Marcus, Family, Company
At the telegraph office
   "The Fourth Telegram"....................................... Spangler, Mr. Grogan
   "Give Me All the Money" .... Thief, Spangler

At home
"Everything Is Changed"..................................... Homer, Mrs. Macauley
"The World Is Full of Loneliness"................................. Mrs. Macauley
"Hi Ya, Kid" (Reprise)................................. Trainman, Ulysses, Company

ACT II

At the debarkation center
"How I Love Your Thingamajig"... Soldiers
"Everlasting"... Tobey
"An Orphan I Am"... Tobey
"I'll Tell You About My Family" .... Marcus
At home
"I Wish I Were a Man" .... Mary Arena
War front
"Marcus, My Friend" .... Tobey
"My Sister Bess" .... Marcus
Home front
"I've Known a Lot of Guys" .... Diana Steed
"Diana"... Spangler
At war and at home
"Dear Brother"... Homer, Marcus
"The Birds in the Trees/A Lot of Men" .... Diana Steed, Spangler
"Parting"................. Mrs. Macauley, Wives, Sweethearts, Mothers, Friends, Soldiers
At the telegraph office
"Mr. Grogan, Wake Up"... Homer
"Hello, Doc".. Spangler
In the park
"What Am I Supposed to Do?" .... Homer, Spangler
Home
"Long Past Sunset" (Reprise)............................... Mrs. Macauley, Company
"I'm Home" .... Tobey
"Somewhere, Someone".. Bess
"I'll Always Love You"................................... Mary Arena, Company
"Hi Ya, Kid" (Reprise)................................. Trainman, Ulysses, Company
"Fathers and Mothers (And You and Me)" .... Company

The Golden Age (29). By A.R. Gurney Jr.; suggested by *The Aspern Papers* by Henry James. Produced by Nicholas Benton, Stanley Flink, Brent Peek and Force Ten Productions, Inc. at the Jack Lawrence Theater. Opened April 12, 1984. (Closed May 6, 1984)

Virginia................ Stockard Channing   Isabel Hastings Hoyt.......... Irene Worth
Tom .... Jeff Daniels

Directed by John Tillinger; scenery, Oliver Smith; costumes, Jane Greenwood; lighting, Arden Fingerhut; production stage manager, Franklin Keysar; stage manager, Judy Boese; press, David Powers, Leo Stern.

Time: Spring and summer, today. Place: The front room of the second floor of a brownstone house on the Upper East Side of New York City. The play was presented in two parts.

Scholar in search of a manuscript manages to gain access to the home and lives of a dowager and her granddaughter. Previously produced at Kennedy Center, Washington, D.C.

Shirley MacLaine on Broadway (47). Variety show with original music and lyrics by Marvin Hamlisch and Christopher Adler; additional material by Larry Grossman and Buz Kohan. Produced by Guber/Gross Productions and The Nederlander Organization at the Gershwin Theater. Opened April 19, 1984. (Closed May 27, 1984)

CAST: Shirley MacLaine, Mark Reina (dance captain), Larry Vickers, Jamilah Lucas, Antonette Yuskis.

Musicians: Jack French musical director, John Spooner drums, John Smith bass, Rick Marvin keyboards.

Directed and choreographed by Alan Johnson; costumes, Pete Menefee; lighting, Ken Billington; associate lighting designer, Jeffrey Schissler; produced by Michael Flowers; press, Mark Goldstaub.

Showcase designed to display Shirley MacLaine in dancing, singing and monologue, presented without intermission.

MUSICAL NUMBERS: Overture; "Now" (original music and lyrics by Marvin Hamlisch and Christopher Adler); Harold Arlen Medley (arranged by Marvin Hamlisch); Hooker Medley; "In the Movies" (original music and lyrics by Marvin Hamlisch and Christopher Adler); Choreographers; "Life Is Just a Bowl of Cherries" (new lyrics by Christopher Adler); "Nobody Does It Like Me" (new lyrics by Buz Kohan); "Cockeyed Optimist/Imagine"; "Friends/Now" (Reprise).

Beethoven's Tenth (25). By Peter Ustinov. Produced by Robert A. Buckley, Douglas Urbanski and Sandra Moss in association with the Baltimore Center for Performing Arts at the Nederlander Theater. Opened April 22, 1984. (Closed May 13, 1984)

Stephen Fauldgate	George Rose	Dr. Collis Jagger	Gwyllum Evans
Jessica Fauldgate	Mary Jay	Father	Anderson Matthews
Irmgard	Gina Friedlander	Countess Giulietta Guiccardi	Leslie O'Hara
Pascal Fauldgate	Adam Redfield	Count Robert Wenzel	
Ludwig	Peter Ustinov	Gallenberg	Neil Flanagan

Understudies: Mr. Ustinov—John Messenger; Messrs. Rose, Flanagan—John Swindells; Miss Jay —Victoria Boothby; Messrs. Redfield, Matthews—Richard DeFabees; Misses Friedlander, O'Hara —Marietta Mead; Mr. Evans—Neil Flanagan.

Directed by Robert Chetwyn; scenery, Kenneth Mellor; costumes, Madeline Ann Graneto; lighting, Martin Aronstein; sound, Jim Morris; production associate, Karen Leahy; Mr. Ustinov's costume, John Fraser; musical sequences, Stephen Pruslin; production stage manager, Jake Hamilton; stage manager, Joe Cappelli; press, Marilynn LeVine, Merle Frimark, Meg Gordean.

Place: The London home of Stephen Fauldgate. The play was presented in two parts.

Beethoven comes back to life to straighten out the affairs of a music critic. A foreign play previously produced in London and at the Ahmanson Theater, Los Angeles.

Play Memory (5). By Joanna M. Glass. Produced by Alexander H. Cohen and Hildy Parks at the Longacre Theater. Opened April 26, 1984. (Closed April 29, 1984)

Cam MacMillan	Donald Moffat	Miss Halverson	Marilyn Rockafellow
Ruth MacMillan	Jo Henderson	Mike Melzewski	Tom Brennan
Jean MacMillan	Valerie Mahaffey	Duncan	Rex Robbins
Billy	Jerry Mayer	Ross	Curt Williams
Ken	Edwin J. McDonough	Ernest	Steven Moses
Roy	James Greene		

Understudies: Mr. Moffat—Rex Robbins; Miss Henderson—Marilyn Rockafellow; Mr. Robbins —Edwin J. McDonough; Messrs. Williams, Brennan—Jerry Mayers; Messrs. Greene, Mayer, McDonough—Curt Williams; Mr. Moses—Glen Gardali. Standby: Miss Mahaffey—Lizbeth Mackay.

Directed by Harold Prince; scenery, Clarke Dunham; costumes, William Ivey Long; lighting, Ken Billington; incidental music, Larry Grossman; associate producer, Samuel Klutznick; co-presented by Bernard Gersten; production stage manager, Francis X. Kuhn; stage manager, Marc Schlackman; press, Merle Debuskey, David Roggensack.

Time: 1939 to 1968. Place: The city of Sasketoon, Saskatchewan, Canada. The play was presented in two parts.

Reflections on a family's decline through alcoholism and other problems.

A MOON FOR THE MISBEGOTTEN—Kate Nelligan and Jerome Kilty in a revival of the Eugene O'Neill play

Oliver! (17). Revival of the musical freely adapted from Charles Dickens's *Oliver Twist*; book, music and lyrics by Lionel Bart. Produced by Cameron Mackintosh, Carole J. Shorenstein and James M. Nederlander by arrangement with The Southbrook Group at the Mark Hellinger Theater. Opened April 29, 1984. (Closed May 13, 1984)

Oliver Twist . . . . Braden Danner
At the Workhouse:
  Mr. Bumble . . . . Michael McCarty
  Mrs. Bumble . . . . Elizabeth Larner
At the undertaker's:
  Mr. Sowerberry . . . . Roderick Horn
  Mrs. Sowerberry . . . . Frances Cuka
  Charlotte . . . . Andi Henig
  Noah Claypole . . . . Alan Braunstein
At the Thieves' Kitchen:

Fagin . . . . Ron Moody
The Artful Dodger . . . . David Garlick
Nancy . . . . Patti LuPone
Bet . . . . Sarah E. Litzsinger
Bill Sikes . . . . Graeme Campbell
Bullseye . . . . Vito; Buffy
At the Brownlows':
  Mr. Brownlow . . . . Michael Allinson
  Dr. Grimwig . . . . Louis Beachner
  Mrs. Bedwin . . . . Elizabeth Larner

Workhouse Boys and Fagin's Gang: Robert David Cavanaugh, Samir Chowdhury, Ruben Cuevas, Roshi Handwerger, Cameron Johann, Mark Manasseri, Michael Manasseri, Kipp Marcus, Shawn Morgal, Brian Noodt, Roy Nygaard, R.D. Robb, Dennis Singletary, Zachary A. Stier.

Londoners: Diane Armistead, Louis Beachner, Alan Braunstein, Frances Cuka, W.P. Dremak, Gregg Edelman, Tony Gilbert, Eleanor Glockner, Beth Guiffre, Andi Henig, Roderick Horn, Jan Horvath, Michael McCarty, William McClary, Marcia Mitzman, Martin Moran, Barbara Moroz, Cheryl Russell, Clark Sayre, Jane Strauss, Susan Willis.

Alternate for Oliver Twist—Cameron Johann. Standby: Mr. Moody—Stephen Hanan. Understudies: Mr. Danner—Cameron Johann, Zachary A. Stier; Miss LuPone—Marcia Mitzman; Mr. Campbell—Tony Gilbert; Miss Larner (Mrs. Bumble)—Eleanor Glockner; Mr. Allinson—Louis Beachner; Mr. Garlick—Kipp Marcus, Michael Manasseri; Miss Litzsinger—Andi Henig; Miss Larner (Mrs. Bedwin)—Diane Armistead; Mr. Beachner—W.P. Dremak; Miss Henig—Jane

Strauss; Mr. Horn—William McClary; Mr. Braunstein—Martin Moran; Miss Cuka—Susan Willis; Swings—Edward Prostak, Carrie Wilder, Joe Anthony Wright.

Directed by Peter Coe; musical direction, John Lesko; design, Sean Kenny; lighting, Andrew Bridge; sound, Jack Mann; orchestrations, Eric Rogers; executive producers, R. Tyler Gatchell Jr., Peter Neufeld; associate director, Geoffrey Ferris; production stage manager, Sam Stickler; stage manager, Bethe Ward; press, Fred Nathan, Anne Abrams.

Time: About 1850. Place: North of England and London. Act I: The workhouse, the undertaker's, Paddington Green, the Thieves' Kitchen, streets of London. Act II: The "Three Cripples," the Brownlows', the Thieves' Kitchen, the Brownlows', London Bridge.

Oliver! was originally produced on Broadway 1/6/63 for 774 performances and in a return engagement 8/2/65 for 64 performances. This is its first major New York revival.

The list of musical numbers in *Oliver!* appears on page 293 of *The Best Plays of 1962–63.*

*A Moon for the Misbegotten (36). Revival of the play by Eugene O'Neill. Produced by The Shubert Organization and Emanuel Azenberg at the Cort Theater. Opened May 1, 1984.

Josie Hogan	Kate Nelligan	James Tyrone Jr.	Ian Bannen
Mike Hogan	John Bellucci	T. Stedman Harder	Michael Tolaydo
Phil Hogan	Jerome Kilty		

Standbys: Miss Nelligan—Giulia Pagano; Messrs. Bannen, Tolaydo—Donald Gantry; Mr. Bellucci—Michael Tolaydo; Mr. Kilty—George Hall.

Directed by David Leveaux; scenery and costumes, Brien Vahey; lighting, Marc B. Weiss; original music, Stephen Endelman; production stage manager, Sally J. Jacobs; stage manager, Philip Cusack; press, Bill Evans, Sandra Manley.

Time: Between the hours of noon on a day in early September, 1923, and sunrise of the following day. Place: Connecticut, at the home of tenant farmer Phil Hogan. The play was presented in two parts.

A Moon for the Misbegotten was first produced on Broadway 5/2/57 for 68 performances and was named a Best Play of its season (a 1946–47 Theater Guild production directed by Arthur Shields, played by Mary Welch, James Dunn and J.M. Kerrigan and designed by Robert Edmond Jones closed on the road). Its last major New York revival took place on Broadway 12/29/73 for 314 performances. The 1984 production was previously presented at American Repertory Theater, Cambridge, Mass.

*Sunday in the Park With George (34). Musical with book by James Lapine; music and lyrics by Stephen Sondheim. Produced by The Shubert Organization and Emanuel Azenberg by arrangement with Playwrights Horizons at the Booth Theater. Opened May 2, 1984.

George (Seurat);		Boatman; Charles Redmond	William Parry
George (his grandson)	Mandy Patinkin	Celeste #1; Waitress	Melanie Vaughan
Dot; Marie	Bernadette Peters	Celeste #2; Elaine	Mary D'Arcy
Old Lady; Blair Daniels	Barbara Bryne	Soldier; Alex	Robert Westenberg
Nurse; Mrs.; Harriet Pawling	Judith Moore	Man With Bicycle;	
Franz; Dennis	Brent Spiner	Museum Assistant	John Jellison
Boy; Louise	Danielle Ferland	Little Girl	Michele Rigan
Young Man; Frieda; Betty	Nancy Opel	Woman;	
Man; Louis; Billy Webster	Cris Groenendaal	Photographer	Sue Anne Gershenson
Jules; Bob Greenberg	Charles Kimbrough	Mr.; Lee Randolph	Kurt Knudson
Yvonne; Naomi Eisen	Dana Ivey		

Understudies: Mr. Patinkin—Robert Westenberg; Miss Peters—Joanna Glushak; Misses Bryne, Moore, Ivey—Sara Woods; Messrs. Spiner, Westenberg—Cris Groenendaal, Ray Gill; Miss Ferland—Michele Rigan; Miss Opel—Sue Anne Gershenson; Mr. Groenendaal—Ray Gill, John Jellison; Messrs. Kimbrough, Parry—John Jellison; Misses Vaughan, D'Arcy—Sue Anne Gershenson, Joanna Glushak; Mr. Knudson—Ray Gill.

Musicians: Marilyn Reynolds concert mistress; Cecelia Hobbs violin; Karl Bargen viola; Eileen M. Folson cello; Paul Ford piano, synthesizer; Ted Sperling synthesizer; Beth Schwartz Robinson harp; Ronald Sell French horn; Les Scott, Al Hunt woodwinds; Robert Ayers percussion.

Directed by James Lapine; musical direction, Paul Gemignani; scenery, Tony Straiges; costumes, Patricia Zipprodt, Ann Hould-Ward; lighting, Richard Nelson; special effects, Bran Ferren; sound, Tom Morse; movement, Randolyn Zinn; orchestrations, Michael Starobin; production stage manager, Charles Blackwell; stage managers, Fredric H. Orner, Loretta Robertson; press, Fred Nathan & Associates, Leslie Anderson, Anne Abrams, Ted Killmer, Bert Fink.

Act I: A series of Sundays from 1884 to 1886, alternating between a park on an island in the Seine just outside of Paris and George's studio. Act II: 1984 at an American art museum and on the island.

Though "suggested by the life of Georges Seurat and his painting 'A Sunday Afternoon on the Island of La Grande Jatte' " (a program note states), the characters "Are all products of the authors' imaginations" in the Act I story of a French painter breaking new impressionist ground and (in Act II) his American grandson experimenting with laser effects.

A Best Play; see page 217.

ACT I

"Sunday in the Park With George" .... Dot
"No Life" .... Jules, Yvonne
"Color and Light" .... Dot, George
"Gossip" .... Celeste #1, Celeste #2, Boatman, Nurse, Old Lady, Jules, Yvonne
"The Day Off" .... George, Nurse, Franz, Frieda, Boatman, Soldier, Celeste #1,
    Celeste #2, Yvonne, Louise, Jules, Louis
"Everybody Loves Louis" .... Dot
"Finishing the Hat" .... George
"We Do Not Belong Together" .... Dot, George
"Beautiful" .... Old Lady, George
"Sunday" .... Company

ACT II

"It's Hot Up Here" .... Company
Chromolume #7 .... George, Marie
"Putting It Together" .... George, Company
"Children and Art" .... Marie
"Lesson #8" .... George
"Move On" .... George, Dot
"Sunday" .... Company

A Woman of Independent Means (13). By Elizabeth Forsythe Hailey; based on her novel. Produced by Robert A Buckley, Douglas Urbanski and James Hansen with Della Koenig, Sandra Moss and Warren Cowan at the Biltmore Theater. Opened May 3, 1984. (Closed May 13, 1984)

Bess Steed Garner .... Barbara Rush

Directed by Norman Cohen; incidental music, Henry Mancini; scenery, Roy Christopher; costumes, Garland Riddle; lighting, Martin Aronstein; sound, Jon Gottlieb; production associate, Karen Leahy; associate producers, Robert Michael Geisler, John Roberdeau; production stage manager, Warren Crane; stage manager, Joanne Dalsass; press, Solters/Roskin/Friedman, Inc., Josh Ellis, Louise Ment, Cindy Valk.

Time: A span of a woman's life from 1899 to 1977. The play was presented in two parts.

One-performer play about a Texas matriarch. Previously produced in Los Angeles.

*End of the World (30). By Arthur Kopit. Produced by Kennedy Center and Michael Frazier at The Music Box. Opened May 6, 1984.

Michael Trent .... John Shea
Philip Stone .... Barnard Hughes
Audrey Wood .... Linda Hunt
Paul Cowan .... Richard Seff
Merv Rosenblatt;
  Gen. Wilmer .... David O'Brien

Stella; Ann................. Elaine Petricoff
Stanley Berent .... Jaroslav Stremien
Pete......................... Peter Zapp
Jim .... Nathaniel Ritch
Trent's Son................. Wade Raley

Strangers, Charles, Waiters, Waitress, Attache, Customers: Elaine Petricoff, Nathaniel Ritch, Peter Zapp, Frank Hankey.

Standby: Miss Hunt—Lee Bryant. Understudies: Messrs. Shea, Ritch—Frank Hankey; Messrs. O'Brien, Seff, Stremien—Larry Pine.

Directed by Harold Prince; scenery, Clarke Dunham; costumes, William Ivey Long; lighting, Ken Billington; incidental music, Larry Grossman; sound, Rob Gorton; projections, Clarke Dunham, Lisa Podgur; assistant to Mr. Prince, Ruth Mitchell; production stage manager, Beverley Randolph; stage manager, Steven Kelley; press, Becky Flora.

Act I: The Commission. Act II: The Investigation. Act III: The Discovery.

Mystery millionaire commissions playwright to write a play he hopes will expose an international conspiracy to wage nuclear war.

The Babe (5). By Bob and Ann Acosta. Produced by Corniche Productions, Ltd. at the Princess Theater. Opened May 17, 1984. (Closed May 20, 1984)

George Herman Ruth .... Max Gail

Directed by Noam Pitlik; scenery, Ray Recht; costumes, Judy Dearing; lighting, F. Mitchell Dana; produced by Peter F. Buffa; production stage manager, Doug Laidlaw; stage manager, John O'Neill; press, Max Eisen, Barbara Glenn, Maria Somma.

Scene 1: 1923, the Yankees have just won their first World Series. The Babe is 28 years old, at the top of his game—and on top of the world. Scene 2: 1935, the Babe is 40 years old; his playing days are over. Scene 3: June 13, 1948, as part of the silver anniversary of Yankee Stadium, the oldtimers game is under way; for the last time, Ruth dons the Yankee pinstripes; 60 days later, the Babe will be dead. The play was presented without intermission.

One-character dramatization of the life and career of Babe Ruth.

*****The Wiz** (9). Revival of the musical based on *The Wonderful Wizard of Oz* by L. Frank Baum; book by William F. Brown; music and lyrics by Charlie Smalls. Produced by Tom Mallow, James Janek and The Shubert Organization at the Lunt-Fontanne Theater. Opened May 24, 1984.

Aunt Em .... Peggie Blue
Toto .... Toto
Dorothy .... Stephanie Mills
Uncle Henry;
  Field Mouse .... David Weatherspoon
Tornado .... Daryl Richardson
Addaperle............... Juanita Fleming
Scarecrow............... Charles Valentino
Tinman.................. Howard Porter
Lion .... Gregg Baker
Chief of Field Mice............. Ada Dyer

Field Mouse;
  Lord High Underling... Lawrence Hamilton
Royal Gatekeeper .... Sam Harkness
Head of Society of
  Emerald City .... Sharon Brooks
The Wiz....................... Carl Hall
Evillene...................... Ella Mitchell
Soldier Messenger .... Marvin Engran
Winged Monkey .... Germaine Edwards
Glinda.................... Ann Duquesnay

Munchkins: Carol Dennis, Ada Dyer, Lawrence Hamilton, Sam Harkness, David Weatherspoon. Yellow Brick Road: Alfred L. Dove, Germaine Edwards, Dwight Leon, David Robertson. Sunflowers: Carol Dennis, Ada Dyer, Sam Harkness, David Weatherspoon. Crows: Paula Anita Brown, Marvin Engran, Jasmine Guy. Strangers: Carol Dennis, Sam Harkness, David Weatherspoon. Kalidahs: Marvin Engran, Jasmine Guy, Lawrence Hamilton, Raymond C. Harris, Gigi Hunter, Martial Roumain.

Also Poppies: Sharon Brooks, Paula Anita Brown, Carla Earle, Tanya Gibson, Gigi Hunter, Daryl

Richardson. Emerald City Citizens: Paula Anita Brown, Roslyn Burrough, Carol Dennis, Alfred L. Dove, Ada Dyer, Carla Earle, Germaine Edwards, Marvin Engran, Tanya Gibson, Jasmine Guy, Lawrence Hamilton, Sam Harkness, Raymond C. Harris, Gigi Hunter, Dwight Leon, Daryl Richardson, David Robertson, Martial Roumain, David Weatherspoon.

Understudies: Miss Mills—Ada Dyer; Miss Blue—Ann Duquesnay; Miss Duquesnay, Mr. Richardson—Sharon Brooks; Miss Fleming—Carol Dennis; Miss Mitchell—Juanita Fleming; Mr. Valentino—Germaine Edwards; Mr. Baker—Sam Harkness; Mr. Hall—David Weatherspoon; Mr. Porter—Lawrence Hamilton; Miss Edwards—Alfred L. Dove; Swing Dancers/Singer—Sheri Moore, Eugene Little.

Directed by Geoffrey Holder; choreography and staging of musical numbers, George Faison; musical direction and vocal arrangements, Charles H. Coleman; scenery, Peter Wolf; costumes, Geoffrey Holder; lighting, Paul Sullivan; orchestrations, Harold Wheeler; dance arrangements, Timothy Graphenreed; sound, Gary M. Stocker; assistant musical director, John Simmons; production stage manager, Jack Welles; stage manager Luis Montero; press, Max Eisen, Barbara Glenn, Maria Somma.

The Wiz was originally produced on Broadway 1/5/75 for 1,672 performances. This is its first major New York revival.

The list of scenes and musical numbers in *The Wiz* appears on page 336 of *The Best Plays of 1974–75.*

PLAYS WHICH CLOSED PRIOR TO BROADWAY OPENING

Productions which were organized by New York producers for Broadway presentation but which closed during their production and tryout period are listed below.

Chaplin. Musical with book, music and lyrics by Anthony Newley and Stanley Ralph Ross. Produced by Raymond Katz, Sandy Gallin, James M. Nederlander and Arthur Rubin with David Susskind in a pre-Broadway tryout. Opened at the Music Center Pavilion, Los Angeles, August 12, 1983. (Closed September 24, 1983)

Charlie	Anthony Newley	Matron; Chee Chee San;	
Hannah; Miss Peterson	Mary Leigh Stahl	Lillian	Marsha Bagwell
Young Charlie	Scott Grimes	Grown Sydney	Michael Byers
Young Sydney	Ricky Segall	Teen Charlie	Thom Keeling
M.C.; Mack Sennett; Edwin	Lyle Kanouse	Kamo; Butzi;	
Charles Senior; Hearst	Kenneth H. Waller	Carl Robinson	S. Marc Jordan
Oona; Lita;		Reeves; Fatty Arbuckle; Dubezek;	
Paulette Goddard	Andrea Marcovicci	Oliver Hardy	Ric Stoneback
Victoria	Kathy Andrini	Stan Laurel; Willhartz	Jim MacGeorge
Grudgewick; Picklebrain	Jack Ritschel	Mabel Normand	Sheri Cowart
		Kojo	Thom Sesma

People Who Touched Charlie's Life: Kathy Andrini, K.T. Brown, Sheri Cowart, Nikki D'Amico, Dennis Daniels, Kathleen Dawson, Michael Estes, Michael Jay Lawrence, Aaron Lohr, Bridget Michele, Barbara Moroz, Roger Spivy, Chance Taylor. Swings: Adam Hurley, Frank Kopyc, Alice Anne Oakes, J. Thomas Smith.

Directed and choreographed by Michael Smuin; scenery, Douglas W. Schmidt; costumes, Willa Kim; lighting, Ken Billington; orchestrations, Bill Byers, Chris Boardman, Angela Morley; music supervised, arranged and conducted by Ian Fraser; co-choreographer, Claudia Asbury; production stage manager, Martin Gold; press, Solters/Roskin/Friedman, Josh Ellis, Louise Ment, Cindy Valk.

Musical biography of the great film comedian. The play was presented in two parts.

A SENSE OF HUMOR—Jack Lemmon and Estelle Parsons in
a scene from the play by Ernest Thompson

MUSICAL NUMBERS: Overture, "A Little Bit of Power and Powder and Paint," "Me and You,"
"Joyeux Noel," "Love," "Sydney's Hymn," "Heel and Toe and Away We Go," "Funny Man," "The
American Dream," "Madame Butterfingers," "Doing the Charlie Chaplin," "If Only You Were
Here," "Bonne Nuit, Papa," "My Private Life," "Thanks for Nothing," "Dinner With W.R.," "One
Man Band," "Remember Me."

A Sense of Humor. By Ernest Thompson. Produced by Robert Fryer and Frank Von
Zerneck in association with Center Theater Group/Ahmanson Theater, Los Angeles
in a pre-Broadway tryout. Opened at the Auditorium Theater, Denver, November
16, 1983; at the Ahmanson Theater, Los Angeles, December 4, 1983; and at the Curran
Theater, San Francisco, January 29, 1984. (Closed at the Curran Theater February 26,
1984)

Richard Dale . . . . Jack Lemmon   Abe Manning . . . . Clifton James
Elizabeth Dale . . . . Estelle Parsons   Jean Manning . . . . Polly Holliday

Standbys: Mr. Lemmon—Warren Munson; Misses Parsons, Holliday—Liz Sheridan.
Directed by Robert Greenwald; scenery and lighting, Gerry Hariton, Vicki Baral; costumes, Len
Marcus; Miss Parsons's costumes, Ruth Morley; special artwork, D.J. Hall; associate producer, James
Hansen; production stage managers, A. Robert Altshuler, Jerry Trent; press, Fred Nathan & As-
sociates, Anne Abrams, Leslie Anderson, Bert Fink.
Act I, Scene 1: Nonsense. Scene 2: Innocents. Act II, Scene 1: Ascents of decency. Scene 2: A sense
of humor.
A supermarket manager and his wife cope with a daughter's suicide and a troubled marriage.

Lyndon. By James Prideaux; based on the book *Lyndon* by Merle Miller. Produced by Henry T. Weinstein, Robert W. Whitmore, Yale Wexler and Lester Osterman in association with Warner Brothers, Inc. and Leslie Srager in a pre-Broadway tryout. Opened at the Wilmington, Del. Playhouse January 27, 1984; at the Eisenhower Theater, Washington, D.C. February 2, 1984; at the Shubert Theater, Philadelphia, February 14, 1984. (Closed February 26, 1984)

Lyndon Baines Johnson... Jack Klugman

Directed by George Schaefer; scenery, Roy Christopher; costumes, Al Lehman; lighting, Marcia Madeira; associate producers, Jerry Felix, Brian K. Gendece; production stage manager, Bill McComb; press, Solters/Roskin/Friedman, Inc., Josh Ellis, Milly Schoenbaum, Kevin Patterson.
One-man performance of a biography of the late President. The play was presented in two parts.

PLAYS PRODUCED
OFF BROADWAY

Some distinctions between off-Broadway and Broadway productions at one end of the scale and off-off-Broadway productions at the other were blurred in the New York theater of the 1970s and 1980s. For the purposes of this *Best Plays* listing the term "off Broadway" is used to distinguish a professional from a showcase (off-off-Broadway) production and signifies a show which opened for general audiences in a mid-Manhattan theater seating 499 or fewer and 1) employed an Equity cast, 2) planned a regular schedule of 8 performances a week and 3) offered itself to public comment by critics at a designated opening performance.

Occasional exceptions of inclusion (never of exclusion) are made to take in visiting troupes, borderline cases and a few nonqualifying productions which readers might expect to find in this list because they appear under an off-Broadway heading in other major sources of record.

Figures in parentheses following a play's title give number of performances. These figures do not include previews or extra non-profit performances.

Plays marked with an asterisk (*) were still running on June 1, 1984. Their number of performances is figured from opening night through May 31, 1984.

Certain programs of off-Broadway companies are exceptions to our rule of counting the number of performances from the date of the press coverage. When the official opening takes place late in the run of a play's regularly-priced public or subscription performances (after previews) we count the first performance of record, not the press date, as opening night—and in each such case in the listing we note the variance and give the press date.

In a listing of a show's numbers—dances, sketches, musical scenes, etc.—the titles of songs are identified wherever possible by their appearance in quotation marks (").

Most entries of off-Broadway productions which ran fewer than 20 performances or scheduled fewer than 8 performances a week are somewhat abbreviated, as are entries on running repertory programs repeated from previous years.

HOLDOVERS FROM PREVIOUS SEASONS

Plays which were running on June 1, 1983 are listed below. More detailed information about them appears in previous *Best Plays* volumes of appropriate date. Important cast changes since opening night are recorded in a section of this volume.

THE FANTASTICKS—*Above,* Jerry Orbach as El Gallo, Rita Gardner as The Girl and Kenneth Nelson as The Boy in the original 1960 cast of the record long-run Tom Jones–Harvey Schmidt musical; *below,* Sal Provenza, Virginia Gregory and Howard Paul Lawrence in the same three roles 25 years later in the 1984 cast

*The Fantasticks (10,019; longest continuous run of record in the American theater). Musical suggested by the play *Les Romantiques* by Edmond Rostand; book and lyrics by Tom Jones; music by Harvey Schmidt. Opened May 3, 1960.

Cloud 9 (971). By Caryl Churchill Opened May 18, 1981. (Closed September 4, 1983)

Playwrights Horizons. Sister Mary Ignatius Explains It All for You and **The Actor's Nightmare.** (947) Program of two one-act plays by Christopher Durang. Opened October 21, 1981. (Closed January 29, 1984) **The Dining Room** (511). By A.R. Gurney Jr. Opened February 24, 1982. (Closed July 17, 1983)

*Forbidden Broadway (982). Cabaret revue with concept and lyrics by Gerard Alessandrini. Opened May 4, 1982. Revised version opened October 27, 1983.

*Little Shop of Horrors (756). Musical based on the film by Roger Corman; book and lyrics by Howard Ashman; music by Alan Menken. Opened July 27, 1982.

*True West (685). Revival of the play by Sam Shepard. Opened October 17, 1982.

Greater Tuna (501). By Jaston Williams, Joe Sears and Ed Howard. Opened October 21, 1982. (Closed December 31, 1983)

Upstairs at O'Neals' (308). Cabaret revue conceived by Martin Charnin. Opened October 29, 1982. (Closed July 2, 1983)

Extremities (325). By William Mastrosimone. Opened December 22, 1982. (Closed October 2, 1983)

Quartermaine's Terms (375). By Simon Gray. Opened February 24, 1983 (Closed January 8, 1984)

The Middle Ages (110). By A.R. Gurney Jr. Opened March 23, 1983. (Closed June 26, 1983)

Roundabout Theater Company. Duet for One (96). By Tom Kempinski. Opened March 15, 1983. (Closed June 19, 1983). **Winners** by Brian Friel and **How He Lied to Her Husband** by George Bernard Shaw (193). Opened March 22, 1983. (Closed September 11, 1983)

Win/Lose/Draw (49). Program of three one-act plays: *Little Miss Fresno* by Ara Watson and Mary Gallagher, *Final Placement* by Ara Watson and *Chocolate Cake* by Mary Gallagher. Opened April 24, 1983. (Closed June 5, 1983)

Wild Life (55). Program of three one-act plays by Shel Silverstein: *I'm Good to My Doggies*, *Chicken Suit Optional* and *The Lady or the Tiger Show*. Opened May 2, 1983. (Closed June 19, 1983)

My Astonishing Self (40). Revival of the one-man performance devised by Michael Voysey from the writings of George Bernard Shaw. Opened May 3, 1983. (Closed June 5, 1983)

The Cradle Will Rock (64). Revival of the musical by Marc Blitzstein. Opened May 9, 1983. (Closed May 29, 1983 after 24 performances). Reopened July 12, 1983. (Closed August 14, 1983 after 40 additional performances)

Out of the Night (31). Adapted by Eric Krebs from a book by Jan Valtin. Opened May 11, 1983. (Closed June 5, 1983)

Jacques Brel Is Alive and Well and Living in Paris (48). Revival of the musical conceived by Eric Blau and Mort Shuman. Opened May 15, 1983. (Closed June 26, 1983)

Manhattan Made Me (24). By Gus Edwards. Opened May 17, 1983. (Closed June 5, 1983)

New York Shakespeare Festival. **Egyptology: My Head Was a Sledgehammer** (48). Text and scoring by Richard Foreman. Opened May 17, 1983. (Closed June 26, 1983) **Fen** (43). By Caryl Churchill. Opened May 24, 1983. (Closed July 3, 1983)

Jeeves Takes Charge (83). One-man show conceived, adapted and performed by Edward Duke; based on works of P.G. Wodehouse. Opened May 17, 1983. (Closed June 18, 1983 after 35 performances) Reopened July 26, 1983. (Closed September 4, 1983 after 48 performances)

PLAYS PRODUCED JUNE 1, 1983–MAY 31, 1984

The Light Opera of Manhattan (LOOM). Repertory of one new operetta revival (extended engagement) and 12 running operetta revivals. **Rose Marie** (49). Book and lyrics by Otto Harbach and Oscar Hammerstein II; music by Rudolf Friml and Herbert Stothart. Opened May 4, 1983. (Closed June 19, 1983) Produced by Light Opera of Manhattan, William Mount-Burke producer-director, at the Eastside Playhouse.

Cast and credits of this production of *Rose Marie*, originally scheduled to close 5/29/84 but extended as above, appear on page 398 of *The Best Plays of 1982–83*.

ALL PLAYS: Directed by William Mount-Burke; musical direction, William Mount-Burke; assistant musical director and pianist, Brian Molloy; assistant conductor and organist, Stanley German; choreography, Jerry Gotham; stage manager, Jerry Gotham.

LOOM'S 1983–84 repertory included 12 running productions mounted in previous seasons and presented on the following schedule (operettas have book and lyrics by W.S. Gilbert and music by Arthur Sullivan unless otherwise noted): *The Red Mill* (21), book and lyrics by Henry Blossom, music by Victor Herbert, opened July 20; *The Desert Song* (42), book and lyrics by Otto Harbach, Oscar Hammerstein II and Frank Mandel, music by Sigmund Romberg, opened August 10 and March 14; *The Mikado* (56), opened June 22, September 14, February 1 and April 25; *H.M.S. Pinafore* (28) opened July 6 and October 12; *The Pirates of Penzance* (28), opened August 31 and February 29.

Also *Princess Ida* (14), opened September 28; *The Student Prince* (28), book and lyrics by Dorothy Donnelly, music by Sigmund Romberg, opened October 26; *The Merry Widow* (25), English lyrics by Alice Hammerstein Mathias, based on the book by Victor Leon and Leo Stein, music by Franz Lehar, opened November 23, December 31 and January 4; *Babes in Toyland* (21), book by William Mount-Burke and Alice Hammerstein Mathias, lyrics by Alice Hammerstein Mathias, music by Victor Herbert, opened December 7; *The Gondoliers* (14), opened January 18; *Iolanthe* (14), opened February 15; *A Night in Venice* (21), by William Mount-Burke and Alice Hammerstein Mathias, based freely on an idea by Zell & Genée, lyrics by Alice Hammerstein Mathias, music by Johann Strauss, opened April 4; *The Vagabond King* (28), lyrics by W.H. Post and Brian Hooker, music by Rudolf Friml, opened May 9. (Repertory closed June 3, 1984)

Performers in LOOM repertory during the 1983–84 season included Raymond Allen, Sharon Azrieli, Joyce Bolton, Elizabeth Burgess-Harr, John J. Bonk, Jon Brothers, Bob Cuccioli, William Carter Corson, Buddy Crutchfield, Christina Darnowski, Kelly Fritz, Marilyn Florez, Antonio Garza, Jonathan Geen, Lynn Greene-Brooke, Billy Hester, Lloyd Harris, Gilbert Hervatin, Keith Harmeyer, Karen Hartman, John Patrick Howard, Wendy Hester.

Also Janette Leslie Jones, Joanne Jamieson, Daniel Kim, Randall Klose, Ann J. Kirschner, Sylvia Lanka, Leif Lorenz, Darrell Lormand, Anthony Mellor, Cole Mobley, Gregory Mobley, Jane Malizia, Bruce McKillip, Allan Marks, Georgia McEver, Claudia O'Neill, Dan O'Driscoll, Stephen O'Mara, Susanna Organek.

Also Millie Petroski, Adam Petroski, Paula Pavone, John Palmore, Paul Phinney, Vashek

Pazdera, Gary Pitts, Barbara Rouse, Stephen Rosario, Irma Rogers, Rhanda Spotton, Karen Sussman, Karen Shipp, Jennifer Shepherd, Cheryl Savitt, Lisa Smith, Mary Setrakian, Denyce Texeira, Lance Taubold, Nancy Temple, Stephen Todar, Ernesto Valenzuela, David Wolin, Stanley Wesler, David Zimmerman.

*Fool for Love (432). By Sam Shepard. Produced by Circle Repertory Company, Marshall W. Mason artistic director, Richard Frankel managing director, B. Rodney Marriott acting artistic director, in the Magic Theater of San Francisco production at the Circle Theater. Opened May 26, 1983; see note.

May	Kathy Whitton Baker	Martin	Dennis Ludlow
Eddie	Ed Harris	Old Man	Will Marchetti

Understudies: Miss Baker—Ann Gentry; Messrs. Ludlow, Marchetti—Matthew Loricchio.

Directed by Sam Shepard; scenery, Andy Stacklin; costumes, Ardyss L. Golden; lighting, Kurt Landisman, supervised by Mal Sturchio; sound, J.A. Deane; associate directors, Julie Hebert, Chris Silva; production stage manager, Suzanne Fry; press, Reva Cooper.

Irresistible love/hate relationship between half-brother and half-sister, previously produced in San Francisco. The play was presented without intermission.

NOTE: *Fool for Love* premiered too late in the 1982–83 season for a clear evaluation of its status. On 11/27/83 it moved from the Circle Theater to the Douglas Fairbanks Theater (with John Lion then listed as one of the producers) for a continuing run. It was considered eligible for the 1983–84 best-play Obie Award, which it won. Similarly, we cite it as a 1983–84 Best Play; see page 89.

Will Patton replaced Ed Harris. Bruce Willis replaced Will Patton. Ellen Barkin replaced Kathy Whitton Baker 2/14/84. Moira McCanna Harris replaced Ellen Barkin 3/12/84. Stephen Mendillo replaced Dennis Ludlow.

New York Shakespeare Festival. 1982–83 schedule included **Goodnight Ladies!** (16) Devised by the Hesitate and Demonstrate company. Geraldine Pilgrim artistic director. Opened June 7, 1983. (Closed June 19, 1983). **Orgasmo Adulto Escapes From the Zoo** (60). One-woman performance by Estelle Parsons of a new English version of the original Italian *Tutta Casa, Letto e Chiesa* by Franca Rame and Dario Fo. Opened in two parts August 2 and 3, 1983. (Closed October 2, 1983) Produced by New York Shakespeare Festival, Joseph Papp producer, at the Public Theater (see note).

BOTH PLAYS: Associate producer, Jason Steven Cohen; press, Merle Debuskey, Richard Kornberg, Barbara Carroll, Bruce Campbell.

GOODNIGHT LADIES!

CAST: Lizza Aiken, Alex Mavro, Andrzej Borkowski, Rick Fisher.

Directed by Geraldine Pilgrim; lighting, Tom Donellan; sound tape, John Darling; technicians, Tom Donellan, Victor Kravchenko.

Series of visual images devised by the performers.

ORGASMO ADULTO ESCAPES FROM THE ZOO

Incidental Male Roles—John Masterson.

Directed by Franca Rame and Estelle Parsons; costumes, Ruth Morley; lighting, Jennifer Tipton; scenic consultant, Santo Loquasto; production stage manager, Elizabeth Holloway; stage manager, John Masterson.

Series of eight satirical one-woman plays performed by Estelle Parsons—*Waking Up, A Woman Alone, We All Have the Same Story, Contrasto for a Solo Voice, Monologue of a Whore in a Lunatic Asylum, The Freak Mamma, It Happens Tomorrow, Medea*—presented in two programs of four playlets each on successive evenings. A foreign play previously produced in Italy.

Note: In Joseph Papp's Public Theater there are many separate auditoriums. *Goodnight La-*

dies! played Martinson Hall, *Orgasmo Adulto Escapes From the Zoo* played the Estelle R. Newman Theater.

The American Place Theater. 1982–83 schedule concluded with **Great Days** (21). By Donald Barthelme. Opened June 7, 1983; see note. Closed June 26, 1983. Produced by The American Place Theater, Wynn Handman director, Julia Miles associate director, at American Place Theater.

CAST: Momma—Paul Collins, Robert Stattel; The Conservatory—Penelope Allen, Jeanne Ruskin; Grandmother's House—Collins, James Greene; The Apology—Catherine Byers, Ruskin. (Intermission.) Morning—Stattel, Greene; Great Days—Allen, Byers, Ruskin; The Leap—Stattel, Greene, Collins.

Understudy: Misses Allen, Byers, Ruskin—Deidre Westervelt.

Directed by J Ranelli; scenery, Neil Peter Jampolis; costumes, David C. Woolard; lighting, Arden Fingerhut; production stage manager, Nancy Harrington; press, Jeffrey Richards Associates.

Series of conversations taking a comedy approach to contemporary life and times, presented in two parts.

Note: Press date for *Great Days* was 6/16/83.

Greek (6). By Steven Berkoff. Produced by Mark Beigelman, Susan Albert Loewenberg and L.A. Theater Works at Actors' Playhouse. Opened June 8, 1983. (Closed June 12, 1983)

Directed by Steven Berkoff; scenery and lighting, Gerry Hariton, Vicki Baral; costumes, Peter Mitchell; presented in association with Michael Kleinman Productions and Lorin Theatrical Productions; production stage manager, Duane Mazey; press, Jeffrey Richards Associates, Robert Ganshaw; with Georgia Brown, Ken Danziger, Mary Denham, John Francis Harries.

Time: The present. Place: England.

The Oedipus story as a modern occurrence. A foreign play previously produced in London and elsewhere, including its American premiere in Los Angeles by L.A. Theater Works, Susan Albert Loewenberg producing director.

Taking My Turn (345). Musical conceived by Robert H. Livingston; music by Gary William Friedman; lyrics by Will Holt. Produced by Richard Seader, Joanne Cummings, Maurice Levine, Arleen and Anthony Kane, Sonny Fox and Sally Sears at the Entermedia Theater. Opened June 9, 1983. (Closed January 8, 1984)

Eric	Mace Barrett	Charles	Tiger Haynes
Edna	Marni Nixon	Dorothy	Margaret Whiting
John	Victor Griffin	Benjamin	Ted Thurston
Helen	Cissy Houston	Janet	Sheila Smith

Band: Barry Levitt director, keyboards; Richie Pratt drums; Ron McLure bass; Al Hunt sax, woodwinds; Fred Griffin French horn; Larry Farrell trombone; Peter Calandra assistant to director.

Understudies: Messrs. Barrett, Haynes—Irving Barnes; Messrs. Griffin, Thurston—Edward Penn; Misses Nixon, Houston, Whiting, Smith—Sis Clark.

Directed by Robert H. Livingston; musical staging, Douglas Norwick; musical direction, Barry Levitt; scenery, Clarke Dunham; costumes, Judith Dolan; lighting, David F. Segal; arrangements and orchestrations, Gary William Friedman; production stage manager, Kate Pollock; stage manager, Mimi Wallace; press, Jeffrey Richards Associates, Robert Ganshaw.

Time: During the course of one year . . . this year. Act I: Spring-summer. Act II: Fall-winter.

Billed as "A musical celebration based on writings by people in their prime," a series of musical statements about aging, some of which are credited to the following persons: Elise Brosnan, Diana Collins, Diana Ellman, Frances Feldman, Morton and Elise Goldman, Pauline Goodman, Ethel Greene, Lillian Hendel, Don Herold, Abe Janowitz, Anna Kainen, Gertrude Weil Klein, Bobo Lewis, Mary Lipke, Sara Lipsky, Dorothy Livingston, Esta Wolff March, Ruth Mooney, Janet

Neuman, Anna Popkin, Susan Rifkin, Gertrude Schleier, Rose Schulman, Ida Schiffman, Bea Smith, Rose Snyderman, Bertha Wohl and members of JASA.

ACT I

"This Is My Song"... Company
"Somebody Else"... Company
"Fine for the Shape I'm In"....................................... Dorothy, Edna, Helen
"Two of Me" .... Janet
"Janet Get Up" .... Company
"I Like It" .... Company
"I Never Made Money From Music" .... Charles
"Vivaldi".. Edna, Company
"Do You Remember?"... Ben, Company
"In April".. Dorothy
"Pick More Daisies" .... Company

ACT II

"Taking Our Turn".. Company
"Sweet Longings"... Janet, Company
"I Am Not Old" .... Helen
"Do You Remember?" (Reprise) .... Ben, Company
"The Kite"..John
"Good Luck to You"... Eric, Company
"In the House".. Eric
"Somebody Else" (Reprise).. Company
"It Still Isn't Over" .... Ben, Dorothy
"This Is My Song" (Reprise) .... Company

Roundabout Theater Company. 1982–83 schedule included **Ah, Wilderness!** (48). Revival of the play by Eugene O'Neill. Opened June 14, 1983; see note. (Closed July 24, 1983) **The Knack** (96). Revival of the play by Ann Jellicoe. Opened June 21, 1983; see note. (Closed September 11, 1983) Produced by Roundabout Theater Company, Gene Feist producing director, Todd Haimes managing director, (*Ah, Wilderness!* at the Haft Theater, *The Knack* at Stage One).

AH, WILDERNESS!

Nat Miller	Philip Bosco	David McComber	Joseph Leon
Essie	Dody Goodman	Muriel McComber	Liane Langland
Arthur	John Dukakis	Wint Selby; Bartender	Robert Curtis-Brown
Richard	Scott Burkholder	Belle	Jean Hackett
Mildred	Kelly Wolf	Nora	Bernadette Quigley
(Tommy)	Mark Scott Newman, Tommy Harris	Salesman	Scott Gordon Miller
Sid Davis	Robert Nichols		(Parentheses indicate role in which the
Lily Miller	Laurinda Barrett		performers alternated)

Directed by John Stix; scenery, Kenneth Foy; costumes, Gene K. Lakin; lighting, Ron Wallace; music, Philip Campanella; production stage manager, Victoria Merrill; press, Susan Bloch and Company, Adrian Bryan-Brown, Ron Jewell, Ellen Zeisler.

Act I, Scene 1: The Miller home in a small town in Connecticut, early morning, July 4, 1906. Scene 2: Evening of the same day. Act II, Scene 1: Back room of a bar in a small hotel, 10 o'clock the same night. Scene 2: The Miller home, a little after 10 o'clock the same night. Scene 3: The Miller home, about 1 o'clock the following afternoon. Scene 4: A boathouse on the harbor, about 9 o'clock that night. Scene 5: The Miller home, about 10 o'clock the same night.

The last major New York revival of *Ah, Wilderness!* was by Circle in the Square on Broadway 9/18/75 for 77 performances.

BABES IN TOYLAND—A scene from the Light Opera of Manhattan (LOOM) production of the Victor Herbert musical

THE KNACK

Tom	Daniel Gerroll	Rolen	John Abajian
Colin	Mark Arnott	Nancy	J. Smith-Cameron

Directed by Peter Gordon; scenery, Douglas Stein; costumes, Jane Clark; lighting, Ronald Wallace; sound, Philip Campanella; production stage manager, Kathy J. Faul.

Time: 1962. Place: A room in London, England.

The Knack was first produced off Broadway 5/27/64 for 685 performances. This is its first major New York revival.

Note: Press date for *Ah, Wilderness!* was 6/28/83, for *The Knack* was 8/21/83.

Samuel Beckett's Ohio Impromptu, Catastrophe, What Where (350). Program of three one-act plays by Samuel Beckett. Produced by The Harold Clurman Theater, Jack Garfein artistic director, and Lucille Lortel at the Harold Clurman Theater. Opened June 15, 1983. (Closed April 15, 1984)

Ohio Impromptu		*Catastrophe*	
Reader	David Warrilow	His Assistant	Margaret Reed
Listener	Rand Mitchell	The Director	Donald Davis
		Luke	Rand Mitchell
		Protagonist	David Warrilow

What Where		Bim......................	Rand Mitchell
Bam	Donald Davis	Bem ....~............	Daniel Wirth
Bom	David Warrilow	Voice of Bam...............	Donald Davis

Understudy: Messrs. Warrilow, Mitchell—Daniel Wirth.

Directed by Alan Schneider; scenery and lighting, Marc D. Malamud; costumes, Carla Kramer; production stage manager, Charles Kindl; press, Joe Wolhandler Associates.

Ohio Impromptu stages poetic images of love and death; *Catastrophe*, written for the Czechoslovakian playwright Vaclav Havel, dramatizes martyrdom to tyrannous government; *What Where* is a further examination of victims of an oppressive society. The former was written in 1981 and premiered in connection with the author's 75th birthday celebration at Ohio State University. The latter is a world premiere. *Catastrophe*, written in 1982, was previously produced in France.

Alvin Epstein joined the cast in mid-run as an alternate performer in the principal roles.

A Best Play; see page 191.

Yellow Fever (138). By R.A. Shiomi; story co-conceived by Marc Hayashi. Produced by Pan Asian Repertory Theater, Tisa Chang artistic/producing director, at the 47th Street Theater. Opened June 16, 1983. (Closed October 30, 1983)

Sam Shikaze...................	Donald Li	Nancy Wing...............	Freda Foh Shen
Rosie.....................	Carol A. Honda	Sgt. Mackenzie	Jeffrey Spolan
Goldberg; Supt. Jameson	James Jenner	Capt. Kenji Kadota..........	Ernest Abuba
Chuck Chan..................	Henry Yuk		

Understudies: Misses Shen, Honda—Lynette Chun; Messrs. Yuk, Abuba—Ron Nakahara; Messrs. Spolan, Jenner—Jude Ciccolella.

Directed by Raul Aranas; scenery, Christopher Stapleton; costumes, Eiko Yamaguchi; lighting, Dawn Chiang; stage manager, Eddas Bennett; press, Shirley Herz, Sam Rudy.

Time: March, 1970s. Place: Powell Street in Vancouver, British Columbia. Act I: Rosie's cafe and Sam's office. Act II: The Dover Inn, an English-style pub, and Sam's office.

A Sam Spade-type mystery melodrama with an oriental version of the private detective a la Humphrey Bogart. Previously produced by Asian American Theater Company, San Francisco, and off off Broadway by Pan Asian Repertory Theater 12/1/82 for 58 performances.

Mako replaced Donald Li at evening performances beginning 9/27/83. Gerald Lancaster replaced Jeffrey Spolan 10/83.

New York Shakespeare Festival. Summer schedule of two outdoor programs. **King Richard III** (62). Revival of the play by William Shakespeare. Opened June 30, 1983; see note. (Closed July 31, 1983). **Non Pasquale** (32). Pop opera based on *Don Pasquale* by Gaetano Donizetti and Giovanni Ruffini; new libretto by Nancy Heikin and Anthony Giles; music adapted by William Elliott. Opened August 9, 1983; see note. (Closed September 4, 1983). Produced by New York Shakespeare Festival, Joseph Papp producer, at the Delacorte Theater in Central Park. Both plays: Associate producer, Jason Steven Cohen; press, Merle Debuskey, Richard Kornberg, Barbara Carroll, Bruce Campbell.

KING RICHARD III

Richard, Duke of Gloucester....	Kevin Kline	Berkeley; Friar Penker;	
Clarence.................	Bruce Davison	Urswick..................	Jonathan Croy
Brakenbury; Bishop of Ely;		Halberdier; Lovell.......	Peter Francis-James
Surrey	Maurice Copeland	Elizabeth	Concetta Tomei
Hastings.....................	John Seitz	Rivers; Archbishop of	
Lady Anne..............	Madeleine Potter	Canterbury	Ivar Brogger
Body of Henry VI; Priest........	Ed Rubeo	Grey; Archbishop of York;	
Tressel; Dr. Shaa...........	John Harnagel	Sheriff of Norfolk; Sheriff	Tom Klunis

Dorset...................... Steven Culp
Buckingham............... Gerry Bamman
Derby..................... Mark Hammer
Margaret................... Marian Seldes
Catesby.................. Richard Greene
Murderer; Richmond ..... David Alan Grier
Murderer; Vaughan;
  Messenger............. Christopher Wertz
Keeper of Tower; Messenger;
  Brandon................. Reg E. Cathey
Ratcliffe .... Christopher McCann

Edward IV; Scrivener;
  Tyrell; Blunt........... Terrance O'Quinn
Duchess of York.............. Betty Miller
Boy........................ Ward Saxton
Girl................... Katherine Neuman
Duke of York .... Michael Pearlman
Prince Edward............ Matthew Vipond
Lord Mayor................... Roc Dutton
Mistress Shore............... Sandra Laub
Hastings; Herbert .... Ving Rhames
Messenger................... Paul R. Duke
Page .... Scott Becker

Guards, Halberdiers, Gentlemen, Lords, Citizens, Attendants, Soldiers: Christian Baskous, Jonathan Croy, Paul R. Duke, Roc Dutton, John Harnagel, Brian Jackson, William E. Kennedy, Robert E. Quinn, Ving Rhames, Ed Rubeo, Dana Smith, Malcolm Smith, John C. Talbot, Susan Titman, Jonathan Walker, Christopher Wertz.

Musicians: Jack Bashkow reeds, Richard Clymer trumpet, William Uttley percussionist.

Directed by Jane Howell; scenery and costumes, Santo Loquasto; lighting, Pat Collins; music, Richard Peaslee; fight sequences, B.H. Barry; production stage manager, Bonnie Panson; stage manager, Bill McComb.

The play was presented in two parts. The last major New York revival of *King Richard III* (as it is billed in this production) or *Richard III* (as it is generally styled in these *Best Plays* volumes) took place on Broadway 6/14/79 for 33 performances.

NON PASQUALE

Trumpet..................... Joe Grifasi
Malatesta .... Joe Masiell
Don Pasquale................ Ron Leibman
Piccola .... Maureen Sadusk
Pasquale's Valet.............. Joe Pichette
Ernesto..................... Kipp Tozzi

Nina .... Carol Dennis
Pinta.................... Susan Goodman
Santa Maria................. Marcie Shaw
Norina .... Priscilla Lopez
Cousin Alfredo .... James Rich
Cousin Cesario............. Ernesto Gasco

Pasquale's Servants, Norina's Relatives, Townspeople: Kevin Berdini, Joyce Leigh Bowden, Katharine Buffaloe, Charlotte d'Amboise, Christopher d'Amboise, Carol Dennis, Bruce Falco, Ernesto Gasco, Susan Goodman, N.A. Klein, Paul Nunes, Caroline Peyton, Joe Pichette, James Rich, Kathy Robinson, David Sanders, Alan Sener, Charlie Serrano, Marcie Shaw, Lauren Tom, Michael Willson.

Musicians: Martin Grupp orchestra manager; Amy Berger harp; Neil Capolongo electric drums; John Caruso electric bass; Richard Cohen clarinet, flute, saxophone; Carolyn Dutton violin; Laurie Fink trumpets; Janet Glazener keyboards; Robby Kirshoff guitars, mandolin; George Maniere trumpets; Katherine Mueller flute, alto flute, piccolo; Bill Ruyle percussion; Marc Shaiman keyboards; Vinnie Zummo guitars, accordion.

Understudies: Mr. Grifasi--Charlie Serrano; Mr. Masiell—N.A. Klein; Mr. Leibman—Ernesto Gasco; Miss Sadusk—Susan Goodman; Mr. Tozzi—James Rich; Miss Lopez—Joyce Leigh Bowden, Carol Dennis; Miss Dennis—Kathy Robinson; Miss Goodman—Caroline Peyton; Miss Shaw—Katharine Buffaloe; Mr. Pichette—David Sanders; Mr. Gasco—Michael Willson; Alternates —Nanette Ledet, James Dunne (Dance Captain).

Directed by Wilford Leach; choreography, Margo Sappington; musical direction, vocal arrangements, conductor, William Elliott; music adapted from original arrangements and orchestrations by Tito Schipa Jr. and Gianni Marchetti; scenery, Bob Shaw, Wilford Leach; costumes, Nan Cibula; lighting, Jennifer Tipton; additional orchestrations and music coordination, Roy Moore; assistant musical director and associate conductor, Vincent Fanuele; production stage manager, Stephen McCorkle; stage manager, Ginny Martino.

"Pop Opera" freely adapted from the RCA Italy recording *Er Dom Pasquale,* conceived by Tito Schipa Jr., Gianni Marchetti, Roberto Bonanni and William Herandez.

ACT I

Scene 1: Villa Pasquale
"The House of Don Pasquale" .... Trumpet, Pasquale, Piccola, Malatesta, Ensemble
"Holy and Innocent" .... Malatesta
"Just Like a Young Man"... Pasquale, Piccola
"The Duchess Song" .... Pasquale, Ernesto
"Always".. Ernesto
Scene 2: Norina's souvenir stall
"Love Must Be Delicato" .... Norina
"Pazzo"................................ Norina, Nina, Pinta, Santa Maria, Ensemble
"Recitativo" .... Malatesta
"Ah, Sweet Revenge".. Norina, Malatesta
"Subito (Nearer to the Lire)" .... Nina, Pinta, Santa Maria, Norina, Malatesta, Ensemble
Scene 3: Villa Pasquale
"From the Convent/She's a Virgin"................. Norina, Malatesta, Pasquale, Piccola
"The Wedding Ceremony" .... Trumpet, Malatesta, Pasquale, Piccola, Norina
"The What on Earth Is Going on Tango" .... Ernesto, Pasquale, Malatesta, Norina,
                                                              Piccola, Servants
"Permission"....................................... Norina, Pasquale, Malatesta Piccola
"We Need a Few More Servants" .... Norina, Pasquale, Servants, Ensemble
"Si, Signora"... Valet, Servants, Ensemble
"Oh, What a Wedding!" .... Ensemble

ACT II

Scene 1: Villa Pasquale, three days later
"We Must Talk"... Pasquale, Norina
"Poor Don Pasquale"... Norina, Pasquale
"Lullaby"......................... Pasquale, Norina, Nina, Pinta, Santa Maria, Beaux
Scene 2: Via Andrea Doria
"Softly, Softly to the Garden" .... Malatesta, Pasquale, Trumpet, Ensemble
"Fight to the Death" .... Cesario, Malatesta, Trumpet, Pasquale, Ensemble
Scene 3: Pasquale's garden
"Serenade".. Ernesto, Ensemble
"Tell Me You Love Me".. Ernesto, Norina
"If Only"... Pasquale
"That is Norina?".................................... Pasquale, Malatesta, Ensemble
"La Morale" .... Malatesta, Trumpet
"Finale (Bravo, Bravo)"... Ensemble

Note: Press date for *King Richard III* was 7/13/83, for *Non Pasquale* was 8/24/83.

American Passion (1). Musical with book by Fred Burch; music by Willie Fong Young; lyrics by Willie Fong Young and Fred Burch. Produced by Stuart Ostrow at the Joyce Theater. Opened and closed at the evening performance, July 10, 1983.

Directed and choreographed by Patricia Birch; scenic consultant, Heidi Landesman; costumes, William Ivey Long; lighting, Richard Winkler; sound, Otts Munderloh; orchestrations and arrangements, Timothy Graphenreed; production stage manager, Perry Cline; press, John Springer, Gary Springer. With Rosko, Taryn Grimes, Margie Perez, Laura Dean, Christal Wood, Don Kehr, William Morrison, Sam Slovick, Todd Graff, Liza Lauber, Karl Leff.

Young performers competing in a contest. The show was presented without intermission.

An Evening With Quentin Crisp (61). One-man performance by and with Quentin Crisp. Produced by Ross & Timm Productions and Michael R. Hirtz at the Actors' Playhouse. Opened July 14, 1983. (Closed September 4, 1983)

Scenery, Kenneth Cook; lighting, Pamela C. Ross; stage manager, Pamela C. Ross; press, Patt Dale, Daniel Kellachan.

Subtitled *The Naked Civil Servant* (the title of Crisp's autobiography), this celebration of gay individuality in monologue was previosuly produced off Broadway 12/20/78 for 81 performances. This 1983 version contains new material from the autobiographical sequel *How to Become a Virgin* and was presented in two parts, with the audience invited to ask questions.

Dogs (6). Musical with book by James Stewart Bennett and Charles G. Horne; music and lyrics by James Stewart Bennett. Produced by the Provincetown Theater Ensemble at the Perry Street Theater. Opened August 10, 1983. (Closed August 14, 1983)

Directed by Charles G. Horne; scenery, Jack Kelly; costumes, Jack Kelly, Peyton Smith; lighting, Edward R.F. Matthews; production stage manager, Glen Cruz Mariano; press, Howard Atlee. With Lanny Green, Linda Marie Larson, Caroline Cox, Kathryn Hunter, Terry Blaine, Valerie Santuccio, Nicholas Searcy, Mark Enis, Neil Lyons, D. Jonathan Vaughn.

One of nine dogs escaped from the New York City pound is adopted by the Mayor.

The Brooklyn Bridge (28). Musical with book and lyrics by Dorothy Chansky; music by Scott MacLarty. Produced by Dorothy Chansky with The Bridge Theater Production Company at the Quaigh Theater. Opened August 17, 1983. (Closed September 11, 1983)

Man in the Street . . . . David Higlen	Henry Murphy;	
Mrs. O'Malley; Lady Reporter;	Gen. G.K. Warren . . . . Paul Merrill	
Landlady . . . . Anne Gartlan	John Roebling; Dr. Smith; E.F. Farrington;	
William Kingsley; Eddie . . . . Nick Jolley	Mayor Low . . . . Jack Sevier	
Emily Warren Roebling . . . . Bijou Clinger	Washington Roebling . . . . . John Leslie Wolfe	

Directed by Marjorie Melnick; musical director, Harrison Fisher; scenery, Terry Bennett; costumes, Karen Gerson; lighting, Leslie Spohn; choreography, Missy Whitchurch; production stage manager, Steven Shaw; press, Patt Dale Associates, James Baldassare.

Musical about the building of the Brooklyn Bridge, presented on the occasion of the bridge's 100th anniversary.

ACT I

Prologue: 1983, the Brooklyn Bridge
Scene 1: 1865, a street in Brooklyn
    "Brooklyn" . . . . Company
Scene 2: 1865, a church in Cold Spring, N.Y.
    "Love Means" . . . . Emily
    "Can I Do It All" . . . . Washington
    "Bridge to the Future" . . . . John Roebling
Scene 3: 1866, Murphy's home, Owl's Head, Brooklyn
    "Cash Politics" . . . . Kingsley, Murphy
Scene 4: 1867, the Bridge Company office in Brooklyn
    "The Roebling Plan" . . . . Company
Scene 5: 1869, near the East River; the Roebling house on Columbia Heights in Brooklyn
    "Love Means" (Reprise) . . . . Emily
    "Can I Do It All" (Reprise) . . . . Washington
Scene 6: 1870, a street in Brooklyn
    "Keep Me Out of the Caisson" . . . . Man in the Street
Scene 7: 1872, the Roebling house
    "When You're the Only One" . . . . Emily, Mrs. O'Malley

ACT II

Scene 8: 1872–1876: The bridge construction site
    "Ain't No Women There" . . . . Kingsley, Murphy, Farrington, Man in the Street
    "Every Day for Four Years" . . . . Company

Scene 9: 1876–1881, the Roebling house and the Bridge Company office
"The Man in the Window"..Washington
"All That I Know" ....Emily
Scene 10: 1882, a street in Brooklyn
Scene 11: May 24, 1883 at the Brooklyn Bridge
Finale..Company
Epilogue: 1983, the Brooklyn Bridge

Preppies (52). Musical with book by David Taylor with Carlos Davis; music and lyrics by Gary Portnoy and Judy Hart Angelo. Produced by Anthony Fingleton and Carlos David at the Promenade Theater. Opened August 18, 1983. (Closed October 2, 1983)

Marie Pantry................ Beth Fowler
Joe Pantry .... Michael Ingram
Parker Richardson Endicott III; Admissions
Officer; Headmaster; Majordomo;
Mr. Bonifacio; Bishop .... David Sabin
Bitsy Wingate; Mrs. Atwater..... Tudi Roche
Steffie Palmer.......... Karyn Quackenbush
Lawyer; Jinks Deerborn .... Tom Hafner
Botsworth Norvil Bogswater II;

Bogsy (Botsworth Norvil
Bogswater III) .... Dennis Bailey
Cotty (Parker Richardson
Endicott IV)............... Bob Walton
Muffy (Angelica Livermore
Atwater) .... Kathleen Rowe McAllen
Bookie Bookbinder .... John Scherer
Skipper Seabrook; Mr. Atwater.. James Gedge
Lallie deForest................ Susan Dow

Musicians: Jeffrey Lodin conductor, piano; John Mahoney keyboards; Norbert Goldberg percussion; Dave Dutemple bass.

Understudies: Mr. Walton—James Gedge; Mr. Bailey—Tom Hafner; Misses Roche, Quackenbush, Dow—Tia Riebling; Miss Fowler—Ruth Williamson; Messrs. Hafner, Scherer, Gedge—Robbie McNeill; Messrs. Ingram, Sabin—Sel Vitella.

Directed and choreographed by Tony Tanner; musical direction and vocal arrangements, Jeffrey Lodin; scenery, David Jenkins; costumes, Patricia McGourty; lighting, Richard Winkler; sound, Tom Gould; dance music and orchestrations, Peter Larson; associate producer, Valerie Gordon; originally produced by the Goodspeed Opera House, Michael P. Price executive producer; production stage manager, Melissa Davis; stage manager, Marc Schlackman; press, Jeffrey Richards Associates, C. George Willard.

Farcical machinations over an inheritance in the so-called "preppy" culture. Previously produced at the Goodspeed Opera House.

ACT I

"People Like Us"..Company
"The Chance of a Lifetime" .... Endicott, Joe, Marie, Lawyer
"One Step Away"...Marie
"Summertime" ....Company
"Fairy Tales" .... Cotty, Muffy, Bogsy, Company
"The Parents' Farewell" ....Company
"Bells"...Company
"Moving On" ....Company

ACT II

"Summertime" (Reprise)..Preppy Boys
"Our Night"....................................... Muffy, Cotty, Company
"We've Got Each Other" ....Joe, Marie
"Gonna Run"..Cotty
"No Big Deal" ....Company
"Worlds Apart"...Cotty, Muffy
"Bring on the Loot".......................................Bogsy, Company
"People Like Us" (Reprise)..Company
Finale...Company

A Weekend Near Madison (15). By Kathleen Tolan. Produced by Dasha Epstein at the Astor Place Theater. Opened September 13, 1983. (Closed September 25, 1983)

Jim	Randle Mell	Nessa	Mary McDonnell
Doe	Robin Groves	Samantha	Holly Hunter
David	Bill Mesnik		

Directed by Emily Mann; scenery, Thomas Lynch; costumes, Karen Gerson; lighting, Craig Miller; sound, Tom Gould; stage manager, Neal Ann Stephens; press, Solters/Roskin/Friedman, Inc., Milly Schoenbaum.

Reunion of 1960s college friends, presented in two acts. Previously produced at Actors Theater of Louisville.

Basement Tapes (15). By Erik Brogger. Produced by Christopher Hart, Mike Houlihan and Eileen McMahon at the Top of the Gate. Opened September 14, 1983. (Closed September 25, 1983).

Directed by Robert Engels; scenery, Mark Haack; costumes, Kristina Watson; lighting, Bonnie Ann Brown; production stage manager, Kevin Mangan; press, Patt Dale Associates, Jim Baldassare. With Michael Laskin, Bill Schoppert, David Wohl.

Time: The present. Place: Gerald Ford's basement recreation room in Palm Springs. The play was presented in two acts.

Political satire, an imaginary meeting of G. Gordon Liddy, Gerald R. Ford and Richard M. Nixon.

*Roundabout Theater Company. Schedule of four revivals. **The Master Builder** (88). By Henrik Ibsen; adapted by Gene Feist. Opened September 20, 1983; see note. (Closed December 4, 1983) **The Killing of Sister George** (190). By Frank Marcus. Opened September 27, 1983; see note. (Closed March 18, 1984) **Old Times** (90). By Harold Pinter. Opened December 20, 1983; see note. (Closed March 4, 1984) ***On Approval** (76). By Frederick Lonsdale. Opened March 27, 1984; see note. Produced by Roundabout Theater Company, Gene Feist producing director, Todd Haimes managing director, *The Master Builder* and *Old Times* at Stage One and *The Killing of Sister George* and *On Approval* at the Susan Bloch Theater.

THE MASTER BUILDER

Halvard Solness	Edward Seamon	Ragnar Brovik	Keith Reddin
Aline Solness	Joan Potter	Kaia Fosli	Susan Pellegrino
Dr. Herdal	Tom Klunis	Hilda Wangel	Laurie Kennedy
Knut Brovik	Maury Cooper		

Directed by David Hammond; scenery, Roger Mooney; costumes, Eloise Lunde; lighting, Judy Rasmuson; sound, Philip Campanella; production stage manager, Kathy J. Faul; press, Susan Bloch & Company, Adrian Bryan-Brown, Bill Gosewisch, Ellen Zeisler.

Time: Autumn, 1892. Place: The Solness's home, Christiana, Norway. Act I: Early evening. Act II, Scene 1: The next morning. Scene 2: That evening.

The last major New York revival of *The Master Builder* took place off Broadway by the Roundabout Repertory Company 10/17/71 for 64 performances.

THE KILLING OF SISTER GEORGE

Alice "Childie" McNaught	Tandy Cronyn	Mrs. Mercy Croft	Ruby Holbrook
June Buckridge		Madame Xenia	Elizabeth Owen
(Sister George)	Aideen O'Kelly		

Directed by Allen R. Belknap; scenery, Roger Mooney; costumes, Susan A. Cox; lighting, Ron Wallace; sound, Philip Campanella: production stage manager, Kurt Wagemann.

Time: The late 1950s. Place: The living room of June Buckridge's flat, Devonshire Street, London. Act I: Tuesday afternoon, later September. Act II, Scene 1: A week later, 4 A.M. Scene 2: Late afternoon of the same day. Act III: Two weeks later, morning.

The Killing of Sister George was produced on Broadway 10/5/66 for 205 performances and was named a Best Play of its season. This is its first major New York revival.

OLD TIMES

Deeley................. Anthony Hopkins   Anna...................... Jane Alexander
Kate .... Marsha Mason

Directed by Kenneth Frankel; scenery, Marjorie Bradley Kellogg; costumes, Linda Fisher; lighting, Judy Rasmuson; musical direction, Philip Campanella; production stage manager, Kathy J. Faul.

Time: An autumn night. Place: A converted farmhouse in England. The play was presented in two parts.

Old Times was produced on Broadway 11/16/71 for 119 performances and was named a Best Play of its season and received a special citation from the New York Drama Critics Circle. This is its first major New York revival.

ON APPROVAL

Helen .... Cynthia Dozier   George .... Mark Capri
Maria .... Jane Summerhays   Richard................. John Cunningham

Directed by Daniel Gerroll; scenery, Holmes Easley; costumes, Richard Hieronymus; lighting, Ronald C. Wallace; musical direction, Philip Campanella; production stage manager, Mimi Apfel.

On Approval was first produced on Broadway 10/18/26. This is its first major New York revival.

Act I: Helen's house in Mayfair, London, September 1926, an autumn evening. Act II: Helen's house in Scotland, October 1926. Scene 1: Early afternoon. Scene 2: Three hours later.

Note: Press date for *The Master Builder* was 10/12/83, for *The Killing of Sister George* was 11/1/83, for *Old Times* was 1/12/84, for *On Approval* was 5/8/84.

The Roundabout also offered (but never presented to the press in an announced premiere) a revival of *Desire Under the Elms* by Eugene O'Neill, directed by Terry Schreiber, with Lenny Von Dohlen, Tom Spiller, Patrick Meyers, Lee Richardson, and Kathy Whitton Baker, at stage One 3/20/84–6/3/84 for 82 performances.

Serious Bizness (189). Cabaret revue written by Jennifer Allen, David Babcock, Don Perman and Winnie Holzman; music by David Evans. Produced by Jill Larson and Marisa Smith at O'Neals'/43d St. Cabaret. Opened September 26, 1983. (Closed April 21, 1984)

David Babcock   Don Perman
Jill Larson   Nealla Spano

Directed by Phyllis Newman; musical director, Frederick Weldy; scenery, Loren Sherman; costumes, Cynthia O'Neal; lighting, Mal Sturchio; associate producer, Jeffrey Matthews; stage manager, C. Myron Moore; press, Susan L. Schulman.

Comedy sketches on the contemporary scene, presented without intermission. Previously produced off off Broadway in the American Humorists series at American Place.

*Manhattan Theater Club. Schedule of six programs. **The Philanthropist** (64). Revival of the play by Christopher Hampton. Opened September 27, 1983; see note. (Closed November 20, 1983) **Blue Plate Special** (48). Musical with book by Tom Edwards; music by Harris Wheeler; lyrics by Mary L. Fisher. Opened October 18, 1983; see note. (Closed November 27, 1983) **Friends** (48). By Lee Kalcheim. Opened December 13, 1983: see note. (Closed January 22, 1984) **Mensch Meier** (48). by Franz Xaver Kroetz; translated by Roger Downey. Opened February 11, 1984; see note. (Closed March 18, 1984) **Other Places** (48). Program of one-act plays by Harold Pinter: *Victoria Station*, *One for the Road* and *A Kind of Alaska*. Opened April 10, 1984; see note. (Closed

IN REVIVAL AT THE ROUNDABOUT—*Above,* Marsha Mason, Anthony Hopkins and Jane Alexander in Harold Pinter's *Old Times; below,* Cynthia Dozier and Jane Summerhays *(bottom of photo)* with Mark Capri and John Cunningham in Frederick Lonsdale's *On Approval*

May 20, 1984) *The Miss Firecracker Contest (35). By Beth Henley. Opened May 1, 1984; see note. Produced by Manhattan Theater Club, Lynne Meadow artistic director, Barry Grove managing director, *The Philanthropist*, *Friends*, *Mensch Meier* and *Other Places* at DownStage, *Blue Plate Special* and *The Miss Firecracker Contest* at UpStage.

THE PHILANTHROPIST

Philip	David McCallum	Braham	Benjamin Hendrickson
Donald	Anthony Heald	Araminta	Robin Bartlett
John	Brent Spiner	Liz	Cherry Jones
Celia	Glenne Headly		

Standbys: Mr. Spiner—Rob Knepper; Mr. Heald—William Kux; Messrs. McCallum, Hendrickson—Jeremiah Sullivan.

Directed by Andre Ernotte; scenery, Kate Edmunds; costumes, Linda Fisher; lighting, F. Mitchell Dana; sound, Eric Rissler Thayer; production stage manager, Dianne Trulock; stage manager, Mindy K. Farbrother; press, Virginia P. Louloudes, Kim Kuhlmann, Abigail Evans.

The play was presented in two parts. *The Philanthropist* was produced on Broadway 5/15/71 for 72 performances and was named a Best Play of its season. This is its first major New York revival.

William Kux replaced Brent Spiner and Denise Stephenson replaced Robin Bartlett 10/28/83.

BLUE PLATE SPECIAL

Della Juracko	Gretchen Cryer	Preacher Larry Finney	Ron Holgate
Ronnie Frank Flaugher	Gordon Paddison	Connie Sue Day	Mary Gordon Murray
Ricky Jim Robinson	David Strathairn	Ramona Juracko	Tina Johnson

Blue Plate Special Band: Jimmy Roberts keyboards; Steve Mallardi electric and acoustic bass; Kevin McCann guitars, banjo; Karl Schmitt drums.

Directed by Art Wolff; choreography, Douglas Norwick; musical direction, Jimmy Roberts; scenery, David Jenkins; costumes, David Murin; lighting, Arden Fingerhut; orchestrations and arrangements, Robby Merkin; production stage manager, Steven Adler.

Time: Episode 41, in the present. Place: A continuing daytime drama broadcast from Morning Glory Mountain, Tenn.

Country western takeoff of soap operas, as a nuclear waste dump is found beneath the produce garden of a diner.

ACT I

"Morning Glory Mountain" .... Della, Company
"At the Bottom Lookin' Up" .... Connie Sue
"Ramona's Lament" .... Ramona
"Never Say Never" .... Ramona, Ronnie Frank
"Halfway to Heaven" .... Connie Sue, Ramona, Della
"Satisfaction Guaranteed" .... Larry, Della, Company

ACT II

"Blue Plate Special" .... Della, Company
"Twice as Nice" .... Della, Larry
"All American Male" .... Ronnie Frank
"Side of Fires" .... Della, Connie Sue, Ramona
"Honky Tonk Queens" .... Connie Sue, Ramona
"I Ain't Looking Back" .... Connie Sue, Company
"I'm Gonna Miss Those Tennessee Nights" .... Della

FRIENDS

Harold (Okie) Peterson	Craig T. Nelson
Mel Simon	Ron Silver

Directed by Barnet Kellman; scenery, David Jenkins; costumes, Patricia McGourty; lighting, Ian Calderon; sound, Eric Rissler Thayer; fights, B.H. Barry; production stage manager, Karen Armstrong.

College friends meet again in midlife crisis.

MENSCH MEIER

Otto Meier.............. Stephen McHattie   Ludwig Meier .... Thor Fields
Martha Meier .... Barbara Eda-Young

Directed by Jacques Levy; scenery, Ray Recht; costumes, Susan Hilferty; lighting, Robert Jared; paintings, Clayton Campbell; production stage manager, G. Roger Abell.

Time: Recently. Place: Munich, West Germany. The play was presented in two parts.

Western capitalist workers viewed as blue-collar slaves. A foreign play previously produced in Germany.

OTHER PLACES

CAST: *Victoria Station*—Henderson Forsythe, Kevin Conway; *One for the Road*—Kevin Conway, Greg Martyn, David George Polyak, Caroline Lagerfelt; *A Kind of Alaska*—Dianne Wiest, Henderson Forsythe, Caroline Lagerfelt.

Directed by Alan Schneider; scenery, John Lee Beatty; costumes, Jess Goldstein; lighting, Rocky Greenberg; stage manager, James Bernardi.

Victoria Station is an ongoing misunderstanding between a taxi dispatcher and driver. *One for the Road* deals with the persecution of political prisoners in an unidentified country. *A Kind of Alaska* is about a patient who awakens from a 29-year coma. Foreign plays previously produced in London.

THE MISS FIRECRACKER CONTEST

Carnelle Scott .... Holly Hunter   Delmount Williams........ Mark Linn-Baker
Popeye Jackson .... Belita Moreno   Mac Sam .... Budge Threlkeld
Elain Rutledge.......... Patricia Richardson   Tessy Mahoney .... Margo Martindale

Directed by Stephen Tobolowsky; scenery, John Lee Beatty; costumes, Jennifer Von Mayrhauser; lighting, Dennis Parichy; sound, Stan Metelits; production stage manager, Wendy Chapin; stage manager, Daniel Kanter.

Time: The end of June and the beginning of July. Place: Brookhaven, Miss., a small Southern town. The play was presented in two parts.

Members of a small-town family embroiled in the maximum effort of one of them to win a beauty contest. Previously produced in regional theater in Dallas, Detroit, Buffalo and Chicago and in London.

A Best Play; see page 238.

Note: Press date for *The Philanthropist* was 10/13/83, for *Blue Plate Special* was 11/15/83, for *Friends* was 1/10/84, for *Mensch Meier* was 2/26/84, for *Other Places* was 4/17/84. for *The Miss Firecracker Contest* was 5/27/84.

Big Maggie (46). By John B. Keane. Produced by David J. Bell and Louis Roberts in association with Hugh O'Lunney, Lester Osterman executive producer, at the Douglas Fairbanks Theater. Opened September 28, 1983. (Closed November 6, 1983)

Maggie Polpin.............. Robin Howard   Mick Polpin.............. Kevin McGuire
Old Man.................. Scott Schofield   Katie Polpin.................. Terry Finn
Old Woman................ Hope Cameron   Teddy Heelin................ James Handy
Gert Polpin .... Juliana Donald   Mary Madden .... Maura Vaughn
Mr. Byrne .... David Huddleston   Mrs. Madden.................. Anne Clay
Maurice Polpin .... Robert Walsh

Directed by Donal Donnelly; scenery, David Potts; costumes, Judith Dolan; lighting, Andrea Wilson; sound, Tom Gould; production stage manager, Bill McComb; press, Jeffrey Richards Associates, Robert Ganshaw.

Act I, Scene 1: A graveyard, March. Scene 2: Maggie's sitting room, that night. Act II, Scene 1: Maggie's shop, three months later. Scene 2: That evening. Scene 3: The shop, almost a year later. Scene 4: That night.

Comedy, middle-aged widow builds independence for herself and her children. A foreign play previously produced in Dublin.

Donal Donnelly replaced David Huddleston.

Fun House (70). One-man performance by and with Eric Bogosian. Produced by The Gero Organization and Frederick M. Zollo in association with Sheldon Cohen, Jerome R. Corsi and Vincent P. Rigolsi at the Actors Playhouse. Opened September 29, 1983. (Closed November 27, 1983)

Directed by Eric Bogosian; co-directed by Joanne Bonney; design, Eric Bogosian, Jeffrey McRoberts; press, Warren Knowlton.

An actor's portrait gallery of mostly sinister characters. The play was presented in two parts. Previously presented off off Broadway this season at New York Shakespeare Festival.

The American Place Theater. Schedule of four programs. **The Vi-Ton-Ka Medicine Show** (18). Revue assembled from elements of the traditional American medicine show. Opened October 4, 1983. (Closed October 16, 1983) **Do Lord Remember Me** (42). Return engagement of the play by James de Jongh. Opened January 14, 1984. (Closed February 19, 1984) **The Danube** (8). By Maria Irene Fornes. Opened March 11, 1984. (Closed March 18, 1984) **Terra Nova** (14). By Ted Tally. Opened April 25, 1984. (Closed May 6, 1984) Produced by The American Place Theater, Wynn Handman director, Julia Miles associate director (*Terra Nova* co-produced with Playwrights Horizons, Andre Bishop director, Paul Daniels managing director) at the American Place Theater.

THE VI-TON-KA MEDICINE SHOW

Fred F. Bloodgood	Randy Lucas
James "Goober" Buchanan	Dale Madden Sr.
Col. Buster Doss	Dale "Boots" Madden
Susan Gibney	Mary Smith McClain
Ernest W. Hayes	Connie Mills
Dewitt "Snuffy" Jenkins	Homer "Pappy" Sherrill
Tommy Kizziah	Leroy Watts
Harold Lucas	

Project director, Glenn Hinson; associate project director, C. Lee Jenner; staging and design consultant, Brooks McNamara; scenery and lighting, Marco A. Martinez-Galarce; production supervisor, Nancy Harrington; press, Jeffrey Richards Associates, Robert Ganshaw.

Authentic recreation of a medicine show in the American style, including the simulated hawking of an all-purpose curative tonic, presented without intermission.

Overture—Dale Madden organ, Boots Madden drums; Medicine Show Introduction—Col. Buster Doss; The Hired Hands—Snuffy Jenkins banjo, Harold Lucas guitar, Randy Lucas bass, Pappy Sherrill fiddle; The Betting Bit—Connie Mills, Leroy Watts; The Hired Hands ("Dixie Breakdown," "Pig in a Pen," "Alabama Jubilee")—Jenkins banjo, washboard, Harold Lucas guitar, Randy Lucas banjo, bass, Sherrill fiddle; Ventriloquism, "Ace in the Hole"—Doss; "Alabama Jubilee" on the fly spray—Goober Buchanan, Doss; "The Circus Organlog"—Dale Madden.

Also Vi-Ton-Ka Tonic Lecture—Fred F. Bloodgood; The King Bee—Buchanan, Doss, Watts; "Old Blind Fiddler," "Please Don't Talk About Me," "I Love You Because"—Tommy Kizziah, Sherrill fiddle; Chair Dance—Watts; Candy Pitch—Bloodgood; Dance Contest—The Hired Hands; "Don't the Moon Look Lonesome," "St. Louis Blues"—Mary Smith McClain; Wichita Kid Bullwhips and Sharpshooting—Boots Madden, Susan Gibney; "When the Saints Go Marching In"—McClain; "When the Saints Go Marching In" (Reprise)—Company.

DO LORD REMEMBER ME

CAST: Giancarlo Esposito, Frances Foster, Ebony Jo-Ann, Lou Myers, Roger Robinson. Standby: Celestine DeSaussure.

Directed by Regge Life; scenery, Julie Taymor, lighting, Sandra L. Ross; costumes, Judy Dearing; production stage manager, Nancy Harrington; stage manager, Celestine DeSaussure.

This collection of firsthand memories of slavery was produced by American Place 1/23/83 for 127 performances; see its entry in *The Best Plays of 1982–83.*

THE DANUBE

Mr Sandor .... Sam Gray	Kovacs; Waiter; Doctor;	
Paul Green.................. Richard Sale	Barber .... Thomas Kopache	
Eve Sandor-Green .... Kate Collins	English Tape .... W. Scott Allison	
	Hungarian Tape............ Stephan Balant	

Directed by Maria Irene Fornes; scenery, Maria Irene Fornes; costumes, Gabriel Berry; lighting, Anne E. Militello; puppets, Esteban Fernandez; production stage manager, Nancy Harrington.

Romance between a Hungarian and an American in the shadow of nuclear disaster. Previously produced off off Broadway at Theater for the New City.

TERRA NOVA

Scott .... Robert Foxworth	Oates..................... Daniel Gerroll	
Amundsen .... Anthony Zerbe	Wilson .... Simon Jones	
Kathleen................... Christine Healy	Evans .... Michael Countryman	
Bowers .... Ian Trigger		

Directed by Gerald Gutierrez; scenery, Douglas Stein; costumes, Ann Emonts; lighting, Paul Gallo; sound, Scott Lehrer; film design, John Pieplow; production stage manager, Kate Pollock; press, Bob Ullman.

Drama of the doomed Scott Antarctic expedition, previously produced at Yale Repertory Theater (1977), Mark Taper Forum (1979) and elsewhere, somewhat revised in this version. The play was presented in two parts.

A Little Madness (7). By Gerald Zipper. Produced by Bellwether Productions and Bella Rosenberg at the Provincetown Playhouse. Opened October 5, 1983. (Closed October 9, 1983)

Directed by Norman Gevanthor; scenery, John Kasarda; costume supervision, Oleksa; lighting, Spencer Mosse; press, Arthur Cantor, Harvey Elliott. With David Falkner, Pamela Burrell, John LaGioia, Kathleen Doyle, Sam Gray, Ron Siebert, Robert Silver.

Upper New York West Side family in crisis brought on by a son's illegal trade in armaments.

City Stage Company (CSC; formerly Classic Stage Company). Repertory of three programs (also see note), **Big and Little/scenes** (47). By Botho Strauss; translated by Christopher Martin. Opened October 6, 1983. (Closed December 30, 1983) **Hamlet** (41). Revival of the play by William Shakespeare; adapted by Karen Sunde and Christopher Martin. Opened December 15, 1983. (Closed January 29, 1984) **Dance of Death** (16). Revival of the play by August Strindberg; English version by Christopher Martin. Opened May 6, 1984. (Closed May 20, 1984) Produced by City Stage Company, Christopher Martin artistic director, Dan J. Martin (subsequently Will Maitland Weiss) managing director, at City Stage Company.

ALL PLAYS: Director/designer, Christopher Martin; dramaturg, Karen Sunde; costumes, Miriam Nieves; lighting, Rick Butler; stage manager, Bonnie L. Becker; press, Will Maitland Weiss.

BIG AND LITTLE/SCENES

Morocco
Lotte .... Karen Sunde

Nightwatch
Lotte .... Karen Sunde
Woman .... Amy Warner
Man.................... John Camera

Ten Rooms (in 16 scenes)
Lotte .... Karen Sunde
Fat Woman........ Mary Eileen O'Donnell
Tent..................... John Camera
Old Woman .... Helene Rose
Old Man .... Noble Shropshire
Guitar Player .... Thomas Lenz
Woman in Zipped-Up Dress.. Amy Warner
Research Assistants .... Gary Sloan,
Ginger Grace
Paul .... Tom Spiller
Turk............... Charles H. Patterson

Big and Little
Lotte .... Karen Sunde
Meggy .... Amy Warner
Turk............... Charles H. Patterson
Turk's Wife........ Mary Eileen O'Donnell
Man....................... Tom Spiller
Boy .... Gary Sloan
Girl .... Ginger Grace
Tenants: Tom Spiller, Mary Eileen O'Donnell, Ginger Grace, Amy Warner, John Cam-

era, Noble Shropshire, Helene Rose, Thomas Lenz.

Station
Lotte .... Karen Sunde

Family in a Garden
Lotte .... Karen Sunde
Bernard .... Thomas Lenz
Wilhelm.................. John Camera
Josephine......... Mary Eileen O'Donnell
Albert .... Gary Sloan

Wrong Number
Lotte .... Karen Sunde

Dictation
Lotte .... Karen Sunde
Alf.................... Noble Shropshire

Abominable Angel
Lotte .... Karen Sunde
Man in Parka................ Tom Spiller

In Society
Lotte .... Karen Sunde
Doctor.................... John Camera
Patients: Gary Sloan, Ginger Grace, Thomas Lenz, Amy Warner, Charles H. Patterson, Mary Eileen O'Donnell, Helene Rose, Noble Shropshire, Tom Spiller.

A journey through modern society with a Candide-like optimist as a guide. A foreign play (*Gross und Klein*) produced in West Germany (1978), Paris (1982), London (1983) and elsewhere. The play was presented in two parts with the intermission following *Ten Rooms*.

HAMLET

1st Gravedigger................ Tom Spiller
2d Gravedigger .... Thomas Lenz
Hamlet .... Noble Shropshire
Claudius.................. John Camera
Gertrude........... Mary Eileen O'Donnell

Ghost .... Charles H. Patterson
Polonius .... Donn Youngstrom
Laertes .... Gary Sloan
Ophelia..................... Ginger Grace
Duenna.................... Amy Warner

Associate director, Karen Sunde.
Subtitled "After Shakespeare," a free adaptation playing in two hours without intermission. The last major New York revival of *Hamlet* was by New York Shakespeare Festival 12/2/82 for 37 performances.

DANCE OF DEATH

Edgar .... Jerry Whiddon
Alice...................... Karen Sunde

Kurt .... Tom Spackman

Scenery and costumes, Terry A. Bennett; lighting, Christopher Martin; stage manager, Arlene Roseman.
The last major New York Revival of *(The) Dance of Death* was by New York Shakespeare Festival at Lincoln Center 4/4/74 for 37 performances.

Note: The CSC season also included the running repertory productions of *Faust Part One* (13) and *Faust Part Two* (13) by Johann Wolfgang von Goethe, adapted by Christopher Martin from the translations of Bayard Taylor and Philip Wayne, with songs by Frank Wedekind, presented in the repertory 10/21/83–12/31/83, with a cast consisting of Christopher Martin, Gary Sloan, Charles H. Patterson, Noble Shropshire, John Camera, Tom Spiller, Thomas Lenz, Ginger Grace, Donn Youngstrom, Amy Warner and Mary Eileen O'Donnell (see entries in *The Best Plays of 1982–83*).

New York Shakespeare Festival. Schedule of eight programs. **My Uncle Sam** (16). By Len Jenkin. Opened October 11, 1983. (Closed October 23, 1983) **Sound and Beauty** (63). Program of two one-act plays by David Henry Hwang: *The House of Sleeping Beauties* and *The Sound of a Voice*. Opened November 6, 1983. (Closed January 1, 1984.) **A Private View** (95). Program of three one-act plays by Vaclav Havel; translated by Vera Blackwell: *Interview, A Private View* and *Protest*. Opened November 20, 1983. (Closed February 12, 1984) **Lenny and the Heartbreakers** (20). Musical with book by Kenneth Robins; music by Scott Killian and Kim D. Sherman; lyrics by Kenneth Robins, Scott Killian and Kim D. Sherman. Opened December 22, 1983. (Closed January 8, 1984) **The Human Comedy** (79). Musical based on the novel by William Saroyan; book and lyrics by William Dumaresq; music by Galt MacDermot. Opened December 28, 1983. (Closed March 4, 1984 and transferred to Broadway; see its entry in the Plays Produced on Broadway section of this volume)

Also **Cinders** (56). By Janusz Glowacki; translation by Christina Paul. Opened February 20, 1984. (Closed April 8, 1984) **Fen** (59). Revival of the play by Caryl Churchill. Opened March 4, 1984. (Closed April 22, 1984) **Young Playwrights Festival** (12). Program of five one-act plays: *Romance* by Catherine Castellani, *Meeting the Winter Bike Rider* by Juan Nunez, *Fixed Up* by Patricia Durkin, *In the Garden* by Anne Harris and *Tender Places* by Jason Brown. Opened May 9, 1984 in the Foundation of the Dramatists Guild production, Gerald Chapman artistic director, Peggy C. Hansen producing director. (Closed May 20, 1984) Produced by New York Shakespeare Festival, Joseph Papp producer, at the Public Theater (see note).

ALL PLAYS: Associate producer, Jason Steven Cohen; press, Merle Debuskey, Richard Kornberg, Barbara Carroll, Bruce Campbell.

MY UNCLE SAM

CAST: Laura Innes, Olek Krupa, Kathleen Layman, Mark Margolis, John Nesci, Kristine Nielsen, Rocco Sisto, Scott Wentworth, Margaret Whitton, R. Hamilton Wright, Ray Xifo.

Directed by Len Jenkin; scenery, John Arnone; costumes, Kurt Wilhelm; lighting, Frances Aronson; choreography, Catlin Cobb.

Abstract theater of mixed impressions including a chase theme in which a detective-like young man searches for his great uncle, a traveling salesman.

SOUND AND BEAUTY

The House of Sleeping Beauties
Michiko .... Ching Valdes
Kawabata.................... Victor Wong
Girl................. Elizabeth Fong Sung
Time: 1972. Place: Tokyo. Scene 1: Night. Scene 2: Following evening. Scene 3: Evening, several months later. Scene 4: Evening, one week later.

Fantasy, a novelist's suicide after visits to a house in which all the girls are maintained in a drugged state, an attempt to explore the relationship of the real-life Japanese Nobel Prize-winning novelist Yasunari Kawabata's suicide in 1972 with his novella of similar title.

The Sound of a Voice
Man .... John Lone
Woman.................. Natsuko Ohama
Movement .... Ching Valdes, Elizabeth Fong Sung

Recorded music: Lucia Hwong pipa, koto, cheng, synthesizer, biwa, vocal, also co-arranger; Yukio Tsuji shakuhachi, percussion, koto, cheng, biwa, gagaku flute, also arranger; Jack Kripl soprano sax.

Place: A remote corner of the forest.

Ill-fated relationship between a woman living alone in the forest and a wandering samurai.

Directed by John Lone; assisted by Lenore Kletter; music, Lucia Hwong; musical direction and choreography, John Lone; scenery, Andrew Jackness; lighting, John Gisondi; costumes, Lydia Tanji; production stage manager, Alice Jankowiak; stage manager, Morton Milder.

A PRIVATE VIEW

Head Maltster	Barton Heyman	Michael	Nicholas Hormann
Vanek	Stephen Keep	Stanek	Richard Jordan
Vera	Concetta Tomei		

Directed by Lee Grant; scenery, Marjorie Bradley Kellogg; costumes, Carol Oditz; lighting, Arden Fingerhut; production stage manager, Michael Chambers; stage manager, Anne King.

Place: Prague, Czechoslovakia. Part I: Time, 1975. Scene 1: *Interview*. Scene 2: *Private View*. Part II: Time, 1978. Scene 3: *Protest*.

Semi-autobiographical foreign (Czechoslovakian) plays written to be performed in the private apartments of friends, by an author who was at one time imprisoned by the state for human rights activities and whose works are banned for public production in his own country. *Interview* is a comic treatment of a boss's effort to persuade one of his brewery workers to inform on himself. In *Private View*, a threadbare friend is entertained by an affluent couple. *Protest* bares a novelist's moral weakness in the face of state oppression.

LENNY AND THE HEARTBREAKERS

(Lenny)	Michael Brian, Robert Joy	Soprano Saint	Nancy Ringham
J.P. di Medici	Darren Nimnicht	(Angela)	Joanna Glushak, Sally Stotts
Alto Saint	Sally Williams	(Parentheses indicate roles in which the performers alternated)	
Tenor Saint	James Wilson		
Bass Saint	Frank Nemhauser		

Dancers: Michael Blake, Janis Brenner, Betsy Fisher, Robert McWilliams, Margaret Morris, Danial Shapiro, Joanie Smith, Edward Akio Taketa.

Musicians: Hank Levy, vocoder; Robby Kilgore, Linn drum machine; Rob Schwimmer, prophet synthesizer #1; Jeremy Kahn, Jupiter synthesizer #2; Janet Glazener, Jupiter synthesizer #3; Bill Cammarota, prophet synthesizer #4; percussion; Bill Moersch; guitar, Jim Tunnell.

Understudies: Messrs. Brian, Joy, Wilson—Gary Harger; Messrs. Nimnicht, Nemhauser—Raymond Murcell; Miss Williams—Gloria Parker; Misses Glushak, Stotts, Ringham—Janis Brenner; Swing Dancer—Holly Schiffer.

Directed and choreographed by Murray Louis and Alwin Nikolais; conductor, James McElwaine; scenery, Alwin Nikolais with Nancy Winters; costumes, Lindsay W. Davis; lighting, Alwin Nikolais with Peter Koletzke; sound, Bill Dreisbach, John Kilgore; film sequences and computer graphic slides, John Sanborn, Mary Perillo; orchestrations, Kim D. Sherman, Scott Killian; additional orchestrations, James McElwaine, Robert Kilgore; production stage manager, Stephen McCorkle; stage manager, Mitchell Lemsky.

Subtitled "A New American Opera," a rock musical with electronic sound and visual effects, telling of an artist commissioned to create a masterpiece; individual musical numbers not identified.

THE HUMAN COMEDY

Trainman	David Johnson	Bess	Mary Elizabeth Mastrantonio
Ulysses	Josh Blake	Helen	Anne Marie Bobby
Mother	Bonnie Koloc	Miss Hicks	Laurie Franks
Homer	Stephen Geoffreys	Spangler	Rex Smith

Thief............... Christopher Edmonds	Girl...................... Lisa Kirchner
Mr. Grogan............... Gordon Connell	Boy....................... Louis Padilla
Felix....................... Daniel Noel	Toby...................... Joe Kolinski
Beautiful Music............... Delores Hall	Soldiers..... Kenneth Bryan, Michael Willson
Mary Arena............. Caroline Peyton	Neighbor.......... Kathleen Rowe McAllen
Mexican Lady.............. Olga Merediz	Diana Steed.............. Leata Galloway
Voice of Matthew; Marcus....... Don Kehr	

Townspeople: Donna Lee Marshall, Grady Mulligan, Vernon Spencer.

Musicians: Josh Rodriguez, Joel Derovin violins; Gregory Singer viola; Nestor Cybriwsky cello; Doug Shear double bass; Jimmy Madison percussion; Charles C. Brown III guitars; Allen Won, Seldon Powell sax, clarinet, flute; Allen Shawn keyboard; Mac Gollehan trumpet, fluglehorn; Eddie Bert trombone.

Directed by Wilford Leach; musical direction and orchestrations, Galt MacDermot; conductor, Tania Leon; costumes, Rita Ryack; lighting, Stephen Strawbridge; production stage manager, Alan Fox; stage manager, K. Siobhan Phelan.

Act I: Train Crossing, At Home, At School, Telegraph Office, Home, Messages, Telegraph Office, Home, Train Crossing. Act II: A Debarkation Center, Home, War Front, Home Front, Telegraph Office, Home.

Musical version of Saroyan's 1943 novel and screen play about children and adults of a California family deeply affected by World War II, expressed almost entirely in song. The list of musical numbers in *The Human Comedy* (not identified in this version) appears in its entry in the Plays Produced on Broadway section of this volume.

Walter Hudson replaced Rex Smith 2/84.

CINDERS

Inspector; Soundman....... Peter McRobbie	Stepmother.................. Melissa Leo
Principal................... George Guidall	Father...................:. Martha Gehman
Deputy.................. Robin Gammell	1st Ugly Sister............... Anna Levine
Cinderella................ Lucinda Jenney	2d Ugly Sister.............. Johann Carlo
Prince..................... Dori Hartley	Director........... Christopher Walken
Fairy Godmother............ Greta Turken	Electrician.............. Kevin McClarnon
Mouse..................... Eli Marder	Cameraman.............. Jonathan Walker

Directed by John Madden; scenery, Andrew Jackness; costumes, Jane Greenwood; lighting, Paul Gallo; songs, Richard Peaslee; music director, Deena Kaye; production stage manager, James Harker; stage manager, Tracy B. Cohen.

Place: A girls' reform school somewhere in Poland, not that far from Warsaw, really. The play was presented in two parts.

Authorities exploit and harass reform school inmates by permitting a film crew to intrude upon their lives and their production of a version of the Cinderella story. A foreign (Polish) play previously produced in London.

FEN

CAST: Boy Scaring Crows, Angela, Deb, Mrs. Finch—Pamela Reed; Japanese Businessman, Nell, May, Mavis—Concetta Tomei; Wilson, Frank, Mr. Tewson, Geoffrey—David Strathairn; Shirley, Shona, Miss Cade, Margaret—Linda Griffiths; Val, Woman Working in the Field—Ellen Parker; Mrs. Hassett, Becky, Alice, Ivy—Robin Bartlett.

Directed by Les Waters; scenery and costumes, Annie Smart; lighting, Tom Donnellan; original music, Ilona Sekacz; production stage manager, Stephen McCorkle; stage manager, Mitchell Lemsky.

Place: The Fens in the east of England, less than a hundred miles north of London. The play was presented without intermission.

Fen was produced 5/24/83 for 43 performances by New York Shakespeare Festival with a British cast in the Joint Stock Company production.

THE HUMAN COMEDY—Rex Smith, Gordon Connell and Stephen Geoffreys in a scene from the musical presented by Joseph Papp at his Public Theater before its transfer uptown to Broadway

YOUNG PLAYWRIGHTS FESTIVAL

Romance
by Catherine Castellani, age 18
Woman........ Catherine Ann Christianson
Man .... Rob Knepper
   Directed by Elinor Renfield; original music, Louis Rosen. Young man and his girl friend share love and poverty.

Meeting the Winter Bike Rider
by Juan Nunez, age 17
Mark..................... Jeffrey Marcus
Tony...................... Corey Parker
   Directed by Elinor Renfield; original music, Louis Rosen. Conversation and friendship at a small-town gas station.

Fixed Up
by Patricia Durkin, age 16
Laura .... Ellen Mareneck
Jeffrey..................... Marc Epstein

Directed by Shelly Raffle; music recorded by Michael Rubell and Whyte Lyte. A blind date for the high school prom.

In the Garden
by Anne Harris, age 17
Kate .... Etain O'Malley
Mary.............. Pamela Payton-Wright
   Directed by James Milton; original music, Louis Rosen. Two sisters meet in their childhood home after their mother's death.

Tender Places
by Jason Brown, age 13
Mary.................... Carolyn Mignini
Paul .... Stephen Vinovich
Eric.................... Knowl Johnson
Sam.................... Lois Diane Hicks
   Directed by Shelly Raffle. A 12-year-old boy is caught between his divorcing parents.

ALL PLAYS: Scenery, Loren Sherman; costumes, Patricia McGourty; lighting, Mal Sturchio; sound coordinator, Bill Dreisbach; production stage manager, Esther Cohen; stage managers, Morton Milder, Diane Ward.

These five plays by young authors (ages given above at the time of submission of scripts) were selected from over 1,000 entries in the Foundation of the Dramatists Guild's third annual Young Playwrights Festival for this off-Broadway production, the first such under the aegis of New York Shakespeare Festival. In addition to the above productions, this Festival held readings of *Liars* by Joseph Yesutis, *Buddies* by Kevin Hammond, *Always Open* by Rebecca Gilman, *We Three Kings* by Alexander Frere-Jones and *Living in the U.S.A.* by Julie Tayco.

Note: In Joseph Papp's Public Theater there are many separate auditoriums. *My Uncle Sam* played the Other Stage, *Sound and Beauty* and *Cinders* played LuEsther Hall, *A Private View* and *Young Playwrights Festival* played Martinson Hall, *Lenny and the Heartbreakers* and *Fen* played the Estelle R. Newman Theater, *The Human Comedy* played the Anspacher Theater.

Weekend (8). Musical with book, music and lyrics by Roger Lax. Produced by Donald Rubin at the Theater at St. Peter's Church. Opened October 24, 1983. (Closed October 31, 1983)

Directed and choreographed by David H. Bell; musical direction, Clay Fullum; scenery, Ursula Belden; costumes, Sally Lesser; lighting, Toni Goldin; sound, Paul Garrity; orchestrations, Robby Merkin; production stage manager, Tom Capps; press, Solters/Roskin/Friedman, Inc., Milly Schoenbaum, Kevin Patterson. With Justin Ross, Louise Edeiken, Gregg Edelman, Carole-Ann Scott.

Understudy: Miss Edeiken—Rosalyn Rahn.

Boy and girl in facing Manhattan apartments meet and fall in love.

Tallulah (42). Musical with book by Tony Lang; music by Arthur Siegel; lyrics by Mae Richard. Produced by Mark deSolla Price, John Van Ness Philip and Leonard Soloway in association with David Susskind at the West Side Arts Center Cheryl Crawford Theater. Opened October 30, 1983. (Closed December 4, 1983)

Tallulah . . . . Helen Gallagher   John Barrymore; John Emery . . . . . Joel Craig
Will Bankhead . . . . Russell Nype

Men: Tom Hafner, Eric Johnson, Ken Lundie, Patrick Parker, Clark Sterling.

Musicians: Bruce W. Coyle conductor, piano; Peter Hammer percussion; Jim Rice piano II.

Understudies: Mr. Nype—Eric Johnson; Mr. Craig—Ken Lundie; Men—William Alan Coats.

Directed and choreographed by David Holdgrive; musical direction and arrangements, Bruce W. Coyle; scenery and costumes, John Falabella; lighting, Ken Billington; projection graphics, Stanley Topliff; assistant choreographer, William Alan Coats; assistant musical director, Jim Rice; production stage manager, Mark Baltazar; stage manager, Tracy A. Crum; press, Francine L. Trevens, Penny M. Landau, David Lotz.

Revue-style presentation of events in the life of Tallulah Bankhead.

MUSICAL NUMBERS, ACT I: "Darling"—Helen Gallagher, Men; "Tallulah"—Gallagher, Men; "When I Do a Dance for You"—Gallagher, Russell Nype; "Home Sweet Home"—Gallagher, Men; "I've Got to Try Everything Once"—Gallagher, Joel Craig; "You're You"—Gallagher, Tom Hafner, Patrick Parker, Clark Sterling, Ken Lundie; "I Can See Him Clearly"—Gallagher; "Tallulah-baloo"—Men; "The Party Is Where I Am"—Men.

ACT II: "Stay Awhile"—Tallulah, Men; "It's a Hit"—Lundie, Sterling, Hafner, Men; "If Only He Were a Woman"—Gallagher, Johnson, Men; "Tallulah" (Reprise)—Nype; "Love Is on Its Knees"—Gallagher, Craig, Men; "Don't Ever Book a Trip on the IRT"—Gallagher, Men; "You Need a Lift!" Gallagher; Finale—Gallagher, Men.

The unassigned number "I'm the Woman You Wanted" was also included in the score.

Sunset (1). Cabaret revue with music by Gary William Friedman; lyrics by Will Holt. Produced by Diane deMailly at the Village Gate Downstairs. Opened and closed at the evening performance, November 7, 1983.

Directed by Andre Ernotte; choreographed by Buzz Miller; musical direction, Donald York; scenery, Kate Edmunds; costumes, Patricia Zipprodt; lighting, Robert Jared; sound, Paul Garrity; orchestrations and vocal arrangements, Gary William Friedman; press, Solters/Roskin/Friedman, Inc., Milly Schoenbaum. With Tammy Grimes, Walt Hunter, Ronee Blakely, Kim Milford.

The lives of four entertainers, presented in a Hollywood cafe setting.

Leftovers (43). Revue conceived and written by Marcia Kimmell, Deah Schwartz and Anne Wilford. Produced by Judith Finn Haines and John Adams Vaccaro at the Astor Place Theater. Opened November 8, 1983. (Closed December 18, 1983)

Marcia Kimmell	Anne Wilford
Deah Schwartz	

Directorial consultant (New York production), Barbara Harris; directorial consultant (San Francisco production), Kenna White: scenery, Robert F. Strohmeier; costumes, Tamara Melcher, Gregory Reeves; lighting, Arwin Bittern, Vivian Leone; stage manager, Arwin Bittern; press, Betty Lee Hunt, Maria Cristina Pucci, James Sapp.

The adventures and diets of a compulsive eater, improvisationally developed by the performers. The play was presented without intermission. Previously produced in San Francisco and elsewhere.

*Playwrights Horizons. Schedule of three programs (also see note). **Baby With the Bathwater** (84). By Christopher Durang. Opened November 8, 1983. (Closed January 15, 1984) ***Isn't It Romantic** (202). Revised version of the play by Wendy Wasserstein. Opened December 15, 1983. **Fables for Friends** (22). By Mark O'Donnell. Opened February 16, 1984. (Closed March 4, 1984) Produced by Playwrights Horizons, Andre Bishop artistic director, Paul Daniels managing director, at Playwrights Horizons.

BABY WITH THE BATHWATER

Helen	Christine Estabrook	Cynthia; Woman in the Park;	
John	W.H. Macy	Miss Pringle; Susan	Leslie Geraci
Nanny; Woman in the Park;		Young Man	Keith Reddin
Principal	Dana Ivey		

Directed by Jerry Zaks; scenery, Loren Sherman; costumes, Rita Ryack; lighting, Jennifer Tipton; sound, Jonathan Vail; press, Bob Ullman.

Comic treatment of the often-damaging stresses of the parent-child relationship.

Kate McGregor-Stewart replaced Dana Ivey. Mary Louise Wilson replaced Kate McGregor-Stewart 12/6/83.

ISN'T IT ROMANTIC

Janie Blumberg	Cristine Rose	Simon Blumberg	Stephen Pearlman
Harriet Cornwall	Lisa Banes	Lillian Cornwall	Jo Henderson
Marty Sterling	Chip Zien	Paul Stuart	Jerry Lanning
Tasha Blumberg	Betty Comden	Vladimir	Tom Robbins

Telephone Messages: Schlomo—Timmy Geissler; Hart Farrell—Kevin Kline; Julie Stern—Swoosie Kurtz; Tajlei Kaplan Singleberry—Patti LuPone; Operator—Ellis Rabb; Cynthia Peterson—Meryl Streep; Milty Sterling—Jerry Zaks.

Directed by Gerald Gutierrez; scenery, Andrew Jackness; costumes, Ann Emonts; lighting, James F. Ingalls; sound, Scott Lehrer; music coordinator, Jack Feldman; dance sequences, Susan Rosenstock; production stage manager, J. Thomas Vivian; stage manager, Toby Simpkins.

Time: The present. Place: New York. The play was presented in two parts.

Two New York women cope with males, careers and New York City life. Original version was first produced off Broadway by the Phoenix Theater 5/28/81 for 37 performances.

Marge Kotlisky replaced Betty Comden 1/31/84. Peg Murray replaced Jo Henderson 3/6/84. Barbara Barrie replaced Marge Kotlisky 5/11/84.

FABLES FOR FRIENDS

CAST: Paul McCrane, Brian Tarantina, Timothy Daly, Laura Hughes, Debra Cole, Cynthia Darlow.

Directed by Douglas Hughes; scenery, Christopher Nowak; costumes, Linda Fisher; lighting, David Noling; music, Paul Sullivan; production stage manager, Barbara Abel; stage manager, Vincent A. Feraudo.

Nine comedy vignettes of friendship, presented without intermission.

Note: In addition to the programs presented at its theater on Theater Row, Playwrights Horizons co-sponsored an off-Broadway production of *Terra Nova* by Ted Tally with The American Place Theater at the American Place Theater; see its entry in the listing of The American Place Theater schedule in this section of this volume.

Secret Honor (47). One-man performance by Philip Baker Hall in a play by Donald Freed and Arnold M. Stone. Produced by Robert Altman and Sandcastle 5 Productions in the Los Angeles Actors Theater production, Bill Bushnell producing artistic director, at the Provincetown Playhouse. Opened November 8, 1983. (Closed December 18, 1983)

Directed by Robert Harders; scenery and lighting, Russell Pyle; production stage manager, Donald David Hill; press, Jeffrey Richards Associates, Eileen McMahon.

Time: 1980s. Place: The study of Richard M. Nixon. The play was presented without intermission.

Subtitled *The Last Testament of Richard M. Nixon,* the actor as the former President telling his side of the Watergate story to a tape recorder. Previously produced in Los Angeles.

Painting Churches (206). By Tina Howe. Produced by Elizabeth I. McCann, Nelle Nugent, Ray Larsen, Lee Guber and Shelly Gross in the Second Stage production at the Lamb's Theater. Opened November 22, 1983. (Closed May 20, 1984)

Fanny Church . . . . Marian Seldes   Margaret Church . . . . Elizabeth McGovern
Gardner Church . . . . George N. Martin

Standbys: Miss Seldes—Lily Lodge; Miss McGovern—Frances McDormand; Mr. Martin—Wyman Pendleton.

Directed by Carole Rothman; scenery, Heidi Landesman; costumes, Linda Fisher; lighting, Frances Aronson; production stage manager, Loretta Robinson; stage manager, Barbara Schneider; press, Solters/Roskin/Friedman, Inc., Joshua Ellis, Louise Ment.

Time: Several years ago.

Place: Beacon Hill, Boston, Mass. Act I, Scene 1: A bright spring morning. Scene 2: Two days later. Scene 3: 24 hours later. Act II, Scene 1: Three days later. Scene 2: The last day.

Young artist comes home to find her Bostonian parents in crisis over the father's failing health and in turmoil over moving out of their Beacon Hill house. Previously produced last season off off Broadway by Second Stage.

Joanne Camp replaced Elizabeth McGovern 3/24/84.

A Best Play; see page 116.

The Negro Ensemble Company. Schedule of two programs; see note. **Puppetplay** (47). By Pearl Cleage. Opened November 23, 1983. (Closed January 1, 1984) **American Dreams** (27). By Velina Houston. Opened January 28, 1984. (Closed February 19, 1984) Produced by The Negro Ensemble Company, Douglas Turner Ward artistic director, Leon B. Denmark managing director, at Theater Four.

PUPPETPLAY

Saxophonist .... Wendell Brooks	Woman Two .... Phylicia Ayers-Allen
Woman One.................. Seret Scott	Puppeteer................... Brad Brewer

Directed by Clinton Turner Davis; scenery, Llewellyn Harrison; costumes, Judy Dearing; lighting, William H. Grant III; sound, Bernard Hall; production stage manager, Jesse Wooden Jr.; press, Irene Gandy.

Two women share the company of a life-sized puppet in their home.

AMERICAN DREAMS

Manfred Banks .... Count Stovall	Policeman Bill; Military Officer.. Ron August
Freddie Banks .... Sandra Reaves-Phillips	Blue River Banks .... Kim Yancey
Creed Banks............... Reuben Green	Alexis Morgan............... Janet League
Setsuko Banks .... Nancy Hamada	Fumiko Brennan .... Ching Valdes
Lawrence .... Walter Allen Bennett Jr.	

Directed by Samuel P. Barton; scenery, Daniel Proett; costumes, Judy Dearing; lighting, Shirley Prendergast; sound, Bernard Hall; production stage manager, Jerry Cleveland.

Racial frictions between blacks and Asian Americans.

Note: The Negro Ensemble Company also offered (but never presented to the press in an announced premiere) a revival of *Colored People's Time* by Leslie Lee 2/28/84–4/8/84 for 48 performances, directed by Horacena J. Taylor, scenery by Charles McClennahan, costumes by Myrna Colley-Lee, lighting by Shirley Prendergast, sound by Bernard Hall, with a cast including L. Scott Caldwell, Chuck Cooper, Tracy Griswald, Samuel L. Jackson, Carol Maillard, Kim Staunton, Charles Weldon, Robert Aberdeen, Angela Bassett, Kenneth Laron Johnson.

*Circle Repertory Company. Schedule of five programs. **The Sea Gull** (20). Revival of the play by Anton Chekhov; translated by Jean-Claude van Itallie. Opened November 24, 1983. (Closed December 11, 1983) **Full Hookup** (46). By Conrad Bishop and Elizabeth Fuller. Opened December 29, 1983. (Closed January 22, 1984) **Levitation** (46). By Timothy Mason. Opened February 12, 1984. (Closed March 11, 1984) **The Harvesting** (33). By John Bishop. Opened April 1, 1984. (Closed April 29, 1984) ***Balm in Gilead** (1) Revival of the play by Lanford Wilson; co-produced by The Steppenwolf Theater Ensemble, Jeff Perry artistic director, in The Steppenwolf Theater Company of Chicago production. Opened May 31, 1984. Produced by Circle Repertory Company, Marshall W. Mason artistic director, B. Rodney Marriott acting artistic director, Richard Frankel managing director, *The Sea Gull* at American Place Theater, other plays at the Circle Theater.

THE SEA GULL

Medvedenko.................. Michael Ayr	Dorn...................... Dennis Patrick
Masha..................... Robin Bartlett	Arkadina .... Barbara Cason
Sorin..................... Michael Higgins	Trigorin .... Judd Hirsch
Treplev.................. Richard Thomas	Shamraev .... Richard Seff
Yakov..................... Bruce McCarty	Maid................... Colleen Davenport
Nina .... Katherine Cortez	Cook...................... Beryl Towbin
Paulina .... Nancy Killmer	

Understudies: Misses Cortez, Bartlett—Colleen Davenport; Misses Cason, Killmer—Beryl Towbin; Mr. McCarty—David Fellows; Messrs. Higgins, Patrick, Seff—Matthew Lewis.

Directed by Elinor Renfield; production supervised by Tanya Berezin; scenery, John Lee Beatty; costumes, Jennifer Von Mayrhauser; lighting, Dennis Parichy; sound, Chuck London Media/-Stewart Werner; original music, Norman L. Berman; production stage manager, Fred Reinglas; press, Richard Frankel, Reva Cooper.

Time: The turn of the century. Place: Russia. Act I: The park of Sorin's estate. Act II: The lawn

FULL HOOKUP—Jacqueline Brookes and Lynne Thigpen in the Circle Repertory production of the play by Conrad Bishop and Elizabeth Fuller

behind Sorin's house. Act III: The dining room in Sorin's house. Act IV: Two years later, the drawing room in Sorin's house. The play was presented in two parts with the intermission following Act II.

The last major New York revival of *The Sea Gull* took place off Broadway at New York Shakespeare Festival 11/11/80 for 40 performances.

FULL HOOKUP

Ric	Steve Bassett	Joellen	Lynne Thigpen
Beth	Sharon Schlarth	Les	Edward Seamon
Rosie	Jacqueline Brookes		

Understudies: Mr. Bassett—Mick Weber; Mr. Seamon—Tom Smith; Misses Schlarth, Brookes, Thigpen—Colleen Davenport.

Directed by Marshall W. Mason; associate director, B.H. Barry; scenery, David Potts; costumes, Laura Crow; lighting, John P. Dodd; sound, Chuck London Media/Stewart Werner; production stage manager, Ginny Martino.

Time: The present. Place: Omaha, Neb. The play was presented in two parts.

Husband-wife violence leading to murder in a trailer-park setting. Previously produced in Louisville and Dallas.

LEVITATION

Joe	Ben Siegler	Jean	Trish Hawkins
Arthur	Michael Higgins	Inga	Helen Stenborg
Ada	Lenka Peterson	Wright	Matthew Lewis
Michael	Eric Schiff	Tom	Adam Davidson
Ira	Bruce McCarty		

Understudies: Mr. Siegler—Tom Smith; Messrs. Higgins, Lewis—Mick Weber; Misses Peterson, Hawkins, Stenborg—Colleen Davenport; Messrs. Schiff, McCarty—David Fellows.

Directed by B. Rodney Marriott; scenery, David Potts; costumes, Laura Crow; lighting, Dennis Parichy; sound, Chuck London Media/Stewart Werner; original music, Norman L. Berman; production stage manager, Judy Boese.

Time: August 1979. Place: A residential section of Minneapolis. The play was presented without intermission.

Aspiring playwright comes home to his family and confronts his own feelings of love and dread.

THE HARVESTING

Carol Ann Lassiter	Kiya Ann Joyce	Gary Majors	James McDaniel
Tommy Heisler	Timothy Carhart	Bim Miller	Edward Seamon
Curtis Gibson	Lionel Mark Smith	Louise Cline	S. Epatha Merkerson
John Torski	Jimmie Ray Weeks	Police Officers	Colleen Davenport,
Walter Hollins	Paul Butler		Tom Smith
Joyce Miller	Jane Fleiss		

Directed by John Bishop; scenery, Loren Sherman; costumes, Ann Emonts; lighting, Mal Sturchio; sound, Chuck London Media/Stewart Werner; associate director, Chris Silva; dramaturg, Milan Stitt; production stage manager, Fred Reinglas.

Time: Independence Day weekend, 1976. Place: Mansfield, Ohio. The play was presented in two parts.

Detective probes the past while investigating a double murder.

BALM IN GILEAD

John	Paul Butler	Frank	Zane Lasky
Ernesto	Giancarlo Esposito	Al	Burke Pearson
Carlo	Lazaro Perez	Darlene	Laurie Metcalf
Babe	Debra Engle	Dopey	Gary Sinise
Rust	Billie Neal	Kay	Betsy Aidem
Bonnie	Tanya Berezin	Joe	Danton Stone
Fick	Terry Kinney	Terry	Karen Sederholm
Franny	Jeff Perry	Ann	Glenne Headly
David	Brian Tarantina	Xavier	Tom Zanarini
Tig	James McDaniel	Stranger	Tom Irwin
Rake	James Pickens Jr.	Tim	Mick Weber
Martin	Jonathan Hogan	Judy	Charlotte Maier
Bob	Bruce McCarty		

Children: Adam Davidson, Eben Davidson, Erinnisse Heuer, Samantha Kostmayer.

Understudies: David Fellows, Susan Hall, Jodie Markell, Mario Moreno, Michael Rispoli.

Directed by John Malkovich; scenery and lighting, Kevin Ridgon; costume supervision, Glenne Headly; sound, John Malkovich; sound supervision, Chuck London/Stewart Werner; production stage manager, Teri McClure.

Time: October, 1972. Place: An all-night coffee shop and the street corner outside, Upper Broadway, New York City. The play was presented in two parts.

Chicago (Steppenwolf) production of play produced in 1965 at Cafe La Mama. This is its first major New York presentation.

And a Nightingale Sang . . . (177). By C.P. Taylor. Produced by Wayne Adams, Sherwin M. Goldman and Martin Markinson in association with Westport Productions, William Twohill executive producer, at the Mitzi E. Newhouse Theater. Opened November 27, 1983. (Closed April 28, 1984)

Helen Stott....................	Joan Allen	Andie	Robert Cornthwaite
Joyce Stott..........	Moira McCanna Harris	Eric......................	Francis Guinan
George Stott................	John Carpenter	Norman	Peter Friedman
Peggy Stott.................	Beverly May		

Directed by Terry Kinney; scenery, David Jenkins; costumes, Jess Goldstein; lighting, Kevin Rigdon; sound, David Budries; production stage manager, Dorothy J. Maffei; stage manager, Zoya Wyeth; press, Betty Lee Hunt, Maria Cristina Pucci, James Sapp.

Time: During the years of World War II. Place: Newcastle-on-Tyne. Act I, Scene 1: "Oh, Johnnie, How You Can Love" Sunday, Sept. 3, 1939. Scene 2: "We'll Meet Again" June 20, 21, 1940. Scene 3: "Yours" Aug. 12, 1940. Act II, Scene 1: "That Lovely Weekend," Nov. 1942. Scene 2: "The White Cliffs of Dover" June 6, 7, 1944. Scene 3: "A Nightingale Sang in Berkeley Square" May 8, 1945.

A British family carries on with life and loves in the midst of a world war. A foreign play previously produced in Newcastle, London and elsewhere including Chicago and Hartford.

Jeanine Morick replaced Moira McCanna Harris 3/5/84. George Hall replaced Robert Cornthwaite 2/13/84. Jack Bittner replaced George Hall 4/9/84.

A Best Play; see page 131.

The Lady and the Clarinet (39). By Michael Cristofer. Produced by Lucille Lortel, Elizabeth I. McCann, Nelle Nugent and William P. Suter at the Lucille Lortel Theater. Opened November 28, 1983. (Closed December 31, 1983)

Clarinet Player.................	Jay Dryer	Jack.........................	Paul Rudd
Luba.................	Stockard Channing	George	Josef Sommer
Paul	Kevin Geer		

Standbys: Miss Channing—Valorie Armstrong; Mr. Geer—Mark Moses; Mr. Dryer—Ed Gilmore; Messrs. Rudd, Sommer—Eric Booth, Dan Desmond.

Directed by Gordon Davidson; music, Stanley Silverman; scenery, Heidi Landesman; costumes, William Ivey Long; lighting, Beverly Emmons; production stage manager, Franklin Keysar; stage manager, Ron Nguvu; press, Solters/Roskin/Friedman, Inc., Joshua Ellis, Louise Ment.

Woman reminisces about the men in her life to a clarinet player hired for a party. The play was presented without intermission. Previously produced at the Mark Taper Forum, Los Angeles, and the Long Wharf Theater, New Haven, Conn.

*The Mirror Theater. Repertory of five revivals. ***Paradise Lost** (90). By Clifford Odets. Opened December 10, 1983. ***Inheritors** (46). By Susan Glaspell. Opened December 11, 1983. ***Rain** (40). By John Colton. Opened March 6, 1984. ***Ghosts** (15). By Henrik Ibsen; translated by Eva Le Gallienne. Opened May 15, 1984. ***The Hasty Heart** (6). By John Patrick. Opened May 15, 1984. Produced by The Mirror Theater, Sabra Jones artistic director, Barbara Leep administrator, at the Real Stage.

GHOSTS

Regine Engstrand	Sabra Jones	Alternates: Terry Finn (Regine), Matthew
Jakob Engstrand	Baxter Harris	Cowles (Jakob), Michael O. Smith (Manders),
Pastor Manders..............	W.B. Brydon	David Cryer (Manders), Madeleine Sherwood
Mrs. Helene Alving..........	Geraldine Page	(Mrs. Alving), Steven Weber (Osvald).
Osvald Alwing..............	Victor Slezak	

PERFORMER	"PARADISE LOST"	"INHERITORS"	"RAIN"	"THE HASTY HEART"
Mason Adams	Gus Michaels			
Haru Aki			Native	
Margaret Barker		Grandmother Morton		
Peter Bloch	Milton; (Julie)	(Felix II young; Harry)		(Orderly)
W.B. Brydon			(Davidson)	
Frank Camacho			Native	
Randy William Charnin	Policeman; (Milton)	Harry	Pvt. Griggs	
Bryan Clark	Leo Gordon	(Lewis; Felix II)	(Bates)	
Matthew Cowles	Kewpie	(Emil)		Digger
David Cryer	Lucas Pike	Silas Morton	Rev. Davidson	
Francois de la Giroday	Felix			(Kiwi)
Terry Finn	Pearl Gordon; (Lucy)	(Madeline)		(Margaret)
Clement Fowler	Sam Katz; (Leo)	Felix Fejevary I; (Holden)	Qtmstr. Bates	
William Ha'o			Native	
Baxter Harris	Phil Foley	(Felix I)		
Ann Hillary	Bertha Katz	(Grandmother; Aunt Isabel)	Mrs. MacPhail	
Meg Hosey	Lucy; (Pearl, Libby)			
Timothy Jenkins				Tommy
Sabra Jones	Libby Michaels	Madeline Fejevary	Sadie Thompson	
Tad Jones	Ben Gordon	Horace Fejevary	(O'Hara)	Kiwi; (Yank)
Lilah Kan			Native; (Mrs. Horn)	
José Kendall				Blossom
Jim Knobeloch	Schnabel	Emil Johnson		
Sofia Landon				Margaret
David May	Post; Williams; (Paul)	(Smith)	(Hodgson)	Orderly
Clark Middleton	(Williams)			
Camilla Moore			(Mrs. MacPhail)	
F.J. O'Neil	Rogo; Mr. May	Sen. Lewis		Colonel
Jess Osuna	(Gus)	Prof. Holden	Dr. MacPhail	
Geraldine Page	Clara Gordon	Aunt Isabel Fejevary	Mrs. Horn (Mrs. Davidson)	
James Pritchett	(Sam; Pike; Rogo; Detective)	Felix Fejevary II	(MacPhail; Davidson)	(Colonel)
James Rebhorn		(Silas)	Sgt. O'Hara	Yank
Charles Regan	Cameraman; Paul; (Mr. May Post)	Ira Morton; (Lewis)		
Madeleine Sherwood	(Clara; Bertha)		Mrs. Davidson	
Victor Slezak				Lachlen
Fred G. Smith	Detective; (Post Cameraman)	Smith		
Michael O. Smith	(Foley; Schnabel)	(Ira)	Trader Horn	(Digger)
John Strasberg	(Felix)	(Silas)		
Steven Weber	Julie Gordon	Felix Fejevary II (young); (Horace)	Cpl. Hodgson	(Lachlen)

(Parentheses indicate roles in which the performers served as alternates)

ALL PLAYS: Directed by John Strasberg (*The Hasty Heart* directed by Porter Van Zandt); scenery, Ron Placzek; costumes, Heidi Hollmann; lighting, Mal Sturchio; sound, Rob Gorton; *Paradise Lost* pianist, Julie Holtzman; stage managers, Alan R. Traynor, Kathleen Blair Costello.

PARADISE LOST: Place: Leo Gordon's home in an American city. Act I: Armistice Day, 1932. Act II: 1934. Act III: April 30, 1935.

Paradise Lost was first produced on Broadway by the Group Theater 12/9/35 for 73 performances. This is its first major New York revival.

INHERITORS: Place: The Illinois-Iowa border. Act I, Scene 1: July 4, 1879, Silas Morton's cabin. Scene 2: 1921, conference room of the college library. Act II: 1921, Silas Morton's cabin.

Inheritors was first produced off Broadway at the Provincetown Playhouse in 1921 and was revived by Civic Repertory Theater 3/15/27 for 17 performances.

RAIN: Time: The rainy season. Place: The front room of Joe Horn's hotel-store on the island of Pago-Pago in the South Seas. Act I, Scene 1: Early morning. Scene 2: Two days later, late afternoon. Act II, Scene 1: Four days later, night. Scene 2: Early the following morning.

The last major New York revival of *Rain* took place off Broadway 3/23/72 for 7 performances.

GHOSTS: Time: The 1880s. Place: A spacious garden-room in Mrs. Alving's country estate on one of the large fjords in the west of Norway. Act I: Middle of the afternoon. Act II: After dinner. Act III Towards dawn.

The last major New York revival of *Ghosts* took place on Broadway 8/30/82 for 40 performances.

THE HASTY HEART: Time: Spring, 1944. Place: The convalescent ward in a temporary British general hospital somewhere to the rear of the Assam-Burma front. Act I: Early morning. Act II, Scene 1: Two weeks later. Scene 2: A few nights later. Act III, Scene 1: The next day. Scene 2: The following morning.

The Hasty Heart was first produced on Broadway 1/3/45 for 207 performances and was named a Best Play of its season. It was revived off Broadway in the 1953–54, 1956–57 and 1959–60 seasons.

One More Song/One More Dance (14). Ballet revue created by Grover Dale. Produced by Lee Gross Associates at the Joyce Theater. Opened December 21, 1983. (Closed December 31, 1983)

Directed by Grover Dale; musical direction and arrangements, Joel Silberman; scenery, Lawrence Miller; costumes, Albert Wolsky; lighting, Richard Nelson; press, Mark Goldstaub. With Ann Reinking, Jeff Calhoun, Gary Chryst, Stephen Joy, Gregory Mitchell, Brian Sutherland, Robert Warners.

Miss Reinking and six male dancers performing a modern ballet with songs.

Dinah! Queen of the Blues (7). One-woman performance by Sasha Dalton; written by Sasha Dalton and Ernest McCarty. Produced by Woodie King Jr., Raymond L. Gaspard, Martin Markinson and Mary Card, Ashton Springer executive producer, at the Westside Arts Center. Opened January 11, 1984. (Closed January 15, 1984)

Directed by Woodie King Jr.; scenery and lighting, Llewellyn Harrison; costumes, Judy Dearing; sound, Brian Penny; musical direction, Bross Townsend; arrangements, Corky McLerkin; additional arrangements, Ernest McCarty; production stage manager, Richard Douglass; press, Michael Alpert, Ruth Jaffe.

Musical tribute to Dinah Washington, with Miss Dalton portraying her in a biographical sketch and in performance as a singer. The play was presented in two parts. Previously produced in Chicago and in New York in a night club version.

The Living Theater (32). Repertory of four programs. **The Archeology of Sleep** (10). By Julian Beck. Opened January 17, 1984. **The Antigone of Sophokles** (7). Revival of the play by Bertolt Brecht; based on the German translation of Frederich Hölderlin; English translation by Judith Malina. Opened January 20, 1984. **The Yellow Methuselah** adapted by Hanon Reznikov from George Bernard Shaw's *Back to Methuselah* and Wassily Kandinsky's *The Yellow Sound*. (7). Opened January 24, 1984. **The One and the**

Many (8). Revival of the play by Ernest Toller; translated by Judith Malina. Opened January 28, 1984. (Repertory closed February 12, 1984). Produced by The Living Theater, Julian Beck and Judith Malina directors, at the Joyce Theater.

PERFORMER	"THE ARCHEOLOGY OF SLEEP"	"THE ANTIGONE OF SOPHOKLES"	"THE ONE AND THE MANY"
Isha Manna Beck	The Sleeping City: New York	Messenger; Theban	Masses; Worker; Phantom
Julian Beck	Doctor	Kreon; Theban	
Raaja Fischer		Polyneikes; Theban	Masses; Banker; Worker; People's Guard; Phantom
Rain House	Divine	Theban	Guide
Mina Lande	Amuh		
Henriette Luthi	Pandora	Theban	Masses; Woman; Phantom
Judith Malina		Antigone; Theban	Sonja Irene L.
Catherine Marchand	Catherine		
Antonia Matera	Antonia	Ismene; Theban	Masses; Worker; Comrade; Phantom; 1st Prisoner
Maria Nora	Liza	Theban	Masses; Comrade; Worker; Phantom
Horacio Martin Palacios	Dandelion	Eteokles; Theban; Elder	Masses; Banker; Worker; Guard; Phantom; Executioner
Hanon Reznikov	Hanon	Tiresias; Theban	Nameless One
Stephan Schulberg	Rabbi Krazy Kat	Megareus; Theban; Elder	Masses; Worker; Phantom; Officer
Dirk Szuszies	Mister X	Theban	Masses; Worker; Phantom
Ilion Troya	Sabuhl	Hamon; Theban	Masses; Comrade; Banker; Worker; Guard; Phantom
Serena Urbani		Theban	
Christian Vollmer	Christian	War Horse; Theban; Elder	Husband
Thomas Walker	Tom	Guard; Theban; Elder	Masses; Banker; Worker; Priest

THE ARCHEOLOGY OF SLEEP—Directed by Judith Malina; scenery, costumes, lighting, Julian Beck; music, Raaja Fischer; press, Shirley Herz, Sam Rudy.

Exploration of the phenomena of sleep and dreaming, occasionally making direct contact with the audience in this troupe's usual style. The play was presented without intermission, in more than 70 scenes. Previously presented in Nantes (1983).

THE ANTIGONE OF SOPHOKLES: Directed by Judith Malina and Julian Beck. Previously produced in Living Theater repertory at the Brooklyn Academy of Music 10/10/68.

THE ONE AND THE MANY—Directed by Judith Malina; scenery, costumes and lighting by Julian Beck; choral music, Raaja Fischer. American premiere of 1920 German expressionist drama *Masse Mensch*, previously produced in 1980 in Living Theater repertory in Europe.

THE YELLOW METHUSELAH

CAST: Red/Gray-green Creature, Voice, Yellow Figure, Longlived Native, Chloe—Antonia Matera; Eve, Voice, Green Figure, Ethel, Cleopatra-Semiramis—Catherine Marchand; Cain, Joyce

WOZA ALBERT!—Percy Mtwa and Mbongeni Ngema in a scene from their South African play

Burge, Barnabas, Emperor, Strephon—Christian Vollmer; Red/Gray-green Creature, Voice, Red Figure, Longlived Native, Penelope—Henriette Luthi; Yellow Giant, Yellow Figure, Zozim, Phineas —Horacio Martin Palacios; Red/Gray-green Creature, Conrad Barnabas, Yellow Figure, Ambrose, Martellus—Ilion Troya.

Also Serpent, Recorder, Mrs. Lutestring, Oracle, The She/Ancient Lilith—Judith Malina; Red Creature, George Bernard Shaw, Confucius, Elderly Gentleman, The He-Ancient—Julian Beck; Red/Gray-green Creature, Voice, Purple Figure, Molly, Daphne—Maria Nora; Blue Figure, Wassily Kandinsky, Zoo, Ecrasia—Mina Lande; Fawn, Voice, Yellow Figure, Longlived Native, Amaryllis —Raaja Fischer; Red/Gray-green Creature, Voice, Orange Figure, Longlived Native, Pygmalion— Rain House; Yellow Giant, George Lubin, Burge-Lubin, Longlived Native, Acis—Stephan Schulberg; Adam, Franklyn Barnabas, Archbishop, Longlived Native, Ozymandias—Thomas Walker.

Directed by Hanon Reznikov; music, Alvin Curran; scenery, costumes, lighting, Julian Beck; musical direction, Raaja Fischer; lighting technician, Nicolas Serrano; masks and props, Ilion Troya, Anthony Johnopoulos.

Prologue—The Six Days of Creation: Prelude, Voice and Vision. Day 1: Wind Over Water. Day 2: Gravity/Mass. Day 3: Land and Sea. Day 4: Firmament. Day 5: Birds and Fishes. Day 6: The Creatures of Eden. Act I: In the Beginning (4004 B.C.). Act II: The Gospel of the Brothers Barnabas (present day). Act III: The Thing Happens (2234 A.D.). Act IV: An Elderly Gentleman's Progress (3000 A.D.). Act V: As Far as Thought Can Reach (31,984 A.D.). The play was presented in two parts with the intermission following Act IV.

American premiere of a melange of material adapted from Shaw and Kandinsky. Previously produced in Living Theater repertory in 1982 in Europe.

Nostalgic for the Future (1). One-man show created and performed by Steve Ben Israel. Produced by the Westside Arts Theater at the Westside Arts Theater. Opened and closed at the evening performance, February 9, 1984.

Directed by Steve Ben Israel; press, Shirley Herz, Sam Rudy, Pete Sanders.
Series of character sketches by a former member of the Living Theater.

Babalooney (24). Musical revue created through improvisation by the company; original music by Larry Schanker and the Practical Theater Co. Produced by Arthur Cantor, Brad Hall, Bruce Ostler, Paul Barrosse and Bonnie Nelson Schwartz in the Practical Theater Co. production at the Provincetown Playhouse. Opened February 15, 1984. (Closed March 4, 1984)

CAST: Rush Pearson (Chip and The Skipper Too), Jamie Baron (Rob and The Millionaire and His Wife), Bekka Eaton (Ernie and The Rest), Uncle Charlie (Himself and Gilligan), Jane Muller (Steve and The Movie Star), Paul Barrosse (Doug, Our Smelly Little Cousin).

The Bababalooney Band: Larry Schanker piano, synthesizers; Ronny Crawford drums, etc.

Directed by Brad Hall; scenery, Louis DiCrescenzo; costumes, Iwo Jima, Jen Crawford; lighting, Tom Larson; overtures arranged by Larry Schanker and Ronny Crawford; other arrangements, Larry Schanker; stage manager, Wolf Larson; press, Harvey Elliott, Tom Siracusa.

Visiting Evanston, Ill. troupe presenting comic and musical numbers developed by the company.

Rockaby (78). Program of three one-act plays by Samuel Beckett: *Enough*, *Footfalls* and *Rockaby*. Produced by the Harold Clurman Theater, Jack Garfein artistic director, and Lucille Lortel at the Samuel Beckett Theater. Opened February 16, 1984. (Closed April 22, 1984).

Enough
Reader . . . . Billie Whitelaw

Footfalls
May . . . . Billie Whitelaw
Mother's Voice . . . . Sybil Lines

Rockaby
Woman and Voice . . . . Billie Whitelaw

Understudy: Miss Whitelaw—Virginia Kay White.

Directed by Alan Schneider; scenery and lighting, Rocky Greenberg; costumes, Carla Kramer; production stage manager, Thom Mangan; press, Jeffrey Richards Associates, Richard Dahl.

Enough (written in 1966) is a dramatic reading of a short story about a relationship between a young woman and an old man. In *Footfalls* (1976), a daughter taking care of her helpless mother is herself confused about where and who she is, in a production based on the original as directed by Samuel Beckett at the Royal Court Theater in London. In *Rockaby* (1980), a very old woman is drawing out the last gasps of her life, a playlet written by Beckett for Miss Whitelaw. Previously produced in London.

A Best Play; see page 191.

Street Theater (31). By Doric Wilson. Produced by Jack Ross, Charles C. Timm and Ken Cook at the Actors Playhouse. Opened February 22, 1984. (Closed March 18, 1984)

CAST: Louis Affenito, Curt Baker, Beth Berman, Peter Bruno, Tom Cahill, John Canning, Julia Dares, David Drake, Tibor Feldman, Daniel Holmberg, Michael Lynch, Gary Sharder, Tony Torres, Casey Wayne.

Directed by Ken Cook; scenery, Robert Merkel; lighting, Pamela Ross; press, Michael Alpert, Ruth Jaffe.

The June 1959 gay bar riot on Christopher Street in New York City. Previously produced off off Broadway.

Woza Albert! (79). By Percy Mtwa, Mbongeni Ngema and Barney Simon. Produced by Elliot Martin, Arnold Bernhard and Columbia Artists Theatricals Corp., Gary McAvay executive producer, in association with Lucille Lortel in the Market Theater

Company production at the Lucille Lortel Theater. Opened February 23, 1984. (Closed May 6, 1984)

CAST: Percy Mtwa, Mbongeni Ngema.
Directed by Barney Simon; scenery, Barney Simon; lighting, Manny Manim; stage managers, Joseph De Pauw, Dixon Setlare Malele; press, Jeffrey Richards Associates, Robert Ganshaw.
Series of acidulously comic scenes developed by the performers and director on the subject of the black man's life in contemporary South Africa. A foreign play previously produced in Johannesburg and elsewhere, including the U.S.

*A . . . My Name Is Alice (81). Musical revue conceived by Joan Micklin Silver and Julianne Boyd. Produced by Rosita Sarnoff, Anne Wilder and Douglas F. Goodman by special arrangement with The Women's Project (Julia Miles director) at the American Place Theater. Opened February 24, 1984; closed March 11, 1984 and reopened at The Village Gate Upstairs April 8, 1984.

Roo Brown   Alaina Reed
Randy Graff   Charlaine Woodard
Mary Gordon Murray

Understudies: Misses Graff, Murray, Woodard—Christine Anderson; Messrs. Brown, Reed—Jackee Harry.
Directed by Joan Micklin Silver and Julianne Boyd; choreography, Edward Love; musical director, Michael Skloff; scenery, Ray Recht; costumes, Ruth Morley; lighting, Ann Wrightson; sound, Tom Gould; orchestrations, Doug Katsaros; associate producers, Frederick D. Offenberg, Mark Teschner; stage manager, Renee F. Lutz; press, Shirley Herz, Sam Rudy, Peter Cromarty.
Mildly feministic topical revue which began as part of American Place's Women's Project.

MUSICAL NUMBERS AND SCENES, ACT I: "All Girl Band" (music by Doug Katsaros, lyrics by David Zippel)—Company; A . . . My Name Is Alice Poems (by Marta Kauffman and David Crane)—Company; "At My Age" (music by Glen Roven, lyrics by June Siegel)—Roo Brown, Randy Graff; "Trash" (music by Michael Skloff, lyrics by Marta Kauffman and David Crane)—Company; For Women Only Poems (by Marta Kauffman and David Crane)—Brown; "Good Thing I Learned to Dance" (music by Stephen Lawrence, lyrics by Mark Saltzman)—Charlaine Woodard.
Also "Welcome to Kindergarten" (music by Michael Skloff, lyrics by Marta Kauffman and David Crane)—Mary Gordon Murray, Brown; "I Sure Like the Boys" (music by Lucy Simon, lyrics by Steve Tesich)—Graff; Ms. Mae (by Cassandra Medley)—Alaina Reed; Good Sports (Detroit Persons, Susan Rice; Educated Feet, Carol Hall)—Company; "The Portrait" (music and lyrics by Amanda McBroom)—Murray; "Bluer Than You" (music by David Evans, lyrics by Winnie Holzman)—Graff, Reed, Brown.
ACT II: "Pretty Young Men" (music by Lucy Simon, lyrics by Susan Birkenhead)—Murray, Reed, Brown; Demigod (by Richard LaGravanese)—Woodard; "The French Song" (music and lyrics by Don Tucker, monologue by Art Murray)—Murray; "Pay Them No Mind" (music and lyrics by Calvin Alexander and James Shorter)—Reed; Hot Lunch (by Anne Meara)—Murray, Woodard; "Emily, the M.B.A." (music by Stephen Lawrence, lyrics by Mark Saltzman)—Graff, Reed, Woodard, Murray; "Sisters" (music by Cheryl Hardwick, lyrics by Maggie Bloomfield)—Brown; "Honeypot" (music by Stephen Lawrence, lyrics by Mark Saltzman)—Graff, Reed.

Hey, Ma . . . Kaye Ballard (62). One-woman musical with and by Kaye Ballard; concept and original music and lyrics by David Levy and Leslie Eberhard. Produced by Karl Allison and Bryan Bantry at the Promenade Theater. Opened February 27, 1984. (Closed April 22, 1984)

Directed by Susan H. Schulman; special appearance by Arthur Siegel; scenery, Linda Hacker; costumes, William Ivey Long; lighting, Ruth Roberts; musical direction and supervision, Robert Billig; orchestrations, Robby Merkin; associate producer, Paul Bellardo; production stage manager, Marjorie Horne; press, Henry Luhrman Associates, Terry M. Lilly.

Miss Ballard telling her life story and singing a group of songs, both new numbers and standards, some of which she introduced in the course of her career.

MUSICAL NUMBERS, ACT I (by David Levy and Leslie Eberhard unless otherwise noted): "Up There," "Someone Special" (by David Schaefer and Joseph Connolly), "Nana" (by Jerry Goldberg and Danny Sachs), "You Made Me Love You" (by James Monaco and Joe McCarthy), "Thinking of You" (by Harry Ruby), "Supper Club," "Without a Song" (by Vincent Youmans, Billy Rose and Edward Eliscu), "Nobody But You" (by George Gershwin, Arthur Jackson and B.G. DeSylva), "Teeny Tiny (by Kaye Ballard, Marshall Baerer and David Walker), "Hey, Ma."

ACT II: "Down There" (Reprise), "Lazy Afternoon" (by John Latouche and Jerome Moross), "Always, Always You" (by Bob Merrill), "Hey, Ma" (Reprise), "You Don't Need It", "Down in the Depths" (by Cole Porter), "Cookin' Breakfast for the One I Love" (by Henry Tobias and William Rose), "Old Tunes" (by Charles Strouse and Lee Adams), "All the Magic Ladies."

*Orwell That Ends Well (105). Musical revue by and with The Original Chicago Second City Company; music by Fred Kaz. Produced by Bernard Sahlins and Art D'Lugoff in the Second City production at the Village Gate Downstairs. Opened March 4, 1984.

Meagan Fay	John Kapelos
Mike Hagerty	Richard Kind
Isabella Hofmann	Rick Thomas

Directed by Bernard Sahlins; associate producer, Joyce Sloane; stage manager, Craig Taylor; press, Max Eisen, Maria Somma, Madelon Rosen.

Social satire in skits and songs, previously produced in Chicago.

ACT I: Reunion—Cast; Job Interview—Meagan Fay, Rick Thomas; Rendezvous—Cast; Editorial —Fay, John Kapelos; Nothingness and Being—Richard Kind, Mike Hagerty; "Culture Quiz"— Thomas; Oh America!—Cast; Personals—Fay, Kapelos; "Pirates"—Cast.

ACT II: Bernardin—Thomas; Love Story—Fay, Kapelos, Kind; Oh Chicago!—Cast; Double Exposure—Isabella Hofmann, Thomas, Kapelos; Domesticity—Hofmann, Kind; Home Study— Hagerty, Fay, Kind; The Uses of Television—Thomas, Kapelos, Fay, Hofmann; Growing Up—Fay, Hofmann; "Margaret Thatcher"—Hofmann, Thomas; "Who Gives a Damn"—Cast.

Pieces of Eight (7). Program of eight one-act plays: *The Unexpurgated Memoirs of Bernard Mergendeiler* by Jules Feiffer, *The Black and White* by Harold Pinter, *The Tridget of Greva* by Ring Lardner, *The Sandbox* by Edward Albee, *The (15 Minute) Dogg's Troupe Hamlet* by Tom Stoppard, *Come and Go* by Samuel Beckett, *Foursome* by Eugene Ionesco, *I'm Herbert* by Robert Anderson. Produced by Joseph Papp in The Acting Company production, John Houseman producing artistic director, Margot Harley executive producer, Michael Kahn and Alan Schneider artistic directors, at the Public Theater (Martinson Hall). Opened March 7, 1984. (Closed March 11, 1984)

The Unexpurgated Memoirs of Bernard Mergendeiler
Naomi.................. DeLane Matthews
Bernard...................... Jack Kenny

The Black and White
1st Old Woman............ Laura Brutsman
2d Old Woman .... Libby Colahan

The Tridget of Greva (translated from the Squinch)
Laffler, a Wham Salesman .... Gregory Welch
Corby, a Corn Vitter.......... David Manis
Barhooter, the Tridget ... Richard S. Iglewski

The Sandbox
Mommy .... Libby Colahan
Daddy....................... Jack Kenny
Young Man .... Anthony Powell
Musician..................... Phil Meyer
Grandma .... Laura Brutsman

The (15 Minute) Dogg's Troupe Hamlet
Shakespeare; Polonius.... Richard S. Iglewski
Bernardo; Marcellus;
  Gravedigger; Osric............ Jack Kenny
Francisco; Horatio.......... Gregory Welch
Claudius.................... David Manis

Hamlet	Anthony Powell	Vi	DeLane Matthews
Gertrude	Libby Colahan	Ru	Laura Brutsman
Ghost; Fortinbras	Phil Meyer		
Ophelia	Laura Brutsman	*Foursome*	
Laertes	Terrence Caza	Dupont	Jack Kenny
Players: Terrence Caza, Jack Kenny, DeLane		Durand	Terrence Caza
Matthews, Phil Meyer, Gregory Welch.		Martin	David Manis
		Lady	DeLane Matthews
Come and Go		*I'm Herbert*	
Flo	Libby Colahan	Herbert	Richard S. Iglewski
		Muriel	Libby Colahan

Conceived and directed by Alan Schneider; scenery, Mark Fitzgibbons; costumes, Carla Kramer; *Come and Go* costumes by John David Ridge; lighting, Richard Riddell; music for *The Sandbox* by William Flanagan; production stage manager, Giles F. Colahan; stage manager, Michael S. Mantel; press, Merle Debuskey, Richard Kornberg, Barbara Carroll, Bruce Campbell.

The program was subtitled "an evening of eight modern one-act plays" and presented in two parts with the intermission following *The (15 Minute) Dogg's Troupe Hamlet*. Previously produced at Keene, N.H. State College and the University of Iowa and herewith presented on tour for the John F. Kennedy Center, Washington, D.C., with a repertory also including *The Cradle Will Rock*, *The Merry Wives of Windsor* and *Pericles*.

Dracula, or A Pain in the Neck (2). By Phil Woods and Michael Bogdanov. Produced by Kazuko Hillyer in association with the Concert Arts Society in the New Vic Theater of London production, Michael Bogdanov artistic director, at the Beacon Theater. Opened March 19, 1984. (Closed March 22, 1984)

Directed by Michael Bogdanov; press, Shirley Herz. With Anthony Milner, Michael Bogdanov.

Adaptation of the Dracula story. A foreign play previously produced in London.

To Gillian on Her 37th Birthday (46). By Michael Brady. Produced by M Square Entertainment, Inc. (Mitchell Maxwell, Alan J. Schuster, Fred H. Krones) and The Ensemble Studio Theater (Curt Dempster artistic director, David S. Rosenak managing director) at Circle in the Square Downtown. Opened March 22, 1984. (Closed April 29, 1984)

David	David Rasche	Paul	Richmond Hoxie
Cindy	Noelle Parker	Esther	Jean DeBaer
Rachel	Sarah Jessica Parker	Gillian	Cheryl McFadden
Kevin	Frances Conroy		

Directed by Pamela Berlin; music composed by Robert Dennis; scenery, Robert Thayer; costumes, Deborah Shaw; lighting, Allen Lee Hughes; sound, Bruce Ellman; associate producer, Andrew R. Morse; production stage manager, Richard Costabile; press, Bruce Cohen.

Widower and his family adjusting to his beloved wife's death. The play was presented in two parts. Previously produced off off Broadway.

The Flight of the Earls (25). By Christopher Humble. Produced by Hendrix Productions, Inc. and John Van Ness Philip at the Westside Arts Theater (Downstairs). Opened March 25, 1984. (Closed April 15, 1984)

Ian Earl	Guy Paul	Brigitte Earl	Christine Estabrook
Timothy Strain	Reed Birney	Claire Strain	Peggy Schoditsch
Michael Earl	Timothy Landfield	Keith Earl	Kenneth Meseroll
Kate Earl	Carol Teitel		

NITE CLUB CONFIDENTIAL—Fay DeWitt and
Stephen Berger in the "Love Isn't Born, It's Made"
number from the cabaret musical

Directed by Allen R. Belknap; scenery, Lawrence Miller; costumes, Susan A. Cox; lighting, Richard Winkler; production stage manager, Mark Baltazar; stage manager, Tracy Crum; press, Betty Lee Hunt, Maria Cristina Pucci, James Sapp, Robert Larkin.

Time: September, 1971. Place: The Earl family home in County Tyrone, Act I, Scene 1: Late afternoon. Scene 2: An hour later. Scene 3: Half an hour later. Act II, Scene 1: Immediately following. Scene 2: Early the next morning. Scene 3: An hour later.

Melodrama of a violently anti-British family in Ireland.

The Actors' Delicatessen (8). By Murray Mednick and Priscilla Cohen. Produced by Yentl Productions/George A. Schapiro with Chris Silva and Sari E. Weisman at the Provincetown Playhouse. Opened March 26, 1984. (Closed April 1, 1984)

Directed by Julie Hebert; scenery, Ernest Allen Smith; costumes, Dona Granata; lighting, Novella T. Smith; sound, Aural Fixation; press, Burnham/Callaghan Associates. With Marilyn Sokol, David Garfield.

Comedy about two vaudeville stars.

A Hell of a Town (16). By Monte Merrick. Produced by The Gero Organization in association with Michael Benahum at the Westside Arts Theater (Upstairs). Opened March 27, 1984. (Closed April 8, 1984)

Directed by Allan Carlsen; scenery, Ray Recht; costumes, Pamela Scofield; lighting, F. Mitchell Dana; sound, Nic Minetor; production stage manager, Louis D. Pietig; stage manager, Jason Gero; press, Shirley Herz, Sam Rudy, Pete Sanders. With Joanna Gleason, Peter Riegert.

Comedy, after nuclear cataclysm two people find themselves the only ones left in New York City.

The Vampires (23). By Harry Kondoleon. Produced by Stephen Graham at the Astor Place Theater. Opened April 11, 1984. (Closed April 29, 1984)

Directed by Harry Kondoleon; scenery, Adrianne Lobel; costumes, Rita Ryack; lighting, William Armstrong; sound, Paul Garrity; fight direction, Randy Kovitz; production stage manager, David K. Rodger; press, David Powers, Leo Stern. With John Vickery, Jayne Haynes, Anne Twomey, Graham Beckel, Elizabeth Berridge, Paul Guilfoyle.

Comedy about a crazily eccentric suburban family. The play was presented in two parts.

Love (17). Musical based on the play *Luv* by Murray Schisgal; book by Jeffrey Sweet; music by Howard Marren; lyrics by Susan Birkenhead. Produced by Haila Stoddard, Joy Klein and Maggie Minskoff at the Audrey Wood Theater. Opened April 15, 1984. (Closed April 29, 1984)

Harry .... Nathan Lane   Ellen .... Judy Kaye
Milt .... Stephen Vinovich

Musicians: Uel Wade piano, conductor; Bernie Berger reeds; Ian Finkel percussion; Jack Gale trombone.

Understudy: Messrs. Lane, Vinovich—Gus Kaikkonen.

Directed by Walton Jones; musical staging, Ed Nolfi; musical direction, vocal and dance arrangements, Uel Wade; scenery and costumes, Kevin Rupnik; lighting, Ruth Roberts; orchestrations, Robby Merkin; associate producers, John Kenley, Vincent Curcio, Tarquin Jay Bromley; stage manager, Richard Lombard; press, Solters/Roskin/Friedman, Inc., Josh Ellis, Louise Ment, Cindy Valk.

Place: A bridge. Act I: An October evening. Act II: One year later.

Musical version of the comedy originally produced on Broadway 11/11/64 for 901 performance and named a Best Play of its season.

ACT I

"Sincerely, Harold Berlin".. Harry
"Polyarts U".. Milt, Harry
"Paradise"... Milt, Harry
"Carnival Ride"... Milt, Harry
"The Chart".. Ellen
"Paradise" (Reprise).. Ellen, Harry
"Ellen's Lament"... Ellen, Harry
"Somebody"... Harry, Ellen
"Yes, Yes, I Love You"... Harry, Ellen
"Carnival Ride" (Reprise)... Milt, Harry, Ellen

ACT II

"Love"... Ellen
"What a Life!"... Ellen, Milt
"Paradise" (Reprise)... Ellen, Milt
"Lady"... Milt, Ellen
"If Harry Weren't Here".. Ellen, Milt
"My Little Brown Bag".. Harry, Ellen, Milt
"Do I Love Him?"... Harry, Ellen
"Harry's Resolution"... Harry, Ellen, Milt
"Love" (Reprise) .... Ellen, Milt
"Carnival Ride" (Reprise).. Harry

*'night, Mother (50). Transfer from Broadway of the play by Marsha Norman. Produced by Dann Byck, Wendell Cherry, The Shubert Organization and Frederick M. Zollo at the Westside Arts Theater. Opened April 18, 1984.

Thelma Cates .... Anne Pitoniak
Jessie Cates .... Kathy Bates

Standbys: Miss Pitoniak—Helen Harrelson; Miss Bates—Phyllis Somerville.
Directed by Tom Moore; scenery and costumes, Heidi Landesman; lighting, James F. Ingalls; associate producer, William P. Suter; production stage manager, Larry Forde; press, Betty Lee Hunt, Maria Cristina Pucci.
Place: A relatively new house built way out on a country road. The play was presented in two parts.
This production of *'night, Mother* appeared on Broadway 3/31/83 for 380 performances through 2/26/84, after which it reopened off Broadway. It was named a Best Play of the 1982–83 season and won the Pulitzer Prize.

Spookhouse (6). By Harvey Fierstein. Produced by Terry Allen Kramer and Harry Rigby at Playhouse 91. Opened May 2, 1984. (Closed May 6, 1984)

Directed by Eric Concklin; scenery, Bill Stabile; costumes, Randy Barcelo; lighting, Craig Miller; sound design and special effects consultant, Bran Ferren; sound design, Bob Kerzman; associate producer, Frank Montalvo; production stage manager, James Long; press, Henry Luhrman Associates, Terry M. Lilly, Keith Sherman, Kevin P. McAnarney. With Ron Meier, Court Miller, Anne Meara, Dawn Kreizer, Tom Noonan.
Time: A Friday morning in June. Place: An apartment above the Spookhouse at Coney Island. Act I: 10 A.M. Act II: 11 A.M.
A mother defends her family from its black sheep, a son who has raped and killed.

*Nite Club Confidential (25). Musical with book by Dennis Deal; new songs by Dennis Deal. Produced by CHS Productions and Greentrack Entertainment, Ltd. in association with Sidney L. Schlenker, Joseph Stein Jr. and Barbara M. Friedman at the Ballroom Theater. Opened May 10, 1984.

Buck Holden .... Stephen Berger   Mitch Dupre .... Steve Gideon
Sal........................ Tom Spiroff   Kay Goodman............... Fay DeWitt
Dorothy Flynn.............. Denise Nolin

Musicians: Joel Raney piano, leader; Rudolph Biro bongos; Matthew Patuto drums; Faun Stacy bass.
Directed by Dennis Deal; conceived by Dennis Deal with Albert Evans and Jamie Rocco; music supervision, Albert Evans; scenery, Christopher Cole; costumes, Stephen Rotondaro; lighting, Richard Latta; sound, Stuart Schwartz; arrangements, Dennis Deal; stage manager, David K. Black; press, Francine L. Trevens, Andrew Shearer, John Fisher, Caroline Cornell.
Time: The Eisenhower era.
1950s cabaret performers in night club settings, previously produced off off Broadway at Riverwest.

ACT I

Asterisk (*) signifies a new song by Dennis Deal and Albert Evans
Prologue .... Company
Sutton Place
    *"Nite Club".. Ensemble
Cafe High Society
    "Comment Allez-Vous?" .... High Hopes
        (by Murray Grand)
    "Something's Gotta Give"... Kay, High Hopes
        (by Johnny Mercer)

"Love Isn't Born, It's Made" .... Kay, Buck
    (by Arthur Schwartz and Frank Loesser)
Limbo
    "Comment Allez-Vous?" (Reprise) .... High Hopes
The Silver Rocket Lounge
    "Goody, Goody" .... High Hopes
    (by Matt Malneck and Johnny Mercer)
A radio studio
    "Goody, Goody" (continued) .... High Hopes
    "Nothing Can Replace a Man" .... Dorothy
    (by Dan Shapiro and Sammy Fain)
A street corner
    "I Thought About You" .... Buck
    (by Johnny Mercer and Jimmy Van Heusen)
A Hollywood sound stage
    *"Put the Blame on Mamie" .... Kay, High Hopes
A prosperous New York club
    *Dorothy's "Opener" .... Dorothy
    *"The Canarsie Diner" .... Dorothy, High Hopes
    "Saturday's Child" .... Dorothy
    (by Baldwin Bergersen and Phyllis McGinley)
A chic club in Paris
    *"Bonjour" .... Kay, High Hopes
    "French With Tears" .... Kay
    (by Harold Rome)
    "That Old Black Magic" .... Kay, High Hopes
    (by Harold Arlen and Johnny Mercer)

ACT II

A street in Paris .... Buck, Sal, Dorothy, Mitch
A Village jazz club
    *"Crazy New Words" .... Mitch
The Steel Pier
    "Black Slacks" .... Sal
    (by Joseph Bennett and Jimmy Denton)
Club Top of the Top
    "Something's Gotta Give" (Reprise) .... Dorothy
    *"The Long Goodbye" .... Kay
Club Au Revoir
    "Nite Club" (Reprise) .... Buck, Ensemble
    "Ev'rybody's Boppin' " .... New High Hopes
    (by Jon Hendricks)
    "Cloudburst" .... New High Hopes
    (by Jon Hendricks, Leroy Kirkland and Jimmy Harris)
    "The Other One (Darling)" .... Kay
    (by June Carroll and Arthur Siegel)
    "Yodelin' Dixieland" .... Sal, Mitch, Dorothy
    (by Wally Schmied and Fred Rauch)
    *"Dressed to Kill" .... Kay
    *"Dead End Street" .... Kay, Ensemble
Epilogue .... Company

*The Shadow of a Gunman (11). Revival of the play by Sean O'Casey. Produced by Irish Arts Center in association with Ross and Timm Productions, Carol Glannone, Charlotte Moore and Bruce Saul at the Actors' Playhouse. Opened May 22, 1984.

Davoren	Ciaran O'Reilly	Tommy Owens	Shane O'Neill
Shields	Chris O'Neill	Mrs. Henderson	Carmel O'Brien
McGuire; Auxiliary	Mickey Kelly	Mr. Gallagher	Chris Keeley
Landlord	John William Short	Mrs. Grigson	Terry Donnelly
Minnie	Freda Cavanaugh	Mr. Grigson	Maurice Kehoe

Directed by Jim Sheridan; scenery, David Raphel; costumes, Randall Ouzts, Mary G. Dixon; lighting, Victor En Yu Tan; stage manager, Patrick Folan; press, Francine L. Trevens, Andrew Shearer.

The last major New York revival of *The Shadow of a Gunman* took place off off Broadway 2/29/72 for 72 performances. Transfer of Irish Arts Center production from off off Broadway.

PLAYS PRODUCED
OFF OFF BROADWAY

AND ADDITIONAL PRODUCTIONS

Here is a comprehensive sampling of off-off-Broadway and other experimental or peripheral 1983–84 productions in New York, compiled by Camille Croce. There is no definitive "off-off-Broadway" area or qualification. To try to define or regiment it would be untrue to its fluid, exploratory purpose. The listing below of hundreds of works produced by more than 80 OOB groups and others is as inclusive as reliable sources will allow, however, and takes in all leading Manhattan-based, new-play-producing, English-language organizations.

The more active and established producing groups are identified in **bold face type,** in alphabetical order, with artistic policies and the name of the managing director(s) given whenever these are a matter of record. Each group's 1983–84 schedule is listed with play titles in CAPITAL LETTERS. Often these are works-in-progress with changing scripts, casts and directors, sometimes without an engagement of record (but an opening or early performance date is included when available).

Many of these off-off-Broadway groups have long since outgrown a merely experimental status and are offering programs which are the equal in professionalism and quality (and in some cases the superior) of anything in the New York theater, with special contractual arrangements like the showcase code, letters of agreement (allowing for longer runs and higher admission prices than usual) and, closer to the edge of the commercial theater, a so-called "mini-contract." In the list below, all available data on opening dates, performance numbers (with a plus sign + in the case of a show still running) and major production and acting credits (almost all of them Equity members) is included in the entries of these special-arrangement offerings.

A large selection of lesser-known groups and other shows that made appearances off off Broadway during the season appears under the "Miscellaneous" heading at the end of this listing.

Amas Repertory Theater. Dedicated to bringing all people regardless of race, creed, color or economic background together through the creative arts. Rosetta LeNoire, founder and artistic director.

THE BUCK STOPS HERE (16). Conceived by Richard A. Lippman; book, Norman J. Fedder; music and lyrics, Richard A. Lippman, additional lyrics, Norman J. Fedder. October 27, 1983. Director, Regge Life; choreographer, Tim Millett; musical director, Lea Richardson; scenery, Kalina Ivanov; lighting, Gregg Marriner; costumes, Eiko Yamaguchi. With Harris Store, Alexana Ryer, Jacqueline Trudeau, Scott Banfield, Mary Dunn, Kimberly Mucci, Brian Pew, Peter Piekarski, Laurel Lockhart.

SING ME SUNSHINE (16). Book, Robert E. Richardson and Johnny Brandon; music and lyrics, Johnny Brandon, based on *Peg O' My Heart* by J. Hartley Manners. February 9, 1984. Director,

AMAS REPERTORY THEATER—The entire company in a
scene from *Blackberries* by Joseph George Caruso

Jack Timmers; choreographer, Henry Le Tang; musical director, Thom Birdwell; scenery, Robert
Lewis Smith; lighting, Paul Sullivan; costumes, Gail Cooper-Hecht. With Andrea Frierson, Scott
Willis, Sal Biagini, Leonard Drum, Jan Horvath, Rose Roffman.

BLACKBERRIES (16). Concept and book, Joseph George Caruso; sketches, Billy K. Wells;
additional material, dialogue, direction and choreography, Andre De Shields. April 19, 1984.
Musical director, John McMahon; scenery, Edward Goetz; lighting, Deborah Tulchin; costumes,
Mardi Philips. With Steven Bland, Clent Bowers, Christina Britton, Marion Caffey, Ellia English, Cynthia Pearson, Mardi Philips, Gary Sullivan, Tug Wilson, Andrew Wright.

American Place Theater. In addition to the regular off-Broadway subscription season,
cabaret and other special projects are presented. Wynn Handman, director, Julia
Miles, associate director.

American Humorists Series
BREAKFAST CONVERSATIONS IN MIAMI (21). By Reinhard Lettau. January 6, 1984.
Director, Gordon Edelstein; scenery, Neil Peter Jampolis; lighting, Jane Reisman; costumes,
David C. Woolard. With William Meyers, Jeremiah Sullivan, Pierre Epstein, Humbert Allen
Astredo, Arthur Brooks, Tom Carson, Robert Silver.

PAY ATTENTION (20). Text and music, Doug Skinner. April 24, 1984. Slide show drawings,
Doug Roesch. With Doug Skinner, Eddie Gray.

The Women's Project

HEART OF A DOG (12). Cabaret written and performed by Terry Galloway. June 1, 1983. Scenery, Maxine Willi Klein; lighting, Joni Wong; costumes, Mimi Maxmen.

TERRITORIAL RITES (13). By Carol K. Mack. June 2, 1983. Director, Josephine Abady; scenery, David Potts; lighting, Frances Aronson; costumes, Mimi Maxmen. With Robin Groves, Michael Gross, Kim Hunter, Penelope Milford.

A . . . MY NAME IS ALICE (12). Conceived and directed by Joan Micklin Silver and Julianne Boyd. November 2, 1983. Choreographer, Yvonne Adrian; musical director, Jan Rosenberg; scenery, Adrianne Lobel; lighting, Ann Wrightson; costumes, Mimi Maxmen. With Lynnie Godfrey, Randy Graff, Polly Pen, Alaina Reed, Grace Roberts.

A FESTIVAL OF ONE-ACT PLAYS (33). SPECIAL FAMILY THINGS by Ara Watson and Mary Gallagher, directed by Page Burkholder, with Lois Smith, Sharon Chatten; THE ONLY WOMAN GENERAL by Lavonne Mueller, directed by Bryna Wortman, with Colleen Dewhurst, John P. Connolly; OLD WIVES TALE by Julie Jensen, directed by Alma Becker, with Kenna Hunt, Helen Stenborg, Jane Hickey, Donna Davis; AYE AYE AYE I'M INTEGRATED by Anna Deavere Smith, directed by Billie Allen, with Seret Scott, Elba Kenney; CANDY & SHELLEY GO TO THE DESERT by Paula Cizmar, directed by Carey Perloff, with Mary Catherine Wright, Lisa Goodman, Chris Baskous; THE LONGEST WALK by Janet Thomas, directed by Claudia Weill, with Frances Chaney, Sol Frieder, Kevin Tighe, Rino Thunder, Peter Yoshida, Freda Foh Shen, Garrett M. Brown; TO HEAVEN IN A SWING written and performed by Katharine Houghton. March 20–April 1, 1984.

Circle Repertory Projects in Progress. Developmental programs for new plays. Marshall W. Mason, artistic director.

THE HARVESTING written and directed by John Bishop. October 31, 1983.
DYSAN by Patrick Meyers. November 14, 1983. Directed by B. Rodney Marriott.
LISTEN TO THE LIONS by John Ford Noonan. November 28, 1983. Directed by John Bishop.
SAVE THE WORLD by Berilla Kerr. December 12, 1983. Directed by Dan Bonnell.
DANNY AND THE DEEP BLUE SEA by John Patrick Shanley. January 9, 1984. Directed by Barnet Kellman.
HUBBARD, OHIO by Steve Nelson. February 6, 1984. Directed by David Irvine.
THE EARLY GIRL by Caroline Kava. April 2, 1984. Directed by Claudia Weill.
A LITTLE GOING AWAY PARTY by Sybille Pearson. May 22, 1984. Directed by Maureen Shea.

Ensemble Studio Theater. Nucleus of playwrights-in-residence dedicated to supporting individual theater artists and developing new works for the stage. Almost 300 projects each season, initiated by E.S.T. members. Curt Dempster, artistic director.

TO GILLIAN ON HER 37TH BIRTHDAY. By Michael Brady. October 23, 1983. Director, Pamela Berlin; scenery, Robert Thayer; lighting, Allen Lee Hughes; costumes, Deborah Shaw. With James Rebhorn, Sarah Jessica Parker, Noelle Parker, Heather Lupton, Richmond Hoxie, Jean DeBaer, Cheryl McFadden.

BROKEN EGGS. By Eduardo Machado. February 10, 1984. Director, James Hammerstein; scenery, Keith Gonzales; lighting, Cheryl Thacker; costumes, Deborah Shaw. With Leonardo Cimino, Julie Garfield, Baxter Harris, Karen Kondazian, Theresa Saldana, Michael Sandoval, Ann Talman.

MARATHON '84 (one-act play festival). Schedule included: HOUSE by Danny Cahill, directed by Bruce Ornstein; BITE THE HAND by Ara Watson, directed by David Margulies; REMEMBER CRAZY ZELDA? by Shel Silverstein, directed by Art Wolff; BLOOD BOND by Gina Barnett, directed by Melodie Somers; AT HOME by Richard Dresser, directed by Jerry Zaks; FINE LINE by Janice Van Horne, directed by Harris Yulin; SLAM! by Jane Willis, directed by Shirley Kaplan; JAZZ by Elizabeth Albrecht, directed by Elaine Petricoff; BEEN TAKEN by Roger Hedden, directed by Billy Hopkins; A SENSE OF LOSS by Mark Malone, directed by Robin Saex; VERMONT SKETCHES by David Mamet, directed by Gregory Mosher; SAXOPHONE MUSIC by Bill Bozzone; ARIEL BRIGHT by Katharine Long; RAVING by Paul Rudnick. April 26–June 18, 1984.

Equity Library Theater. Actors' Equity sponsors a series of revivals each season as showcases for the work of actor-members and an "informal" series of original, unproduced material. George Wojtasik, managing director.

THE LADY'S NOT FOR BURNING by Christopher Fry. September 22, 1983. Directed by Kip Rosser; with Stephen Burks, Leonard Kelly-Young, Peggy Harmon, James Leach, Lynn Archer, Charles Michael Howard, Robert Molnar, Lisabeth Bartlett, Zeke Zaccaro, Gerald Lancaster, Callan Egan.

THE MUSIC MAN (musical) book, music and lyrics by Meredith Willson; story by Meredith Willson and Franklin Lacey. October 27, 1983. Directed by Worth Howe; with James Anthony, Sarah Rice, Ari Gold, Leonard Drum, Mary Rausch, Mollie Smith, Cheryl Montelle, Skip Zipf, Irma Larrison, Terry Runnels, Lowell Alecson, Jessica Houston, John Barone, Joanna Beck, Suzanne Lukather, Alan Stuart, Brett Larson, Whitney Anne Savage.

FOR THE USE OF THE HALL by Oliver Hailey. December 1, 1983. Directed by Margaret Denithorne; with Helen Lloyd-Breed, William Wise, Nancy Linehan, Myra Turley, Linda Christina-Jones, John P. Connolly.

RED, HOT AND BLUE! (musical) book by Howard Lindsay and Russel Crouse, music and lyrics by Cole Porter, adapted by Gerry Matthews. January 5, 1984. Directed by Christopher Catt; with Susan Cella, A.C. Weary, Tom Flagg, Gordon Stanley, Christine Anderson.

A THURBER CARNIVAL by James Thurber, music by Don Elliott. February 9, 1984. Directed by J. Barry Lewis; with Peter Bartlett, Joy Bond, Linda Gelman, Stephen Gleason, Mitchell Greenberg, Evelyn Joan Halus, Jim McNickle, Hardy Rawls, Kate Weiman.

UP IN CENTRAL PARK (musical) book by Herbert and Dorothy Fields, music by Sigmund Romberg, lyrics by Dorothy Fields. March 8, 1984. Directed by John Sharpe; with Barbara McCulloh, James Judy, Meredith Murray, Nick Corley, Judy Anne Nelson, Richard Blair, Jim Donahoe, Nick Jolley, David Bryant.

Informal Series: 3 performances each

BE STILL THUNDER by Shirley Hardy-Leonard. September 26, 1983. Directed by Shelly Raffle; with W. Benson Terry, Edythe Davis, Minnie Gentry, David Sotolongo, Joan Valentina, Allen Barone, Mitchell Bonta.

THE MEN'S GROUP by David St. James. October 17, 1983. Directed by Kent Thompson; with Janet Aldrich, Jeffrey West, Jonathan Slaff, Leo Schaff, Jerry Lee.

TRADING PLACES (musical revue) conceived and performed by Jeff Veazey and Susan Stroman. November 21, 1983. Directed by Dennis Deal.

THE MIDDLEMAN by Glen Merzer. January 16, 1984. Directed by David Dorwart; with Pattie Tierce, Kent Thompson, Stan Lachow, Paul Edwards, Arthur Strimling.

DICKENS'S REFLECTIONS ON THE CAROL (musical) adapted by Philip William McKinley, music and lyrics by Suzanne Buhrer and Philip William McKinley. January 19, 1984. Directed by Stephen Bonnell; with Frank Ventura, David Trim, Thomas Ikeda, Michael Shane Rogers, Kathryn Wilson, Michele Rigan.

ROMANTIC ARRANGEMENTS by Alan M. Brown. February 27, 1984. Directed by Morgan Sloane; with Lachlan Macleay, Linda Cook, Stephen Ahern, Nona Waldeck, Daniel Allen Kremer.

A GOOD YEAR FOR THE ROSES by Susan Kander. March 26, 1984. Directed by Stan Lachow; with Rosemary McNamara, Kathleen Claypool, William R. Riker, Jay Devlin, Dee Ann McDavid.

A TOUCH OF THE POET by Eugene O'Neill. April 12, 1984. Directed by Yvonne Ghareeb; with Andrew Gorman, Don Perkins, Kay Walbye, Helen-Jean Arthur, Gerald J.

NEW FEDERAL THEATER—Lanyard Williams
and Brenda Denmark in Nubia Kai's *Parting*

Quimby, John F. Degen, Carl A. Northgard, Rod Houts, Joanne Dorian, John Armstrong.
PAL JOEY (musical) book by John O'Hara, music by Richard Rodgers, lyrics by Lorenz
Hart. May 10, 1984. Directed by Bill Herndon; with Mark Fotopoulos, Spence Ford, Cathy
Brewer-Moore, Greg Ganakas, Marijane Sullivan, Mary Lou Shriber.
AMERICAN POWER PLAY by Judith Brussell. May 21, 1984. Directed by Dinah Gravel; with
J.D. Cedillo, Lynne Charnay, Eileen Engel, Doug Franklin, Nancy Hamada, Laura Neal, Nicho-
las Saunders, Robin Westphal, Steve Wise.

Hudson Guild Theater. Presents plays in their New York, American, or world premieres.
David Kerry Heefner, producing director, Daniel Swee, associate director.

28 performances each

SAND DANCING. By Kenneth Pressman. October 12, 1983. Director, Robert Moss; scenery
and lighting, Paul Wonsek; costumes, Jeanne Button. With John Abajian, Stephen Burleigh,
Kristin Griffith, Lynn Milgrim, Michael Earl O'Connor, Willie Reale.

WEDNESDAY. By Julia Kearsley. November 22, 1983. Director, Geraldine Fitzgerald; scenery,
Ron Placzek; lighting, Phil Monat; costumes, Mariann Verheyen. With John Bowman, Mia
Dillon, John Cunningham, Sada Thompson.

GETTING ALONG FAMOUSLY. By Michael Jacobs. January 25, 1984. Director, Joan Darling; scenery, James Leonard Joy; lighting, Phil Monat; costumes, Mariann Verheyen. With Tom Aldredge, Ted Flicker, Beverly Nero, Edward Power.

LOVE LETTERS ON BLUE PAPER. By Arnold Wesker. March 28, 1984. Director, Kenneth Frankel; scenery, Paul Wonsek; lighting, Jeff Davis; costumes, Mariann Verheyen. With Christopher Curry, Pauline Flanagan, Jeffrey Jones, Josef Sommer.

BROWNSTONE. Musical by Josh Rubins, Peter Larson and Andrew Cadiff; music, Peter Larson and Josh Rubins; lyrics, Josh Rubins. May 23, 1984. Director, Andrew Cadiff; choreographer, Cheryl Carty; musical director, Yolanda Segovia; scenery and lighting, Paul Wonsek; costumes, Tom McKinley. With Loni Ackerman, Ralph Bruneau, Kimberly Farr, Maureen McGovern, Lenny Wolpe.

INTAR. Innovative culture center for the Hispanic American community of New York City, focusing on the art of theater. Max Ferra, artistic director, Dennis Ferguson-Acosta, managing director.

35 performances each

SARITA. Book, lyrics and directed by Maria Irene Fornes; music, Leon Odenz. January 18, 1984. Scenery, Donald Eastman; lighting, Anne E. Militello; costumes, Gabriel Berry. With Blanca Camacho, Michael Carmine, Sheila Dabney, Rodolfo Diaz, Tom Kirk, Carmen Rosario.

EQUINOX. By Mario Diament, translated by Simone Z. Karlin and Evelyn Strouse. March 7, 1984. Director, Moni Yakim; scenery, Don Coleman; lighting, Lisa Grossman; costumes, K.L. Fredericks. With Fran Anthony, Maria Cellario, Judith Granite, Lindanell Rivera, Ricardo Velez, Lisa Vidal.

THE CUBAN SWIMMER and DOG LADY. By Milcha Sanchez-Scott. April 25, 1984. Director, Max Ferra; scenery, Ming Cho Lee; lighting, Anne E. Militello; costumes, Connie Singer. With Carlos Carrasco, Carlos Cestero, Lillian Hurst, Graciela Lecube, Jeannette Mirabal, Elizabeth Pena, Manuel Rivera, Marcella White.

Staged readings

SPANISH EYES written and directed by Eduardo Ivan Lopez. October 9, 1983.
KING WITHOUT A CASTLE by Candido Tirado. October 11, 1983. Directed by Guillermo Gentile.
CENTRAL AMERICA by Ana Maria Simo. October 16, 1983. Directed by Livia Perez.
THE CUBAN SWIMMER and DOG LADY by Milcha Sanchez-Scott. October 18, 1983. Directed by Julie Arenal.
EQUINOX by Mario Diament. October 23, 1983. Directed by Moni Yakim.
THE COCKROACHES written and directed by Guillermo Gentile. October 25, 1983.
SARITA written and directed by Maria Irene Fornes. October 30, 1983.

Interart Theater. A professional environment primarily for women playwrights, directors, designers and performers to participate in theatrical activity. Margot Lewitin, artistic director.

RANGE (24). Written and performed by Joanne McEntire. July 27, 1983. Director, Jeannine Haas; lighting, Susan Chute; costumes, Betty LaRoe; projections, Loette McCay.

THROUGH THE LEAVES (53). By Franz Xaver Kroetz, translated by Roger Downey. March 16, 1984. Director, JoAnne Akalaitis; dramaturg, Colette Brooks; scenery, Douglas Stein; lighting, Frances Aronson; costumes, Kurt Wilhelm. With Ruth Malaczech, Frederick Neumann. (Coproduced with Mabou Mines.)

NOTES FROM THE MOROCCAN JOURNALS (2). Solo performance by Nancy duPlessis. May 3, 1984.

LaMama Experimental Theater Club (ETC). A busy workshop for experimental theater of all kinds. Ellen Stewart, founder; Wesley Jensby, artistic director.

Schedule included:

THE LIGHT OPERA. Conceived and composed by Charlie Morrow. June 7, 1983. Director, Tom O'Horgan; choreographer, Min Tanaka; scenery, Jun Maeda; lighting, Harry Primeau; costumes, Gabriel Berry. With the Western Wind.

TOUR OF HELL written and directed by Tom Murrin. June 15, 1983.

UNCLE VANYA by Anton Chekhov, translated by Jean-Claude van Itallie. August 30, 1983. Directed by Andrei Serban.

THE ARBOR. By Andrea Dunbar. September 1, 1983. Director, Leonardo Shapiro; scenery, Bil Mikulewicz; lighting, Arden ·Fingerhut; costumes, Sally Lesser. With Helen Nicholas, Leslie Lyles.

THE SAD LAMENT OF PECOS BILL ON THE EVE OF KILLING HIS WIFE and SUPERSTITIONS. By Sam Shepard. September 8, 1983. Director, Julie Hebert. With Mark Petrakis, O-Lan Shepard.

DIVERSIONS, OR PROOF THAT IT'S IMPOSSIBLE TO LIVE. By Aubrey Simpson. October 10, 1983. Director, John-Michael Tebelak.

ONCE IN DOUBT. By Ray Barry. November 3, 1983. Director, David Saint.

DAMNEE MANON, SACREE SANDRA. By Michel Tremblay, translated by John Van Burek. December 1, 1983. Director, George Ferencz; scenery, Bill Stabile; lighting, Blu; costumes, Sally J. Lesser. With Priscilla Smith, Ray Wise.

HAPPY DAYS by Samuel Beckett. December 28, 1983. Directed by Rick Lonon.

ALL STRANGE AWAY. By Samuel Beckett. January 2, 1984. Director, Gerald Thomas; scenery, Daniela Thomas; lighting, Blu; costumes, Sally J. Lesser. With Ryan Cutrona.

DOG'S EYE VIEW. Written and directed by John Jesserun. January 7, 1984.

HOT TIME written, directed and choreographed by Donald Byrd. January 12, 1984.

STREET DREAMS. Lyrics by Eve Merriam; music by Helen Miller. February 2, 1984. Lighting, Lance Miller. With Chiara Peacock, Stephanie Keyser, Meredith Rutledge, Rick Negron, Daniel Parker, John Braswell, Lucy Pendleton.

A RACE. Created and directed by Ping Chong. February 11, 1984. Designer-in-chief, Paul Krajniak; lighting, Blu; costumes, Mel Carpenter. With Rob List.

LA FIN DU CIRQUE. By Kenneth Bernard; directed by John Vaccaro.

HOT LUNCH APOSTLES and PEDRO PARAMO, from Juan Rulfo's novel. March 20, 1984. Director, Paul Zimet; music, Sybille Hayn, Ellen Maddow, Harry Mann; scenery, Marjorie Bradley Kellogg; lighting, Blu; costumes, David Carl Robinson. With The Talking Band.

I'LL BE RIGHT BACK. By Spiderwoman Theater. April 4, 1984. Director, Muriel Miguel; music, Ellen Haag.

BRECHT'S ASHES 2 and THE MILLION. Text and direction by Eugenio Barba. April 26, 1984. With Odin Teatret.

THE SHOEMAKERS. translated by Regina Gelb with David Weisberg. May 3, 1984. Director, Bradford Mays.

JERUSALEM (musical). Written and directed by Elizabeth Swados. May 23, 1984.

FUN CITY. Written and directed by Matthew Maguire.

FIVE OF US. By Len Jenkin.

Manhattan Punch Line. Comedy theater. Steve Kaplan, Mitch McGuire, Jerry Heymann, Richard Erickson, producing directors.

A KISS IS JUST A KISS (20). By Paul Foster. June 6, 1983. Director, Don Scardino; scenery, Production Values; costumes, Julie Schwolow; lighting, Joshua Dachs. With Steve Ahern, Beth Austin, Shelby Brammer, Kevin O'Connor.

IN DEEPEST SYMPATHY (24). By Dana Coen. November 3, 1983. Director, Steven D. Albrezzi; scenery, Production Values; lighting, Joshua Dachs; costumes, Julie Schwolow. With Laurie Heineman, Bernard Barrow, Joan Kaye, Frances Chaney, Gil Kashkin, Susan Heldfond, Lee Shepherd, Stephen Singer.

JUNE MOON by Ring Lardner and George S. Kaufman. December 9, 1983. Directed by Steve Kaplan; with Stephan Weyte, Michael Countryman, Susan Dow, Mercedes Ruehl, Joanne Camp, David Berk, F.L. Schmidlapp, Joel Bernstein, Laura Margolis.

THE RIVALS by Richard Brinsley Sheridan. February 3, 1984. Directed by Tom Costello; with Wendy Rosenberg, Debora Pressman, Angela Pietropinto, Michael P. Moran, Larry Pine, John Michalski, Arthur Erickson.

HACKERS (24). By Mike Eisenberg. March 2, 1984. Director, Jerry Heymann; scenery, Jane Musky; lighting, Scott Pinkney; costumes, David Loveless. With Tim Choate, Michael Curran, Peter Basch, Sabrina LeBauf.

LAUGHING STOCK: GOODBY, HOWARD, F.M. and TENNESSEE (24). By Romulus Linney. April 6, 1984. Director, Ed Howard; scenery, Paul Bryan Eads; lighting, Judy Rasmuson; costumes, Sally Lesser. With Frances Sternhagen, Jane Connell, Helen Harrelson, Harold Guskin, Peggity Price, Timothy Wilson.

RICH GIRLS (24). By Philip Magdalany. May 17, 1984. Director, Robert Moss; scenery, Rick Dennis; lighting, Gregory Macpherson; costumes, Michael Krass. With Gwyda Donhowe, Lisa Lonergan, Louise Troy.

Manhattan Theater Club. In addition to its regular season, MTC has inaugurated a developmental plays-in-progress series of staged readings. Lynne Meadow, artistic director, Barry Grove, managing director.

In-the-Works series

AMERICANS ABROAD by Andrew Foster. April 24, 1984.
WARNING SIGNALS by Nancy Donohue. May 15, 1984.

New Dramatists. An organization devoted to playwrights; member writers may use the facilities for anything from private cold readings of their material to public script-in-hand readings. Casey Childs, program director.

Staged readings

PARTIAL OBJECTS by Sherry Kramer. October 6, 1983. Directed by John Pynchon Holms; with John Getz, Maria Maxwell, Christopher McCann, Katherine Neuman.
I DARE YOU TO RESIST ME by Pedro Juan Pietri. October 20, 1983. Directed by Livia Perez; with Theresa Saldana, Michael Morin, Donavan Diez, Joseph Taro, Ben Kelman.
THE TRAVELLING SQUIRREL by Robert Lord. November 10, 1983. Directed by Jack Hofsiss; with Michael Murphy, Jill Eikenberry, Nicholas Martin, Tom Cashin, Suzanne Lederer, Jeffrey Jones, Joyce Reehling Christopher.
DER INKA VON PERU by Jeffrey M. Jones. November 15, 1983. Directed by John Pynchon Holms; with Ron Vawter, Richard M. Davidson, Barbara Somerville, Richard Sale, Tracey Ellis, Karen Young.
BULLY by Paul D'Andrea. November 22, 1983. Directed by David Feldshuh; with Leon Russom, Caitlin Hart, Jacqueline Knapp, John Lagici, Ivar Brogger.
THE DAY OF THE PICNIC by Russell Davis. December 2, 1983. Directed by Tony Giordano; with Mary Alice, Margaret Hilton, Keith David, Ron Faber, Lori Tan Chinn, Carl Low, John Peterson.
THE MILL HAND'S LUNCH BUCKET by August Wilson. December 7, 1983 and February 8, 1984. Directed by Claude Purdy; with Roc Dutton, Leonard Jackson, Reg E. Cathey, Nick Smith.
A HARD LOOK AT OLD TIMES by John Nassivera based on the writings of Walter Hard. Directed by Jill Charles; with Andrew Macmillan.
CARELESS LOVE by John Olive. December 19, 1983. Directed by Robert Falls; with Randle Mell, Laura Innes.
ZONES OF THE SPIRIT (one-act plays) by Amlin Gray. January 13, 1984. Directed by Gideon Y. Schein; with Bob Blackburn, Monique Fowler, Richard Zobel, Lance Davis.

MARJORIE by Lee Blessing. January 23, 1984. Directed by Howard Dallin; with Diane Martella, Peter DeMaio.

THE FRED AND GINGER CONTEST (musical) book by Peter Dee, music and lyrics by John O'Donnell. January 27, 1984. With Sheila Ellis, Robert Stillman, Mara Beckerman, Douglas Fisher, Joyce Leigh Bowden, Robert Anderson.

THE BULLDOG AND THE BEAR by Richard Gordon. February 2, 1984. With James Earl Jones, Barnard Hughes.

MORTALLY FINE by William J. Sibley. February 15, 1984. Directed by Peter Masterson; with Bill Hardy, Gil Rogers, Valerie Mahaffey, Carlin Glynn, Ruth Nelson, Paige Johnson, Roxie Lucas, Kevin Cooney.

JAY by Anthony Giardina. February 27, 1984. Directed by Lynda Lee Burks; with Mary Joy, Frances Chaney, Natalija Nogulich, Marcel Rosenblatt, Jennifer Marcot, Mark Blum.

SOUL OF A TREE and WHY THE LORD CAME TO SAND-MOUNTAIN (one-act plays) by Romulus Linney. March 7, 1984. Directed by Leon Russom; with Pirie MacDonald, Jacqueline Brooks, Lee Croghan, Kari Jenson.

HOLDING PATTERNS words and music by Jeffrey Sweet. March 9, 1984. Directed by William Alton; with Jack Gilpin, Colleen Dodson, Bruce Jarchow, Lynne Kadish, Nancy McCabe-Kelly.

THE NAIN ROUGE by Mac Wellman, music by Michael Roth and HARM'S WAY by Mac Wellman, music by Bob Jewett. March 15, 1984. Directed by Jim Simpson; with Susan Berman, Reg E. Cathey.

THE BALLAD OF JOHNNY AND ABDUHL by Roger Nieboer. March 26, 1984. Directed by Amy Brosnahan; with Roger Nieboer, Amy Brosnahan, Gerald Arbinder.

DEFINE SUCCESS by William J. Sibley. March 30, 1984. Directed by Gideon Y. Schein; with Sally Faye Reit, Lois Smith, Michael Ayr, Munson Hicks.

BANG by Laura Cunningham. April, 1984. Directed by Casey Childs; with Maria Cellario, Mark Blum, Gina Rogak, David Rasche.

SYLVIE libretto by Norah Holmgren. April 11, 1984. Directed by Ben Krywosz; with Ruth Golden, Roger Saylor, Deidre Kingsbury, Frank Nemhauser.

AMERICA WAS by Jack Heifner. April 26, 1984. Directed by Will MacAdam; with Cly Fowkes, Richard Voigts, Bill Tatum, Mark Hamilton, Sharon Laughlin.

SHARON AND BILLY by Alan Bowne. May 4, 1984. Directed by Mark D'Alessio; with Phyllis Somerville, Bryan Clark, Lynda Kavy, Peter Berkrot.

New Federal Theater. The Henry Street Settlement's training and showcase unit for playwrights, mostly black and Puerto Rican. Woodie King Jr., producer.

BASIN STREET (15). Book, G. William Oakley and Michael Hulett; music, Turk Murphy; lyrics, Michael Hulett. September 8, 1983. Director, G. William Oakley; choreographer, Michael Gorman; musical director, Thom Bridwell; scenery, Robert Edmonds; lighting, Jeremy Johnson; costumes, Judy Dearing. With Charles H. Patterson, Tamara Tunie, Sandra Reaves-Phillips, Clebert Ford, J. Lee Flynn, Lawrence Vincent.

SHADES OF BROWN (12). By Michael Picardie. October 6, 1983. Director, Joan Kemp-Welch; scenery, Loren Sherman. With Count Stovall, Michael O'Hare. (Co-production with Chelsea Theater Center.)

THE TRIAL OF ADAM CLAYTON POWELL JR. (12). By Billy Graham. October 20, 1983. Director, Dianne Kirksey; scenery, Billy Graham; lighting, Zebedee Collins; costumes, Karen Perry. With Timothy Simonson, Eldon Bullock, Dan Barbaro, Richard Mooney, Bill Canyon, Charles Harley, Barry Ford, Christine Campbell, Mizan Nunes.

SEA ROCK CHILDREN IS STRONG CHILDREN (15). Written and directed by Paul Webster. December 1, 1983. Choreographer, Gora Singh; music, Ricardo Cadogan; scenery, Terry Chandler; lighting, Pam Demont; costumes, Jane Milligan. With Annice Carew, Jeannette Sims, Desmond Coryatt, Maureen Denton.

BECOMING GARCIA (15). By Tato Laviera. February 2, 1984. Director, Esteban Vega; scenery, Pete Caldwell; lighting, William H. Grant III; costumes, Karlos. With Carlos Carrasco,

THEATER OF THE OPEN EYE—Mark Johannes, Graeme
Malcolm and Heather Hollingsworth in Molière's *Scapin*

Raul Davila, Gerta Grunen, Geisha Otero, Ilka Tanya Payan, Elizabeth Pena, Hector Qui-
nones.

SELMA (15). Book, music and lyrics, Tommy Butler. February 16, 1984. Director, Cliff
Roquemore; choreographer, Charles Lavont Williams; musical director, Neal Tate; lighting,
William H. Grant III; costumes, Judy Dearing. Tommy Butler, Rita Graham-Knighton, Sherrie
Strange, Ernie Banks, Cora Lee Day, Ronald Wyche.

TWENTY YEAR FRIENDS (15). By J.E. Gaines. March 15, 1984. Director, Andre
Mtume; scenery, Terry Chandler; lighting, Jeffrey Richardson; costumes, Celia Bryant. With
Juanita Clark, Clebert Ford, Jack Neal, Roscoe Orman, Louise Stubbs, Joyce Walker-Joseph.

FRATERNITY (15). By Jordan Budde. March 22, 1984. Director, Gideon Y. Schein; scenery,
Jane Clark; lighting, Victor En Yu Tan; costumes, Judy Dearing. With Mark Moses, Donald E.
Fischer, Kevin Carrigan, Robert Downey, Steve Hofvendahl.

THE LAST DANCEMAN (15). By Alan Foster Friedman. May 3, 1984. Director, John Pynchon Holms; scenery and lighting, Richard Harmon; costumes, Sheila Kehoe; music, Alan Foster Friedman; choreography, Lynnette Barkley. With Joel Rooks, Hy Anzel, Anthony Inneo, Norma Novak, Jerry Matz, Steve Coats, Leslie Carroll.

THE HOOCH (15). By Charles Michael Moore. May 4, 1984. Director, Chuck Smith; scenery, Llewellyn Harrison; lighting, William H. Grant III; costumes, Karen Perry. With Aran, Kevin Hooks, Cortez Nance, Hubert B. Kelly Jr., Jaime Perry, Clifton C. Powell, Jeffrey Howard Kaufman, Neal Arluck, Ching Valdes.

THE WOMAN'S SERIES (four new black playwrights). GAMES by Joyce Walker Josephs, directed by Elizabeth Van Dyke. July 20, 1983. PARTING by Nubai Kai, directed by Bette Howard. July 21, 1983. HOSPICE by Pearl Cleage, directed by Frances Foster. July 22, 1983. INCANDESCENT TONES by Rise Collins, directed by Rise Collins. July 23, 1983.

New York Shakespeare Festival Public Theater. Schedule of workshop productions and guest residencies, in addition to its regular productions. Joseph Papp, producer.

FUNHOUSE written, designed and performed by Eric Bogosian. July 3, 1983.

EMMETT: A ONE MORMON SHOW by and with Emmett Foster. July 7, 1983; reopened August 11, 1983.

COMPANY by Samuel Beckett; directed and performed by Honora Fergusson and Frederick Neumann; reopened November 15, 1983.

No Smoking Playhouse. Emphasis on new plays and adaptation of classics, stressing the comedic. Norman Thomas Marshall, artistic director.

A MAN IN THE HOUSE (24). By John von Hartz. October 6, 1983. Director, Norman Thomas Marshall; scenery, Beate Kessler; lighting, Leslie Ann Kilian; costumes, Marla R. Kaye. With Alan Bluestone, George Wolf Reily, Peter Jolly, June Ballinger.

BHUTAN. By Jane Stanton Hitchcock. November 15, 1983. Director, John Bird; scenery, Tom Barnes; lighting, Betsy Adams; costumes, Cynthia O'Neal. With Marcus Smythe, Cynthia Crumlish, Patricia Hodges, N. Erick Avari.

The Open Space Theater Experiment. Emphasis on experimental works. Lynn Michaels, Harry Baum, directors.

20 performances each

ANOTHER PARADISE. By Donna Spector. March 28, 1984. Director, Nancy Gabor; scenery and lighting, Robert E. Briggs; costumes, Mary Huessy; music, Carolyn Dutton. With Allison Brennan, Ralph Elias, Lauren Klein, Anne O'Sullivan.

ALL THE NICE PEOPLE. By Hugh Leonard. April 5, 1984. Director, Alex Dmitriev; scenery, James Morgan; lighting, Ann Wrightson; costumes, Barbara Weiss. With Kathleen Chalfant, David Clarke, Mildred Clinton, Eric Hall, James Harper, Cara Duff-MacCormick, W.T. Martin, Jaime McIntosh, Marilyn McIntyre, Dermot McNamara, Peter Rogan, Dan Strimer.

Pan Asian Repertory Theater. Aims to present professional productions which employ Asian American theater artists, to encourage new plays which explore Asian American themes and to combine traditional elements of Far Eastern theater with Western theatrical techniques. Tisa Chang, artistic director.

A SONG FOR A NISEI FISHERMAN (24). By Philip Kan Gotanda. November 30, 1983. Director, Raul Aranas; scenery, Atsushi Moriyasu; lighting, Victor En Yu Tan; costumes, Eiko Yamaguchi. With Stanford Egi, Wai Ching Ho, Mariye Inouye, Alvin Lum, Tom Matsusaka, Ron Nakahara, Barbara Pohlman, Ann C. Stoney, Ronald Yamamoto.

THE FACE BOX (28). By Wakako Yamauchi. February 29, 1984. Director, Ron Nakahara; scenery, Ronald Kajiwara; lighting, Toshiro Ogawa; costumes, Eiko Yamaguchi. With Natsuko Ohama, Michael G. Chin, Kati Kuroda, Koji Okamura.

EMPRESS OF CHINA (42). By Ruth Wolff. April 25, 1984. Director, Tisa Chang; scenery, Bob Phillips; lighting, Victor En Yu Tan; costumes, Eiko Yamaguchi. With Ernest Abuba, Tina Chen, Mel G. Gionson, Carol A. Honda, Lester J.N. Mau, Alvin Lum, Tom Matsusaka, Mary Lee.

Playwrights Horizons. Dedicated to the development of American playwrights, composers and lyricists through the production of their work in readings, workshops and full-scale productions. Andre Bishop, artistic director.

CHRISTMAS ON MARS by Harry Kondoleon. June 2, 1983. Director, Andre Ernotte; scenery, Andrew Jackness; costumes, Rita Ryack; lighting, James F. Ingalls. With Michael O'Keefe, Harriet Harris, Joe Pichette, Marie Cheatham.

THAT'S IT, FOLKS by Mark O'Donnell. June 26, 1983. Director, Douglas Hughes; scenery, Loren Sherman; costumes, Ann Emonts; lighting, Rachel Budin; sound, Gary Harris. With Alice Playten, David Pierce, Cynthia Darlow, Peter G. Morse, Jerome Collamore, James McDonnell.

Workshops
SUNDAY IN THE PARK WITH GEORGE (musical) by Stephen Sondheim and James Lapine, suggested by Georges Seurat's painting, *A Sunday Afternoon on the Island of La Grande Jatte.* July 6, 1983. With Mandy Patinkin, Bernadette Peters, Dana Ivey.
AMERICA KICKS UP ITS HEELS (musical) book by Charles Rubin, music and lyrics by William Finn. March 9, 1984. Directed by Mary Kyte and Ben Levit; with Patti LuPone, Robin Boudreaux, I.M. Hobson, Dick Latessa, Rodney Hudson, Alexandra Korey, Lenora Nemetz.

Puerto Rican Traveling Theater. Professional company presenting bilingual productions primarily of Puerto Rican and Hispanic playwrights, emphasizing subjects of relevance today. Miriam Colon Edgar, founder and producer.

THE MASSES ARE ASSES (28). By Pedro Pietri, translated by Alfredo Matilla. January 11, 1984. Director, Alba Oms; scenery and lighting, Robert Strohmeter. With Alex Colon, Ivonne Coll, Mike Robelo.

O.K. (42). By Isaac Chocron, translated by Pilar Zalamea. February 22, 1984. Director, Alba Oms; scenery, Carl A. Baldasso; lighting, Craig Kennedy. With Sheila MacRae, Isabel Segovia, Christofer De Oni, Elisa de la Roche.

THE ACCOMPANIMENT by Carlos Gorostiza and THE MANAGEMENT WILL FORGIVE A MOMENT OF MADNESS by Rodolfo Santana (42). April 18, 1984. Director, Vicente Castro; scenery, Carl A. Baldasso; lighting, Craig Kennedy; costumes, Paul Harold Gindhart. With Freddy Valle, Jorge Luis Ramos, Sully Diaz, Norman Briski, David Zuniga.

Quaigh Theater. Primarily a playwrights' theater, devoted to the new playwright, the established contemporary playwright and the modern (post-1920) playwright. Will Lieberson, artistic director.

CHRISTOPHER BLAKE by Moss Hart. July 13, 1983. Directed by June Prager; with Herman O. Arbeit, Michael Eliot Cooke, Richard Marr, Andrew Cassese, Lee Moore, Leslie Lyles, Susan Orem, David Lanton.

DRAMATHON '83 (one-act plays in marathon). Schedule included: BEWARE THE RABBITS (musical) music by Burt Conrad, lyrics by Bill Donnelly, directed by Ken Lieberson; CHANEL by T. Wayne Moore, directed by Phyllis Guarnaccia; THE GREAT RAGE OF PHILIP HOTZ by Max Frisch, directed by Charlie Otte; LOVE ALWAYS written and directed by Tony Marinelli; CENTRAL PARK by William Inge, directed by Anne Cowett; COF-FEE by Herbert Hartig and Lois Balk Korey and THOUGHTS ON THE INSTANT OF GREETING A FRIEND ON THE STREET by Jean-Claude van Itallie, directed by Gail Leondar; THE ORIENTAL LADY AND THE DENVER GAL by Tom Dunn, directed by Pam Rubinfield; IN THE WINGS by Bruce T. Paddock and Phil Morton, directed by Cash Tilton; THERE'S NO UPSTAIRS AT THE RED DOG by John Fiero; SNOW LEOPARD by Lisa Humbertson, directed by Joe Banno.

Also DISPATCH by Alfred Tessler, directed by Melanie Sutherland; DARLENE AND HER MIRROR IMAGE by Paul T. Nolan; MUSIC OF THE SOUL conceived and directed by Olivia Faison; ACTION PAINTING by Steve Shilo, directed by Ted Mornel; LONG TIME NO SEE by C. Dumas; WEDDING DAY TRAGEDY by Tom Dunn, directed by Liz Wright; VAN GOGH'S EAR by Matt Swann directed by Tom Tift; THE DRESSING ROOM by Robert Sugarman, directed by Greg Petitti; SWORDPLAY by Steve Shilo, directed by Stuart Schwartz; CECILE, OR THE SCHOOL FOR FATHERS by Jean Anouilh, directed by Shela Xoregos; VITAL STATISTICS written and directed by Charles Gemmill; LOTTERY WIN-NERS ANONYMOUS by Abraham Markus, directed by Peter Von Berg; OVERTONES by Alice Gerstenberg, directed by Dennis McLernon; STARTING OVER (musical) lyrics and directed by Charles Paul Gollnick, music by Bruce Levine.

Also SCHTICS AND SCHTONES (revue sketches) directed by Robin Schuman; DID YOU EVER GO TO P.S. 43? by Michael Schulman, directed by Keith Batten; IT'S VERY DARING . . . THE CONTINENTAL by James Himelsbach, directed by G. Michael Trupiano; FOUR QUARTETS by T.S. Eliot, directed by Jim Curran; GENESIS II by David Thibodaux; TALK SHOW by William Manger, directed by Mitchell Kobren; DIVERS' WORLD by Bruce Bradley; ROUNDELAY by Morna Murphy, directed by Eni Ativie; FUNNYHOUSE OF A NEGRO by Adrienne Kennedy, directed by Susan E. Watson; THE DAY THEY CANCELLED "LOVE BOAT" by Adam Kraar, directed by Maura Tighe; ANY CORNER by Richard Corey, directed by Sara Poster; THE LIMIT by Susan Haga; MARASMUS by Charles Waxburg, directed by Peter Gordon; THE BROOKLYN REVUE by Chuck Reichenthal, directed by Barbara Paris.

Also I'M HERBERT by Robert Anderson, directed by Lee Davis Knight; RUBBINGS by Mark St. Germain, directed by E.M. Christian; SOMETHING TO EAT written and directed by Norman Rhodes; BASIC NEEDS by William Thompson, directed by Craig Butler; HOME AT LAST by Mark Robson; TOP LOADING LOVER libretto by Glenn Allen Smith, music by Raymond Allen, directed by Ted Mornel; FALLING LEAVES, MR. ROSE'S BIRD and WIE GEHT'S ICEK by E. Michael Benedict, directed by E. Michael Benedict, Michael Reil, Barbara Summerville; THE MAN WHO ATTEMPTED TO CLIMB TO THE TOP OF MT. KILI-MANJARO by Sonny Hyles; MEADOW LARKING by Marc-Steven Dear, directed by Keith David. December 30, 1983–January 3, 1984.

BITTERSUITE (23). Musical by Mike Champagne and Elliott Weiss. January 20, 1984. Director, Bert Michaels; scenery, Geoffrey Hall; lighting, Eric Cornwell; costumes, Eric Newland. With Claudine Casson, Del Green, Anthony Mucci, Theresa Rakov, Richard Roemer.

YEATS (one-act plays): AT THE HAWK'S WELL, THE DREAMING OF THE BONES and THE KING OF THE GREAT CLOCK TOWER. By William Butler Yeats. May 16, 1984. Directed by Sam McCready; with Todd Oleson, Brooke Myers, Michael Stacy, Kevin Gardiner.

Lunchtime Series

BREAKING IN by James T. McCartin. October 30, 1983. Directed by Christopher Jones; with Eileen McCabe, Christine Solazzi.
CLEAN TIME (musical) book and lyrics by Guy C. Coleman, music by David Brown. November 14, 1983. Directed by Guy C. Coleman; with Donna Sue Chase, Michele Riley, Rochelle Matthewson, Lavenson Lockhart, Guy C. Coleman.
AUTO-EROTIC MISADVENTURE by F.J. Hartland. November 28, 1983. Directed by Peter Gordon; with Portia Kamons, Paul Zappala, Jon Wool.
DEAR BRUTUS by J.M. Barrie. December 5, 1983. Directed by Dianne Busch; with Estelle J. Greene, Susan Ball, Patti Specht, James Harter, John Moon.

WPA THEATER—Roxanne Hart and Peter Riegert
in *La Brea Tarpits* by Alan Gross

CARDSHARKS by F.J. Hartland. January 9, 1984. Directed by Peter Gordon; with Elaine Bush, Barbara Shannon, Jon Wool, Paul Zappala.
CECILE, OR THE SCHOOL FOR FATHERS by Jean Anouilh, translated by Luce and Arthur Klein. January 23, 1984. Directed by Shela Xoregos; with Anna Becker.
SWORDPLAY by Steve Shilo; directed by Stuart Schwartz and I'M HERBERT by Robert Anderson; directed by Lee Davis Knight. February 6, 1984. With Mary Jo Anderson, Steve Pesola, Arthur Anderson, Fay Gold.
BIRDSONG by James Saunders. February 20, 1984. Directed by Sara Louise Lazarus; with Steve Wise, Robert Biggs, Lisa Goodman, Karen Biggs.
ANY CORNER by Richard Cory. March 5, 1984. Directed by Sarrala Poster.
VITAL STATISTICS by Bryan Patrick Harnetiaux. March 12, 1984. Directed by Charles Gemmill; with Betty Burrows, R. MacCallum, David McDonald, Charles Gemmill.
BASIC NEEDS by William A. Thompson. March 26, 1984. Directed by Craig Butler; with Paula de Caro, Scott Sherman.
OFFICE MISHEGOSS by Adam Kraar. April 9, 1984. Directed by Maura Tighe; with Yvette Edelhart, Anna Heins.
IN THE WINGS by Bruce T. Paddock and Phil Morton; directed by Cash Tilton and SOMETHING TO EAT written and directed by Norman Rhodes. April 23, 1984. With Katy Piel, Sims Wyeth.
BEANSTOCK by David Shawn Klein. May 7, 1984. Directed by Dennis McLernon; with Richard Dahlia, Garrison Phillips, Genevieve Hall.
I GOT SHOES by Jill Maynard. May 28, 1984. Directed by Anne Cowett; with Jacqueline Barnett, George Himes, Roz Dunn, Constance Kane.

The Ridiculous Theatrical Company. Charles Ludlam's camp-oriented group devoted to productions of his original scripts and broad adaptations of the classics. Charles Ludlam, artistic director and director of all productions.

GALAS (190). By Charles Ludlam. September 13, 1983. Scenery, Jack Kelly; costumes, Everett Quinton; lighting, Lawrence Eichler; original music, Peter Golub; production assistant, Sarah Jenkins. With Charles Ludlam, Emilio Cubeiro, Everett Quinton, John Heys, Deborah Petti, Black-Eyed Susan, Bill Vehr, Julian Craggs, Edward McGowan, Fred Segilia.

The Second Stage. Committed to producing plays of the last ten years believed to deserve another chance, as well as new works. Robyn Goodman, Carole Rothman, artistic directors.

SERENADING LOUIE by Lanford Wilson. January 17, 1984. Directed by John Tillinger; with Jimmie Ray Weeks, Dianne Wiest, Peter Weller, Lindsay Crouse.

ALL NIGHT LONG (28). By John O'Keefe. March 6, 1984. Director, Andre Gregory; scenery, Adrianne Lobel; lighting, James F. Ingalls; costumes, Susan Hilferty. With Michael Riney, Mary McDonnell, Gerry Bamman, Catherine Coray, Alyssa Jayne Milano.

LANDSCAPE OF THE BODY by John Guare. April 19, 1984. Directed by Gary Sinise; with Christine Lahti, Dann Florek, Mary Copple, Ted Sod, Christian Slater, Eddie Castrodad, Alison Bartlett, Maddie Corman, Reg E. Cathey, Frank Maraden.

LINDA HER and THE FAIRY GARDEN (one-act plays) (28). By Harry Kondoleon. May 31, 1984. Director, Carole Rothman; scenery, Andrew Jackness; lighting, Frances Aronson; costumes, Mimi Maxmen. With Brooke Adams, Brenda Currin, John Glover, Carol Kane, Anne Lange, Staci Love, Rick J. Porter, Mark Soper, Robert Weil.

Shelter West. Aims to offer an atmosphere of trust and a place for unhurried and constructive work. Judith Joseph, artistic director.

FLESH, FLASH AND FRANK HARRIS (16). By Paul Stephen Lim. October 27, 1983. Director, Judith Joseph; scenery and costumes, Tatiana DeStempel; lighting, David Tasso. With Norma Jean Giffin, Ray Iannicelli, David Kerman, John David Barone, Margot Avery, Perry Barden, June White, Judith Joseph, Rita McCaffrey, Bruce Mohat, Richard Boddy, Anthony Dinovi, Martin Thompson.

BYRON IN HELL (6). Adapted from Lord Byron's writings by Bill Studdiford. January 24, 1984. With Ian Frost.

Soho Rep. Infrequently or never-before-performed plays by the world's greatest authors, with emphasis on language and theatricality. Marlene Swartz, Jerry Engelbach, artistic directors.

Schedule included:

UNDER THE GASLIGHT by Augustin Daly. October 28, 1983.

THE WOOD PAINTING by Ingmar Bergman, YES IS FOR A VERY YOUNG MAN by Gertrude Stein, GEORGE WASHINGTON CROSSING THE DELAWARE and BERTHA, QUEEN OF NORWAY by Kenneth Koch. December 2-18, 1983.

THE DWARFS by Harold Pinter. March 16, 1984. Directed by Jerry Engelbach.

MANDRAKE. Book and lyrics by Michael Alfreds, based on Machiavelli's *Mandragola,* music by Anthony Bowles. April 13, 1984. Director, Anthony Bowles; musical director, Michael Rafter; scenery, Joseph A. Varga; lighting, David Noling; costumes, Steven L. Birnbaum. With Steve Sterner, Andrew Barnicle, Tory Alexander, Mary Testa, Suzanne Ford, Mary Eileen O'Donnell.

LENZ. By Mike Stott, based on Georg Buchner's story. May 18, 1984. Director, Alma Becker.

Theater for the New City. Developmental theater, incorporating live music and dance into new American experimental works. George Bartenieff, Crystal Field, artistic directors.

SELF: A SELF IMPORTANT MUSICAL (street theater) (14). Written and directed by Crystal Field; music, Mark Hardwick. August 3, 1983.

THE DREAM KEEPER SPEAKS: THE WORLD OF LANGSTON HUGHES (12). October 6, 1983. Director, Ernest Parham. With John S. Patterson.

MUD (20). Written and directed by Maria Irene Fornes. November 10, 1983.

SUCCESS AND SUCCESSION (20). By Ronald Tavel. November 10, 1983. Director, Michael Hillyer; scenery, Rick Dennis; lighting, Craig Kennedy; costumes, Natalie B. Walker. With John Fitzgibbon, Tony Hoty, Lola Pashalinski, Elizabeth Chin, John Henry Redwood, Tom Mardirosian, Joan Matthiessen.

ART FOLLOWS REALITY (12). By Daryl Chin. November 10, 1983. Director, Larry Qualis.

THE MARTHA PLAY (12). By Patricia Cobey. December 22, 1983. Director, Saskia Hegt.

TROPICAL FEVER IN KEY WEST: THE CAKE and AN OLD TUNE (one-act plays). By Robert Heide. December 22, 1983. Director, Sebastian Stuart; scenery, John Eric Broaddus; lighting, Craig Kennedy. With John Uecker, Chris Tanner, Jeremy Brooks, Regina David, Harvey Perr, J.P. Dougherty, Dorsey Davis.

KAREER SUICIDE (12). By Stephen Holt. January 19, 1984. Director, Bob Plunkett.

GREEK FIRE (12). By Ron Faber. January 19, 1984. Director, Jacques Chwat.

THE LAST OF HITLER (16). Written and directed by Joan Schenkar. March 1, 1984.

THE PANEL (12). By Kenneth Bernard. March 15, 1984. Director, John Albano.

JOURNEY INTO HAPPINESS (12). By Franz Xaver Kroetz. April 12, 1984. Director, Akim Nowack.

PLAY WITH AN ENDING, OR COLUMBUS DISCOVERS THE WORLD (12). By Kenneth Bernard. April 19, 1984. Director, John Vaccaro.

ZONES OF THE SPIRIT: OUTLANDERS and WORMWOOD (12). By Amlin Gray. May 17, 1984. Director, Sharon Ott; scenery, Kate Edmunds; lighting, Rachel Budin, David Higham; costumes, Colleen Muscha. With Bill Moor, Leslie Geraci, Peter Crook, James Pickering.

DELICATE FEELINGS (20). By Rosalyn Drexler. May 24, 1984. Director, George Ferencz.

Theater of the Open Eye. Total theater involving actors, dancers, musicians and designers working together, each bringing his own talents into a single project. Jean Erdman, producing artistic director, Amie Brockway, associate artistic director.

THE CRICKET ON THE HEARTH (12). Adapted from Charles Dickens's novel. December 17, 1983. Director, Amie Brockway; scenery and lighting, Jean Doherty; costumes, Patricia Mink. With Sal Brienza, Gwen Cassel, Diana DeMayo, Tom Grasso, William Isaacs, Joyce Korn, Vicki Kulkin, T. Wayne Moore, Jon Nichols, Dana Bell Thrush, Brenda Vicary, Barbara Wiechman, Lori Wilner.

UNDER HEAVEN'S EYE . . . TIL COCKCROW (24). By J.E. Franklin. February 2, 1984. Director, Thelma Carter; scenery, Ernest Allen Smith; lighting, Robert F. Strohmeier; costumes, Lynn P. Hoffman. With Rosanna Carter, Cynthia Martels, Charles Nelson, Freda Scott, Olivia Williams.

PRESQUE ISLE (24). By Joyce Carol Oates. March 22, 1984. Director, Sallie Brophy; music, Paul Shapiro; scenery, Thomas Stoner; lighting, Matt Ehlert; costumes, Linda Vigdor. With Bridget Brophy, Douglas Day, Graeme Malcolm, Elizabeth Perry, Meg Van Zyl.

SCAPIN by Molière. May 18, 1984. Directed by Amie Brockway. With Susan Banks, Anne Fox, Richard Henson, Heather Hollingsworth, Edward Hyland, Mark Johannes, Mark Kapitan, Graeme Malcolm, Rita Nachtman, Raymond Anthony Thomas.

Theater Off Park. Provides Murray Hill-Turtle Bay residents with a professional theater, showcasing the talents of new actors, playwrights, designers and directors. Bertha Lewis, producing director, Albert Harris, artistic director, Trevor Thomas, managing director.

16 performances each

PROMENADE. Book and lyrics by Maria Irene Fornes; music by Al Carmines. October 11, 1983. Director, Albert Harris; musical director, John R. Williams; scenery, Leo B. Meyer; lighting, Martin Friedman; costumes, Tony Chase. With Regina O'Malley, Georgia Creighton, Jason Graae, Tim Ewing, Mitchell Jason.

FIRST TIME ANYWHERE (one-man show). By Leo Meyer. November 8, 1983. Director, Louis Rackoff; scenery, Philip Louis Rodzen; lighting, Todd Lichtenstein. With Ted Van Griethuysen.

A PORTRAIT OF HENRY CHINASKI (from the works of Charles Bukowski). December 9, 1983. Music and lyrics, John Roby; directed and performed by Mina E. Mina; scenery and lighting, James Knight.

PUNCH IN/PUNCH OUT (one-act plays): UNTIL FURTHER NOTICE . . . TOMORROW IS CANCELLED by Elyse Nass and James Struthers, directed by Bob Luke; THE REAL WIFE BEATER by Elyse Nass, directed by Toni Dorfman. March 8, 1984. With Edward Canaan, Steven Field, Timothy Hall, Diane Jean-George, Barbara Nicoll, Thom Zimerle.

WPA Theater. Produces neglected American classics and new American plays in the realistic idiom. Kyle Renick, artistic director, Wendy Bustard, managing director, Edward T. Gianfrancesco, resident designer.

THE ALTO PART (25). By Barbara Gilstrap. October 20, 1983. Director, Zina Jasper; scenery, Edward T. Gianfrancesco; lighting, Craig Evans; costumes, Don Newcomb. With Kit Flanagan, Marisa Morell, Carole Manferdini, Elizabeth Council, Jane Hoffman, Jennifer Walker.

LA BREA TARPITS (30). By Alan Gross. January 4, 1984. Director, Stephen Zuckerman; scenery, James Fenhagen; lighting, Phil Monat; costumes, Mimi Maxmen. With Roxanne Hart, Peter Riegert.

THIN ICE (25). By Jeffrey Haddow. March 15, 1984. Director, Dann Florek; scenery, Tom Schwinn; lighting, Phil Monat; costumes, Don Newcomb. With William Carden, Caitlin Clarke, Dave Florek, Anne DeSalvo.

MR. & MRS. (30). By Kevin Wade. May 3, 1984. Director, David Trainer; scenery, David Gropman; lighting, Paul Gallo; costumes, David Murin. With Peter Friedman, Mark Metcalf, Polly Draper, Pamela Brook.

York Theater Company. Each season, productions of classic and contemporary plays are mounted with professional casts, providing neighborhood residents with professional theater. Janet Hayes Walker, producing director.

NUDE WITH VIOLIN by Noel Coward. November 16, 1983. Directed by Bill Prosser; with Edward Conery, Janet Hayes Walker, Kevin Anderson, Jacqueline Barnett, Jeffrey D. Eiche, Lynne Charney.

MASS APPEAL (11). By Bill C. Davis. January 17, 1984. Director, Austin Pendleton; scenery, James Morgan; lighting, Mary Jo Dondlinger; costumes, Robert Swasey. With E.G. Marshall, Scott Burkholder.

PACIFIC OVERTURES (20). Book by John Weidman; music and lyrics by Stephen Sondheim; additional material by Hugh Wheeler. March 22, 1984. Director, Fran Soeder; choreography, Janet Watson; musical director, James Stenborg; scenery, James Morgan; lighting, Mary Jo Dondlinger; costumes, Mark Passerell. With Ernest Abuba, Tony Marino, Henry Ravelo, Thomas Ikeda, Tom Matsusaka, Eric Miji, Ronald Yamamoto, Tim Ewing, John Baray, Khin-Kyaw Maung, Kevin Gray, Lester J.N. Mau, Alan Tung, John Bantay, Francis Jue.

ELIZABETH AND ESSEX (16). Book by Michael Stewart and Mark Bramble, based on Maxwell Anderson's *Elizabeth the Queen*; music by Douglas Katsaros; lyrics by Richard Engquist. May 17, 1984. Director, Sondra Lee; choreography, Onna White; musical director, Douglas Katsaros; scenery, James Morgan; lighting, Mary Jo Dondlinger; costume consultant, Willa Kim. With Evelyn Lear, Dennis Parlato, David Bryant, Nora Colpman, Willy Falk, Paul David Richards, Gordon Stanley, D. Peter Samuel, George Dvorsky, Jan Pessano, Sally Yorke, Paul Blankenship, Lisa Vroman, Barbara Scanlon.

Miscellaneous

In the additional listing of 1983–84 off-off-Broadway productions below, the names of the producing groups or theaters appear in CAPITAL LETTERS and the titles of the works in *italics*. This list consists largely of new or reconstituted works and excludes most revivals, especially of classics. It includes a few productions staged by groups which rented space from the more established organizations listed previously.

ACTORS AND DIRECTORS THEATER. *Forbidden Copy* by Percy Granger; directed by Miguel Ten and *The Wig Lady* by Leslie Lee; directed by Robert Maitland (one-act plays). July 15, 1983. With Yvonne Villarini, Lynne Marie Brown, Judith Granite, Susan Jeffries. *Eve Is Innocent* by Leonard Melfi. September 24, 1983. Directed by Alice Spivak; with Peggy Bruen, Ellen Foley, Steve Beach. *Willie* by Leslie Lee. January 13, 1984. With Herb Downer, Thomas Anderson.

ACTOR'S OUTLET. *Marmalade Skies* by M.Z. Ribalow. October 2, 1983. Directed by Thomas Babe; with Mark Arnott, Chris Lutkin, Catherine Butterfield, Kathryn Dowling, Alanna Hamill. *A Song for a Nisei Fisherman* by Philip Kan Gotanda. December 6, 1983. Directed by Raul Aranas; with Ron Nakahara, Mariye Inouye.

AMERICAN JEWISH THEATER. *Made in Heaven* by Edward Belling. October 1, 1983. Directed by Stanley Brechner; with Vera Lockwood, Maurice Sterman, Estelle Kemler, Reuben Schafer, Lauren White, David Chandler. *It's Hard to Be a Jew* by Sholem Aleichem, translated by Isaiah Sheffer. February 11, 1984. Directed by Dan Held; with Steven Gilborn, Avi Hoffman.

AMERICAN RENAISSANCE THEATER. *Home Again Kathleen* by Thomas Babe. September 21, 1983. Directed by Nyla Lyon; with Rebecca Darke, Jacqueline Schultz, Pamela Tucker-White, Colin Lane, Anne Swift. *Savage Amusement* by Peter Flannery. February, 1984. Directed by Pierre Epstein; with Christopher Wells, Marc Epstein, Rob Knepper, Kelly Pino, Brenda Daly.

AMERICAN THEATER ALLIANCE. *Suzanna Andler* by Marguerite Duras, translated by Barbara Bray. April 25, 1984. Directed by Aaron Levin.

AMERICAN THEATER OF ACTORS. *The Last of the Knucklemen* by John Powers. October 26, 1983. Directed by Peter Masterson and Carlin Glynn; with Kevin O'Connor, Dennis Quaid, Ben George. *My Father's House* by James Jennings. January 17, 1984. Directed by Ed Setrakian; with Henderson Forsythe, Joanne Hamlin, James Nixon, Ted Zurkowski, Katie Grant.

AMISTAD WORLD THEATER INTAR STAGE II. *Split Second* by Dennis McIntyre. February 1984. Directed by Samuel P. Barton; with John Danielle, Michele Shay, Norman Matlock, Peter Jay Fernandez, Bill Cwikowski, Helmar Augustus Cooper.

APPLE CORPS. *Appointment With Death* by Agatha Christie. July 14, 1983. Directed by John Raymond; with Charlotte Jones, Debra Whitfield, Bob Del Pazzo, Mary Orr, Robert McFarland. *The Strange Case of Dr. Jekyll and Mr. Hyde* by Colston Corris from Robert Louis Stevenson's story. August 25, 1983. Directed by Christopher Catt; with Orson Bean, Val Dufour, Jeremy Stuart, Debra Whitfield, Rica Martens.

ARK THEATER COMPANY. *The Man Who Could See Through Time* by Terri Wagener. March 11, 1984. Directed by Carey Perloff; with Bob Gunton, Leslie Geraci. *The Transposed Heads* adapted from Thomas Mann's novella by Sidney Goldfarb and Julie Taymor. May 10, 1984. Directed by Julie Taymor; with Sheila Dabney, Harry Streep, Mark Morales, Yamil Borges.

BASEMENT WORKSHOP. Ntozake Shangé and Jane Miller (poetry reading). December 20, 1983.

BILLIE HOLIDAY THEATER. *Friends* by Samm-Art Williams. September 22, 1983. Directed by Mikell Pinkney; with Valera Drummond, Helmar Augustus Cooper, Avan Littles, Carol Mitchell-Smith.

BREAD AND PUPPET THEATER. *The Insurrection Opera and Oratorio* by and with The Bread and Puppet Theater. February 15, 1984. *Josephine* adapted from Franz Kafka's novel, by and with The Bread and Puppet Theater. March, 1984.

BROOKLYN ACADEMY OF MUSIC. *The Way of How* created and directed by George Coates, music by Paul Dresher. October 14, 1983. Collaborative work with John Duykers, Rinde Eckert, Leonard Pitt, Paul Dresher. *The Gospel at Colonus* adapted and directed by Lee Breuer from Sophocles, music by Bob Telson. November, 1983. With Clarence Fountain, Martin Jacox, Kevin Davis, Isabell Monk, Jevetta Steele, Carl Lumbly, Robert Earl Jones. Both pieces performed as part of the Next Wave Festival.

C H S PRODUCTIONS. *The Patrick Pearse Motel* by Hugh Leonard. March, 1984. Directed by Robert Bridges; with James Gleason, Richard Merrell, Janet Bell, Judith Tillman, William Ferriter, Madelyn Griffith-Haynie, Ron Randell.

CARTER THEATER. *Please Don't Take My Rhythms and Blues* written and directed by Titus Walker. August, 1983. With the Ujamaa Black Theater Company.

CLASSIC THEATER. *A New Way to Pay Old Debts* by Philip Massinger. September 24, 1983. Directed by Maurice Edwards; with Owen S. Rackleff, Arlene Nadel, Edward Baran, Sid R. Gross, Harry H. Kunesch. *The Life I Gave You* by Luigi Pirandello, translated by Frederick May. November 23, 1983. Directed by Maurice Edwards; with Vera Lockwood, Virginia Aquino, Elizabeth De Ono, Patricia Mauceri, Maurice Sterman. *Tosca 1943* by Victorien Sardou, adapted and directed by Owen S. Rackleff. April 21, 1984. With Martitia Palmer, Edward Baran, Dan Lutzky.

COCTEAU REPERTORY. *Judas* by Robert Patrick. September 23, 1983. Directed by Eve Adamson; with Coral Potter, Craig Smith, John Emmett.

DOUGLAS FAIRBANKS THEATER. *A Christmas Carol* by Charles Dickens, adapted and performed by Rob Inglis. December, 1983.

DUPLEX CABARET THEATER. *The Nunsense Story* (musical) conceived by Dan Goggin, book by Steve Hayes, music and lyrics by Dan Goggin. Directed by Felton Smith; with Marilyn Farina, Nanette Gordon, John Hatchett, Suzanne Hevner, Roger Keller.

18TH STREET PLAYHOUSE. *And Baby Makes Seven* by Vi Bremen. January 5, 1984. Directed by Paula Vogel; with Sondra Allen, Cary Bickley, Ted Montague. *Across the Pond* by George Joshua. February, 1984. Directed by Randy Frazier; with Joe David, Kelle LeMar, Jack Rose, L. Anthony Williams, Rhobye Wyatt.

GREENE STREET THEATER. *Ball* (musical) book and lyrics by John Jiler, music by Richard Vitzhum. January 19, 1984. Directed by Daniel Wilson; choreographer, Margarite Winer; with Phillip Goodman, Martha Horstman, Mary Irey, Mike Lisenco, Marcia McIntosh.

IRISH ARTS CENTER. *The Shadow of a Gunman* by Sean O'Casey. April 9, 1984. Directed by Jim Sheridan; with Chris O'Neill.

JEWISH REPERTORY THEATER. *Up from Paradise* (musical) book and lyrics by Arthur Miller, music by Stanley Silverman. October 25, 1983. Directed by Ran Avni; with Len Cariou, Austin Pendleton, Alice Playten, Lonny Price, Paul Ukena Jr., Avery J. Tracht, Richard Frisch, Raymond Murcell, Walter Bobbie. *Gifted Children* by Donald Margulies. November 26, 1983. Directed by Joan Vail Thorne; with Zohra Lampert, Dinah Manoff, Ben Siegler. *The Homecoming* by Harold Pinter. February 21, 1984. Directed by Anthony McKay; with Joe Silver, Charles Randall, Mark Arnott, Howard Sherman, William McNulty, Cheryl McFadden. *Escape from Riverdale* by Donald Wollner. April, 1984. Directed by Lynn Polan; with Stephen Hamilton, Lisa Goodman, Michael Albert Mantel, Peter Berkrot, Rob Morrow, David Saint.

LAMB'S THEATER COMPANY. *Courage* by John Pielmeier. May, 1984. Directed by Susan Gregg; with Paul Collins.

MEDICINE SHOW THEATER ENSEMBLE. *Paris* (musical) by Cole Porter, based on Martin Brown's play. September 8, 1983. Directed by Barbara Vann; with Ray O'Conner, Katherine Burger, James Barbosa, Barbara Vann. *Annajanska* by George Bernard Shaw; directed by Paul Murphy and *A Sensation Novel* by W.S. Gilbert, music by David Hollister; directed by Peter Schlosser. March 21, 1984.

MODERN TIMES THEATER. *Freedom Days* by Steve Friedman. February 2, 1984. Directed by Danny Partridge; with Bruce Butler, Peggy Pettit, Joan Rosenfels, Steve Friedman.

MUSIC-THEATER GROUP/LENOX ARTS CENTER. *The Garden of Earthly Delights*, based on Hieronymus Bosch's painting, conceived and directed by Martha Clarke in collaboration with Robert Barnett, Felix Blaska, Robert Faust, Marie Fourcaut, Margie Gillis, Polly Styron, music by Richard Peaslee in collaboration with Eugene Friesen, Bill Ruyle, Steven Silverstein. April 4, 1984.

NAMELESS THEATER. *The Jungle*, created by The Irondale Ensemble, adapted from Upton Sinclair's novel. November 30, 1983. Directed by James Louis Niesen; with The Irondale Ensemble. *Ethan Frome* by Owen and Donald Davis, adapted from the novel by Edith Wharton. March 21, 1984. Directed by James Louis Niesen; with David Finklestein, Barbara Mackenzie-Wood, Christina Sluberski and The Irondale Ensemble.

NEIGHBORHOOD GROUP THEATER. *Forever Yours Marie-Lou* by Michel Tremblay, translated and directed by Merwan P. Mehta. April 13, 1984. With Paul Scott, Harriet Miller, Susan Swindell, Sharon Shahinian.

NEW AMSTERDAM THEATER COMPANY. *One Touch of Venus* (musical) book by Ogden Nash and S.J. Perelman, music by Kurt Weill, lyrics by Ogden Nash. October 15, 1983. With Jim Dale, Susan Lucci, Peggy Cass, Lee Roy Reams, David Garrison, Paige O'Hara, Jack Dabdoub. *Sweethearts* (operetta) book by Harry B. Smith and Fred de Gresac, music by Victor Herbert, lyrics by Robert B. Smith. December 12, 1983. With Jane Powell, Elaine Bonazzi, Judy Kaye, Christopher Hewett, Roderick Cook, Cris Groenendaal. *Roberta* (musical) book by Otto Harbach, based on Alice Duer Miller's novel, *Gowns by Roberta*, music by Jerome Kern. April 15, 1984. With Russ Thacker, Loni Ackerman, David Carroll, Judith Blazer, Paula Lawrence.

NEW THEATER OF BROOKLYN. *Artists and Admirers* by Alexander Ostrovsky, translated by Alex Bayer and Deborah J. Pope. April 26, 1984. Directed by Deborah J. Pope; with Gayle Harbor, Alex Paul, Michael Sutton, Hal Studer.

NEW YORK CLOWN-THEATER FESTIVAL. *Avner the Eccentric* (mime) with Avner Eisenberg; *A Beautiful Friendship* with Fred Yockers and John Towsen; clown-theater pieces with Karen McCormick, Stanley Allan Sherman, Valerie Dean, Don Reider, Ronlin Foreman, Michael Davis. June 7–July 10, 1983.

NEW YORK GILBERT & SULLIVAN PLAYERS. *Princess Ida* December 29, 1983; *Ruddigore* April 5, 1984; *H.M.S. Pinafore* May 31, 1984. Operettas by W.S. Gilbert and Arthur Sullivan; conductor, Beverly Bullock; co-music director, Jeffrey Kresky.

NEW YORK PUBLIC LIBRARY "THEATER IN THE LIBRARY" SERIES. *Hughie* (one-act play) by Eugene O'Neill. July 11, 1983. With Jason Robards, Jack Dodson. *On the Fifth Great Day of God: A Celebration in Praise of Creatures, Taken From the Works of Major Writers* (reading). September 19, 1983. With George Rose.

NEW YORK THEATER WORKSHOP AND NEW YORK THEATER STUDIO. *Souvenirs* by Sheldon Rosen. May, 1984. Directed by Stephen Katz; with Ellen Barber, Larry Block, David Purdham, John Milligan, Delphi Lawrence, Gilbert Cole.

NEW YORK UNIVERSITY THEATER. *The Human Voice* by Jean Cocteau, translated and performed by Susannah York. May 23, 1984.

O'NEALS'/43D ST. CABARET. *Banned in France* (revue) by and with Terry Sweeney, Carey Cromelin, Ginger Donelson, Lanier Laney, Walter Thomas. July, 1983. Directed by Arthur Collis.

SOUTH STREET THEATER—N. Erick Avari and Zach
Grenier in *Bhutan* by Jane Stanton Hitchcock

OUR STUDIOS. *A Trunk Full of Memories* by Ward Morehouse III. January 26, 1984. Directed by Lise Liepmann; with John Farrell, Frances Ford, Eleanor Cody Gould, Heidi Miller, William Morino. *Chaturanga* written and directed by Nancy Putnam Smithner. March 9, 1984. With the Ensemble of Movement Theater.

PERFORMING GARAGE. *North Atlantic* (mixed-media work) by the Wooster Group, book by Jim Strahs, music by Eddy Dixon. January, 1984. Directed by Elizabeth LeCompte; with Willem Dafoe, Spalding Gray, Anna Kohler, Nancy Reilly, Peyton Smith, Michael Stumm, Ron Vawter, Ann Pusey, Kate Valk.

PERRY STREET THEATER. *Second Prize: Two Months in Leningrad* by Trish Johnson. October 17, 1983. Directed by Gus Kaikkonen; with Edmond Genest, Mark Soper, J. Smith-Cameron. *Clean Sweep* by Joel Gross. February 16, 1984. Directed by Brian Hurley; with Robin Thomas, Kathy McNeil, Tom Ligon, Carole Chase. *The Fetishist* by Michel Tournier. May 30, 1984. Directed by Francoise Kourilsky with Honora Fergusson; with Frederick Neumann.

PLAYHOUSE 46. *Pahokee Beach* by Leo Rost. November 15, 1983. Directed by Georgia McGill; with Ted Farlow, Nancy Deering, Sylvia Davis, Joe Mulligan, Chris Seiler.

PRODUCTION COMPANY. *Dementos* (musical) concept and lyrics by Robert I., book by Sebastian Stuart and Robert I., music by Marc Shaiman. October 13, 1983. Directed by Theodore Pappas; with Charlaine Woodard, Jimmy Justice, Joanne Beretta, Patrick Jude, Jane Galloway, Roger Lawson. *Second Lady* (monodrama) by M. Kilburg Reedy. November 12, 1983. Directed by Carey Perloff; with Judith Ivey. *Criminal Minds* by Robin Swicord. January 15, 1984. Directed by David Trainer; with Pamela Reed, Leo Burmester, John Glover. *The Road to Hollywood* (musical) book by Michael Pace, music by Rob Preston, lyrics by Michael Pace and Rob Preston. April,

1984. Directed by Word Baker; with Michael Pace, Gary Herb, Bebe Neuwirth, Nora Mae Lyng, Kay Cole.

RACHEL'S. *I Can't Give You Anything but Lyrics by Dorothy Fields* (cabaret of Dorothy Fields's songs). May, 1984. With David Lahm, Judy Kreston, Harvey Granat.

RICHARD ALLEN CENTER FOR CULTURE AND ART. *Take Me Along* (musical) adapted from Eugene O'Neill's *Ah, Wilderness!* by Robert Merrill, Joseph Stein and Robert Russell, book by Joseph Stein, music and lyrics by Robert Merrill. March 23, 1984. Directed by Geraldine Fitzgerald and Mike Malone; with Duane Jones, Mary Alice, Rhetta Hughes, Mario Van Peebles, Marchand Odette, Mark Wade, Robert Kya-Hill, Vanessa Bell, Sandy Williams, Olivia Ward.

RIVERSIDE SHAKESPEARE COMPANY. *The Merry Wives of Windsor* by William Shakespeare. July 15, 1983. Directed by Timothy Oman; with Joseph Reed, Norma Fire. *Under Milk Wood* by Dylan Thomas, *The Tarnished Phoenix*, from D.H. Lawrence's works and *The Merchant of Venice* by William Shakespeare. October 18–22, 1983. (Presented as part of The Shakespeare Project with actors from the Royal Shakespeare Company.) *The Tempest* by William Shakespeare. November, 1983. Directed by Robert Mooney; with Bertram Ross. *Henry V* by William Shakespeare. May 11, 1984. With Frank Muller.

RIVERWEST THEATER. *Nite Club Confidential* (cabaret) by Dennis Deal and Al Evans. September, 1983. Directed by Dennis Deal; with Fay DeWitt. *The Ninth Step* by Tom Ziegler. February 6, 1984. Directed by Roderick Cook; with Kim Ameen, Lynne Goodwin, Karen Tull, Jennie Ventriss.

ROADSIDE THEATER. *South of the Mountain* written and directed by Ron Short. September 7, 1983. With Ron Short, Tom Bledsoe, Nancy Jeffrey.

SILVER LINING. *The Great American Backstage Musical* book by Bill Solly and Donald Ward, music and lyrics by Bill Solly. September 15, 1983. Directed by Bob Talmadge; with Mark Fotopoulos, Suzanne Dawson, Joe Barrett, Paige O'Hara, Bob Amaral, Maris Clement.

SOUTH STREET THEATER. *Brass Birds Don't Sing* by Samm-Art Williams. October 21, 1983. Directed by Samm-Art Williams; with Joseph Jamrog, Richard Portnow, Herbert Reubens, Janet Sarno, Susan Stevens. *Bhutan* by Jane Stanton Hitchcock. November 29, 1983. Directed by John Bird; with Marcus Smythe, Cynthia Crumlish, Patricia Hodges, Doug Stender, N. Erick Avari. *Mademoiselle* by Arthur Whitney. February 7, 1984. Directed by Cliff Goodwin; with Sylvia Davis, David Carlyon, Peter Filiaci.

THEATER AT ST. CLEMENT'S. *Time Was* by Shannon Keith Kelley. June 8, 1983. Directed by Lynn Thomson; with Kyra Sedgwick, Delphi Harrington, John J.D. Swain, Page Moseley, Ron Harper. *The Guitarron* by Lynne Alvarez. June 10, 1983. Directed by Stephen Berwind; with N. Erick Avari, Paul Butler, Joseph Montalbo, Michael Morin, Lionel Pina, Manuel Yesckas. *Dr. Selavy's Magic Theater* (co-production of Music Theater Group/Lenox Arts Center and Ontological-Hysteric Theater); music by Stanley Silverman; lyrics by Tom Hendry. January, 1984. Directed by Richard Foreman; with Jessica Harper, Roy Brocksmith, Annie Golden, John Vining, Kathi Moss, Dara Norman, Charlie O'Connell, Michael Ward, David Patrick Kelly.

T.O.M.I. THEATER. *Tallulah* (musical) book by Tony Lang, music by Arthur Siegel, lyrics by Mae Richard. June 13, 1983. Directed by David Holdgreiwe; with Helen Gallagher, Robert Dale Martin, Joel Craig. *Mighty Fine Music* (revue of Burton Lane's music) written and directed by Brent Wagner. August 26, 1983. With Jennifer S. Myers, Leslie Klein, Ted Kociolek, James Pietsch. *November Soul: The Odyssey of Young Herman Melville,* adapted and performed by Michael Finnerty. November 14, 1983. Directed by Anthony Alicata. *All the Nice People* by Hugh Leonard. April 9, 1984. With Marilyn McIntyre, Cara Duff-MacCormick. *Family Snapshots* by Sam Henry Kass. May, 1984. Directed by Peter Kass; with Roger Serbagi, Kevin Gray.

TOP OF THE VILLAGE GATE. *Cummings and Goings* poetry by e.e. cummings, music by Ada Janik, additional songs by Steven Margoshes. January 15, 1984. Directed by Nina Janik; with Sharon Brown, Elisa Fiorillo, Nina Hennessey, Raymond Patterson.

VINEYARD THEATER. *Faith Healer* by Brian Friel. October 21, 1983. Directed by Dann Florek; with J.T. Walsh, Kathleen Chalfant, Martin Shakar.

WEST BANK CAFE THEATER. *Dick Deterred* (musical) book and lyrics by David Edgar, music by William Schimmel. September 24, 1982. Directed by George Wolf Reily; with Steve Pudenz, Richard Litt, Mary Kay Dean, Sylvester Rich.

WEST END THEATER. *Barbara & Ruth* by Jerry Koegel. July 7, 1983. Directed by Marc Le-Blond; with Virginia Ashton, Steve Borton, Jennifer White, Lewis Morgan, Ray Proscia.

WRITERS THEATER. *The Other Shore* by José Lopez Rubio, translated by Marion Peter Holt. February 23, 1984. Directed by Walter Bobbie.

CAST REPLACEMENTS AND TOURING COMPANIES

Compiled by Stanley Green

The following is a list of the more important cast replacements in productions which opened in previous years, but were still playing in New York during a substantial part of the 1983–84 season; or were still on a first-class tour in 1983–84, or opened in New York in 1983–84 and went on tour during the season (casts of first-class touring companies of previous seasons which were no longer playing in 1983–84 appear in previous *Best Plays* volumes of appropriate years).

The name of each major role is listed in *italics* beneath the title of the play in the first column. In the second column directly opposite appears the name of the actor who created the role in the original New York production (whose opening date appears in *italics* at the top of the column). Indented immediately beneath the original actor's name are the names of subsequent New York replacements, together with the date of replacement when available.

The third column gives information about first-class touring companies, including London companies (produced under the auspices of their original New York managements). When there is more than one roadshow company, #1, # 2, etc., appear before the name of the performer who created the role in each company (and the city and date of each company's first performance appears in *italics* at the top of the column). Their subsequent replacements are also listed beneath their names, with dates when available.

AGNES OF GOD

	New York 3/30/82	*#1 London 8/2/83* *#2 San Francisco 8/17/83*
Dr. Martha Livingstone	Elizabeth Ashley Diahann Carroll 9/27/82 Elizabeth Ashley 10/11/82 Diahann Carroll 5/2/83	#1 Susannah York #2 Elizabeth Ashley
Mother Miriam Ruth	Geraldine Page	#1 Honor Blackman #2 Mercedes McCambridge
Agnes	Amanda Plummer Mia Dillon 9/7/82 Amanda Plummer 9/14/82 Carrie Fisher 1/3/83 Maryann Plunkett 4/12/83 Lily Knight 7/19/83	#1 Hilary Reynolds #2 Maryann Plunkett

AMADEUS

	New York 12/17/80	*Los Angeles 12/9/82*
Antonio Salieri	Ian McKellen John Wood 10/31/81 Frank Langella 4/13/82 David Dukes 11/16/82	John Wood

413

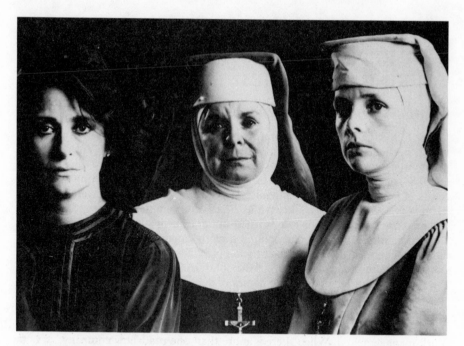

AGNES OF GOD—Elizabeth Ashley, Mercedes McCambridge and Maryann Plunkett in the national touring company of the 1981–82 Best Play

	David Birney 5/24/83	
	John Horton 9/20/83	
	Daniel Davis 9/27/83	
Wolfgang Amadeus Mozart	Tim Curry	Mark Hamill
	Peter Firth 7/7/81	John Pankow 4/28/83
	John Pankow 3/10/82	
	Dennis Boutsikeris 4/13/82	
	John Pankow 11/16/82	
	John Thomas Waite 4/19/83	
	Mark Hamill 4/28/83	
	John Thomas Waite 8/2/83	
	Peter Crook 9/27/83	
Constanze Weber	Jane Seymour	Michele Seyler
	Caris Corfman 5/26/81	
	Amy Irving 7/7/81	
	Caris Corfman 2/16/82	
	Michele Farr 3/23/82	
	Suzanne Lederer 4/13/82	
	Maureen Moore 5/24/83	

BRIGHTON BEACH MEMOIRS

	New York 3/27/83	*Ft. Lauderdale 11/26/83*
Eugene	Matthew Broderick	Jonathan Silverman
	Fisher Stevens 8/2/83	
	Matthew Broderick 2/7/84	
	Fisher Stevens 5/1/84	

Stanley	Zeljko Ivanek	Mark Nelson
	J. Patrick Breen 8/2/83	
Nora	Jodi Thelen	Elizabeth Perkins
	Marissa Chibas	
Jack	Peter Michael Goetz	Charles Cioffi
Kate	Elizabeth Franz	Joan Copeland
	Marilyn Chris	
Laurie	Mandy Ingber	Olivia Laurel Mates
	Elizabeth Ward	
Blanche	Joyce Van Patten	Barbara Caruso
	Kathleen Widdoes	

THE CAINE MUTINY COURT-MARTIAL

New York 5/5/83

Lt. Greenwald	John Rubinstein
	Michael Moriarty 8/2/83
Lt. Cmdr. Queeg	Michael Moriarty
	Philip Bosco 8/2/83
Lt. Cmdr. Challee	William Atherton
	Kent Broadhurst 9/30/83
Lt. Maryk	Jay O. Sanders
	James Widdoes
	Joe Namath 9/20/83

CATS

	New York 10/7/82	*Boston 12/21/83*
Bombalurina	Donna King	Cindi Klinger
	Marléne Danielle	
Bustopher Jones/Asparagus/	Stephen Hanan	Sal Mistretta
Growltiger	Timothy Jerome	
Cassandra	René Ceballos	Charlotte d'Amboise
	Christina Kumi Kimball	
Coricopat/Mungojerrie	René Clemente	Allen Hidalgo*
	Guillermo Gonzalez	Ray Roderick*
	Joe Antony Cavise 3/84	
Demeter	Wendy Edmead	Pamela Blasetti
	Marléne Danielle	
	Wendy Edmead	
	Jane Bodle 3/84	
Grizabella	Betty Buckley	Laurie Beechman
	Laurie Beechman 4/9/84	Diane Frantantoni 2/23/84
Jennyanydots	Anna McNeely	Cindy Benson
Mistoffelees	Timothy Scott	Jamie Torcellini
Old Deuteronomy	Ken Page	Kevin Marcum
Plato/Macavity/Rumpus Cat	Kenneth Ard	Russell Warfield
	Scott Wise	

Rum Tum Tugger	Terrence V. Mann	Rich Hebert
Rumpleteazer	Christine Langner Paige Dana 3/84	Kelli Ann McNally
Skimbleshanks	Reed Jones Michael Scott Gregory	Anthony Whigas
Tantomile	Janet L. Hubert Sundy Leigh Leake	Tori Brenno

*Mr. Hidalgo played *Coricopat*, Mr. Roderick played *Mungojerrie.*

A CHORUS LINE

N.Y. Off Bway 4/15/75
N.Y. Bway 7/25/75

Kristine	Renee Baughman Christine Barker 10/81
Sheila	Carole Bishop (name changed to Kelly Bishop 3/76) Jane Summerhays 9/82 Kelly Bishop 10/19/83 Jane Summerhays 11/1/83 Kelly Bishop 3/84 Kathryn Ann Wright 4/84
Val	Pamela Blair Mitzi Hamilton 7/81
Mike	Wayne Cilento Danny Herman 4/83
Larry	Clive Clerk Brad Jeffries 11/82 J. Richard Hart 8/83
Maggie	Kay Cole Pam Klinger 9/81
Richie	Ronald Dennis Kevin Chinn 1/81 Reggie Phoenix 10/83
Judy	Patricia Garland Melissa Randel 12/81
Don	Ron Kuhlman Michael Danek 12/82
Bebe	Nancy Lane Pamela Ann Wilson 1/82
Connie	Baayork Lee Lily-Lee Wong 10/81 Sachi Shimizu 11/83 Lauren Tom 4/84
Diana	Priscilla Lopez Loida Santos (previously know as Loida Iglesias) 3/83
Zach	Robert LuPone Steve Boockvor 8/23/82 Eivind Harum 7/83

Mark	Cameron Mason Chris Marshall 4/83
Cassie	Donna McKechnie Pamela Sousa 11/81 Cheryl Clark 10/83
Al	Don Percassi Buddy Balou' 3/83
Greg	Michel Stuart Ronald A. NaVarre 9/82 Justin Ross 10/83
Bobby	Thomas J. Walsh Matt West 9/80
Paul	Sammy Williams Tommy Aguilar 5/82 Sammy Williams 10/19/83

Note: On September 29, 1983 *A Chorus Line* gave its 3,389th performance and became the longest running production in Broadway history. Performers who appeared in the show for any part of the 1983–84 season are listed above under the names of the original cast members. The many previous replacements in these roles are listed on pages 437–440 of *The Best Plays of 1982–83.* Original casts of the three touring companies of *A Chorus Line* appear on pages 472–473 of *The Best Plays of 1978–79.*

DREAMGIRLS

	New York 12/20/81	Los Angeles 3/20/83
Effie Melody White	Jennifer Holliday Vanessa Townsell 12/6/82 Julia McGirt 11/83	Jennifer Holliday Lillias White 12/6/83
Lorrell Robinson	Loretta Devine	Arnetia Walker
C.C. White	Obba Babatunde Tony Franklin 1/84	Lawrence Clayton
James Thunder Early	Cleavant Derricks Hinton Battle 7/25/83 Clinton Derricks-Carroll Cleavant Derricks 11/83 David Alan Grier 3/84	Clinton Derricks-Carroll
Curtis Taylor Jr.	Ben Harney	Larry Riley
Deena Jones	Sheryl Lee Ralph Linda Leilani Brown Sheryl Lee Ralph 11/83	Linda Leilani Brown
Michelle Morris	Deborah Burrell Terry Burrell 3/83 Ethel Beatty 3/84 Terry Burrell 4/84	Deborah Burrell
Marty	Vondie Curtis-Hall	Weyman Thompson

Note: On June 20, 1983, changes instituted in the West Coast company of *Dreamgirls* (a refurbishing of the first number in Act II and seven minutes of Act II cuts) were incorporated into the New York company.

EXTREMITIES

	New York 12/22/82
Marjorie	Susan Sarandon
	Karen Allen 3/29/83
	Farrah Fawcett 5/24/83
Terry	Ellen Barkin
	Glenne Headly
	Priscilla Lopez 4/7/83
	Lorna Luft 7/5/83

THE FANTASTICKS

	New York 5/3/60
El Gallo	Jerry Orbach
	Roger Neil 5/17/83
	Sal Provenza 8/9/83
Luisa	Rita Gardner
	Virginia Gregory 12/7/82
Matt	Kenneth Nelson
	Howard Lawrence 12/29/81
	(name changed to Howard Paul Lawrence)

Note: On May 3, 1984 *The Fantasticks*, the longest running New York production of all time, began its 25th year. As of May 31, 1984, 30 actors had played the role of El Gallo, 26 actresses had played Luisa and 22 actors had played Matt during the musical's more than 10,000 performances. Performers who appeared in the show for any part of the 1983–84 season are listed above under the names of the original cast members. The many previous replacements in these roles are listed on pages 442–444 of *The Best Plays of 1982–83*.

42ND STREET

		#1 *Chicago 1/1/83*
		#2 *Philadelphia 11/13/83*
	New York 8/25/80	#3 *Los Angeles 2/10/84*
Julian Marsh	Jerry Orbach	#1 Ron Holgate
		#2 Barry Nelson
		#3 Jon Cypher
Dorothy Brock	Tammy Grimes	#1 Elizabeth Allen
	Milicent Martin 10/28/81	Milicent Martin 4/26/83
	Elizabeth Allen 4/26/83	#2 Dolores Gray
	Milicent Martin 9/6/83	#3 Milicent Martin
	Anne Rogers 12/13/83	
Peggy Sawyer	Wanda Richert	#1 Nancy Sinclair
	Nancy Sinclair 10/15/80	#2 Clare Leach
	Karen Prunczik 10/20/80	#3 Nana Visitor
	Wanda Richert 10/25/80	
	Lisa Brown 7/26/82	
	Karen Zimba 11/15/83	
Billy Lawlor	Lee Roy Reams	#1 Jim Walton
	James Brennan 12/13/83	#2 Jim Walton
		Lee Roy Reams 12/13/83
		Jim Walton
		#3 Lee Roy Reams

| *Maggie Jones* | Carole Cook
Peggy Cass 9/81
Jessica James 10/4/82 | #1 Bibi Osterwald
#2 Bibi Osterwald
#3 Carole Cook |
| *Bert Barry* | Joseph Bova | #1 William Linton
#2 Don Potter
#3 Matthew Tobin |

GREATER TUNA

	New York 10/21/82	*Houston 8/17/83*
	Joe Sears Ronn Carroll 6/2/83 Ron Lee Savin 9/20/83	Joe Sears
	Jaston Williams Michael Jeter 6/2/83	Jaston Williams

MASTER HAROLD . . . AND THE BOYS

	New York 5/4/82	*Boston 3/15/83*
Sam	Zakes Mokae	James Earl Jones Hugh Hurd 9/30/83 John Amos 10/1/83 Zakes Mokae 10/4/83
Willie	Danny Glover Delroy Lindo 2/3/83	Delroy Lindo
Hally	Lonny Price	Charles Michael Wright

MY ONE AND ONLY

	New York 5/1/83
Capt. Billy Buck Chandler	Tommy Tune Ron Young 1/10/84 Tommy Tune 1/17/84
Edith Herbert	Twiggy Stephanie Ely 1/3/84 Twiggy 1/10/84

NINE

	New York 5/9/82	*Washington 3/27/84*
Guido Contini	Raul Julia Bert Convy 1/10/83 Raul Julia 1/24/83 Sergio Franchi 5/9/83	Sergio Franchi
Luisa Contini	Karen Akers Maureen McGovern 12/6/82 Eileen Barnett 11/83	Diane M. Hurley
Liliane La Fleur	Liliane Montevecchi Priscilla Lopez 11/8/82 Liliane Montevecchi 11/22/82	Jacqueline Douguet

Carla	Anita Morris Beth McVey 8/15/83 Wanda Richert 9/12/83	Karen Tamburrelli
Claudia	Shelly Burch Kim Kriswell 1/31/83 Barbara Stock Beth McVey	Lauren Mitchell
Saraghina	Kathi Moss Jennifer Light	Camille Saviola
Guido's Mother	Taina Elg	Leigh Beery

ON YOUR TOES

	New York 3/6/83	*Miami Beach 3/22/84*
Vera Baronova	Natalia Makarova Galina Panova 6/14/83 Valentina Kozlova 1/17/84 Galina Panova 1/31/84	Leslie Caron*
Junior Dolan	Lara Teeter	Michael Kubala
Sergei Alexandrovitch	George S. Irving David Gold 8/30/83 George S. Irving 9/6/83	Stephen Pearlman
Peggy Porterfield	Dina Merrill Kitty Carlisle 6/14/83 Dina Merrill 7/26/83 Kitty Carlisle 12/20/83	Frances Bergen
Konstantine Morrosine	George de la Pena Leonid Kozlov 1/17/84 George de la Pena 1/31/84 Sandor Nemethy 3/6/84 Leonid Kozlov 3/13/84 Terry Edlefsen 3/27/84	Alexander Filipov

*Because of an injury, Miss Caron alternated performances during the first week with Natalia Makarova. Miss Caron's subsequent hospitalization caused the tour to end in Dallas April 28, 1984.

PRIVATE LIVES

	New York 5/8/83	*Philadelphia 7/24/83*
Amanda Prynne	Elizabeth Taylor	Elizabeth Taylor
Elyot Chase	Richard Burton	Richard Burton

QUARTERMAINE'S TERMS

	New York 2/24/83
St. John Quartermaine	Remak Ramsay Lee Richardson
Anita Manchip	Caroline Lagerfelt Caitlin Clarke
Mark Sackling	Kelsey Grammer John Christopher Jones

Henry Windscape	John Cunningham
	Jack Ryland
Melanie Garth	Dana Ivey
	Barbara Caruso 10/83

SISTER MARY IGNATIUS EXPLAINS IT ALL FOR YOU

New York 10/21/81

Sister Mary Ignatius	Elizabeth Franz
	Kathleen Chalfant
	Nancy Marchand 9/28/82
	Mary Louise Wilson 3/15/83
	Lynn Redgrave 8/9/83
	Patricia Gage 8/30/83
Aloysius Benheim	Jeff Brooks
	Christopher Durang 7/13/82
	Jeff Brooks 7/27/82
	Christopher Durang 12/24/82
	Jeff Brooks 12/28/82
	Brian Keeler 6/28/83
	Jeff Brooks 9/13/83
Dame Ellen Terry	Mary Catherine Wright
	Deborah Rush 5/24/82
	Alice Playten 7/13/82
	Mary Catherine Wright
Meg	Polly Draper
	Carolyn Mignini 5/24/82
	Brenda Curtin

TORCH SONG TRILOGY

N.Y. Off Bway 1/15/82
N.Y. Bway 6/10/82   *San Francisco 7/6/83*

Arnold Beckoff	Harvey Fierstein	Donald Corren
	Harvey Fierstein	Jonathan Hadary 1/10/84
	Donald Corren (mats.) 4/83	Donald Corren 1/31/84
	Jonathan Hadary (mats.) 6/8/83	Jonathan Hadary 2/28/84
	David Garrison (eves.) 6/13/83	Harvey Fierstein 5/8/84
	Jonathan Hadary (eves.) 8/10/83	
	Philip Astor (mats.) 8/24/83	
	Harvey Fierstein (eves.) 1/10/84	
	Philip Astor (alternate)	
	(eves.) 1/30/84	
	Jonathan Hadary (eves.) 5/8/84	
Ed	Joel Crothers	Brian Kerwin
	Court Miller	Jared Martin 5/8/84
	Court Miller	
	Robert Sevra 2/83	
	Peter Ratray 8/83	
	Court Miller 1/10/84	
	Jared Martin 1/31/84	
	Court Miller 5/8/84	
	Raymond Baker (eves.)	
	Peter Ratray (mats.)	

TORCH SONG TRILOGY—Jonathan Hadary in the Harvey
Fierstein role with Estelle Getty in the Broadway company

Mrs. Beckoff

Estelle Getty
Estelle Getty
  Barbara Barrie 1/31/83
  Estelle Getty 2/14/83
  Chevi Colton 6/21/83

Sylvia Kauder
  Estelle Getty 6/21/83

David

Matthew Broderick
  Fisher Stevens 3/21/82
Fisher Stevens
  Matthew Vipond

Christopher Collet
  Lawrence Monoson

TRUE WEST

New York 10/17/82

Lee

John Malkovich
  Bruce Lyons 4/26/83
  Jim Belushi
  Dennis Quaid 11/15/83
  Daniel Stern 3/6/84

Austin

Gary Sinise
  Richmond Hoxie
  Dan Butler 4/17/83
  Gary Cole
  Randy Quaid 11/15/83
  Jere Berns 3/6/84
  Tim Matheson 3/23/84

WOMAN OF THE YEAR

	New York 3/29/81	Los Angeles 6/9/83
Tess Harding	Lauren Bacall	Lauren Bacall
Sam Craig	Harry Guardino	Harry Guardino
Jan Donovan	Marilyn Cooper	Marilyn Cooper

Note: For New York cast changes of Woman of the Year, see pages 449–450 of The Best Plays of 1982–1983.

YOU CAN'T TAKE IT WITH YOU

	New York 4/4/83
Martin Vanderhof	Jason Robards Eddie Albert 8/23/83
Penelope Sycamore	Elizabeth Wilson Frances Sternhagen 9/27/83
Boris Kolenkhov	James Coco Ellis Rabb 6/20/83 Rex Robbins 7/26/83 George Rose 9/6/83
Olga	Colleen Dewhurst Eva Gabor 10/11/83 Colleen Dewhurst 12/6/83
Alice Vanderhof	Maureen Anderman Sandy Faison 7/5/83 Monique Fowler 12/6/83
Mrs. Kirby	Meg Mundy Betty Miller 8/30/83

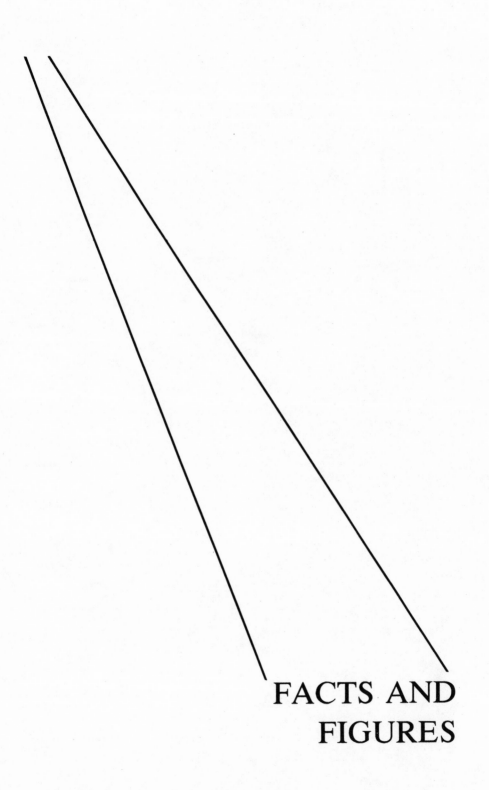

FACTS AND
FIGURES

LONG RUNS ON BROADWAY

The following shows have run 500 or more continuous performances in a single production, usually the first, not including previews or extra non-profit performances, allowing for vacation layoffs and special one-booking engagements, but not including return engagements after a show has gone on tour. In all cases the numbers were obtained directly from the shows' production offices. Where there are title similarities, the production is identified as follows: (p) straight play version, (m) musical version, (r) revival.

THROUGH MAY 31, 1984

(PLAYS MARKED WITH ASTERISK WERE STILL PLAYING JUNE 1, 1984)

Plays	Number Performances	Plays	Number Performances
*A Chorus Line	3,669	How To Succeed in Business Without Really Trying	1,417
Grease	3,388	Hellzapoppin	1,404
*Oh! Calcutta! (r)	3,308	The Music Man	1,375
Fiddler on the Roof	3,242	Funny Girl	1,348
Life With Father	3,224	Mummenschanz	1,326
Tobacco Road	3,182	Angel Street	1,295
Hello, Dolly!	2,844	Lightnin'	1,291
My Fair Lady	2,717	Promises, Promises	1,281
Annie	2,377	The King and I	1,246
Man of La Mancha	2,328	Cactus Flower	1,234
Abie's Irish Rose	2,327	Sleuth	1,222
Oklahoma!	2,212	1776	1,217
Pippin	1,944	Equus	1,209
South Pacific	1,925	Sugar Babies	1,208
The Magic Show	1,920	Guys and Dolls	1,200
Deathtrap	1,793	Amadeus	1,181
Gemini	1,788	Cabaret	1,165
Harvey	1,775	Mister Roberts	1,157
Dancin'	1,774	Annie Get Your Gun	1,147
Hair	1,750	The Seven Year Itch	1,141
The Wiz	1,672	Butterflies Are Free	1,128
Born Yesterday	1,642	Pins and Needles	1,108
The Best Little Whorehouse in Texas	1,639	Plaza Suite	1,097
Ain't Misbehavin'	1,604	They're Playing Our Song	1,082
*42nd Street	1,572	Kiss Me, Kate	1,070
Mary, Mary	1,572	Don't Bother Me, I Can't Cope	1,065
Evita	1,567	The Pajama Game	1,063
Barefoot in the Park	1,530	Shenandoah	1,050
Mame (m)	1,508	The Teahouse of the August Moon	1,027
Same Time, Next Year	1,453	*Dreamgirls	1,019
Arsenic and Old Lace	1,444	Damn Yankees	1,019
The Sound of Music	1,443		

427

Plays	Number Performances	Plays	Number Performances
Never Too Late	1,007	Bubbling Brown Sugar	766
Any Wednesday	982	State of the Union	765
A Funny Thing Happened on		The First Year	760
the Way to the Forum	964	You Know I Can't Hear You	
The Odd Couple	964	When the Water's Running	755
Anna Lucasta	957	Two for the Seesaw	750
Kiss and Tell	956	Joseph and the Amazing	
Dracula (r)	925	Technicolor Dreamcoat (r)	747
Bells Are Ringing	924	Death of a Salesman	742
The Moon Is Blue	924	For Colored Girls, etc.	742
Beatlemania	920	Sons o' Fun	742
The Elephant Man	916	Candide (mr)	740
Luv	901	Gentlemen Prefer Blondes	740
Chicago	898	The Man Who Came to Dinner	739
Applause	896	Nine	739
Can-Can	892	Call Me Mister	734
Carousel	890	West Side Story	732
Hats Off to Ice	889	High Button Shoes	727
Fanny	888	Finian's Rainbow	725
Children of a Lesser God	887	Claudia	722
Follow the Girls	882	The Gold Diggers	720
Camelot	873	Jesus Christ Superstar	720
I Love My Wife	872	Carnival	719
The Bat	867	The Diary of Anne Frank	717
My Sister Eileen	864	I Remember Mama	714
No, No, Nanette (r)	861	Tea and Sympathy	712
Song of Norway	860	Junior Miss	710
Chapter Two	857	Last of the Red Hot Lovers	706
A Streetcar Named Desire	855	Company	705
Barnum	854	Seventh Heaven	704
Comedy in Music	849	Gypsy (m)	702
Raisin	847	The Miracle Worker	700
You Can't Take It With You	837	That Championship Season	700
La Plume de Ma Tante	835	Da	697
Three Men on a Horse	835	The King and I (r)	696
The Subject Was Roses	832	Cat on a Hot Tin Roof	694
*Torch Song Trilogy	827	Li'l Abner	693
Inherit the Wind	806	Peg o' My Heart	692
No Time for Sergeants	796	The Children's Hour	691
Fiorello!	795	*Cats	689
Where's Charley?	792	Purlie	688
The Ladder	789	Dead End	687
Forty Carats	780	The Lion and the Mouse	686
The Prisoner of Second Avenue	780	White Cargo	686
Oliver!	774	Dear Ruth	683
The Pirates of Penzance (1980 r)	772	East Is West	680
Woman of the Year	770	Come Blow Your Horn	677
Sophisticated Ladies	767	The Most Happy Fella	676

Plays	Number Performances	Plays	Number Performances
The Doughgirls	671	Kismet	583
The Impossible Years	670	Detective Story	581
Irene	670	Brigadoon	581
Boy Meets Girl	669	No Strings	580
Beyond the Fringe	667	Brother Rat	577
Who's Afraid of Virginia Woolf?	664	Pump Boys and Dinettes	573
Blithe Spirit	657	Show Boat	572
A Trip to Chinatown	657	The Show-Off	571
The Women	657	Sally	570
Bloomer Girl	654	Golden Boy (m)	568
The Fifth Season	654	One Touch of Venus	567
Rain	648	Happy Birthday	564
Witness for the Prosecution	645	Look Homeward, Angel	564
Call Me Madam	644	Morning's at Seven (r)	564
Janie	642	The Glass Menagerie	561
The Green Pastures	640	I Do! I Do!	560
Auntie Mame (p)	639	Wonderful Town	559
A Man for All Seasons	637	Rose Marie	557
The Fourposter	632	Strictly Dishonorable	557
Two Gentlemen of Verona (m)	627	Sweeney Todd, the Demon	
The Tenth Man	623	Barber of Fleet Street	557
Is Zat So?	618	A Majority of One	556
Anniversary Waltz	615	The Great White Hope	556
The Happy Time (p)	614	Toys in the Attic	556
Separate Rooms	613	Sunrise at Campobello	556
Affairs of State	610	Jamaica	555
Oh! Calcutta!	610	Stop the World—I Want to Get	
Star and Garter	609	Off	555
The Student Prince	608	Florodora	553
Sweet Charity	608	Ziegfeld Follies (1943)	553
Bye Bye Birdie	607	Dial "M" for Murder	552
Irene (r)	604	Good News	551
Broadway	603	Peter Pan (r)	551
Adonis	603	Let's Face It	547
Street Scene (p)	601	Milk and Honey	543
Kiki	600	Within the Law	541
Flower Drum Song	600	The Music Master	540
A Little Night Music	600	Pal Joey (r)	540
Agnes of God	599	What Makes Sammy Run?	540
Don't Drink the Water	598	The Sunshine Boys	538
Wish You Were Here	598	What a Life	538
A Society Circus	596	Crimes of the Heart	535
Absurd Person Singular	592	The Unsinkable Molly Brown	532
Blossom Time	592	The Red Mill (r)	531
A Day in Hollywood/A Night		A Raisin in the Sun	530
in the Ukraine	588	Godspell	527
The Me Nobody Knows	586	The Solid Gold Cadillac	526
The Two Mrs. Carrolls	585	Irma La Douce	524

Plays	Number Performances	Plays	Number Performances
The Boomerang	522	The Rothschilds	507
Follies	521	On Your Toes (r)	505
Rosalinda	521	Sugar	505
The Best Man	520	Shuffle Along	504
Chauve-Souris	520	Up in Central Park	504
Blackbirds of 1928	518	Carmen Jones	503
The Gin Game	517	The Member of the Wedding	501
Sunny	517	Panama Hattie	501
Victoria Regina	517	Personal Appearance	501
Fifth of July	511	Bird in Hand	500
Half a Sixpence	511	Room Service	500
The Vagabond King	511	Sailor, Beware!	500
The New Moon	509	Tomorrow the World	500
The World of Suzie Wong	508		

LONG RUNS OFF BROADWAY

Plays	Number Performances	Plays	Number Performances
*The Fantasticks	10,019	The Mad Show	871
The Threepenny Opera	2,611	Scrambled Feet	831
Godspell	2,124	The Effect of Gamma Rays on Man-in-the-Moon	
Jacques Brel	1,847	Marigolds	819
Vanities	1,785	A View From the Bridge (r)	780
You're a Good Man Charlie Brown	1,547	The Boy Friend (r)	763
The Blacks	1,408	*Little Shop of Horrors	756
One Mo' Time	1,372	The Pocket Watch	725
Let My People Come	1,327	The Connection	722
The Hot l Baltimore	1,166	The Passion of Dracula	714
I'm Getting My Act Together and Taking It on the Road	1,165	Adaptation & Next	707
Little Mary Sunshine	1,143	Oh! Calcutta!	704
El Grande de Coca-Cola	1,114	Scuba Duba	692
One Flew Over the Cuckoo's Nest (r)	1,025	The Knack	685
The Boys in the Band	1,000	*True West	685
*Forbidden Broadway	982	The Club	674
Cloud 9	971	The Balcony	672
Sister Mary Ignatius Explains It All for You & The Actor's Nightmare	947	America Hurrah	634
		Hogan's Goat	607
Your Own Thing	933	The Trojan Women (r)	600
Curley McDimple	931	Krapp's Last Tape & The Zoo Story	582
Leave It to Jane (r)	928	The Dumbwaiter & The Collection	578
		Dames at Sea	575

Plays	Number Performances	Plays	Number Performances
The Crucible (r)	571	The Dirtiest Show in Town	509
The Iceman Cometh (r)	565	Happy Ending & Day of	
The Hostage (r)	545	Absence	504
Six Characters in Search of an		Greater Tuna	501
Author (r)	529	The Boys From Syracuse (r)	500
The Dining Room	511		

NEW YORK CRITICS AWARDS, 1935–36 to 1983–84

Listed below are the New York Drama Critics Circle Awards from 1935–36 through 1983–84 classified as follows: (1) Best American Play, (2) Best Foreign Play, (3) Best Musical, (4) Best, regardless of category (this category was established by new voting rules in 1962–63 and did not exist prior to that year).

1935–36—(1) Winterset
1936–37—(1) High Tor
1937–38—(1) Of Mice and Men, (2) Shadow and Substance
1938–39—(1) No award, (2) The White Steed
1939–40—(1) The Time of Your Life
1940–41—(1) Watch on the Rhine, (2) The Corn Is Green
1941–42—(1) No award, (2) Blithe Spirit
1942–43—(1) The Patriots
1943–44—(2) Jacobowsky and the Colonel
1944–45—(1) The Glass Menagerie
1945–46—(3) Carousel
1946–47—(1) All My Sons, (2) No Exit, (3) Brigadoon
1947–48—(1) A Streetcar Named Desire, (2) The Winslow Boy
1948–49—(1) Death of a Salesman, (2) The Madwoman of Chaillot, (3) South Pacific
1949–50—(1) The Member of the Wedding (2) The Cocktail Party, (3) The Consul
1950–51—(1) Darkness at Noon, (2) The Lady's Not for Burning, (3) Guys and Dolls
1951–52—(1) I Am a Camera, (2) Venus Observed, (3) Pal Joey (Special citation to Don Juan in Hell)
1952–53—(1) Picnic, (2) The Love of Four Colonels, (3) Wonderful Town
1953–54—(1) Teahouse of the August Moon, (2) Ondine, (3) The Golden Apple
1954–55—(1) Cat on a Hot Tin Roof, (2) Witness for the Prosecution, (3) The Saint of Bleecker Street

1955–56—(1) The Diary of Anne Frank, (2) Tiger at the Gates, (3) My Fair Lady
1956–57—(1) Long Day's Journey Into Night, (2) The Waltz of the Toreadors, (3) The Most Happy Fella
1957–58—(1) Look Homeward, Angel, (2) Look Back in Anger, (3) The Music Man
1958–59—(1) A Raisin in the Sun, (2) The Visit, (3) La Plume de Ma Tante
1959–60—(1) Toys in the Attic, (2) Five Finger Exercise, (3) Fiorello!
1960–61—(1) All the Way Home, (2) A Taste of Honey, (3) Carnival
1961–62—(1) The Night of the Iguana, (2) A Man for All Seasons, (3) How to Succeed in Business Without Really Trying
1962–63—(4) Who's Afraid of Virginia Woolf? (Special citation to Beyond the Fringe)
1963–64—(4) Luther, (3) Hello, Dolly! (Special citation to The Trojan Women)
1964–65—(4) The Subject Was Roses, (3) Fiddler on the Roof
1965–66—(4) The Persecution and Assassination of Marat as Performed by the Inmates of the Asylum of Charenton Under the Direction of the Marquis de Sade, (3) Man of La Mancha
1966–67—(4) The Homecoming, (3) Cabaret
1967–68—(4) Rosencrantz and Guildenstern Are Dead, (3) Your Own Thing

1968–69—(4) The Great White Hope, (3) 1776
1969–70—(4) Borstal Boy, (1) The Effect of Gamma Rays on Man-in-the-Moon Marigolds, (3) Company
1970–71—(4) Home, (1) The House of Blue Leaves, (3) Follies
1971–72—(4) That Championship Season, (2) The Screens, (3) Two Gentlemen of Verona (Special citations to Sticks and Bones and Old Times)
1972–73—(4) The Changing Room, (1) The Hot l Baltimore, (3) A Little Night Music
1973–74—(4) The Contractor, (1) Short Eyes, (3) Candide
1974–75—(4) Equus, (1) The Taking of Miss Janie, (3) A Chorus Line
1975–76—(4) Travesties, (1) Streamers, (3) Pacific Overtures
1976–77—(4) Otherwise Engaged, (1) American Buffalo, (3) Annie
1977–78—(4) Da, (3) Ain't Misbehavin'
1978–79—(4) The Elephant Man, (3) Sweeney Todd, the Demon Barber of Fleet Street
1979–80—(4) Talley's Folly, (2) Betrayal, (3) Evita (Special citation to Peter Brook's Le Centre International de Créations Théâtrales for its repertory)
1980–81—(4) A Lesson From Aloes, (1) Crimes of the Heart (Special citations to Lena Horne: The Lady and Her Music and the New York Shakespeare Festival production of The Pirates of Penzance)
1981–82—(4) The Life & Adventures of Nicholas Nickleby, (1) A Soldier's Play
1982–83—(4) Brighton Beach Memoirs, (2) Plenty, (3) Little Shop of Horrors (Special citation to Young Playwrights Festival)
1983–84—(4) The Real Thing, (1), Glengarry Glen Ross, (3) Sunday in the Park With George (Special citation to Samuel Beckett for the body of his work)

NEW YORK DRAMA CRITICS CIRCLE VOTING, 1983–84

The New York Drama Critics Circle voted Tom Stoppard's *The Real Thing* the best play of the season on the first ballot by a simple majority of 14 votes (Clive Barnes, John Beaufort, Mel Gussow, Richard Hummler, Howard Kissel, Don Nelsen, William Raidy, Frank Rich, John Simon, Marilyn Stasio, Allan Wallach, Douglas Watt, Edwin Wilson, Linda Winer) to 4 for David Mamet's *Glengarry Glen Ross* (Michael Feingold, Brendan Gill, Jack Kroll, Edith Oliver) and 1 for Ted Tally's *Terra Nova* (Julius Novick).

Having named a foreign play its best of bests, the Circle proceeded to vote on a best American play. *Glengarry Glen Ross* won on the first ballot with a simple majority of 14 votes (Barnes, Feingold, Gill, Gussow, Hummler, Kissel, Kroll, Nelsen, Oliver, Raidy, Rich, Stasio, Wallach, Winer) to 2 for *Terra Nova* (Novick, Simon), 2 for Arthur Kopit's *End of the World* (Beaufort, Wilson) and Watt abstaining.

Sunday in the Park With George, with book by James Lapine and music and lyrics by Stephen Sondheim, was voted the best musical of the season on the first ballot with a simple majority of 10 votes (Beaufort, Gill, Kissel, Kroll, Novick, Oliver, Rich, Wallach, Wilson, Winer) to 4 for *La Cage aux Folles* by Harvey Fierstein and Jerry Herman (Barnes, Hummler, Raidy, Stasio) and 3 for *The Gospel at Colonus* by Lee Breuer and Bob Telson (Feingold, Nelsen, Gussow).

A special citation was proposed and voted to Samuel Beckett for the body of his work, including the two programs of one-act plays during the past season.

CHOICES OF SOME OTHER CRITICS

Critic	Best Play	Best Musical
Judith Crist WOR-TV, *TV Guide*	Glengarry Glen Ross	Sunday in the Park With George
John Gambling Broadcaster, WOR-AM	The Real Thing	La Cage aux Folles
Alvin Klein WNYC Radio, New York *Times*	Glengarry Glen Ross	La Cage aux Folles
Stewart Klein WNEW-TV	The Real Thing	La Cage aux Folles
Richard J. Scholem Radio Long Island	The Real Thing and Glengarry (tie)	La Cage aux Folles
Joel Siegel WABC-TV	Glengarry Glen Ross	La Cage aux Folles
Leida Snow WINS-TV	The Real Thing	Sunday in the Park

PULITZER PRIZE WINNERS, 1916–17 to 1983–84

1916–17—No award

1917–18—Why Marry?, by Jesse Lynch Williams

1918–19—No award

1919–20—Beyond the Horizon, by Eugene O'Neill

1920–21—Miss Lulu Bett, by Zona Gale

1921–22—Anna Christie, by Eugene O'Neill

1922–23—Icebound, by Owen Davis

1923–24—Hell-Bent fer Heaven, by Hatcher Hughes

1924–25—They Knew What They Wanted, by Sidney Howard

1925–26—Craig's Wife, by George Kelly

1926–27—In Abraham's Bosom, by Paul Green

1927–28—Strange Interlude, by Eugene O'Neill

1928–29—Street Scene, by Elmer Rice

1929–30—The Green Pastures, by Marc Connelly

1930–31—Alison's House, by Susan Glaspell

1931–32—Of Thee I Sing, by George S. Kaufman, Morrie Ryskind, Ira and George Gershwin

1932–33—Both Your Houses, by Maxwell Anderson

1933–34—Men in White, by Sidney Kingsley

1934–35—The Old Maid, by Zoë Akins

1935–36—Idiot's Delight, by Robert E. Sherwood

1936–37—You Can't Take It With You, by Moss Hart and George S. Kaufman

1937–38—Our Town, by Thornton Wilder

1938–39—Abe Lincoln in Illinois, by Robert E. Sherwood

1939–40—The Time of Your Life, by William Saroyan

1940–41—There Shall Be No Night, by Robert E. Sherwood

1941–42—No award

1942–43—The Skin of Our Teeth, by Thornton Wilder

1943–44—No award

1944–45—Harvey, by Mary Chase

1945–46—State of the Union, by Howard Lindsay and Russel Crouse

1946–47—No award

1947–48—A Streetcar Named Desire, by Tennessee Williams

1948–49—Death of a Salesman, by Arthur Miller

1949–50—South Pacific, by Richard Rodgers, Oscar Hammerstein II and Joshua Logan

1950–51—No award

1951–52—The Shrike, by Joseph Kramm

1952–53—Picnic, by William Inge

1953–54—The Teahouse of the August Moon, by John Patrick

1954–55—Cat on a Hot Tin Roof, by Tennessee Williams

1955–56—The Diary of Anne Frank, by Frances Goodrich and Albert Hackett

1956–57—Long Day's Journey Into Night, by Eugene O'Neill

1957-58—Look Homeward, Angel, by Ketti Frings
1958-59—J.B., by Archibald MacLeish
1959-60—Fiorello!, by Jerome Weidman, George Abbott, Sheldon Harnick and Jerry Bock
1960-61—All the Way Home, by Tad Mosel
1961-62—How to Succeed in Business Without Really Trying, by Abe Burrows, Willie Gilbert, Jack Weinstock and Frank Loesser
1962-63—No award
1963-64—No award
1964-65—The Subject Was Roses, by Frank D. Gilroy
1965-66—No award
1966-67—A Delicate Balance, by Edward Albee
1967-68—No award
1968-69—The Great White Hope, by Howard Sackler
1969-70—No Place To Be Somebody, by Charles Gordone

1970-71—The Effect of Gamma Rays on Man-in-the-Moon Marigolds, by Paul Zindel
1971-72—No award
1972-73—That Championship Season, by Jason Miller
1973-74—No award
1974-75—Seascape, by Edward Albee
1975-76—A Chorus Line, by Michael Bennett, James Kirkwood, Nicholas Dante, Marvin Hamlisch and Edward Kleban
1976-77—The Shadow Box, by Michael Cristofer
1977-78—The Gin Game, by D.L. Coburn
1978-79—Buried Child, by Sam Shepard
1979-80—Talley's Folly, by Lanford Wilson
1980-81—Crimes of the Heart, by Beth Henley
1981-82—A Soldier's Play, by Charles Fuller
1982-83—'night, Mother, by Marsha Norman
1983-84—Glengarry Glen Ross, by David Mamet

THE TONY AWARDS, 1983-84

The American Theater Wing's Antoinette Perry (Tony) Awards are presented annually in recognition of distinguished artistic achievement in the Broadway theater. The awards are voted by members of the governing boards of the four theater artists organizations: Actors' Equity Association, The Dramatists Guild, The Society of Stage Directors and Choreographers and the United Scenic Artists, plus the members of the first and second night theater press, the board of directors of the American Theater Wing and the membership of the League of New York Theaters and Producers, from a list of four nominees in each category.

The nominations (Broadway shows only) are made by a committee of theater professionals appointed by the Tony Awards Administration Committee. The 1983-84 Nominating Committee was composed of Jay P. Carr, critic of the Boston *Globe;* Schuyler Chapin, dean of the arts of Columbia University; Richard L. Coe, critic emeritus of the Washington *Post;* George Cuttingham, president of the American Academy of Dramatic Arts; William Glover, former drama critic for the Associated Press; Mary C. Henderson, curator of the Theater Collection of the Museum of the City of New York; Henry Hewes of the American Theater Critics Association; Norris Houghton, former president of the National Theater Conference; Elliot Norton, former drama critic of the Boston *Herald American;* David Oppenheim, dean of the New York University's Tisch School of the Arts; Seymour Peck of the New York *Times,* and George C. White, president of the O'Neill Theater Center.

The list of 1983-84 nominees follows, with winners in each category listed in **bold face type.**

BEST PLAY (award goes to both producer and author). *Glengarry Glen Ross* by David Mamet, produced by Elliot Martin, The Shubert Organization, Arnold Bernhard and The Goodman Theater; *Noises Off* by Michael Frayn, produced by James Nederlander, Robert Fryer, Jerome Minskoff, Kennedy Center, Michael Codron, Jonathan Farkas and MTM Enterprises, Inc.; *Play Memory* by Joanna M. Glass, produced by Alexander H. Cohen and Hildy Parks; **The Real Thing** by **Tom Stoppard**, produced by **Emanuel Azenberg, The Shubert Organization, Icarus Productions, Byron Goldman, Ivan Bloch, Roger Berlind** and **Michael Codron.**

BEST MUSICAL (award to producers). *Baby* produced by James B. Freydberg, Ivan Bloch, Kenneth-John Productions, Inc., Suzanne J. Schwartz and Manuscript Productions; **La Cage aux Folles** produced by **Allan Carr, Kenneth D. Greenblatt, Marvin A. Krauss, Stewart F. Lane, James M. Nederlander, Martin Richards, Barry Brown** and **Fritz Holt**; *Sunday in the Park With George* produced by The Shubert Organization and Emanuel Azenberg; *The Tap Dance Kid* produced by Stanley White, Evelyn Barron, Harvey J. Klaris and Michel Stuart.

BEST BOOK OF A MUSICAL. *Baby* by Sybille Pearson; *La Cage aux Folles* by **Harvey Fierstein**; *Sunday in the Park With George* by James Lapine; *The Tap Dance Kid* by Charles Blackwell.

BEST SCORE OF A MUSICAL. *Baby*, music by David Shire, lyrics by Richard Maltby Jr.; **La Cage aux Folles**, music and lyrics by **Jerry Herman**; *The Rink*, music by John Kander, lyrics by Fred Ebb; *Sunday in the Park With George*, music and lyrics by Stephen Sondheim.

OUTSTANDING ACTOR IN A PLAY. Rex Harrison in *Heartbreak House*, **Jeremy Irons** in *The Real Thing*, Calvin Levels in *Open Admissions*, Ian McKellen in *Ian McKellen Acting Shakespeare*.

OUTSTANDING ACTRESS IN A PLAY. **Glenn Close** in *The Real Thing*, Rosemary Harris in *Heartbreak House*, Linda Hunt in *End of the World*, Kate Nelligan in *A Moon for the Misbegotten*.

OUTSTANDING ACTOR IN A MUSICAL. Gene Barry in *La Cage aux Folles*, **George Hearn** in *La Cage aux Folles*, Ron Moody in

Oliver, Mandy Patinkin in *Sunday in the Park With George*.

OUTSTANDING ACTRESS IN A MUSICAL. Rhetta Hughes in *The Amen Corner*, Liza Minnelli in *The Rink*, Bernadette Peters in *Sunday in the Park With George*, **Chita Rivera** in *The Rink*.

OUTSTANDING FEATURED ACTOR IN A PLAY. Philip Bosco in *Heartbreak House*, **Joe Mantegna** in *Glengarry Glen Ross*, Robert Prosky in *Glengarry Glen Ross*, Douglas Seale in *Noises Off*.

OUTSTANDING FEATURED ACTRESS IN A PLAY. **Christine Baranski** in *The Real Thing*, Jo Henderson in *Play Memory*, Dana Ivey in *Heartbreak House*, Deborah Rush in *Noises Off*.

OUTSTANDING FEATURED ACTOR IN A MUSICAL. **Hinton Battle** in *The Tap Dance Kid*, Stephen Geoffreys in *The Human Comedy*, Todd Graff in *Baby*, Samuel E. Wright in *The Tap Dance Kid*.

OUTSTANDING FEATURED ACTRESS IN A MUSICAL. Martine Allard in *The Tap Dance Kid*, Liz Callaway in *Baby*, Dana Ivey in *Sunday in the Park With George*, **Lila Kedrova** in *Zorba*.

OUTSTANDING DIRECTION OF A PLAY. Michael Blakemore for *Noises Off*, David Leveaux for *A Moon for the Misbegotten*, Gregory Mosher for *Glengarry Glen Ross*, **Mike Nichols** for *The Real Thing*.

OUTSTANDING DIRECTION OF A MUSICAL. James Lapine for *Sunday in the Park With George*, **Arthur Laurents** for *La Cage aux Folles*, Richard Maltby Jr. for *Baby*, Vivian Matalon for *The Tap Dance Kid*.

OUTSTANDING SCENIC DESIGN. Clarke Dunham for *End of the World*, Peter Larkin for *The Rink*, **Tony Straiges** for *Sunday in the Park With George*, Tony Walton for *The Real Thing*.

OUTSTANDING COSTUME DESIGN. **Theoni V. Aldredge** for *La Cage aux Folles*, Jane Greenwood for *Heartbreak House*, Anthea Sylbert for *The Real Thing*, Patricia Zipprodt and Ann Hould-Ward for *Sunday in the Park With George*.

OUTSTANDING LIGHTING DESIGN. Ken Billington for *End of the World*, Jules Fisher for

La Cage aux Folles, **Richard Nelson** for *Sunday in the Park With George*, Marc B. Weiss for *A Moon for the Misbegotten*.

OUTSTANDING CHOREOGRAPHY. Wayne Cilento for *Baby*, Graciela Daniele for *The Rink*, **Danny Daniels** for *The Tap Dance Kid*, Scott Salmon for *La Cage aux Folles*.

OUTSTANDING REPRODUCTION OF A PLAY OR MUSICAL. *American Buffalo* produced by Elliot Martin and Arnold Bernhard;

Death of a Salesman produced by **Robert Whitehead** and **Roger L. Stevens**; *Heartbreak House* produced by Circle in the Square; *A Moon for the Misbegotten* produced by The Shubert Organization and Emanuel Azenberg.

SPECIAL TONY AWARDS. **The Old Globe Theater**, San Diego; **Peter Feller**; **La Tragédie de Carmen**; The Brooks Atkinson Award to **Al Hirschfeld**; **A Chorus Line** for performance 3,-389 when it became the longest-running show in Broadway history.

TONY AWARD WINNERS, 1947–1984

Listed below are the Antoinette Perry (Tony) Award winners in the categories of Best Play and Best Musical from the time these awards were established (1947) until the present.

1947—No play or musical award
1948—Mister Roberts; no musical award
1949—Death of a Salesman; Kiss Me, Kate
1950—The Cocktail Party; South Pacific
1951—The Rose Tattoo; Guys and Dolls
1952—The Fourposter; The King and I
1953—The Crucible; Wonderful Town
1954—The Teahouse of the August Moon; Kismet
1955—The Desperate Hours; The Pajama Game
1956—The Diary of Anne Frank; Damn Yankees
1957—Long Day's Journey Into Night; My Fair Lady
1958—Sunrise at Campobello; The Music Man
1959—J.B.; Redhead
1960—The Miracle Worker; Fiorello! and The Sound of Music (tie)
1961—Becket; Bye Bye Birdie
1962—A Man for All Seasons; How to Succeed in Business Without Really Trying
1963—Who's Afraid of Virginia Woolf?; A Funny Thing Happened on the Way to the Forum
1964—Luther; Hello, Dolly!
1965—The Subject Was Roses; Fiddler on the Roof
1966—The Persecution and Assassination of Marat as Performed by the Inmates of the Asylum of Charenton Under the Direction of the Marquis de Sade; Man of La Mancha
1967—The Homecoming; Cabaret
1968—Rosencrantz and Guildenstern Are Dead; Hallelujah, Baby!
1969—The Great White Hope; 1776
1970—Borstal Boy; Applause
1971—Sleuth; Company
1972—Sticks and Bones; Two Gentlemen of Verona
1973—That Championship Season; A Little Night Music
1974—The River Niger; Raisin
1975—Equus; The Wiz
1976—Travesties; A Chorus Line
1977—The Shadow Box; Annie
1978—Da; Ain't Misbehavin'
1979—The Elephant Man; Sweeney Todd, the Demon Barber of Fleet Street
1980—Children of a Lesser God; Evita
1981—Amadeus; 42nd Street
1982—The Life & Adventures of Nicholas Nickleby; Nine
1983—Torch Song Trilogy; Cats
1984—The Real Thing; La Cage aux Folles

THE OBIE AWARDS, 1983–84

The *Village Voice* Off-Broadway (Obie) Awards are given each year for excellence in various categories of off-Broadway (and frequently off-off-Broadway) shows, with close distinctions between these two areas ignored in Obie Award-giving. The Obies were voted by a panel of *Village Voice* critics (Eileen Blumenthal, Michael Feingold, Erika Munk, Julius Novick and Ross Wetzsteon), plus Lanford Wilson as a guest judge.

BEST AMERICAN PLAY. **Fool for Love** by Sam Shepard.

BEST MUSICAL. **The Gospel at Colonus**, book by Lee Breuer, music by Bob Telson.

BEST PERFORMANCES. **Kathy Baker, Ed Harris** and **Will Patton** in *Fool for Love*, **F. Mur-** **ray Abraham** in *Uncle Vanya*, **Sheila Dabney** in *Sarita*, **Morgan Freeman** in *The Gospel at Colonus*, **George Guidall** in *Cinders*, **Richard Jordan** in *A Private View*, **Ruth Maleczech** and **Frederick Neumann** in *Through the Leaves*, **Stephen McHattie** in *Mensch Meier*, **Dianne Wiest** in *Serenading Louie* and *Other Places*.

ADDITIONAL PRIZES AND AWARDS, 1983–84

The following is a list of major prizes and awards for achievement in the theater this season. In all cases the names of winners appear in **bold face type.**

MARGO JONES AWARD. To the producer and producing organization whose continuing policy of producing new theater works has made an outstanding contribution to the encouragement of new playwrights. **Bill Bushnell** and the **Los Angeles Actors' Theater.**

1984 JOSEPH MAHARAM FOUNDATION AWARDS. For distinguished theatrical design for original American productions presented in New York (selected by a committee comprising Tish Dace, Mel Gussow, Henry Hewes, Patricia MacKay and Edward F. Kook). Design collaboration: **Tony Straiges** and **Bran Ferren** (scenery and special effects), **Patricia Zipprodt** and **Ann Hould-Ward** (costumes) and **Richard Nelson** (lighting) for *Sunday in the Park With George*. Scenery: **Bill Stabile** for *Spookhouse*. Costumes: **Theoni V. Aldredge** for *La Cage aux Folles*. Lighting: **Paul Gallo** for *The Garden of Earthly Delights*.

Other nominations for outstanding scene design: Richard Foreman and Nancy Winters for *Dr. Selavy's Magic Theater*, Linda Hartinian for *Imagination Dead Imagine*, Peter Larkin for *Doonesbury*, Santo Loquasto and Ken Kobland for *The Photographer*, James Morgan for *Pacific Overtures*, Kevin Rigdon for *Balm in Gilead*, Douglas Stein for *Through the Leaves*, Alison Yerxa for *The Gospel at Colonus*.

Other nominations for outstanding costume design: Santo Loquasto for *The Photographer*, Mark Passerell for *Pacific Overtures*, Everett Quinton for *Galas*, Kurt Wilhelm for *Through the Leaves* and *My Uncle Sam*.

Other nominations for outstanding lighting design: Marc D. Malamud for *Ohio Impromptu, Catastrophe, What Where*, Jennifer Tipton for *The Photographer*, Marc B. Weiss for *A Moon for the Misbegotten*.

40th ANNUAL THEATER WORLD AWARDS. For outstanding new talent in Broadway and off-Broadway productions in the 1983–84 season (selected by a committee comprising Clive Barnes, Douglas Watt and John Willis). **Martine Allard** in *The Tap Dance Kid*, **Joan Allen** in *And a Nightingale Sang . . .*, **Kathy Baker** in *Fool for Love*, **Mark Capri** in *On Approval*, **Laura Dean** in *Doonesbury*, **Stephen Geoffreys** and **Bonnie Koloc** in *The Human Comedy*, **Todd Graff** in *Baby*, **Glenne Headly** in *The Philanthropist*, **J.J. Johnston** in *American Buffalo*, **Calvin Levels** in *Open Admissions*, **Robert Westenberg** in *Zorba*.

4th ANNUAL RICHARD L. COE AWARD. For an individual who has made a significant contribution to the development of original material for the theater. **Roger L. Stevens.**

49th ANNUAL DRAMA LEAGUE AWARD. For distinguished performing. **Jeremy Irons** in *The Real Thing*.

OUTER CRITICS CIRCLE AWARDS. For distinguished achievement in the 1983–84 New York theater season, voted by critics of foreign and out-of-town periodicals. Broadway play: **The Real Thing.** Broadway musical: **La Cage aux**

Folles. Off-Broadway play: **Painting Churches**. Revival: **Death of a Salesman**. Revue: **A . . . My Name Is Alice**. Actor: **George Hearn** in *La Cage aux Folles*. Actress: **Marian Seldes** in *Painting Churches*. Book of a musical: **Jeffrey Sweet** for *Love*. Music and lyrics: **Howard Marren** and **Susan Birkenhead** for *Love*, **Gary William Friedman** and **Will Holt** for *Taking My Turn* (tie). Direction: **Michael Blakemore** for *Noises Off*. Costumes: **Theoni V. Aldredge** for *La Cage aux Folles*. Debut performances: **Joan Allen** in *And a Nightingale Sang . . .* and **John Malkovich** in *Death of a Salesman*. John Gassner Playwriting Award: **Tina Howe** for *Painting Churches*. Special Awards: **The Roundabout Theater Company** for outstanding productions; **Twiggy** and **Tommy Tune** for sustained peak performances in *My One and Only*.

CLARENCE DERWENT AWARDS. For the most promising male and female actors on the metropolitan scene during the 1983–84 season. **Joan Allen** in *And a Nightingale Sang . . .* and **Peter Gallagher** in *The Real Thing*.

EUGENE O'NEILL BIRTHDAY MEDAL. Awarded annually by the Theater Committee for Eugene O'Neill. **Jason Robards** "for enriching universal understanding of the United States."

DRAMA DESK AWARDS. For outstanding achievement, voted by an association of New York drama reporters, editors and critics. Play: **The Real Thing**. Musical: **Sunday in the Park With George**. Director, play: **Michael Blakemore** for *Noises Off*. Director, musical: **James Lapine** for *Sunday in the Park With George*. Actor, play: **Dustin Hoffman** in *Death of a Salesman*. Actress, play: **Joan Allen** in *And a Nightingale Sang . . .* Actor, musical: **George Hearn** in *La Cage aux Folles*. Actress, musical: **Chita Rivera** in *The Rink*. Featured actor, play: **John Malkovich** in *Death of a Salesman*. Featured actress, play: **Christine Baranski** in *The Real Thing*. Featured actor, musical: **Martin Vidnovic** in *Baby*. Featured actress, musical: **Catherine Cox** in *Baby*; **Lila Kedrova** in *Zorba*. Score; **Jerry Herman** for *La Cage aux Folles*. Lyrics, **Stephen Sondheim** for *Sunday in the Park With George*. Book of a musical: **James Lapine** for *Sunday in the Park With George*. Orchestration: **Michael Starobin** for *Sunday in the Park With George*. Revival: **Death of a Salesman**. Scenery: **Tony Straiges** for *Sunday in the Park With George*. Costumes: **Theoni V. Aldredge** for *La Cage aux Folles*. Lighting: **Richard Nelson** for *Sunday in the Park With George*.

One-person show: **Ian McKellen Acting Shakespeare**. Special effects: **Bran Ferren** for *Sunday in the Park With George*. Unique theatrical experience: **La Tragédie de Carmen**. Special awards: **Michael Bennett, Joseph Papp** and **The Shubert Organization** for "extraordinary achievement in the presentation of the 3,389th performance of *A Chorus Line*; **Alan Schneider** for "his integrity in successfully serving a wide range of playwrights"; the **casts** of *Noises Off* and *Glengarry Glen Ross* for outstanding ensemble work; **Equity Library Theater** for "more than four decades of showcasing theater professionals"; **B.H. Barry** for "consistent excellence in fight staging"; **Interart Theater** for "discovering and nurturing contemporary women theater artists and for exploring women's issues in a non-adversary manner."

11th ANNUAL JOSEPH JEFFERSON AWARDS. For outstanding work in Chicago theater in the 1982–83 season, nominated by a 40-member committee. Production of a play. *And a Nightingale Sang . . .* and *Cloud 9* by Steppenwolf Theater Company, **Moby Dick** by **Remains Theater**, *Translations* by The Body Politic, *You Never Can Tell* by the Court Theater. Production of a musical: **Brigadoon** by **Marriott's Lincolnshire Theater**, *Camelot* by Candlelight Dinner Playhouse. Direction of a play: Pauline Brailsford for *Taking Steps*, **Terry Kinney** for *And a Nightingale Sang . . .*, Nicholas Rudall for *You Never Can Tell*, Steven Rumbelow for *Moby Dick*, Art Wolff for *Gorilla*. Direction of a musical: **David H. Bell** for *Brigadoon*, *Chicago* and *Give My Regards to Broadway*, William Pullinsi for *Camelot*. Direction of a revue, **Bernard Sahlins** for *Exit Pursued by a Bear*. Principal actor, play: **Robert Drivas** in *The Man Who Had Three Arms*, Frank Galati in *Endgame*, John Mahoney in *Taking Steps*, Jack McLaughlin in *Who's Afraid of Virginia Woolf?*, Ron Silver in *Gorilla*. Principal actress, play: **Joan Allen** and Moira Harris in *And a Nightingale Sang . . .*, Elaine May in *Hot Line*, Sophie Schwab in *The Comedy of Errors*, Mary Seibel in *The Whales of August*. Principal actor, musical: David Dunbar and Bud Nease in *Camelot*, Robert Neches in *They're Playing Our Song*, James W. Sudik in *Give My Regards to Broadway*. Principal actress, musical: Mary Ernster in *Brigadoon*, **Barbara Robertson** in *Chicago*, Patty Lombard in *They're Playing Our Song*, Hollis Resnik in *Camelot*.

Also principal actor, revue: **Douglas Wood** in *The Fine Line*. Principal actress, revue, **Cheryl Rhoads** in *The Fine Line*, Delores in *Street*

DEATH OF A SALESMAN—Kate Reid as Linda, Dustin Hoffman as Willy Loman and John Malkovich as Biff in the multi-award-winning revival of Arthur Miller's drama

Dreams. Supporting actor, play: Scott Jaeck in *Tribute* and *Awake and Sing!*, **Roger Mueller** in *Taking Steps*, Kenneth Northcott in *You Never Can Tell*, Jeff Perry in *Cloud 9*. Supporting actress, play: **Glenne Headly** in *The Miss Firecracker Contest*, Laurie Metcalf in *And a Nightingale Sang . . .*, Rondi Reed in *Cloud 9*, Lucy Childs in *Translations*, Charlotte Maier in *You Never Can Tell*. Supporting actor, musical: Dale Benson in *Camelot*, Michael Dunn in *Funeral March for a One Man Band*, **Vince Viverito** in *Chicago*. Supporting actress, musical: **Alene Roberts** in *Chicago*. Scene design: **Kevin Rigdon** for *Moby Dick*. Lighting design, **Mary McAuliffe** and **Kevin Rigdon** for *Moby Dick*. Sound effects: **Christian Petersen** for *Moby Dick*. Choreography: **David H. Bell** for *Chicago*. Ensemble: **Joan Allen, Francis Guinan,**

Terry Kinney, Laurie Metcalf, Jeff Perry, Rondi Reed and **Alan Wilder** in *Cloud 9*. Costumes: **Jessica Hahn** for *You Never Can Tell*. Original incidental music: **Douglas Wieselman** for *The Comedy of Errors*. New work: **Shel Silverstein** for *Gorilla*. Special Awards: **Claudia Cassidy**; Rep. **Sidney Yates** (Dem.-Ill.) and House Speaker **Michael Madigan** for support of the National Endowment and the Illinois Arts Council; **Fred Fine** "as a public and private advocate of the performing arts."

1983 COMMONWEALTH AWARD. For distinguished service in the dramatic arts. **Jessica Tandy** and **Hume Cronyn**.

GEORGE JEAN NATHAN AWARD. For drama criticism. **Herbert Blau** for his books

Take Up the Bodies and *Blooded Thought: Occasions of Theater*.

15th ANNUAL LOS ANGELES DRAMA CRITICS CIRCLE AWARDS. For distinguished achievement in Los Angeles theater. Production: **The Playboy of the Western World** by **South Coast Repertory**, **Cloud 9** by **L.A. Stage Company**. Original or adaptation for a Los Angeles premiere: **Harvey Fierstein** for *Torch Song Trilogy*, **John Kostmayer** for *On the Money*, **Caryl Churchill** for *Cloud 9*. Direction: **Martin Benson** for *The Playboy of the Western World*, **Don Amendolia** for *Cloud 9*, **Michael Peretzian** for *A Life*. Lead performance: **Jeffrey Combs** in *The Playboy of the Western World*, **Donald Corren** in *Torch Song Trilogy*, **Barbara Rush** in *A Woman of Independent Means*, **Jean Smart** in *Last Summer at Bluefish Cove*, **Ray Stricklyn** in *Vieux Carre*. Featured performance: **Megan Cole** and **Laurie Waters** in *The Playboy*

of the Western World. Ensemble performance: **Jack Bannon, Paul Eiding, Laurence Guittard, Nancy Lane, Marnie Mosiman, Christine Pickles** and **Charles Steak** in *Cloud 9*. Creation and performance: **Ian McKellen** for *Ian McKellen Acting Shakespeare*; **Bill Irwin, M.C. O'Connor** and **Doug Skinner** for *The Regard of Flight*. Scenery. **Mark Donnelly** for *The Playboy of the Western World*, **D. Martyn Bookwalter** for *On the Money*, **Ralph Funicello** for *A Month in the Country*. Costumes, **Barbara Cox** for *The Playboy of the Western World*, **Robert Blackman** for *A Month in the Country*. Lighting: **Cameron Harvey** for *The Playboy of the Western World*, **Martin Aronstein** for *A Month in the Country*. Choreography: **Michael Bennett** and **Michael Peters** for *Dreamgirls*. Vocal arrangements: **Cleavant Derricks** for *Dreamgirls*. Puppet creation: **Martin P. Robinson** for *Little Shop of Horrors*.

1983–84 PUBLICATION
OF RECENTLY-PRODUCED PLAYS

Abigail's Party and *Goose-Pimples.* Mike Leigh. Penguin (paperback).
After the Lions. Ronald Harwood. Amber Lane Press (paperback).
Babes in the Wood. Rick Besoyan. Broadway Play Publishing (paperback).
Baby With the Bathwater. Christopher Durang. Nelson Doubleday.
Billy Bishop Goes to War. John Gray with Eric Peterson. Talonbooks (paperback).
Blood and Ice. Liz Lochhead. Salamander Press (paperback).
Brighton Beach Memoirs. Neil Simon. Random House.
Bugler Boy and his Swish Friend, The. Stanley Eveling. Salamander Press (paperback).
Cloud 9: Revised American Edition. Caryl Churchill. Methuen (paperback).
Code Breaker, The. Pauline C. Conley. Anchorage Press (paperback).
Coming Clean. Kevin Elyot. Faber & Faber (paperback).
Communication Cord, The. Brian Friel. Faber & Faber (paperback).
Custom of the Country, The. Nicholas Wright. Methuen (paperback).
Cuttin' a Rug. John Byrne. Salamander Press (paperback).
Decadence/Greek. Steven Berkoff. Riverrun Press/John Calder (paperback).
Derek/Chorus from After the Assassinations Collection. Edward Bond. Methuen (paperback).
Fen. Caryl Churchill. Methuen (paperback).
Fool for Love. Sam Shepard. City Lights, 1983 (also in paperback).
Fugue. Rona Munro. Salamander Press (paperback).
Genius, The. Howard Brenton. Methuen (paperback).
Glengarry Glen Ross. David Mamet. Grove Press (also in paperback).
K2. Patrick Meyers. Nelson Doubleday.
Lent. Michael Wilcox. Methuen (paperback).
Man Who Had Three Arms, The. Edward Albee. Atheneum.
Master Class. David Pownall. Faber & Faber (paperback).
Masterpieces. Sarah Daniels. Methuen (paperback).

Molly Bailey's Traveling Family Circus: Featuring Scenes from the Life of Mother Jones. Megan Terry and Jo Anne Metcalf. Broadway Play Publishing, 1983 (paperback).
Night Just Before the Forest/Struggle of the Dogs and the Black. Bernard-Marie Koltes. UBU Repertory Theater, 1984 (paperback).
'night, Mother. Marsha Norman. Hill and Wang (paperback).
Noises Off: Revised Version. Michael Frayn. Methuen (paperback).
Not About Heroes. Stephen MacDonald. Faber & Faber (paperback).
Not Waving. Catherine Hayes. Faber & Faber (paperback).
Office, The. Jean-Paul Aron. UBU Repertory Theater (paperback).
Ohio Impromptu, Catastrophe and *What Where.* Samuel Beckett. Grove.
On the Razzle. Tom Stoppard. Faber & Faber.
Other Worlds. Robert Holman. Methuen.
Passion. Peter Nichols. Methuen (paperback).
Plenty. David Hare. Plume/New American Library (paperback).
Quiet in the Land. Anne Chislett. Coach House Press (paperback).
Real Thing, The. Tom Stoppard. Faber & Faber (paperback).
Sailmaker. Alan Spence. Salamander Press (paperback).
Slab Boys. John Byrne. Salamander Press (paperback).
Soft Cops. Caryl Churchill. Methuen (paperback).
Space Invaders. Alan Spence. Salamander Press (paperback).
Street Theater. Doric Wilson. The Sea Horse Press.
Still Life. John Byrne. Salamander Press (paperback).
Sufficient Carbohydrate. Dennis Potter. Faber & Faber (paperback).
Summit Conference. Robert David MacDonald. Broadway Play Publishing (paperback).
Swimming Pools at War. Yves Navarre. Ubu Repertory Theater (paperback).
Tales from Hollywood. Christopher Hampton (paperback).
Three Plays by Samuel Beckett. Samuel Beckett. Grove Press (paperback).
Torch Song Trilogy. Harvey Fierstein. Villard Books/Random House.
Victory: Choices in Reaction. Howard Barker. Riverrun Press/John Calder (paperback).
Woza Albert! Percy Mtwa and Mbongeni Ngema, Barney Simon. Methuen (paperback).
Zorba book by Joseph Stein, music by John Kander, lyrics by Fred Ebb. Nelson Doubleday.

A SELECTED LIST OF OTHER PLAYS PUBLISHED IN 1983–84

Best Short Plays, 1983. Ramon Delgado, editor. Chilton.
Disjecta: Miscellaneous Writings and a Dramatic Fragment. Samuel Beckett. Grove Press.
Dog It Was That Died and Other Plays, The. Tom Stoppard. Faber & Faber (also in paperback).
Five Plays by Galsworthy. John Galsworthy. Methuen (paperback).
Gammer Gurton's Needle: In Three Acts. I.E. Clark (paperback).
Harvest Festival, The. Sean O'Casey. New York Public Library.
Home/The Changing Room/Mother's Day. David Storey. Penguin (paperback).
Luv and Other Plays. Murray Schisgal. Dodd, Mead (paperback).
Molière's Tartuffe. Translated by Christopher Hampton. Faber & Faber (paperback).
Plautus: The Darker Comedies. Translated by James Tatum. Johns Hopkins University Press.
Sicilian Comedies. Luigi Pirandello. Performing Arts Journal.
Strindberg: Five Plays. August Strindberg. University of California Press (also in paperback).
Three Sisters. Anton Chekhov. New translation by Michael Frayn. Methuen (paperback).
Wesker, Trilogy, The. Arnold Wesker (four volumes each containing three plays). Penguin.

MUSICAL RECORDINGS OF NEW YORK SHOWS

Title and publishing company are listed below. Each record is an original cast album unless otherwise indicated. An asterisk (*) indicates recording is also available on cassettes. Two asterisks (**) indicate availability on digital, three (***) on compact disk.

Baby. Polygram.
Candide. 1956 OC. CBS Melodiya. (*)
Joseph and the Amazing Technicolor Dreamcoat. Chrysalis. (*)
La Cage aux Folles. RCA. (*). (**).
My One and Only. Atlantic. (*). (2 albums)
On Your Toes. 1983 Broadway Cast. Polygram. (*)
Rink, The. Polygram. (*)
Stephen Sondheim Evening, A. RCA. (*) (2 albums).
Sunday in the Park With George. RCA (*). (**). (***)
Tallulah. Painted Smiles.
Upstairs at O'Neals' (1982 original cast). Painted Smiles.
Zorba. Original cast with Anthony Quinn. RCA. (*).
Zorba. 1968 Original cast with Herschel Bernardi (re-issue). Capitol. (*)

NECROLOGY

MAY 1983–MAY 1984

PERFORMERS

Agnew, Robert (84)—November 8, 1983
Ahern, Will (86)—May 16, 1983
Ahmed, Fayza (52)—September 21, 1983
Alexander, Georgea Backus (82)—September 7, 1983
Alexander, Marion W. (71)—July 31, 1983
Alvarado, Croz (73)—January 28, 1984
Anderson, Bettye (79)—May 29, 1983
Apaka, Alfred (87)—January 25, 1984
Archer, Osceola Adams (93)—November 20, 1983
Armstrong, Lucille (69)—October 3, 1983
Arne, Peter (62)—August 1, 1983
Atwood, William L. (71)—November 9, 1983
Azama, Ethel (48)—March 5, 1984
Baille, Isobel (88)—September 24, 1983
Barisano, James (75)—September 7, 1983
Barnes, Paul J. (64)—May 16, 1983
Barry, Jack (66)—May 2, 1984
Basile, Louis (48)—March 2, 1984
Bennett, Boyd (69)—July 16, 1983
Benson, Lucille (69)—February 17, 1984
Berenger, Anne (53)—July 18, 1983
Berk, Sammy (88)—August 5, 1983
Bernabe, Amalia (88)—September 10, 1983
Berry, Robert (76)—January 1984
Bester, Rolly (66)—January 12, 1984
Bierne, Michael (46)—June 20, 1983
Bing, Nina Schelemskaya-Schelesnaya (86)—December 21, 1983
Birckhead, Muriel (66)—February 8, 1984
Bittan, Anne C. (28)—December 17, 1983
Blaney, Norah (90)—Winter 1984
Bogaert, Lucienne (90)—February 4, 1984
Bonus, Ben (63)—April 6, 1984
Boxer, Herman (80)—November 5, 1983
Boyer, Lucienne (82)—December 6, 1983
Brandon, Peter (57)—November 27, 1983
Brengel, George (69)—November 22, 1983
Brennan, Dennis (55)—June 17, 1983

Briarhopper, Homer (61)—May 18, 1983
Brignone, Lila (70)—March 24, 1984
Brito, Nina (42)—January 30, 1984
Brooks, Jack (49)—May 6, 1984
Bull, Peter (72)—May 20, 1984
Busch, LeRoy E. (74)—September 16, 1983
Byrd, Glen (70)—Summer 1983
Caine, Joan-ellen (57)—August 22, 1983
Cameron, Rod (73)—December 21, 1983
Campbell, Wishart (82)—November 5, 1983
Campina, Fidela (90)—Spring 1984
Cano, Fanny (38)—December 8, 1983
Canova, Judy (66)—August 5, 1983
Carignan, Lee Maurice (73)—March 26, 1984
Carpenter, Frederick L. (62)—March 31, 1984
Carruthers, Ben (48)—September 27, 1983
Carson, Violet (85)—December 26, 1983
Case, Anna (95)—January 7, 1984
Casman, Nellie (88)—May 27, 1984
Castro, Estrellita (71)—July 10, 1983
Caubisens, Henri Jean (82)—January 23, 1984
Chamlee, Ruth Miller (90)—June 28, 1983
Chase, Chaz (81)—August 4, 1983
Chauvel, Elsa (85)—August 22, 1983
Christensen, Norman—July 31, 1983
Clark, Jameson (76)—January 4, 1984
Clayton, Jan (66)—August 28, 1983
Coffield, Peter (37)—November 19, 1983
Colson, Robert Crozy—July 19, 1983
Conrad, Michael (58)—November 22, 1983
Coogan, Jackie (69)—March 1, 1984
Cooper, Edwin (89)—February 2, 1984
Cooper, Tommy (62)—April 15, 1984
Cordero, Victor (69)—December 8, 1983
Corona, Margarita (72)—October 13, 1983
Cortesina, Helena (73)—Winter 1984
Costello, Anthony (42)—August 15, 1983
Cou, Santiago Gomez (81)—Spring 1984
Courter, Madeleine Janis—June 15, 1983
Crisman, Nino (72)—Fall 1983
Cross, Glenn B. (74)—August 13, 1983
Culver, Ronald (83)—February 29, 1984

Dalio, Marcel (83)—November 20, 1983
Dana, Leora (60)—December 13, 1983
Darnell, Larry (54)—July 3, 1983
Davis, Pesha Paul (60)—February 10, 1984
Dawson, Ronald (81)—January 24, 1984
de Brailly, Alexandre Bugny (83)—November 15, 1983
De Haven, Sue (72)—October 24, 1983
Delaney, John J. (59)—March 21, 1984
del Castillo, Enrique (50)—February 7, 1984
deLeon, Elizabeth Ann Stears (69)—June 12, 1983
Demarest, William (91)—December 28, 1983
de Remer, Rubye—March 18, 1984
Dexter, Alan (65)—December 19, 1983
Dial, Auzie Russel (83)—September 28, 1983
Dobbs, Kenneth—September 2, 1983
Dolin, Anton (79)—November 25, 1983
Donald, Duck (32)—April 22, 1984
Dooley, Ray (93)—January 28, 1984
Donner, Ral (41)—April 6, 1984
Dors, Diana (52)—May 4, 1984
D'Orsay, Fifi (79)—December 2, 1983
Driscoll, Robert Miller (55)—December 5, 1983
Dudan, Pierre (68)—February 5, 1984
Dudley, Peter (47)—October 20, 1983
Dunn, Judith (49)—July 1, 1983
Durant, Jack (78)—January 7, 1984
Eby, Eleanor Swindell (49)—September 4, 1983
Edwards, Scott (58)—September 9, 1983
Elliott, William David (49)—September 30, 1983
El Mligi, Mahmoud (73)—Summer 1983
Farden, Carl (82)—June 10, 1983
Field, Franklin (93)—April 8, 1984
Fix, Paul (82)—October 14, 1983
Fleischmann, Herbert (59)—April 5, 1984
Flinn, June McNulty (70)—January 5, 1984
Fontanne, Lynn (95)—July 30, 1983
Ford, David Conant (58)—August 7, 1983
Foy, Eddie Jr. (78)—July 15, 1983
Francis, Derek (60)—March 28, 1984
Fraser, Mary R. Dacy (72)—April 15, 1984
Friedkin, Harold (47)—June 18, 1983
Furman, Roger (59)—November 27, 1983
Fu Sing (29)—July 7, 1983
Gaillard, Edwin C. (76)—October 4, 1983
Gardner, Dave (57)—September 22, 1983
Gary, Harold (77)—January 21, 1984
Gaye, Marvin (44)—April 1, 1984
Gilpin, John (55)—September 5, 1983
Gobbi, Tito (68)—March 5, 1984
Godfrey, Derek (59)—June 18, 1983
Gomes, Elza (73)—May 17, 1984

Gonzalez, Jose Orejas (77)—December 16, 1983
Gordon, David M. (75)—August 22, 1983
Gramm, Donald (54)—June 2, 1983
Grant, Shauna (20)—March 21, 1984
Granville, Rosina (91)—March 26, 1984
Graves, Ernest (64)—June 1, 1983
Gray, Christine Ursula (84)—May 19, 1983
Green, Gilbert (68)—April 15, 1984
Grimes, Marcella (83)—August 4, 1983
Groot, Kenneth—June 24, 1983
Guild, Jean—August 25, 1983
Haage, Karin—August 20, 1983
Hackett, Joan (49)—October 8, 1983
Halsema, Frans (44)—February 24, 1984
Hannaike, Gilbert (49)—September 12, 1983
Hannen, Hermione (70)—October 1, 1983
Hardwick, Paul (64)—October 22, 1983
Hartley, Russell (61)—October 2, 1983
Hartman, Johnny (60)—September 15, 1983
Hartnett, Kathleen (48)—April 3, 1984
Heard, Daphne (77)—June 22, 1983
Heijermans, Hermine (80)—August 8, 1983
Heinrich, Lois (69)—August 9, 1983
Henderson, Jack E. (88)—August 31, 1983
Heyward, Jenifer DuBose (54)—March 27, 1984
Higgins, Edward C. (54)—May 18, 1983
Holland, Jack (91)—July 20, 1983
Holmes, Nancy Ryan (79)—May 23, 1983
Huerta, Rodolfo Guzman (64)—February 5, 1984
Hurndall, Richard (73)—April 13, 1984
Ireton, Glenn F. (77)—September 23, 1983
Jackson, Devon (57)—March 11, 1984
Jaffe, Sam (93)—March 24, 1984
Jefferson, Lauretta (76)—November 3, 1983
Johnson, E. Lamont (29)—February 14, 1984
Jonah, Dolly (53)—July 14, 1983
Jones, Carolyn (54)—August 3, 1983
Junco, Tito (69)—December 9, 1983
Kane, Byron (60)—April 10, 1984
Kaufman, Andy (35)—May 16, 1984
Kavanaugh, Dorriet (38)—December 31, 1983
Kellin, Mike (61)—August 26, 1983
Kenworthy, Edward (64)—June 15, 1983
Kidder, Walter H. Jr. (66)—March 24, 1984
Kingsley, Susan (37)—February 6, 1984
Kinser, Patrick (30)—October 26, 1983
Kitchell, Iva (75)—November 19, 1983
Klavun, Walter (77)—April 13, 1984
Lambetti, Ellie (57)—September 2, 1983
Lancaster, Robert (70)—August 31, 1983
LaRue, Jack (80)—January 11, 1984
Leavitt, Ruth M. (93)—April 26, 1984
Leeb, Natalie (85)—May 30, 1983

Leeds, Andrea (70)—May 21, 1984
Lestocq, Humphrey (65)—January 29, 1984
Le Mesurier, John (71)—November 15, 1983
Levinoff, Joseph (73)—January 2, 1984
Lind, Gillian (79)—Fall 1983
Link, Frank (46)—December 31, 1983
Livingstone, Mary (77)—June 30, 1983
Loffman, Constance Reed (55)—February 25, 1984
Logan, Jacqueline (78)—April 4, 1984
Long, Avon (73)—February 15, 1984
Lontere, Jolene (46)—October 30, 1983
Loo, Richard (80)—November 20, 1983
Lowry, Ed (87)—August 17, 1983
Mace, Paul (33)—August 12, 1983
MacFarlane, Laura (late 40s)—May 28, 1983
Madden, Kate (33)—April 25, 1984
Maddern, Merle (96)—January 15, 1984
Mallett, Jane (84)—April 14, 1984
Mander, Raymond (72)—December 20, 1983
Manulis, Katharine Bard (66)—July 28, 1983
Marchal, Arlette (82)—Winter 1984
Marisse, Anne (48)—February 18, 1984
Markham, David (70)—December 15, 1983
Marley, John (77)—May 22, 1984
Marlowe, June (81)—March 10, 1984
Marshall, Marjorie Ward (75)—December 22, 1983
Massey, Raymond (86)—July 29, 1983
Mayo, Nick (60)—September 11, 1983
McAvoy, May (83)—April 26, 1984
McLaughlin, Henry (90)—July 24, 1983
McLean, Don (44)—February 11, 1984
McNab, Dorothy Cumming (84)—December 10, 1983
McPherson, Don (61)—February 15, 1984
McWilliams, Paul (79)—March 12, 1984
Mercer, Mabel (84)—April 20, 1984
Merman, Ethel (76)—February 15, 1984
Michaels, Loretta R. (45)—July 22, 1983
Middleton, Ray (77)—April 10, 1984
Millard, Paul Martin—August 9, 1983
Milner, Jessamine (88)—July 9, 1983
Modi, Schrad (86)—January 28, 1984
Mokotow, Fay (38)—February 20, 1984
Monleon, Luis Sancho (66)—June 16, 1983
Monteux, Doris Hodgkins (89)—March 13, 1984
Moore, Kathryn (96)—October 14, 1983
Moore, Robert (56)—May 10, 1984
Morecambe, Eric (58)—May 28, 1984
Murphy, Dorothy Day (72)—September 16, 1983
Niven, David (73)—July 29, 1983
Nordmark, Harry C. (74)—April 8, 1984
Nossen, Bram (87)—December 25, 1983

Oakland, Simon (61)—August 29, 1983
O'Brien, Pat (83)—October 15, 1983
Ode, Erik (72)—July 19, 1983
Olds, Margaret (70)—May 21, 1983
Oliver, Bette (52)—May 16, 1983
Omens, Estelle (early 50s)—December 4, 1983
O'Moore, Patrick (74)—December 10, 1983
Orr-Yamada, Jennifer Susan (26)—Fall 1983
Owen, Terence (62)—September 14, 1983
Palacios, Margarita (72)—Summer 1983
Papayannopoulos, Dionyssis (72)—April 17, 1984
Parsons, Charlie (76)—Summer 1983
Paulson, Viola (Jones)—April 13, 1984
Peddie, Eddie (64)—October 6, 1983
Penrose, John (69)—May 22, 1983
Perras, Margherita (76)—February 2, 1984
Phillips, Lillian (95)—Fall 1983
Pickens, Slim (64)—December 8, 1983
Pierce, Madeleine (82)—October 8, 1983
Podesta, Maria Esther (87)—September 18, 1983
Ponyman, John Kuhner (41)—February 4, 1984
Popov, Andrei (66)—Summer 1983
Porel, Marc (34)—Summer 1983
Powell, William (91)—March 5, 1984
Raglyn, Cynthia (46)—January 14, 1984
Rees, Joan (60)—July 29, 1983
Retschy, Gerhard (64)—June 12, 1983
Richardson, Ralph (80)—October 10, 1983
Rickard, Vernon Edward (80)—October 25, 1983
Ridley, Arnold (88)—March 12, 1984
Rigaud, Georges (78)—January 17, 1984
Roberts, Cliff (65)—July 15, 1983
Roberts, Helen Mortenson (61)—March 30, 1984
Roberts, Roy (57)—Fall 1983
Rossi, Tino (76)—September 27, 1983
Roth, Joe (88)—September 1, 1983
Rounds, David (40)—December 9, 1983
Rowland, Henry (70)—April 26, 1984
Sack, Susan (45)—August 30, 1983
Sandor, Alfred (64)—September 22, 1983
Scanlon, Arthur (67)—February 11, 1984
Scholl, Danny (61)—June 21, 1983
Scholten, Hank (63)—June 22, 1983
Schutte, Sanford K. (49)—June 27, 1983
Seckler, Bill (78)—October 3, 1983
Shaw, Marguerite (66)—September 23, 1983
Shayne, Tamara (80)—October 23, 1983
Shearer, Norma (80)—June 12, 1983
Shephard, Shelly (55)—January 2, 1984
Shuttleworth, Edyth (76)—Winter 1984
Sinclair, Betty (76)—September 20, 1983

Singerman, Paulina (72)—Winter 1984
Skeaping, Mary (81)—February 9, 1984
Sklar, Michael Joel (39)—March 5, 1984
Smeage, Linda (39)—February 14, 1984
Smith, Ada (Bricktop) (89)—January 31, 1984
Smith, Chief Elmer Tug (63)—November 19, 1983
Smith, Walter (84)—November 4, 1983
Somack, Jack (64)—August 24, 1983
Spainard, Earl (70)—June 2, 1983
St. Angel, Michael (67)—January 13, 1984
Stanley, Mike (65)—January 14, 1984
Stanley, Poppy (76)—July 11, 1983
Sternberg, Sam (75)—July 22, 1983
Suhrawardy, Vera Vlasova (81)—October 12, 1983
Sullivan, Frank R. (76)—June 17, 1983
Swindell, Eleanor Eby (49)—September 4, 1983
Tannen, Blanche Ruth Shwed (77)—July 4, 1983
Taylor, Eve—August 29, 1983
Tenley, Theodore (79)—July 27, 1983
Thatcher, Leora (89)—March 5, 1984
Thomsen, Robert (70)—October 28, 1983
Thorson, Ethel (63)—October 11, 1983
Tilley, Sandra (38)—September 9, 1983
Tobin, Gail (40)—February 10, 1984
Torrisi, Joseph (37)—October 27, 1983
Tracy, Louise Treadwell (87)—November 13, 1983
Travis, Bernie (49)—March 10, 1984
Travis, Merle (65)—October 20, 1983
Tripolino, Joseph III (43)—December 18, 1983
Van Heesvelde, Willy (50)—August 27, 1983
Victor, Dee (57)—December 18, 1983
Vivyan, John (67)—December 20, 1983
Wallgren, Gunn (69)—June 5, 1983
Waverly, Frances (81)—January 10, 1984
Wehlin, Robert (64)—September 4, 1983
Weil, Helen (69)—October 8, 1983
Weir, Olive (86)—June 9, 1983
Weissmuller, Johnny (79)—January 20, 1984
West, Brooks (67)—February 7, 1984
Whitney, Michael (52)—November 30, 1983
Wiedemeyer, Peter (50)—July 1, 1983
Wilcoxon, Henry (78)—March 6, 1984
Wilkes, Edmund C. (77)—February 27, 1984
Williams, Louise Blow (63)—June 12, 1983
Williams, Ken (69)—February 16, 1984
Wilson, Frank (84)—Winter 1984
Wilson, Jackie (49)—January 21, 1984
Wolfe, Edwin R. (90)—September 22, 1983
Woods, Maurice (45)—November 1, 1983
Youngman, David (79)—July 8, 1983
Zampese, Alan (53)—April 14, 1984

Zilles, Mary Esther Lawson (63)—October 22, 1983

PLAYWRIGHTS

Allen, David Richard (29)—September 5, 1983
Anderson, Thelma D. (45)—October 4, 1983
Andrade, Jorge (62)—March 13, 1984
Aulicino, Armand (63)—May 16, 1983
Baker, Herbert (62)—June 30, 1983
Berns, Julie (84)—December 28, 1983
Bosworth, Francis (78)—May 15, 1983
Boylan, Mary (70)—February 18, 1984
Clark, Dorothy Park (83)—June 22, 1983
Colmar, Andrew (43)—May 31, 1983
de Murat, Ulyses Petit (76)—August 20, 1983
Dodson, Owen (68)—June 21, 1983
Goodrich, Frances (93)—January 29, 1984
Goyen, William (68)—August 19, 1983
Guerrico, Silvia (79)—September 15, 1983
Haight, George (79)—April 17, 1984
Halper, Albert (79)—January 19, 1984
Hamilton, Wallace (64)—September 1, 1983
Higley, Philo (82)—May 11, 1983
Kantor, Leonard (59)—April 13, 1984
Lambert, Betty (50)—November 4, 1983
Llewellyn, Richard (76)—November 30, 1983
Lorimer, Graeme (80)—September 6, 1983
Magnier, Claude (62)—June 22, 1983
Melville, Alan (73)—December 23, 1983
Raphaelson, Samson (87)—July 16, 1983
Schrank, Joseph (83)—March 23, 1984
Scotland, James (65)—August 14, 1983
Shaw, Irwin (71)—May 16, 1984
Warwick, James (89)—August 15, 1983
Wells, Win Delaine (43)—December 6, 1983
Wibberley, Leonard (68)—November 23, 1983
Xantho, Peter (78)—August 11, 1983
Younin, Wolf (76)—May 31, 1984

COMPOSERS, LYRICISTS

Adam, Claus (66)—July 4, 1983
Amfitheatrof, Daniele (82)—June 7, 1983
Auric, Georges (84)—July 23, 1983
Babadyanyan, Arno (63)—Fall 1983
Ben-Haim, Paul (86)—January 14, 1984
Bernier, Buddy (73)—June 18, 1983
Bishop, Walter—January 8, 1984
Bojanowski, Jerzy (88)—September 10, 1983
Bruns, George (69)—May 23, 1983
Cohan, Mary (74)—September 11, 1983
Dietz, Howard (86)—July 30, 1983
Dragon, Carmen (69)—March 28, 1984

Eager, Mary Ann (78)—January 18, 1984
Egk, Werner (82)—July 10, 1983
Ellison, Ben (81)—February 1, 1984
Estrada, Claudio (73)—January 22, 1984
Freed, Fred (79)—August 31, 1983
Gentry, Bo (41)—July 1, 1983
Gershwin, Ira (86)—August 17, 1983
Ginastera, Alberto (67)—June 25, 1983
Goldman, Maurice (73)—February 2, 1984
Greene, Walter W. (73)—December 23, 1983
Hastings, Martha (84)—November 9, 1983
Heppner, Sam (69)—June 1, 1983
Herzog, Arthur J. Jr. (82)—September 1, 1983
Hess, Johnny (68)—November 14, 1983
Hossein, Andre (78)—August 9, 1983
Hoy, Bonnee H. (47)—November 6, 1983
Huergo, Maruja Pacheco (67)—September 14, 1983
Jenkins, Gordon (73)—May 1, 1984
Kahn, Grace LeBoy (92)—Spring 1983
Kennedy, Jimmy (81)—April 6, 1984
Kohlman, Churchill (77)—May 22, 1983
Leigh, Carolyn (57)—November 19, 1983
Leip, Hans (89)—June 6, 1983
Mennin, Peter (60)—June 17, 1983
Mikulskis, Alfonsas (74)—October 18, 1983
Moon, William H. (75)—January 5, 1984
Moross, Jerome (68)—July 25, 1983
Mundy, Jimmy (75)—April 24, 1984
Newman, Greatrex (91)—January 19, 1984
Olman, Abe (95)—Winter 1984
Pontier, Armando (65)—Spring 1984
Powell, Edward (74)—February 28, 1984
Stock, Larry (87)—May 3, 1984
Szmathmary, Irving (76)—October 29, 1983
Tailleferre, Germaine (91)—November 7, 1983
Wade, James (53)—August 1, 1983
Webster, Paul Francis (76)—March 22, 1984

Donohue, Jack (75)—March 27, 1984
Engel, Samuel G. (79)—April 7, 1984
Farquhar, Robroy (70s)—October 4, 1983
Fishburn, Alan M. (69)—June 22, 1983
Gibson, Charles (77)—October 10, 1983
Hooper, Alan (36)—July 13, 1983
Kaufman, Sidney (73)—July 30, 1983
Levin, Jack (53)—May 26, 1984
Liese, Oscar (77)—July 27, 1983
Lindtberg, Leopold (82)—April 18, 1984
Lucia, Luis (70)—March 1984
Mack, Irving (89)—November 10, 1983
Macy, Gertrude (79)—October 18, 1983
Meth, Max (83)—January 3, 1984
Moyer, Billy (81)—February 14, 1984
Nash, Gene (54)—May 18, 1983
O'Sullivan, Eugene (62)—December 1, 1983
Oumansky, Alexander N. (88)—July 10, 1983
Parella, Anthony J. (68)—November 14, 1983
Peate, Patricia Flynn (72)—October 25, 1983
Prinz, LeRoy (88)—September 15, 1983
Putch, William H. (60)—November 23, 1983
Rachmil, Lewis J. (75)—February 19, 1984
Radin, Roy (33)—June 12, 1983
Schelb, Frederick J. (89)—July 3, 1983
Schlom, Herman (79)—November 2, 1983
Schneider, Alan (66)—May 3, 1984
Smith, Thomas C. (39)—August 17, 1983
Straus, Ann Marlow (77)—May 26, 1984
Thomas, Jerome B. (63)—July 12, 1983
Thomas, William C. (80)—April 2, 1984
Toobin, Jerome (64)—January 22, 1984
Tors, Ivan (67)—June 4, 1983
Traube, Shepard (76)—July 23, 1983
White, Stuart (33)—July 5, 1983
Woodruff, Frank (77)—September 16, 1983
Young, Marshall T. (65)—January 16, 1984

PRODUCERS, DIRECTORS, CHOREOGRAPHERS

Aldrich, Robert (65)—December 5, 1983
Alexander, Stephen (63)—June 18, 1983
Andre, Thomas J. (78)—July 14, 1983
Andrew, Thomas (52)—January 11, 1984
Archibald, James (63)—July 25, 1983
Benedict, Richard (64)—April 25, 1984
Bernstein, Richard (61)—October 29, 1983
Box, Sydney (76)—May 25, 1983
Buckley, Allen F. (60)—April 3, 1984
Burgess, Walter (50s)—April 28, 1984
Cohen, Norman (47)—October 26, 1983
D'Arcy, Wilbur Lyle (59)—September 10, 1983
Dickinson, Thorold (80)—April 14, 1984

CONDUCTORS

Allan, Tommy (67)—October 30, 1983
Antonini, Alfredo (82)—November 3, 1983
Arnold, Geoffrey (53)—August 24, 1983
Basie, Count (William) (79)—April 26, 1984
Begbie, J. Mouland—May 19, 1983
Boechler, Guy Joseph (34)—January 8, 1984
Carnevale, Anthony (67)—August 7, 1983
Caruso, Frank (87)—October 28, 1983
Coleman, Earl M. (81)—September 24, 1983
Davis, Johnny (73)—November 24, 1983
Dods, Marcus (66)—April 30, 1984
Ferrin, Harold C. (68)—July 25, 1983
Gray, Hollis M. (82)—March 16, 1984
Grillo, Frank (75)—April 15, 1984
Groob, Jacob (64)—Spring 1984
Harwood, C. William (36)—April 26, 1984

Hawn, Edward Rutledge (73)—June 6, 1983
Hopkins, Claude (80)—February 19, 1984
Hubler, David G. (56)—October 4, 1983
Hutton, Ina Ray (67)—February 19, 1984
James, Harry (67)—July 5, 1983
Jedeerby, Thore (70)—January 10, 1984
Lewis, Anthony (68)—June 5, 1983
Liberace, George (71)—October 16, 1983
MacMahon, Samuel (70)—September 25, 1983
Maples, Nelson (85)—July 15, 1983
Martin, Freddy (76)—September 30, 1983
Martin, Thomas (74)—May 14, 1984
Mazzu, Joe (58)—August 12, 1983
Milton, Roy (76)—September 18, 1983
Moeckel, Hans (61)—October 6, 1983
Neighbors, Paul (65)—August 26, 1983
O'Conner, Terry (85)—September 15, 1983
Prado, Perez (57)—December 4, 1983
Russell, Howard H. (78)—September 18, 1983
Salter, Harry (85)—March 5, 1984
Shirali, Vishnudas (77)—February 26, 1984
Spialek, Hans (89)—November 20, 1983
Spigler, William (74)—February 26, 1984
Stafford, William (65)—March 7, 1984
Thompson, Leon (55)—June 21, 1983
White, Albert (77)—November 9, 1983

CRITICS

Atkinson, Brooks (89)—January 13, 1984
Currie, Donald Glenne (57)—January 4, 1984
Denby, Edwin (80)—July 12, 1983
Drew, Bernard (57)—January 24, 1984
Dumas, Greg (53)—May 6, 1984
Freustic, Jean (69)—June 5, 1983
Hannah, Peggy Conway (66)—March 13, 1984
Kallai, Sandor (54)—April 24, 1984
Koopmans, Rudy (50)—April 26, 1984
Kragh-Jacobsen, Svend (74)—May 5, 1984
Lawson, Evelyn (76)—January 19, 1984
Locklair, Wriston (59)—March 3, 1984
Lowens, Irving (67)—November 14, 1983
Malcolm-Smith, George—February 23, 1984
Meccoli, Domenico (70)—November 21, 1983
Olimsky, Fritz (88)—December 1983
Rich, Allen (80)—January 1, 1984
Thurston, Chuck (72)—May 7, 1984
Williams, Alexander W. (74)—August 9, 1983
Yanni, Nicholas A. Jr. (40)—February 15, 1984

DESIGNERS

Barthram, Reginald (57)—June 26, 1983
Coltellacci, Giulio (67)—June 26, 1983
Cutting, Blair (71)—April 2, 1984

Foote, Dan (52)—January 29, 1984
Ganeau, Francois (71)—Fall 1983
Greenwell, Robert (65)—October 27, 1983
Herndon, Walter (55)—January 21, 1984
Howard, Donald (57)—September 27, 1983
Karinska, Barbara (97)—October 18, 1983
Mack, Adele (83)—October 9, 1983
Novarese, Vittorio Nino (76)—October 17, 1983
Verhille, Guy C. (53)—July 11, 1983
Wakevitch, Georges (76)—February 11, 1984

MUSICIANS

Bobo, Willie (49)—September 15, 1983
Bonati, Joseph (52)—August 12, 1983
Booker, James (43)—November 8, 1983
Brewster, Herbert (48)—April 23, 1984
Brilhart, Verlye Milles (71)—October 2, 1983
Brooks, Gladys Rice (97)—January 19, 1984
Brown, Frank (50)—May 13, 1983
Bryan, Georgia A. (85)—May 7, 1983
Dorfmann, Ania (84)—April 21, 1984
Douglass, Stephen (33)—January 12, 1984
Dudley, Allen P. (64)—December 11, 1983
Easton, Jack (55)—April 10, 1984
Essig, Thelma A. (82)—April 30, 1984
Ewell, Don (66)—August 9, 1983
Fennimore, Arthur C. (42)—February 18, 1984
Fitzer, Juanita (83)—May 18, 1983
Foilb, Samuel (early 60s)—June 21, 1983
Forbes, Graham (66)—May 22, 1984
Friedman, Henry (86)—August 18, 1983
Fry, Leta Williams (85)—February 23, 1984
Gardner, Samuel (92)—January 23, 1984
Garland, William (60)—April 23, 1984
Genge, Dan (18)—January 8, 1984
Golden, Jimmy (66)—May 17, 1984
Gottschalk, Edgar (89)—March 24, 1984
Haeussler, Theodore (84)—May 20, 1983
Hakim, Sadik (60)—Summer 1983
Henderson, Raymond (54)—April 18, 1984
Higgins, Jack (62)—January 31, 1984
Hollister, Carroll (82)—October 1, 1983
Houff, Bruno (74)—July 12, 1983
Howard, Merle (70)—December 12, 1983
Jackson, Preston (81)—November 13, 1983
Jacobi, Irene (93)—May 25, 1984
Jacobs, Paul (53)—September 25, 1983
Johnson, Marion—July 10, 1983
Jones, Roger (70)—June 30, 1983
Kelly, Luke (44)—January 30, 1984
Kirkpatrick, Ralph (72)—April 13, 1984
Kitchen, Inez Blackstone (94)—October 7, 1983
Klein, Irving (66)—February 7, 1984

Landauer, Walter (73)—August 3, 1983
Langdon, Dorothy (81)—June 21, 1983
Levitan, Sam (64)—March 28, 1984
Lynch, Johnny (66)—August 9, 1983
Mann, Paul (72)—May 27, 1983
McCurdy, Alexander Jr. (77)—June 1, 1983
Mehegan, John (67)—April 3, 1984
Messina, Frank (62)—September 1, 1983
Miner, Frank (67)—December 6, 1983
Moore, Russell (70)—December 15, 1983
Morgan, Neil (22)—January 8, 1984
Mosse, Sany (54)—July 2, 1983
Neve, Herb (78)—September 27, 1983
Nickerson, Albert C. (72)—November 14, 1983
Olsen, Frank (72)—September 4, 1983
Orchard, Frank (69)—December 27, 1983
Pecora, Santo (82)—May 29, 1984
Platt, Lew (75)—December 25, 1983
Polisi, William (76)—February 16, 1984
Pollikoff, Max (80)—May 13, 1984
Raymond, Rose (94)—January 9, 1984
Reed, Waymon (43)—November 25, 1983
Reisenberg, Nadia (78)—June 10, 1983
Richmond, Bernice (84)—December 26, 1983
Ripoll, Tony (40)—October 30, 1983
Ross, Nathan (61)—March 2, 1984
Schafer, Jack (76)—March 27, 1984
Schoute, Rutger (74)—April 20, 1984
Schwarz, Boris (77)—December 31, 1983
Shapiro, Lydia Ita (78)—November 28, 1983
Smith, Maurice S. (65)—January 14, 1984
Sonju, Russell (62)—April 15, 1984
Suggs, Edward W. (74)—May 23, 1983
Sykes, Roosevelt (77)—July 11, 1983
Taylor, Leslie Jr. (52)—November 16, 1983
Tizol, Juan (84)—April 23, 1984
Vassilis, Tsitsanis (68)—January 18, 1984
Vivier, John (26)—September 21, 1983
Welch, Gordon Ward (78)—March 25, 1984
Werner, William K. (64)—March 7, 1984
Wheeler, Marion C. (76)—June 20, 1983
Williams, E.P. (64)—July 29, 1983
Williams, Francis (72)—October 2, 1983
Wilson, Dennis (39)—December 28, 1983
Wilson, J. Donald (69)—January 26, 1984
Winston, Harry (87)—September 15, 1983
Winters, Bill (71)—July 24, 1983
Wood, Chris (39)—July 12, 1983
Woodward, Kenneth V. (82)—November 24, 1983
Zazofsky, George—August 19, 1983

OTHERS

Abelson, Rosemarie (37)—July 11, 1983
Stage manager, publicist

Abrahams, Mark (85)—June 20, 1983
Stage Door Canteen
Ahmed, Ahmed Iskandar (39)—Winter 1984
Information Minister
Albright, Ivan Le Lorraine (86)—November 18, 1983
Painter
Antonello, Joe Jr. (72)—June 1, 1983
Booking agency
Arden, Dorothy—September 23, 1983
Rockette
Argent, Jack (60)—May 25, 1983
Leeds Music
Arons, Max (79)—March 27, 1984
Attorney
Bacharach, Bert (85)—September 15, 1983
Syndicated columnist
Barnes, Gloria—April 18, 1984
Runyon-Winchell Cancer Fund
Barry, Jack (66)—May 2, 1984
TV producer
Barton, G.S. (39)—July 27, 1983
Daily Variety reporter
Barzini, Luigi Jr. (75)—March 30, 1984
Journalist
Beaupre, Lee (42)—May 17, 1984
Publicist
Bishop, Harold (82)—October 22, 1983
Broadcast pioneer
Blackstone, Milton (77)—October 29, 1983
Publicist
Bloch, Harold J. (56)—August 4, 1983
Restaurateur
Bolton, Kenyon C. (71)—July 14, 1983
Cleveland Play House
Bondy, Edward Joseph (51)—December 17, 1983
William Morris Agency
Bouchard, Thomas (89)—March 5, 1984
Photographer
Bowser, John A. (47)—August 22, 1983
Theater owner
Bradley, Jenny (97)—June 3, 1983
Literary agent
Brett, George P. Jr. (91)—February 11, 1984
Publisher
Breytenbach, P.P.B. (80)—March 2, 1984
South African theater
Brown, Monte Charles (57)—January 5, 1984
Electrician
Bryant, Hazel (44)—November 7, 1983
Richard Allen Center
Burg, Mary Lou (53)—May 16, 1983
Copyright Royalty Tribunal
Cadwell, Paul (94)—October 4, 1983
Attorney
Campbell, Robert R. (66)—July 15, 1983
Publisher

Candela, Christina Marie (50s)—April 13, 1984
Actors' agent

Cargill, Jerome H. (84)—February 28, 1984
Agent

Coe, Christine Sadler (81)—June 25, 1983
Wife of Richard L. Coe

Cole, Edward C. (79)—March 24, 1984
Yale University Drama School

Conrad, Anthony Lee (62)—January 9, 1984
RCA Corporation

Cornell, Phyllis Langner (66)—January 7, 1984
Country Playhouse

Corning, Erastus II (73)—May 28, 1983
Arts partron

David, Jenkin Reese (75)—March 14, 1984
Park College Drama Department

Davis, Richard (84)—March 14, 1984
Film exhibitor

de la Renta, Francoise (62)—June 17, 1983
Magazine editor

Dempsey, Jack (87)—May 31, 1983
Prize fighter, restaurateur

Dorn, Norman K. (67)—August 14, 1983
Publicist

Eldridge, Carleton G. Jr. (61)—September 4, 1983
Attorney

Fielding, Nancy (70)—October 31, 1983
Literary agent

Finney, Charles G. (78)—April 16, 1984
Author

Fiore, James M. Jr. (36)—January 22, 1984
Company and general manager

Flame, Ditra (78)—February 1984
Original Lady in Black

Ford, John Anson (100)—November 3, 1983
Hollywood Arts Council

Forward, James D. Jr. (72)—November 9, 1983
California Arts Commission

Gallo, Michael—November 18, 1983
Carpenter

Geltman, Max (78)—May 16, 1984
Stage manager

Giannelli, Enrico (70)—November 30, 1983
Editor

Glass, George (73)—April 1, 1984
Publicist

Goldman, Irving (73)—May 20, 1983
Shubert executive

Goldstein, Hal (61)—September 21, 1983
Theater equipment

Goode, Gerald (84)—November 28, 1983
Publicist

Graves, Madge D. (74)—April 16, 1984
Production assistant

Green, Bernie (74)—June 15, 1983
Publicist ¯

Gross, Harvey (78)—November 2, 1983
Casino, hotel operator

Harper, Joe (61)—August 5, 1983
TV anchorman

Harris, Clyde J. (74)—July 17, 1983
Waldorf-Astoria

Hathaway, Ralph M. (72)—February 21, 1984
Theater manager

Hemsley, Gilbert V. Jr. (47)—September 4, 1983
Lighting director

Hertz, Aleksander (87)—May 16, 1983
Author

Hinkel, Cecil E. (69)—May 20, 1983
Univ. of Conn. Theater Dept.

Holmes, Joseph R. (55)—May 27, 1983
Reagan's Hollywood agent

Horowitz, Al (78)—February 24, 1984
Publicity director

Hoskwith, Arnold K. (66)—February 14, 1984
Agent

Houghland, James A. (56)—May 4, 1983
Publicist

Hunt, Harry T. (78)—January 24, 1984
Hunt's Circus

Ishimoto, Fred (58)—September 5, 1983
Talent agent

Johnson, James A. Jr. (39)—May 18, 1983
Publicist

Kammins, Jack (77)—November 5, 1983
Attorney

Kane, Walter (82)—May 27, 1983
Talent agent

Kelley, F. Beverly (78)—April 3, 1984
Theater, circus advance man

Kelley, Tom (72)—January 6, 1984
Marilyn Monroe calendar shot

Kilgore, Al (55)—August 15, 1983
Caricaturist

Krawitz, Seymour (59)—September 20, 1983
Publicist

Krushen, Morris (79)—July 15, 1983
Reporter

Langley, Adria Locke (84)—August 14, 1983
Author

Lasky, Lawrence G. (77)—March 22, 1984
Theater manager

Letter, Ben (75)—June 27, 1983
Cleveland Play House

Lido, Serge (77)—March 2, 1984
Photographer

Litchfield, Mary Jane (40)—August 25, 1983
Stage manager

McCaffery, John K.M. (69)—October 3, 1983
  Newscaster
Meltzer, Jack (81)—November 12, 1983
  Authority on records
Mitchell, Jack (65)—February 28, 1984
  Theater manager
Morosoff, Olga (36)—May 16, 1983
  Hampton Playhouse
Neill, Frank (67)—April 15, 1984
  Publicity director
Neumann, Kurt (81)—March 18, 1984
  Ballet company manager
Newman, Robert B. (65)—October 2, 1983
  Acoustics
Olevsky, Ben (77)—February 10, 1984
  Chief projectionist
Parkinson, Edward (66)—January 28, 1984
  Publicist
Paskman, Joseph (83)—September 2, 1983
  Company manager
Perry, Charlotte (93)—October 28, 1983
  Teacher
Pew-Bandy, Roberta (75)—March 21, 1984
  Arts patron
Pitts, Richard (71)—May 29, 1983
  Entertainment editor
Prince, Frank C. (47)—October 11, 1983
  Production associate
Proctor, James D. (77)—February 4, 1984
  Publicist
Raskoff, Max L. (75)—December 23, 1983
  Attorney
Reeves, Rosser (73)—January 24, 1984
  Ted Bates ad agency
Reid, Anthony (63)—April 28, 1983
  American Educational Theater Ass'n
Reynolds, Frank (59)—July 20, 1983
  ABC-TV anchorman
Russell, Carroll (85)—October 12, 1983
  Modern dance patron
Russell, Jack (76)—November 20, 1983
  Agent
Seidel, A. Kurt (89)—January 6, 1984
  Master violin-maker

Shapiro, Nat (61)—December 15, 1983
  Music editor
Share, Robert (54)—April 5, 1984
  Berklee School of Music
Sharp, Charles S. (68)—January 16, 1984
  Dallas Summer Musicals
Silver, Jack (83)—September 15, 1983
  Supplied costumes
Smith, William J. (83)—October 8, 1983
  Publicist
Stark, Eliot (72)—June 28, 1983
  Reporter
Stein, Doris (82)—April 7, 1984
  Philanthropist
Steinhoff, Irving (67)—Winter 1984
  Purple Onion night club
Stiefel, Milton (83)—November 14, 1983
  Ivoryton Playhouse
Taylor, Albert (77)—April 16, 1984
  Talent agent
Treloar, Dorothy (65)—October 31, 1983
  Entertainment columnist
Vinci, Ernesto (85)—November 7, 1983
  Voice teacher
Ventura, Marcel (80s)—January 2, 1984
  Artists' manager
Wait, Newman E. Jr. (61)—December 18,
  1983
  Saratoga Performing Arts Center
Wattenbarger, W.W. (62)—February 9, 1984
  Stage manager
Wechsler, James (67)—September 15, 1983
  Columnist, editor
Weinberg, Curt (67)—October 20, 1983
  Publicist
Weinberg, Herman G. (75)—November 7,
  1983
  Translator
Weinberger, Andrew D. (82)—May 13, 1984
  Attorney
Weyerhaeuser, Vivian O'Gara—June 6, 1983
  Metropolitan Opera
Wright, Louis (84)—February 26, 1984
  Folger Shakespeare Library

THE BEST PLAYS, 1894–1983

Listed in alphabetical order below are all those works selected as Best Plays in previous volumes in the *Best Plays* series. Opposite each title is given the volume in which the play appears, its opening date and its total number of performances. Two separate opening-date and performance-number entries signify two separate engagements off Broadway and on Broadway when the original production was transferred from one area to the other, usually in an off-to-on direction. Those plays marked with an asterisk (*) were still playing on June 1, 1984 and their number of performances was figured through May 31, 1984. Adaptors and translators are indicated by (ad) and (tr), the symbols (b), (m) and (l) stand for the author of the book, music and lyrics in the cast of musicals and (c) signifies the credit for the show's conception.

NOTE: A season-by-season listing, rather than an alphabetical one, of the 500 Best Plays in the first 50 volumes, starting with the yearbook for the season of 1919–1920, appears in *The Best Plays of 1968–69.*

PLAY	VOLUME	OPENED	PERFS
ABE LINCOLN IN ILLINOIS—Robert E. Sherwood	38–39	Oct. 15, 1938	472
ABRAHAM LINCOLN—John Drinkwater	19–20	Dec. 15, 1919	193
ACCENT ON YOUTH—Samson Raphaelson	34–35	Dec. 25, 1934	229
ADAM AND EVA—Guy Bolton, George Middleton	19–20	Sept. 13, 1919	312
ADAPTATION—Elaine May; and NEXT—Terrence McNally	68–69	Feb. 10, 1969	707
AFFAIRS OF STATE—Louis Verneuil	50–51	Sept. 25, 1950	610
AFTER THE FALL—Arthur Miller	63–64	Jan. 23, 1964	208
AFTER THE RAIN—John Bowen	67–68	Oct. 9, 1967	64
AGNES OF GOD—John Pielmeier	81–82	Mar. 30, 1982	486
AH, WILDERNESS!—Eugene O'Neill	33–34	Oct. 2, 1933	289
AIN'T SUPPOSED TO DIE A NATURAL DEATH—(b, m, l) Melvin Van Peebles	71–72	Oct. 7, 1971	325
ALIEN CORN—Sidney Howard	32–33	Feb. 20, 1933	98
ALISON'S HOUSE—Susan Glaspell	30–31	Dec. 1, 1930	41
ALL MY SONS—Arthur Miller	46–47	Jan. 29, 1947	328
ALL OVER TOWN—Murray Schisgal	74–75	Dec. 12, 1974	233
ALL THE WAY HOME—Tad Mosel, based on James Agee's novel *A Death in the Family*	60–61	Nov. 30, 1960	333
ALLEGRO—(b,l) Oscar Hammerstein II, (m) Richard Rodgers	47–48	Oct. 10, 1947	315
AMADEUS—Peter Shaffer	80–81	Dec. 17, 1980	1,181
AMBUSH—Arthur Richman	21–22	Oct. 10, 1921	98
AMERICA HURRAH—Jean-Claude van Itallie	66–67	Nov. 6, 1966	634
AMERICAN BUFFALO—David Mamet	76–77	Feb. 16, 1977	135
AMERICAN WAY, THE—George S. Kaufman, Moss Hart	38–39	Jan. 21, 1939	164
AMPHITRYON 38—Jean Giraudoux, (ad) S. N. Behrman	37–38	Nov. 1, 1937	153
ANDERSONVILLE TRIAL, THE—Saul Levitt	59–60	Dec. 29, 1959	179
ANDORRA—Max Frisch, (ad) George Tabori	62–63	Feb. 9, 1963	9
ANGEL STREET—Patrick Hamilton	41–42	Dec. 5, 1941	1,295
ANGELS FALL—Lanford Wilson	82–83	Oct. 17, 1982	65
	82–83	Jan. 22, 1983	64
ANIMAL KINGDOM, THE—Philip Barry	31–32	Jan. 12, 1932	183
ANNA CHRISTIE—Eugene O'Neill	21–22	Nov. 2, 1921	177
ANNA LUCASTA—Philip Yordan	44–45	Aug. 30, 1944	957
ANNE OF THE THOUSAND DAYS—Maxwell Anderson	48–49	Dec. 8, 1948	286

PLAY	VOLUME	OPENED	PERFS
ANNIE—(b) Thomas Meehan, (m) Charles Strouse, (l) Martin Charnin, based on Harold Gray's comic strip "Little Orphan Annie"	76–77	Apr. 21, 1977	2,377
ANOTHER LANGUAGE—Rose Franken	31–32	Apr. 25, 1932	344
ANOTHER PART OF THE FOREST—Lillian Hellman	46–47	Nov. 20, 1946	182
ANTIGONE—Jean Anouilh, (ad) Lewis Galantiere	45–46	Feb. 18, 1946	64
APPLAUSE—(b) Betty Comden and Adolph Green, (m) Charles Strouse, (l) Lee Adams, based on the film *All About Eve* and the original story by Mary Orr	69–70	Mar. 30, 1970	896
APPLE TREE, THE—(b,l) Sheldon Harnick, (b, m) Jerry Bock, add'l (b) Jerome Coopersmith, based on stories by Mark Twain, Frank R. Stockton and Jules Feiffer	66–67	Oct. 18, 1966	463
ARSENIC AND OLD LACE—Joseph Kesselring	40–41	Jan. 10, 1941	1,444
AS HUSBANDS GO—Rachel Crothers	30–31	Mar. 5, 1931	148
ASHES—David Rudkin	76–77	Jan. 25, 1977	167
AUTUMN GARDEN, THE—Lillian Hellman	50–51	Mar. 7, 1951	101
AWAKE AND SING—Clifford Odets	34–35	Feb. 19, 1935	209
BAD MAN, THE—Porter Emerson Browne	20–21	Aug. 30, 1920	350
BAD HABITS—Terrence McNally	73–74	Feb. 4, 1974	273
BAD SEED—Maxwell Anderson, based on William March's novel	54–55	Dec. 8, 1954	332
BARBARA FRIETCHIE—Clyde Fitch	99–09	Oct. 23, 1899	83
BAREFOOT IN ATHENS—Maxwell Anderson	51–52	Oct. 31, 1951	30
BAREFOOT IN THE PARK—Neil Simon	63–64	Oct. 23, 1963	1,530
BARRETTS OF WIMPOLE STREET, THE—Rudolf Besier	30–31	Feb. 9, 1931	370
BECKET—Jean Anouilh, (tr) Lucienne Hill	60–61	Oct. 5, 1960	193
BEDROOM FARCE—Alan Ayckbourn	78–79	Mar. 29, 1979	278
BEGGAR ON HORSEBACK—George S. Kaufman, Marc Connelly	23–24	Feb. 12, 1924	224
BEHOLD THE BRIDEGROOM—George Kelly	27–28	Dec. 26, 1927	88
BELL, BOOK AND CANDLE—John van Druten	50–51	Nov. 14, 1950	233
BELL FOR ADANO, A—Paul Osborn, based on John Hersey's novel	44–45	Dec. 6, 1944	304
BENT—Martin Sherman	79–80	Dec. 2, 1979	240
BERKELEY SQUARE—John L. Balderston	29–30	Nov. 4, 1929	229
BERNARDINE—Mary Chase	52–53	Oct. 16, 1952	157
BEST LITTLE WHOREHOUSE IN TEXAS, THE—(b) Larry L. King, Peter Masterson, (m,l) Carol Hall	77–78	Apr. 17, 1978	64
	78–79	June 19, 1978	1,639
BEST MAN, THE—Gore Vidal	59–60	Mar. 31, 1960	520
BETRAYAL—Harold Pinter	79–80	Jan. 5, 1980	170
BEYOND THE HORIZON—Eugene O'Neill	19–20	Feb. 2, 1920	160
BIG FISH, LITTLE FISH—Hugh Wheeler	60–61	Mar. 15, 1961	101
BILL OF DIVORCEMENT, A—Clemence Dane	21–22	Oct. 10, 1921	173
BILLY BUDD—Louis O. Coxe, Robert Chapman, based on Herman Melville's novel	50–51	Feb. 10, 1951	105
BIOGRAPHY—S. N. Behrman	32–33	Dec. 12, 1932	267
BLACK COMEDY—Peter Shaffer	66–67	Feb. 12, 1967	337
BLITHE SPIRIT—Noel Coward	41–42	Nov. 5, 1941	657
BOESMAN AND LENA—Athol Fugard	70–71	June 22, 1970	205
BORN YESTERDAY—Garson Kanin	45–46	Feb. 4, 1946	1,642
BOTH YOUR HOUSES—Maxwell Anderson	32–33	Mar. 6, 1933	72
BOY MEETS GIRL—Bella and Samuel Spewack	35–36	Nov. 27, 1935	669
BOY FRIEND, THE—(b, l, m) Sandy Wilson	54–55	Sept. 30, 1954	485
BOYS IN THE BAND, THE—Mart Crowley	67–68	Apr. 15, 1968	1,000

PLAY	VOLUME	OPENED	PERFS
TENTH MAN, THE—Paddy Chayefsky......................	59–60	Nov. 5, 1959	623
THAT CHAMPIONSHIP SEASON—Jason Miller...............	71–72	May 2, 1972	144
	72–73	Sept. 14, 1972	700
THERE SHALL BE NO NIGHT—Robert E. Sherwood..........	39–40	Apr. 29, 1940	181
THEY KNEW WHAT THEY WANTED—Sidney Howard........	24–25	Nov. 24, 1924	414
THEY SHALL NOT DIE—John Wexley.....................	33–34	Feb. 21, 1934	62
THOUSAND CLOWNS, A—Herb Gardner...................	61–62	Apr. 5, 1962	428
THREEPENNY OPERA—(b, l) Bertolt Brecht, (m) Kurt Weill, (tr) Ralph Manheim, John Willett	75–76	Mar. 1, 1976	307
THURBER CARNIVAL, A—James Thurber..................	59–60	Feb. 26, 1960	127
TIGER AT THE GATES—Jean Giraudoux's *La Guerre de Troie n'aura pas lieu,* (tr) Christopher Fry	55–56	Oct. 3, 1955	217
TIME OF THE CUCKOO, THE—Arthur Laurents..............	52–53	Oct. 15, 1952	263
TIME OF YOUR LIFE, THE—William Saroyan	39–40	Oct. 25, 1939	185
TIME REMEMBERED—Jean Anouilh's *Léocadia,* (ad) Patricia Moyes......................................	57–58	Nov. 12, 1957	248
TINY ALICE—Edward Albee............................	64–65	Dec. 29, 1964	167
TOILET, THE—LeRoi Jones	64–65	Dec. 16, 1964	151
TOMORROW AND TOMORROW—Philip Barry...............	30–31	Jan. 13, 1931	206
TOMORROW THE WORLD—James Gow, Arnaud d'Usseau.....	42–43	Apr. 14, 1943	500
*TORCH SONG TRILOGY—Harvey Fierstein *(The International Stud, Fugue in a Nursery, Widows and Children First)*	81–82	Jan. 15, 1982	117
	82–83	June 10, 1983	827
TOUCH OF THE POET, A—Eugene O'Neill	58–59	Oct. 2, 1958	284
TOVARICH—Jacques Deval, (tr) Robert E. Sherwood	36–37	Oct. 15, 1936	356
TOYS IN THE ATTIC—Lillian Hellman.....................	59–60	Feb. 25, 1960	556
TRANSLATIONS—Brian Friel............................	80–81	Apr. 7, 1981	48
TRAVESTIES—Tom Stoppard............................	75–76	Oct. 30, 1975	155
TRELAWNY OF THE WELLS—Arthur Wing Pinero	94–99	Nov. 22, 1898	131
TRIAL OF THE CATONSVILLE NINE, THE—Daniel Berrigan, Saul Levitt..	70–71	Feb. 7, 1971	159
TRIBUTE—Bernard Slade..............................	77–78	June 1, 1978	212
TWO BLIND MICE—Samuel Spewack	48–49	Mar. 2, 1949	157
UNCHASTENED WOMAN, THE—Louis Kaufman Anspacher....	09–19	Oct. 9, 1915	193
UNCLE HARRY—Thomas Job............................	41–42	May 20, 1942	430
UNDER MILK WOOD—Dylan Thomas.....................	57–58	Oct. 15, 1957	39
VALLEY FORGE—Maxwell Anderson......................	34–35	Dec. 10, 1934	58
VENUS OBSERVED—Christopher Fry......................	51–52	Feb. 13, 1952	86
VERY SPECIAL BABY, A—Robert Alan Aurthur	56–57	Nov. 14, 1956	5
VICTORIA REGINA—Laurence Housman..................	35–36	Dec. 26, 1935	517
VIEW FROM THE BRIDGE, A—Arthur Miller...............	55–56	Sept. 29, 1955	149
VISIT, THE—Friedrich Duerrenmatt, (ad) Maurice Valency	57–58	May 5, 1958	189
VISIT TO A SMALL PLANET—Gore Vidal	56–57	Feb. 7, 1957	388
VIVAT! VIVAT REGINA!—Robert Bolt	71–72	Jan. 20, 1972	116
VOICE OF THE TURTLE, THE—John van Druten.............	43–44	Dec. 8, 1943	1,557
WAGER, THE—Mark Medoff	74–75	Oct. 21, 1974	104
WAITING FOR GODOT—Samuel Beckett	55–56	Apr. 19, 1956	59
WALTZ OF THE TOREADORS, THE—Jean Anouilh, (tr) Lucienne Hill	56–57	Jan. 17, 1957	132
WATCH ON THE RHINE—Lillian Hellman..................	40–41	Apr. 1, 1941	378
WE, THE PEOPLE—Elmer Rice..........................	32–33	Jan. 21, 1933	49
WEDDING BELLS—Salisbury Field.......................	19–20	Nov. 12, 1919	168
WEDNESDAY'S CHILD—Leopold Atlas	33–34	Jan. 16, 1934	56

INDEX

Play titles appear in **bold face**. *Bold face italic* page numbers refer to those pages where complete cast and credit listing for New York productions may be found.